Hemingway and Africa

Hemingway's two extended African safaris, the first in the 1930s and the second in the 1950s, gave rise to two of his best-known stories ("The Snows of Kilimanjaro" and "The Short Happy Life of Francis Macomber"), a considerable amount of journalism and correspondence, and two non-fiction books, *Green Hills of Africa* (1935), about the first safari, and *True at First Light* (1999; longer version, *Under Kilimanjaro*, 2005), about the second. Africa also figures largely in his important posthumous novel *The Garden of Eden* (1986). The variety and quantity of this literary output indicate clearly that Africa was a major factor in the creative life of this influential American author. But surprisingly little scholarship has been devoted to the role of Africa in Hemingway's life and work. To start the long-delayed conversation on this topic, this book offers historical, theoretical, biographical, theological, and literary interpretations of Hemingway's African narratives. It also presents a wide-ranging introduction, a detailed chronology of the safaris, a complete bibliography of Hemingway's published and unpublished African works, an up-to-date, annotated review of the scholarship on the African works, and a bibliography of Hemingway's reading on natural history and other topics relevant to Africa and the world of the safari.

Studies in American Literature and Culture

Hemingway's two African safaris produced journalistic essays, short fiction, parts of a novel, and two volumes of creative nonfiction.

Photo Courtesy of Earl Theisen Archives, Roxann Livingston / John F. Kennedy Library.

Hemingway and Africa

Edited by
Miriam B. Mandel

Rochester, New York

Copyright © 2011 by the Editor and Contributors

All Rights Reserved. Except as permitted under current legislation, no part of this work may be photocopied, stored in a retrieval system, published, performed in public, adapted, broadcast, transmitted, recorded, or reproduced in any form or by any means, without the prior permission of the copyright owner.

First published 2011 by Camden House
Transferred to digital printing 2013
Reprinted in paperback 2016

Camden House is an imprint of Boydell & Brewer Inc.
668 Mt. Hope Avenue, Rochester, NY 14620, USA
www.camden-house.com
and of Boydell & Brewer Limited
PO Box 9, Woodbridge, Suffolk IP12 3DF, UK
www.boydellandbrewer.com

Paperback ISBN-13: 978-1-57113-967-2
Paperback ISBN-10: 1-57113-967-2
ISBN-13: 978-1-57113-483-7
ISBN-10: 1-57113-483-2

Library of Congress Cataloging-in-Publication Data

Hemingway and Africa / edited by Miriam B. Mandel.
    p. cm. — (Studies in American literature and culture)
Includes bibliographical references and index.
ISBN-13: 978-1-57113-483-7 (hardcover: alk. paper)
ISBN-10: 1-57113-483-2 (hardcover: alk. paper)
    1. Hemingway, Ernest, 1899–1961—Travel—Africa. 2. Hemingway, Ernest, 1899–1961—Knowledge—Africa. 3. Hemingway, Ernest, 1899–1961—Religion. 4. Americans—Africa—History—20th century. 5. Africa—Description and travel. 6. Big game hunting—Africa. 7. Safaris—Africa. 8. Africa—In literature.   I. Mandel, Miriam B. II. Title. III. Series.

PS3515.E37Z617913 2011
813'.52—dc22

2011018418

This publication is printed on acid-free paper.
Printed in the United States of America.

This one is for

Pablo Pésaj Adí

Contents

List of Illustrations	xi
Acknowledgments	xiii
A Note on the Texts	xv
Hemingway's African Narratives	xvii
Hemingway in Africa: Chronology	xxi
Introduction Miriam B. Mandel	1

I: Knowing What Hemingway Knew

1:	Hemingway's Reading in Natural History, Hunting, Fishing, and Africa *Miriam B. Mandel and Jeremiah M. Kitunda*	41
2:	Ernest Hemingway on Safari: The Game and the Guns *Silvio Calabi*	85
3:	"Love is a dunghill.... And I'm the cock that gets on it to crow": Hemingway's Farcical Adoration of Africa *Jeremiah M. Kitunda*	122

II: Approaches to Reading

4:	Canonical Readings: Baudelaire's Subtext in Hemingway's African Narratives *Beatriz Penas Ibáñez*	151
5:	Tracking the Elephant: David's African Childhood in Hemingway's *The Garden of Eden* *Suzanne del Gizzo*	176

6: An Elephant in the Garden: Hemingway's Africa in
   The Garden of Eden Manuscript   199
   Chikako Tanimoto

7: Between Ngàje Ngài and Kilimanjaro: A Rortian Reading of
   Hemingway's African Encounters   212
   Frank Mehring

III: On Religion and Death

8: Memorial Landscapes: Hemingway's Search for Indian Roots   239
   Philip H. Melling

9: Hemingway's African Book of Revelations: Dawning of a
   "New Religion" in *Under Kilimanjaro*   273
   Erik G. R. Nakjavani

10: Barking at Death: Hemingway, Africa, and the
    Stages of Dying   299
    James Plath

IV: What Others Have Said

11: On Safari with Hemingway: Tracking the Most
    Recent Scholarship   323
    Kelli A. Larson

Notes on the Contributors   385

Index   389

List of Illustrations

Frontispiece. Hemingway on Safari: Writing	iv
Fig. I.1. Camp Life: The Dining Tent	20
Fig. I.2. Camp Life: The Bath Tent	21
Fig. I.3. Safari Life: No Roads	22
Fig. I.4. Safari Life: No Bridges	23
Fig. I.5. Writing, Always Writing	24
Fig. I.6. Dismantled Tent	25
Fig. 2.1. Second Safari: The Scott Shotgun	97
Fig. 2.2. First Safari: The Springfield .30-06	102
Fig. 2.3. The Young Hemingway: The Colt Woodsman	113
Fig. 3.1. Kenya's Coat of Arms	132
Fig. 7.1. Kilimanjaro	228

Acknowledgments

This is the second book I have edited for Camden House, and I am happily indebted to James Hardin, who first brought me into this happy connection, and to James Walker, whose kind and intelligent guidance has made this work a pleasure. My well-informed contributors also taught me much and, in the end, shaped this book. I thank them for their good humor in dealing with the larger and smaller tasks demanded of them, for their witty comments and correspondence, and for their participation on my panel on Africa at the 14th Biennial Hemingway Society Conference in Lausanne, Switzerland in June of 2010.

I would also like to thank Susan Wrynn, curator of the Hemingway Collection at the John F. Kennedy Presidential Library and Museum, Boston, and the small army of Hemingway Collection interns who answered my many queries. Thanks also to Arthur Waldhorn and Earl Rovit, who read an early draft of my introduction and offered helpful advice; and to the in-house and external readers who read the entire manuscript for Camden House and whose intelligent suggestions were incorporated into all our essays. Mary Petrusewicz, our excellent copy-editor, also deserves our thanks for her sharp eyes and clear thinking.

For the illustrations, we are grateful to Roxann Livingston, who generously gave permission to reproduce photographs taken by her father, Earl Theisen, during Hemingway's second safari; to Maryrose Grossman, curator of the Audiovisual Archives at the JFK Library, who prepared the prints; and to Silvio Calabi, who helped me choose and caption them. Special thanks also to Tony Bly and Ryan Staples of Appalachian State University for the image of Kenya's coat of arms. At Camden House, Jane Best prepared the manuscript for publication and Sue Smith managed the design of our handsome cover: thanks to both.

Pablo Adí and my two daughters, Jessica and Naomi Mandel, add pleasure to every aspect of my life. I am grateful beyond words.

M. B. M.
Ra'anana, Israel
March 2011

A Note on the Texts

ERNEST HEMINGWAY'S WORK was, for practically all of his career, published by Charles Scribner's Sons, all of whose editions and reprints bear the same page numbers. We have, therefore, used Scribner's texts for references to the novels and the volumes of nonfiction. For the short stories, which have been frequently reprinted and collected, we have taken the pagination of *The Short Stories of Ernest Hemingway* (New York: Scribner's, 1938), feeling that this edition, which represents the texts as Hemingway himself supervised them into print, is the most authoritative and widely available. It contains all the African stories except for "The Good Lion," which was first published in 1951 (see below).

Most of the journalism, although published in a variety of newspapers and magazines, has been collected into two books, both edited by William White, which also carry the Scribner's imprint: *By-Line: Ernest Hemingway. Selected Articles and Dispatches of Four Decades* (1967), and *Ernest Hemingway. Dateline: Toronto. The Complete Toronto Star Dispatches, 1920–1924* (1985). For the letters, we have used what is currently available: *Ernest Hemingway: Selected Letters 1917–1961*, edited by Carlos Baker (New York: Scribner's, 1981); *The Only Thing That Counts: The Ernest Hemingway–Maxwell Perkins Correspondence*, edited by Matthew J. Bruccoli, with the assistance of Robert W. Trogdon (New York: Scribner's, 1996); and *At the Hemingways: With Fifty Years of Correspondence Between Ernest and Marcelline Hemingway, Centennial Edition*, by Marcelline Hemingway Sanford, with a Foreword by Michael Reynolds (Moscow: University of Idaho Press, 1999).

The narrative of Hemingway's first safari was serialized in *Scribner's Magazine* in seven monthly installments ranging in length from six to eleven pages and illustrated by Edward Shenton, May–November 1935. All our references, however, are to the more complete version, the book *Green Hills of Africa*, published by Scribner's on 25 October 1935.

The narrative of Hemingway's second safari has appeared in three different forms: as "African Journal," a three-part magazine publication edited by Ray Cave and published in *Sports Illustrated* (1971–1972); as a book edited by Patrick Hemingway, *True at First Light* (New York: Scribner's, 1999); and as another, longer book, *Under Kilimanjaro*, edited by Robert W. Lewis and Robert E. Fleming (Kent: Kent State University Press, 2005). Because *Under Kilimanjaro* is the more complete text, we have consistently used it in all our essays.

Citations to all of Hemingway's texts are given parenthetically in the text, with full title at the first mention and initials thereafter.

Hemingway's African Narratives

This chronological list identifies those of Hemingway's published works that discuss Africa or that are set, wholly or in part, in Africa. They include book reviews, journalism, short fiction, and book-length nonfiction.

The unpublished materials are in the Hemingway Collection, the John F. Kennedy Presidential Library and Museum, Columbia Point, Boston, Massachusetts.

Published Works

1922

"Prize-Winning Book Is Centre of Storm." Review of *Batouala*, by René Maran. *Toronto Star Weekly*, 25 March 1922, 3. Reprinted as "Black Novel a Storm Center," in *Dateline: Toronto. The Complete Toronto Star Dispatches, 1920–1924*, edited by William White, 112–13. New York: Scribner's, 1985. *Batouala*, which Hemingway much admired for both its content and its style, is set in Africa.

1934

"A.D. in Africa: A Tanganyika Letter." *Esquire*, 1 April 1934, 19, 146. Reprinted in *By-Line: Ernest Hemingway. Selected Articles and Dispatches of Four Decades*, edited by William White, 159–61. New York: Scribner's, 1967.

"Shootism Versus Sport: The Second Tanganyika Letter. *Esquire*, June 1934, 19, 150. Reprinted in *By-Line: Ernest Hemingway. Selected Articles and Dispatches of Four Decades*, 162–66.

"Notes on Dangerous Game: The Third Tanganyika Letter." *Esquire*, July 1934, 19, 194. Reprinted in *By-Line: Ernest Hemingway. Selected Articles and Dispatches of Four Decades*, 167–71.

1935

"Sailfish Off Mombasa: A Key West Letter." *Esquire*, March 1935, 21, 156.

"Green Hills of Africa." Illustrations by Edward Shenton. Serialized in *Scribner's Magazine*, May–October 1935.

Green Hills of Africa. New York: Scribner's, 1935.

1936

"Wings Always Over Africa: An Ornithological Letter." *Esquire*, January 1936, 31, 174–75. Reprinted in *By-Line: Ernest Hemingway. Selected Articles and Dispatches of Four Decades*, 229–35. The interesting material on hyenas and vultures in East Africa is relevant to "The Snows of Kilimanjaro."

"The Snows of Kilimanjaro." *Esquire*, August 1936, 27, 194–201. Reprinted in *The Short Stories of Ernest Hemingway*, 52–77. New York: Scribner's, 1938.

"The Short Happy Life of Francis Macomber." *Cosmopolitan*, September 1936. Reprinted in *The Short Stories of Ernest Hemingway*, 3–37. New York: Scribner's, 1938.

1951

"The Good Lion." *Holiday*, March 1951. Reprinted in *The Complete Short Stories of Ernest Hemingway: The Finca Vigía Edition*, 482–84. New York: Scribner's, 1987. Its companion fable, "The Good Bull," has a parallel publication history.

"Préface." Translated into French by Paule de Beaumont. In François Sommer, *Pourquoi ces bêtes sont-elles sauvages?* Paris: Nouvelle Éditions de la Toison d'Or, 1951.

1953

"Foreword." Original English version of "Préface," in Sommer, *Pourquoi ces bêtes sont-elles sauvages?* In François Sommer, *Man and Beast in Africa.* Translated by Edward Fitzgerald. London: Jenkins [1953]; New York: Citadel, 1954. Reprinted as "Foreword" in *Hemingway and the Mechanism of Fame: Statements, Public Letters, Introductions, Forewords, Prefaces, Blurbs, Reviews, and Endorsements*, edited by Matthew J. Bruccoli, with Judith S. Baughman, 126–28. Columbia: South Carolina UP, 2006.

Text of "Foreword" also available at http://books.google.co.il/boo ks?id=0iCYVqAMnfkC&pg=PA126&lpg=PA126&dq=man+and +beast+in+africa&source=bl&ots=l3Pex2z7z8&sig=8CTP1hNds pLAzoNPD1CmH6y7Fzg&hl=en&ei=ZdiPSrzaMKLAmgPNh-GmAQ&sa=X&oi=book_result&ct=result&resnum=3#v=onepage& q=&f=false (accessed 25 October 2009).

1954

"Safari." With Photographs by Earl Theisen. *Look*, 26 January 1954, 19–34. The first section is reprinted in *Hemingway on Hunting*, edited and with an introduction by Seán Hemingway, foreword by Patrick Hemingway, 205–9. Guilford, CT: The Globe Pequot Press, 2001.

"The Christmas Gift." Part I, *Look*, 20 April 1954, 29–37; Part II, *Look*, 4 May 1954, 79–89. Reprinted in in *By-Line: Ernest Hemingway. Selected Articles and Dispatches of Four Decades*, 425–69.

Posthumous Publications

1971–1972

African Journal. Edited and introduction by Ray Cave. Illustrated by Jack Brusca. "Part One: Miss Mary's Lion." *Sports Illustrated*, 20 December 1971; "Part Two: Miss Mary's Lion." *Sports Illustrated*, 3 January 1972; "Part Three: Imperiled Flanks." *Sports Illustrated*, 10 January 1972.

1986

The Garden of Eden. Edited by Tom Jenks. New York: Scribner's, 1986. Kibo's story, included in this novel, is reprinted separately as "An African Story" in *The Complete Short Stories of Ernest Hemingway: The Finca Vigía Edition*, 545–54.

1999

True at First Light. Edited and with an excellent introduction by Patrick Hemingway. New York: Scribner's, 1999.

2005

Under Kilimanjaro. Edited by Robert W. Lewis and Robert E. Fleming. Kent: Kent State UP, 2005.

Unpublished Works

The manuscripts, notes, and fragments listed below are all connected, in one way or another, to Hemingway's African safaris. Susan Wrynn, the curator of the Hemingway Collection, JFK Library, and her assistant, Marti Verso, generously helped me identify and collect them. The items range from one to several pages. Additional unidentified items may exist in this and perhaps other archives.

"Filet of Lion." Undated one page typescript, single-spaced, on Finca Vigía stationery. Humor-laced recipe for butchering, aging, cooking, and garnishing lion tenderloin steaks, followed by a defense of the meat's taste and edibility and a relevant quote from F. C. Selous, *A Hunter's Wanderings in Africa*. The reference to "my wife" is probably to Mary. JFK Item 376.

"had waked him." Undated handwritten fragment, one page, bearing circled number two, description of Thomas Gill building a fire and speaking to his dog. Probably but not necessarily set in Africa. JFK Item 826.

"I made an operational plan. . . ." Photocopy of undated typescript fragment, nine lines of dialogue with Keiti, one page. JFK Item 488.

"Kilimanjaro." Undated handwritten fragment, seven numbered pages, divided into titled sections and presenting a series of noun phrases describing, in turn, "Kilimanjaro," "Camp," "After rain," "In a field," "Camp," "Camp in the drought," and "On the mud flat." The references to Charo and Mary (p. 5) date this to the second safari. JFK Item 534.5.

Marginalia, six pages, hunting notes and diary for 14–28 December 1933 (first safari), on the last two pages and the endpapers of Frederick Jackson's *Notes on the Game Birds of Kenya and Uganda*.

"What did they say?" Undated handwritten fragment, two numbered pages, mostly of dialogue between Thomas Gill and an unnamed man wearing a shawl. JFK Item 826.

Hemingway in Africa: Chronology

First Trip to Africa, 1933–1934

ERNEST AND PAULINE HEMINGWAY spend about eighty days in areas officially known then as the Colony and Protectorate of Kenya (formerly British East Africa) and the Tanganyika Territory (formerly German East Africa), which are today Kenya and Tanzania. About sixty days were dedicated to safari, from 20 December 1933 to 19 February 1934, of which about two weeks in January were lost to illness.

1933

8 December, Friday: Pauline and Ernest Hemingway arrive in Mombasa on board the *General Metzinger*, which they had boarded in Marseille, with Charles Thompson, on 22 November. They had traveled through the Suez Canal and the Indian Ocean to reach Mombasa.

9–10 December: Depart Mombasa to spend the weekend with Charles and Katherine Fannin on the mainland.

10 December: Travel three hundred miles by train and check into the New Stanley Hotel, Nairobi.

14 December: Stay with Philip Percival at his farm at Potha Hills in Machakos District (in what is now the Eastern Province of Kenya). They begin hunting in the Kapiti Plains (Baker, 248).

20 December: Depart Nairobi to begin the safari, spending the night at a rest camp.

21 December: Drive to Arusha (Tanzania), stopping at the Hotel Arusha for a swim in the pool and dinner.

22 December: Hunting in the afternoon from the Arusha camp.

24 December: Overnight on "the Crater" (Ngorongoro Crater, in today's Arusha National Park, Tanzania, a Masai game reserve, supposedly rich in lion).

25 December: Descending from the Crater, they encounter a lioness. A gun goes off, the bullet narrowly missing Hemingway's head.

30 December: They move camp.

1934

ca. 2 January: Hemingway falls ill with amoebic / tropical dysentery (Bruccoli, 206).

6 January: Move camp, Hemingway still ill.

7 January: Move camp again.

8, 9 January: Hemingway ill, unable to hunt.

10 January: Hemingway ill, but goes hunting.

11 January: Move camp.

12 January: Hemingway ill, unable to hunt.

13 January: Hemingway ill, unable to sit in the car, stands on the running boards when they go hunting.

14 January: The decision is made to transfer the weak Hemingway to Arusha Hospital by plane instead of by car (to avoid a three hour ride over rough terrain).

15 January: Waiting for plane to arrive.

16 January: Hemingway flown to Arusha. But instead of going into hospital, he continues to Nairobi, checking into the New Stanley Hotel. Expects to rejoin the safari on 21 January, at Ngorongoro Crater.

17 January: Percival ill with indigestion.

18 January: They move camp to Ngorongoro.

20 January: They break camp and descend from Ngorongoro. Thompson hunts kudu, but Percival and Pauline Hemingway drive to Arusha, to discover Hemingway is not there.

21 January: Pauline in Arusha, exchanges telegrams with Hemingway.

22 January: Hemingway joins her.

24 January: They depart Arusha, camp at Mosquito River,[1] begin hunting.

28 January: Move camp to the Mbulumbulu[2] District.

29 January: Hemingway kills a rhinoceros.

31 January: Break camp and continue hunting for rhino.

1 February: Hemingway kills a buffalo.

4 February: Move camp to Babati[3] and thence to Dick Cooper's estate.

5 February: Depart Cooper's estate, go through Babati and set up camp in Gallapo.[4]

9 February: Break camp.

10 February: Move camp to Kijungo, reputedly rich in kudu.

11 February: Thompson kills kudu.

12 February: Koritschoner (prototype for Kandinsky in *Green Hills of Africa*) first appears.
13 February: Koritschoner joins them for lunch and dinner.
14 February: Koritschoner departs early in the morning.
17 February: Hemingway returns to camp late at night with two kudu and a sable cow.
18 February: Break camp and travel to Tanga.[5]
19 February: Depart Tanga and go to Mombasa, stay at Tudor House.
20 February: Depart Mombasa.
21 February: Begin fishing in "a little island off Lamu at the mouth of the Tanu river where have hired an empty Arab House to fish for swordfish" with Alfred Vanderbilt who "would rather fish than do anything" (Ernest Hemingway, quoted in Bruccoli, 206).
28 February: Depart Mombasa for Villefranch (via Suez Canal and Palestine) on the *Gripsholm*.

Second Trip to Africa, 1953–1954

Ernest and Mary Hemingway spend seven months in what were then the Colony of Kenya and Tanganyika Territory, and are now Kenya and Tanzania. They also flew as far east as Uganda and the Congo. About four months were spent on safari: from 1 September to 13 October, and from about 1 November to 15 January.

1953

22 August, Saturday: Hemingways arrive in Mombasa, on the *SS Dunnottar Castle*, having journeyed two weeks from Marseille "up the Mediterranean, through the Suez Canal, and around the Horn of Africa to Mombasa" (Reynolds, *Final Years*, 266). They stay in the Manor Hotel (Mary Hemingway, 341).
23 August: Depart Mombasa, to spend a week in Philip Percival's Kitanga Farm, near Machakos in the Kajiado district (Kenya), where the Hemingways meet their safari staff and are joined by Mayito Menocal, Earl Theisen, and Denis Zaphiro.
1 September: Depart Kitanga Farm and set up their first safari camp, by the Salengai River, Kajiado District. They see many elephants, shoot a rhino and track the wounded beast on the first day.
2 September: Find the dead rhino.
5 September: Stop at a Masai settlement, where they hear complaints about marauding lions.

6 September: Sight herds of elephants feeding.

9 September: Shoot lion (Mary Hemingway, 347).

10 September: Arrive at their second camp, at the foothills of Mount Kilimanjaro, in "a game reserve opened only to the Hemingway safari, for the government was determined to keep them supplied with abundant animals and ample photo opportunities" to reassure the world that in spite of the Mau Mau uprising, the area was safe for tourism (Reynolds, *Final Years*, 267). During the course of the safari "Hemingway was appointed acting game ranger of the concession, and managed the safari when Pop [Percival] left for personal business" (Boese, 114).

19 September: Move camp to Salengai River (in today's Rift Valley Province, Kenya).

ca. 22 September: Break camp, spend a night at "Olorgasa[i]lie Camp on the eastern edge of the Great Rift Valley" and continue through "the ugly, treeless town of Magadi" (Mary Hemingway, 356).

24 September: Set up camp in Figtree Camp (Baker, 517), in today's Masai Mara Game Reserve, Kenya.

4 October: Theisen departs for Nairobi and thence home to the United States, Mayito Menocal goes to hunt in Tanganyika, Percival departs for Kitanga Farm, the Hemingways remain at Fig Tree Camp.

13 October: Depart Fig Tree Camp, drive to Nairobi to stay with the Percivals: "we declared the first part of our safari formally ended" (Mary Hemingway, 361).

ca. 15 October: Hemingway flies by himself to Tanganyika to visit his son Patrick at John's Corner, staying there into November. At about this time, Mayito Menocal visits him there before departing for Cuba.

ca. 24–27 October. Mary and Percival drive to John's Corner to join Hemingway.

ca. 27–29 October: Mary and Hemingway with Patrick and his wife Henrietta (Mary Hemingway, 361).

Early November: Mary, Patrick, Percival, and Ernest Hemingway set up camp at the Bahora Flats of Ruaha River (Tanzania).

ca. 5 November: Rain forces them to break camp; they travel north to Kenya.

ca. 5–12 November: With Denis Zaphiro at Kajiado.

ca. 12 November: Set up camp at Kimana Swamp, which will be their base for the next fifty days (Mary Hemingway, 363). [I count sixty-plus days until 15 January.] Their safari guide is Zaphiro, with occasional visits from Percival.

5 December: Mary and Zaphiro kill a lion (Mary Hemingway, 363–64).

12 December: Mary and Ernest do an hour's aerial sightseeing with Roy Marsh, who flies Mary to Nairobi for Christmas shopping.

15 December: Hemingway kills a leopard at noon, takes Debba and her friends into Loitokitok (Kenya), buys them dresses and then, back in the camp, parties with them.

ca. 16 December:[6] Mary returns to camp and "found that Ernest had been going native with a vengeance," dyeing his clothes and going hunting with a spear (Baker, 518).

19 and 20 December: Hemingway writes entries in Mary's diary celebrating their sex life.

21 December: Mary and Hemingway visit the Wakamba village where Debba lives, but don't see her (Mary Hemingway, 370).

24 December: Preparations for Christmas guests.

25 December: The Hemingways' Christmas party is attended by William Hale, Denis Zaphiro, Debba, her aunt, their safari staff of thirteen, and other visiting Wakamba and Masai (Mary Hemingway, 371).

30 December: Hale departs, appointing Hemingway honorary game warden (Mary Hemingway, 372).

31 December: "They marked New Year's Eve quietly with tea and mince pies, brought down by the Percivals" (Baker, 518).

1954

1 January: Hemingway receives "a beautiful King's stick . . . carved from the Altiasiga tree . . . The elders of the local tribes carry such sticks as emblems of their authority" (Mary Hemingway, 373).

15 January: Safari ends, the Hemingways leave Kimana for Nairobi.

15–21 January: In Nairobi.

21 January: Aerial sightseeing tour: "they took off from West Nairobi airport . . . with Roy Marsh at the controls. . . . They flew southwest to Figtree Camp . . . explored the Rift Escarpment from the air, and marveled at the color of Lake Natron, pink with immense flocks of flamingoes. That afternoon they turned west over Ngorongoro Crater and the Serengeti Plain. . . . They set down briefly at Mwanza [Tanzania] to refuel, and by sundown had reached [Lake] Kivu" (between Congo and Rwanda). They spent the night at Bukavu (eastern Congo) (Baker, 519).

22 January: Aerial tour continues: "they turned north, threading the chain of Lakes Edward, George, and Albert, and descending that evening at Entebbe on the northwest shore of [Lake] Victoria Nyanza" (Baker, 519).

23 January: Aerial tour continues: "they saw the White Nile . . . and detoured eastward along the Victoria Nile," the lakes and the Murchison Falls, where they had their first crash; Hemingway hurt his back, right arm, and shoulder, and Mary suffered two cracked ribs (Baker, 519; Reynolds, *Final Years*, 272–73). They spend the night outdoors.

24 January: They are taken aboard the *Murchison*, on which they reach Butiaba (Uganda) late that afternoon. There they board "a twelve-seater De Havilland Rapide . . . to fly . . . to Entebbe." Attempting takeoff, the plane catches fire; both are seriously injured while escaping the burning plane, Hemingway suffering a broken skull, two crushed lumber vertebrae, multiple internal injuries (kidney, liver, intestines), burns, and smoke inhalation, and Mary an injured knee. A policeman drives them to Masindi, where they spend the night at the Railway Hotel (Baker, 520–21; Reynolds, *Final Years*, 273–74).

25 January: Drive one hundred miles to Entebbe.

26 January: Patrick arrives at Entebbe.

28 January: Hemingway is flown to Nairobi for treatment.

2 February: Hemingway flies from Nairobi to fishing camp, suffers burns at fishing camp.

17 February: Start fishing the Pemba Channel, living in Shimoni (southeastern Kenya, near the Tanzania border).

ca. 8 March: Depart fishing camp.

10 March: Depart Mombasa for Venice on *SS Africa*.

Notes

[1] The name of today's Tanzanian town of Mto wa Mbu translates as "River of Mosquitoes" or "Mosquito River." Founded in the late 1920s, it was an oasis village encampment when the Hemingways camped there (or nearby). It is about 120 km from Arusha.

[2] Today Mbulumbulu is one of the thirteen administrative wards in the Karatu District of the Arusha Region of Tanzania.

[3] Babati is now a district in the Manyara Region of Tanzania.

[4] Gallapo is in the Kongwa District of the Dodoma Region of Tanzania, to the south of Manyara.

[5] Tanga Region is on the eastern coast of Tanzania; Tanga is the country's most northerly seaport city (near Kenya).

[6] Mary writes that she returned to camp the day after the leopard was killed (368), which would be the 16th. A collect cable sent from Nairobi and signed Papa and Mary arrived in New York at 8:49 AM, 17 December; it may have been sent by Marsh, who flew her back to camp on the 16th ("the next day") and received instructions to send the cable when he returned to Nairobi, which he probably did late on the 16th or on the 17th.

Works Cited and Consulted

Baker, Carlos. *Ernest Hemingway: A Life Story.* 1969. New York: Collier Macmillan, 1988.

Boese, Gil K. "*Under Kilimanjaro:* The Other Hemingway." *Hemingway Review* 25, no. 2 (2006): 114–18.

Bruccoli, Matthew J., ed., with the assistance of Robert W. Trogdon. *The Only Thing That Counts: The Ernest Hemingway–Maxwell Perkins Correspondence.* New York: Scribner's, 1996.

Chamberlin, Brewster, comp. "A (Preliminary) Chronology of the Life and Times of Ernest Hemingway." Key West Art and Historical Society (unpublished), compiled 2008, revised 2010.

Hemingway, Ernest. *Ernest Hemingway: Selected Letters 1917–1961.* Edited by Carlos Baker. New York: Scribner's, 1981.

Hemingway, Mary. *How It Was.* New York: Knopf, 1976.

Hemingway, Pauline Pfeiffer. *1933–1934 Diary of Safari to Africa with Ernest Hemingway.* M1344, Department of Special Collections and University Archives, Stanford University Libraries, Stanford, California.

Martin, Lawrence H. "Safari in the Age of Kenyatta." *Hemingway Review* 25, no. 2 (2006): 101–6.

Reynolds, Michael. *An Annotated Chronology: An Outline of the Author's Life and Career, Detailing Significant Events, Friendships, Travels, and Achievements.* Omni Chronology Series 1. Detroit: Omnigraphics, 1991.

———. *Hemingway: The Final Years.* New York: Norton, 1999.

———. *Hemingway: The 1930s.* New York: Norton, 1997.

Introduction

Miriam B. Mandel

ERNEST HEMINGWAY WAS PERHAPS the most peripatetic of the authors who shaped American literature. He traveled at home and abroad, on ship, train, car, and plane, spending a good bit of time not just on the travel itself but also on the myriad details that attend it: checking timetables, booking passage, obtaining visas, making reservations at hotels, arranging for letters of credit and money in various currencies, requesting and organizing payment for fishing permits, hunting licenses, and tickets for bullfights, making arrangements for the handling of personal mail, bills, and, even more important, manuscripts, publishing contracts, and page proofs that needed to be mailed back and forth within set deadlines. He also supervised details like the ordering and proper packing of the necessary hunting and fishing gear and, another important item in Hemingway's travels, the boxes and trunks of books that always accompanied him.

Hemingway was interested in and careful about all these details, as we learn from his letters to his friends, in which he reports how busy he is with arrangements, comments on the equipment he is acquiring, updates them on his frequently modified itineraries, instructs them how best to write or cable him (usually through his bank or his editor, Max Perkins), and urges them to meet up with him somewhere. Traveling so often and so much, checking in and out of hotel rooms and rented apartments, hunting or fishing for months on end and, in addition, frequently derailed by marital and romantic complications, periodic bouts of depression, a series of serious accidents, and frequent fevers and infections — where did this man find the time and concentration needed for reading and writing? But somehow, in spite of or more probably because of the chaos and upheaval that characterized so much of his life, he read entire libraries on a variety of subjects and wrote poetry, a play, two volumes of journalism, five books of nonfiction,[1] nine novels, and about fifty short stories, many of them masterpieces.

Travel is of course a complex process: one leaves one place or condition in order to reach another, but what is one seeking? The leaving of a place might be what motivates the journey (as in, I need to get away from this heat and humidity), the specific destination might be what drives it (I have to get to Spain by May), or it might be that the journey itself — that indeterminate, fertile, liminal space of change and process, of becoming instead of being — is in fact what one needs and seeks. In the case of Hemingway, for whom travel was a major occupation and preoccupation, all three factors — the starting or "home" place, the destination or "away" place, and the travel itself — need to be considered, for they help us understand what and how he wrote.

The places that Hemingway left — that is, his homes in the United States and Cuba — are curiously underrepresented in his books. But the countries that he came to, especially Italy, Spain, and France, are quite familiar territory to his readers, for they provide the settings for much of his work. For an author who repeatedly said that he invented out of knowledge, this is odd, because these European countries were the places that he knew the least, the places that he knew only as a visitor, a guest, a foreigner. It is also odd — and very interesting — that these away-from-home places themselves eventually became, like his home places, points of departure, as Hemingway went on to explore one country after another. It may be that as Hemingway acquired the idiom and learned the history and customs of a new locale, as he developed homely habits and a history of his own in it — in short, as it became more familiar and started to approximate the stable condition of "home" — it became a site he needed to leave. If to Robert Frost home is the place one can always come back to,[2] for Hemingway it is the place that one always has to leave.

This holds true for every place except Africa. On his first safari (to the Colony and Protectorate of Kenya and to Tanganyika Territory, today's Kenya and Tanzania), Hemingway can't get enough of Africa: "Now, being in Africa, I was hungry for more of it" (*Green Hills of Africa*, 73). So much so that even while he is there, he dreads going away: "All I wanted to do now was get back to Africa. We had not left it, yet, but when I would wake in the night I would lie, listening, homesick for it already" (72). Knowing that at some point soon he will certainly have to leave, he vows to return: "I would come back to Africa" (285). And years later, when he does return, he realizes that "I never knew of a morning in Africa when I woke that I was not happy" and concludes that "I had been a fool not to have stayed on in Africa" (*Under Kilimanjaro*, 16, 205).

The journey that took Hemingway from his view of home as a place or condition that he needs to leave to the recognition that Africa is a place or condition that he wants *not* to leave, is a long and complicated one — long enough, in fact, to permit us to see, retrospectively, the many repetitions and variations that give it shape, rhythm, and definition. To unravel its complications, we must start at the beginning, looking at the places that were Hemingway's homes: the points of departure.

Hemingway's Homes

Oak Park (1899–1919). Hemingway was born, on 21 July 1899, in the family home headed by his widowed maternal grandfather, Ernest Hall, at 439 North Oak Park Avenue, Oak Park, Illinois. "Abba" (Hebrew for father) Hall died in May 1905, and eighteen months later the family moved to a larger eight-bedroom home, not far away, that had been designed by Hemingway's multitalented mother[3] at 600 North Kenilworth Avenue. Here he lived with his parents and five siblings, with his paternal grandparents around the corner, until he graduated from high school and left home, soon after his eighteenth birthday, to work as a cub reporter for the *Kansas City Star* and go to his first war. In January 1919 he returned to Oak Park as a veteran of that war, to recover from his emotional and physical wounds. But he had no intention of staying there: he chafed to get away.

Key West (the 1930s). After an eventful decade spent largely in Europe (discussed below), Hemingway settled in Key West, Florida, and bought, in April 1931, the home at 907 Whitehead Street where he lived with his second wife, Pauline, and their sons, Patrick and Gregory, for almost a decade. (The house was financed by Pauline's wealthy uncle, Gustavus Adolphus Pfeiffer.[4]) Every year, Hemingway traveled from Key West to a variety of destinations: Wyoming and Montana (for the hunting), Arkansas (to visit Pauline's family), Cuba and its waters (for the fishing), Europe (especially Spain, for the bullfights), and East Africa (for his first safari). As his marriage to Pauline foundered, his absences from the Key West home became more frequent.

San Francisco de Paula (the 1940s and 1950s). By 1939, Hemingway and his new love interest, Martha Gellhorn, were renting and refurbishing the Finca Vigía (Lookout Farm), a lovely hilltop estate near the village of San Francisco de Paula, about a half hour's drive from Havana. Here he lived more than twenty years, longer than anywhere else, first with Gellhorn, who became his third wife, and then with Mary Welsh, his fourth wife. From Cuba, Hemingway traveled the world, not only revisiting his favorite European countries but also going as far east as China, as far south as Peru, and as far away as Africa (for the second safari).[5]

Ketchum. In 1958, recognizing that political problems might force him to leave Cuba, Hemingway rented first one and then another house in Ketchum, Idaho, before buying, in April 1959, the large, graceless Topping house (400 Canyon Run Boulevard), where he finally succeeded in killing himself on 2 July 1961.[6]

All of these homes, from Oak Park to Ketchum, were large and comfortable, with rooms for servants and for work. In Oak Park his mother had a large music room and his father a doctor's reception room cum medical library. Hemingway himself always had a study or office of his own in which to write. In Cuba, he actually had four: his bedroom (where he wrote standing up), his study, a library with a large desk, and a third-floor study in a separate building, which his wife set up for him but which he seldom used. All these handsome homes have been carefully preserved, restored, and declared museums or historic landmarks, enabling us to see where and how Hemingway lived and worked for fifty years. Reading his homes, and particularly the three homes that he himself bought, we would conclude that in adulthood Hemingway sought or needed the same suburban comfort and ease his parents had enjoyed, that he wanted a family home in a small community that would provide a stable framework like the one that dominated his formative years.

But in fact, such frameworks irked Hemingway from the very beginning. He broke with Oak Park, his parents, and their values as soon as he could, choosing, for example, not to go to college, as most of his family (including his grandmothers) had done. As an adult, he did not go to church regularly, he married and divorced with shocking frequency, he did not have a "regular job" but instead drank, fished, and traveled extravagantly. He rejected the Victorian strictures imposed by the self-consciously virtuous Village (its official denomination) of Oak Park so vehemently that after he left home, he seldom returned to it. But, as Michael Reynolds pointed out, "Oak Park culture and standards [had] for good or ill . . . become a part of him" ("Oak Park," 34).[7] And so, although he did not go to college, he embarked upon a lifelong course of reading and study. He left his parents' Protestantism, but, as Philip Melling and Erik Nakjavani demonstrate in their essays in this book, he struggled to define a system of belief or ethics. He did not live with one spouse all his life, as Oak Park decreed, but he did not feel comfortable outside marriage, as evidenced by the fact that he was married for all of his adult life, acquiring the next wife as soon as the divorce from the previous one was final. He didn't have a "job," but he got up early every day to write, keeping careful and public track of his productivity and earnings.

Even this briefest of overviews indicates that although Hemingway was uncomfortable in his first home and left it early, his subsequent homes all reflect not just its physical comforts but also a great many of its cultural values. He rejected home but he carried — probably he could not help but carry — Oak Park's and his family's habits with him.

The Oak Park Legacy: Traveling Away from Home

One of those habits was travel. Hemingway was not quite one year old when his parents first took him and his older sister Marcelline away from their home in Oak Park to their new summer cottage in the Upper Peninsula, Michigan. In 1900, such travel was complicated, requiring much advance planning and packing. Marcelline provides details:

The trip, an arduous one, began on the lake steamer *State of Ohio*, which took us from Chicago to Harbor Springs. Here my parents carried their luggage aboard the local train bound for Petoskey; in Petoskey they again unloaded and changed cars for the train to the village of Walloon Lake, where for the last time they tugged out their luggage and transferred it to the little steamer which took them up the lake. This was to be our itinerary for many summers to come. (Sanford, 68)

This annual multistage transplantation took Hemingway away from the busy, tightly scheduled indoor life of home, school, and church, to a more leisured, more pastoral outdoor life devoted to hunting, fishing, farming, and exploring — a life more typical of the nineteenth century that he and his parents were born into than of the twentieth century with which we tend to identify him. Although Michigan is an American setting, for Hemingway it was very much an "away" place, for it signified entry into another time: the slow, rural, romantic past, still populated by Indians and Indian lore, or perhaps a more abstract, Edenic garden that provided privacy, enabled introspection, and offered respite from family constraints and obligations. Bernice Kert writes: "If the prevailing tone on Oak Park Boulevard was Victorian propriety, at Windemere [the lakeside cottage] it was an exultant freedom" (28). Since Michigan was a place repeatedly visited, it eventually became a repository of memories and a site of nostalgia for his own earliest innocence, romance, and freedom, all necessarily lost in time.

Trips to Nantucket, Massachusetts, were also a tradition in the family. In 1909, Grace took her firstborn, Marcelline, to Nantucket. In 1910, she took Ernest and, subsequently and one by one, three more of her children. This was a longer trip, by boat, train, and steamer, that she undertook to expose them to the ocean, to the suffragette movement (many lecturers on women's rights spoke in Nantucket), and to American history (in nearby Boston, Concord, and Lexington). Bernice Kert notes perceptively that "Ernest's first effort at fiction followed the Nantucket holiday" (38–39).[8]

Travel stimulated Hemingway, and travel to the past became a habit with him. In fact, throughout his life he consistently left home to visit and revisit an away place that was less rigid, less industrialized, more removed from modern bustle, more free. Just as he went away from Oak Park to sojourn in Michigan, so he went from Key West to other, more isolated Keys and to the Gulf Stream and, from 1928 onward, to ranches and lodges in the American West.[9] In Cuba, he found a local away place in the small fisherman's village of Cojímar where he moored his cabin cruiser, befriended the local fishermen, and set out on extended fishing trips (the *Pilar* could comfortably sleep crew, family, and guests).[10] Following the pattern established in Michigan, he returned to all these "get away" places often.

It is these places of temporary habitation, and not the owned, lived-in, more demanding permanent home places, that become settings for the work set in Hemingway's two home countries, the United States and Cuba. The first stories that Hemingway published — "Up in Michigan" (*Three Stories and Ten Poems*, 1923), "The Three Day Blow," "The End of Something," "Indian Camp," "The Doctor and the Doctor's Wife," "Big Two-Hearted River" (*In Our Time*, 1925) — as well as his first published novel, *The Torrents of Spring* (1926), are set in Michigan, and not in Oak Park. To emphasize the awayness of this nonhome place, the settings of these works are not homes, but rather a vacation cabin, a cottage, a restaurant, a tent, a campsite, or the outdoors. In his next America-based work, *To Have and Have Not* (1937), the main character Harry Morgan lives in Key West, but the novel generally shows him elsewhere, visiting Havana or traveling and, finally, dying, on a boat. Hemingway set a few stories in the American West, and in these as well the protagonist is not only away from home but also in a place or situation that is, by definition, transient, like a hospital room ("The Gambler, the Nun, and the Radio") or on the road or visiting friends ("Wine of Wyoming"). And *The Old Man and the Sea*, Hemingway's only fully Cuban novel, begins and ends in Hemingway's getaway place, Cojímar, and its main character spends most of the novel on his skiff, constantly moving along the surface of the Gulf Stream. In these American and Cuban books, then, it is the away place, not the home place, that provides the setting. "Home" is banished from Hemingway's written work, even when that work is set in a country Hemingway lived in for decades on end.

This pointed absence of the permanent place of residence generally, and of Hemingway's own homes in particular,[11] invites the question of the relationship between the place of habitation and the place depicted in art. Some writers, like William Faulkner, need to stay put and to write about a place that, even if invented, descends from the familiar habitat. Other writers and artists, like James Joyce and Joan Miró, need to be elsewhere in order to be able to depict the home place that rules memory. Hemingway's frequent travels suggest that he too needed distance from his home places, but not in order to write about them. He wrote *at* home — he wrote everywhere — but he did not write *about* home. We can only speculate about why this is so,[12] but we can say with certainty that the lived-in home places are strikingly absent from his creative output, and that the visited or away places are just as insistently its focus. And the condition of travel — the liminal space between one place or condition and another — is no less central.

The Pattern of Travel

Hemingway's travels to his away places display striking similarities. The trip is usually envisioned as an extended absence from home, requiring extensive planning and serious amounts of luggage (which grow to mountainous size as Hemingway's finances improve); and it increasingly takes him farther away, to various European destinations and then to East Africa, the most away (in terms of distance and culture) of his many away places. Arrival at each new setting invariably elicits contagious enthusiasm for this "good country," and Hemingway exhorts his friends (via letters) and his readers (via sensuous descriptions of landscapes and adventures) to visit and see for themselves. Even before the crowds arrive, however, Hemingway himself has moved on to a new, farther away place.

An important aspect of Hemingway's travel is repetition. His first visit to his away places, whether in the United States, Cuba, or Europe, was generally followed by several closely spaced return visits, and, in the case of foreign countries, as we shall see below, by a second round of visits anywhere from twenty to thirty years after the first. When he returns to these places, he finds them quite changed, not only because of the passage of time but also because of his own writing about them: Pamplona after *The Sun Also Rises* is not what it was when Hemingway first saw it. And Hemingway himself is not the same: he is richer, more famous, has a new wife and, unfortunately, worse health.

In both the earlier and later periods of his life, Hemingway's European settings — Italy, France, and Spain — mark stages in the journey that culminated in Kenya. Both the first and second time that Hemingway went to Africa, he traveled through these other important countries of his biography, as if recapitulating or retracing the several stages of his repeated journeys away from home or from those places that, as they become familiar through repeated visits and increased knowledge of their language, literature, and history, threaten to become home. This pattern I have outlined is not without exceptions and irregularities, but it is a pattern, and a strong one.

The complicated, frequent, time-consuming travel that interrupted the continuity of his home life did not, somehow, derail or disrupt his creative life. And the foreign getaway places, doubly antithetical to home, became central to his work. Italy, France, Spain, and Eastern Africa each became the setting for at least two books, the first the result of his initial encounters with the new setting, and the second one, colored by nostalgia, of the visits of his middle and late years. Here also a pattern emerges. The first or earlier books of each pair were written relatively soon and relatively quickly, and were all published within nine years, between 1926 and 1935. The later books were written more slowly, over a period of twenty years, and some were published posthumously. Although the earlier and later books that emerge from each country are separated by decades, they are strikingly connected to each other, not just in terms of setting but also in terms of the definition and situation of the main characters. Beatriz Penas Ibáñez argues, elsewhere and in the essay we include in this book, that the later book is often a reexamination or a comment on the first.

Rejection of Oak Park: Travel to Foreign Lands

Hemingway's away places have become permanently associated with him (biographers study Pamplona to find Hemingway) and with his main characters (for readers, Pamplona inevitably recalls Jake Barnes, Brett Ashley, and Robert Cohn). But the association is, in fact, accidental and impermanent: there is no necessary, legal, or lasting connection between the author or character and the setting. Just as Hemingway was not Spanish, so his main characters are seldom French, Italian, Spanish, or African. Instead, they are (mostly) Americans who intend to keep that citizenship, although they have left their homes and countries and are now abroad, somewhere or other. They generally like where they are, but they have no intention of staying there. For most of the time we spend with them, they are unsettled, in transit, ready to move on to the next city or battlefield or bullfight festival or hunting site or fishing spot. They are sojourners — a less kind word would be *drifters* — and not expatriates, or people who have decided to settle down in a foreign country.[13] Having gone abroad, they wander quite readily from one foreign city and country to another, almost indefinitely, and not more than a handful of them finally decide to go back home. If and when they do, they are unable to live there.[14]

These characters' housing, like their lives, is impermanent: they eat, sleep, make love, and part from each other in commandeered villas, rented apartments, hotel rooms, bars, hospitals, gondolas, sailboats, trains, caves, and tents. While abroad, they even tend to die in impermanent places — in an impersonal, inefficient Swiss hospital (Catherine Barkley) — or, even more often, while traveling: in Spain, Robert Jordan is doomed to face an enemy bullet when his horse falls on him; in Italy, Colonel Cantwell has his fatal heart attack in the back seat of a car; in France, Thomas Hudson's two sons and their mother are killed in a car crash.

As we noted earlier, three factors define travel — the place of departure, the place of arrival, and the space or condition that exists between them. But in Hemingway's art, home (the place of departure) is absent, and the destination (the place of arrival) inevitably and very quickly becomes a place of departure; departure is practically built into arrival. Of the three factors, then, only two are visible: the away place, and the travel that leads away from it to the next away place. By means of characters that are insistently (one is tempted to use the word *permanently*) unsettled and transient, Hemingway was able to investigate the matters and mores that necessarily attend the concept of home: matters of civil, familial, social, political, sexual, and religious responsibility.

These matters, and the institutions that have been devised to regulate them, were first defined for Hemingway in Oak Park, where family and church were closely intertwined and where the values of one generation were accepted by the next. Hemingway and his parents lived with his grandfather, Ernest Hall, "a gentle, godly man who worshipped on Sundays at Grace Episcopal Church, knelt on the Brussels carpet in the parlor to lead evening prayer, and softly asked the blessing at the dinner table" (Baker, 2). His daughter supervised bedtime prayers and made sure that her children went regularly to church and participated in church activities. Hemingway's paternal grandfather, Anson Tyler Hemingway, who lived nearby, was also a religious man: he founded the Chicago YMCA and served as its general secretary for ten years. Anson's son Clarence (Ed) not only adopted these attitudes but also, in 1920, pressed his own son "to associate with YMCA men, strong Christians all" (qtd. in Mandel, *Complete Annotations*, 472). Hemingway joined, but not happily.

Early and consistently, Hemingway chafed at the values that Oak Park, like most of middle-class America, rather rigidly subscribed to at that time. In today's parlance, he was at odds with that normative narrative, although he could not absolutely discard it. The resultant discordance and discomfort led to an examination of marriage and church, the institutions on which the Oak Park concept of home rested. To achieve as clear and uncontaminated an attitude towards them as possible, Hemingway took them out of their original context via transplanted characters living elsewhere, anywhere *but* home. By going away, his characters have achieved some degree of detachment from home; and by refusing to settle in their host countries, they avoid attachment to them as well. And so we have American characters and narrators that are in Italy, in France, in Spain, and, finally, in Kenya and Tanganyika. East Africa offered maximum distance from Middle America's powerful normative narrative. And the safari situation, being the most unsettled, made the least demands in these areas. It is not surprising, then, that Africa became for Hemingway (via his self-referent narrators) the one place that he insisted he did not need or want to leave.

Africa not only broke or ended the centrifugal pattern of travel I have suggested, it also broke a self-imposed taboo. Reynolds was among the first to notice that "Oak Park remains beneath the surface, invisible and inviolate. It was his first world . . . the one he never wrote about" (*Young Hemingway*, 5, 15). That absence, as Hemingway's own iceberg theory insists, is meaningful. When the full text of *Under Kilimanjaro* was published, several years after Reynolds's death, an oblique reference to his childhood in Oak Park surfaced. This suggests that, having achieved the ultimate away place, the place that one does *not* have to leave, Hemingway was free or able to write about "his first world," albeit briefly and indirectly.

Before we come full circle to Oak Park, however, a look at Hemingway's European travels will clarify his insistent and intensifying need not just to travel to an away place (repeating the experience of Oak Park) but to travel to a different, farther and farther away place (rejecting the experience of Oak Park). Looking at these factors as they recur in his European travels and writings will help us understand how and why Africa generally and the African safari in particular are so central to our understanding of Hemingway's life and work.

Italy: Two Rounds of Visits, 1918 and 1948[15]

In 1917, the young Hemingway's aim to join the war effort was frustrated by defective vision in his left eye. Unable to enlist, he accepted the suggestion of his friend, Theodore Brumback, who had lost the sight of one eye in an accident, that he volunteer, as Brumback had already done, for the Red Cross ambulance service on the Italian front. The ploy worked, and in May 1918, Hemingway sailed for Europe on the *SS Chicago*.[16] He served in northern Italy, was wounded at Fossalta di Piave on 8 July 1918, and recovered at the American Red Cross Hospital in Milan, falling in love with Agnes von Kurowsky in the process. By January 1919, he was well enough to be discharged. His outlook was now international, his affection for Italy strong, and, repeating the pattern established in Michigan, he returned to Italy often, for short visits in 1922, 1923, and 1927.

Hemingway didn't marry the girl he met in Italy, nor did he settle down in Italy or even make a gesture in that direction. By 1922 he was living in Paris, in 1923 he discovered Spain and the Spanish bullfight, and by the late 1920s he was in love with the Gulf Stream. Italy was his first European away setting. It gave him enough material for several Italian stories and his first and great Italian novel, *A Farewell to Arms*, published in 1929. He left it long before it could become home.

In 1948, thirty years after his first exposure to Italy, Hemingway returned, this time with his fourth wife, Mary. The pattern was the same — a long first visit (from September 1948 to the end of April 1949) followed by shorter ones (about two months in 1950, six weeks in 1954), followed by a novel — but the style was different: this time, Hemingway arrived with a major reputation, abundant luggage, and a brand-new chauffeur-driven car. Hemingway showed Mary the places of his youth and, not incidentally, became infatuated with the eighteen-year-old Adriana Ivancich. All this welter of military nostalgia, lavish lifestyle, and middle-aged romance with youth drives his second Italian novel, *Across the River and into the Trees*, published twenty-one years after the first.

Hemingway's two Italian novels bear a strong family resemblance. Both are set in northern Italy and both feature an American military man who was or is wounded on the battlefield. Both male protagonists have good Italian friends, and both are in love with a non-American girl. In both novels the love affair is central, and the lovers, lacking a home, conduct it in hospitals, restaurants, hotels, small rented boats, and even a gondola. The novels end with the death of one of the lovers. The American protagonists do not return home, either to start a new life or to be buried. These are novels not just of displacement but also of loss.

France: Two Rounds of Visits, 1922 and 1944

On 3 September 1921 Ernest Hemingway married Hadley Richardson, and early in 1922 they went to Europe. He had thought of going back to Italy but, upon Sherwood Anderson's advice, they went to Paris instead.

The so-called Paris years offer a dizzying itinerary of travel to many away places that became the settings for a great deal of fine prose. In 1922, as a freelance foreign correspondent for the *Toronto Star*, Hemingway went to Italy for the Genoa Economic Conference, to Constantinople (now Istanbul) to cover the Greco-Turkish War, and to Switzerland for the Lausanne Peace Conference. To this work-related travel, the couple added vacations: in May and June they hiked in Switzerland, Austria, and Italy; in August they undertook a month-long mountain hike in Bavaria. In the winter of 1922–1923 they skied in Chamby, Switzerland. From February to April, they traveled in Italy: Milan, Genoa, Rapallo, Orbotello, Sirmione, back to Milan, and on to Cortina d'Ampezzo. In March, Hemingway returned to Paris once, and to Germany twice (both times by himself); in April he was back in Cortina d'Ampezzo to pick up Hadley and return to their rented apartment in Paris.

By now, the condition of "home" was approaching, or encroaching: when they returned to Paris, Hadley was three months pregnant. But Hemingway did not slow or settle down. Instead, he set out for a new country, going, in May 1923, to Spain to see bullfights in the company of a friend, Robert McAlmon. By early June he was back in Paris, early in July he returned to Spain (this time with Hadley), and in August they sailed for Canada, where their son, John Nicanor, was born (10 October 1923). At the end of December Hemingway quit his job with the *Toronto Star*, and by the beginning of 1924 the family was on its way back to France; that year they also went back to Spain for the bullfights and to Austria for the skiing, their traveling seemingly unimpeded by the baby (they took a nursemaid).

Travel, movement, and change dominated the next two years, 1925 to 1927. Hemingway fell in love with Pauline Pfeiffer, divorced Hadley, married Pauline (May 1927) and, throughout, continued to travel: a quick trip to New York to negotiate and sign contracts with Scribner's, his new publisher (this involved two trans-Atlantic crossings within three weeks); long winter vacations skiing, first in Austria with Hadley (winter 1926) and then in Switzerland with Pauline (winter 1927); and long summers, lasting into the fall, going to bullfights throughout Spain. From 1923 to 1927, then, Paris gave way to Spain as the away place of choice. Paris had become too domestic: the rented apartment where he lived with Hadley (and the baby) and the much more elegant apartment he shared with Pauline were increasingly abandoned for life in Spanish hotels and pensions, as the fiestas and ferias took him from one city to another. This peripatetic life style was one of the many attractions of Spain.

In spite of — or, more probably, because of — these many geographic and emotional dislocations and displacements, Hemingway established himself as an author during what were actually mostly the *not*-Paris years,[17] publishing (in addition to his journalism) two novels (*The Torrents of Spring* and *The Sun Also Rises*, both in 1926) and three books of short stories: *Three Stories and Ten Poems* in July 1923, *In Our Time* in October 1925, and *Men Without Women* in October 1927. Hemingway's many away places, both in the United States and through so much of Europe, had made their way into literature.

In March 1928, Pauline and Ernest Hemingway returned to the United States. The move was precipitated by their desire to have their son, Patrick, born in the States (he arrived on 28 June 1928) and their decision to live in Key West, Florida. France faded from Hemingway's life: in subsequent visits to Europe, in 1929 and 1931, he visited that country only briefly, for the focus had shifted to Spain and the research he needed to finish *Death in the Afternoon* (1932). In late 1933 and early 1934, France was just a stop on the way to and from Africa; and in 1937 and 1938, again, Paris was only a stopover on Hemingway's journeys to Spain to cover the Spanish Civil War. The first round of visits to France had ended.

It was not until 1944–1945, more than twenty years after his first encounter with Paris, that Hemingway returned to France. As happened with the return visits to Italy, the first visit was the longest, lasting roughly eight months, from July 1944 to March 1945. By now, he had divorced Pauline, was separating from his third wife, Martha Gellhorn, and was in love with Mary Welsh, who became his fourth wife.

The by-now obligatory subsequent visits were, as usual, shorter: Hemingway and Mary were in France again in November and December of 1949; they drove through France to Spain in 1953 (three or four days) and 1954 (one day) before and after their African safari; and they returned for a couple of weeks in 1956, on their way to Spain to see bullfights. In 1959 Hemingway went briefly to Paris and to Aigues-Mortes and Le Grau-du Roi (in Provence) to check details for his two France-based books, both written in the last years of his life and published posthumously: *A Moveable Feast* in 1964 (a longer version appeared in 2009) and *The Garden of Eden* in 1986.

Like the Paris sections of *The Sun Also Rises*, these French books are set in the 1920s, the years of Hemingway's first exposure to France. Both are narratives of physical and emotional displacement: they have multiple settings (France and Austria for *Feast*, France and Spain for *Garden*) and in both the love interest shifts from married monogamy to sexual adventures among a threesome to the destruction of the marriage and the protagonist's commitment to the other woman, who in both cases enters the plot through her relationship with the wife.

France, where Hemingway decided to drop journalism in favor of creative writing, produced books featuring young male American writers living abroad and moving from one away place to another as they learn their craft. We see them working through memory to write about places they have left behind: in *Feast*, we read about the writing of a story we recognize as being set many years earlier, in Michigan ("Big Two Hearted River") and in *Garden* the story being written is set in Africa, where the protagonist spent much of his childhood. Because these characters have no real home, we see them in friends' homes, in hotels, cafes, bookshops, restaurants, cars, the streets, or the outdoors. Both writer-protagonists rent a work room for themselves that is even farther removed from home or domestic life than the foreign, temporary rented quarters that they share with their wives. They definitely need impermanence, transience, and solitude in order to think and write.

Spain: Two Rounds of Visits, 1923 and 1953

By now, the remarkably consistent pattern of repetition is quite visible. Just as the suggestion to volunteer for the Red Cross, which first brought Hemingway to Italy, was sparked by his friend Theodore Brumback, and his first trip to Paris was the result of Sherwood Anderson's recommendation, so Hemingway's first trip to Spain was undertaken on the advice of friends: Gertrude Stein and Alice B. Toklas recommended the bullfight to him and in May 1923, as we have noted, he acted on their advice. As he always did when he found a new away place, Hemingway soon returned to Spain: in July 1923 and 1924, with Hadley, and in 1925, with Hadley and a group of friends (who were fictionalized in *The Sun Also Rises*). In 1927, 1929, and 1931, Hemingway (now married to Pauline) visited Madrid, Pamplona, Valencia, and the other cities on the bullfight calendar, which runs from early spring until October. By 1933, with his big bullfight book written and published, he was ready for a new away place. This time, he paused only briefly in Spain, seeing just a few bullfights before traveling on to Africa.

Political events, his deteriorating home life, and a new romance combined to draw Hemingway back to Spain in 1937 and 1938. Still married to Pauline but accompanied by Martha Gellhorn, Hemingway made four trips to Spain to report on the Spanish Civil War for the North American Newspaper Alliance. He visited Barcelona, Madrid, Teruel, Gandesa, Tortosa, Segorbe, and other places involved in the fighting. After the fall of Spain's Second Republic in 1939, Hemingway went into a self-imposed exile from Spain that lasted seventeen years.

In the early 1950s, thirty years after his first trip to Spain, Hemingway returned. At that point, the isolationist and isolated Spanish dictator Francisco Franco attempted to establish relations with the United States, the United States in turn extended its European Recovery Plan (the Marshall Plan) to Spain, and Spain permitted the construction of American military bases on Spanish soil.[18] American tourism to Spain picked up and late in 1953 Hemingway came for a one month visit on his way to Africa and, early in 1954, another month on his way back. His passion for the bullfight reawakened, he returned for another month in 1956 and for longer stints in 1959 and 1960 to gather material for his second nonfiction essay on the bullfight, published in three installments in *Life* and *Life en español* (1960 and 1961) and posthumously as a book, *The Dangerous Summer* (1985).

There can be no doubt that Hemingway loved Spain. But for all his intense involvement in the country's cultural and political life, he never considered settling down in any of the Spanish cities and towns that he admired. Quite the contrary: it was the nomadic lifestyle required of bullfight aficionados and war correspondents that attracted him. It exposed him to the different regions or "kingdoms" of Spain, each having, in the days before television and good roads, strongly differentiated cultural patterns. (Today, as defined by the post-Franco Constitution of 1978, they are called *comunidades autónomas*, autonomous communities.) Both the frequent travel and the repeated exposure to difference suited his needs, and the Spain he visited in the 1920s and 1930s yielded lively journalism, important stories like "The Undefeated," "Hills Like White Elephants," and "A Clean, Well-Lighted Place," as well as two major novels (*The Sun Also Rises* and *For Whom the Bell Tolls*), his first nonfiction book (*Death in the Afternoon*), and work in two new genres: the movie script for *The Spanish Earth* and his only full-length play, *The Fifth Column*.[19] The second round of visits, in the 1950s, produced *The Dangerous Summer*, the last work he supervised into print.

Hemingway's two Spain-based novels, published fourteen years apart, show striking similarities. Each features an American, apparently in his early or midthirties, who comes to Spain often and for long stretches: the one because he loves the Spanish bullfight, the other because he is a professor of Spanish literature. Both have learned to speak Spanish and both have internalized the violence and idealism central to the country's identity, as expressed in the bullfight, in one novel, and in the civil war, in the other. Both are terribly in love with a beautiful, short-haired non-American girl who is well acquainted with suffering; both endure terrible wounds (one before and the other during the action of the novel) that spell the end of the love affair. Much as they love Spain, neither has, or intends to have, a permanent home there: Jake Barnes lives in hotels in Pamplona and San Sebastian while holding onto his rented apartment in Paris, and Robert Jordan has meals in a cave, sleeps outdoors with Maria, and fantasizes their future together at the University of Montana at Missoula.

Hemingway's two Spanish nonfiction books are even more widely separated in time than the two Spanish novels: *Death in the Afternoon* appeared in 1932 and *The Dangerous Summer*, in its first incarnation, more than a quarter century later. But they are very closely related to each other: both present first-person American narrators who have an American wife vaguely in the background. Neither book gives us an intimate love story, as these narrators focus on the bulls and the bullfighters, but both do offer plenty of technical material, not just about the bullfight but also about the different regions of Spain: where to go and what to see, eat, and drink there. Both narrators are published authors, writers writing in English; both are happy to be in Spain, but only as visitors, living in rented apartments, hotel rooms, or the home of friends.

Our detour through Hemingway's European travels and writings reveals that travel — going away and then away again and again — is basic to Hemingway's life and work, a need that surfaced early and intensified over the years. Hemingway went away to Italy, then to France, and then to Spain, all before he published his first two novels, *Torrents of Spring* and *The Sun Also Rises*, in 1926, at age twenty-seven. During this time, and in the travel of his middle-age as well, his stays in each away city or town became shorter and shorter, for departure, change, and travel to the next away place had become dominant factors in his life.

Going Farthest Away: Africa

Hemingway's first African safari had a longer gestation than his first European trips, which were decided upon rather quickly. Hemingway had hunted birds and other small game most of his life, but when he went to Montana and Wyoming in 1928 he discovered big-game hunting (antelope, mountain sheep, elk, and bear).[20] When Pauline's generous Uncle Gus offered to underwrite an African safari for him, Pauline, and a couple of their friends, Hemingway immediately began planning the trip. In 1930, even as he was writing with enormous passion on Spain and bullfighting, his letters focus on hunting rifles, hunting licenses, and hunting guides. He was already reading up on the new subject, working out schedules and itineraries, convincing friends to come, and outfitting himself with new equipment.

The safari didn't happen in the spring or summer of 1930, and a badly broken right arm suffered in a car crash early in November put his "writing instrument" out of commission for almost six months.[21] This long interruption meant that he needed another full bullfight season in Spain to bring his research up to date: he was there from May to mid-September 1931. The next year, 1932, was also taken up with the postponed work on *Death in the Afternoon* and with writing the short stories for the collection that Scribner's insisted should follow it (*Winner Take Nothing*, 1933). Finally, in August 1933, after years of making and remaking travel plans, Hemingway sailed on the *Reina de la Pacifica* for Spain and, in November, sailed from Marseille to Mombasa on the *General Metzinger*. He landed in East Africa in early December and stayed until the end of February 1934.[22]

In the letters and journalism that followed this first safari, Hemingway showed the usual enthusiasm and the usual desire to return soon to this latest "good country." But this time, the long initial visit was not followed, as generally happened, by a series of return visits. The Spanish Civil War, the divorce from Pauline, the move to Cuba, the marriage to Martha, the Second World War (which took Hemingway away from Cuba for almost a year, from April 1944 to March 1945), the divorce from Martha, the marriage to Mary, the commercial ventures that fame brought him, the short stories, the play, the journalism, and four novels — *To Have and Have Not* (1937), *For Whom the Bell Tolls* (1940), *Across the River and Into the Trees* (1950), *The Old Man and the Sea* (1952) —all intervened. In all those twenty years between safaris, Hemingway continued to travel (he made fifteen transatlantic crossings and one trip to the Far East), but his imagination was not captured by any other new "good country." Africa was the last and best of those, and by 1952 he was chafing to return to it. But problems with the filming of *The Old Man and the Sea* delayed the trip, as did his aggressive negotiations with *Look* magazine, which finally offered $15,000 to cover the expenses of a safari and another $10,000 for a written report illustrated by *Look*'s photographer, Earl Theisen. Hemingway would have preferred to go on his own, but the magazine's offer was too attractive to pass up.

Hemingway's second trip to Africa, delayed even longer than the first, began in late June 1953. With Mary and "593 pounds of necessities stuffed into twenty-four pieces of baggage" (Reynolds, *Final Years*, 264), Hemingway sailed from New York to Le Havre, spent an emotional July in Spain (this was his first trip to Spain since the Civil War, and his first with Mary), and sailed for Mombasa early in August for what turned out to be an almost seven-month stay. It was a tense time: the colony was in the grip of the Mau Mau rebellion against the colonial government, and Jomo Kenyatta, who eventually became independent Kenya's first president in 1964, had been jailed just a few months before Hemingway arrived. Protests were widespread, frequent, and violent. But for Hemingway this was a good time: he was basking in the huge critical, popular, and financial success of *The Old Man and the Sea*, which, among other things, earned him the Pulitzer Prize in fiction one month before he began this journey eastward and strengthened his hopes for the Nobel. And he was, finally, in Africa again.

Although this second safari ended with two airplane crashes and serious burns and injuries, Hemingway wanted, as he usually did, a prompt return visit. In 1956, he was planning an itinerary that would take him through Spain and France on his way to Africa. But he was still affected by injuries from the plane crashes and suffering from practically chronic anemia, hypertension, elevated cholesterol, and other problems, all of them aggravated by alcohol abuse. Doctors advised against the trip, and political events — Egypt nationalized and then restricted travel through the Suez Canal, which complicated his itinerary — finally convinced him, in December 1956, to postpone the trip. Although he crossed the Atlantic again in 1959, he was at that time committed to *Life* magazine for a piece on the bullfight, and no African excursion was planned. By 1960 he was too ill to travel. The second safari was the last.

Hemingway's two African trips share several important characteristics: both were repeatedly postponed and delayed, both were funded by outside sources, both were preceded by European interludes, both began in the same city, Mombasa, both included trips to Nairobi and surrounding areas, both were begun in good health, and both were marred by medical emergencies (amoebic dysentery during the first safari, injuries from airplane crashes after the second). Both were capped by fishing vacations in Kenyan waters (one week's fishing on Lamu Island after the first safari, and about a month in the Pemba Channel, while staying in Shimoni village, after the second). Both were shared with a wife, and each time the wife kept a diary: Pauline's account of the first safari is still unpublished, Mary's diary of the second was incorporated into her memoir, *How It Was* (1976). On both safaris, Hemingway traveled with a friend as well as a wife: Charles Thompson in 1933–1934, and Mario (Mayito) Menocal in 1953–1954. Both safaris were supervised, in whole or in part, by Philip Percival. Hemingway's trips to Africa even share the same difference from Hemingway's other travels, in that the initial visit was not followed, soon after, by a cluster of return visits, as happened with the away places in Hemingway's home countries (the repeated visits to Michigan, the American West, and Cojímar) and with his trips abroad (the clusters of visits to Italy, France, and Spain).

The most important similarity is that the two safaris produced a large body of literature, considering the relatively short time that Hemingway spent there. The first yielded five *Esquire* articles (1934–1936), two of Hemingway's most famous stories, "The Snows of Kilimanjaro" and "The Short Happy Life of Francis Macomber," as well as a book-length narrative, *Green Hills of Africa*. The second produced a short essay, "Safari," with photographs by Earl Theisen, and a short story, "The Christmas Gift," both published in *Look* in 1954, as well as a long narrative that was eventually published, in varying forms, posthumously: "African Journal" appeared in three parts in *Sports Illustrated* in 1971–1972; *True at First Light: A Fictional Memoir*, edited by Patrick Hemingway, appeared in the Hemingway centennial 1999; and *Under Kilimanjaro*, the more complete version of the manuscript, edited by Robert W. Lewis and Robert E. Fleming, came out in 2005. The African safaris also produced the African stories that appear in *The Garden of Eden*, also published posthumously.

All this body of African work emerges from only two visits and a total of nine months that Hemingway spent on that continent. Some of that time, we need to remember, he spent in the cities of Mombasa and Nairobi, or in hospital, or fishing — so that Hemingway was actually in a hunting or safari situation, the sort he depicted in his Africa-based fiction and nonfiction, for a little less than six months.[23] When we compare this to the time spent in Italy, or France, or Spain, we realize that the African trips were, proportionately, perhaps the most productive of Hemingway's long lifetime of travel. What was there about Africa that unleashed this creativity?

Safari Vanquishes the Problem of Home

> Now the lion looked about him at the faces of all the nice people and he knew that he was at home but that he had also traveled. He was very happy.
>
> — Ernest Hemingway, "The Good Lion"

The African narratives are set in a land and situation that are about as far away as one can get, in space and outlook, from the dogmatic Victorian attitudes of Oak Park, and it might be that this distance enabled Hemingway to examine and perhaps even resolve the problem that had troubled him for much of his life — namely, the guilt caused by a lifestyle that looks and feels self-indulgent (lots of travel, reading, hunting, fishing, and drinking), parasitic (allowing someone else to pay for his house, cars, and safaris), and immoral (repeatedly falling in love with women not currently his wives). Hemingway lived a "liberated" modern life and repeatedly claimed that he enjoyed it, but that very insistence suggests the opposite: that he was still struggling against the concept of home, whose values diluted or undercut his pleasure in the lifestyle he had chosen. By writing about all places except home, he avoided the unwholesome prospect of a public rejection or condemnation of his own family, or the equally untenable procustean stance of self-rejection.

The African safari — *safari* is a Swahili word that means journey — is as far as one can get from the very concept of home. It is by definition composed of movement, travel, and impermanence. There is nothing else like it. Even when one is out fishing on the Gulf Stream and one's boat is in motion and its coordinates in flux, one actually lives in a homelike, fixed locale, gear and clothes unpacked and stowed away for the duration of the cruise. Following the bulls or the wars, one is less settled, staying in hotels for the duration of the event, then packing and traveling to the next hotel, feria after feria, battle after battle. And on an African safari, one lives an even less settled life, breaking camp and moving every few days to set up a new series of tents on another site.

On safari, one needs to attend to the details of travel almost constantly: deciding on time of departure and site of destination; packing guns, clothes, books and notebooks; supervising the dismantling of the tents and the loading of everything onto trucks and cars; discussing and deciding how best to manage the usually complicated terrain, and even suffering breakdowns and detours as one goes looking for the next "good country," which, as one knows, one will soon have to leave — because the rains will come or not come, or the animals no longer visit this salt lick, or simply because, once again, the next "good country" beckons. On safari, one's very dwelling is not only portable, constructed to be dismantled, but is also disjointed: one does not live in a tent, but goes from tent to tent to perform the various activities of one's life: there is a tent for cooking, another for sleeping, for dining, for bathing. Safari is the antithesis of home.

Safari denies not just the notion of home, but of place, even of an away place. Perhaps it is not a place at all, but a constant displacement: it represents the act of travel itself, the quintessential condition of impermanence, of departure and seeking. Although it demands a degree of cooperation and civility among fellow travelers, it is not based on the institutions (home, school, church) that society requires for its survival. For Hemingway, this absence of constraints was soothing and liberating. Oxymoronically, then, if being at home means that one doesn't need to look for another place or condition to be in, then the unsettled, liminal situation offered by the African safari was, to Hemingway's restless soul, home.

Hemingway seems to have sensed this during his first safari, when he wrote that he "loved this country and *I felt at home* and where a man feels at home, outside of where he's born, is where he's meant to go" (*Green Hills of Africa*, 283–84, my italics). He recognizes that he needs that feeling of home that Africa gives him: "I would come back to Africa. . . . I would come back to where it pleased me to live; to really live. Not just let my life pass. . . . I knew a good country when I saw one" (285).

Fig. I.1. On the second safari, Hemingway, Philip Percival (with pipe) and Mario (Mayito) Menocal (with hat) relax in the dining tent. The mosquito netting has been pulled aside at the front, for access.

Photo courtesy of John F. Kennedy Library.

Fig. I.2. Hemingway poses next to the bath tent; towels are stored in the basket visible in the foreground.

Photo courtesy Ernest Hemingway Collection / John F. Kennedy Presidential Library and Museum, Boston.

Fig. I.3. Hemingway grasps his rifle as Denis Zaphiro turns his Game Department Land Rover into a shallow ravine. Mary is wedged in between them; the gunbearers sit in the back.

Photo courtesy Ernest Hemingway Collection / John F. Kennedy Presidential Library and Museum, Boston.

Fig. I.4. Fording a stream, Hemingway and his gunbearer look down at the current, to ensure safe footing.

Photo courtesy Ernest Hemingway Collection / John F. Kennedy Presidential Library and Museum, Boston.

Fig. I.5. A comprehensive portrait of camp life.

Photo Courtesy of Earl Theisen Archives, Roxann Livingston / John F. Kennedy Library.

Fig. I.6. The dismantled tent — a recurring moment of transition that is emblematic of safari life.

Photo courtesy Ernest Hemingway Collection / John F. Kennedy Presidential Library and Museum, Boston.

In his second safari narrative, he again makes clear that he needs what Africa has to offer and concludes that "I had been a fool not to have stayed on in Africa" when he first came (*Under Kilimanjaro*, 205). In this book, Hemingway finally feels comfortable enough to break a lifelong silence about his first home: he has his autofictional narrator recall an event from his childhood, when his grandmother encouraged a grandson named Hemingway and repeatedly addressed as "Ern" to "do what you truly want to do" (giving him permission to indulge his desires) while at the same time promising him that "everything will be all right" (suggesting that there would be no conflict between desire and morality). Because she did that for him, the narrator tells us, he "loved my grandmother more than anyone in the world and more than I could love anyone ever again" (368).

This is an extraordinary episode, dealing as it does with the original biological family. Fathers and mothers do not figure largely in Hemingway's work, and when they do appear (mostly in the Nick Adams stories, set in Michigan), they are presented in a negative light. There are no good mothers, and even the most affectionately drawn father (in "Fathers and Sons") is not forgiven the ridiculously ineffectual advice he offers. Grandparents appear even less often, and in the few instances when they are recalled, they are far away, off-stage, and impersonal: in *A Farewell to Arms*, the grandfather simply sends money (76, 135), in *For Whom the Bell Tolls* he is recalled for the American Civil War stories he told (233, 339), and in *Green Hills of Africa* he is associated with disease: he had lived at a time when "Michigan was a malaria ridden state" (384). Grandmothers are even more scarce: Frederic Henry seems to be the only fictional character who had one (*Farewell*, 258).

In *Under Kilimanjaro*, however, the grandmother figure comes to the fore, and in the most positive way. She is the inspiration for the remarkable effort to establish a "new religion" that would combine freedom of action (like drinking and having several wives) with freedom from disapproval or punishment (the feeling that "everything will be all right") — conflicting freedoms that Oak Park could not countenance.

Nomadic safari life, which collapses the place of departure and the place of arrival into the creative and liberating impermanence of travel itself, offered Hemingway the cultural and emotional distance that this fugitive from home needed. Freeing him from the concept of home, safari life enabled reconciliation with the past and, more important, relief from the burden of internal conflict and guilt. It thus freed Hemingway to remember and even to write about Oak Park.

After his second safari, Hemingway left Africa, returned to his home, resumed his pattern of leaving home, traveled again to Italy, to France, and to Spain. He never went back to Africa. But some of the breakthrough experienced in Africa survived, as we see in some of the books that were published posthumously. After Africa, he seems able to revisit guilt-inducing situations more freely, writing autofictionally about his first breaching of monogamy (*A Moveable Feast*) and being able to explore quite openly a variety of sexual matters (*The Garden of Eden*) that had been hidden or excluded in earlier work. The settings, characters, and facts of safari life are most clearly visible in Hemingway's African narratives, of course, but the freedoms offered by the very impermanence built into that life enrich other work as well. More than any of his other travels, Hemingway's safaris freed him from place generally, from the strictures of the home place in particular, and even, for one brief episode, from his self-imposed taboo on Oak Park.

Africa, for Hemingway, was far more than a particular place or time or event. It behooves us, who read him with such pleasure, to study it.

This Book

Geographically titled books on Hemingway tend to be picture books (generally beautiful and rich in contextualizing quotes), guide books (telling us how to find Hemingway locales), or travel books (describing the author's own travels through Hemingway territory, often including photographs and interviews with people who knew or are related to Hemingway). We have titles like *Hemingway in Paris*, *A Guide to Hemingway's Paris*, *Hemingway's Spain* (at last count, no fewer than three books carry this title), *Hemingway in Spain*, *Hemingway's Cuba*, and *Hemingway in Cuba* (also three books), *Hemingway en el Perú*, *Hemingway in Michigan*, *Picturing Hemingway's Michigan*, *Ernest Hemingway in Key West*, *Ernest Hemingway in Idaho*, and so on.[24] Africa is a relative newcomer to this library; Christopher Ondaatje's illustrated first-person narrative, *Hemingway in Africa: The Last Safari*, appeared in 2003.[25]

Some of Hemingway's individual works have been the subject of collections of essays,[26] including Kent State University Press's new series, *Teaching Hemingway*.[27] Similarly, some but not all of Hemingway's home and away places have been the site of international Hemingway conferences and, thereafter, the focus of edited collections of scholarly essays.[28] But two important sites have suffered neglect: Cuba and Africa.[29] Some of the essays in a recent collection, *Ernest Hemingway and the Geography of Memory*, edited by Mark Cirino and Mark P. Ott (Kent: Kent State University Press, 2010), do reference these and other places (those that touch upon Africa have been included in Larson's comprehensive bibliography in chapter 11 of this volume), but that fine book does not focus on any particular place. Forty years earlier, John M. Howell's *Hemingway's African Stories: The Stories, Their Sources, and Their Critics* (New York: Scribner's, 1969) had looked at the Africa-based fiction, but not the nonfiction. It seems quite clear to me that, with the publication of the full second safari narrative in 2005, we have before us a sufficiently large body of material to warrant a scholarly examination of Africa as a site and topic in the life and work of Ernest Hemingway.

I originally thought, when I sent out the call for papers on this topic, that the Africa-based essays would fall into categories according to Hemingway's genres, giving the book a section on the short fiction, another on the book-length nonfiction, and another on the journalism. But books tend to develop a personality of their own, and our contributors went in three quite different directions, some supplying important extratextual background materials, some focusing on techniques and theories of reading, and others addressing philosophical matters. I am happy to report that, in discussing the same text, they often draw quite different conclusions, and that occasionally, in discussing different texts, they come to related conclusions. This gives the book a rich texture. I am only sorry that Hemingway's Africa-based and -themed journalism was neglected, and that no one has yet bothered to say anything about his very funny fable, "The Good Lion," which features a pasta-eating African lion.

As subscribers to Hemingway's oft-quoted iceberg theory — "If a writer of prose knows enough about what he is writing about he may omit things that he knows" (*Death in the Afternoon*, 192) — we start this book with what we figure Hemingway knew. Miriam B. Mandel and Jeremiah Kitunda have compiled a bibliography entitled "Hemingway's Reading in Natural History, Hunting, Fishing, and Africa" — a reading list that is so long, varied, and thorough that one is struck practically speechless (no academic would confess to being totally speechless) by the man's erudition in such nonliterary subjects. The list reminds us that Hemingway's work emerges out of research and reading, and not just out of his experiences, dramatic as these often were.

The next two essays, by Silvio Calabi and Jeremiah Kitunda, offer necessary information that most of us lack. Calabi's "Ernest Hemingway on Safari: The Game and the Guns" gives us historical and technical details about the safari, the animals that are hunted and the weapons that are used. A hunter's shotguns and rifles are personalized items, custom-made or customized to fit their owner's body, purposes, finances, strengths, and shooting style. Thus they help us decipher not only the character or narrator who uses, misuses, forgets, or refuses to use them, but also the man who knew and wrote about them. Calabi's essay will thus be useful to literary critics and to biographers. Equally helpful is Kitunda's "'Love is a dunghill. . . . And I'm the cock that gets on it to crow': Hemingway's Farcical Adoration of Africa," which offers local knowledge, with emphasis on linguistic and folkloric elements. Kitunda discusses the significance of some of the smaller animals that Hemingway mentions, like the cock and the warthog, within the native culture, even giving us a Wakamba folksong, with translation, to illustrate a point. Kitunda also translates and decodes the names and nicknames Hemingway gives his African characters, and evaluates Hemingway's statements on the customs and family relations among the Wakamba, the tribe to which the narrator of *Under Kilimanjaro* was most attracted.[30]

Beatriz Penas Ibáñez, Suzanne del Gizzo, and Chikako Tanimoto look at source texts and manuscripts as they focus on *The Garden of Eden*. Penas Ibáñez's "Canonical Readings: Baudelaire's Subtext in Hemingway's African Narratives" takes us from Hemingway to Baudelaire and thence to Coleridge. Penas Ibáñez also reads Hemingway through Hemingway, seeing his later work and style as a self-reflexive and metatextual commentary and elaboration of his earlier texts (which thus become sources) and arguing that he identified literary style with a female figure and changed styles as his aesthetic needs changed — a process paralleled by his character David Bourne, who moved from one woman to another as part of his writerly growth.

Suzanne del Gizzo begins her essay by tracking the literary sources, direct and indirect, of Hemingway's elephant, of the dog Kibo, and of his treatment of childhood. From this, "Tracking the Elephant: David's African Childhood in Hemingway's *The Garden of Eden*" moves to a close reading of the African stories in *Eden*, with an emphasis on the role of empathy and constructive remembering in David's creative process. "Ultimately," she says, "I attempt to examine the way that Hemingway's portrayal of childhood and his focus on empathy intersect with and illuminate the challenges of authorship and the rigors of the writing process in ways that deepen readers' understanding of David Bourne and his relationship to his African past."

Chikako Tanimoto takes a different scholarly approach: manuscript studies. In "An Elephant in the Garden: Hemingway's Africa in *The Garden of Eden* Manuscript," she tells us that an important phrase, "tribal things" — originally used in reference to changes in skin and hair color and experimental sexual behavior — was cut by Tom Jenks when he carved *The Garden of Eden* out of the much longer manuscript. Jenks turned Africa into a mere geographic background, Tanimoto argues, while in the original, "Africanization," the elephant, and "tribal things" are central not only to the characters of David, Catherine, and Marita, but also to the relationship between Africa and the West that dominates the book, which she sees as a Euro-American story of initiation.

Frank Mehring focuses on a different text, "The Snows of Kilimanjaro," and uses a different technique of reading. Combining Richard Rorty's neopragmatic model with the theories of ecocriticism, Mehring reads authorial silences to uncover "cultural indifference" and its attendant ethical repercussions. In his fine article, "Between Ngàje Ngàje and Kilimanjaro: A Rortian Reading of Hemingway's African Encounters," he provocatively argues that Harry, like many of Hemingway's protagonists, is incurious and inattentive to the environment of wilderness in which he has placed himself. Mehring's close reading of the story's famous italicized vignettes or flashbacks reveals Harry as unredeemedly urban and deconstructs his stated goal of finding salvation in Africa.

In the next section of the book, Philip H. Melling and Erik G. R. Nakjavani look at spiritual and philosophical matters that occupied Hemingway throughout his lifetime: the belief systems of the Ojibwa tribes that he had met in Michigan, the African-based *Santería* that he came to know during his decades in Cuba, and the religious customs and traditions of the Wakamba tribe in Kenya. In "Memorial Landscapes: Hemingway's Search for Indian Roots," Melling proposes that Hemingway recognized and was attracted by the shared belief of these totemistic faiths in "the relationship between the sacred place and the supernatural occasion." He finds that, during Hemingway's second safari, his attempts to perform the ceremonies appropriate to these iconic landscapes and animals were foiled by Western influence and the compromises required of him by his wife, Mary. Nakjavani also finds that "the narrator's 'new and unknown religion' evolves out of his own past religious experiences, his sensitivity and openness to meditative and contemplative responses to other religions," and, in particular, "his keen proclivities for all things genuinely African." In "Hemingway's African Book of Revelations: Dawning of a 'New Religion' in *Under Kilimanjaro*," he argues that the narrator subscribes to "sentient materialism," a system that holds that all that exists, whether organic or inorganic, is sentient and is therefore, in relation to itself, sacred. For Hemingway, as represented by his narrator, this has a productive result: mystical experiences, prophecy, and artistic creativity.

The next essay, by James Plath, "Barking at Death: Hemingway, Africa, and the Stages of Dying," is not about the death of another (as when a bullfighter kills a bull or a soldier kills his enemy), but about something more difficult to grasp: the death of the self. More than a decade ago, Pamela A. Boker, writing about "Snows," examined "the debilitating effects of defensively repressing grief" in the face of one's death, and Daniel Listoe, writing about *The Old Man and the Sea*, discussed the energizing effect of the recognition of death, which enables a character to achieve what he now knows is the final aim of his life.[31] In our volume, Plath takes a more comprehensive approach. Working with psychiatrist Elisabeth Kübler-Ross's now-classic study *On Death and Dying* (1969), he finds that the five stages she identifies can be seen in Hemingway's work, all the way from denial in the early work, where Hemingway presents death as a distant, totally imagined event, to acceptance, as seen in the last novels. Plath argues that the African excursions, during which Hemingway himself faced death, were a turning point in his treatment of the topic.

This book ends as it began, with a bibliography. It journeys from a list of what Hemingway read to a list of how others have read Hemingway. From the beginning, Hemingway's work has invited readers to fill the narrative gaps, make sense of his laconic style, and generally try to decipher his open, ambiguous, and generally minimalistic texts. Linda W. Wagner surveyed five decades of this criticism in *Ernest Hemingway: A Reference Guide*, compiled in 1975 and published in 1977. Kelli A. Larson continued Wagner's work, publishing her annotated bibliography, *Ernest Hemingway: A Reference Guide 1974–1989*, in 1990. This included eleven pieces on *Green Hills of Africa*, twenty-two on "Snows" (of which four were source studies), and fifty-five on "The Short Happy Life" (including four source studies). From 1986, when *The Garden of Eden* was published, to 1989, when Larson's survey ended, *Garden* generated fifty-three articles and reviews. In the bibliographic essay she contributes to this book, "On Safari with Hemingway: Tracking the Most Recent Scholarship," she brings the entire African branch of Hemingway scholarship up to date, listing and annotating, year by year, scholarly work done on African texts from 1989 to 2010. She includes, of course, all the work elicited by the publication of *True at First Light* (1999) and *Under Kilimanjaro* (2005). Following Albert J. DeFazio III as bibliographer to *Hemingway Review*, she is up to date on the ever-growing body of criticism and biography that continues to accumulate around Ernest Hemingway.

Criticism is always a work in progress, and much African material still needs to be examined. Pauline Pfeiffer's and Mary Hemingway's original safari diaries, full of information and probably consulted by Hemingway as he wrote, are unpublished. We could use a complete annotation of *all* the animals that Hemingway mentions in his African texts, and of the flora as well. Man-made items, like books and brands that are mentioned in these narratives, also need historical contextualization and evaluation, along the model of Calabi's essay on guns. As Tanimoto has demonstrated, the manuscripts at the Hemingway Collection in Boston contain fragments, false starts, revisions, and excisions that can help us read. Linguistic studies of the languages Hemingway employs in his African texts — Spanish, French, German, Swahili, and other African languages — could help us become educated readers: Kitunda's essay has begun this work. Comparative readings and source studies are time-honored techniques whose application, as Penas Ibáñez and del Gizzo demonstrate, enriches our reading. We need more of them. The essays by Mehring, Melling, and Nakjavani amply prove that critical theory and interdisciplinary studies open up these texts in new ways. The forthcoming multivolume publication of Hemingway's correspondence will undoubtedly give us much new material about Hemingway's travels to Africa and the composition of the resultant narratives. Africa is still an understudied area in Hemingway studies, and many resources and approaches can be used to explore it. This book is only a beginning.

Notes

[1] I use the word *nonfiction* because it is the one used most often to describe writing that is not "pure" fiction, whatever that is. In 1980, Ronald Weber attacked the problem of terminology, mentioning alternatives like "art-journalism, nonfiction novel, essay-fiction, factual fiction, journalit" and "New Journalism" before finally choosing "literary nonfiction" (1). Patrick Hemingway, who edited the 1999 version of Hemingway's unpublished safari manuscript, subtitled it *A Fictional Memoir*. Most recently, Richard Rhodes argued for "verity writing" (12–13). The terminology, like the genre, remains vexing. Hemingway's five volumes of nonfiction are *Death in the Afternoon* (1932), *Green Hills of Africa* (1935), *The Dangerous Summer* (1960, 1985), *A Moveable Feast* (1964, 2009), *and Under Kilimanjaro* (2005).

[2] "Home is the place where, when you have to go there, / They have to take you in." Robert Frost, "The Death of the Hired Man" (1914).

[3] At various stages of her life, Grace Hall Hemingway was a singer, architect, music teacher, and painter (many landscapes).

[4] Childless Uncle Gus also gave the Hemingways new cars and expensive vacations. In turn, Hemingway dedicated *A Farewell to Arms* to him.

[5] During his lifetime, Hemingway visited a great many other countries, e.g., Austria, Canada, China, England, Germany, Guam (then under U.S. naval administration), Hong Kong (a British Crown Colony at the time), Mexico, Palestine (later Israel), the Philippines, Peru, Switzerland, and Turkey. Some of these became settings for a journalistic essay, a short story, or a few pages in a longer work. Hong Kong, where he stayed a few days, shows up in *Islands in the Stream* (290–93); Turkey, which he also visited only briefly in order to report the Greco-Turkish War, is the setting for the beautifully complex "On the Quai at Izmir" (*In Our Time*). Switzerland appears in one short story, "Homage to Switzerland" (*Winner Take Nothing*), and in the last five chapters of *A Farewell to Arms*. But I am more interested in the countries Hemingway visited repeatedly and used intensively in his writing, including book-length works of fiction and nonfiction as well as short stories.

[6] When he died, Hemingway still owned all three of his homes (in Key West, San Francisco de Paula, and Ketchum). He also owned the Windemere property in Michigan, which his mother had signed over to him and Pauline in 1935 (Kert, 323), although after spending his honeymoon with Hadley there, Hemingway never lived (or even vacationed) in Windemere.

[7] Many critics have supported Reynolds's statements about the importance of Oak Park values and ideology. In another context, I argued the same point: that Hemingway's travel and tourism, although focused on foreign countries, were in fact shaped by the ideology of the "See America First" movement, to which he was exposed during his formative years in Oak Park, and which explains his "penchant for unfamiliar landscapes and for energetic, physical involvement with

rough, untamed terrain" ("Configuring There as Here," 102–3, 93). His persistent search for that terrain was one of the factors that brought him, finally, to Africa.

[8] Kert reports that Hemingway's "first effort at fiction [was] a short story entitled 'My First Sea Vouge.' . . . In the story the young hero's mother dies when he is four years old." The story is based on the experiences of a great-uncle who had gone "around the world with his widowed father, the sea captain, after his mother's death" (39). See also Baker, 11 (for the complete text of the story, see 12).

[9] While living in Key West, Hemingway visited the Folly Ranch and then the Lower Ranch, both in Wyoming (in 1928), and in the 1930s he repeatedly lodged at the L-T Ranch, also in Wyoming. While living in Cuba, in the 1940s, he spent several autumns at the Sun Valley Lodge in Idaho.

[10] Hemingway wrote Arnold Gingrich, the publisher of *Esquire* who had advanced Hemingway almost half the boat's cost, that she "sleeps six in cabin and two in cockpit" (*Selected Letters*, 404).

[11] Although some of the Michigan stories may derive from the Windemere cottage, this is a vacation or away place, and not Hemingway's "home." Only once, as best I can figure, do we see a Hemingway character in a space that resembles any of the author's own homes. This is at the very beginning and end of the "Cuba" section of *Islands in the Stream,* when Thomas Hudson walks through rooms that seem to derive from the Finca Vigía.

[12] Perhaps he needed travel as an antidote to the familiar, repetitive details and predictable schedules of home life, which may have deadened creativity for him. Or perhaps he needed to escape the opposite aspect of the home place — the emotional turmoil, conflicts, frictions, complications, and compromises that eat up so much energy. Perhaps he couldn't separate home from the people who shared it with him and about whom he preferred to keep silent, protecting their and his secrets. It seems that the stimuli offered by displacement into a different environment enabled him to shunt aside both familial boredom and familial chaos and pain, even if only temporarily, and to focus on artistic activity.

[13] That classification, so often used in Hemingway criticism, really applies to only one of Hemingway's characters, Santiago (*The Old Man and the Sea*), who is from the Canary Islands but who settled down in Cuba, where he has lived most of his life and where he will die.

[14] In "Soldier's Home," Harold Krebs returns to his parents' home after the war, but cannot build a life there. In *Torrents of Spring,* we also have returned veterans, one of whom cannot settle down: "somehow, he was not satisfied. Somewhere, somehow, there must be something else. Something else." He finally goes away, shedding his clothes as he goes "out into the night" (86). In *Islands in the Stream*, Thomas Hudson comes home after several days at sea (he has just heard about his son's death), but he soon leaves home for the bar and the boat. Hemingway's characters have generally left home to live, for a while, elsewhere; in they few cases where they do have a home, or are at home, they need to leave it. As Nick Adams says at the end of "The Killers," "I'm going to get out of this town" (289).

[15] The dates reflect the beginning of Hemingway's two periods in each country.

[16] For Hemingway's failed attempts to enlist and his relationship to Brumback, see Baker, 36–41. Sanderson offers an excellent, detailed review of Hemingway's relations with Italy (1–37). She notes that "Hemingway's visits to Italy fall into two clear categories. The first group of visits in 1918, 1922, 1923, and 1927 occurred in his youth. . . . The second cluster of visits took place in 1948–1949, 1949–1950, and 1954, when the prematurely aging Hemingway returned . . . after many personal changes and losses" (2). This pattern was to dominate most of his subsequent foreign travel.

[17] Reynolds details the years 1922–1926 in *Hemingway: The Paris Years*, ending his account with Hemingway's return to Europe in February 1926, after his short trip to New York to sign contracts with Scribner's. Reynolds discusses the years 1926–1928 in his next volume, *Hemingway: The American Homecoming*, although Hemingway was mostly living in Paris during those years and the actual homecoming occurred in 1928. Reynolds ends *The American Homecoming* in April 1929, with the Hemingways traveling once again to Paris on their way to Spain.

[18] The Pact of Madrid, signed in 1953 between Spain and the United States, marked the beginning of the end of Spain's isolation. The pact enabled to the building of American military bases on Spanish soil: a naval base in Rota (near the Straits of Gibraltar), and air bases in Morón (near Seville), Zaragoza, and Torrejón (near Madrid). For a concise list of agreements on visas, mutual defense, and other aspects of the relationship between Spain and the United States in the 1950s, see http://madrid.usembassy.gov/.

[19] In 2000, Spain launched the "Recovery of Historical Memory" project, to recover information about the Spanish Civil War and the subsequent thirty-five years of dictatorship, during which Francisco Franco repressed information about the Civil War and about populations that opposed his regime. In a talk presented at Cuba's Coloquio Hemingway, Vicente González Vincente reported that Hemingway's writing about the Spanish Civil War — his novel, short stories, play, and, most particularly, his wartime despatches — are now the subject of intense study in Spain. González Vicente is a Spanish social researcher and member of the Association of Friends of the International Spanish Brigades.

[20] In addition to five African trophies, taken during the first safari, the dining room of the Finca Vigía displays "a wapiti or American elk (Cervus canadensis), most likely taken in Wyoming, in 1930; and two pronghorn American antelopes (Antilocapra americana), both taken in Idaho 1941." There are several other heads in the house (Rodríguez Ferrero, 27; see also 20 and 23).

[21] The crash occurred on 1 November 1930. Hemingway was hospitalized for almost two months and didn't recover the full use of his writing arm until April 1931.

[22] Henry Strater and Archibald MacLeish were also invited to join the first safari, but in the end only Charles Thompson, a friend from Key West, and Hemingway's wife Pauline went with him to Africa.

[23] The first safari lasted sixty days, from 20 December 1933 to 20 February 1934, of which about two weeks were lost to illness. The second lasted four months and three weeks, from 1 September 1953 to 21 January 1954, with a break in the middle to visit his son Patrick at John's Corner (see Chronology).

24 *Hemingway in Paris* is by Noel Riley Fitch and *A Guide to Hemingway's Paris* is by John Leland. The three books titled *Hemingway's Spain* were written or compiled by Barnaby Conrad, Robin Gajdusek, and Robert Markham, respectively; *Hemingway in Spain*, a collection of poems and photographs, is the work of David P. Reiter. Two more books that focus on their authors' experiences in connecting Hemingway and Spain are Castillo-Puche's anecdotal first-person account, *Hemingway in Spain: A Personal Reminiscence of Hemingway's Years in Spain by his Friend* (1974); and Edward F. Stanton's wider-ranging *Hemingway and Spain: A Pursuit* (1989). *Hemingway's Cuba* is a picture book by Gérard de Cortanze and Jean-Bernard Naudin, and of the three titled *Hemingway en [in] Cuba*, one is a personal account by Yuri Paporov (translated into Spanish by Armando Partida); another, by Norberto Fuentes, is similarly anecdotal; and the third, produced jointly by Hilary Hemingway and Carlene Brennan, has beautiful pictures. Although Hemingway visited Perú only for a couple of weeks, the journalist who interviewed him there, Mario Saavedra-Piñón Castillo, recently put out a short book of photographs and texts called *Hemingway en el Perú*. We also have *Hemingway e Venezia* (by Sergio Perosa), and *Hemingway in Toronto* (by David Donnell), to name just a few of the books that focus on Hemingway's connection to particular cities. Enrique Cirules's *Ernest Hemingway in the Romano Archipelago* (which is off the northern coast of Cuba) was translated into English by Douglas Edward LaPrade. For the United States, *Hemingway in Michigan* is by Constance Cappel; *Picturing Hemingway's Michigan* is by Michael R. Federspiel; and *Ernest Hemingway in Key West* and *Ernest Hemingway in Idaho* are both by Marsha Bellavance-Johnson. Many more books connect Hemingway to a specific locale, but very few collections of scholarly essays have adopted this approach.

25 Ondaatje romantically undertook to "stop where he [Hemingway] stopped and look where he looked, in a quest for the heart of his strange and profound affection for Africa" (20). In her 2006 review of Ondaatje's book, Suzanne del Gizzo describes it as a "pilgrimage-based," "associative," and "derivative" "field-based effort." She regrets his "lack of critical engagement with . . . new [scholarly and theoretical] material — a missed opportunity" (124–26). I agree with her remarks, which reinforce his own claim that "Africa's role in his [Hemingway's] life and work remains intriguing and under-explored territory" (20).

26 For example, *Twentieth Century Interpretations of "The Old Man and the Sea*," ed. Katharine T. Jobes (1968), and my own *Companion to Hemingway's "Death in the Afternoon"* (2004).

27 Two volumes are already published, both in 2008: *Teaching Hemingway's "The Sun Also Rises,"* edited by Peter Hays, and *Teaching Hemingway's "A Farewell to Arms,"* edited by Lisa Tyler.

28 We have, for example, *Hemingway in Italy and Other Essays*, edited by Robert W. Lewis (1990) and *Hemingway's Italy: New Perspectives*, edited by Rena Sanderson (2006), both of which present scholarly essays read at international conferences in that country. *Hemingway's Spain: New Essays*, edited by Carl P. Eby (forthcoming), collects essays from an international Hemingway conference held in Ronda and Málaga, 25–30 June 2006: this will be the first collection of scholarly essays with Spain in the title (email communication from Carl P. Eby, 21 March 2011).

[29] Fortunately, a collection called *Hemingway and Cuba*, edited by Lawrence Grimes and Bickford Sylvester, is scheduled for winter 2012 (email communication from Lawrence Grimes, 17 March 2011).

[30] The narrator of *Green Hills of Africa*, on the other hand, is more impressed by the strength, beauty, self-confidence, and generosity of spirit of the Masai villagers he meets in the rich kudu country (218–21, 286–87), although he describes the northern Masai as "sullen . . . contemptuous" (219). In that book, the Wakamba are neglected.

[31] See Larson's bibliographic essay in this volume, s.v. 1996 and 1997.

Works Cited

Baker, Carlos. *Ernest Hemingway: A Life Story.* 1969. Reprint, New York: Macmillan Collier, 1988.

Chamberlin, Brewster, comp. "A (Preliminary) Chronology of the Life and Times of Ernest Hemingway." Key West Art and Historical Society (unpublished), 2008, revised 2010.

del Gizzo, Suzanne. Review of Christopher Ondaatje's *Hemingway in Africa: The Last Safari. Hemingway Review* 26, no. 1 (Fall 2006): 124–27.

González Vincente, Vicente. "Hemingway at the Battle of Madrid." Paper read at Coloquio Hemingway, 21–24 June 2007, La Habana, Cuba.

Hemingway, Ernest. *Death in the Afternoon.* 1932. Reprint, New York: Scribner's, 1960.

———. *Ernest Hemingway: Selected Letters: 1917–1961.* Edited by Carlos Baker. 1981. Reprint, London: Panther Books, 1985.

———. *A Farewell to Arms.* 1929. Reprint, New York: Scribner's, 1957.

———. *For Whom the Bell Tolls.* New York: Scribner's, 1940.

———. "The Good Lion." In *The Complete Short Stories of Ernest Hemingway: The Finca Vigía Edition*, 482–84. New York: Scribner's, 1987. First published 1951 in *Holiday*.

———. *Islands in the Stream.* New York: Scribner's, 1970.

———. "The Killers." In *The Short Stories of Ernest Hemingway*, 279–89. 1938. Reprint, New York: Scribner's, 1966. First published 1927 in Hemingway's *Men Without Women*.

———. *To Have and Have Not.* 1937. Reprint, New York: Scribner's, 1970.

———. *The Torrents of Spring.* 1926. Reprint, New York: Simon & Schuster, 1998.

———. *True at First Light: A Fictional Memoir.* Edited and with an introduction by Patrick Hemingway. New York: Scribner's, 1999.

———. *Under Kilimanjaro.* Edited by Robert W. Lewis and Robert E. Fleming. Kent: The Kent State UP, 2005.

Hemingway, Mary. *How It Was.* New York: Knopf, 1976.

Hemingway, Seán. "Introduction" to *Hemingway on Hunting*, edited by Seán Hemingway, foreword by Patrick Hemingway, xxi–xxxvi. Guilford CT: The Globe Pequot Press, 2001.

Kert, Bernice. *Hemingway's Women*. New York: Norton, 1983.

Mandel, Miriam B. "Configuring There as Here: Hemingway's Travels and the 'See America First' Movement." *Hemingway Review* 19, no. 1 (Fall 1999): 92–105.

———. *Hemingway's "Death in the Afternoon": The Complete Annotations*. Lanham, MD: The Scarecrow Press, 2002.

———. "Internal Structures: The Conservatism of *A Farewell to Arms*." In Sanderson, *Hemingway's Italy*, 174–84.

Ondaatje, Christopher. *Hemingway in Africa: The Last Safari*. New York: HarperCollins, 2003.

Reynolds, Michael. *Hemingway: The American Homecoming*. Cambridge, MA: Blackwell, 1992.

———. *Hemingway: The Final Years*. New York: Norton, 1999.

———. *Hemingway: The Paris Years*. New York: Basil Blackwell, 1989.

———. "Oak Park Before the Great War." In *Ernest Hemingway: The Oak Park Legacy*, edited by James Nagel, 23–36. Tuscaloosa: The U of Alabama P, 1996.

———. *The Young Hemingway*. New York: Basil Blackwell, 1986.

Rhodes, Richard. "PEN Hemingway Prize Keynote Address." *Hemingway Review* 29, no. 1 (2009): 9–15.

Rodríguez Ferrero, Gladys. "Museo Finca Vigía Celebrates Its 45th Birthday." *Hemingway Review* 27, no. 2 (2008): 16–34.

Sanderson, Rena. "Hemingway's Italy: Paradise Lost." In *Hemingway's Italy: New Perspectives*, edited by Rena Sanderson, 1–37. Baton Rouge: Louisiana State UP, 2006.

Sanford, Marcelline Hemingway. *At the Hemingways: With Fifty Years of Correspondence Between Ernest and Marcelline Hemingway. Centennial Edition*. Foreword by Michael Reynolds. Moscow: U of Idaho P, 1999.

Scholes, Robert, and Nancy R. Comley. *Hemingway's Genders: Rereading the Hemingway Text*. New Haven: Yale UP, 1994.

Theisen, Earl. Published photographs from the 1953–54 safari by permission of Roxann Livingston. Unpublished photographs from The Hemingway Collection at the John F. Kennedy Presidential Library and Museum, Boston.

Weber, Ronald. *The Literature of Fact: Literary Nonfiction in American Writing*. Athens: Ohio UP, 1980.

I: Knowing What Hemingway Knew

1: Hemingway's Reading in Natural History, Hunting, Fishing, and Africa

Compiled by Miriam B. Mandel and Jeremiah M. Kitunda

> *He was always reading, reading. Carried soft covers and papers and magazines in his pockets all the time. He read whenever the pace slowed.*
>
> — Denis Zaphiro, describing Hemingway on safari
> (Meyers, *Hemingway: A Biography*)

THIS BIBLIOGRAPHY BEGAN with Jeremiah Kitunda's tracking down of the "twenty-three rare volumes on African hunting" (Reynolds, *The 1930s*, 168) that Hemingway ordered from Brentano's in Paris as he returned from his first safari.[1] The Brentano list is interesting on a number of counts. It is historically oriented, almost half of it consisting of books published in the nineteenth century, with the earliest (Harris) being published almost a century before Hemingway undertook his own first safari. Clearly, at this time Hemingway was not looking for practical up-to-date advice or technical information, but rather, as he prepared to write about his experiences, for historical depth (e.g., Greener's 1881 book on the history of weapons). This is an attitude we recognize in his fiction, in which details like the names of characters or places are historically resonant. The past was always relevant to Hemingway.

It is also interesting that the Brentano list, although short, has room for personal accounts of individual explorers and adventurers (e.g., Baldwin, Selous, Stanley), for books about animals that he did not intend to hunt, like the chamois (Boner) and the elephant (Stigand's *Hunting the Elephant in Africa* and Neumann's *Elephant-hunting in East Equatorial Africa*), and also for a surprisingly large number of volumes about hunting in countries other than the ones he had visited in East Africa (Harris), and even in continents other than Africa (e.g., Aflalo, Dane, Darrah, Highton, Kinloch, Leveson, Niedieck). This suggests that although Hemingway had, by this time, hunted specific animals in a particular area of Africa, he was interested in something wider: not merely the experience of hunting, but the *genre* of writing about exploration and hunting. Just as the protagonist of *Green Hills of Africa* is a competitive hunter, so the author of that book is a competitive writer, one who jealously keeps track of the competition and announces, in his epigraph, his intention to overtake and surpass it, by taking the genre onto a different level. Similarly, he read many books about elephants, not because he was interested in hunting them, but because they might be an interesting subject to write about. The two elephant books ordered from Brentano's share the shelf with many others (e.g., Bell, Blunt, De Watteville, Lewis [about circus elephants!], Oberjohann, Ranking, Sanderson, Scott), some of which still need to be studied as possible source materials for his magnificently complex African elephant story (or stories) included in *The Garden of Eden*. Hemingway wrote out of his reading, not just out of his experiences.

After we found the relevant bibliographical details of the twenty-three volumes mentioned in the original Brentano list, and taking the inclusiveness of that list as our guiding light, we decided to expand the scope of our bibliography to include as many as possible of the books we know Hemingway owned or read on the topics of Africa, natural history, hunting, fishing, weapons, tackle, the professional vocabulary necessary for these activities (in English, Spanish, and Swahili), local customs, and the memoirs and biographies of people interested in the topics that interested him (namely, the accounts of or by fishermen, hunters, explorers, historians, naturalists). As the bibliography expanded, we were increasingly impressed by the number and quality of the books on natural history, which emphasize Hemingway's bent for the precise scientific and technical detail. Natural history was, as Susan Beegel so cogently demonstrated in "A Guide to the Marine Life in Ernest Hemingway's *The Old Man and the Sea*," a lifelong interest for Hemingway and an integral part of his writing.

Fishing and hunting in a variety of waters and habitats — in the United States, in the Caribbean, in South America, in several European countries, and in Kenya — Hemingway collected a practical sportsman's library that included dictionaries, phrasebooks, guide books, catalogues that advertise weapons, ammunition, tents, and tackle, and books offering instruction on how different game is to be hunted in different terrain (e.g., Denis David Lyell's *The Hunting and Spoor of Central African Game: with life-size Illustrations of most of the Game Tracks*). His library shows him reading about all categories of animals: it includes standard nineteenth-century volumes on ichtyology and fishing (La Blanchère, Marburg, Norris, Roosevelt, Sauvage, Yale), on ornithology (Osborn, Stanley and White), as well as twentieth-century books on wonderfully varied and specific topics, like Augusta Foote Arnold's *The Sea-beach at Ebb-tide: A Guide to the Study of the Seaweeds and the Lower Animal Life Found Between Tidemarks* (1901), Jordan and Gilbert's *Fossil Fishes of Diatom Beds of Lompoc, California* (1920), Herbert Lee Stoddard's *The Bobwhite Quail: Its Habits, Preservation and Increase* (1932), R. Tenniel

Evans's *The Butterfly Collector's Handbook for East Africa* (1946), and Marston Bates's *The Natural History of Mosquitoes* (1949).

Hemingway's father, Clarence (Ed) Hemingway — a medical doctor, amateur natural historian, and founding member of the Agassiz Club of Oak Park — had early on inspired and encouraged an interest in natural history and environmental awareness, as well as responsible hunting and fishing.[2] Pictures of a very young Hemingway show him with a fishing rod, and, as Silvio Calabi points out in his essay in this volume, Hemingway acquired his first weapon at what would seem to us now a shockingly young age.[3] In addition to offering equipment, practical knowledge, and inspiration about hunting, Dr. Hemingway encouraged his son to read more generally about Africa, the hunter's paradise, recommending specific pamphlets and books (they are included in the list below, s.v. "Come Over to Africa" and "Weber"). These recommendations elicited no resistance from Hemingway, who is reputed to have read a book a day. As the titles and dates of his library indicate, he bought and read books about hunting, fishing, natural history, and Africa until the very last year of his life.

And as his father had done for him, so Hemingway did for his sons, instilling in them so strong a love for these outdoor sports that his oldest son, John Nicanor (Jack) Hemingway, titled his memoir *Misadventures of a Fly Fisherman*; his second son, Patrick, worked for many years as a game warden in Africa; and his youngest son, Gregory, was an expert shot even as a child. Some of the most beautiful pictures taken of Hemingway and his handsome sons show them holding guns or fishing rods.

And he attempted to transmit this passion to his readers as well by including hunting and fishing episodes in so much of his work. We are fortunate that these writings have been gathered and reissued in two collections: Nick Lyons's *Hemingway on Fishing*, with a foreword by Jack Hemingway, and *Hemingway on Hunting*, edited and with an introduction by his grandson, Seán Hemingway, and a foreword by Patrick Hemingway. The bibliography below could serve as a reference tool for readers wanting the intellectual backgrounds underlying these beautiful, often symbolic episodes collected from Hemingway's evocative journalism, fiction, and nonfiction.

Most of the books and pamphlets in Hemingway's library are in English, but a good number are in French, some are in Italian and Spanish, and there is even the occasional volume in Dutch, German, or Portuguese. The books were published in Belgium, Britain, Cuba, France, India, Spain, the United States, and several African countries.

As befits the scientific and historic nature of the subject, most of the publications listed below are nonfiction. Some boast diagrams, drawings, maps, photographs, and other types of illustrations. Many are rare editions; some are specialized government publications not widely available.

Occasionally, as in the case of W. H. Hudson, a naturalist wrote fiction, and if Hemingway owned these works of fiction they are included in the bibliography. Some novelists (e.g., Forester, Hanley, and Kessel) set their books in Kenya, and if Hemingway owned these works, we include them as well. Like the Brentano list, our more complete safari-oriented bibliography indicates clearly that Hemingway's interest in Africa was continent-wide and included South Africa and countries he never visited or hunted in. As was his wont on any topic that interested him, Hemingway acquired an eclectic, technical, historical, international, practical, comprehensive, and scholarly library.

What follows is necessarily an incomplete listing. We can never know all that Hemingway read on any subject that he loved and intended to write about.

Hemingway's Reading in Natural History, Hunting, Fishing, and Africa

This bibliography is grounded on Michael S. Reynolds's *Hemingway's Reading, 1910–1940: An Inventory* and its "Supplement," which together catalogue his reading from childhood through the Paris and Key West years; and on James D. Brasch and Joseph Sigman's *Hemingway's Library: A Composite Record*, which also includes the contents of Hemingway's library at Finca Vigía, his Cuban home from 1939 to 1960. Because this is a historical bibliography, we have also, like our sources, retained the original spelling, punctuation, and capitalization of the titles, even when these look odd to modern eyes. When place or date of publication are absent from these sources, we provide the information relevant to the book's first edition, enclosing this — and any other information not provided by Reynolds, Brasch, and Sigman — in brackets. For several of the books, the first was the only edition, and therefore necessarily the one Hemingway owned.

When Hemingway owned two or more copies of the same book, or differently dated reissues, we note this after the earlier publication date. When he owned different editions, we list them separately. Catalogues and books of records, which carry the same title for several years but offer different or updated information, are also listed individually.

An asterisk preceding the listing indicates that the item was ordered from Brentano's Book Shop, Paris, shortly after the first safari. The marker (Fitch) at the end of an entry indicates that the item was noted in the cards of Sylvia Beach's lending library. Our thanks to Carl P. Eby and Larry Grimes for identifying items we had missed.[4] Patrick Hemingway identified Olive Schreiner, Doris Lessing, and other writers as literary influences,[5] and Scribner's records at Princeton University Library indicate that they sent, and Hemingway received, books by Corbett and Siemel.⁶

Hemingway's enormous reading on bulls, their anatomy and breeding, is not included here, so as not to repeat bibliographical information provided in Miriam B. Mandel's "Subject and Author: The Literary Backgrounds of *Death in the Afternoon*."

Adams, Ramon Frederick. *Western Words: A Dictionary of the Range, Cow Camp, and Trail.* Norman: University of Oklahoma, 1944.

*Aflalo, Frederick George, ed. *Sport in Europe.* London: Sands, 1901.

Akeley, Carl Ethan. *In Brightest Africa.* [Garden City, NY: Garden City Publishing Co.,] 1923.

Akeley, Mary L. *Carl Akeley's Africa: The Account of the Akeley-Eastman-Pomeroy African Hall Expedition of the American Museum of Natural History.* Foreword by Henry Fairfield Osborn. New York: Blue Ribbon Books, 1932.

Alexander, Hermann (Graf von Keyserling). *The Travel Diary of a Philosopher.* 2 vols. London: Cape, 1925. (Fitch)

Alexander, Wilfrid Backhouse. *Birds of the Ocean: A Handbook for Voyagers Containing Descriptions of All the Sea-Birds of the World, with Notes on Their Habits and Guides to Their Identification.* New York: Putnam, 1928. Hemingway also owned a second printing with the same title, New York: Putnam, 1954.

American Kennel Club. *Toy Dogs: The Breeds and Standards As Recognized by the American Kennel Club.* Introduction by Charles T. Inglee. New York: Watt, 1935.

American Museum of Natural History. *Birds of Paradise.* By Ernst Mayo. New York: American Museum of Natural History, 1945.

———. *General Guide to the American Museum of Natural History.* New York: Man and Nature Publications, American Museum of Natural History, 1956. Hemingway owned two copies of this book.

———. *On the Biology of the Atlantic Marlins: Makaira Ampla and Makaira Albida.* New York, 1958.

Andersson, Karl Johan. *Lake Ngami; or, Explorations and Discoveries, during Four Years' Wanderings in the Wilds of South Western Africa.* London: Hurst & Blackett, 1856.

Arnold, Augusta Foote. *The Sea-beach at Ebb-tide: A Guide to the Study of the Seaweeds and the Lower Animal Life Found Between Tidemarks.* New York: Century, 1901.

Ashton, Ethel O. *Swahili Grammar, Including Intonation.* London: Longmans, 1951.

Askins, Charles. *Modern Shotguns and Loads, Together with Treatise on the Art of Wing-shooting*. Marshallton, DE: Small-Arms Technical Publishing Co., 1929.

———. *Wing and Trap Shooting*. New York: Macmillan, 1948.

Audubon, John James. *The Birds of America*. Foreword and descriptive captions by William Vogt. New York: Macmillan, 1946.

Austin, A. B., comp. *An Angler's Anthology*. [London: Country Life Ltd., 1931.]

Aymar, Gordon Christian. *Bird Flight*. [A collection of two hundred photographs. Garden City, NY: Garden City Publishing Co., 1938.] Hemingway owned two copies.

Babcock, Havilah. *My Health Is Better in November: Thirty-five Stories of Hunting and Fishing in the South*. New York: Greenberg, 1952.

Back, Howard. *The Waters of Yellowstone with Rod and Fly*. New York: Dodd, Mead, 1938.

Baker, Samuel White. *The Albert N'Yanza, Great Basin of the Nile and Explorations of the Nile Sources*. 2 vols. London: Macmillan, 1867. Hemingway also owned the one-volume edition: London: Macmillan, 1874.

———. *Ismailïa: A Narrative of the Expedition to Central Africa for the Suppression of the Slave Trade. Organized by Ismail, Khedive of Egypt*. New York: Harper, 1875.

———. *The Nile Tributaries of Abyssinia and the Sword Hunters of the Hamran Arabs*. 1869.

———. *The Rifle and the Hound in Ceylon*. London: Longmans, 1890.

———. *Wild Beasts and Their Ways: Reminiscences of Europe, Asia, Africa and America*. London: Macmillan, 1891.

*Baldwin, William Charles. *African Hunting and Adventure from Natal to the Zambezi, including Lake Ngami, the Kalahari Desert, & etc., from 1851 to 1860*. London: Bentley, 1863.

Bandini, Gian Andrea. *Il libro del mare: Prose e poesio marinaresche*. Milan: Trevesini, ca. 1954.

Bandini, Ralph. *Men, Fish and Tackle: The Story of J. A. Coxe As Told to Ralph Bandini*. Bronson, MI: Published privately by Bronson Reel Co., 1936.

Barbellion, Pierre. *Lancer léger et poissons de sport*. Paris: Malaine, 1941.

Barbour, Thomas. *Naturalist at Large*. Boston: Little, Brown, 1945.

———. *A Naturalist in Cuba*. Boston: Little, Brown, 1945.

———. *That Vanishing Eden: A Naturalist's Florida*. Boston: Little, Brown, 1945.

Barisoni, Eugenio. *Cacciatore de fussagno.* Florence: Olimpia, 1944.

Barnard, Keppel Harcourt. *A Beginner's Guide to South African Shells.* Cape Town: Miller, 1951.

———. *A Pictorial Guide to South African Fishes, Marine and Freshwater.* Cape Town: Miller, 1947.

Bascom, William R., and Paul Gebauer. *Handbook of West African Art.* Assembled and edited by Robert E. Ritzenthaler. Milwaukee: Bruce, 1953.

Bates, Henry Walter. *The Naturalist on the River Amazons: A Record of Adventures, Habits of Animals, Sketches of Brazilian and Indian Life, and Aspects of Nature under the Equator, during Eleven Years of Travel.* London: Murray, 1864.

Bates, Marston. *The Natural History of Mosquitoes.* New York: Macmillan, 1949.

———. *The Nature of Natural History.* New York: Scribner's, 1954.

Batten Pooll, A. H. *Some Globe-trottings with a Rod.* Eton: Spottiswoode, 1937.

Beebe, William, ed. *The Book of Naturalists: An Anthology of the Best Natural History.* New York: Knopf, 1945.

Bell, Walter Dalrymple Maitland. *The Wanderings of an Elephant Hunter.* London: Spearman, 1958.

Bent, Newell. *Jungle Giants.* Norwood, MA: Printed for friends of the author by the Plimpton Press, 1936. About Tanganyika.

Bergman, Ray. *Just Fishing.* [The first edition is 1935; later printings are by Outdoor Life (1941) and Knopf (1943, 1945).]

———. *Trout.* New York: Knopf, 1947.

Betten, Henry Lewis. *Upland Game Shooting.* Philadelphia: Penn, 1940.

Biguet, Fernand. *La pêche à la ligne d'aujourd'hui.* Paris: Bornemann, 1929.

———. *Pour apprendre à pêcher les petits poissons: Ablette, chabot, goujon, vairon, vandoise.* Paris: Bornemann, 1935.

Birch, D. Percival Lea. *Sea Fishing.* [Vol. 3 of the Sportman's Libary, n.d.]

Birds in Natural Colors: A Monthly Serial (bound edition). Chicago: Mumford, 1899. This may be the "large bound volumes of a monthly serial called *Birds of Nature,*" with which Hemingway became familiar as a child (Baker, 4).

Birkby, Carel. *It's a Long Way to Addis.* London: Muller, 1942.

———. *Native Life in South Africa.* Pretoria: South African Tourist Corp., 1954.

Blaikie, William Garden. *The Personal Life of David Livingstone, Chiefly from His Unpublished Journals and Correspondence in the Possession of His Family*. Philadelphia: Potter, 1881.

Blixen-Finecke, Bror von. *African Hunter*. Translated by F. H. Lyon. New York: Knopf, 1938.

Blunt, David Enderby. *Elephant*. London: East Africa, 1933.

Boisset, L. de. *Les mouches du pêcheur de truites*. Paris: Champs-Elysées, 1939.

———. *L'ombre, poisson de sport*. Paris: Champs-Elysées, 1941.

———. *La truite, poisson de grand sport*. Paris: Champs-Elysées, 1942.

Boisset, L. de, and Richard Vibert. *La pêche fluviale en France: Son état, son avenir*. Paris: Champs-Elysées, 1944.

*Boner, Charles. *Chamois Hunting in the Mountains of Bavaria and in the Tyrol*. London: Chapman & Hall, 1860.

Bonner, Paul Hyde. *Amanda. The Glorious Mornings: Stories of Shooting and Fishing*. New York: Scribner's, 1954.

The Book of Fishes: Game Fishes, Food Fishes, Shellfish and Curious Citizens of American Ocean Shores, Lakes and Rivers. Washington, DC: The National Geographical Society, 1924. Hemingway owned two copies.

Boyes, John. *The Company of Adventurers*. London: East Africa, 1928.

Breder, Charles Marcus. *Field Book of Marine Fishes of the Atlantic Coast from Labrador to Texas; Being a Short Description of Their Characteristics and Habits with Keys for Their Identification*. [New York: G. P. Putnam's Sons, 1929, 1948.]

Briggs, Ellis O. *Shots Heard Round the World: An Ambassador's Hunting Adventures on Four Continents*. New York: Viking, 1957.

Brown, Pete. *Guns and Hunting*. New York: Barnes, 1955.

Bruette, William Arthur. *American Duck, Goose, and Brant Shooting*. New York: Scribner's, 1934.

Bucciantini, Pier Luigi. *Vita all'aperto: Novelle di caccia e di pesca*. Turin: Società Editrice Internazionale, 1953.

Bulpin, Thomas Victor. *South Africa's Animal Kingdom*. Pretoria: South African Tourist Corp., 1954.

Burnand, Tony. *Bec bleu, la grise, et quelques autres*. Paris: Stock, 1942.

———. *Grosse bête et petit gibier*. Paris: Gallimard, 1937.

Burnand, Tony, and Charles C. Ritz. *A la mouche: Méthods et matériel modernes pour la pêche à la mouche, de la truite, de l'ombre, du poisson blanc*. La théorie solunaire de J. A. Knight. Préfaces du J. de Neuflize et de Lord Glanusk. Paris: Champs-Elysées, 1939. For an explanation of John Alden Knight's solunar (sun and moon) theory of fishing and hunting, see http://www.kingsoutdoorworld.com/hunting-guide/deer_activity.htm.

———. *Vade Mecum du pêcheur à la mouche: Résumé de ce qu'il faut savoir sur le matériel et la technique modernes pour pecher, à la mouche, truites, ombres et poissons blancs.* Paris: Au Bord de L'eau, 1941.

Burns, Eugene. *The Complete Book of Fresh and Salt Water Spinning.* New York: Barnes, 1955.

Burrard, Gerald. *The Modern Shotgun.* 3 vols. London: Jenkins, 1951. Hemingway also owned an earlier edition of the first volume: *The Modern Shotgun.* Vol. 1: *The Gun.* New York: Scribner's, 1931.

Burton, Richard Francis. *First Footsteps in East Africa* [; *Or, an Exploration of Harar.* London: Longman, Brown, Green, and Longmans,] 1856.

———, trans. *The Arabian Nights' Entertainment; or, The Book of a Thousand Nights and a Night: A Selection of the Most Famous and Representative of These Tales from the Plain and Literal Translations by Richard F. Burton.* 1885. Chosen and arranged by Bennett A. Cerf. Introductory essay by Ben Ray Redman. New York: Modern Library, 1932.

Buxton, Earl. *Fishing and Shooting.* London: Murray, 1924.

Buxton, Edward North. *Two African Trips, with Notes & Suggestions on Big Game Preservations in Africa.* London: Stanford, 1902.

Buzzacott, Francis Henry. *The Complete American and Canadian Sportman's Encyclopedia of Valuable Instruction.* Brasch and Sigman don't identify which edition of this popular book Hemingway owned.

Caine, Louis S. *Game Fish of the South and How to Catch Them.* New York: Houghton Mifflin, 1935.

Calder-Marshall, Arthur. *At Sea.* [New York, 1934.]

Camp, Raymond Russell, ed. *The Fireside Book of Fishing: A Selection from the Great Literature of Angling.* New York: Simon & Schuster, 1959.

———, ed. *The Hunter's Encyclopedia.* New York: Stackpole & Heck, 1948. Brasch and Sigman list this twice: once under the editor's name, and once under the title. Hemingway may have owned two copies.

Carrère, Louis. *Mouche noyée: Pêche sportive de la truite dans les rivières et les torrents.* Préface de Tony Burnand. Toulouse: Boisseau, 1942.

———. *Technique du lancer léger.* Préface de S. Massé. Toulouse: Boisseau, 1942.

Carson, Rachel Louise. *The Sea Around Us*. New York: Oxford, 1951.

———. *Under the Sea-wind: A Naturalist's Picture of Ocean Life*. New York: Oxford, 1952.

Casciano, Rocca. *Caccie e viaggi del conte Giovanni Macchetti dall'Africa al Camciatca*. N.p., n.d. Rocca Casciano, or Rocca San Casciano, seems to be a place, not a person. I have found no trace of this book.

Caswell, John. *Sporting Rifles and Rifle Shooting*. New York: Appleton, 1920.

Chalmers, Patrick Reginald. *The Angler's England*. Philadelphia: Lippincott, 1938.

Chapin, James Paul. *The Preparation of Birds for Study: Instructions for the Proper Preparation of Bird Skins and Skeletons for Study and Future Mounting*. New York: American Museum of Natural History, 1957.

*Chapman, Abel. *Savage Sudan; Its Wild Tribes, Big-game, and Bird-life*. London: Gurney & Jackson, 1921.

Chapman, Abel, and Walter J. Buck. *Wild Spain: Records of Sport with Rifle, Rod, and Gun; Natural History and Exploration*. London: Gurney & Jackson, 1893.

Chapman, Frank Michler. *Handbook of Birds of Eastern North America*. New York: Appleton, 1928.

Chapman, Wilbert McLeod. *Fishing in Troubled Waters*. New York: Lippincott, 1949.

Claflin, Bert. *Muskie Fishing*. New York: Knopf, 1948.

Cloete, Stuart. *The African Giant: The Story of a Journey*. Boston: Houghton Mifflin, 1955.

———. *Against These Three: A Biography of Paul Kruger, Cecil Rhodes, and Lobengula, Last King of the Matabele*. Boston: Houghton Mifflin, 1945.

———. *Congo Song*. Derby, CT: Monarch Books, 1958.

———. *The Mask*. Boston: Houghton Mifflin, 1957.

Cole, Sonia Mary. *The Prehistory of East Africa*. Harmondsworth: Penguin, 1954.

Collins, Henry Hill. *Complete Field Guide to American Wildlife: East, Central, and North*. New York: Harper, 1959.

Collis, William Robert Fitz-Gerald. *African Encounter: A Doctor in Nigeria*. New York: Scribner's, 1960.

"Come Over to Africa" and "Harvest is Ripe." Pamphlets about Africa, written by missionaries, that Hemingway's father recommended to him in 1921. In the nineteenth and early twentieth centuries, missionaries and churchmen often wrote about natural history, seeing it as an expression of divinity. See, for example, Stanley (a bishop), White and Wood (both reverends), and Weber (a medical missionary), whose books Hemingway owned. Hemingway's opinions on this mix of natural history and religion are expressed most vividly in his attack on the pious Scottish explorer Mungo Park (*Death in the Afternoon,* 134, 138, 139), whose books, however, do not appear in Hemingway's library.

Connett, Eugene Virginius, ed. *American Big Game Fishing.* Presents essays by Mrs. Oliver C. Grinnell, Francis H. Low, Herman P. Gray, and others. New York: Derrydale, 1935.

Conrad, Joseph. *The Complete Short Stories of Joseph Conrad.* It is difficult to know which edition Hemingway owned. Reynolds remarks that "by 1924, Hemingway had read most, if not all, of Conrad" (*Hemingway's Reading,* 18), including *Heart of Darkness,* which details the ironies of colonialism in the Belgian Congo in the 1880s.

Constantin-Weyer, Maurice. *La chasse au brochet.* Paris: Champs-Elysées, 1941.

Cook, Beatrice Gray. *Truth Is Stranger than Fishin'.* New York: Morrow, 1955.

Cook, Melville Thurston, and William Titus Horne. *Coffee Leaf Miner and Other Coffee Pests.* Santiago de las Vegas, Cuba: Estación Central Agronómica, 1905.

———. *Insects and Diseases of Vegetables.* Santiago de las Vegas, Cuba: Estación Central Agronómica, 1908.

Cooper, Eric, ed. *Sea Fishing.* Philadelphia: Lippincott, 1934. Hemingway owned two copies.

Copley, Hugh. *The Game Fishes of Africa.* London: Witherby, 1952.

———. *Small Mammals of Kenya.* Nairobi: Highway Press, 1950.

———. *When Dragons Roamed East Africa: A Little Guide to Very Remote Chapter of the History of East Africa.* Nairobi: Highway Press, 1948.

———. *Wonders of the Kenya Seashore: A Short Guide to the Birds, Fishes, Shells, and Other Forms of Life Found on the Seashore.* Nairobi: Highway Press, 1946.

Corbett, Edward James [Jim Corbett]. *Jungle Lore.* Oxford: Oxford UP, 1953. This book was shipped by Scribner's to Hemingway when he was on safari and receipt was confirmed by cable from Nairobi on 17 December 1954. It is not listed by Reynolds or Brasch and Sigman.

———. *Man-Eaters of India.* New York: Oxford, 1957.

———. *My India.* New York: Oxford, 1952.

———. *The Temple Tiger, and More Man-eaters of Kumaon.* New York: Oxford, 1955.

Cordeiro, Arsénio. *Espadartes de Sesimbra.* Lisbon: Diana, 1959.

Cotlow, Lewis N. *Zanzabuku (Dangerous Safari).* New York: Rinehart, 1956.

Cousteau, Jacques-Yves, P. Tailles, and F. Dumas. *Par dix-huit mètres de fond: Histoire d'un film.* Paris: Durel, 1946.

Covarrubias, Miguel. *The Eagle, the Jaguar, and the Serpent: Indian Art of the Americas. North America: Alaska, Canada, the United States.* New York: Knopf, 1954. Hemingway owned two copies.

Craighead, John Johnson, and Frank C. *Hawks, Owls, and Wildlife.* Harrisburg, PA: Stackpole, 1956.

Cross, Reuben R. *Tying American Trout Lures: A Practical Guide to the Production of Dry Flies, Wet Flies, Nymphs and Bucktails for Pleasure and Profit.* New York: Dodd, Mead, 1940.

Cuba. Department of Agriculture. *Almanaque agrícola nacional.* Havana, 1941.

Curtis, Charles P. [Jr., and Richard C. Curtis.] *Hunting in Africa East and West.* [Boston: Houghton Mifflin, 1925.]

Curtis, Paul Allan. *American Game Shooting.* New York: Dutton, 1927.

———. *Sporting Firearms Today in Use.* New York: Dutton, 1922.

Daly, Marcus. *Big Game Hunting and Adventure, 1877–1936.* London: Macmillan, 1937.

*Dane, Richard Morris. *Sport in Asia and Africa.* London: Melrose, 1921.

*Darrah, Henry Zouch. *Sport in the Highlands of Kashmir.* London: Rowland Ward, 1898.

Davidson, Basil. *The Lost Cities of Africa.* Boston: Little, Brown, 1959.

Dean, Harry, and Sterling North. *The Pedro Gorino: The Adventures of a Negro Sea-captain in Africa and on the Seven Seas in His Attempts to Found an Ethiopian Empire.* Boston: Houghton Mifflin, 1929.

Dean, Roy B. *Light Tackle Fishing for Sailfish in Acapulco Waters.* N.p., n.d.

De Guingand, F. W. *African Assignment.* London: Hodder & Stoughton, 1953.

De Watteville, Vivienne. *Out in the Blue.* London: Methuen, 1937.

———. *Speak to the Earth: Wanderings and Reflections among Elephants and Mountains.* Preface by Edith Wharton. New York: Smith & Haas, 1935.

Dimock, Anthony Weston. *The Book of the Tarpon.* New York: Outing, 1911.

Dinesen, Isak [Karen von Blixen-Finecke]. *Out of Africa.* New York: Random House, 1938.

———. *Out of Africa.* With an introduction by Bernardine Kielty. New York: Modern Library, 1952.

Dodge, Natt Noyes. *Poisonous Dwellers of the Desert.* Brasch and Sigman are uncertain about bibliographic details. Santa Fe, NM: Southwestern Monuments Association, 1947? [Year, 1947, confirmed in Library of Congress Catalog of Copyright Entries, 3rd Series.]

Doughty, Charles Montagu. *Passages from Arabia Deserta.* Selected by Edward Garnett. [With a Portrait of the Author. London: Jonathan Cape,] 1931. Doughty's *Travels in Arabia Deserta* was first published in 1888 and went through many editions and printings. Hemingway's early correspondence with his editor Max Perkins indicates his awareness of this book as early as April 1925 when, thinking of what would become *Death in the Afternoon,* he wrote: "I hope some day to have a sort of Doughty's Arabia Deserta of the Bull Ring" (*Selected Letters,* 156). However, the surviving copies in his library were published in 1931 and 1937 (see next item).

———. *Travels in Arabia Deserta.* Introduction by T. E. Lawrence. New York: Random House, 1937.

Doukan, Gilbert. *La chasse sous-marine: Précis de pêche au fusil harpon.* Paris: Chantenay, 1946. Hemingway owned two copies.

Duguid, J. *Tiger-man: An Odyssey of Freedom.* New York: Century, 1932.

Eastman, George. *Chronicles of an African Trip.* Privately printed for the author, 1927.

Edminster, Frank Custer. *American Game Birds of Field and Forest; Their Habits, Ecology, and Management.* New York: Scribner's, 1954.

Edwards, Ernest Preston. *Finding Birds in Mexico.* Amherst, VA: Edwards, 1955.

Elliot, Russell W. *Your Shotgun vs. You.* Kansas City, MO: Brown-White-Lowell, 1955.

Emil, Ludwig. [Translated by Mary H. Lindsay]. *The Nile: The Life-Story of a River.* [New York: Viking Press, 1937.]

Esquire's First Sports Reader. Edited by Herbert Graffis. New York: Barnes, 1945.

Esquire's Second Sports Reader. Edited with an introduction by Arnold Gingrich. New York: Barnes, 1946.

Evanoff, Vladimir. *Surf Fishing.* New York: Barnes, 1948.

Evans, R. Tenniel. *The Butterfly Collector's Handbook for East Africa.* [Illustrated by R. E. Bush.] Nairobi: [Ndia Kuu,] 1946.

Farrington, Sara Houston (Chisie). *Women Can Fish.* New York: Coward-McCann, 1951.

Farrington, Selwyn Kip. *Atlantic Game Fishing.* Introduction by Ernest Hemingway. New York: Kennedy, 1937. Hemingway also owned a 1957 reprint of this book.

———. *A Book of Fishes.* Philadelphia: Blakiston, 1946.

———. *Fishing the Pacific.* New York: Coward-McCann, 1953.

———. *Pacific Game Fishing.* New York: Coward-McCann, 1942.

Farson, Negley. *Going Fishing.* New York: Harcourt, Brace, 1943. Hemingway owned two copies.

Fichter, George S., ed. *The Fisherman's Handbook for 1954–1955.* Oxford, OH: Fisherman Press, 1955.

Field and Stream (periodical). *The Sportman's World; for Every Hunter and Fisherman: A Richly Illustrated Guide to Sport in Seventeen Areas of the United States and Abroad.* By the editors of *Field and Stream.* New York: Holt, 1959.

Fisher, James, and R. N. Lockley. *Sea-birds: An Introduction to the Natural History of the Sea-birds of the North Atlantic.* Boston: Houghton Mifflin, 1954.

Fishes of Cuba and the Atlantic Coasts of Tropical America. Museo Carlos de la Torre y Huerta. Havana, 1946.

Fishing and Hunting in Cuba. 4th ed. N.p., n.d.

The Fishing Gazette (periodical). Hemingway's issues of this magazine are stored in the Finca Vigía, Cuba.

Fitz, Grancel. *North American Head Hunting.* New York: Oxford, 1957. A contemporary account calls this "an engaging personal account of experiences in obtaining big-game trophies" (*The Rotarian,* April 1958).

Fitzpatrick, James Percy. *Jock of the Bushveld.* London: Longman, Green, 1954.

Ford Treasury of the Outdoors. Edited by Ford Motor Company, Publications Dept. New York: Simon & Schuster, 1952.

Forester, C. S. *The African Queen.* New York: Modern Library, 1940. Popular romantic novel, set during WWI in Africa. Reynolds notes that a 1936 letter from Hemingway to Mr. Reed indicates that Hemingway had read and enjoyed the book by that date (*Hemingway's Reading,* 126).

Forester, Frank. *See* Herbert, Henry William

France. Union des fédérations des syndicats d'initiative de France. *La chasse en France: Premier inventaire des lieux de chasse.* Paris, 1927.

———. *La pêche en France.* Paris, 1925.

Francis, Francis. *A Book on Angling; Being a Complete Treatise on the Art of Angling in Every Branch with Explanatory Plates, etc.* Edited by Sir Herbert Maxwell. London: Jenkins, 1920.

Frémont, Isabelle Victorine. *Some Birds of East Africa.* Nairobi: Highway, 1951.

Gérard, Jules. *La chasse au lion.* Paris: Michel Lévy, 1874.

Ghidini, Luigi, ed. *Nuovo manuale del cacciatore.* Milan: Hoepli, 1946.

Gibb, Hamilton Alexander Rosskeen, Edward Denison, and Eileen Power, eds. *Muhammad Ibn 'Abd Allah Called Ibn Batutah: Travels in Asia and Africa 1325–1354.* Translated by H. A. R. Gibb. London: Routledge, 1929.

Gilpatric, Guy. *The Complete Goggler, Being the First and Only Exhaustive Treatise on the Art of Goggle Fishing.* New York: Dodd, Mead, 1938. In Hemingway's *Islands in the Stream,* Thomas Hudson's son Andy is fearful about goggle fishing (done underwater with spears) and stays on board while his brother David does it. The blood of the fish David catches attracts a shark (54, 56, 70–71, 78–88).

Gladstone, Hugh Stewart. *Record Bags and Shooting Records, Together with Some Account of the Evolution of the Sporting Gun, Marksmanship, and the Speed and Weight of Birds.* London: Witherby, 1922.

Godfrey, Joseph Charles. *Popular Mechanics' Guide to Good Hunting and Trapping.* Chicago: Popular Mechanics, 1952.

Godfrey, Joseph Charles, and Frank Dufresne. *The Great Outdoors: The Where, When, and How of Hunting and Fishing, Including a New Dictionary of Sportsmen's Terms.* New York: Whittesey House, 1949.

Golding, Harry, ed. *The Wonder Book of the Wild.* London: Ward, Lock, 1924. (Fitch)

Goode, George Brown. *American Fishes: A Popular Treatise upon the Game and Food Fishes of North America with Especial Reference to Habits and Methods of Capture.* New edition, completely revised and largely extended by Theodore Gill. Boston: Page, 1903.

Gorer, Geoffrey. *Africa Dances: A Book about West African Negroes.* New York: Knopf, 1935.

Graham, B. N. Gordon. *Hunter at Heart.* [Illustrated by A. I. Cameron and from photos by the author and others.] London: Jenkins, 1950. About hunting in Sri Lanka.

Graham, Joseph Alexander. *The Sporting Dog*. [1904.] New York: Macmillan, 1924.

Graham, Robert Bontine Cunninghame. *Rodeo: A Collection of the Tales and Sketches of R. B. Cunninghame Graham*. Selected and with an introduction by A. F. Tschiffely. [Heinemann, 1936.]

Gray, Prentiss Nathaniel, ed. *Records of North American Big Game*. New York: Derrydale, 1932.

———, ed. *Records of North American Big Game*. New York: Scribner's, 1952.

Green, Roland. *Wing-tips: The Identification of Birds in Flight*. London: Black, 1947.

Greene, Graham. *Journey without Maps*. Garden City, NY: Doubleday, Doran, 1936.

*Greener, William Welllington. *The Gun and Its Development, with Notes on Shooting*. London: Cassell, Petter, Galpin, 1881.

*Greenwood, James. *Wild Sports of the World: A Book of Natural History and Adventure*. London: Ward, Lock & Tyler, 1880. Hemingway owned two copies of this book.

Gregg, William H. [assisted by Capt. John Gardner]. *Where, When and How to Catch Fish on the East Coast of Florida*. [With One Hundred Engravings, and Twelve Colored Illustrations of Fishes. New York, 1902.]

Gregory, William K., and Francesca La Monte. *The World of Fishes: A Survey of Their Habits, Relationships and History and a Guide to the Fish Collections of the American Museum of Natural History*. New York: American Museum of Natural History, 1947.

Grey, Edward. *The Charm of the Birds*. [New York: Frederick A. Stokes, 1927.]

Grey, Romer C. *Adventures of a Deep-sea Angler*. New York: Harper, 1930.

Grey, Zane. *An American Angler in Australia*. New York: Harper, 1937.

———. *Tales of the Angler's Eldorado: New Zealand*. [First published in 1926 or 1927.]

———. *Tales of Swordfish and Tuna*. London: Hodder & Stoughton, 1927.

———. *Tales of Tahitian Waters*. New York: Harper, 1931.

Grogan, Ewart Scott, and Arthur H. Sharp. *From the Cape to Cairo: The First Traverse of Africa from South to North*. London: Nelson, n.d. (ca. 1900). Grogan was resident on the foothills of Kilimanjaro at the time of Hemingway's two trips. The two might have met, as Grogan lived not very far from Hemingway's camp site.

Guinot, Robert. *La chasse: Les armes; les chiens; les gibiers de plaine et de montagne; la sauvagine; le gros gibier; les animaux nuisibles; l'organisation des chasse; la legislation.* Paris: Larousse, 1939.

Günther, Klaus, and Kurt Deckert. *Creatures of the Deep Sea.* New York: Scribner's, 1956.

Haig-Brown, Roderick L. *Fisherman's Winter.* New York: Morrow, 1954.

———. *The Western Angler: An Account of Pacific Salmon and Western Trout.* New York: Morrow, 1947.

Hakkenberg van Gaasbeek, H. C. M. *Caraïbisch Steekspel. Omslag en tekeningen van Paul Erkelens.* Assen: Van Gorcum, 1955.

Hall, Henry Marion. *A Full Creel.* New York: Longmans, Green, 1946.

———. *The Ruffed Grouse.* New York: Oxford, 1946.

———. *Woodcock Ways.* New York: Oxford, 1946.

Hanley, Gerald. *The Consul at Sunset.* [Hanley wrote novels set in Kenya and other African countries. The first British edition of this book, which Hemingway praises, seems to be London: Collins, 1951]. *The Consul at Sunset* is praised in *Under Kilimanjaro* (208).

———. *The Year of the Lion.* [The first British edition of this book, which Hemingway reads during his second safari, seems to be London: Collins, 1953.] The narrator of *Under Kilimanjaro* reads this book (209, 224).

Hardy, Alister Clavering. *The Open Sea: Its Natural History.* Vol. 1: *The World of Plankton.* Vol. 2: *Fish and Fisheries.* Boston: Houghton Mifflin, 1956, 1959.

———. *Hardy's Angler's Guide.* London, 1924.

———. *Hardy's Angler's Guide.* London, n.d.

———. *Hardy's Angler's Guide.* London, n.d.

*Harris, William Cornwallis. *The Wild Sports of Southern Africa; Being the Narrative of a Hunting Expedition from the Cape of Good Hope, through the Territories of the Chief Moselekatse, to the Tropic of Capricorn.* London: Murray, 1839. Hemingway also owned a later edition: London: Pickering, 1841.

Harroy, Jean Paul. *Afrique, terre qui meurt: La dégradation des sols africains sous l'influence de la colonisation.* Brussels: Hayez, 1949.

Hately, T. L., and Hugh Copley. *Angling in Africa;* [*With Some Account of East African Fish.* London: East Africa], 1933.

Hausman, Ethel Hinckley. *Beginner's Guide to Wild Flowers*. New York: Putnam, 1948.

Hausman, Leon Augustus. *Field Book of the Eastern Birds*. New York: Putnam, 1946.

Hawker, Peter. *Instructions to Young Sportsmen in All That Relates to Guns and Shooting*. Edited with an introduction by Eric Parker. London: Jenkins, 1922. Hemingway owned two copies.

Hedin, Sven Anders. *My Life as an Explorer*. Translated by Alfhild Huebsch. New York: Boni & Liveright, 1925.

Heilner, Van Campen. *A Book on Duck Shooting*. [ca. 1939.]

———. *Our American Game Birds*. Foreword by Col. Theodore Roosevelt. Garden City, NY: Doubleday, Doran, 1941.

———. *Salt Water Fishing*. New York: Knopf, 1945. Hemingway also owned the Knopf 1953 edition.

Herbert, Henry William [Frank Forester]. *The Complete Manual for Young Sportsmen, with Directions for Handling the Gun, the Rifle and the Rod; The Art of Shooting on the Wing; The Breaking, Management and Hunting of the Dog; The Varieties and Habits of Game; River, Lake and Seafishing, etc*. New York: Stringer & Townsend, 1857.

———. *Frank Forester's Fish and Fishing of the United States and British Provinces of North America*. New York: Townsend, 1864. Hemingway owned two copies of this book.

"Harvest is Ripe." *See* "Come Over to Africa."

Hewitt, Edward Ringwood. *Better Trout Streams: Their Maintenance, with Special Reference to Trout Habits and Food Supply*. New York: Scribner's, 1931. Hemingway owned two copies of this book.

———. *Telling on the Trout*. New York: Scribner's, 1930.

———. *A Trout and Salmon Fisherman for Seventy-five Years*. New York: Scribner's, 1948.

Hickey, Joseph James. *A Guide to Bird Watching*. London: Oxford, 1943.

Hicks, James Ernest. *What the Citizen Should Know about Our Arms and Weapons*. New York: Norton, 1941.

*Highton, Hugh Percy. *Shooting Trips in Europe and Algeria, Being a Record of Sport in the Alps, Pyrenees, Norway, Sweden, Corsica and Algeria*. London: Witherby, 1921.

Hill, Howard. *Wild Adventure*. Harrisburg, PA: Stackpole, 1954. About archery hunting.

Hill, William Charles Osman, et al. *The Elephant in Central Africa*. London: Rowland Ward, 1953. Donated by Mary Hemingway to the Hemingway Collection, JFK Library.

Hoffmann, Ralph. *Birds of the Pacific States*. Boston: Houghton Mifflin, 1927.

Holder, Charles Frederick. *The Big Game Fishes of the United States*. New York: Macmillan, 1924.

Holland, Robert, Daniel Holland, and Raymond Holland. *Good Shot! A Book of Rod, Gun and Camera*. New York: Knopf, 1946.

Hollingsworth, Lawrence William. *A Short History of the East Coast of Africa*. London: Macmillan, 1951.

Hornell, James. *Fishing in Many Waters*. Cambridge, England: UP, 1950.

Hudson, W[illiam] H[enry]. *Adventures Among Birds*. London: Dent, 1928.

———. *Afoot in England*. [First edition was London: Dent, 1909.]

———. *Birds in London*. London: Dent, 1924.

———. *Birds in Town and Village*. [First published in 1920.]

———. *The Book of a Naturalist*. [First published in 1919.]

———. *Dead Man's Plack and Old Thorn & Poems*. [First published in 1920 or 1924.]

———. *Far Away and Long Ago* [: *A Childhood in Argentina*. First published in 1917. A 1918 edition is subtitled *A History of My Early Life*.] Hemingway's character David Bourne seems to own several of W. H. Hudson's books; he admires *Far Away and Long Ago* and *Nature in Downland* (*Garden of Eden* 94–95, 194).

———. *Hampshire Days*. London: Dent, 1925.

———. *A Hind in Richmond Park*. [First edition, London: Dent, 1922.]

———. *Idle Days in Patagonia*. London: Dent, 1924. The narrator of Hemingway's *Death in the Afternoon* claims he admires Hudson's "charming and sound" descriptions of Patagonia's plant and animal life (133).

———. *The Land's End: A Naturalist's Impressions in West Cornwall*. London: Dent, 1926.

———. *The Naturalist in La Plata*. [First edition, 1892.] London: Dent, 1929.

———. *Nature in Downland*. London: Dent, 1925.

———. *Le pays pourpre*. Paris: Plon, 1927. [Translation of *The Purple Land that England Lost*, 1885.] Hemingway's characters Robert Cohn and Jake Barnes have read Hudson's *The Purple Land* (*The Sun Also Rises*, 9–10).

———. *Rare, Vanishing, and Lost British Birds.* Compiled by Linda Gardiner. London: Dent, 1923.

———. *A Traveller in Little Things.* [First published in 1921.]

———. *W. H. Hudson's South American Romances.* [A posthumous collection of previously published works, including *The Purple Land* and *Green Mansions.* London: Duckworth, 1930.]

Hughes-Parry, Jack. *Fishing Fantasy: A Salmon Fisherman's Note-book.* London: Eyre & Spottiswoode, 1949.

Hunt, Lynn Bogue. *An Artist's Game Bag.* [First edition, New York: Derrydale Press, 1936.]

Huntingford, George Wynn Brereton, and C. R. V. Bell. *East African Background.* London: Longmans, Green, 1950.

Hureau, Jean. *Plein air et camping: Manuel practique.* Paris: Éditions de la Revue "Camping," 1942.

*Hutchinson, Horatio Gordon, ed. *Big Game Shooting, Volumes 1 and 2.* London: Newnes, 1905. In the Brentano list, the title *Big Game Shooting* appears twice: once with no further identification, and once identified as consisting of two volumes and attached to the name Bodminton (*sic*), a reference to the *Badminton Library of Sports and Pastimes* (1824–1899), of which Volumes XX and XXI were titled *Big Game Shooting* and were edited by Phillips-Wolley, q.v. Hemingway also owned other books with the same or similar titles: see the entries for Maydon, and Whelen.

Huxley, Elspeth Joscelin. *Four Guineas: A Journey through West Africa.* London: Chatto & Windus, 1954.

———. *Murder on Safari.* New York: Harper, 1938. A detective novel set in Kenya.

———. *White Man's Country: Lord Delamere and the Making of Kenya.* 2 vols. London: Chatto & Windus, 1953.

Huxley, Julian. *Africa View.* New York: Harper, 1931.

Imaz Baume, Arturo. *Cacería.* Mexico City: Talleres Gráficos de la Nación, 1938. About Mexican game birds.

International Game Fish Association. *Organization and Rules.* New York: American Museum of Natural History, 1945.

———. *Organization and Rules.* New York: American Museum of Natural History, 1948.

———. *Organization and Rules.* New York: American Museum of Natural History, n.d.

———. *World Record, Marine Game Fishes.* Miami, 1959.

———. *World Record, Marine Game Fishes.* Miami, 1960.

———. *Yearbook*. New York: American Museum of Natural History, 1952.

Jackson, Frederick John. *Notes on the Game Birds of Kenya and Uganda (Including the Sand-grouse, Pigeons, Snipe, Bustards, Geese, and Ducks)*. London: William & Norgate, 1926. Jackson was one of the early colonial administrators of Ukambani and wrote extensively about Akamba. Hemingway took this book with him on his first safari and kept records of game on its pages.

Jaques, Harry Edwin. *How to Know the Land Birds*. Dubuque, IA: Brown, 1947.

Jearey, Bertram Frederick. *Pride of Lions*. Foreword by J. Wentworth Day. London: Longmans, Green, 1936.

Johnson, David. *The Proud Canaries*. New York: Sloane, 1959.

Johnson, Eldridge Reeves. *Tarpomania & Buck Fever*. Camden, NJ: Privately printed, 1928.

Johnson, Isaac Charles. *Sport on the Blue Nile; or, Six Months of a Sportsman's Life in Central Africa*. London: Banks, 1903.

Johnson, Martin, and Osa Johnson. Although Hemingway's letters indicate that he was familiar with the work of this American husband-wife team of explorers and photographers who documented Africa in the 1920s, their books are not mentioned in any of the inventories of his library.

Johnson, Melvin Maynard. *Rifles and Machine Guns: A Modern Handbook of Infantry and Aircraft Arms*. New York: Morrow, 1944.

Johnson, Melvin Maynard, and Charles T. Haven. *Ammunition: Its History, Development and Use, 1600–1943*. New York: Morrow, 1943.

Jordan, David Starr. *The Fish Fauna of the California Tertiary*. Stanford: Stanford UP, 1921.

———. *Fishes*. New York: Appleton, 1925.

Jordan, David Starr, and Carl Leavitt Hubbs. *Studies in Ichthyology: A Monographic Review of the Family of Atherinidae or Silver-sides*. Stanford: Stanford UP, 1919.

Jordan, David Starr, and James Z. Gilbert. *Fossil Fishes of Diatom Beds of Lompoc, California*. Stanford: Stanford UP, 1920.

Jouenne, Lucien. *Pendant vos vacances, pêchez au bord de la mer*. Paris: Flammarion, 1922.

Jouenne, Lucien, and J. H. Perreau. *La pêche au bord de la mer*. [Librairie J. B. Baillière & fils, 1927.]

Kaplan, Moise N. *Big Game Angler's Paradise*. [The first edition is Tallahassee, FL: Rose Printing Co., 1936; the second edition was published in New York: Liveright, 1937.] It is not clear which edition Hemingway owned.

———. *Big Game Fisherman's Paradise: A Complete Treatise on Angling Philosophy, Sidelights and Scenes in Florida Salt-water Fishing Ventures*. Tallahassee, FL: Department of Agriculture, 1956.

Kephart, Horace. *The Book of Camping and Woodcraft: A Guide for Those Who Travel in the Wilderness*. Kephart first gathered his how-to essays for *Field and Stream* into a book in 1906; a second edition was published in 1921. It is not clear which edition Hemingway owned.

Kessel, Joseph. *The Lion*. Translated from the French by Peter Green. New York: Knopf, 1959. Hemingway owned two copies of this popular novel, which is set in Kenya.

Kieran, John. *A Natural History of New York City: A Personal Report after Fifty Years of Study & Enjoyment of Wildlife within the Boundaries of Greater New York*. Boston: Houghton Mifflin, 1959.

*Kinloch, Alexander Angus Airlie. *Large Game Shooting in Thibet, the Himalayas, and Northern India*. Calcutta: Thacker, Spink, 1885.

Kipling, Rudyard. Hemingway owned Kipling's *Collected Verse*, six volumes of the *Compact Edition of Rudyard Kipling*, ten volumes of the *Works*, and individual editions of several Kipling books.

Klein, Herb. *Lucky Bwana: The Adventures of a Big Game Hunter in British East Africa*. Dallas, 1953.

Klingel, Gilbert C. *Inagua, Which Is the Name of a Very Lonely and Nearly Forgotten Island*. New York: Dodd, Mead, 1940. The story of a shipwrecked scientific expedition, illustrated with photographs by the author.

Knight, John Alden. *Field Book of Fresh Water Angling*. New York: Putnam, 1944.

———. *Modern Fly Casting*. New York: Scribner's, 1942.

———. *The Theory and Technique of Fresh Water Angling*. New York: Harcourt, Brace, 1940.

La Blanchère, Henri de. *La pêche et les poissons: Nouveau dictionnaire général des pêches*. Paris: Delagrave, 1868.

La Branche, George Michel Lucien. *The Dry Fly and Fast Water: Fishing with the Floating Fly on American Trout Streams*. New York: Scribner's, 1914.

La Chevasnerie-Libault, Antoine de. *Gibiers et chasses d'Europe*. Paris: Payot, 1939.

Lake, Alexander. *Hunter's Choice: True Stories of African Adventure*. New York: Doubleday, 1954.

———. *Killers in Africa: The Truth about Animals Lying in Wait and Hunters Lying in Print.* Garden City, NY: Perma-books, 1954.

La Monte, Francesca Raimonde. *Marine Game Fishes of the World.* Garden City, NY: Doubleday, 1953.

———. *North American Game Fishes.* Garden City, NY: Doubleday, Doran, 1945. Hemingway owned three copies of this book.

———. *A Review and Revision of the Marlins, Genus Makaira.* New York: American Museum of Natural History, 1955.

La Monte, Francesca Raimonde, and Donald E. Marcy. *Ichthyological Contributions to the International Game Fish Association.* New York, 1941.

Landor, Arnold Henry Savage. *An Explorer's Adventures in Tibet.* New York: Harper, 1910.

Large, Laura Antoinette. *Little Stories of Famous Explorers.* New York: Platt & Munk, 1935.

Lawrence, D. H. Without specifying titles, Patrick Hemingway identifies "D. H. Lawrence's later work" as a literary influence for Hemingway's *Under Kilimajaro*. According to Brasch and Sigman, Hemingway owned several books by Lawrence, including *The Plumed Serpent* (1926), *The Ladybird* (1927), *The Prussian Officer and Other Stories* 1927), *The Lovely Lady* (1946), *The Portable D. H. Lawrence* (1947 and 1954). He also had a copy of the poem "The Triumph of the Machine." "Hemingway mentions D. H. Lawrence in this memoir [*True at First Light*] I think specifically to justify the invention in this book of his own religion which was meant to apply simply to himself and the people he was on safari with" (Patrick Hemingway, 14).

Leakey, Louis Seymour Bazett. *Animals in Africa.* London: Harvill, 1953.

———. *Mau Mau and the Kikuyu.* London: Methuen, 1953.

Le Breton, F. H. *Up-country Swahili Exercises for the Soldier, Settler, Miner, Merchant, and Their Wives, and All Who Deal with Up-country Natives without Interpreters.* Richmond, Surrey: Simpson, 1949. Hemingway also owned a later edition by the same publisher and title (it may be a reprint): Richmond, Surrey: Simpson, 1956.

Legrand, Maurice. *Au fil de l'eau: Souvenirs d'un pêcheur.* Tours: Arrault, 1943.

Leigh, William Robinson. *Frontiers of Enchantment: An Artist's Adventures in Africa.* New York: Simon & Schuster, 1938.

Lenz, Ellis Christian. *Muzzle Flashes: Five Centuries of Firearms and Men.* Huntington, WV: Standard, 1944.

Leopold, Aldo. *Game Management.* New York: Scribner's, 1933.

Lessing, Doris. *Martha Quest.* 1952. This is the first of the five novels featuring Martha Quest, the child of colonial parents, who was born in Central Africa. The others are *A Proper Marriage* (1954), *A Ripple from the Storm* (1958), *Landlocked* (1965), and *The Four-Gated City* (1969). Together, these five novels are called *Children of Violence.* Patrick Hemingway defined "the marvelous series of novels, the so-called Martha Quest novels" as a literary influence on Hemingway as he wrote about the second safari (14). He must have been referring to the first three, as the last two were published after Hemingway died. No Lessing work appears in Reynolds's or Brasch and Sigman's bibliographies.

Lettow-Vorbeck, Paul Emil von. *My Reminiscences of East Africa.* London: Hurst & Blackett, 1920.

*Leveson, Henry Astbury (H. A. L.). *Sport in Many Lands: Europe, Asia, Africa and America, etc. etc.* London: [Frederick] Warne, n.d. [ca. 1877].

Lewis, George Washington. *Elephant Tramp.* Edited by Byron Fish. Boston: Little, Brown, 1955. Modern editions of what seems to be this book are called *I Loved Rogues: The Life of an Elephant Tramp,* and seem to be about training elephants for the circus.

Lhote, Henri. *Le Niger en kayak: Histoires de navigation, de chasse, de pêche et aventures.* Paris: Susse, 1943.

Lincoln, Frederick Charles. *The Migration of American Birds.* Illustrated by Louis Agassiz Fuertes. Garden City, NY: Doubleday, Doran, 1939.

Locke, Arthur. *The Tigers of Trengganu.* New York: Scribner's, 1954.

Lutz, Frank Eugene. *Field Book of Insects of the United States and Canada.* New York: Putnam, 1935.

Lydekker, Richard. *Animal Portraiture: Fifty Studies by Wilhelm Kuhnert.* London: Warne, 1912.

―――. *The Game Animals of Africa.* [London: R. Ward, 1908.] Brasch and Sigman attribute this book to Lyell.

Lyell, Denis David. *The Hunting and Spoor of Central African Game [with life-size Illustrations of most of the Game Tracks].* London: Seely, Service & Co., 1929. Brasch and Sigman indicate that Hemingway owned two copies. For a contemporary review of the book, see http://www.jstor.org/stable/1784702.

―――, ed. *African Adventure: Letters from Famous Big Game Hunters.* New York: Dutton, 1935.

Lynn-Allen, Bulkeley Garbutt. *Shot-gun and Sunlight: The Game Birds of East Africa*. London: Batchworth, 1951.

MacDowell, Syl [Tom Gunn]. *Western Trout*. New York: Knopf, 1948.

Mackworth-Praed, Cyril Winthrop, and C. H. B. Grant. *African Handbook of Birds*. Series I: *Birds of Eastern and Northeastern Africa*. 2 vols. London: Longmans, Green, 1952, 1955. Hemingway owned a later edition, also in two volumes and carrying the same title: London: Longmans, Green, 1957. The narrator of *Under Kilimanjaro* took this "good new book" with him (probably volume 1 of the earlier edition) (224). For a contemporary description of "the bird book" (*Under Kilimanjaro*, 225), see http://afraf.oxfordjournals.org/cgi/reprint/52/207/168.pdf.

Madan, Arthur C. *English-Swahili Dictionary*. [2nd ed. Oxford: Clarendon Press,] 1902.

Major, Harlan. *Salt Water Fishing Tackle*. New York: Funk & Wagnalls, 1948.

Malcolm, George, and Aymer Maxwell. *Grouse and Grouse Moors*. London: Black, 1910.

Malet, Rawdon. *Unforgiving Minutes*. [With illustrations. London: Hutchinson & Co., 1934].

Manore, Jean [Emmanuel Gallus]. *Choses de chasse*. Paris: Emile Nourry, 1904.

Maran, René. *Batouala*. [Paris: A. Michel, 1921.] Hemingway's glowing 1922 review of this book is reprinted as "Black Novel a Storm Center" in *Ernest Hemingway. Dateline: Toronto. The Complete Toronto Star Dispatches, 1920–1924*, edited by William White, 112–13. New York: Scribner's, 1985.

Marbury, Mary Orvis. *Favorite Flies & Their Histories*. Boston: Houghton Mifflin, 1892.

Markham, Beryl. *West with the Night*. New York: Farrar, Strauss and Giroux, 1942.

Marron, Eugenie. *Albacora: The Search for the Giant Broadbill*. New York: Random House, 1957.

Marryat, Frederick. *Capt. Marryat's Works*. 24 vols. Boston: Estes, 1896–1898. Reynolds identifies Africa as the setting of one of Marryat's novels, *Jacob Faithful*.

Mathews, Ferdinand Schuyler. *Field Book of American Trees and Shrubs*. New York: Putnam, 1915.

———. *Field Book of American Wild Flowers*. New York: Putnam, 1929.

———. *Field Book of Wild Birds and Their Music*. [First edition was Kessinger Publishing, 1902.]

Matout, Louis. *Méthode nouvelle de pêche practique. Comment réussir de grosse pêches*. Paris: Hachette, 1924.

Matthiessen, Peter. *Wildlife in America*. New York: Viking, 1959.

*Maydon, Hubert Conway, ed. *Big Game Shooting in Africa*. Philadelphia: Lippincott, n.d. [ca. 1929]. The book is now in the Hemingway Collection, JFK. Hemingway took notes in the margins of the last two pages and the endpapers, with references to Pauline, Charles [Thompson], and Alfred [Vanderbilt], which date to the first safari. Although this American edition is the only one that was included in the books that Mary Hemingway donated to the Hemingway Collection, she claims to have read a British edition (*How It Was*, 313); this would have been vol. 14 of the Lonsdale Library (London: Seeley, Service & Co., 1932). For a review, see http://www.jstor.org/stable/1784052.

McDermand, Charles. *Waters of the Golden Trout Country*. New York: Putnam, 1946. Hemingway owned two copies.

Meeker, Oden. *Report on Africa*. New York: Scribner's, 1954.

Millet, Fernand Victor. *Les grands animaux sauvages de l'Annam, leurs moeurs, leur chasse et leur tir*. Paris: Plon, 1930.

Milne, Lorus Johnson, and Margery J. Milne. *The Life of the Water Film*. New York, 1947.

———. *A Multitude of Living Things*. N.p., 1947.

Mitchell-Hedges, Frederick Albert. *Battles with Giant Fish* [with illustrations from photographs by Lady Richmond Brown. First edition was published in London by Duckworth & Co., 1923. A second edition followed in 1926.] Brasch and Sigman do not indicate which edition Hemingway owned.

Mitchell-Henry, L. *Tunny Fishing at Home & Abroad*. London: Rich & Cowan, 1934. Hemingway owned two copies.

Molloy, Peter. *The Cry of the Fish Eagle: The Personal Experiences of a Game Warden and His Wife in the Southern Sudan*. London: Joseph, 1957.

Money, Albert William. *Pigeon Shooting*. Edited by A. C. Gould. New York: Shooting and Fishing Publishing Co., 1896.

Monfreid, Henri de. *La croisière du hachich*. [Grasset, 1933.]

———. *Le drame éthiopien*. [Grasset, 1935.]

———. *L'enfant sauvage*. [N.p., n.d.]

———. *Le lépreux*. [Grasset, 1935.]

———. *Le masque d'or; ou, Le dernier négus.* [Grasset, 1936.]

———. *La poursuite du Kaïpan.* 1 vol. [of 2. Grasset, 1934.]

———. *Les secrets de la Mer Rouge.* Paris: Grasset, 1931.

———. *Vers les terres hostiles de l'Ethiopie.* Paris: Grasset, 1933.

Moore, Audrey. *Serengeti.* New York: Scribner's, 1939. Hemingway owned two copies.

Moore, Ernst D. *Ivory: Scourge of Africa.* New York: Harper, 1931.

Moreno, Abelardo. *Estudio anatómico del género polynista beck.* Havana, 1950. Brasch and Sigman suggest this anatomical study is about *Polinices picta*, or Baracoa, although in the index they list this book under "Snails."

Moreno, Abelardo, and Ramona Fernández. *La fauna de Cuba.* Havana: Fernández, 1945.

Morris, Percy A. *A Field Guide to the Shells of Our Atlantic Coast.* Boston: Houghton Mifflin, 1947.

Muldoon, Guy. *Leopards in the Night.* London: Hart-Davis, 1955.

———. *The Trumpeting Herd.* London: Hart-Davis, 1957.

Myers, Arthur Bowen Richards. *Life with the Hamran Arabs: An Account of a Sporting Tour of Some Officers of the Guards in the Soudan, during the Winter of 1874–1875.* London: Smith, Elder, 1876.

Naether, Carl Albert. *The Book of the Pigeon.* [Philadelphia: David McKay, 1939. A fourth, completely revised edition was issued by the same publisher in 1958. Brasch and Sigman do not identify the edition Hemingway owned.]

Naintré, Loïc, C. Oddenino, and M. Laurens. *La pêche en mer.* Paris: Prisma, 1948.

[Naylor, Wilson S. *Daybreak in the Dark Continent.* The Young People's Missionary Movement, 1905.]

Needham, Paul Robert. *Trout Streams: Conditions That Determine Their Productivity and Suggestions for Stream and Lake Management.* Ithaca, NY: Comstock, 1938.

Nesbitt, Lewis Mariano. *Hell-hole of Creation: The Exploration of Abyssinian Danakil.* New York: Knopf, 1935.

*Neumann, Arthur H. *Elephant-hunting in East Equatorial Africa; Being an Account of Three Years' Ivory-hunting under Mount Kenia and among the Ndorobo Savages of the Lorugi Mountains, including a Trip to the North End of Lake Rudolph.* London: Ward, 1898.

New Zealand Birds and Flowers: A Selection of Colour Plates. Wellington, New Zealand: Reed, 1955.

*Niedieck, Paul. *With Rifle in Five Continents*. Translated from the original German by H. B. Stanwell. London: Ward, 1908.

Norman, John Roxborough. *A History of Fishes*. New York: Wyn, 1948.

Norris, Thaddeus. *The American Angler's Book, Embracing the Natural History of Sporting Fish, and the Art of Taking Them, with Instructions in Fly-fishing, Fly-making, and Rod-making, and Directions for Fish-breeding, to Which Is Added Dies Discatoriae, Describing Noted Fishing-places, and the Pleasure of Solitary Fly-fishing*. Philadelphia: Porter & Coates, 1864.

Norton, Mortimer. *Salt Water Sports Fishing, by Old Ai*. N.p., 1948.

Nyabongo, Akiki K. *The Story of an African Chief*. Introduction by William Lyon Phelps. New York: Scribner's, 1935.

Oberjohann, Heinrich. *Komoon! Capturing the Chad Elephant*. Translated by Rhoda de Terra. New York: Pantheon, 1952.

Oberthür, Joseph. *Gibiers de notre pays: Histoire naturelle pour les chasseurs*. Ouvrage publié sous le haut patronage du Saint-Hubert Club de France. Paris: Champs-Elysées, 1941. Hemingway owned three copies of this book.

———. *Poissons et fruits de mer de notre pays: Pêche, histoire naturelle, cuisine*. Paris: Nouvelle Edition, 1944.

Osborn, Robert Chesley. *How to Catch Trout*. New York: Coward-McCann, 1941. Hemingway owned two copies.

———. *How to Shoot Ducks*. New York: Coward-McCann, 1941.

———. *How to Shoot Quail*. New York: Coward-McCann, 1941.

Oudard, Georges. *Chasses féodales d'aujourd'hui: U.R.S.S. Pologne–Roumanie*. Paris: Plon, 1934.

Pardo García, Luis. *Cuestiones de pesca fluvial*. Valencia: Vives Mora, 1934.

———. *Cuestiones de pesca y caza acuática*. Valencia: Vives Mora, 1935.

Parker, Eric. *Elements of Shooting*. London: Field, 1924.

———, ed. *Shooting by Moor, Field, and Shore: A Practical Guide to Modern Methods*. By Eric Parker, Leslie Sprake, Major Portal, and others. Philadelphia: Lippincott, 1929. Hemingway seems to have owned two copies of this first American edition; the book was also published in Britain in the same year.

———, ed. *Shooting by Moor, Field, and Shore*. [In The Lonsdale Library Series.] London: Seeley Service, 1951.

Paton, Alan. *The Land and People of South Africa*. Philadelphia: Lippincott, 1955.

———. *South Africa in Transition*. New York: Scribner's, 1956.

———. *Too Late the Phalarope*. London: Cape, 1953.

Patterson, John Henry. *The Man-eaters of Tsavo and Other East African Adventures*. Foreword by Frederick Courteney Selous. London: Macmillan, 1908.

———. *The Man-eating Lions of Tsavo*. Chicago: Field Museum of Natural History, 1925.

Pearson, Haydn Sanborn. *Sea Flavor*. New York: McGraw-Hill, 1948. [Vignettes describing the flora, fauna, and daily life of the New England coast.]

*Pease, Alfred Edward. *The Book of the Lion*. London: Murray, 1914.

Peattie, Donald Culross. *Forward the Nation*. New York: Putnam, 1942.

———. *Green Laurels: The Lives and Achievements of the Great Naturalists*. [New York: Simon & Schuster, 1936.]

Peattie, Roderick, ed. *A Gathering of Birds: An Anthology of the Best Ornithological Prose*, [1939. Attributed to Doanald Culross Peattie.]

Les pêches sportives [*étude et vulgarisation des meilleurs procédés de pêche au lancer, pêche au trainer, etc.*]. N.p.: L'Édition Française, 1929. This is a classified as a catalogue.

Penwill, D. J. *Kamba Customary Law: Notes Taken in the Machakos District of Kenya Colony*. London: Macmillan, 1951.

Percival, Arthur Blayney. *A Game Ranger on Safari*. London: Nisbet, 1928.

———. *A Game Ranger's Note Book*. London: Nisbet, 1927.

Pérez Ramos, A. Carlos. *Caza y pesca en América: Manual práctico de caza y pesca publicado en español e inglés. La ley de gangsterismo y nuevas instrucciones sobre licencias a armas*. Havana: Lex, 1948. Hemingway owned three copies of this bilingual manual on hunting and fishing that also discusses the "gangster law" and the licensing of weapons.

———. *Caza y pesca en Cuba: Manual práctico de cazadores y pescadores; leyes, decretos-leyes y disposiciones sobre licencias de armas, reglamentos guarda jurados, vigilantes nocturnos y asuntos de los municipios*. Havana: Lex, 1945.

Pernau, G. de. *Pour réussir du tir aux pigeons: Education, entraînement, conseils*. Monaco: Chêne, 1913.

Perrott, Daisy Valerie. *Teach Yourself Swahili*. London: English Universities Press, 1951.

Peterson, Roger Tory. *Birds over America*. New York: Dodd, Mead, 1948.

———. *Field Guide to the Birds.* [First published in 1934, this influential book helped shape the genre of field guides.]

———. *A Field Guide to Western Birds.* Boston: Houghton Mifflin, 1941.

———. *How to Know the Birds.* New York: New American Library, 1957.

Peterson, Roger Tory, Guy Mountford, and P. A. D. Hollom. *A Field Guide to the Birds of Britain and Europe.* Boston: Houghton Mifflin, 1954.

Pettingill, Olin Sewall. *A Guide to Bird Finding East of the Misissippi.* New York: Oxford, 1951.

———. *A Guide to Bird Finding West of the Mississippi.* New York: Oxford, 1953.

*Phillipps-Wolley, Clive. *Big Game Shooting;* [*with contributions by Sir Samuel W. Baker et al.; with illustrations by Charles Whymper, J. Wolf and H. Willink, and from photographs.*]. 2 vols. London: Longmans, Green, 1894. [Volumes XX and XXI of the *Badminton Library of Sports and Pastimes.*]

Pigot, Robert. *Twenty-Five Years' Big Game Hunting.* London: Chatto & Windus, 1928.

Pinchot, Gifford. *Just Fishing Talk.* New York: Telegraph, 1936.

Poli, François. *Pesca de tiburones.* Barcelona: Hispano-Europea, 1958. About shark fishing.

Pollard, Hugh Bertie Campbell. *Game Birds: Rearing, Preservation, and Shooting.* London: Eyre & Spottiswoode, 1929.

———. *The Gun Room Guide.* [London: Eyre & Spottiswoode, 1930.]

———. *Wildfowl & Waders: Nature & Sport in the Coastlands.* Depicted by the late Frank Southgate, R. B. A., and described by Hugh B. C. Pollard. London: Country Life, 1928.

Pope, Clifford Hillhouse. *Turtles in the U.S. and Canada.* [New York: Knopf, 1939.]

Popowski, Bert. *Crow Shooting.* New York: Barnes, 1946.

Potous, Paul L. *My Enemy, the Crocodile: The Strange Story of Africa's Deadliest Business.* New York: Funk, 1957.

Pough, Richard Hooper. *Audubon Bird Guide: Small Land Birds of Eastern & Central North America from Southern Texas to Central Greenland.* Garden City, NY: Doubleday, 1949.

———. *Audubon Water Bird Guide: Water, Game and Large Land Birds, Eastern and Central North America, from Southern Texas to Central Greenland.* Garden City, NY: Doubleday, 1951. Hemingway owned two copies.

Pretorius, Philip Jacobus. *Jungle Man: The Autobiography of Major P. J. Pretorius.* Foreword by J. C. Smuts. New York: Dutton, 1948.

Puxley, W. Lavallin. *Deep Seas and Lonely Shores.* New York: Dutton, 1936.

Radcliffe, William. *Fishing from the Earliest Times.* London: Murray, 1926.

Ranking, John. *Historical Researches on the Wars and Sports of the Mongols and Romans, in Which Elephants and Wild Beasts Were Employed or Slain and the Remarkable Local Agreement of History with the Remains of Such Animals Found in Europe and Siberia.* London: Privately printed, and sold by Longmans, Rees, Orme, Brown, Green, etc., 1826.

Ransome, Arthur. *"Racundra's" First Cruise.* London: Cape, 1927.

———. *Rod and Line.* London: Cape, 1940.

Raswan, Carl Reinhard. *The Black Tents of Arabia: My Life among the Bedouins.* [London: Hutchinson, 1935.]

Ratcliffe, B. J., and Howard Elphinstone. *A New English-Swahili Phrase Book.* Nairobi: East African Standard, 1952. Hemingway owned two copies of this book.

Reed, Chester Albert. *Bird Guide.* Part 2: *Land Birds East of the Rockies.* New York: Doubleday, Page, 1909.

Reed's Seamanship. [This widely used guidebook for professional seamen and yachtsmen, first published in the 1830s, evolved into an even more popular *Reed's Nautical Calendar.*] See http://www.reed-salmanac.com/index.cfm?fuseaction=About&AboutPages=yes.

Reeve, J. Stanley. *Fox Hunting Formalities.* Issued as a supplement to *The Sportsman.* Boston: The Sportsman, 1929.

Reid, Mayne. *The Boy Hunters; or, Adventures in Search of a White Buffalo.* Novel, ca. 1855.

Reid, Victor Stafford. *The Leopard.* New York: Viking, 1958. Novel by a Jamaican author set in Kenya during the Mau Mau rebellion.

Reignac, Jean. *La chasse pratique: Droits et devoirs du chasseur, choix des az-mes et des munitions, le tir, les chiens de chasse; races, élevage, dressage, le gibier; de plaine, des bois, du marais, de la Montaigne, du bord de la mer, comment on le chasse, protection du gibier, destruction des rapaces, conseils.* [Librairie Hachette, 1928.]

Reitz, Deneys. *Afrikander.* New York: Minton, [Balch & Co.], 1933. About Namibia.

———. *Trekking On*. [Preface by J. C. Smuts. London: Faber & Faber, 1933, rpt. 1934, 1947]. Hemingway seems to have had the 1934 version. About South and East Africa.

Richards, Coombe. *El Salmón*. Barcelona: Hispano-Europea, 1958. [Probably a translation of Richards, *Salmon: How to Catch Them*, first published in 1956.]

Richardson, Wyman. *The House on Nauset Marsh [A Cape Cod Memoir]*. New York: Norton, 1955. Describes animal life in Cape Cod, with focus on fishing and duck hunting.

Ritz, Charles C. *Erlebtes Fliegenfischen: Kunst und Technik des Fliegenfischens auf äschen, forellen und lashse*. Mit einer Einführung von Ernest Hemingway, einem Vorwort von L. de Boisset. Ruschlikon-Zurich: Muller, 1956.

[Rivas, Luis Rene et al.], University of Miami, Institute of Marine Science. *Lou Marron-University of Miami Pacific Billfish Expedition: Preliminary Report for 1954*. Coral Gables, FL, 1955.

Robinson, James Merlen. *Forty Years of Hunting*. Minneapolis: Robinson, 1947.

Rodgers, Walter R. *Huntin' Gun: Men, Gun Feel and Game*. Washington: Infantry Journal, 1949.

Roig Montserrat, Juan. *Pesca de la trucha y del salmón*. [N.p., n.d.]

———. *Pesca marítima*. Barcelona: Juventud, [1958].

Roosevelt, Robert Barnwell. *Superior Fishing; or, The Striped Bass, Trout, Black Bass and Blue-Fish of the Northern States*. New York: Orange Judd, 1884.

Roosevelt, Theodore. *African Game Trails: An Account of the African Wanderings of an American Hunter-Naturalist*. London: Murray, 1910.

Roosevelt, Theodore, and Kermit Roosevelt. *Trailing the Giant Panda*. New York: Scribner's, 1929.

Roosevelt, Theodore, T. S. Van Dyke, D. C. Elliot, and A. J. Stone. *The Deer Family*. New York: Macmillan, 1924.

Roughley, Theodore Cleveland. *Wonders of the Great Barrier Reef*. New York: Scribner's, 1947.

Roule, Louis. *Fishes: Their Journeys and Migrations*. Introduction by William Beebe. Translated by Conrad Elphinstone. New York: Norton, 1933.

Rouquet, Louis. *Au bord de l'eau*. Lyon: Masson, 1924.

Royal East African Automobile Association. *Road Book for 1952*. Nairobi, 1951.

Royal Institute of International Affairs. *Abyssinia and Italy* (1935).

Royal Tsavo National Park. Kenya, 1954.

Ruark, Robert. *Horn of the Hunter.* Garden City, NY: Doubleday, 1953.

———. *Something of Value.* Garden City, NY: Doubleday, 1955. Hemingway disparages this best-selling novel, set in Kenya during the Mau Mau uprising, in *Under Kilimanjaro* (309). He owned three other Ruark works, but they do not deal with hunting, natural history, safaris, or Africa. Ruark's *Uhuru* (London: Hamish Hamilton, 1962), a novel set in Kenya, was published after Hemingway died.

Sánchez Roig, Mario, and Federico Gómez de la Maza. *La pesca en Cuba.* Havana: Seoane, Fernández, 1947.

Sanderson, George P. *Thirteen Years among the Wild Beasts of India: Their Haunts and Habits from Personal Observations; with an Account of the Modes of Capturing and Taming Elephants.* London: Allen, 1879.

Sanderson, Ivan Terence. *Animal Treasure.* New York: Viking, 1937.

———. *Follow the Whale.* Boston: Little, Brown, 1956.

———, ed. *Animal Tales: An Anthology of Animal Literature of All Countries.* New York: Knopf, 1946.

Sandys, Edwyn, and Theodore Strong Van Dyke. *Upland Game Birds.* New York: Macmillan, [1902]. Hemingway owned two copies.

Sanford, Leonard Cutler, Louis Bennet Bishop, and Theodore Strong Van Dyke. *The Water-fowl Family.* New York: Macmillan, 1924. Hemingway seems to have owned two copies.

Sauvage, Henri Emile. *La grande pêche (Les poissons).* Paris: Jouvet, 1891.

Schenck, Hilbert Van Nydeck, and Henry Kendall. *Shallow Water Diving and Spearfishing.* Cambridge, MD: Cornell Maritime, 1954.

Schillings, Karl Georg. *In Wildest Africa.* Translated by Frederic Whyte. 2 vols. London: Hutchinson, 1907.

Schmidt, Karl Patterson, and Delbert Dwight Davis. *Field Book of Snakes of the United States and Canada.* New York: Putnam, 1941.

Schreiner, Olive. *The Story of An African Farm.* 1883. A three-part narrative, set in South Africa, identified by Patrick Hemingway as a literary source for *Under Kilimanjaro* (14). The book does not appear in Reynolds's or Brasch and Sigman's bibliographies, either under the author's name or under her pseudonym, Ralph Iron.

Schrenkeisen, Raymond Martin, ed. *Fishing for Salmon and Trout.* Garden City, NY: Doubleday, 1937.

Scott, Jack Denton. *Forests of the Night.* New York: Rinehart, 1959. [A book of photographs about hunting in India, apparently coauthored with Mary Lou Scott.]

Scott, Peter. *Wild Chorus.* [Illustrated by the author. Country Life, 1939.]

Scott, Robert Lee. *Between the Elephant's Eyes!* New York: Dodd, Mead, 1954.

———. *Look of the Eagle.* New York: Dodd, Mead, 1955.

Self, Margaret Cabell. *The Horseman's Encyclopedia.* New York: Barnes, 1946.

———. *Your First Pony.* London: Kaye, 1950.

Seligman, Charles Gabriel. *Races of Africa.* London: Butterworth, 1939.

*Selous, Frederick Courteney. *A Hunter's Wanderings in Africa; Being a Narrative of Nine Years Spent amongst the Game of the Far Interior of South Africa, Containing Accounts of Explorations beyond the Zambesi, on the River Chobe, and in the Matabele and Mashuna Countries, with Full Notes upon the Natural History and Present Distribution of All the Large Mammalia.* London: Bentley, 1881. Hemingway also owned a later edition with the same title, London: Macmillan, 1925.

———. *Travel and Adventure in South-east Africa; Being the Narrative of the Last Eleven Years Spent by the Author on the Zambesi and Its Tributaries, with an Account of the Colonization of Mashunland and the Progress of the Gold Industry in That Country.* London: Ward, 1893.

Seton, Ernest Thompson. *The Library of Pioneering and Woodcraft.* [This was published in several volumes, intended for children in general and boy scouts in particular, of which *Rolf in the Woods* (below) was the first. Garden City, NY: Doubleday, Doran, 1930.]

———. *Life-histories of Northern Animals: An Account of the Mammals of Manitoba.* 2 vols. [New York: Scribner's, ca. 1909.]

———. *Rolf in the Woods: The Adventures of a Boy Scout with Indian Quonab and Little Dog Skookum.* [The first in the series entitled *The Library of Pioneering and Woodcraft.* Doubleday, 1927.]

———. *Trail of an Artist-naturalist.* New York: Scribner's, 1940.

———. *Wild Animals at Home.* [Doubleday, 1913.]

———. *Woodcraft.* [Probably *The Book of Woodcraft and Indian Lore.* Garden City, NY: Doubleday, Page & Company, 1926.]

———. *Woodland Tales.* [Children's stories, 1905.]

Sheldon, Charles. *The Wilderness of Denali: Explorations of a Hunter-naturalist in Northern Alaska.* [Edited by C. Hart Merriam and Edward

Nelson and published posthumously by Sheldon's widow. New York: Scribner's, 1930.]

Shortt, Angus Henry, and Bertram William Cartwright. *Sports Afield Collection of Know Your Ducks and Geese.* Minneapolis: Sports Afield, 1948. Hemingway owned two copies.

Siemel, Sasha. *Tigrero!* New York: Prentice-Hall, 1953. This book was shipped by Scribner's to Hemingway when he was on safari and receipt was confirmed by cable from Nairobi on 17 December 1954. It is not listed by Reynolds or Brasch and Sigman.

Smith, Lawrence Breese. *Dude Ranches and Ponies.* [Illustrated with photographs; Foreword by Philip Ashton Rollins. New York: Coward-McCann, 1936.]

———. *Shotgun Psychology: Theory and Practice Regarding Shotguns, Their Construction and Functioning, and How to Learn to Shoot Them Correctly.* New York: Scribner's, 1938.

Solanes Ragull, Benito. *Manual des pescador aficionado (rio y mar).* Barcelona: Sintes, 1953.

Solar, Antonio C. *The Guide to Hunting & Fishing in Cuba; Published to Give Visiting Sportsmen the Knowledge and Experience of the Cubans.* Havana, 1958. Hemingway owned two copies.

Sommer, François. *Man and Beast in Africa.* Foreword by Ernest Hemingway. Translated from the French by Edward Fitzgerald. London: Jenkins, 1953.

———. *Pourquoi ces bêtes sont-elles sauvages?* Préface de Ernest Hemingway. Paris: Toison d'Or, 1951.

Sommer, Jacqueline and François. *Le safari la gâchette.* Paris: Laffont, 1956. Hemingway owned two copies.

The South and East African Year Book 1933. [The 40th edition of this popular guide book, published in 1934, was edited by A. Samler Brown and G. Gordon Brown (for the Union Castle Mail Steamship Company) and published in London by Sampson Low, Marston & Co. For a contemporary description of the book, see http://www.jstor.org/stable/1785508. Hemingway seems to have owned the 39th edition.]

Southard, Charles Zibeon. *The Evolution of Trout and Trout Fishing in America.* [The first edition is New York: E. P. Dutton & Co., 1928.] Brasch and Sigman do not indicate which edition Hemingway owned.

Spain. Department of Agriculture. *Concurso de trofeos venatorios y exposición de caza en el arte.* Madrid: Sociedad Española de Amigos del Arte, Ministerio de Agricultura, 1950.

———. *Vocabulario español de la caza.* Madrid: Ministerio de Agricultura, 1950.

Sparrow, Walter Shaw. *Angling in British Art through Five Centuries: Prints, Pictures, Books.* [London: The Bodley Head, 1923.]

Sports Afield, Sports Illustrated (periodicals). Hemingway subscribed to these magazines and some issues are stored in his Cuban home, the Finca Vigía.

A Standard English-Swahili Dictionary. London: Oxford, 1953. Hemingway also owned the 1955 Oxford edition. These are probably based on A. C. Madan's work (above), reissued under the editorship of Frederick Johnson.

Stanley, Edward. *A Familiar History of Birds* [*, their Nature, Habits, and Instincts.* 2 vols. 1835; reissued in one volume in 1865]. In *Death in the Afternoon*, Hemingway names and disparages this book of Bishop Stanley (134).

*Stanley, Henry Morton. *How I Found Livingstone: Travels, Adventures and Discoveries in Central Africa, Including Four Months' Residence with Dr. Livingstone.* London: Low, Marston, n.d. [The first edition is 1872, but the book was popular and went through many editions.]

Stefansson, Vilhjalmur. *The Friendly Arctic: The Story of Five Years in the Polar Regions.* London: Harrap, 1921.

———, ed. *Great Adventures and Explorations from the Earliest Times to the Present, As Told by the Explorers Themselves.* With the collaboration of Olive Rathbun Wilcox. New York: Dial, 1947.

Stevenson-Hamilton, James. *South African Eden, from Sabi Game Reserve to Kruger National Park.* London: Cassell, 1952.

———. *Wild Life in South Africa.* London: Cassell, 1950.

*Stigand, Chauncey Hugh. *Game of British East Africa.* [London: H. Cox], 1909.

*———. *Hunting the Elephant in Africa and Other Recollections of Thirteen Years' Wanderings.* Introduction by Colonel Theodore Roosevelt. New York: Macmillan, 1913.

Stoddard, Herbert Lee. *The Bobwhite Quail: Its Habits, Preservation, and Increase.* New York: Scribner's, 1932.

Streever, Fred. *A New Fishing Technique: Deep Trolling with Fine Wire.* New York, n.d.

Sturgis, Bertha. *Field Book of Birds of the Panama Canal Zone.* [New York: G. P. Putnam's Sons, 1928.]

Sutton, George Miksch. *Mexican Birds: First Impressions. Based upon an ornithological expedition to Tamaulipas, Nuevo León and Coahuila.* Norman: U of Oklahoma P, 1951.

Sutton, Richard Lightburn. *Tiger Trails in Southern Asia.* St. Louis: Mosby, 1926.

Sverdup, Harold Ulrik, Martin W. Johnson, and Richard H. Fleming. *The Oceans: Their Physics, Chemistry, and General Biology.* New York: Prentice-Hall, 1942.

Tanganyika Territory Game Preservation Department. *Game Preservation Department Annual Report, 1932; Including Map of the Tanganyika Territory.* Dar es Salaam: Government Printer, 1933. The pamphlet is in the Hemingway Collection, JFK.

Taverner, Eric. *Trout Fishing from All Angles.* London: Seeley, 1929. Hemingway also owned the 1933 Seeley edition.

Taylor, John. Pondoro. *Last of the Ivory Hunters.* New York: Simon & Schuster, 1955.

Teale, Edwin Way. *Adventures in Nature: Selections from the Outdoor Writings of Edwin Way Teale.* New York: Dodd, Mead, 1959.

———. *Journey Into Summer: A Naturalist's Record of a 19,000-mile Journey through the North American Summer.* New York: Dodd, Mead, 1960.

Teasdale-Buckell, George Teasdale. *The Complete Shot.* Fifth edition revised by A. F. Randall. London: Methuen, 1924.

Tee-Van, John, and others, eds. *Fishes of the Western North Atlantic.* New Haven: Sears Foundation for Marine Research, Yale University, 1948.

Tennyson, Julian. *Rough Shooting for the Owner-keeper, Month by Month.* London: Black, 1938.

Tenzing, Norkey. *Tiger of the Snows: The Autobiography of Tenzing of Everest.* Written in collaboration with James Ramsey Ullman. New York: Putnam, 1955.

Thomas, George Clifford, and George C. Thomas III. *Game Fish of the Pacific, Southern Californian and Mexican Coastline.* Philadelphia: Lippincott, 1930.

Thomazi, Auguste Antoine. *Histoire de la pêche des âges de la pierre à nos jours.* Paris: Payot, 1947.

Thommen, George S. *Spinning Reels and Tackle.* New York: Durrell, 1949.

Tomlinson, Henry Major. *The Sea and the Jungle.* London: Duckworth, 1912; New York: Dutton, 1913. (Fitch)

Towner Coston, Harry Ernest. *Speckled Nomads: A Tale of Trout in Two Rivers.* New York: Macmillan, 1939.

Towner Coston, Harry Ernest, F. T. K. Pentelow, and R. W. Butcher. *River Management: The Making, Care & Development of Salmon & Trout Rivers.* Philadelphia: Lippincott, 1936.

Truesdell, Stephen Riggs. *The Rifle: Its Development for Big Game Hunting.* Harrisburg, PA: Military Service, 1947.

United States Bureau of Navigation and Steamboat Inspection. *Pilot Rules for Certain Inland Waters of the Atlantic and Pacific Coasts and of the Coast of the Gulf of Mexico (Revised to July 5, 1933).* Washington: U.S. Gov't. Print. Off., 1933.

United States Coast and Geodetic Survey. *Inside Route Pilot: Intracoastal Waterway, New York to Key West.* Washington: U.S. Gov't. Print. Off., 1936.

———. *Inside Route Pilot: New York to Key West.* Washington: U.S. Gov't. Print. Off., 1931.

———. *Supplement to United States Coast Pilot, Atlantic Coast. Section D: Cape Henry to Key West.* Washington: U.S. Gov't. Print. Off., 1933.

———. *Tide Tables, East Coast, North and South America (Including Greenland).* Washington: U.S. Gov't. Print. Off., 1951.

———. *United States Coast Pilot, Atlantic Coast. Section D: Cape Henry to Key West.* Washington: U.S. Gov't. Print. Off., 1928.

———. *United States Coast Pilot, Gulf Coast. Key West to the Rio Grande.* Washington: U.S. Gov't. Print. Off., 1926.

———. *United States Coast Pilot, Gulf Coast. Key West to the Rio Grande.* Washington: U.S. Gov't. Print. Off., 1936.

United States Department of the Interior. *Fading Trails: The Story of Endangered American Wildlife.* Prepared by a Committee of the United States Department of the Interior, National Park Service. New York: Macmillan, 1942.

United States Hydrographic Office. *Azimuths of the Sun for Latitudes Extending to 70 Degrees from the Equator.* Washington: U.S. Gov't. Print. Off., 1934. Hemingway owned two copies.

———. *Central America and Mexico Pilot (East Coast) from Galinas Point, Colombia to the Rio Grande.* Washington: U.S. Gov't. Print. Off., 1927.

———. *Mexico and Central America Pilot (West Coast) from the United States to Colombia, Including the Gulfs of California and Panama.* Washington: U.S. Gov't. Print. Off., 1928.

———. *Navigation Tables for Mariners and Aviators.* Washington: U.S. Gov't. Print. Off., 1937.

———. *Sailing Directions for the Mediterranean.* Washington: U.S. Gov't. Print. Off., 1945.

———. *Sailing Directions for the West Indies.* Issued under the authority of the Secretary of the Navy. Washington: U.S. Gov't. Print. Off., 1936.

———. *Tables of Computed Altitude and Azimuth, Latitudes 200 to 290 Inclusive.* Washington: U.S. Gov't. Print. Off., 1941. Hemingway owned two copies.

———. *Tables of Computed Altitude and Azimuth, Latitudes 301 to 391 Inclusive.* Washington: U.S. Gov't. Print. Off., 1940.

———. West Indies Pilot. Vol. 2. Washington: U.S. Gov't. Print. Off., 1929.

United States Nautical Almanac Office. *The American Air Almanac, 1945.* Washington: U.S. Gov't. Print. Off., 1945.

———. *The American Ephemeris and Nautical Almanac, 1951.* Washington: U.S. Gov't. Print. Off., 1951.

———. *The American Nautical Almanac, 1942.* Washington: U.S. Gov't. Print. Off., 1942.

———. *The American Nautical Almanac, 1947.* Washington: U.S. Gov't. Print. Off., 1947.

United States Navy Dept. *The 1931 International Code of Signals.* Washington: U.S. Gov't. Print. Off., 1937, 1943.

United States War Dept. *Basic Field Manual: U.S. Rifle, Caliber .30, M1903.* Washington: U.S. Gov't. Print. Off., 1943.

———. *Browning Automatic Rifle, Caliber .30, M1918, without Bipod.* Washington: U.S. Gov't. Print. Off., 1940.

———. *Shotguns, All Types.* Washington: U.S. Gov't. Print. Off., 1942.

Vale, Robert B. *Wings, Fur and Shot: A Grass-roots Guide to American Hunting.* Foreword by Seth Gordon. New York: Stackpole, 1936.

Van der Post, Laurens. *The Dark Eye in Africa.* New York: Morrow, 1955.

———. *Flamingo Feather.* New York: Morrow, 1955. Hemingway owned two copies.

———. *The Lost World of the Kalahari.* New York: Morrow, 1958.

———. *Venture to the Interior.* New York: Morrow, 1951.

Vavon, Antoine Joseph. *La truite: Ses moeurs, l'art de la pêcher.* Etampes (Seine-et-Oise): Dormann, 1927.

Venesmes, Jean. *Les songeries d'un pêcheur sportif.* Paris: Chaubon, 1946.

Verrill, Alpheus Hyatt. *Great Conquerors of South and Central America.* [New York: New Home Library, 1943.]

———. *Strange Sea Shells and Their Stories.* Boston: Page, 1936.

Vesey-Fitzgerald, Brian Seymour, ed. *The Book of the Horse.* London: Nicholson & Watson, 1946.

Vesey-Fitzgerald, Brian Seymour, and Francesca La Monte, eds. *Game Fish of the World.* New York: Harper, 1949.

Vezes, Henri [Ryvez]. *Les pêches au Lancer: Mouches et cuillers truites et brochets.* Paris: Bornemann, 1936.

———. *La truite de rivière: Ses diverses pêches à la ligne.* Paris: Bornemann, 1936.

Viertel, Peter. *White Hunter, Black Heart.* Garden City, NY: Doubleday, 1953. Set in Africa, this novel is based on Viertel's experiences as screenwriter for the movie *The African Queen,* based on C. S. Forester's book of the same title, which Hemingway also owned. In *Under Kilimanjaro,* Hemingway disparages *White Hunter, Black Heart* (309), of which he owned two copies.

Walsingham, Thomas De Gray, and Ralph Payne-Gallwey. *Shooting.* London: Longmans, Green, 1887.

Walden, Howard Talbot. *Upstream & Down.* New York: Macmillan, 1938.

Walton, Isaak. *The Complete Angler; or, The Contemplative Man's Recreation of Izaak Walton and Charles Cotton.* Boston: Little, Brown, 1912.

Wang, Wen-hsien [J. Wong-Quincey]. *Chinese Hunter.* Foreword by Lin Yutang. New York: Day, 1939. [A contemporary review of the British edition of this book identifies the author as J. Wong-Quincey and its subject as hunting in northern China.] See http://www.jstor.org/stable/1788659.

Ward, Rowland. *Rowland Ward's Records of Big Game with Their Distribution Characteristics, Dimensions, Weights and Horn and Tusk Measurements.* Edited by Guy Dollman and J. B. Burlace. London: Ward, 1928.

———. *Rowland Ward's Sportman's Handbook to Collecting and Preserving Trophies and Specimens.* Edited by J. B. Burlace. London: Ward, 1923.

———. *The Sportsman's Handbook to Collecting, Preserving, and Setting-up Trophies & Specimens, Together with a Guide to the Hunting Grounds of the World.* [A popular book by a famous British taxidermist; the 3rd edition was 1883, the tenth was 1911.] Brasch and Sigman don't specify which edition Hemingway owned.

Watkins-Pitchford, Denys James [B. B.]. *Manka, the Sky Gipsy: The Story of a Wild Goose*. New York: Scribner's, 1939.

——, comp. *The Fisherman's Bedside Book*. New York: Scribner's, 1946. Hemingway owned two copies.

——, comp. *The Shooting Man's Bedside Book*. New York: Scribner's, 1948.

——, comp. *The Sportsman's Bedside Book*. London: Eyre Spottiswoode, 1948.

Waugh, Evelyn. *Waugh in Abyssinia*. [1936].

Webb, Walter Freeman. *United States Mollusca: A Descriptive Manual of Many of the Marine, Land and Fresh Water Shells of North America, North of Mexico*. Rochester, NY: Bookcraft, 1942.

Weber, H. L. "Driver Ants." African pamphlet recommended to Hemingway by his father in 1920.

——. "Native Customs." Another such pamphlet.

Whelen, Townsend. *American Big Game Shooting*. Illinois: Western Cartridge, 1925.

——. *Wilderness Hunting and Wildcraft, with Notes on the Habits and Life Histories of Big Game Animals*. [Small Arms Technical Pub. Co., 1927.]

——, ed. *Hunting Big Game: An Anthology of True and Thrilling Adventures*. 2 vols. Harrisburg, PA: Military Service Publishing, 1946.

White, Gilbert. *The Natural History of Selborne, with Observations on Various Parts of Nature; and the Naturalist's Calendar*. Additions and supplementary notes by Sir William Jardin. Edited with further illustrations, a biographical sketch of the Author, and a complete index by Edward Jesse. London: Bohn, 1854. In *Death in the Afternoon*, Hemingway notes that White wrote "most interestingly" about the hoopoe bird (133).

Wilson, Christopher James. *The Story of the East African Mounted Rifles*. Nairobi: [The East African Standards, 1938.]

Winegate, F. R. *Fire and Sword in the Sudan* (1896).

Wise, Hugh Douglas. *Tigers of the Sea*. New York: Derrydale, 1937. About sharks.

Wood, John G[eorge]. *The Popular Natural History*. New York: Burt, n.d. [The first edition of this book was published in London by

Routledge & Sons in 1867. I can find no date for this American edition that Hemingway owned.]

Woodruff, Frank Morley. *The Birds of the Chicago Area*. Chicago: Jennings & Graham, 1907.

Wulff, Lee. *Leaping Silver*. New York: [G. W.] Stewart, 1940.

The Yachtsman's Annual Guide and Nautical Calendar. New York: Motor Boating, 1940.

Yale, Leroy Milton, and others. *Angling*. New York: Scribner's, 1897.

The Year Book and Guide to East Africa, with Atlas, Folding Map, Town Plans, Route Maps. London: Hale, 1954.

Zim, Herbert Spencer, and Robert H. Baker. *Stars: A Guide to the Constellations, Sun, Moon, Planets and Other Features of the Heavens*. New York: Simon & Schuster, 1951.

Zim, Herbert Spencer, and Ira N. Gabrielson. *Birds: A Guide to the Most Familiar American Birds*. New York: Simon & Schuster, 1949.

Zim, Herbert Spencer, and Donald F. Hofmeister. *Mammals: A Guide to Familiar American Species*. New York: Simon & Schuster, 1955.

Zim, Herbert Spencer, and Lester Ingel. *Seashores: A Guide to Animals and Plants along the Beaches*. New York: Simon & Schuster, 1955.

Zim, Herbert Spencer, and Alexander C. Martin. *Flowers: A Guide to Familiar American Wildflowers*. New York: Simon & Schuster, 1950.

———. *Trees: A Guide to Familiar American Trees*. New York: Simon & Schuster, 1952. Hemingway owned two copies.

Zim, Herbert Spencer, and Hurst H. Shoemaker. *Fishes: A Guide to Fresh and Salt-water Species*. New York: Simon & Schuster, 1956. Hemingway owned two copies.

Zim, Herbert Spencer, and Hobart M. Smith. *Reptiles and Amphibians: A Guide to Familiar American Species*. Sponsored by the Wildlife Management Institute. New York: Simon & Schuster, 1956.

Notes

[1] The original Brentano list, dated 23 March 1934, was provided by Samuel Smallidge, Ernest Hemingway Collection Intern, J. F. Kennedy Library and Museum, Boston.

[2] In his short story "Fathers and Sons," Hemingway writes that his character Nick "was very grateful to him [to Nick's father] for two things: fishing and shooting . . . now, at thirty-eight, he loved to fish and shoot exactly as much as when he first had gone with his father. It was a passion that had never slackened and he was very grateful to his father for bringing him to know it" (490).

3 He was given a single-shot twenty-gauge shotgun on either his tenth (according to his grandson, Seán Hemingway, "Introduction," xxv) or twelfth birthday (according to his biographer Carlos Baker, *Life*, 12).

4 Carl P. Eby, e-mail communications to Jeremiah Kitunda, 13 August and 25 September 2005, and to Miriam B. Mandel, 13 March 2010. Lawrence Grimes, e-mail communication to Miriam B. Mandel, 27 March 2010.

5 In Patrick Hemingway, "An Evening with Patrick Hemingway," p. 14.

6 A letter from Wallace Meyer to Ernest Hemingway, 27 November 1953, informs Hemingway that he has been sent eight books that he had requested and six more that might interest him; of those six, only the two by Corbett (*Jungle Lore*) and Siemel (*Tigrero!*) are relevant to this bibliography.

Works Cited and Consulted

Baker, Carlos. *Ernest Hemingway: A Life Story*. 1969. Reprint, New York: Collier Macmillan, 1988.

Beegel, Susan F. "A Guide to the Marine Life in Ernest Hemingway's *The Old Man and the Sea*." *Resources for American Literary Study* 30 (2005): 236–315.

Brasch, James D., and Joseph Sigman. *Hemingway's Library: A Composite Record*. New York: Garland, 1981.

Brentano's Book List, 23 March 1934. Other Materials Series: Book Lists, Misc., Hemingway Collection, John F. Kennedy Presidential Library and Museum, Boston.

Fitch, Noel. "Ernest Hemingway — c/o Shakespeare and Company." *Fitzgerald / Hemingway Annual* (1977): 157–81.

Hemingway, Ernest. *Death in the Afternoon*. New York: Scribner's, 1932.

———. "Fathers and Sons." In *The Short Stories of Ernest Hemingway*, 488–99. 1938. Reprint, New York: Scribner's, 1966. First published 1933 in Hemingway's *Winner Take Nothing*.

———. *Hemingway on Hunting*. Edited and with an introduction by Seán Hemingway. Foreword by Patrick Hemingway. Guilford CT: The Globe Pequot Press, 2001.

———. *Selected Letters 1917–1961*. Edited by Carlos Baker. New York: Scribner's, 1981.

Hemingway, Mary. *How It Was*. New York: Knopf, 1976.

Hemingway, Patrick. "An Evening with Patrick Hemingway." *Hemingway Review* 19, no. 1 (1999): 8–16.

Hemingway, Pauline Pfeiffer. 1933–1934 Diary of Safari to Africa with Ernest Hemingway, M1344, Department of Special Collections and University Archives, Stanford University Libraries, Stanford, California.

Layman, Richard. "Hemingway's Library Cards at Shakespeare and Company." *Fitzgerald / Hemingway Annual* (1975): 191–207.

Mandel, Miriam B. "Subject and Author: The Literary Backgrounds of *Death in the Afternoon*." In *A Companion to Hemingway's "Death in the After-*

noon," edited by Miriam B. Mandel, 79–119. Rochester, NY: Camden House, 2004.

Meyer, Wallace. Typed letter to Ernest Hemingway, 27 November 1953. The original letter is in the Archives of Charles Scribner's Sons, Manuscripts Division, Department of Rare Books and Special Collections, Princeton University Library.

Meyers, Jeffrey. *Hemingway: A Biography*. 1985. London: Paladin Grafton Books, 1987.

Reynolds, Michael S. *Hemingway: The 1930s*. New York: Norton, 1997.

———. *Hemingway's Reading, 1910–1940: An Inventory*. Princeton: Princeton UP, 1981.

———. "A Supplement to *Hemingway's Reading: 1910–1940*." *Studies in American Fiction* 14, no. 1 (1986): 99–108.

2: Ernest Hemingway on Safari: The Game and the Guns

Silvio Calabi

ERNEST HEMINGWAY WAS a very experienced and skilled lifelong hunter and shooter. He started early. His mother, Grace Hall Hemingway, noted that "Ernest was taught to shoot by Pa when $2^1/_2$ and when 4 could handle a pistol" (Hotchner, 49). His grandson, Seán Hemingway, specifies that by the time his grandfather was three years old, he "had learned to load, cock and shoot a gun by himself, and at four he was trekking as much as seven miles on hunting expeditions with his father, carrying his own gun over his shoulder" (xxiv). He adds that Ernest Hemingway received his first firearm, an inexpensive single-shot 20-gauge shotgun, from his grandfather, Anson Hemingway, on his tenth birthday, 21 July 1909 (xxv).[1] In all this, Hemingway was typical of Americans of the first half of the twentieth century, whose familiarity with firearms derived from the settling of the West, two world wars, and a host of smaller armed conflicts. This knowledge began to wane as, for a growing portion of American society, guns devolved from useful and necessary tools in common use to symbols of cultural primitivism. In the twenty-first century, many if not most of Hemingway's readers are strangers to the culturally and technically complicated world of shooting for sport or for food, firearms that are used for hunting, and the African safari.

Hemingway often remarked that he invented from knowledge. He acquired his knowledge of guns and shooting over decades of serious and varied hunting in North America, Cuba, Europe, and East Africa, and if we are to read his "inventions," his narratives, we have to read from that knowledge as well. A few facts and definitions will help us to do so.

The Game

Dangerous game in Africa usually means the "Big Five": lion, leopard, Cape buffalo, rhino, and elephant. Their body weight varies from less than two hundred pounds for the leopard to six or seven tons for a mature elephant bull. All of the Big Five can be killed with deer-size calibers, provided a well-made bullet penetrates the heart or brain. But if one misses the vital spot, the situation can become formidably dangerous, as the attacked or injured animal, suddenly fortified by adrenaline, looks for a fight. Now, the lion's massive chest muscles become hard as plywood and it can cover a hundred yards in four or five seconds. An oncoming elephant often requires a difficult high-angle shot to the forehead, where the brain lies behind a foot or more of resilient, spongy bone. The leopard, although physically the smallest of the five by far, becomes perhaps the most fearsome when wounded: its unearthly speed and small size make it a difficult target. An attacking Cape buffalo leads with its thick, heavy horns, which are difficult if not impossible to penetrate. The two African species of rhinoceros, black and white, are dangerous because of their size (two or three tons, give or take), their thick hide (nearly two inches in places), and their occasional nearsighted belligerence, but they are generally regarded as the least difficult to stop in a charge.[2] The single-minded violence of a fight to the finish with any one of these creatures can be stunning.

To survive a charge the hunter must put a heavy bullet where it will stop the animal short, either by killing it outright or by knocking it down long enough to deliver a follow-up coup de grâce. This is a mortal test of not only the weapon and ammunition, but even more of the shooter's marksmanship, presence of mind, coolness under pressure, and courage.

In each of his two trips to East Africa, Hemingway collected four of the Big Five, but never the biggest of them, the elephant. For a man of Hemingway's bravura personality, this is initially surprising, but maybe less so in context. Elephants were still being shot legally for the commercial value of their ivory in the 1950s, but any kind of market gunning was highly unethical to Roosevelt era conservationists such as Hemingway, and he may have wanted to distance himself from any possible taint of shooting for profit. In addition, many hunters then and now have ambivalent feelings about elephants — which are intelligent, sensitive, social, and sometimes extremely dangerous — as game. Mary Hemingway writes that her husband "had no wish to shoot an elephant" because, he said, elephants are "'too big, too important, too noble'" (400).[3]

The opportunity was certainly there. Elephants are mentioned often in *Under Kilimanjaro* and in Mary Hemingway's chapter about that safari in her memoir, and the Hemingway Collection at the John F. Kennedy Library has an unpublished image of the author gazing at a mature bull with long, symmetrical, bragging-class tusks, well within range. And the desire may have been there as well: Earl Theisen, the *Look* photographer who accompanied the Hemingways in 1953, wrote to his wife that Hemingway "got a little mad with me last night when I turned down an all-night vigil on a 'bad elephant' that he and the game ranger were going to take."[4] After that safari Hemingway himself wrote that he was planning "to go out again to Kenya for six months next year to try to get a really good" elephant ("Notes on Dangerous Game," 171). But he never returned to Africa and never shot an elephant.[5]

The Big Five may be the essence of safari but they're hardly all of it. Two other dangerous animals, the hippopotamus and crocodile, still today account for thousands of human lives every year across the African continent, but they are not widely accepted as "game" (i.e., top-shelf trophies) by hunters. Plains game, the hoofed species that include kudu, eland, impala, springbuck, zebra, hartebeest (kongoni, to Hemingway), warthog, wildebeest, gazelle, bongo, blesbuck, waterbuck, reedbuck, steenbuck, duiker, dik-dik, bushbuck, nyala, sable, roan, and oryx (or gemsbuck) in all their variations, present their own challenges. Although wounded or cornered plains game, in particular sable, oryx, and zebra, can turn and fight, hunting them puts a premium on stalking. These are prey animals and nothing is more difficult to creep up on than a herd of antelope, wary eyes watching in all directions. The Big Five are generally shot at less than a hundred yards — sometimes much less — but plains game may require shooting at three or four hundred yards, which calls for exceptional accuracy.

A word about trophy hunting: In its pure form, it means finding and killing the best-possible example of a certain species of game. This requires either fantastic luck (to stumble on an elephant with outstanding tusks, for example, just outside camp) or sometimes going to the necessary extremes: weeks in the field, repeat trips, hard work and sweat, frequent frustration and disappointment. Hemingway was not a trophy hunter who wanted his name in the record books. Rather, he hunted for high-quality examples of desirable species (especially kudu, lion, leopard, and Cape buffalo), and the bigger, the better. Some of his trophies, from Africa and North America, still adorn the walls of his Cuban home, the Finca Vigía.

Today a trophy hunter can essentially buy his way into certain record books by spending whatever it takes at a game ranch that has bred an outsize example of whatever he's looking for. Most hunters believe in fair chase and don't do this. Philip Percival, Hemingway's hunting guide on safari, was known to say: "If you want to have a nice hunt, leave the tape measure at home."[6]

Going on Safari, Then and Now

The Europeans who settled and farmed southern Africa in the seventeenth and eighteenth centuries necessarily did plenty of shooting, game and otherwise, but before about 1890 most Europeans who hunted in eastern Africa focused on the dangerous but lucrative elephant ivory trade (sometimes "a pound for a pound"), similar in many ways to commercial whaling. British big-game sportsmen, however, were more likely to go to India, where tiger was the top trophy.[7] Africa's first sporting safari is attributed to William Cornwallis Harris, a British military engineer from India who in 1837 had been sent on convalescent leave to the Cape Colony (now South Africa). Instead of resting, however, Harris launched a remarkable five-month hunting trek north beyond the Limpopo River into what became Rhodesia and is now Zimbabwe. News of his, and others', hunting exploits spread, and soon more adventure-seeking British military men, spurred by tales of wild tribes, vast unexplored lands, and astoundingly abundant game, came to Africa (accessible from India via the Indian Ocean) to hunt.

By the time of the First World War, the safari — Swahili for "journey," from an Arabic word — was becoming popular among the British aristocracy, which traditionally loved to shoot. East Africa (especially the area that is now Kenya) became the romantic destination of choice. Theodore Roosevelt's eleven-month hunting and natural history expedition (1909–1910), took place in Kenya, where he hired a dashing British expatriate, the twenty-three-year-old Philip Percival, as one of his guides.[8] When Hemingway followed suit, in 1933, he chose the same region and the same guide, who became "Pop" in *Green Hills of Africa*.

Even through the Great Depression, safaris were often deluxe expeditions that lasted months, as both of Hemingway's did. The wealthy gentlemen adventurers who went on safari for up to a year at a time may or may not have been experienced hunters when they set out, may or may not have been in good physical condition, and may or may not have been familiar with their guns and rifles, but they had the time to become so in the field — after a leisurely journey by ship and train (Hemingway's mode of travel also). With the advent of Imperial Airways' flying boat service from Britain to East Africa in the 1930s, the pace began to quicken, but until about 1970 the normal safari still lasted at least thirty days. Today's hunters are hard pressed to set aside two weeks, and many begin their hunts while still dealing with jet lag and the other stresses of commercial air travel. They are often on a tight schedule and interrupted by phone calls and email. Going on safari is not what it was.

The Costs of a Safari

An African hunting safari was always expensive and is becoming more so. Costs typically include a per diem for the camp or lodge as well as fees for government ministries and local jurisdictions plus a payment for each animal. Today these range from a few hundred dollars for a warthog or an impala to many thousands of dollars for an elephant or lion, while a rhino may demand six figures. The cost in Hemingway's time was much less, even accounting for inflation. However, Gus Pfeiffer reportedly supplied $25,000 in stock (nearly $400,000 in 2009) to underwrite Hemingway's first safari (Reynolds, *The 1930s*, 150). The trip surely cost far less than that, $20,000 being the generally accepted figure (Raeburn, 33). Even that seems high, but it may have included ancillary expenses such as guns and clothing, even taxidermy afterward.

In the 1950s a client paid about $75 to $100 per day for the services of a white hunter and his camp and staff, while a Full Class A 1953 visitor's game license good for thirty-eight species (up to six specimens of each, depending on the animal) as well as game birds cost 1,000 Kenyan shillings ($140 at the time),[9] with additional special licenses required for lion, leopard, elephant, and buffalo. These costs varied by district and by the game, ranging from a second elephant at 2,000 shillings ($280 then) to as little as 20 shillings, in some places, for up to four buffalo. Normally, hunters could not buy extra animals on top of these licenses, but in the 1950s, the Hemingways did — something that William Hale, the chief game warden, would have had to authorize. Mary wrote: "We were paying $58.57 for having killed fifty-one animals, including some shot by [Ernest's son] Patrick and Bill Lowe, [editor] of *Look* magazine" (470). In fact, *Look* more than paid for the safari, giving Hemingway $15,000 ($120,000 in 2009) for expenses (and therefore not taxable income) and another $10,000 ($80,000 in 2009) for a 3,500-word story. Hemingway earned an additional $20,000 ($160,000 in 2009) from *Look* for "The Christmas Gift," the story of his two plane wrecks at Murchison Falls in January 1954, after his safari had ended, and another $5,000 ($40,000 in 2009) for a sequel, photographed by Earl Theisen in Cuba, thirty months after the accidents.

In the 1950s, a deluxe thirty-day safari might have topped out at $7,000 for a couple (the Hemingways stayed for several months), excluding travel, clothing, guns and gear, tips, personal supplies, and taxidermy. Today, the equivalent month in neighboring Tanzania,[10] but without a rhino, would exceed $140,000 — an increase of nearly three times over simple inflation. For Hemingway, going on safari was quite profitable, even in his ultra-high income tax bracket.

The Guns

Both in the 1930s and the 1950s, the Hemingways brought large quantities of clothing, medicines, items for personal hygiene and comfort, favorite food and drink, gifts for friends and staff, photographic and writing materials, and many boxes of books to last them through the long months and unexpected difficulties, accidents, and breakdowns of their safaris. But most important were the firearms and ammunition they would need: these items (and the peripheral gear: cleaning supplies, cases, etc.) are mentioned often in the African narratives, and it is useful to have some information about them and their terminology and history. Some basic terms:

Ammunition: Cartridge, Caliber, Gauge

Cartridge

A single unit of ammunition is a cartridge: it consists of a bullet wedged into the mouth of a metal case, or shell, that holds the gunpowder and, in its base, a primer. The cartridge is a precise fit in the chamber, the first section of the gun barrel. The gun's firing pin or hammer strikes the cartridge primer, which ignites the powder that propels the bullet downrange. After a cartridge has been fired, the empty shell is left behind in the chamber and must be removed before the chamber can be reloaded. There are at least five different "actions," the basic mechanisms that accomplish this clearing-reloading process in modern rifles and shotguns, and each has its pros and cons as well as its fans and detractors.

By law and by sporting tradition and ethics, a hunting arm (whether rifle, shotgun, or handgun) fires one round at a time; the trigger has to be pulled once per shot. A firearm that shoots as long as its trigger is held back is an automatic weapon — a machine gun, forbidden to unauthorized civilians in America since the National Firearms Act of 1934.

Caliber

The diameter of the bullet/bore is the caliber, expressed in millimeters for Continental rifles or modern military weapons (8mm, say, or 5.56mm) and in decimal fractions of an inch (.308, for example, or .303) for American and British rifles. There may be many proprietary "chamberings" for a given caliber, such as .300 Weatherby Magnum, .300 Winchester Magnum, .300 H&H Magnum, .300 Dakota, and so on, all different in certain dimensions and performance and none interchangeable.

Gauge

Shotguns are measured in "gauge." While for a rifle a higher caliber means a bigger bore diameter, on a shotgun a higher gauge number is a smaller bore. Gauge is the number of balls that could be made from one pound of lead that each just fit the inside diameter of the barrel. This comes from early cannon designation. A "12-pounder" cannon (a cannon is a gun — no rifling in the barrel; see below, s.v. "Rifles" [Single Projectile]) fired a 12-pound ball; a 12-gauge gun is a 1/12-pounder. Twelve is the most popular shotgun gauge and the one favored by Hemingway in Africa. A 1/12-pound lead ball is 0.729 inches in diameter. Hence 12 gauge measures .729 caliber — nearly three-quarters of an inch, far larger than any sporting rifle bore because of the need to accommodate the several hundred shot pellets in a typical bird-shooting cartridge.

There is, it hardly needs saying, a tremendous variety of guns, gauges, and calibers available to American and European hunters (and target shooters). Ammunition should be considered in tandem with any discussion or definition of a firearm.

Shotguns, Rifles, and Handguns

Shotgun (Multiple Projectiles)

Loosely speaking, the word *gun* refers to any firearm, but strictly speaking it means a shotgun, not a rifle (see below, "Rifles,") or handgun. A shotgun is a "smoothbore" — no rifling in the barrel — meant to shoot cartridges that contain pellets, usually lead, that spread out in flight. This makes it easier to hit a bird on the wing. Shotguns are inherently short-range weapons. While a high-velocity rifle bullet will carry for far more than a mile, given optimal muzzle elevation, even the largest birdshot pellets fall to earth within three or four hundred yards. At very close range the ounce or so of pellets in a typical shot cartridge doesn't have time to spread out much, so inside thirty feet a shotgun blast is highly lethal and destructive, no matter whether the gun was loaded with fine birdshot or large buckshot. Beyond that distance the spread of the pellets can be controlled somewhat by "choking" the barrel at the muzzle — constricting its inside diameter slightly. A "full-choke" barrel delivers a tighter cloud of pellets downrange than an open barrel — putting most of the shot inside a two-foot circle, approximately, at forty yards. Shotguns can be single-barreled or double-barreled.

Rifles (Single Projectile)

Whether designed for sporting, police, or military use, a rifle fires a single projectile: a bullet. The term comes from "rifling," the half-dozen or so grooves cut along the bore, the inside of the rifle barrel, in long spirals. The bullet is a tight fit in the bore; the rifling makes it spin in flight, for stability and accuracy. A hunting rifle should put its bullets into a one-inch circle at a hundred yards, but in the field the shooter's skill and steadiness contribute more to accuracy than the rifle's mechanical consistency. Like shotguns, rifles can be single- or double-barreled as well as single-shot or repeating.

Pistols

Normally handguns (pistols and revolvers) are not useful on safari, being too inaccurate for meat hunting and not powerful enough for big game, but some hunters use them to finish off wounded animals. A handgun fires a single bullet, just as a rifle does. There's no evidence in his published writings that Hemingway took a pistol with him on his first safari. He did, however, take two .22-caliber Colt Woodsman pistols with him on the second: one dating from about 1919, and the other an updated model he bought at Abercrombie & Fitch on June 25, 1953, the day he and Mary sailed from New York to Le Havre en route to Kenya.

The Battery

The choice of one's safari battery — the shotguns and rifles for the trip — is a matter that has puzzled, pleased, and intrigued hunters since the beginning. At one level it's just a matter of selecting the right tools for the job, the job being the game and the distances and cover at which and in which the shooting is expected to occur. Big, thick-skinned animals such as elephant and rhinoceros require heavy bullets made for penetration; smaller species, the various antelope and other so-called plains game, are less heavily muscled and boned and can be killed with less powerful cartridges and smaller-caliber, lighter bullets. Dangerous game — animals that "run both ways" (away from or at the hunter, though it is impossible to predict which) — sometimes has to be met with extra force delivered by rifles that function reliably and quickly at close range.

Robert Ruark, the American journalist and novelist of the 1950s and 1960s who wrote much about Africa, coined the phrase "Use enough gun" — enough to kill quickly and cleanly, that is. "Too much" gun, on the other hand, is punishing to carry (because it's heavy) and to shoot (because of excessive recoil).

At another level the choice of safari battery can be intensely personal, an expression of wealth, status, education, experience, skill, and personal style. An experienced professional hunter (PH)[11] can often form a close picture of a client based almost entirely on "reading" his or her battery. Are the guns brand new or well used? Have they been cared for? What kind of sights do they have? Are they traditional, classic calibers with walnut gunstocks or the latest in ultravelocity performance on synthetic stocks? How many did the client bring? Are they custom made? Gold-inlaid and profusely engraved or plain? American, British, German, Austrian, Belgian, Italian, Spanish, other? Bolt-action, single-shot, double-barreled, other? All these details signify.

Hemingway's well-used and practical battery would have suitably impressed his PH on both safaris ("here is a man who knows what he's about"), while his marksmanship, at least on the second trip, might have left the hunter thinking, "I'll have to be ready on the big stuff."

Hemingway's Battery (Including Guns Used By Friends and Family)

The Shotguns

Hemingway took his favorite shotgun, the single-barreled Winchester Model 12 repeater, on both safaris. Pauline Hemingway used a French-made

Darne 28-gauge double-barreled shotgun on the first safari; it gets an exceedingly brief mention in *Green Hills of Africa* (129). On the second safari, Hemingway also took his English double-barreled Scott gun. As photographs of that safari reveal, Patrick Hemingway had an Italian-made Beretta over-under shotgun with him when he visited his father in camp, but it is not mentioned in the post-second-safari texts.[12] There likely were other shotguns too.

The Rifles

Hemingway liked bolt-action rifles and brought his favorite — the G&H Springfield .30-06 — on both safaris. On the second safari, Hemingway also brought a Model 61 Winchester .22 pump-action rifle, but he does not mention it in *Under Kilimanjaro*. Both Hemingway wives used bolt-actions as well: Austrian-made 6.5mm Mannlicher-Schoenauer rifles. Mayito Menocal, the wealthy friend from Cuba who came along for part of the second trip, used a Weatherby bolt-action. (At the time, these rifles and their proprietary calibers were the latest thing in American high tech, and somewhat controversial, and there were surely discussions on the subject — one that stirs up hunters to this day — around the campfire [e.g., *Under Kilimanjaro*, 276]). In contrast to Menocal, Hemingway was a traditionalist who preferred proven, even classical, guns and cartridges from established American, British, Italian, German, and Austrian makers. Hemingway doesn't tell us what his friend "Karl" (based on Charles Thompson) carried in the first safari, but Leicester Hemingway reports that he too had a Springfield (142).

Although double-barreled rifles (the "big guns") are a critical element of the classical safari, Hemingway seems not to have been overly attached to his. In the first safari, the "big guns" were a .470 Nitro Express (allegedly rented) and Percival's .450 No. 2 Nitro Express. On the second safari, Hemingway's "big gun" was a .577 Nitro Express (*UK*, 20) made by Westley Richards (Mary Hemingway, 398) and Denis Zaphiro had a .470 Nitro Express double rifle (Mary Hemingway, 420), maker unknown.

The Pistol

Hemingway took two Colt Woodsman pistols on the second safari.

In what follows, I discuss most of these (and a few other) guns, and their ammunition, in some detail. I have organized the discussion in terms of what I perceived to be the weapons' importance to Hemingway, expressed mostly by how long he had owned and used them and how much detail he provided about them in his writings. Thus I discuss the Winchester Model 12 (his favorite shotgun) and the Springfield .30-06 (a favorite rifle) at the beginning of their sections.

Hemingway's Pump-Action Shotgun: The 12-Gauge Winchester Model 12

The Model 1912 pump-action shotgun, made in New Haven, Connecticut, by the Winchester Repeating Arms Company, made its debut in that year; the name was shortened to Model 12 in 1919. Unlike traditional double-barreled shotguns from Britain or Europe, which could fire only two rounds before reloading, multishot pump guns are a uniquely American design. They have a single barrel with another tube, usually shorter, underneath: this is the magazine, where cartridges are stored. The gun's wooden foregrip is attached to an actuating bar that slides back and forth. After a shot is fired, pulling the foregrip back a few inches ejects the spent shell through a port on the side of the action, lets a fresh round feed backward out of the magazine tube, and recocks the gun; pushing the grip ahead again brings the new cartridge up and into the firing chamber and locks the action, so that the gun is ready to shoot once more. A skilled hand can work this pull-push pumping action in an eye blink.

Winchester's Model 12 held up to five rounds in the magazine (in the civilian 12-gauge version) plus one in the chamber and was arguably the best pump gun ever made. Before the First World War much of the United States was a still-raw land of vast wild-bird populations, commercial market hunting and no bag limits, and many people still relied on shotguns for self-defense as well as food, not mere sport. The more cartridges a gun could fire between reloadings, the better. Thanks to its handling, speed, build quality, and reliability, the Model 12 became known as the Perfect Repeater. The M12 could even be "slam fired," simply pumped as fast as possible while the trigger was held back. This feature didn't much benefit hunters, but it helped make the Model 12 a favorite also with police officers and soldiers who relied on shotguns in buildings, trenches, tunnels, and other close quarters.[13] The Model 12 had another feature, particularly useful to the traveling hunter: without tools, in seconds it could be taken apart into two sections for easier packing in a case or duffle.

From 1912 to 1963, when Winchester discontinued regular production of it, close to two million M12s were made in a wide variety of gauges and styles. They were used mostly to shoot gamebirds (a moving target) such as grouse, pheasants, ducks, and geese. The Model 12, like all successful shotguns, had a certain balance and liveliness that suited this kind of dynamic gunning. Shotguns have no sights and are generally pointed rather than aimed.

In Hemingway's time almost every serious American hunter owned a Model 12, had owned one, or wanted one, a situation that Winchester encouraged by sending professional shooters around the country to demonstrate the gun's capabilities. It was not an inexpensive gun: in 1914 a field-grade 12-gauge version cost about $32 ($685 in 2009), a working man's weekly wage. By 1963, the final year of regular production, the same gun cost $110 ($765) — slightly more, adjusted for inflation. By then, Winchester was losing money on several of its best shotguns and rifles, and the company, instead of raising prices, decided to cut quality. In 1964 the standard Model 12 was replaced by a more cheaply built Model 1200. A few Model 12s were made as late as 2006, but the old craftsmanship was gone. Today a pre-1964 serial number on any Winchester adds to its value and original Model 12s are prized.

Hemingway, a hunter since childhood, apparently acquired his Model 12 as a young man. In December 1931, however, a fire at the Pfeiffer family's home in Arkansas destroyed Hemingway's typewriter, some boots and clothing, and several of his guns. If this "once burnt-up, three times restocked" Model 12 (*UK*, 329) was one of them, its steel parts survived the fire and Hemingway fitted a new wooden buttstock and forend, a simple repair typical of the "waste not, want not" Depression years. A hunter and shooter of Hemingway's upbringing would not junk a good gun lightly, especially a "well-loved . . . worn smooth old Winchester Model 12 pump gun that was faster than a snake and was, from thirty-five years of us being together, almost as close a friend and companion with secrets shared and triumphs and disasters not revealed as the other friend a man has all his life" (329).

There is no specific mention of his Model 12 in *Green Hills of Africa*, but he does shoot guinea fowl (35–36) and ducks (132–33) and in one passage Hemingway is trying to "pump a wet shell in" (133),[14] suggesting that he had this gun with him on his first safari as well as the second one. In *Under Kilimanjaro* Hemingway describes the "loading [of] the Winchester 12-gauge pump with SSG which is buckshot in English" (326).

This smooth-operating, well-broken-in gun was greatly admired by the trackers and gunbearers in *Under Kilimanjaro*: "They all believed it was an automatic weapon since it could be fired faster than any automatic shotgun . . . it was regarded as a straight witchcraft gun and it was never used unless we needed meat badly or for backing up or for going in as for the leopard. It was a goose, guinea, and leopard gun and a back-up gun on lion" (391–92) — clearly useful and central to Hemingway's hunting life, in Africa and in Idaho, where it appeared in many photographs.[15]

Hemingway's Double-Barreled Shotguns: Side-by-Side and Over-Under

The Side-by-Side W&C Scott (aka "the Purdey")

Hemingway's double-barreled 12-gauge gun in the 1953–1954 safari was made by a now-defunct Birmingham (England) company called

W. & C. Scott & Son. Scott produced double guns that were of high quality (a great deal of handcraftsmanship) but of lesser repute than Purdey guns. Hemingway describes his Scott as a "live-pigeon" gun, that is, one made for competitions where a lot of cash and prestige often hang on the shooter's ability to kill a hard-flying pigeon before it can escape over a penalty line. Such guns generally have tightly choked barrels, designed to throw a dense pattern of shot at relatively long range. Photographs show that Hemingway used it in pigeon shoots at the Club de Cazadores del Cerro, near the Finca Vigía, and later in Idaho. Such Scott (and Purdey) guns (as well as the big-game rifles on Hemingway's safaris) have their paired, single-shot barrels arranged horizontally, side by side.

Near the end of *Under Kilimanjaro*, there is a single paragraph about the Scott (fig. 2.1), its provenance, and its nickname:

> "Put the three rifles and the Purdey in the car," I told Ngui. The Purdey was not a Purdey but a straight-stocked long-barreled Scott live-pigeon full choke in both barrels that I had bought from a lot of shotguns a dealer had brought down from Udine to the Kechlers' villa in Codroipo. The Scott and a very beautiful twenty-eight inch barrel over-and-under Merkel had fitted me and I had shot them both for many years. Ngui and Charo called the Scott the Purdey[16] and so the Purdey it was. It was a lovely shooting gun whoever made it. (392)

Mary Hemingway writes that Hemingway had bought a new gun (probably a Beretta S3 over-under) in Italy in the fall of 1948 (258), but a history of Beretta dates the transaction to the fall of 1949 (Wilson, 336). The Scott was probably bought at the same time, joining at least two other side-by-side shotguns, American-made Winchester Model 21s in 20 gauge, that saw use in Cuba and Idaho, but not, apparently, in Europe or Africa.[17]

The Merkel (and Other) Over-Unders

The passage also mentions a Merkel. This was a German double gun with its barrels stacked vertically: "over-and-under" (O/U). Hemingway evidently owned other Merkels as well. He had bought a 12-gauge O/U shotgun from Abercrombie & Fitch on 12 March 1945 (G&H Book 9, 59), when he returned from London at the end of the Second World War. Patrick Hemingway, who was with him at the time, recalls it as an "ugly cadmium-plated Merkel 12-gauge over-under" (telephone interview). Abercrombie & Fitch records, however, show that Hemingway bought a matched pair of Merkels on that date, which could bring to three the number of Merkels that Hemingway owned, although there is no textual or photographic evidence that any of them went with him to Africa.

Fig. 2.1. Hemingway on his second safari, cradling his Scott shotgun. The snowcapped summit of Kilimanjaro has emerged from the clouds behind him.

Photo courtesy Ernest Hemingway Collection / John F. Kennedy Presidential Library and Museum, Boston.

Practically speaking, there would have been little or no reason for him to bring three 12-bore guns to Africa, and we know for certain that he had his Model 12 Winchester and the Scott side-by-side double. Those two are quite different in form and function and would have served all safari needs well.

In addition to the Merkels, Hemingway had over-under shotguns by Browning (an American firm, but made in Belgium) and the Beretta (Italian) mentioned above. These, like the side-by-side Scott and Winchester Model 21s, were all "upper middle-class" double-barreled shotguns: not as expensive as a Purdey, but still beyond the reach of a blue-collar sportsman.

Toward the end of his life, having passed through all the stages of a hunter's evolution, Hemingway remained a shotgunner. He said: "Killing cleanly and in a way that gives you esthetic pride and pleasure has always been one of the greatest enjoyments of a part of the human race. At seventeen you would rather kill a grizzly bear than any other thing. At forty-five, having killed many, you would not kill a bear under any circumstances because you have learned over the years that he is your brother. But you will continue to kill your pheasants high and clean as long as you have eyes to do so" (Hotchner, 54). Hemingway killed only perhaps three grizzly bears, in Wyoming or Montana, but possibly thousands of pheasants. In spite of his battery of more expensive double-barreled guns, side-by-side and over-under, it was the single-barrel Winchester Model 12 pump, worn smooth and silvery by decades of use, that remains the iconic Hemingway shotgun.

The Rifles

In addition to his shotguns, Hemingway owned a number of useful and high-quality rifles. The single-barreled repeating rifles that went to Africa included a Springfield .30-06 modified by Griffin & Howe, a Mannlicher-Schoenauer 6.5mm / .256, and a pump-action, .22-caliber Model 61 Winchester. Griffin & Howe records show that he bought a bolt-action Mauser .505 Gibbs in 1941 (G&H Ledgers, Book 8), but the only mention of such a rifle comes in "The Short Happy Life of Francis Macomber." The double-barreled rifles will be discussed towards the end of this section.

The Springfield .30-06

Hemingway's Springfield, which he used in the American West and on both safaris, was a modified version of the American 1903 military rifle — officially the United States Rifle, Caliber .30, Model 1903 — which was designed and initially produced by the government armory in Springfield, Massachusetts. Its manually operated turn-bolt action was based on the Mauser design perfected in Germany a decade earlier: after a shot is fired, lifting the handle on the side recocks the rifle and unlocks the breech bolt; pulling the bolt backward a few inches on its rails then extracts the empty shell from the barrel and kicks it away to the side. With the bolt slid back out of the way, a fresh round can rise, under spring pressure, from the magazine beneath. When the shooter shoves the bolt forward again, it scoops up the new cartridge and rams it into the chamber. Pushing the bolt handle downward once more relocks everything, ready for firing.

The Springfield rifle and its cartridge were developed more or less together as the U.S. Army's primary infantry weapon. The round was officially designated by the War Department as "Cartridge, Ball, Caliber .30, Model of 1906," hence .30-06 (sometimes called the .30 Government). By military standards, the .30-06 is a relatively large, powerful round that generates considerable recoil and demands a fairly heavy rifle. In at least sixteen variations ranging from ordinary "ball" to armor-piercing and tracer, it was so effective that it survived the army's transition from the Springfield and Enfield bolt-action rifles of the First World War to the semiautomatic M1 Garand rifle of World War II and Korea. It also served brilliantly in full-automatic weapons such as the fabled Browning Automatic Rifle (BAR) and many tripod-, vehicle-, and aircraft-mounted machine guns up until about 1970.

The Springfield rifle served "officially" only from 1903 till 1936, but it saw much use in World War II, since production of the new M1 Garand rifle fell behind demand, and snipers used them even in Vietnam.[18] In short, several generations of American soldiers had been indoctrinated in shooting the .30-06,[19] and when the Doughboys and GIs came home and returned to hunting, it was with the beloved "ought-six."

The .30-06 thus became, in the twentieth century, the most popular hunting cartridge in North America, if not the world. But military ammunition, designed to leave behind fairly clean, one-diameter holes[20] (which somewhat reduce the carnage on a battlefield), is generally counterproductive on game, where the need is to kill as quickly as possible, and not to permit medical intervention and survival. Most hunting bullets are therefore designed to penetrate the skin and then "mushroom": to expand on contact with tissue to cut as many blood vessels and organs as possible. Ammunition companies began to make such bullets for the .30-06 very early on. Dozens, if not hundreds, eventually were developed, in weights ranging from 55 to 250 grains, which with different powder charges let the '06 handle everything from rodents to moose and bear. Theodore Roosevelt was probably the first American to bring a .30-06 to Africa, in 1909, and before long it had proven itself on all plains game and even, with reservations, the Big Five.

The rifle moved easily from the battlefield into civilian life. In 1903, the U.S. Congress had established the National Board for the Promotion of Rifle Practice, to keep American citizens proficient in shooting against any future need to defend the country, either in uniformed service or as partisans fighting an invader.[21] In 1905, Congress passed Public Law 149, which authorized the sale, at cost, of surplus military rifles, ammunition, and equipment to accredited civilian shooting clubs such as the National Rifle Association (the NRA, established in 1871). While many of these surplus rifles were kept in original form and used for target practice, many others went hunting.

During the Depression, surplus Springfields cost anywhere from $15 to $50, depending on grade and condition. In 1934 the NRA member price for a standard Springfield was $32.75 plus a packing charge of $1.35 and $3.41 in federal tax, for a total of $37.51.[22] Military rifles, however, generally are no more suitable for hunting than military ammunition (discussed above), and by 1930, when Hemingway acquired his Springfield through the NRA, many American gunsmiths specialized in converting mass-produced ex-government Springfields into hunting rifles of some style and balance as well as high function — a process that became known as "sporterizing." One such commercial converter was a company called Griffin & Howe, founded by Seymour Griffin, a cabinetmaker, who had bought a Springfield in 1910 and, inspired by Roosevelt's statement that he had had his own rifle "stocked and sighted to suit myself" (22), did the same for himself. Friends then asked Griffin to modify their Springfields, which led to a full-service gunsmithing and sales firm that in 1930 became part of Abercrombie & Fitch, the Madison Avenue sporting-goods store that Hemingway patronized.[23] In 1932, Griffin & Howe advertised (in numerous American outdoor magazines) that it could turn a customer's sow's-ear army rifle into a silk-purse sporter for $52.50 (about $800 in 2009).

Letters in the Princeton University Library show that in 1930 Hemingway discussed with his friend Milford Baker having a Springfield rifle modified by Griffin & Howe.[24] He supplied Baker his measurements and asked also for a cleaning kit and leather cases for both the rifle and a scope.[25] In total, Hemingway acquired a first-class hunting rifle for $256.50, about $3,400 today.[26] It was an important, useful, and, finally, wise investment. Griffin & Howe Springfields have become collectors' items.

For all his passion as a hunter and his considerable income, Hemingway was not a collector of fine guns and rifles. He generally bought function, not purely esthetic touches such as extra engraving or fancy wood, and clearly he appreciated the familiarity he'd built up with certain weapons over time. By the mid-1950s both his Springfield and the Model 12, though well cared for, were missing much of their bluing (metal finish) from decades of handling and obviously were favorites. A. E. Hotchner commented that Hemingway "didn't like automatic guns. He liked the simple, 'pure' (to use his word) guns he had used all his life. He liked a simple, pure approach to hunting, especially birds. If there was anything he taught me, it was that — respect for good, simple, well-fitted equipment, and a simple, 'primitive' attitude toward hunting itself" (*True*).

Hemingway took his Springfield on safari and, when he came home, wrote it into his books. In *Green Hills of Africa*, he writes that M'Cola carries the Springfield and hands it to him when the moment comes to shoot the rhinoceros (76–78). Hemingway opened the bolt to make sure the rifle was loaded with "solids," i.e., the nonexpanding bullets he favored for big game. Hemingway knew that a soft-nose bullet would probably deform and stop before doing much damage to such a massive animal, so he opted for one that would stay in one piece and, he hoped, go deep.[27] The Springfield holds five rounds in the magazine and one in the chamber, and a practiced rifleman can empty a Springfield in well under a minute with accurate fire. But Hemingway succeeded with his first shot.

That a .30-06 bullet, even a 220-grain solid, caused a fatal wound on a thick-skinned, massively boned animal at "all of three hundred" yards is surprising on several counts. First, the distance: dangerous game is normally "engaged" at less than a hundred yards, which allows more accurate shooting and lets the shooter see where the animal goes if the shot doesn't fell it. Second, with the open (i.e., nontelescopic) sights on Hemingway's Springfield, even a rhinoceros is half-obscured by the front bead at three hundred yards, and precise shooting is not possible. Hemingway was a very capable rifle shot when he was in his thirties, but at that range — especially without the magnification of a scope — this would have to qualify as a very lucky shot (fig. 2.2).[28] Or perhaps Hemingway gauged the distance incorrectly (not unusual even for experienced hunters), or he was embellishing the truth. In any case, it is clear that he relied on the Springfield and had enough confidence in it to use it even in such a marginal situation.

Another section of this same episode, if read carefully, shows Hemingway in a more negative light. After that shot, a charge by the wounded rhino seemed imminent, whereupon Pop cautioned the narrator to "Take the big gun" (*GHA*, 78) — apparently a double-barreled .470 Nitro Express (discussed below, a much more effective short-range stopper than the .30-06.) At this point, Hemingway handed the Springfield to M'Cola, exchanging it for the big gun M'Cola had been carrying for him. After finding the rhino down, he takes the Springfield back. The narrator reports that at this point he "noticed it was cocked. . . . 'He had that damned Springfield cocked,' I said to Pop. The cocked gun behind my back made me black angry" (78), and rightly so, since a cocked gun

Fig. 2.2. Hemingway on his first safari, with his military-surplus Springfield .30-06. The rhino hunt is described in Green Hills *of* Africa.

Photo courtesy Ernest Hemingway Collection / John F. Kennedy Presidential Library and Museum, Boston.

can go off. However, Hemingway himself is to blame: the rifle cocked automatically when he opened the bolt and worked the action to reload — and, clearly in a hurry, he did not decock it before swapping with M'Cola for the "big gun." Decocking a bolt-action is a deliberate two-handed movement that is almost impossible to do while running. It seems that, in the heat of the moment, Hemingway unthinkingly handed his cocked Springfield to someone unfamiliar with firearms. Accidents with guns are more common on safari than being mauled by animals;[29] that an experienced hunter like Hemingway could make such a mistake shows why.

The Springfield also appears in *Under Kilimanjaro*, in the climactic hunt for lion. Mary shoots at the lion and misses. As the story unfolds, Hemingway fires his Springfield and misses three times. On his fourth shot the lion, now "beginning to look small in the sights and almost certain to make the far cover," goes down. Hemingway's bullet has broken its spine at a distance so great that Hemingway and G. C. (or "Gin Crazed," a character based on Denis Zaphiro) later measured it with the odometer of the Land Rover and then promised each other that they would "never, never tell anybody" how long a shot it was, whether "drunk or sober with shits or decent people" (257).[30]

The Mannlicher-Schoenauer 6.5mm / .256

Late in the nineteenth century, the modern bolt-action repeating rifle appeared in two variations in Europe. While Peter Paul Mauser's more adaptable German design eventually won worldwide popularity, Ferdinand Ritter von Mannlicher's Austrian bolt-action of 1893 bettered it in several technical aspects. In conventional bolt-action rifles, including the original Mannlicher, the reserve cartridges lie one atop the other in the magazine (the well beneath the bolt). Otto Schönauer designed a rotary magazine (five rounds fit neatly into a horizontal spool that turns to feed each cartridge upward, where the bolt can grab it and slide it forward into the breech) and thus the Mannlicher-Schoenauer (the name was anglicized when applied to the rifle) was born in 1903. It's a mechanically beautiful instrument, but the rotary magazine, which restricts the size of the cartridge that can be accommodated, made it less popular among big-game hunters than the Mauser-type bolt-action, whose vertical box magazine can be made roomy enough to stack even the cigar-size .505 Gibbs cartridges. In contrast, the Mannlicher-Schoenauer was ideal for slender cartridges such as the 6.5x54-millimeter round, which was to this rifle as the .30-06 was to the Springfield.

Both the Mauser and the original Mannlicher were developed for military use[31] and then adapted to hunting (like the Springfield, discussed above). The Mannlicher, however, and especially the Schoenauer version, proved too sophisticated for a military weapon, which should be inexpensive to manufacture and impervious to dirt and human error.[32] But the 6.5 Mannlicher cartridge was a technological breakthrough that suddenly changed the rules on medium-size game. It fired a deadly accurate smallish bullet at about 2,300 feet per second — performance that was spectacular a century ago and is still respectable today. The high-quality, svelte, beautiful-handling Mannlicher-Schoenauer was adopted by many European sportsmen, achieving fame as a "gentleman's rifle."

The British called it by its inch-equivalent diameter, the .256, and it made many friends in Africa. Professionals saw no reason to shoot big, expensive, hard-recoiling Express cartridges when lighter, cheaper ammunition would do. The .256's fast-moving (for the time) 160-grain bullet, small in cross-section and disproportionately long, could reach the vitals of even a big animal, provided the shooter placed it precisely. It was perfect for camp meat, too, but it was too light for protecting clients, who couldn't be counted on to kill dangerous game with one shot or who spooked the animals into wariness. The .30-06 cartridge, however, became more popular than the .256 because its greater size made it adaptable to more kinds of game and shooting, and by 1924 Mannlicher-Schoenauer rifles were available in .30-06 as well as half a dozen other calibers.

A light, easy-recoiling, accurate rifle with a jewel-like trigger and bolt mechanism was also ideal for women, and both Hemingway wives who went on safari used a Mannlicher, although not the same one. Pauline's, in 1933–1934, was a compact Schoenauer carbine (*GHA*, 36, 70) that Hemingway may have acquired in Paris (Leicester Hemingway, 142), where Pauline's Darne shotgun came from. Had he bought it in the United States, the retail price in the early 1930s would have been $100, double the cost of a comparable American rifle. This rifle, Patrick recalled, spent much of its later years in an oil-soaked sheepskin case aboard Hemingway's fishing boat, the *Pilar* (telephone interview). (It, or the second Schoenauer carbine that Hemingway acquired in a raffle in Idaho in 1941 [Arnold, 120], appears in photographs taken long after Ernest and Pauline's divorce.) Twenty years later, Mary Welsh Hemingway also carried a Mannlicher-Schoenauer .256. Photographs from that safari show that it had nonfactory sights, a conventional three-quarter-length stock and a longer barrel, and had been converted to a take-down style — the barrel and forend could be disassembled from the action and buttstock. According to Patrick, this rifle was borrowed from Percival, who had received it as a gift from a client, a member of the Rothschild family, before the Second World War (telephone interview). Photographs show that its stock was too long for Mary, who was only 5' 2" tall (*Under Kilimanjaro*, 40), and this undoubtedly contributed to her erratic marksmanship.

The Model 61 Winchester

Although it is absent from Hemingway's narratives, a Model 61 Winchester .22-caliber rifle was included in the 1950s safari: it appears in several photographs.[33] Like its Winchester sibling, the Model 12 shotgun, the little Model 61 rifle was a slick-operating, high-quality single-barreled pump-action type that could also be taken apart quickly for transport. By 1953 the M61 had already been in production for twenty-one years; by the time manufacture ceased, in 1963, more than 342,000 61s had been sold. On its debut, in 1932, the basic model cost $24.20 ($375 in 2009) and by 1956 the price had climbed, just slightly ahead of inflation, to $55.15 ($435).[34] Unlike the same caliber Colt pistol (discussed below), the M61 rifle could shoot .22 Short, Long, and Long Rifle ammunition interchangeably, one more feature that made it so resoundingly popular. Photographs and Griffin & Howe sales records show that Hemingway owned at least two other Winchester .22 rifles as well, a Model 61A and a Model 77.

The .505 Gibbs

The only "big gun" in Hemingway's African writings that is not a double-barreled rifle (double rifles and their cartridges are discussed below) is a .505 Magnum, and it belonged to a fictional character, Robert Wilson: "Wilson came up then carrying his short, ugly, shockingly big-bored .505 Gibbs and grinning" ("The Short Happy Life of Francis Macomber," 13). This weapon was brought to market in 1912 by George Gibbs, a gunmaker in Bristol, England, whose name soon became attached to his creation. All but one of the big Nitro Express cartridges — among them the .450, .465, .470, .500, .577, and .600 — were developed between 1898 and about 1905 for double or single-shot rifles. The .505 was conceived right afterward for the new Mauser rifle, to create a bolt-action repeater powerful enough for dangerous game. Today there are many dangerous-game cartridges for bolt rifles, but the Gibbs was one of the first. According to Griffin & Howe records, Hemingway bought a Griffin & Howe Mauser chambered for .505 Gibbs in 1941, but there is no mention of it in any of his published writings.

Double-Barreled Rifles (the Big Guns)

With the one exception of Wilson's single-barreled .505, all the "big guns" that Hemingway writes about are large-bore doubles — that is, very powerful rifles with two single-shot barrels that fire fingertip-size bullets and deliver energy measured in tons. They are designed specifically for dangerous game and there is no faster way to fire two aimed shots.

A double rifle differs greatly from a single-barrel repeater such as a bolt-action. It is more akin to a fine shotgun, a balanced and often custom-fitted firearm that can perform brilliantly in certain situations and in certain hands. Depending on caliber, it typically weighs ten to fifteen pounds, almost half again as much as a conventional rifle. Proper stock fit and balance not only improve shooting, but also reduce felt recoil and muzzle jump, which can be severe with big calibers. Big-bore double rifles, meant for shooting at close range, usually have rudimentary open sights and rarely are fitted with scopes or carrying slings. (A bolt-action rifle generally is better suited to deliberate shooting against a more distant, barely moving target.)

Like double-barreled shotguns, double rifles break open in the middle. Pushing a thumb-lever unlocks a hinge and lets the barrels pivot downward, which exposes the breeches. The empty shells are mechanically extracted or ejected; the shooter drops a new cartridge into each barrel and closes the gun again, thus recocking the hammers. An experienced shooter can do this quickly, without looking, and even at a trot. Often he will have the two fresh rounds ready between the fingers of his off hand.

An expert needs six-plus seconds to cycle the action and fire a second well-placed shot from a heavy-recoiling bolt-action rifle. If more than two shots are needed, the big-bore bolt rifle, with its typical four-round capacity (one in the chamber and three in the magazine), would seem to have the edge over a double. However, an expert can reload a double, using the two spare rounds in his fingers, in less than five seconds and then fire those shots in three more seconds, for a total of less than twelve seconds — while the bolt-action shooter needs twenty seconds for four rounds. That eight-second difference can seem like eternity when a Cape buffalo or elephant is in full charge.

As Hemingway understood, a double rifle is a relatively short-range weapon. This is due to inherent limitations in accuracy, not because of its caliber or cartridge. Persuading one rifle barrel to shoot consistently to the very same place is difficult enough; regulating two barrels to do it together is not possible. (There are complex issues involving barrel "flip," bullet speed, and even rifling twist, plus the fact that the barrel tubes converge somewhere downrange.) Instead, a heavy double should put its two bullets well within a handspan at fifty yards. Since an inch one way or the other is almost irrelevant in the matter of killing anything larger than a groundhog, for a hunter shooting offhand at close range this is fine. Long-range accuracy is moot anyway because dangerous game should be attacked inside a hundred yards, to make it easier to place the bullet and then keep tabs on the beast after it's been hit.

The capacity to put big bullets rapidly and accurately onto a fast-approaching target has to be backed up by fail-safe mechanical reliability, since on safari the nearest gunsmith is often hundreds of miles away and breakdowns are a serious, even life-threatening matter. Double rifles address this problem, since they basically offer two guns on one stock: if one fails, the other may still work. The design has proven itself, and mechanically the double gun has changed little since about 1875.

If the bolt-action .30-06 is the most popular hunting rifle, with the widest variety of uses, the heavy double is the rarest of them all, produced in very small numbers for a narrow set of circumstances that only a handful of hunters ever encounter. They have always been astonishingly expensive because they require a great deal of handcraftsmanship to make. (Bolt-action rifles can be mass produced and so are far less costly.) In the mid-1930s a largely handmade, best-grade double rifle from Holland & Holland of London cost £170, equivalent to $850 or about fifteen times as much as an American factory-made bolt-action sporting rifle. Twenty years later, at the time of Hemingway's second safari, the same rifle cost £325, but, thanks to a much stronger postwar American economy, this was only about $910. Still, the importer's markup roughly doubled the price and in 1955 America $1,800 would buy a new Ford or Chevrolet. (Today, the price of a new, best-grade London double rifle will buy a top-of-the-range Mercedes-Benz.) But working PHs who specialize in taking clients after the Big Five often scrape together the money for a heavy double, perhaps a secondhand one, perhaps one from a less expensive maker. It's insurance. As Hemingway noted, "if you make a fool of yourself all that you get is mauled but the white hunter who has a client wounded or killed loses, or seriously impairs, his livelihood" ("Notes on Dangerous Game," 167). Whatever the client is armed with, the PH, who has to protect him when things go wrong, needs a big stopper.

Although many more people hunted in America than in Britain (where, as in Europe, hunting was reserved for the landed gentry), relatively few Americans traveled to Africa or Asia to do so until after the Second World War. It was then that American companies began producing rifles and cartridges more powerful than anything they'd ever made before. In 1956 Winchester debuted its .458 Magnum Model 70 "African" rifle — at $295, the first American bolt-action that was equal in power to the big, costly double guns of the British and Continental makers. (Trouble with early .458 ammunition, however, which took several years to sort out, led to some serious "incidents" in Africa.) Two years later the Weatherby company debuted its even more powerful .460 Magnum. Today virtually every U.S. gunmaker has some sort of rifle suitable for the Big Five.

Ammunition for the "Big Guns": The Nitro Express Cartridges

The ideal calibers for big double rifles are the unique Nitro Express cartridges developed in Britain around 1900, which generate massive shock and — with the right bullets — penetrate the thickest skin, muscle, and bone. By the 1930s, when Hemingway was introduced to them in East Africa, they were time-tested killers whose every detail (there are many, including case wall thickness, length, taper, capacity and rim, chamber pressure and powder) had been refined for performance and dependability in double rifles. Their name can be traced back to a London gunmaker, James (the Younger) Purdey, who in 1850 applied the term "Express Train" to his new rifles, to equate them to the powerful, high-speed trains that were then beginning to crisscross Great Britain. The label was shortened to "Express" and, in the 1870s and 1880s, was applied to newer cartridges such as the .450 Black Powder Express (BPE). But blackpowder ammunition throws out a cloud of smoke, which usually obscures the target for a few critical seconds. Late in the nineteenth century came nitrocellulose gunpowder, which was not only smokeless but also made much more energy and thereby drove a bullet faster and harder. This led to an entirely new series of cartridges, dubbed Nitro Express. To get power adequate to stop charging elephant and such, blackpowder rifles had to be of enormous calibers, which made them extremely heavy and cumbersome, and along with the thick smoke came fearsome recoil that sometimes broke collarbones and gunstocks. Nitro Express rifles, even double-barreled ones, weighed half as much as the BPE monsters, made no smoke, were far easier to shoot and yet were more powerful. All this revolutionized big-game hunting.

The first of the Nitro Express cartridges, the successful .450 NE, was introduced by the London firm of John Rigby & Co. in 1898. The following year, however, the British government of India, attempting to keep army rifles from falling into the hands of rebellious populations, began to regulate .450-caliber military ammunition. By 1902, it was illegal for anyone visiting India to bring .450 rifles or ammunition, sporting or military, Nitro Express or blackpowder. Since virtually every British gunmaker was building rifles for the many .450 cartridges then available, and since India was still the British sportsman's Mecca, the ban was problematic for hunters and for the gunmakers who supplied them.

British firms rushed to make cartridges of different calibers, such as Nitro Express cartridges ranging from .465 up to .600 caliber. The most successful of these, still in relatively wide use today, was the .470 Nitro Express.[35] It used smokeless cordite (a form of nitroglycerine) propellant; generating more than five thousand foot-pounds of energy at the muzzle, it was an "express train" by any standard. Despite the larger caliber, however, its performance did not significantly exceed that of the .450 NE, which did not completely disappear.

Although illegal in India, .450-diameter ammunition was never illegal in Africa, which eventually became an even more popular hunting ground for Europeans than India. We can see this in the lion hunt in *Green Hills of Africa*, where Percival's "stopping" double rifle (which he didn't have to use) carries a cartridge that performs like the .450 NE but is larger: "He opened the breech and took out the two big .450 No. 2's" (41, 37).

Hemingway himself used at least two double-barreled rifles: a .470 Nitro Express, on the first safari, and a .577 Nitro Express, made by Westley Richards, which he took on the second. His professional hunters had similar weapons: on the first safari Percival carried a .450 No. 2 Nitro Express (made by Jos. Lang of London), and on the second, Denis Zaphiro had some sort of .470 Nitro Express.

The .470 Nitro Express

In Hemingway's day few Americans had ever seen a double rifle — a product of British and European gunmakers whose clients visited colonies in Asia and Africa — much less owned one. American big game was deer in the East, elk in the Rocky Mountains, and bear and moose up north, and none of these requires such formidable weaponry. Hemingway much preferred his .30-06, which he said he liked to use "as a surgeon uses his scalpel" (Zaphiro, 19) but he recognized the Express rifle's far greater shocking power.

The .470 Hemingway refers to as "his" big gun in 1933 evidently was rented. Percival had informed Hemingway "that guns, especially big-game rifles, were to be had at a moderate rental," to which Hemingway is reputed to have said, "I'll own my own guns. I don't want to rent them" because, according to his brother Leicester, "he was damned if he was going to become fond of any firearm that might save his life, and then have to turn it back to the owner" (137). Even so, Leicester reports that "Ernest decided to put off all gun selection until he had reached Paris. He could go to the good armorers there and be outfitted for the expedition ahead" (137). Leicester adds that "Paris had been disappointing as a city in which to buy ideal weapons for African game. They had stuck with their lighter-weight American equipment, adding a .256 Mannlicher rifle with very little recoil as a fine gun for Pauline to shoot," and that Ernest did finally rent, "from the gun shop across from the New Stanley Hotel" (142), the double-barreled .470 that gives him trouble during the rhino hunt in *Green Hills of Africa* (75).

Hemingway doesn't identify the maker of the rifle, but on an East African safari of the 1930s any .470 was surely British made, probably with double triggers (one for each barrel), a mechanism that is generally preferable to the single trigger, which typically fires first the right barrel and then (with another pull) the left, with the serious disadvantage that the heavy recoil of the first shot could jar off the second one almost simultaneously, a painful experience that leaves the shooter stunned and empty handed at usually exactly the wrong moment. With double triggers, the second barrel should not fire unless the second trigger is pulled. In such weapons, the first barrel (the right side of the gun) and its trigger and lockwork usually get the most wear.

The problem Hemingway describes — "metal stuck against metal" (*Green Hills of Africa*, 101) — could stem from faulty manufacture or serious wear, although both these problems are unlikely in such costly, handcrafted weapons and with ammunition that is too expensive to shoot casually. Since the .470 became commercially available in about 1907, such a rifle could not have been more than about twenty-six years old in 1933, when Hemingway shoots it. Even if it had been on full-time professional safari or control duty for that long, it would not have fired more than two thousand rounds — not nearly enough to cause a trigger sear to fail, even if all had been fired through just one barrel. Other possible explanations — a foreign body in the lockwork, over-tightened screws, rust — are not impossible in a rental gun. But by far the most likely cause, and the one that PHs immediately think of when they read this passage, was that in the heat of the moment Hemingway simply forgot to slip off the safety; the triggers were blocked.[36] This was a classic blunder that can be embarrassing or, in a charge, fatal to the shooter. Hemingway chose not to explain it — or he may not even have been aware of what he had done. Eventually he got off a shot and then had no difficulty firing the second barrel; presumably he had figured out the problem and deactivated the safety.

In *Under Kilimanjaro*, another anomaly appears, in the same kind of weapon. The narrator recalls a lion hunt from the first safari and comments on the safety catch on Percival's big double rifle: "And I heard your safety click and I was surprised you would have a safety that clicked" (48). A mechanical sound, however faint, is so alien in a natural environment that it not only alerts the game, it may also — in a staring contest with a lion, for instance — provoke a nasty reaction. A safety catch on any hunting rifle should slide on or off silently.

The .577 Westley Richards

The .577 (like the .450 and .470 NEs) was a "break-action" double rifle that could rapidly be taken apart into two sections, the buttstock and the barrels, for cleaning or storage. (High-end doubles come from the maker disassembled and in handsome leather cases that resemble fine luggage.) Hemingway's .577 was a Nitro Express, not the obsolete nineteenth-century blackpowder cartridge of the same caliber on which the NE version was based. Fully a tenth of an inch greater in diameter than the .470, the .577 NE's standard bullet is 50 percent larger — 750 grains v. 500; nearly two ounces — and, traveling at only slightly lower velocity, it generates a devastating 6,600-plus foot-pounds of striking energy and more than 100 foot-pounds of recoil. Shooting it from the prone position is, as Hemingway knew, asking for trouble, since the body can't absorb some of the awful recoil by flexing backward: "Shooting prone I knew the .577 could break my shoulder but probably only the collarbone. . . . With the safety on I squeezed on him," clearly not intending to shoot (*Under Kilimanjaro*, 321).

The .577 was favored by some professional (white) ivory hunters, but even they tended to save it for times when they were facing an aggressive elephant in thick cover or at close range and needed overwhelming shocking power. As with the .470 in *Green Hills of Africa* twenty years earlier, Hemingway provides no clues about this .577, but Mary Hemingway identified it as a Westley Richards (398), and photos from that safari bear this out.[37] The rifle, somewhat battered and in its leather case bearing a Hemingway travel tag, was consigned to James D. Julia Auctioneers for sale on 14 March 2011.

The gunmaking firm of Westley Richards was established in 1812 in Birmingham, England, is still in business today, and is known for a number of gunmaking advancements and patents. Their records indicate that

.577 serial no. 17425, the rifle in the auction, was made with the so-called droplock action type and completed in 1913. Its original owner, a Mr. Stephen H. Christy, had ordered it with a single trigger, a mechanism that may (as discussed above) lead to problems.[38] Westley Richards's single-trigger system, however, has a reputation for reliability.

The .577 is mentioned often in *Under Kilimanjaro* (20, 62, 106, 329): "Charo and Ngui came and pulled the guns in their full-length cases[39] out from under the cots and Ngui assembled the big .577. They were finding shells and counting them and checking on solids for the Springfield and the Mannlicher. It was the first of the fine moments of the hunt" (62).

Hemingway's Pistol: The Colt Woodsman .22 Caliber

The Patent Arms Manufacturing Company, founded in 1836, was reorganized as The Colt's Patent Firearms Manufacturing Company in 1854 and first achieved fame during the Civil War with its revolvers, later known as Peacemakers or Equalizers (from the saying "God made men; Samuel Colt made men equal"). In 1911 the company produced a just-as-illustrious .45-caliber semiautomatic pistol, which was carried by the American military through two world wars, Korea and Vietnam, and is still in wide use today.

The Colt Woodsman model was designed by the firearms genius John Moses Browning, which virtually guaranteed high functioning. On its debut, in 1915, it was simply called the Colt Automatic Pistol, Target Model, and it cost the substantial sum of $32 ($675 in 2009). The Woodsman name was attached to it in 1927 and remained for the rest of the gun's production life, until 1977. A Woodsman is narrow and lightweight and its grip is set at a rakish angle, like a Luger pistol's. The gun points naturally, which, with its excellent trigger mechanism, makes it unusually precise in offhand use. Many variations were made. Hemingway's was a "Match" version, which would have had a better barrel for greater accuracy. Regardless of model or price, the mechanism was the same, while overall weight, barrel length and weight, grip styles, finishes, and sights varied. The Woodsman was a high-quality weapon and is still popular today.

All "automatic" (semiautomatic, to be precise; a true automatic is a machine gun) pistols operate essentially the same way: one inserts a loaded magazine into the grip; pulls back the spring-loaded slide, which cocks the hammer; releases the slide, which, as it springs forward, shoves the first cartridge into the chamber and locks everything up; and squeezes the trigger. The energy of the shot cycles the slide backward to eject the empty case and recock the hammer. The spring then shoves the slide forward again, to scoop up a fresh round and relock the action, ready for firing again. This happens automatically with each pull of the trigger until the magazine is empty (ten times, in the case of a Woodsman).

There are three standard sizes of .22-caliber rimfire ammunition — Short, Long, and Long Rifle — and any number of variants, many of which are now obsolete (BB, CB, Extra Long, WRF, WMR, Winchester Automatic, and so on). The Woodsman was chambered only for the so-called Long Rifle version, which despite its name is also used in pistols. The cartridges are small; the standard 40-grain bullet itself is smaller than an aspirin tablet. The basic rimfire .22 is by far the most popular of all cartridges and very widely used in both rifles and handguns. Even today, the ammunition costs just pennies per round (compared to as much as $25 each for the Nitro Express calibers), which makes it ideal for target practice. Just about every shooter begins with a .22, which is a low-power weapon good mostly for "plinking" (informal target-shooting) or potting small game for the kitchen.

Based on an early photograph of Hemingway with what appears to be a Woodsman in a shoulder holster (fig. 2.3), Hemingway seems to have acquired his Woodsman around 1920, which is consistent with its serial number. He said of the ".22 caliber Colt automatic pistol, shooting a bullet weighing only 40 grains and with a striking energy of only 51 foot pounds at 25 feet from the muzzle" that "this is the smallest caliber pistol cartridge made; but it is also one of the most accurate and easy to hit with, since the pistol has no recoil. I have killed many horses with it, cripples and for bear bait, with a single shot, and what will kill a horse will kill a man. . . . Yet this same pistol bullet fired at point-blank range will not even dent a grizzly's skull, and to shoot at a grizzly with a .22-caliber pistol would simply be one way of committing suicide" ("My Pal the Gorilla Gargantua," 189).

Although Hemingway seems not to have taken a pistol with him on his first safari, he did take two Woodsman pistols on the second, perhaps for self-defense in the Mau Mau uprising.[40] The Mau Mau Rebellion peaked in 1954, while the Hemingways were in-country. If Hemingway truly brought his little pistols to Kenya for protection, he didn't take the terrorist threat seriously. His Model 12 shotgun would have been far better than any handgun as a close-quarters defense weapon (and he mentions tucking it into his cot at night — e.g., *Under Kilimanjaro*, 73 — which is standard procedure in any safari camp against troublesome lion, leopard, or hyena, not just Mau Mau). More likely, Hemingway brought the pistols just for fun and took the local situation as an excuse to wear one as part of his Bwana persona.

The uprising seriously dented East African tourism. To try to undo some of the bad publicity with upbeat stories in American magazines, the

Fig. 2.3. Hemingway in Michigan around 1920, with fly rod, knife, and his first .22-caliber Colt Automatic pistol.

Photo courtesy Ernest Hemingway Collection/John F. Kennedy Presidential Library and Museum, Boston.

Kenyan government took the unusual step of opening a game reserve in the Kajiado District for the Hemingways' exclusive use; this was their first camp.[41] Here, there is a Mau Mau "scare" when escaped insurgents are thought to be heading toward the safari camp, but Hemingway makes light of it — and again underscores his own manliness — by poking fun at the earnest young British policeman who brings the news (*UK*, 54). According to Ian Parker, a Kenya game warden at the time, "southern Kajiado was hardly a Mau Mau area — so much so that, as at the coast, one left one's holstered weapon locked up in a safe."[42]

Hemingway used his little pistols almost as toys, to shoot guinea fowl for the kitchen (*UK*, 51) as well as camp pests such as jackals and even scorpions crawling out of the firewood (272). Patrick recalled that he and his father went out at night in the Land Rover, with Denis Zaphiro (nicknamed the "Stirling Moss of the Land Rover," as well as "G. C.") doing the driving, to shoot at spring hares with a pistol (telephone interview). One Woodsman pistol stayed in Africa: Hemingway gave it to Zaphiro, who had become a good friend of the family. Considering how often and in what contexts it appears in *Under Kilimanjaro* and other texts, it was a meaningful gift.[43]

Even if not useful for shooting game or Mau Mau, the Colt pistol serves in *Under Kilimanjaro* as a metaphor or stand-in for masculinity. In Africa, Hemingway wrote, he carried his little Colt in a well-worn leather holster with a leg tie-down (*UK*, 50), which Debba, his Kamba "fiancée," caressed, no doubt symbolically (171). To clarify or reinforce the equivalence, Hemingway also wrote that "in the old days we never carried pistols and it would have been very bad form in the days when we were pukka sahibs. But now you put the pistol on as naturally as you buttoned the flap of your trousers" (50–51). And not just the Colt pistol: the Winchester Model 12 also takes on phallic undertones when Hemingway describes it as being "faster than a snake" and writes that it "was, from thirty-five years of us being together, almost as close a friend and companion with secrets shared and triumphs and disasters not revealed as the other friend a man has all his life" (329).

Hemingway begins his first book-length exploration of hunting by presenting his semifictional persona hunkered down with two trackers by a salt lick, waiting patiently for a kudu, a great and elusive spiral-horned trophy that he has pursued for ten days. He has already refused to shoot a lesser bull, so as "not to frighten the greater kudu that should surely come at dusk" (5).

Hunters live in this sort of optimism. But even still hunting from a blind is not necessarily easy or even comfortable. Mosquitoes and flies soon arrive. Muscles cramp up. Concentration fails. It begins to rain. And if the wind doesn't shift and ruin hours of waiting, there's always that overwhelming need to sneeze or cough at the worst possible moment. Or the beast simply never appears. (Fifteen years later, the same situation and the same themes open and close Hemingway's *Across the River and Into the Trees*.)

But in this case, in East Africa, Hemingway's careful setup is ruined by the unexpected racket of a truck on a nearby road. One of the trackers stands up and says, "It is finished" (3). In fact it is finished, as any hunter knows. But Hemingway motions the tracker back down and they stay till it's too dark to see the front sight of the rifle and then finally even the rear sight. Superstition, or instinct, or merely a sense of life's perversities outscores logic in the hunting fields. Only a beginner has never unloaded and put away his gun, or otherwise relaxed his attentions, just in time to see his heart's desire step into view at that moment. Hemingway knew this too, or he would not have been a hunter.

Hemingway had absorbed the hunting ethic into his skin as a boy. By the time he first went on safari, an experience that most hunters can only dream of, he was only thirty-four years old, but he was well versed in the outdoors. Hunters bring all that they have learned to Africa, and that ancient continent shows them a new world. Hemingway took much from Africa, but he knew there would always be more yet. A hunter never escapes the gravitational pull of that land: "All I wanted to do now was get back to Africa. We had not left it, yet, but when I would wake in the night I would lie, listening, homesick for it already" (*GHA*, 72).

Notes

My thanks to Griffin & Howe historian Bob Beach, Ian Parker of Nairobi, Aaron Edward Hotchner (who prefers to be known as Hotch), and Patrick Hemingway for their invaluable input and assistance. This essay is copyright © Silvio Calabi 2011. Much of the information in it was published in different form in *Hemingway's Guns: The Sporting Arms of Ernest Hemingway* by Silvio Calabi, Steve Helsley, and Roger Sanger (Camden, ME: Down East Books, 2010). Used here by permission of the authors.

[1] Editor's note: This claim is contradicted by Hemingway biographer Carlos Baker, who writes that Ernest's "grandfather Anson had made him a gift of a single-barrel 20-gauge shotgun" on his twelfth birthday, 21 July 1911 (*Life*, 12).

[2] After near extinction due to poaching for their horns, which are in demand as dagger handles in Yemen and in parts of Asia as folk medicine, rhino populations are slowly recovering on game ranches and preserves in a few southern African countries, and limited trophy hunting is again possible, although wildly expensive. During Hemingway's first safari, in the mid-1930s, rhino were common on the East African plains.

[3] The emotional description of the arduous hunting and killing of an old bull (for his ivory) in *The Garden of Eden* is a loss-of-innocence passage that perfectly expresses these feelings (as well as the difficulties in taking such a trophy).

⁴ This would have been in the category of animal control work, not trophy hunting, and is not mentioned by either Hemingway or his wife.

⁵ Today elephant numbers are rising steadily in many parts of sub-Saharan Africa where there is good habitat, and populations in some regions are well beyond sustainable levels.

⁶ Patrick Hemingway, telephone interview, 18 September 2009.

⁷ Asian elephants were generally off limits because of Hindu religious beliefs and because they had been domesticated for centuries. Indeed, tiger hunters often rode elephant-back.

⁸ Roosevelt actually hired famous hunters Leslie Tarlton and R. J. Cunninghame, who in turn brought Percival aboard as a young assistant.

⁹ Here and throughout I have used the conversion table of the Federal Reserve Bank of Minneapolis to convert foreign currency into U.S. dollars, and to convert U.S. dollars from Hemingway's days into 2009 values. http://www.minneapolisfed.org/.

¹⁰ The Kenyan trophy hunting industry was abruptly shut down in 1977 under President Jomo Kenyatta. It marked the end of an era. However, controlled trophy hunting, with quotas carefully managed by government ministries, still thrives in many southern African countries.

¹¹ The etymology of the term *Professional Hunter* is interesting. Brian Herne, a retired PH, wrote that when Hugh Cholmondeley, the third Lord Delamere, settled in Kenya in the 1890s, he hired two professional hunters: Alan Black, who was to help out on his safaris, and a nameless Somali, who shot for meat for the employees of his ranch: "To differentiate between the two hunters, as well as on account of Black's surname, the Somali hunter was referred to as 'the black hunter,' while Alan Black was always called 'the white hunter,' and from this difference, or so the story goes, 'white hunter' came into common usage" (6). The term came to define any white man in Africa who organized and led hunting parties. The best of them grew into legends and the smart set derived as much cachet from hiring them as they did from bagging a trophy lion. Today they are called PHs, government-licensed professional hunters, and their social status remains much the same in certain circles.

¹² The gun cannot be identified as a Beretta from the photographs. Patrick Hemingway provided the information (telephone interview, 18 September 2009).

¹³ Slam-firing was deemed a safety hazard, or at least a legal liability, in the 1970s. Thereafter all pump-action guns were fitted with interruptors so the trigger has to be pulled separately for each shot.

¹⁴ In those days, shotgun cartridges had waxed-paper cases and brass bases. Water could eventually penetrate the wax coating and the paper would begin to swell, making loading and chambering the round difficult. Since the 1960s most shotshell rounds have plastic bodies (and brass or steel bases), which makes it easier to obey the maxim, "keep your powder dry."

¹⁵ The Model 12 was consigned to Abercrombie & Fitch for sale by Mary Hemingway on 3 July 1963, and sold to "John Nodop" on 2 August 1963. Winchester production records (Schwing) date its serial number, 525488, to 1928.

[16] The gunmaking firm of James Purdey & Sons, Ltd. was established in 1816, is still in business in London, and occupies the same exalted position in gunmaking as Rolls-Royce does in automobiles. Apparently, enough clients brought Purdey guns on safari, and made enough fuss about them, that to Ngui and Charo any double-barreled shotgun was a "Purdey."

[17] One of these he bought from Abercrombie & Fitch in June 1940 (for $117.30; Abercrombie & Fitch Ledgers, Book 8, 285). The second, with a silver escutcheon in the buttstock engraved "M.G.H.," was almost certainly for Martha Gellhorn, his third wife. Mary Hemingway willed both these guns to a friend in Los Angeles. They next surfaced at the James D. Julia auction house, in Maine, where they were sold in one lot, labeled as Hemingway guns, for $23,000 the pair on 9 October 2007. http://www.juliaauctions.com.

[18] Many military or cadet drill teams still carry Springfields in twenty-first century Independence Day parades.

[19] In the early 1960s U.S. forces began to shift to smaller cartridges in lighter, so-called assault rifles capable of both semi- and full-automatic fire.

[20] The Hague Convention of 1899 prohibited "the use of bullets which expand or flatten easily in the human body." Ever since, military bullets have been solid or steel-jacketed types that do not mushroom or expand inside the body.

[21] National rifle associations were established in Britain in 1859 and America in 1871 for almost the same purpose. Target shooting was a popular recreation at the turn of the nineteenth century, in which both Queen Victoria and Theodore Roosevelt took part.

[22] Off-the-rack bolt-action .30-06 sporting rifles from Winchester and Remington cost about $53 at the time, while a commercial Mauser .30-06 from Germany (available, if not common, in the United States at the time) was $110 (see advertisements recurring in period issues of *American Rifleman*, the NRA magazine).

[23] G&H was split off in 1964; A&F closed its doors in 1977, and G&H survives as an independent company to this day. The basement of their present headquarters, in New Jersey, has a floor-to-ceiling rack of ledgers — sixty books with almost twelve thousand pages annotating the firearms that moved through G&H, A&F, and VL&A (Von Lengerke & Antoine) from 1901 into 1977. The pages carry the names of financiers, potentates, celebrities, and plain folk. Bob Beach, a retired high school physics teacher with a yen for good guns, took on the monumental task of sorting out this mountain of information.

[24] This involved much more than restocking: considerable handwork was done to the action and magazine to make them operate smoothly, and precision sights, either open "iron" sights or telescopic sights, were installed. The entire rifle was lightened and spruced up. The final result was indeed "as good, or better, than anything a British firm could have turned out at the time" (Patrick Hemingway, quoted in Seán Hemingway, xvii).

[25] In one letter to Milford Baker, Hemingway refers to a 2.5-power scope on his Springfield; in another he describes watching a bear in Wyoming through the scope. However, Patrick Hemingway recalled that when his father first used the rifle, hunting elk in Montana and Wyoming, he complained that "all he could

see through the scope was a patch of hair." In addition, Hemingway's eyeglasses made using a scope more difficult. He removed the sight and never again used it (telephone interview). In all the photographs of this rifle, taken on safaris twenty years apart as well as in Idaho, it carries no scope.

[26] To compare: A high-grade .30-caliber bolt-action by premier English makers such as Holland & Holland and Rigby retailed for about £35 (or $175) in 1934. Importers doubled the United Kingdom price in the United States. By 1940 inflation in Britain and a weakening of the American dollar tripled the price of such rifles in the United States.

[27] Today a .30-06 is considered nowhere near enough gun for rhino (at least in the hands of an amateur), and even in 1934 it was well on the light side of such proven heavy-game loads as the .375 Holland & Holland Magnum, which debuted in 1912. The .375, however, was an English caliber developed for Africa and India and was uncommon in America.

[28] However, in describing Hemingway's second safari, twenty years later, Denis Zaphiro wrote that Hemingway killed a gazelle at four hundred yards with this same .30-06 — after spurning Zaphiro's offer of a scope-sighted rifle. "Take that away, boy," he reportedly said; "those are for nuns and virgins" (20).

[29] Pauline recorded in her journal an incident early in the safari when Ernest's rifle — she doesn't specify which one — fell off the car top and, supposedly uncocked and safe, discharged next to her husband's head when it hit the ground. She thought he'd been killed (Reynolds, *The 1930s,* 159).

[30] Mary Hemingway's own account of this episode is much less dramatic if a bit unkosher: she steadies her rifle on the Land Rover fender and the fatal shot, at fairly close range, is from G. C.'s rifle (419). Shooting from a vehicle is today frowned upon, if not outright illegal.

[31] The German Mauser influenced the design of the American Springfield rifle to such an extent that the American War Department had to pay Mauser about $1 million in royalties as they developed the rifle that would be used against the Mauser on the battlefields of both world wars.

[32] Nonetheless, the Mannlicher-Schoenauer served in the Greek army through World War II.

[33] One shows Hemingway attempting to shoot, at very close range, a cigarette out of Earl Theisen's outstretched hand with this rifle, while several Masai watch in bemusement. (Mary Hemingway took the picture with Theisen's camera.)

[34] By contrast, the Woodsman pistol then cost about $70.

[35] The colossal .700 Nitro Express, an exercise in one-upmanship and wretched excess, appeared in 1988.

[36] Most doubles, rifles and shotguns, have the safety catch on the top of the stock wrist, right at the shooter's hand, and most of them engage automatically when the gun is loaded. An experienced double-gunner instinctively slides the button forward, off, with his thumb as he raises the gun to his shoulder. (The safety catches of Hemingway's bolt-action Springfield rifle and his pump-action Winchester shotgun lie in very different places, and they don't engage automatically.)

[37] Patrick Hemingway recalled (telephone interview) that the .577 rifle had been given to his father by Winston Guest, in Cuba, and that it had been aboard *Pilar* during the Caribbean patrols of 1942–1943. The thinking was that the powerful bullet might penetrate the conning tower of a German submarine in close combat. (Highly unlikely.)

[38] Anthony Tregear, employee of Westley Richards & Co. Ltd., e-mail communication, 30 June 2009.

[39] When not in use, rifles should be cased to protect them and their vital sights from dust and dirt, bumps and bruises. Most bolt-actions — Hemingway's Springfield, for example — are of one-piece construction and need long cases.

[40] The Mau Mau Uprising, begun by members of the Kikuyu tribe in 1952, took the lives of "only" thirty-two white civilians (http://www.globalsecurity.org/military/library/report/1984/HRD.htm), but the fear of slaughter was pervasive: units of the King's African Rifles and the Kenya Regiment were mobilized; a militia was raised, settlers organized freelance commando raids, and Britain sent a detachment of Royal Marines, the cruiser HMS *Kenya*, and thousands of regular troops. In attempts to root out insurgent camps in the Aberdare Mountains, the Royal Air Force even carried out WWII-style carpet-bombing attacks. Officially, 10,527 Mau Mau were reported killed in action, largely by bush-savvy Kenya and tribal police and the loyalist Kikuyu Home Guard, black and white. Kenyan whites took to carrying guns everywhere, even on social occasions or shopping trips. Ian Parker, a Kenya game warden at the time, commented that "there was a huge element of machismo involved and, to a degree, it was the last flaring of Hollywood's wild west image" (email communication, 15 June 2009).

[41] They later hunted in Machakos, the adjacent district, which contains the Masai and Wakamba tribal lands south and east of Nairobi.

[42] E-mail communication, 15 June 2009. Ian Parker (Nairobi; Kenya Game Department ranger 1956–1964; contemporary and friend of Denis Zaphiro; email communications, June–October 2009).

[43] According to Ian Parker, records of the Police Firearms Bureau, in Nairobi, confirm that the pistol was transferred to the possession of Denis Zaphiro on 12 July 1954. In 1996 it was turned over to Kenya Bunduki, a Nairobi gun shop, by Zaphiro's neighbor and friend, Pat Smith (interviewed by Parker), as Zaphiro had descended into Alzheimer's. Since then it has been sold and has disappeared.

Works Cited

Arnold, Lloyd R. *High on the Wild with Hemingway*. Caldwell, ID: The Caxton Printers, 1968.

Baker, Carlos. *Ernest Hemingway: A Life Story*. 1969. Reprint, New York: Collier Macmillan, 1988.

Baker, Max. "Rifles in India." *Arms & Explosives*, September 1899, 135.

Bull, Bartle. *Safari: A Chronicle of Adventure*. New York: Carroll & Graf, 1988.

Butterfields Auctioneers, San Francisco: Sporting Guns Sale Catalog, 17 November 1997.
Calabi, Silvio. "The .470 Nitro Express." *Sports Afield*, June/July 2007, 69–73.
Capstick, Peter Hathaway. *Safari, the Last Adventure*. New York: Macmillan, 1984.
Dallas, Donald. *Holland & Holland, The Royal Gunmakers*. London: Quiller Press, 2003.
Griffin & Howe (G&H), Bernardsville, New Jersey. Gun-sales Ledgers, Books 8 (1 February 1940–31 January 1943) and 9 (1 February 1943–31 January 1946). Edited by Robert Beach. Unpublished.
Griffin & Howe (G&H), New York. *Rifle Makers and Sportsmen's Equipment Catalog, 1928*. Reprinted in *Gun Digest*, vol. 12, edited by John Amber. Chicago: The Gun Digest Co., 1958.
Haven, Charles T., and Frank A. Belden. *A History of the Colt Revolver*. New York: Bonanza Books, 1940.
Hemingway, Ernest. "The Christmas Gift." Part I, *Look*, 20 April 1954, 29–37; Part II, *Look*, 4 May 1954, 79–89. Reprinted in *By-Line: Ernest Hemingway. Selected Articles and Dispatches of Four Decades*, edited by William White, 425–69. New York: Scribner's, 1967.
———. *The Garden of Eden*. 1986. Reprint, New York: Collier Books, 1987.
———. *Green Hills of Africa*. 1935. Reprint, New York: Collier MacMillan, 1987.
———. *Hemingway on Hunting*. Edited and with an introduction by Seán Hemingway. Foreword by Patrick Hemingway. Guilford CT: The Globe Pequot Press, 2001.
———. "My Pal the Gorilla Gargantua." *Ken* (28 July 1938). Reprinted in *Hemingway on Hunting*, 187–91.
———. "Notes on Dangerous Game: The Third Tanganyika Letter." *Esquire*, July 1934, 19, 194. Reprinted in *By-Line: Ernest Hemingway. Selected Articles and Dispatches of Four Decades*, 167–71.
———. "Safari." With Photographs by Earl Theisen. *Look*, 26 January 1954, 19–34. The first section is reprinted in *Hemingway on Hunting*, 205–9.
———. "The Short Happy Life of Francis Macomber." In *The Short Stories of Ernest Hemingway*, 3–37. 1938. Reprint, New York: Scribner's, 1966. First published 1936 in *Cosmopolitan*.
———. *Under Kilimanjaro*. Kent: Kent State UP, 2005.
Hemingway, Hilary, and Jeffry P. Lindsay. *Hunting with Hemingway: Based on the Stories of Leicester Hemingway*. New York: Riverhead Books, 2000.
Hemingway, Leicester. *My Brother, Ernest Hemingway*. Cleveland, OH: The World Publishing Company, 1961.
Hemingway, Mary Welsh. *How It Was*. New York: Knopf, 1976.
Herne, Brian. *White Hunters*. New York: Henry Holt, 1999.
"The Hero of the Code." *Time*, 14 July 1961.
Hotchner, A. E. "The Guns of Hemingway." *True*, September 1971, 48–56.
Johnson, Paul. *Intellectuals*. New York: HarperCollins, 1990.

Kerasote, Ted. "The Untouchable Wild." *Audubon Magazine*, September–October 1999, 82.
Livingston, Roxanne Theisen (Agoura Hills, CA). Email communications and telephone interviews, April–July 2009.
Lyons, Leonard. "A Day in Town with Hemingway." *New York Post*, 26 June 1953.
Madis, George. *Winchester Dates of Manufacture, 1849–1984*. Brownsboro, TX: Art & Reference House, 1984.
Ondaatje, Christopher. *Hemingway in Africa*. New York: The Overlook Press, 2004.
Raeburn, John. *Fame Became of Him: Hemingway as Public Writer*. Bloomington: Indiana UP, 1984.
Reynolds, Michael. *Hemingway: The 1930s*. New York: Norton, 1997.
———. *Hemingway: The Final Years*. New York: Norton, 2000.
———. *The Young Hemingway*. Oxford: Basil Blackwell, 1986.
Roosevelt, Theodore. *African Game Trails*. New York: Scribner's, 1910.
Schwing, Ned. 2001 Standard Catalog of Firearms. Iola, WI: Krause, 2000.
Sommer, François. *Man and Beast in Africa*. 1922. Translated by Edward Fitzgerald. London: Herbert Jenkins, 1953.
Steinhart, Edward I. *Black Poachers / White Hunters*. Athens: Ohio UP, 2006.
Stoeger, A. F., ed. *Arms, Ammunition, and Shooting Accessories Catalog*. New York: Stoeger Arms Corp., 1940.
———. *Shooter's Bible*. New York: Stoeger Arms Corp., 1940.
Theisen, Earl. "The Last Safari." *Audubon Magazine*, September–October 1999, 73–81.
———. Unpublished photographs from the 1953–1954 safari. The Hemingway Collection at the John F. Kennedy Presidential Library and Museum, Boston.
Walker, John Frederick. *Ivory's Ghosts*. New York: Atlantic Monthly Press, 2009.
Whelen, Townsend. "United States Rifles, Caliber .30." *American Rifleman*, August 1934, 21–24.
Wilson, R. L. *The World of Beretta*. New York: Random House, 2000.
Zaphiro, Denis, as told to Worth Bingham. "Hemingway's Last Safari." *Rogue*, February 1963, 18–20, 87–88.

3: "Love is a dunghill. . . . And I'm the cock that gets on it to crow": Ernest Hemingway's Farcical Adoration of Africa

Jeremiah M. Kitunda

> *All I wanted to do now was to get back to Africa. . . . I loved the country so that I was happy as you are after you have been with a woman that you really love, when, empty, you feel it welling up again and there it is and you can never have it all. . . . Now being in Africa, I was hungry for more of it.*
>
> — Ernest Hemingway, *Green Hills of Africa*

WHEREAS ERNEST HEMINGWAY'S CONTRIBUTION to Africa's image is indisputable, his debt to Africa as a contributor to his life and career remains unexplored. In the 1930s and 1950s, the renowned American writer made two major well-documented excursions to Eastern Africa. These two African excursions, both centered at the foot of Kilimanjaro (Africa's highest and most massive mountain),[1] inspired an important body of texts that includes essays in magazines (*Esquire*, *Look*, and *Sports Illustrated*), a good-sized correspondence, two very fine short stories ("Snows of Kilimanjaro" and "The Short Happy Life of Francis Macomber"), another two short stories embedded in a novel (the African stories in *The Garden of Eden*), and two (or three, depending on how one counts) full-length books (*Green Hills of Africa*, *True at First Light*, and *Under Kilimanjaro*).[2] My title and epigraph, taken from "The Snows of Kilimanjaro" and *Green Hills of Africa*, respectively, encapsulate the centrality of Kilimanjaro and Africa in Ernest Hemingway's African writings.

This large body of work not only attests to the centrality of Africa to Hemingway's biography and bibliography, but it also helped shape the image of Africa in the minds of a very large public. It is important, therefore, to examine the bases of these African texts, or, more precisely, the intersection of Hemingway's intellectual background and the African lore he acquired on safari. What were the sources of his inspiration as a writer and how are those inspirational sources connected to Africa?

In *Fame Became of Him: Hemingway as Public Writer*, John Raeburn argues that Hemingway's rise to "personal fame" in the 1930s (as opposed to the "literary eminence" he achieved in the 1920s) was buttressed by his nonfiction work: *Death in the Afternoon* in 1932 and *Green Hills of Africa* in 1935.[3] Hemingway's self-portrayal as a stalwart hunter of fierce African beasts as well as a pioneer native writer remained one of the vivid and dramatic elements of his personal fame.[4]

As my epigraph reveals, Hemingway was strongly attracted to the culture and landscape of Africa, but it is not clear from his writing whether or not he really respected Africa. Hemingway is complex and as multilayered as an onion. Every time you peel off a layer, another appears, so that it is difficult to pin him down. Is he loving, satiric, or cynical in his attitude to Africa? Having examined Hemingway's work on Africa, I conclude Hemingway is farcical about Africa. The farce in Hemingway's African writings is intentional and at the service of satire, and not the unintentional (as some may interpret it) result of Hemingway's ignorance of East Africa or of its languages and customs. Regardless, let us examine this question in terms of three broad areas: (1) love, sex, and power relationships; (2) intertextuality (African sources, including African languages); and (3) the matters of utopia and ecology. All three themes highlight a Hemingway-Africa symbiosis.

Love, Sex, and Marital Power Struggles in Hemingway's African Works

Farce and satire served Hemingway well as a writer. These two stylistic devices helped him to communicate with humor to his African and Western readers. Africa seems to have offered Hemingway a substitute for bullfighting, with the cock replacing the bull as a symbol of power and sexuality. Hemingway not only declares his literary stand-in (the protagonist or first-person narrator) "the cock," but also has the other (both African and Western) characters address that personage with epithets that credit his authority: "old cock" ("Snows," 75), "brother," "sir," and "the law" (*Under Kilimanjaro*, 35–36). Hemingway's use of the term *cock* in a symbolic context in these pieces invites us to ponder Harry's statement: "Love is a dunghill. . . . And I'm the cock that gets on it to crow" ("Snows," 57).

Africa also offered Hemingway the opportunity to refresh both his marriage and his writing. In Africa, he could work out his thoughts on marital relationships in terms of social satire and comic tragedy. Margot and Francis Macomber, for instance,

> were known as a comparatively happily married couple . . . as the society columnist put it, they were adding more than a spice of

adventure to their much envied and ever-enduring *Romance* by a *Safari* in what was known as *Darkest Africa* until the Martin Johnsons lighted it on so many silver screens where they were pursuing *Old Simba* the lion, the buffalo, *Tembo* the elephant and as well collecting specimens for the Museum of Natural History. . . . They had a sound basis of union. Margot was too beautiful for Macomber to divorce her and Macomber had too much money for Margot ever to leave him. ("Short Happy Life," 22)

This passage, taken together with Harry's attack on wealth and capitalism, suggests that Hemingway was trying to condemn the power of women and money as sources of discord in Western society. "The Snows of Kilimanjaro" and "The Short Happy Life of Francis Macomber" satirize Western capitalism and Western marriage in narratives where evil triumphs. With subtle irony, Hemingway uses African episodes in these marriages as a mirror to drive his point home. Instead of presenting the safari as a shared adventure, which can add "more spice" to a relationship, the narrative reports the end of a marriage. Through Margot's sexual affair with Robert Wilson and the resultant degeneration of the Macombers' marriage to spousal murder,[5] the narrative gives the woman and the European colonialist equal blame. Given that the white hunter, whose physical appearance satirizes Europeans in Kenya, thrived on taking the adventurers' wives, his role in the collapse of Macombers' marriage may also signify the moral decay of Western or colonialist white society. This argument is stronger when we consider that Hemingway generally does not treat colonial society favorably in his writings.

Hemingway quickly noticed that, in Africa, hunting was a testing ground for masculinity; this knowledge appeared in his creation of the character Francis Macomber. Both in this context and according to the Western norms of the 1930s, the power structure of marriage was well defined. Wilson cynically dubs the murder "the end of cuckoldry" after eleven years of tension that could not find relief in adventure ("Short Happy Life," 33). It appears that in Hemingway's view, the marriages in "Snows" and "Short Happy Life" collapsed not only because one party in the marriage had exhausted the capacity for love, but also because in the context of Africa, the rigid Western materialist definition of love and of the marriage bond were revealed as insufficient.

Twenty years later, aging rapidly and with three failed marriages behind him, Hemingway seems to be asking, does cuckoldry really have to lead to the graveyard? Why should infidelity end with murder, or why should it kill marriage? I take it that Hemingway was calling upon the reader to compare two ways of dealing with infidelity, the fatal one presented in "Short Happy Life" and the more tolerant one presented in *Under Kilimanjaro,* which ended with enhanced love.

The "infidelity" in *Under Kilimanjaro* is interesting, and quite different from that in "Short Happy Life." Rather than conducted among Westerners who are on African soil, here it also involves the local population. Hemingway did not hide his admiration for native girls: "African girls . . . are really wonderful and all that nonsense about they can't love you is not true. It is only that they are more cheerful than the girls at home" (*Selected Letters*, 827). He pictured Debba (Ndemba)[6] as very tender and compliant. Many Hemingway scholars have cast Ernest Hemingway in very bad light as a sexist or racist. But, on the basis of his relationships with Debba and other natives, I strongly disagree with such viewpoints. Instead, we need to see him as sensitive and receptive to the African context.

When Margot in the 1936 story was unfaithful to Francis, we hear the remark that "women *are* a nuisance on safari" ("Short Happy Life," 25). But no such castigation was leveled against any woman (or man) when infidelity appears in the narrative about the 1953–54 trip. Here, the reader ought to notice that as a *Mzee* (Mũkamba elder), Hemingway does not portray himself as unfaithful or promiscuous, but simply as attached to two women, Mary and Debba. In African terms, this is legitimate sexual behavior. That is to say, polygamy in African culture is acceptable to both men and women and sometimes it is even the first wife who persuades the husband to marry a second wife for reasons that are as varied as there are individuals in Africa.

During his second safari, Hemingway, who seems to have been unhappy with the rigid Western rules of monogamy, allowed himself a purely African perspective of love and marriage. It looks like self-indulgence, but it is an "adoption" of African polygamy. In a letter to Bernard Berenson, he reported that N'Gui (Ngũi),[7] who was thirty years old and had five wives, would add two with the proceeds of the trip (*Selected Letters*, 827). Seeing these customs as rather liberating to the individual, Hemingway contemplated taking Debba as a second wife, a situation that, remarkably enough, Mary accepted.

However, the story of Debba is even more complex than *Under Kilimanjaro* suggests. Notwithstanding the claims Hemingway made in *Under Kilimanjaro*, it is still questionable whether he really flirted with Debba. Perhaps we need to understand the narrative in the context of Kamba culture relating to romance, lovemaking, flirting, and marriage. I think that Debba is a *joke wife*, not a real one. Within Kamba culture such joke relationships could exist between an old man and a young girl, and even an older woman and a young man, but no sexual intercourse was ever contemplated. When Hemingway turned that joke into reality, he threw his readers into confusion.

Furthermore, Hemingway seems to contradict or misrepresent local customs when he claims that his Kamba brother N'gui would marry Hemingway's fiancée, and that "he and I are brothers so it is OK" (*Selected Letters*, 827). But this claim has two weaknesses. First, he does not treat N'Gui's father, M'Cola (Mūkola), as his father. And although friends and brothers within Kamba and Masai societies could share sexual partners, this could happen only on certain special and well-defined occasions and contexts, and not, as Hemingway suggests, as a matter of course.

For African readers, then, Hemingway seems to be inaccurate or perhaps ignorant of local customs and laws. But for Western readers, Debba may function as Hemingway's mouthpiece to revisit the issue of infidelity and to expose something of African social life, which is tolerant of polygamy. As an adopted Mūkamba, he was free to engage in extramarital sex without jeopardizing his original marital bond with Mary.

Hemingway's bequest to Debba's family communicates (whether consciously or unconsciously) both sarcasm and a positively comic element. In one comic-ironic situation, for example, Hemingway gives Debba's family "a pound of lard and a haunch of a warthog Miss Mary shot" (*Selected Letters*, 826). But these things and actions carried negative meaning for the Kamba, signifying that his relationship with Debba was as stinky and unproductive as the ground-destroying warthog. Contrary to the praise that Hemingway heaps on the warthog in *Under Kilimanjaro*,[8] that animal is not highly esteemed among the Akamba, who associate it with witchcraft, black magic, and anything that is retrogressive. Giving such meat to in-laws would be farcical, since consuming the meat of a warthog is the last thing a Mūkamba would contemplate! A more appropriate present would have been a goat or a chicken, locally regarded as a delicacy and the most respectful treat for in-laws and friends. If, as the English saying goes, actions speak louder than words, then giving warthog meat to Debba's family reduced the Hemingway-Debba (Ndemba) courtship to a farce, ridicule, cynicism, derision, and any other form of insolence we can find for it in English or Kamba language.[9]

Moreover, the fact that Mary had killed the warthog that Hemingway shared with Debba's family figuratively indicates that Mary sanctioned (albeit sneeringly) Hemingway's infidelity — recognizing, perhaps, that what is seen as cuckoldry in the West is simply life in Africa. Infidelity, Hemingway appears to suggest, can be played down through farcical symbolism to avoid such a fate as the Macombers'. In African lore, Hemingway seems to suggest, love and sex are commodities that ought to be shared to enhance community and family cohesion (e.g., that of the Hemingways), but not to rend it asunder as did the Macombers.

Other gender-related subjects also show both Hemingway's awareness of African lore and his refusal to lock himself into any value system.

The publications of the 1930s seem to follow an African- and Western-gendered division of labor, where men are the principal hunters. Not only are there fewer gun-wielding female characters, but they also either stay in the car while the men go hunting (as Margot Macomber does) or hunt far less than the male protagonists, as P. O. M. does in *Green Hills of Africa*. However, in *Under Kilimanjaro*, Mary is the key hunter (246–58). With this character, Hemingway broke both the Western gender constraints and African gender-centered hunting ethics, expressing his rejection of social rigidity, regardless of the culture that promotes it.

Hemingway displays his familiarity with African lore about African gender and social frameworks. When Francis Macomber bolts, he fails to follow the African lore packaged into a Swahili maxim "Asie sikia la mkuu huvunjika guu" (he who listens not to his elders/superiors breaks his leg). Hemingway also has Wilson quote a Somali proverb ("in Africa no woman ever misses her lion and no white man ever bolts"), and make reference to another: "A brave man is always frightened three times by a lion; when he first sees his track, when he first hears him roar, and when he first confronts him" ("Short Happy Life," 7, 11). In spite of his high financial and social status in the West, in Africa Macomber is ignorant of local hunting lore and is weak as a hunter; he is placed at the lowest rank of masculinity, what locals call "a girl of the male sex" (Mwangi, 59). By matching Macomber and the warrior-world of East Africa with a warrior woman (Mary never bolts, unlike Macomber), Hemingway again pours cold water on the very source of pride of the Masai, Kamba, and Western men. But he also reflects the trend, current in Africa after World War II, of decolonization (the decline of Western hegemony in Africa) as well as the postwar feminist challenge to male domination. Mary appears to be the social epitome of these sweeping changes from the old to the new world order of gender and social equality. Africa was for Hemingway the best place to work out such themes. In a 1953 letter, Hemingway wrote: "Mary is very well here and has finally found a country that is as tough as she is" (*Selected Letters*, 825).

In contrast to the troubled marriages described in the works following the first safari, the works emerging from the second safari represent a more settled picture of romance. Even so, the multilayered Hemingway cannot be credited with feminist sentimentality or gender sensitivity, for the narrative of Mary's hunting of the big black-maned lion is rolled into a package of suspense, farce, and ridicule. It is not clear who really kills the lion. It appears that Hemingway's "long-drawn shot," as he puts it, along with those of other men, brings down the lion. In the process of trying to lift the woman up in the new world sensitivity, Hemingway does not stay within clearly discernible frameworks. As elsewhere, here he adopts a principle of praise, praise, and dump!

Intertextuality of Hemingway's African Writings

It is well known that Hemingway was widely read and that his work is highly literate and intertextual. He took many of the titles of his books from existing literature,[10] and his characters and situations are often rooted in the Western canon. As Michael Reynolds informs us, "when Hemingway's interest focused on new materials or a new genre, he read broadly and deep" (*The 1930s*, 169). But hunting and natural history were lifelong interests, and Africa had figured largely in his mind for decades. He had been reading about Africa and African exploration long before he traveled to Africa, and the reading intensified before his first trip. In Paris he had purchased "twenty-three rare volumes on African hunting" (168).[11] Governed by his life-long passion for natural history and ecology, these topics figured in much of his reading about Africa. Hemingway did not always accept or agree with the Western authors he read, and it is instructive to see which authors he disliked and which he approved of.

In *Death in the Afternoon* Hemingway shows his familiarity with the worshipful attitude of an early nineteenth-century explorer of Africa and natural historian, Mungo Park: "When that persevering traveler, Mungo Park, was at one period of his course fainting in the vast wilderness of an African desert, naked and alone, considering his days as numbered and nothing appearing to remain for him to do but to lie down and die, a small mossflower of extraordinary beauty caught his eye," renewed his faith, and gave him hope and strength (134) — an attitude that Hemingway mocks and derides. Mungo Park's reports of his exploration of west and northern Africa in the 1790s were inaccurate and hyperbolic, probably designed to capture a particular audience. Although Hemingway rejects this religious approach to natural history, he is clearly familiar enough with Park's work to quote him.

In addition to Mungo Park, Hemingway was probably familiar with other writers with religious attitudes. Missionaries like Johannes Krapf wrote passionately about the African landscape. In 1848, after news spread across Europe about these East African snowcapped mountains and green hills, rhymester Cecil Frances Humphreys Alexander composed her famous hymn, "There is a green hill far away," as she sat up one night with her sick daughter:

> There is a green hill far away,
> Outside a city wall,
> Where the dear Lord was crucified,
> Who died to save us all.
>
> Refrain:
> O dearly, dearly, has He loved,
> And we must love Him, too,
> And trust in His redeeming blood,
> And try His works to do.[12]

Although Alexander's work[13] is as religious and optimistic as Mungo Park's, which Hemingway ridiculed, he may have been, at some level, influenced by her popular hymn. Although the hill she was seeing is outside her city of Derry (Ireland), and she makes it refer to the hills of Jerusalem, the coincidence of contemporary popular missionary reports of snowcapped mountains and green hills in distant East Africa is too tempting for me not to conclude that Cecil was consciously or unconsciously responding to the popular discourse about these newly found distant African hills and the psychological comfort they potentially held for Europe. The mother's ordeal (in the hymn) is, I believe, comparable to Helen's ordeal under the shadows of Kilimanjaro's House of God, as she nurses her delirious husband, Harry. The snow dome of Kilimanjaro symbolically takes the position of a mother soothing her child (Harry) as he endured pain in the plains of Kilimanjaro. Locally the mountain, its foothills and surrounding plains, are given feminine and divine attributes.

The hill reminded Cecil of Calvary, and it is noteworthy that missionaries recommended the African hills as potential future settlements for European patients. In fact, several locations in Africa were by then already recipients of consumptives and lepers from Europe. At the time, Africa (in addition to the Caribbean islands and Australia) was dubbed "a dunghill whereon England doth cast forth its rubbish" (Linebaugh and Rediker, 124). From as far back as the late seventeenth century, thousands of unlucky people, dubbed *undesirables*, were banished to Africa. These English exiles included deported Irish, Liverpool beggars, lepers, royalist prisoners from Scotland, highwaymen caught on the Scottish borders, pirates caught on the English high seas, exiled Huguenots and Frenchmen, outlawed religious dissenters and the captured prisoners of various uprisings and plots against the king. These groups were settled in Ranter Bay (Madagascar), the Cape Province sanitarium in South Africa, and the St. Helena, McCarthy, and Robben Islands. Even though evidence may be hard to adduce, the circumstances within which Cecil's lyric was composed indicate a muted connection with East African hills, which caught the Western imagination and inspired much poetry.

Hemingway was of course familiar with the work of Mark Twain, about whom he said: "All modern American literature comes from one book by Mark Twain called *Huckleberry Finn*... it's the best book we've had" (*Green Hills of Africa*, 22). Twain was quite familiar with Africa — he toured southern Africa (South Africa, Mauritius, and other Indian Ocean Island nations) in the 1890s. He was not driven by religious sentiment, and he was sympathetic to Africans, being one of the few writers about Africa who castigated British colonialist practices in South Africa and Belgian colonial atrocities in the Congo. "To the Person Sitting in Darkness" and "King Leopold's Soliloquy" stand out as his finest satires; they express the tragedy of imperialism anywhere in the world. It is also remarkable that Mark Twain was a member of the Congo Reform

Association, led by E. D. Morel and Sir Roger Casement, which called for the dissolution of King Leopold's Congo Free State on the grounds of the king's abuse of human rights. Hemingway admired other colonial artists[14] as well, praising Rudyard Kipling as the most talented prose writer, and Gustave Flaubert[15] — who satirized French imperialism in Northern Africa — as the most disciplined. These artists displayed a marked aversion for anything imperial. They produced popular satires on European imperialism by means of narratives that were accessible to the general reader. They loudly condemn the vices of European colonialism.

Hemingway's admiration for Mark Twain and writers of his ilk raises several questions: How successfully did he himself address African issues? How did cultural, political, and natural conditions in Africa influence his writing? How did he view Africans who were at the time under British colonial rule? In other words, how accurately did he capture a true African image and how real was Africa to Hemingway? It is difficult to think that his admiration for Twain, Kipling, and Flaubert did not give him entry into the native African culture. In addition, I would argue that African lore and classical traditions also supplied significant inspiration to Hemingway's writings.

African Lore: The Cock and the Hyena

Hemingway was influenced not only by his wide reading but also by what he learned during his travels. He learned the power of symbolism in African culture and set out to weave these African symbols into his own work. From the Akamba, one of the East African ethnic groups that adopted him, Hemingway learned not only about the warthog but also about cock symbolism, which he integrated with classical cognates. Like the bull in Spain, the cock is, in East Africa and in other countries, a symbol of unchangeable prowess, so that declaring one's self the cock is an act of placing oneself in authority to do anything that concerns the subject in question. In addition to its dietary and ornamental value, the cock is the indispensable clock of Africa, announcing the coming of dawn, the end of day, and the coming of a new age. No doubt Hemingway was figuratively doing exactly that when he has his character Harry declare that "love is a dunghill" and "I am the cock that gets on it to crow,"— perhaps the cock of literate Africa.[16]

Like Kilimanjaro, the cock has been the subject of poetry and lyrics in Africa and carries many sexual allusions. Hemingway probably heard the Kamba sing one of their popular folksongs alluding to the cock, which was dedicated to a famous colonial chief of the Kamba people of the Kitui District of Kenya, and widely sung in the 1950s. The Kamba language is very rich and has many words, including slang words and figurative expressions, to mean the same thing. The several words that mean *cock* appear in darker print, for easier recognition:

Akamba Folksong: **Nzokolo** Ndikoaiwe Mweeni

Ndūmane ngethi kwa sivū Mūnyasya
Ndūmane **ngūkū**[17] ndĩkoaĩwe mweeni
Ndūmane ngethi kwa sivū Mūnyasya
Ndūmane **ngūkū** ndĩkoaĩwe mweeni
Wethĩwa ve mbũi na ng'ombe ni ng'elwe
Ĩĩ wethĩwa ve mbũi na ng'ombe ni ng'elwe
We sivū nĩwĩsĩ **ngūkū** nĩ mũndũ
Ĩĩ nĩ wĩsĩ **ngūkū** nĩ mũndũ
Nzokolo[18] kyayo nĩ kwamũkya mũndũ
Akomete vandũ akũyĩta mwanake
Tumũa na **nzamba**[19] na wethĩwa ndĩkwenda
Nzambane na nondo kũkũkya ngevithe
Nzokolo ndyasye kũkũkya kũkye ngwilita nondonĩ!

Translation: Slaughter no **Cock** for the Guest

I send greetings to chief Mũnyasya
For a **cock** not to be slaughtered for a guest
I send greetings to chief Mũnyasya
For a **cock** not to be slaughtered for a guest
If there is a goat and a cow let them be slaughtered instead
Yes, if there is a goat and a cow, let them be slaughtered instead
You chief know that the **cock** is a man
Yes, you know that the **cock** is a man
The duty of a **cock** is to wake up a man
Sleeping somewhere calling himself a lad
Alert the **cock** and if it doesn't want
I cuddle the breasts till dawn to hide
The **cock** crows at dawn while I am cuddling breasts.

This song signifies the power of the cock as a symbol and its widespread allegorical use in African romance and friendship, as well as in the social, political, and economic realm. Just as Kilimanjaro is the crest of Africa, the cock (*nzamba* in Kamba) represents sex and power. The figure of the cock, for instance, is embedded into Kenya's flag, currency, and the crest of the KANU party, which not only supported the Mau Mau anticolonial movement but also ousted the colonial regime in 1963 and ruled Kenya for forty years. KANU chose the image of the cock to signify its prowess and triumph over colonialism, in the same way that the cock overpowers hens.

Fig. 3.1. Kenya's coat of arms displays the national colors: red, black, green, and white. The lions, spears, and shield represent protection and valor, and the rooster with an axe symbolizes arbitration and justice. The word Harambee *is Swahili for "Pull together." Most local, regional, and national developments after independence were done through self-help cooperative events that were dubbed* Harambee.

Moreover, Congolese army chief Joseph Désiré Mobutu renamed himself *Mobutu sese seko kūkū*[20] *ngbendu wa za banga*, variously translated as "the **cock** who leaves no hen untouched," "the only **cock** among the chickens," or "the **rooster** who sings victory, the **warrior** who moves from one conquest to another and no one can stop him" (Schatzberg, 49). These names symbolized his victory over various competing forces within the Congo Civil War of the 1960s.

At one point, the narrator of *Under Kilimanjaro* reports that N'Gui's "father once saw me changed into a snake" (93), probably during a drinking session. More "magic" occurs when Hemingway caught some roosters, "putting them to sleep by some form of magic and laying them asleep in front of her [Debba's] family's lodge"— actions that the narrator calls "a mistake" and "not magic. It is a trick. Catching them is only a trick too" (35, 372). Nevertheless, catching the roosters and putting them to sleep was interpreted, in the context of Kamba customs, to signify that Hemingway had taken away all power and authority from the village elders, and was now the ruler. No wonder that later the Informer crowned him "the law" to the natives of Kilimanjaro (35).

Hemingway also understood and followed African law concerning the lion or, more accurately, the shooting of lion. He took care not to shoot lions from the safety of a motorcar or while they were sleeping. "For a man to shoot a lion from the protection of a motor car, where the lion cannot even see what it is that is attacking him, is not only illegal but is a cowardly way to assassinate one of the finest of all game animals" ("Shootism," 163). Nonetheless, he enjoyed killing the game and shows little remorse, but claims that he killed cleanly — his sense of killing as another dunghill.

In contrast to this is Hemingway's treatment of the hyena (*fisi* in Swahili, *mbiti* in Kikamba). Hemingway's graphic details about the killing of hyenas and his suggestion in *Green Hills of Africa* that his Kamba assistant enjoyed the ordeal sound unconvincing to African readers. Within Kamba lore, the killing of hyenas and similar species of animals was practically taboo, as the hyena is not only vermin but also a ritual animal, killed only if their predatory activities grow out of proportion. Even so the killing of the hyena was to be conducted by special hunters and in ways different from normal hunting. The Kamba maxim **kwaa mana ta musyi wathite mbiti** (*vanished aimlessly like an arrow that shot a hyena*) encodes the nature of the Kamba view of the hyena in hunting narratives. An arrow that shot the hyena, owl, or crocodile was by law irretrievable, for it was believed it could bring misfortune to the hunter's family. The wounded hyena was simply allowed to escape with the arrow, which would deter his return to the village and symbolically take away misfortune from the human arena. Readers will recall that when the hyena whimpered towards the end of "The Snows of Kilimanjaro," calamity struck — Harry presumably died.

The Kamba and neighboring Kilimanjaro linguistic groups traditionally held the hyena, the owl, the woodpecker, and the bush baby as harbingers of death. Although neither profane nor sacred, these creatures were carefully treated, for they represented a bad omen; careless interaction with them was tantamount to inviting bad luck. If the Kamba within Hemingways' party[21] enjoyed the feat (*GHA*, 37–38), then we must consider that three things had happened by the time of his visit. First, that there had been a shift in traditional Kamba practices (this is not likely, since, in general, the Kamba still handle the hyena with care). Second, that *Green Hills of Africa* presents a particular group of Akamba in East Africa who, as Hemingway puts it, were spoiled by Western cultures. The Kamba enclaves domiciled around the Kilimanjaro region had lost some of their original culture and it will be understandable for a "spoiled dispersed colony" to flout the customs of their parent group. That is, they were likely to have changed their attitudes towards hyenas due to external influence. Thus, their actions, as reported in *Green Hills*, did not represent the Kamba ethnic group as a whole. The third (and most compelling) possibility is that Hemingway was distorting or misrepresenting Kamba practice in order to amuse his audience.

These animals, then, connect to important concepts such as symbolic power, religion, luck, sexuality, and romance within an unprofaned natural world. It is clear that Hemingway had acquired some of the Kamba lore and symbolism attached to several animals — the frozen leopard on top of Kilimanjaro, the whimpering hyena, the ground-damaging warthog, and the cock. Consciously or unconsciously, literally or ironically, he incorporated these classical Kamba traditions and African lore into his own transgressive work.

African Languages

There is no doubt that Hemingway had a good ear for languages. In Europe he acquired, in descending order of fluency, more than a smattering of French, Spanish, Italian, and German. Even in German, which he knew least well, he could distinguish among various local dialects, as evidenced in "Out of Season." During his few months in East Africa, Hemingway took the trouble to learn the rudiments of Swahili and of Kamba languages, and this knowledge appears in his writing. Although one applauds the effort to acquire the language, the many grammatical and spelling errors tells his East African readers that he understood the local languages but was not fluent. It seems that Hemingway used his knowledge to increase his authority and, more complexly, to amuse his readers who could not understand the Kamba language and culture.

In *Under Kilimanjaro*, for example, we have a passage in which the Swahili is entirely incorrect:

> "Hapana simba kubwa sana," Keiti said to me his eyes mocking but apologetic and absolutely confident. He knew it was not the big lion that we had heard so many times. "N'anyake," he said to make an early morning joke. This meant, in Kamba, a lion old enough to be a warrior and marry and have children but not old enough to drink beer. His saying it and making the joke in Kamba was a sign of friendliness, made at daylight when friendliness has a low boiling point, to show, gently, that he knew I was trying to learn Kamba with the non-Moslem and alleged bad element and that he approved or tolerated. (42)

As a speaker of both Swahili and the Kamba languages, I don't see any joke in Keiti's words. The first phrase, "Hapana simba kubwa sana," means in Swahili: "It was not a big lion." However, the second compound word, *N'anyake* (*na inyaake*),[22] means "with its mother" and not as Hemingway translates it. (In Kamba *na* is a conjunction meaning *with* or *and*, whereas *nyaake* means "its mother," "his mother," "her mother" or "their mother.") Keiti does not mention warriorship or beer drinking, as Hemingway suggests. I do not believe that Hemingway erred here through a lack of basic vocabulary. And in any case, he could have simply asked his literate native companions to correct him. Instead, I think that he deliberately inserted these errors to pull the leg of Western readers who, lacking any knowledge of the original languages, would take him at face value and be impressed with his knowledge. I reiterate here that the farce in Hemingway's African writings is intentional and at the service of satire, and not the unintentional result of Hemingway's ignorance of East Africa or his disregard for its languages and its ways. Even though he was not extremely eloquent or fluent in East African languages, Hemingway had at his disposal men who could have corrected his errors.

In other instances, however, Hemingway's language skills were clearly imperfect and incomplete. In both *Green Hills of Africa* and *Under Kilimanjaro*, there is reference to *faro* (rhinoceros, *GHA*, 78, 103) and *faru* (*UK*, 147). But the word should be *kĩfarũ*. Interestingly enough, this fairly obvious mistake (which no native speaker would make) is not corrected, an indication that the native speakers were unwilling to make such a correction when the word was spoken, and that Hemingway did not seek correction when the word was written.

Similarly, *Manamouki*, which is not a word, but is used as such in *Green Hills of Africa* (99), should be *mwanamke* (the Swahili word for female or woman).[23] However, the context in which this Swahili word is used is incorrect with reference to a female rhino. The Swahili speaker would not personify an animal in that manner, but would rather say *kifaru wa kike* (*kike* means *femininity*) or *kifaru mke* (*mke* means woman or wife). *N'dio* ("ndio," 101), which simply means "yes," needs to be contextualized if it is to mean "they are the ones." For example, if one is asked specifically, Are these the ones you were looking for? Are they the ones?, then the answer could well be, "ndio (yes)." But without the contextualizing question, one would have to say *ndio awa* to mean "they are the ones."

Doumi (*GHA*, 101), which is not a word, should be *dume* (male). Droopy's insistence that the narrator refrain from shooting indicates his adherence to the traditional ethics of hunting in which female mammals, especially when they had young ones, must be spared: "Droopy was whispering, 'Manamouki! Manamouki! Manamouki!' very fast and he and M'Cola [Mũkola] were frantic that I should not shoot. It was a cow rhino with a calf and as I lowered the gun, she gave a snort, crashed in the reeds, and was gone" (99). To put it briefly, in stark contrast to European colonizers, Hemingway displayed a rather unsettled attitude towards Africans. Although he seems to have felt comfortable among them and learned their languages, cultures, and lore in a considerably short time, it seems to me that he did not fully identify with or respect the knowledge he had acquired. As we have seen, he was not above using that knowledge, even when it was incomplete or imperfect, to aggrandize himself and to impress and amuse his Western audience.

Romanticism, Utopia, and Ecology

Hemingway's generation saw human society in developmental stages and to them Africa was a reminder of how their own preindustrial ancestors lived. Africa is therefore used to illuminate Western social crises and as a place to revitalize oneself and one's family life. Robert Stephens places Hemingway in this nostalgic tradition, arguing that that the destruction of the American landscape during Hemingway's childhood propelled him into a lifelong search for pristine lands outside America. Hemingway was not the first to see in Africa a solution to Western dystopia. Almost a century before Hemingway's first safari, missionary Johannes Krapf had seen the "republic" of East Africa as more peacefully and democratically promising than the revolutions and counterrevolutions that had characterized the European political landscape by the 1840s. But for Hemingway, it was the physical, not political, African landscape that was the ideal place for him to pursue happiness and innocence, a happiness rooted in the idyllic past. In "The Snows of Kilimanjaro," Hemingway's narrator explicitly says of Harry that "Africa was where he had been happiest in the good time of his life, so he had come out here to start again. . . . [To] work the fat off his soul the way a fighter went into the mountains to work and train in order to burn it out of his body" (59–60). While on safari, the narrator and his wife read books set in Russia and Spain (both of which can be considered frontiers to Europe), which captured the Western nostalgia for lost natural glory. It is telling that after discussing his reading, the narrator in *Green Hills of Africa* declares, in one short and one very long paragraph: "All I wanted to do now was to get back to Africa" (72–73).

Throughout his letters and solid publications, Hemingway presents the African environment in an amorous, idealistic, or sentimental way that leaves a lot of questions in the minds of candid readers. Although Hemingway refused to insert Western religious ecstasy into the African landscape (as Mungo Park did), Hemingway did, to some extent, share in the tendency to romanticize the African environment, as earlier imperialist travel writers had done. In part, this was due to his strong rejection of the destruction of the natural habitat he had, in his early years, witnessed in the Upper Peninsula of Michigan. In part it was due to his need, as a writer, for isolation. While Africa becomes a setting for his sardonic and sarcastic views of love, sex, and power relationships, its landscapes are excessively romanticized — the green hills of Africa are beautifully serene under the shadows of "the mountain" (as if there was only one mountain in Africa), the snows of Kilimanjaro are eternally pure and white, and the fossilized leopard works to immortalize nature in Africa. Like earlier travel writers, then, he painted Africa not only as a place for recreation, renewal, and an escape from the industrialized, overcrowded Western world, but also as a retreat, a better atmosphere for writing. In the Depression years, Hemingway also needed distance from the pressure put upon him to take up social issues, as so many of his generation (Dos Passos, Steinbeck) were doing. All these factors led him to write:

> Naturalists should all work alone. . . . Writers should work alone. They should see each other only after their work is done, and not too often then. Otherwise they become like writers in New York. All angleworms in a bottle, trying to derive knowledge and nourishment from their own contact and from the bottle. Sometimes the bottle is shaped art, sometimes economics, sometimes economic-religion. But once they are in the bottle they stay there. (*GHA*, 21–22)

Hemingway hoped to find a pristine landscape, empty of Western corruption, where he would be free to hunt and write. His need for such a landscape appears in these words: "I had loved country all my life; the country was always better than the people. I could only care about people a few at a time" (*GHA*, 73).

In the process, Hemingway glamorizes or idealizes the African landscape — it is noteworthy that this idyllic view of Africa is not echoed by the locals. Actually, he seems to romanticize a rather sordid period of African environmental experience, when unsupervised hunters broke laws and codes. Hemingway probably hoped that on a safari the social environment would be reduced so that the landscape and the animals could occupy center stage, the focus being on what, when, and how to hunt. As a lifelong hunter and fisherman, and as a writer who wrote about hunting and fishing, this was an ethical and technical problem that Hemingway loved to consider. In "Big Two Hearted River," he wrote about how to fish for trout in an ecological way. In the western United States and in eastern Africa, he subscribed to ecological hunting: as the passage cited above (about *manamouki*) indicates, he refrained from shooting female game.

The hunter's instinct to preserve his hunting environment (in part, perhaps, to ensure future hunting pleasure) gives the hunter a special sensitivity to ecology, to the environment, and particularly to the degradation of the environment. Although Africa was less industrialized than the Western countries Hemingway knew, it was not as ideal an environment as romantic travelogues suggested. Hemingway found environmental degradation even in this faraway continent, leading him to generalize that the only eternity is to be found in writing: "A country, finally, erodes and the dust blows away, the people all die and none of them were of any importance permanently, except those who practiced the arts. . . . A thousand years makes economics silly and a work of art endures forever" (*GHA*, 109).

In *Green Hills of Africa* we read about several ecological problems (soil erosion, the menace of the tsetse fly and locust invasion). While the British colonial regime blamed the natives for environmental change, Hemingway held Western colonialism responsible:

> A continent ages quickly once we come. The natives live in harmony with it. But the foreigner destroys, cuts down the trees, drains the water, so that the water supply is altered and in a short time the soil, once the sod is turned under, is cropped out and, next, it starts to blow away as it has blown away in every old country and as I had seen it start to blow in Canada. The earth gets tired of being exploited. . . . A country was made to be as we found it. We are the intruders and after we are dead we may have ruined it but it will still be there and we don't know what the next changes are. (284–85)

Here, Hemingway captures not only the environmental reality of 1930s Africa but also echoes the words of the eminent nineteenth-century pioneer of ecology, George Perkins Marsh:

> Man is everywhere a disturbing agent. Wherever he plants his foot, the harmonies of nature are turned to discords. The proportions and accommodations which insured the stability of existing arrangements are overthrown. Indigenous vegetable and animal species are extirpated, and supplanted by others of foreign origin, spontaneous production is forbidden or restricted, and the face of the earth is either laid bare or covered with a new and reluctant growth of vegetable forms, and with alien tribes of animal life. These intentional changes and substitutions constitute, indeed, great revolutions; but vast as is their magnitude and importance, they are . . . insignificant in comparison with the contingent and unsought results which have flowed from them. (36)

Hemingway specifically noted the effects of British imperial environmental practices in regard to the tsetse flies. By the 1930s, the tsetse fly (a disease carrier to both man and beast in tropical Africa) had become a major challenge to the colonists. Local oral traditions recall a period when large chunks of land were cleared of vegetation in a bid to tame the menace of the tsetse fly. Hemingway writes, "Droopy's country . . . looked awful. . . . [A]ll the trees had been girdled to kill the tsetse flies. . . . The soil was red and eroded and seemed to be blowing away" (*GHA*, 90). With the decline in vegetation cover, other agents of denudation set in and blew away the top soil, turning East Africa into a wasteland. Droughts and clouds of locusts overwhelmed the remaining natural vegetation and ruined crops, causing a steady migration of natives, which Hemingway also noted.

> [A]ll along the road we passed groups of people making their way to the westward. Some were naked except for a greasy cloth knotted over one shoulder, and carried bows and sealed quivers of arrows. Others carried spears . . . and their women walked behind them, with their pots and pans. Bundles and loads of skins were scattered along ahead on the heads of other natives. All were travelling away from the famine. (34–35)

These were catastrophic years of ecological collapse across colonial Africa. East Africa experienced such severe environmental degradation that Colin Maher, the British director of soil conservation in Kenya in 1937, described the land of the Kamba as

> an appalling example of a large area of land which has been subjected to uncoordinated and practically uncontrolled development by natives whose multiplication and increase of stock has been permitted, free from the checks of war and largely from those of disease, under benevolent British rule. Every phase of misuse of land is vividly and poignantly displayed in this Reserve, the inhabitants of which are rapidly drifting to a state of hopeless and miserable poverty and their land to a parching desert of rocks, stones and sand. (Tiffen, 3)

These ecological problems had become a major preoccupation of the colonial regimes across Africa. The truth is that a severe worldwide environmental degradation punctuated Hemingway's two visits to East Africa. Real environmental recovery (as one Boserupian scholar, Mary Tiffen, observed recently) was never realized until the natives resumed control over their environment through political independence in the 1960s.

Whereas adverse ecological changes caused some native unrest in the 1930s, a combination of ecological and political problems set in motion serious uprisings in the 1950s. On his second visit to the region, Hemingway found Kenya in a state of emergency following an outburst of violence that came to be called the Mau Mau insurgency — for their war cry *Musungu Arundi Ulaya Mwafrika Apate Uhuru*, meaning "let the Europeans go back to Europe for Africans to be free." The colonial regime played it down as a tribal uprising and so did Hemingway, but the fact that several battalions had to be recalled from Malaysia and England points to the magnitude of the problem.[24] The Mau Mau were feared outside of central Kenya and as far away as Tanzania, indicating the strength and power of the insurgency. Hemingway's appointment as honorary game warden indicates a shortfall in white staff as all settlers were called to active military duty against the Mau Mau rebels (*Selected Letters*, 825).

Apart from political turmoil and environmental degradation, Africa of the 1950s was rent apart by racial tensions, which Hemingway downplays. In this, he did not follow Mark Twain's example. As Maxwell Geismar observed, Hemingway's writing is "a total renunciation of all social frameworks, the separation of the writer from the activity of his time; the acceptance of a profound isolation as the basis for the writer's achievement" (37). John Atkins in *The Art of Ernest Hemingway* and Christopher Ondaatje in *Hemingway in Africa* echo the same refrain. Generally speaking, one can say that Hemingway was a frontiersman who kept his distance from metropolitan cities, who claimed that writing was a solitary activity, and who rejected writers who espoused social causes. Focused on himself, on hunting and on writing, Hemingway remained at the periphery of the colonial system and therefore failed to capture the essence of the ongoing political crisis in East Africa. Although his writings were contemporary to books and movies like Isak Dinesen's *Out of Africa* (1937), Jomo Kenyatta's *Facing Mount Kenya* (1938), François Sommer's *Man and Beast in Africa* (1953), Robert Ruark's *Something of Value* (1955) and *Uhuru* (1962), Hemingway's work doesn't reflect the social awareness that drove these works. He did not turn the story of Kenya's environmental degradation into a dramatic development leading to a shocking end, as John Steinbeck did in his classic novel of the American dustbowl, *The Grapes of Wrath*.

Although Hemingway was obviously aware of the social and racial hierarchy of the colonial society of East Africa (which placed Europeans on the top, Indians in the intermediate position, and the native at the lowest rung), he did not give much detail about the Asians and their threat to European colonialism. The Asians who had come to Africa as colonial pacification troops, public works builders, clerks and subordinate staff, confronted the danger of "the man-eaters of Tsavo" — the African lion — as they built the Kenya-Uganda railway. Construction was considerably delayed by lion attacks on "coolies" at Tsavo, halfway between Mombasa and Nairobi in the vicinity of Kilimanjaro, and by armed anticolonial resistance of various natives of inland Kenya — the Masai, the Kamba, the Kikuyu in eastern-central Kenya, and the Nandi and Kisii halfway between Nairobi and Lake Victoria. Lieutenant Colonel John Henry Patterson was commissioned to kill the lions, while Colonel Paul Meinertzhagen was commissioned to quell the Nandi resistance. These events are reflected in the stuffed animals in Chicago's Field Museum of Natural History and are reported in Patterson's colonial classic *The Man-Eaters of Tsavo* (which Hemingway owned), Paul Meinertzhagen's *Kenya*

Diary, and Philip Caputo's *Ghosts of the Tsavo*. Hemingway was obviously aware of all this, but, apparently intent on keeping his distance from colonial politics, chose not to write about it.

The imperial regime was unable to pay for the Asians' passage back to their original homelands and so many settled down in East Africa as traders. In *Green Hills of Africa*, Hemingway had Kandinsky explain their arrival in Kenya (Pop seems to disagree with Kandinksy's version of the events) and their current condition: "They live on nothing and they send all the money back to India. When they have made enough to go home, they leave bringing out their poor relations to take over from them and continue to exploit the country" (30). This is a typical colonial sentiment and is not necessarily true. It is an accusation that East African Asians have had to bear even into the postcolonial era in the contest for economic prominence along racial and class line. To the extent that Hemingway did not argue against social frameworks and take an antiestablishment position (as Twain did), he became a colonial conformist.

Even so, I would say that Hemingway was generally sympathetic to the local populations as he described their migration over a landscape that was being adulterated by Western culture. I strongly disagree with the widespread opinion within Hemingway scholarship that Hemingway's depiction of the natives is marked by bigotry. On the contrary, I see Hemingway's treatment of African reality and people as complex to the point of contradiction: generally sympathetic, but sometimes sarcastic, superficial (as in the matter of the Mau Mau), and even falling into the easy romanticism of travelogues. Thus, for example, the Masai live in the unspoiled country and are "the tallest, best-built, handsomest people I had ever seen and the first truly light-hearted happy people I had seen in Africa" (*GHA*, 219). But generally, realism dominates and individuals are individually treated, sometimes sympathetically, sometimes satirically (especially in the matter of nicknames), and often with a combination of sympathy and satire. The sarcastically nicknamed David Garrick is further mocked by being described as a "theatrical," "bloody ostrich-plume[d] . . . bastard" (2, 186) whom the narrator would love "to shoot . . . in the behind, just to see the look on his face" (178). In contrast, the driver Kamau is not only allowed to keep his own name, but is also presented as someone whose "modesty, pleasantness and skill I admired so much now": "I looked at him, . . . and thought how, when we first were out, he had nearly died of fever, and that if he had died it would have meant nothing to me . . . while now whenever or wherever he should die I would feel badly" (177–78). The native tracker ignominiously nicknamed Droopy was to Hemingway simultaneously "a real savage with lids to his eyes that nearly covered them" and "handsome, with a great deal of style, a fine hunter and a beautiful tracker . . . a great stylist in everything he did" (46, 48).

And with M'Cola (Mũkola), Hemingway inserts typically African humor into his writing. He wears a U.S. Army khaki tunic and a bird-shooting coat given to him by Pop and Papa, and sandals cut from old motorcar tires — an outfit that to this day would inspire giggles among native observers. To a Swahili speaker, his name would be significant (*mũkola* means *robber*). This is not in my view bigotry, but an attempt to individualize the character by giving him a nickname.

The general native superstition and vulnerability to foreign mythmaking is highlighted through the narrative about the adventurer Bror Blixen (the husband of Danish writer Baroness Karen Blixen, whose home is now the well-known Karen Estate of Nairobi), about whom "many say it is not true that [he] is dead. They say that he has disappeared until the death of his creditors and that then he will come again to earth like the Baby Jesus" (*UK*, 244). This reflects a common trend of great colonial demagogues who loot state resources and then use natives to help them escape and to construct a myth of their invisibility and immortality, perhaps copied from colonialist, Christian myth construction. There is, for example, a myth about a man known variously as Bwana Mackenzie or Bwana Ngao (meaning Lord Shield), who, according to legends, fought the British. When he was defeated, he ducked into the Indian Ocean leaving behind a note to the British that he will come to overthrow them at noon. The legend holds that the British habitually shot a cannon ball into the sea every day at noon to keep the challenger away from the British East Africa Empire. The truth is, the legendary Bwana Ngao was a pioneer British imperial merchant named William Mackenzie, a partner of Sir William Mackinnon, the owner of the Imperial British East Africa Company, which ruled what is now Kenya from 1888 to 1920. When the company went bankrupt, the crown took over the territory, forcing Mackenzie and Mackinnon to retire to England — hence the confusion among the natives over what happened in the transfer from company rule to crown rule.

The native perception of the West, derived from *Life* photographs, wonderfully mirrors the equally naïve western perception of Africa, derived from the media and travelogue. Hemingway says that after he gave the Informer "some more penicillin . . . [and] silver nitrate," he "left [him] with two old copies of *Life* to divert him" (*UK*, 267). He also gave Debba's family "a copy of *Life*" (*Selected Letters*, 826) which seems to have made a great impression on her: she cut out pictures and hung them on the wall above her bed.[25] The natives' interpretation of American life via the photographs of *Life* is intelligently employed here to show to the reader how much damage the media can do to misinform and underinform others about distant lands and cultures. The warning goes both ways: here Hemingway seems to admonish Western readers to approach safari reports with caution.

We need to read Hemingway's own safari reports this way. They present a complex view of Africa — or actually, two complex views, separated by two decades. Depending on how one reads these African narratives — through the prism of previous literature, or from the political or biographic or linguistic or psychological perspective — one gets a different reading of each one of his African books. Knowing some of the background facts can help us begin the task of deciphering the literature that emerged from Hemingway's encounter with the dream and reality of Africa.

Notes

I would like to thank my colleagues at Appalachian State University, especially Ralph E. Lentz II and Dick Bruce, who read this article and suggested changes. Special thanks also to Carl P. Eby, of the University of South Carolina, Beaufort, for initiating me into Hemingway studies and for encouraging this particular endeavor; and to Miriam B. Mandel, our editor, for her extreme patience, substantive comments, corrections, and guidance throughout the whole process.

[1] Hemingway correctly refers to this mountain as *Kilimanjaro* as opposed to *Mount Kilimanjaro*. In local languages (Kĩkamba, Kĩchagga, and Kĩswahilĩ), *Kilima* means "Mount," to which is added the name, *Njaro*, to produce *Kilimanjaro* (Mount Njaro). It is therefore redundant to say *Mount Kilimanjaro*, as it is redundant to say "the Sahara desert," since *Sahara* means desert in Arabic.

[2] For more detail on these publications, see chapter 4, "Canonical Readings: Baudelaire's Subtext in Hemingway's African Narratives."

[3] Jeffrey Hart's review of Raeburn's book, "The Unbecoming of an Artist," shares Edmund Wilson's disapproval of this development.

[4] I use the term "native writer" to include one who writes about Africa, even if he or she is not African.

[5] It is noteworthy that Margot's name closely resembles the word "maggot," suggesting that she enlarged family feuds (and made them disappear) the same way blowflie maggots enlarged native wounds and cleaned them of infection *(UK,* 29). She made the feud "disappear" by murdering her spouse.

[6] Hemingway misspelled the name of his fiancée, Debba. If this name is Kamba, as Hemingway claims, in that language the rule is simple: the letter d must be preceded by a capital letter N. The letter b must be preceded by the letter m. Kamba language does not employ double b as Hemingway presents in the word Debba. The name doesn't make sense in the Kamba language, although its pronounciation is very close to "Debba." All Bantu names including Swahili have a meaning derived from place names, natural things, events, or from actions. This name, Debba, can be anything from Ndemba, Nthemba, Nthembwa, or Ndembwa. Otherwise, and probably more interesting or most likely, since Hemingway's native names are derisive or sarcastic, I suspect that the word Debba was a corruption/misspelling of the Kamba word Ndimba, which means buttocks. This appears very likely if we consider the manner of depicting the natives that Hemingway presents in African writings — some are droopy or theatrical, and others have lids

covering their eye balls. I discussed misspellings and other errors in Hemingway's African works in "Ernest Hemingway's African Book: An Appraisal" and "Ernest Hemingway's Safari into Kamba Culture and Language: A Note on the Geographical and Temporal Setting of Under Kilimanjaro." Out of respect for Hemingway's text I use his spelling, but include the correct form in parentheses to help East African readers who may not recognize the misspelled words.

In fact, Hemingway misspelled almost all native names in his African writings except the driver's name — Kamau, who is from the Kĩkũyũ linguistic group of the Mount Kenya region hundreds of miles north of Kĩlĩmanjaro. Mary's gun bearer, Charo, should be spelled *Kyalo* (meaning journey) because Kamba phonology has no letter *c*; nonetheless this character might have been from Taita, a linguistic group that dwells around Kĩlĩmanjaro and has the letter *c* in its phonology.

7 Hemingway's N'Gui should be Ngũi (meaning singer). In Kamba language/phonology the apostrophe cannot come between two consonants, but only between a consonant and a vowel. My personal experience with American readers is that they like to pronounce letter *n* in African names (e.g., Ngũi) as in *ngo*. But in all African languages that I know of, letter *n* combines with letter *g* to form a sound as in *go*, *goose*, or *good*.

8 According to Hemingway, "A warthog is a brave, gallant [I agree], and extremely attractive animal with a fine serious-minded trot. But he is excellent to eat [I part company with Hemingway on this] and I shot him as he trotted across a meadow his tail held high. There was no nonsense about halalling him as the Mohammedans could not eat him and I stuck him with the spear to bleed him. The blade slipped in like going into butter and I wiped the spear on his back, dust gray and with coarse black hairs, and then slipped it back in its sheath" (175).

9 The Swedish ethnographer Gerhard Lindblom, in his monograph *The Akamba in British East Africa*, offers excellent information on Kamba lore and wild animals in the late nineteenth and early twentieth century. See also Hobley.

10 The title *In Our Time* (1925), for example, was culled from the English Book of Prayer ("Give us peace in our time, O Lord"); *For Whom the Bell Tolls* is from John Donne's famous sonnet "No man is an Island" ("Never send to know for whom the bell tolls; it tolls for thee").

11 The Hemingway Collection at the JFK Library holds the Brentano book list Reynolds refers to. The twenty-three titles on that list were supplied by Samuel Smallidge, Ernest Hemingway Collection intern. The list is subsumed in Mandel and Kitunda's bibliography of "Hemingway's Reading in Natural History, Hunting, Fishing, and Africa" in chapter 1 of this volume.

12 The complete text is available at http://www.cyberhymnal.org/htm/t/i/tiagreen.htm.

13 Cecil Alexander is the author of such well-known songs as "All Things Bright and Beautiful" and "Once in Royal David's City."

14 I am using the term "colonial writer" or "colonial artist" as it is used, loosely and sometimes arbitrarily, in African scholarship to refer generically to writers who write about the colonial era in Africa in the nineteenth and twentieth centuries. With

notable exceptions such as Flaubert and Twain, these writers were Eurocentric, glorifying European political, economic, cultural, and intellectual domination of Africa.

[15] Flaubert toured the northern part of the continent (Egypt, Tunisia, and Algeria) in the 1850s, at the height of French imperialism in those parts.

[16] The cock and the dunghill inspired several writers before Hemingway. *The Diary of Samuel Pepys* featured cockfighting and dunghills; and of all the birds of the farmyard, William Shakespeare gave special attention to the cock, especially as a chronometer of the morning hours of Elizabethan time. But Hemingway seems to me to be the first Western writer to be aware of *African* cock symbolism.

[17] *Ngũkũ* is a generic term for fowl, whether male or female, and often whether young or old, but in the context of the song, *ngũkũ* means cock.

[18] *Nzokolo* is a more specific word, and simply means cock. Other Bantu languages also use this word to mean cock, albeit with variant spellings. There are variations in spellings even within Kamba itself. Kĩkamba as a language is divided into at least two major sections, Machakos and Kĩtui. If spellings vary (for instance, *Nthamba* instead of *Nzamba*), it should be attributed to this variation. The dialect variation itself is a result of geographical distance between the two section of Ũkambanĩ and influence by other linguistic groups.

[19] *Nzamba* also specifically means cock. However, this word might also figuratively mean a powerful, invincible male, a hero, bull, victor, etc., depending on the context. *Ngũkũ ya Nzamba* in Kĩkamba specifically means a male fowl. Of the three terms used to mean *cock* in the poem, this is the only word with strong connotations of masculinity, virility, prowess, sexual power, sexual potency, etc.

[20] *Kũkũ* means cock in Kĩkongo, a Bantu language spoken by more than ten million Bakongo and Bandundu people who reside in the tropical forests of the Democratic Republic of Congo, Congo Brazzaville, Angola, and Gabon. Although this language is akin to my first language, so that I could estimate what it means, I am not an expert in Kĩkongo. I therefore consulted native speakers to verify that in this phrase *kũkũ* means cock. It carries the same meaning in Kĩkamba (with variation in spelling) in Kenya, thousands of miles to the east of Congo. In Swahili, which Hemingway used most, *kũkũ* means chicken/hen, and as in Kĩkamba it can be a generic term for both male and female fowl — thus the logic of employing it to mean cock.

[21] In *Green Hills of Africa*, Hemingway is working with Kamba speaking guides, but the party is speaking Swahili. In that context, Hemingway's use of *fisi* is correct.

[22] A consonant and an apostrophe cannot go together in Kamba language. The word should be spelled *na inyaake*.

[23] The word *mwana* means child or offspring, but it changes meaning when used as part of a compound word: *mwanadamu* translates as human being, *mwanariadha* as an athlete, *mwanamke* as woman/female, *mwanamme* as male/man, *mwanainchi* as citizen or native, etc.

[24] The native unrest, Asian threat to colonial regime, and environmental degradation are mentioned as causes for the uprising, but Hemingway's treatment of these events is terse and the reader is not informed how such events came to happen. Hemingway probably expected the reader to be cognizant of contemporary political events.

25 The narrator seems to have given Debba another copy of the same magazine, for "she has on the walls of the lodge the pictures from *Life* magazine of the great beasts of America and of the washing machine, the cooking machines and miraculous ranges, and the stirring machines" (*UK*, 35). In a later chapter, more detail is offered about the pictures Debba cut out of the magazine: "she had a large picture of her [Marlene Dietrich] wearing what looked to me like nothing on the wall above her bed along with an advertisement for the washing machine and garbage disposal units and the two-inch steaks and cuts of ham and the paintings of the mammoth, the little four-toed horse, and the saber-toothed tiger that she had cut from *Life* magazine. These were the great wonders of her new world" (383).

Works Cited

Alexander, Cecil Frances Humphreys. "There is a green hill far away." http://www.cyberhymnal.org/htm/t/i/tiagreen.htm. Accessed October 8, 2009.

Atkins, John. *The Art of Ernest Hemingway: His Work and Personality*. London: Peter Nevill, 1952.

Caputo, Phillip. *Ghosts of Tsavo: Stalking the Mystery Lions of East Africa*. Washington, DC: Adventure Press, National Geographic, 2002.

Dinesen, Isak (Karen Blixen). *Out of Africa*. 1937. Reprint, New York: Vintage Books, 1972.

Dunn, Richard. *Sugar and Slaves: The Rise of the Planter Class in the English West Indies, 1624–1713*. Chapel Hill: U of North Carolina P, 1972.

Geismar, Maxwell. *Writers in Crisis: The American Novel, 1925–1940*. Boston: Houghton Mifflin, 1942.

Hart, Jeffrey. "The Unbecoming of an Artist." Review of John Raeburn's *Fame Became of Him: Hemingway as Public Writer. National Review* (14 December 1984): 48–49.

Hemingway, Ernest. "A.D. in Africa: A Tanganyika Letter." *Esquire*, April 1934, 19, 146. Reprinted in *By-Line: Ernest Hemingway*, 159–61.

———. *By-Line: Ernest Hemingway. Selected Articles and Dispatches of Four Decades*. Edited by William White. New York: Scribner's, 1967.

———. *Death in the Afternoon*. 1932. Reprint, New York: Scribner's, 1960.

———. *Ernest Hemingway: Selected Letters 1917–1961*. 1981. Edited by Carlos Baker. Reprint, New York: Scribner's, 2003.

———. *Green Hills of Africa*. New York: Scribner's, 1935.

———. "Notes on Dangerous Game: The Third Tanganyika Letter." *Esquire*, July 1934, 19, 194. Reprinted in *By-Line: Ernest Hemingway*, 167–71.

———. "Sailfish off Mombasa." *Esquire* 3, March 1935, 21, 156.

———. "Shootism Versus Sport: The Second Tanganyika Letter. *Esquire*, June 1934, 19, 150. Reprinted in *By-Line: Ernest Hemingway*, 162–66.

———. "The Short Happy Life of Francis Macomber." In *The Short Stories of Ernest Hemingway*, 3–37. 1938. Reprint, New York: Scribner's, 1966. First published 1936 in *Cosmopolitan*.

———. "The Snows of Kilimanjaro." In *The Short Stories of Ernest Hemingway*, 52–77. 1938. Reprint, New York: Scribner's, 1966. First published 1936 in *Esquire*.
———. *Under Kilimanjaro*. Kent: Kent State UP, 2005.
———. "Wings Always Over Africa: An Ornithological Letter." *Esquire*, January 1936, 31, 174–75. Reprinted in *By-Line: Ernest Hemingway*, 229–35.
———. *True at First Light*. New York: Simon & Schuster, 1999.
Hobley, Charles William. *Ethnology of A-Kamba and Other East African Tribes*. 1910. Reprint, London: Frank Cass & Co., 1971; London: H. F. & G. Witherby, 1992.
Kenyatta, Jomo. *Facing Mount Kenya*. London: Vintage Books, 1938.
Kitunda, Jeremiah M. "Ernest Hemingway's African Book: An Appraisal." *Hemingway Review* 25, no. 2 (2006): 107–13.
———. "Ernest Hemingway's Safari into Kamba Culture and Language: A Note on the Geographical and Temporal Setting of *Under Kilimanjaro*." *North Dakota Quarterly* 73, nos. 1–2 (2006): 156–72.
Krapf, Johannes. *Travels, Researches, and Missionary Labours, During an Eighteen Years' Residence in Eastern Africa: Together with Journeys to Jagga, Usambara, Ukambani, Shoa, Abessinia and Khartum; and a Coasting Voyage from Mombaz to Cape Delgado*. London: Trubner, 1860.
Lindblom, Gerhard. *The Akamba in British East Africa: An Ethnological Monograph*. 2nd ed. Uppsala: Appelberg, 1920.
Linebaugh, Peter, and Marcus Buford Rediker. *The Many-Headed Hydra: Sailors, Slaves, Commoners, and the Hidden History of the Revolutionary Atlantic*. Harrisonburg, VA: R. R. Donnelley & Son, 2000.
Lumumba. Directed by Raoul Peck. Zeitgeist Films. United States, 2000.
Marsh, George P. *Man and Nature: or, Physical Geography as Modified by Human Action*. New York: Scribner's, 1864.
Meinertzhagen, Richard. *Kenya Diary 1902–1906*. London: Hippocrene Books, 1985.
Mwangi, Meja. *Carcase for Hounds*. Nairobi: Heinemann Educational, 1974.
Ondaatje, Christopher. *Hemingway in Africa: The Last Safari*. Woodstock, NY: Overlook Press, 2004.
Patterson, John Henry. *The Man-Eaters of Tsavo and Other East African Adventures*. London: MacMillan, 1908.
Pepys, Samuel. *The Diary of Samuel Pepys*. Vol. 4. 1663. Reprint, Berkeley and Los Angeles: U of California P, 1970 and 2000.
Raeburn, John. *Fame Became of Him: Hemingway as Public Writer*. Bloomington: Indiana UP, 1984.
Reynolds, Michael S. *Hemingway: The 1930s*. New York: Norton, 1997.
———. *Hemingway's Reading, 1910–1940: An Inventory*. Princeton: Princeton UP, 1981.
Ruark, Robert. *Something of Value*. Garden City, NY: Doubleday, 1955.
———. *Uhuru, A Novel of Africa Today*. New York: McGraw-Hill, 1962.

Schatzberg, Michael G. *Political Legitimacy in Middle Africa: Father, Family, Food*. Bloomington: Indiana UP, 2001.
Steinbeck, John. *Grapes of Wrath*. 1939. Reprint, New York: Penguin, 1987.
Tiffen, Mary, et al. *More People, Less Erosion: Environmental Recovery in Kenya*. Chichester: John Wiley & Sons, 1994.
Twain, Mark. *The Adventures of Huckleberry Finn*. 1884. Reprint, New York: Tom Doherty, 1985.

II: Approaches to Reading

4: Canonical Readings: Baudelaire's Subtext in Hemingway's African Narratives

Beatriz Penas Ibáñez

THIS ESSAY DEVELOPS several interlocking arguments to explain the changes in Ernest Hemingway's writing between the 1930s and the 1950s. It is my contention that Hemingway's attention to the work of Charles Baudelaire — an attention practically neglected or unnoticed by Hemingway's critics[1] — can explain these changes. My second contention is that Ernest Hemingway was aware of the need for him as an artist to keep changing his style of writing according to new aesthetic needs. Third, I contend that from the 1930s onward, Hemingway explored new forms of writing in his African narratives, and that he did this in two phases, or two sets of African narratives, each phase following a safari (the two safaris were twenty years apart). The specific characteristic differentiating the writing after the second safari from the preceding one was Hemingway's reframing of characters as allegories of styles of writing. The great poet Baudelaire used precisely this kind of allegory in his poetry, calling it a correspondence.

Hemingway's connection to Baudelaire is clear. He was familiar with *Les Fleurs du Mal*[2] and, in a letter to Archibald MacLeish dated 14 March 1931, he quotes a line from Poem 100 of the first edition (1857), "La servante au grand cœur dont vous étiez jalouse": "I hope youze know your Baudelaire: Les morts, les pauvres morts[,] ont de grandes douleurs, I wd like to be gt writer but same very difficult" (*Selected Letters*, 338). He playfully drops Baudelaire's name to let MacLeish know the quality of his reading, and simultaneously — by placing the reference next to his statement that he would like to be a great writer — connects his desire to the master figure of Baudelaire as a model. Annotating this letter, Carlos Baker misattributes the line Hemingway quotes to Poem 98, "L'Amour du mensonge" (*Selected Letters*, 339), perhaps because these two poems, 98 and 100, stand in close spatial proximity within *Les Fleurs du Mal* and are strongly connected as regards their symbolic themes — the passing of time and its effect on art, which is basically reflected in the need for art to change in order to keep producing convincing illusions of reality.

Baudelaire's Poem 98 prefers artifice to nature, as it argues for that artifice of beauty that emerges from an illusion of color, created by light (both natural and artificial) that is projected on the morbid face of an aging woman. That artifice is symbolic of art, and this preference of artifice, or the artificial, rather than natural beauty is constant in Baudelaire. In his critical prose writings, for example, Baudelaire insists on an aesthetics that relies on makeup (*maquillage*), arguing that artifice is so essential to beauty and art as to exclude the need to either imitate or refer to nature:

> painting the face is not to be used with the vulgar, unavowable intention of imitating the fair face of nature, or competing with youth. It has, moreover, been observed that artifice does not embellish ugliness, and can only serve beauty. Who would dare assign to art the sterile function of imitating nature? Make-up has no need of concealment, no need to avoid discovery; on the contrary, it can go in for display, if not with affectation, at least with a sort of disingenuousness. (Baudelaire, "Éloge du Maquillage," 428)

Baudelaire's Poem 100 mourns and celebrates the dead woman (aesthetics) who once nursed the now grown-up poet. The woman servant nourished the masterful artist whose persuasive illusions of reality influence his generation and nourish future generations. The anxieties (in Bloom's parlance) or jealousies (in Baudelaire's terms) that the old masters cause in the young artists, before the latter become respected authors themselves, can only end when the young members of the new literary school are able to "make up" their own illusions of life — literary *mensonges*,[3] in Baudelaire's sense of the term in Poem 98 — by means of their new, personal ways of writing. When Hemingway quotes Baudelaire to his poet friend, then, he is declaring a filiation line back to Baudelaire's ideas on art, beauty, and aesthetic creation.

Hemingway argued repeatedly that creation requires destruction, that the creation of an innovative aesthetics requires the destruction of old patterns and styles. In his letter to MacLeish, Hemingway presents this idea indirectly. He declares it more directly in *Death in the Afternoon* (1932). At that time, Hemingway was aligned with Ezra Pound and T. E. Hulme, whose critical writings on language and literary representation stressed the importance of a textuality stripped of inessentials, a "top-to-bottom" narrativity,[4] which Hemingway describes in terms of the iceberg metaphor and which I like to call Hemingway's "iceberg writing":

> If a writer of prose knows enough about what he is writing about he may omit things that he knows and the reader, if the writer is writing truly enough, will have a feeling of those things as strongly as though the writer had stated them. The dignity of movement of an

iceberg is due to only one-eighth of it being above water. A writer who omits things because he does not know them only makes hollow places in his writing. (192)

In other words: what the text says literally, the meaning of the words and sentences visible on the textual surface, is, in Hemingway's metaphor, only the tip of his textual iceberg, a clue to all that remains unsaid, a clear pointer to the existence of hidden meanings that are in the bottom and invisible seven-eighths of the iceberg. Thus, Hemingway's iceberg principle represents a radicalization of the Pound-Hulme modernist manifestoes, and seeks to produce a distinctively laconic style that relies for its power on a rich although textually absent subtext. The visible tip of Hemingway's "laconic" kind of text — the told narrative — signals the existence of another, hidden narrative. Because the relation between the surface and the submerged narratives is disproportionate — one eighth of the text showing and seven-eighths hidden — the narratives require a high standard of reading by a reader aware of the schemas and intertexts that Hemingway was working with when he designed his textual icebergs. The result is a complex kind of narrative coproduction that actively involves the reader. This is *the* Hemingway style of the 1920s and early 1930s, the style that has become a brand, an identity, both to the author and his texts of high modernism.

Shortly after this articulation of his literary credo, Hemingway and his wife Pauline went on a safari to East Africa, from December 1933 to February 1934. The resultant texts — *Green Hills of Africa* (1935), "The Snows of Kilimanjaro" (1936), and "The Short Happy Life of Francis Macomber" (1936) — continue to adhere to the basic iceberg principle, but they shift literary allegiances, deemphasizing the Pound-Hulme literary principles in order to engage in a dialogue with the Baudelairian ethic/aesthetic critical concerns (the status of the literary work of art as a desirable lie, an unconcealed illusion, and an enjoyable artificial paradise). They develop a set of ideas on art and time on and against which Hemingway could refashion himself and his style around 1935 (after his first African safari). It is a second creative phase in Hemingway's career.

After this sea change Hemingway's narrativity reconfigures within a newly defined subtextual constellation and produces a different kind of text, not as laconic and stripped of inessentials as before, but freer (in the 1930s) and quasi-"logorrheic" (in the 1940s and 1950s). Even after undergoing editing by foreign hands (for posthumous publication), the Hemingway texts composed in this period tend to show a pronounced taste for the bizarre and for intertextual patterning and counterpatterning. Of these, I will focus on two that are set in Africa: *Under Kilimanjaro* (composed 1954–61, published 2005) and the "African stories" in *The Garden of Eden* (composed 1954–58, published 1986).

These new texts still adhere to the iceberg theory, although the surface textual tip now tells a story in a more detailed way, not as laconically as before. Because explicitness was atypical of the first (and revered) Hemingway style, its presence in the postsafari writing has been interpreted as a sign of decline in Hemingway's creative powers. Against this stereotype, I mean to show that the apparently digressive details are, in Hemingway's expression, "architectural reforms" of the textual space, necessary for the readers to recover the hidden subtexts that lend theoretical weight to the new "mirror-refracted" narrativity of his iceberg texts. The new and the older structural intertextualities interact in order to create a branching text (Ryan, 336), a virtual space that can be described as a multidimensional network of possible routes. This is the space that Hemingway's readers must navigate, as they move through his postmodernist text. The increased complexity of his new textual and fictional constructions affects the kind and degree of inferential work that readers must perform in order to achieve a suitably complex interpretation.

The African Narratives as Iceberg Texts

Hemingway's Africa-based narratives are iceberg texts that exploit a thematic bifurcation of their surface-to-bottom intertextual narrativity. Their surfaces (the visible tips of the iceberg) report the events of an African safari. They address the matters of color and race symbolically rather than explicitly, offering an idiosyncratic version of American Africanism[5] whose peculiarity rests on its combining three elements — the literal, physical, geographic displacement of white Americans to Africa (on safari), the symbolic displacement of the issue of specifically American Africanness (United States and Cuban Africanism) to a more global kind of treatment of black-white colonial power relations, and the allegorization of Africa — so that the dark continent becomes a setting and a metaphor for art and creativity. The appropriation of Africa by the white colonist allegorizes the artistic appropriation of "the real" by the white writer. In that symbolic country, the African narratives share a metanarrative interest in the creative process.

As I noted earlier, the second-phase iceberg narrativity of the postsafari texts reinscribes Hemingway's Pound-Hulme iceberg narrativity in Baudelairian terms. The more complicated bottom or submerged seven-eighths represent an intertextual exploration of and comment on Baudelaire's aesthetics, especially Baudelaire's love of illusion and makeup, or the aesthetics of lies and artificial beauty, as the writer develops his literary credo. In this submerged space, he explores his craft and its harmonization of contraries, like the creative/destructive nature of the writer's hunt for the real as pursued through a literary representation, or the truthful/illusory nature of the literary product, its truth based on its capacity to deceive the reader and make him or her suspend disbelief in it. These "disillusioned illusions" — in René Girard's terms — that expose their own artificiality are based on Baudelaire's aesthetics as manifested in the Baudelairian praise of lies and makeup in *The Flowers of Evil* — particularly in Poem 98, "L'Amour du mensonge" ("The Love of Lies/Illusion"), and Poem 100, "La servante au grand cœur dont vous étiez jalouse" ("The kind-hearted servant of whom you were jealous"), as well as in the essay "The Painter of Modern Life," especially in its section XI "Éloge du maquillage" ("In praise of makeup"). "L'Amour du mensonge," for example, praises the illusion of rouge created by refracted light on a pale worn-out woman's face, thus inverting stereotypical commonsensical notions about beauty. Beauty is neither in nature nor in the imitation of nature, but in artifice, in the mask, in the obvious makeup, in the artificial color reflected on a discolored face by the touch of light, be it the artificial gaslight projected from a street lamp or the natural light of sunset.

Although the surface narratives of the safaris written after the first and the second safaris show a close family resemblance, their bottom narratives show a quite different weight. In the narratives of the 1930s, the submerged part of the textual iceberg explores the Baudelairian subtext on art by focusing on the writer's creative process and his products as creative illusions, while the surface focuses on safari events and characters (Africanism). In contrast, the African safari narratives of the 1950s explore the creative process both on the surface and the submerged levels, and the correspondences on both levels lead to an extensive parallel reinforcement of the Baudelairian topics. In other words, there is a remarkable difference between the textual formal design of the African narratives written after the first safari, and those written two decades later, after the second one — a difference that does not extend to the thematic component or content itself, but affects the text as regards its length and topic distribution. In the later African narratives the Baudelairian theme replicates from the bottom to the surface narrative, where it is overtly thematized in a series of duplications. This factor changes the external appearance and inner quality of the later African narratives: they become more explicit, playful, and longer than the earlier ones. *Under Kilimanjaro*, for instance, is openly about the difference between telling the truth and telling lies, and about the effects of both these activities in terms of our biographies and in terms of art. Baudelaire's love of illusion and his curiosity about it — so typical of the artist and the child in "The Painter of Modern Life" — are embodied in the Hemingway text by the older white writer, a fictional character, and Hemingway's autobiographical persona. In the narrative, this Hemingway is self-consciously aware of Debba's role as a reservoir of his creativity, but he plays dangerously at love and enjoys his disillusioned illusions — embodied by the black African girl. He says to his skeptical white American wife,

> you can't blame the liars because all a writer of fiction is really is a congenital liar who invents from his own knowledge or that of other men. I am a writer of fiction and so I am a liar too and invent from what I know and what I've heard. I'm a liar. . . . A man who writes a novel or a short story is a liar ipso facto. His only excuse is that he makes the truth as he invents it truer than it would be. That is what makes good writers or bad. (113)

In other words, and to summarize: the first set of African narratives — *Green Hills of Africa*, "The Snows of Kilimanjaro," and "The Short Happy Life of Francis Macomber" — derive from and re-create the experiences of Hemingway's first safari. The African theme in the surface narratives of these works conceals the Baudelairian subtext, the concern with aesthetic principles, by relegating it to the submerged iceberg bottom. The later African writing is based on Hemingway's second safari. In the subsequent narratives — the most complete of which is *Under Kilimanjaro* (composed 1954–61, published 2005) — the theme, stemming again from Baudelaire (the artist's love of lies or illusion produces beauty), has moved into the surface narrative. Thus, the text explicitly tells us that

> almost nothing was true and especially not in Africa. In Africa a thing is true at first light and a lie by noon and you have no more respect for it than for the lovely, perfect weed-fringed lake you see across the sun-baked salt plain. You have walked across that plain in the morning and you know that no such lake is there. But now it is there absolutely true, beautiful and believable. (239)

But there is also a third type of African narrative, a transitional text that Hemingway may have begun in 1945–1947 (Reynolds, 41–44), well after the first safari, and revised in the 1950s. What is clear is that he expanded the African narrative greatly after the second safari, working through several drafts between 1955 and 1961.[6] This januslike text, published posthumously as *The Garden of Eden*, separates the first safari African narratives — "The Snows of Kilimanjaro," "The Short Happy Life of Francis Macomber," and *Green Hills of Africa* — composed in iceberg style à la Baudelaire, from the second safari African narrative, *Under Kilimanjaro*, which is a stylistic experiment in postmodern self-reflexivity and metafictionality. *The Garden of Eden* displays not only the new Hemingway style, in which verbal minimalism and the silencing of essentials cease to be textual priorities, but it also, like most of Hemingway's later work, is first and foremost about representing itself and its intertextuality. That is, *The Garden of Eden* looks at its antecedent formations as if in a mirror, establishes an intertextual archaeology of sources, and refashions itself in terms of both content and form. This intertextual mimetic play produces self-reflexivity and a double textual length, produced by Hemingway's use of an increasing number of metatextual allusions. These are allusions both to Hemingway's own earlier texts[7] and to canonical texts written by early masters. We can find the same textual tendencies in *Under Kilimanjaro*. Among the references to Hemingway's earlier texts, I shall focus here on Hemingway's African stories as mimetized and thematized in *The Garden of Eden*, of which the best example is Kibo's story. Among the allusions to texts of earlier masters, I explore the relevance of Baudelaire's *Flowers of Evil* to Hemingway's African writing, and more particularly to Kibo's story in *The Garden of Eden*.[8]

The Garden of Eden: Baudelairian Correspondences

The Garden of Eden is a complex narrative composed of two well-differentiated fictions: an embedded African fiction, and a frame or enveloping fiction that is non-African. This enveloping narrative is set in Europe: the action starts and ends in the Camargue, France, although the honeymooning American couple of that narrative is also seen in Paris, Hendaye, Madrid, and then back in Cannes. David Bourne, the protagonist, is a young writer whose need to isolate himself to do his writing affects his wife, Catherine, who had expected that her conjugal games[9] and inventions would lead him to write a narrative that features her. In this non-African frame plot, David and Catherine exploit two different kinds of creativity: David manipulates past and present experience into literary matter, and Catherine manipulates their present life in order to provide material for his writing. She eventually fails in her efforts and David stops writing the narrative of their married life in order to write stories based on his own childhood memories of Africa.[10]

It is significant that the African stories in *The Garden of Eden* start flowing from David's imagination only when Marita enters his and Catherine's lives. Only Marita — not Catherine — is allowed to read the stories; she likes them very much and feels they must be protected from third parties (i.e., Catherine, who eventually burns them). There are several textual correspondences — in Baudelaire's sense of the term — between the textual body of the metafictional African short stories and the body of the female character Marita. Marita is short, dark, and has a French background; Hemingway's story is African (dark) and short, with a Baudelairian (French) subtext. Her body corresponds so closely to the textual body of the metafictional African short story that she seems its walking replica. In contrast Hemingway draws Catherine as tall and increasingly blonde, to represent the long non-African narrative that David writes until he abandons it for Marita and the African short stories.

The two women impersonate literary concepts and exemplify Hemingway's taste for symbolistic Baudelairian allegory. Both are beautiful, rich, and dear to the writer: it is only time and tiredness that cause the need for change and novelty. It is in their capacity as allegories of writing, allegories of two styles, that we can understand why in *The Garden of Eden* Catherine and Marita "*seemed,* when he saw them playing, *to be actual human beings* doing something normal *and not figures in some unbelievable play he had been brought unwillingly to attend*" (195, my emphasis). The two women represent the two different aesthetics (Pound-Hulme vs. Baudelaire) and the two different forms — less vs. more explicit and less vs. more authoritative — of narrative characteristic of Hemingway in two different moments of his career (before and after the first safari). *The Garden of Eden*, with its twofold mimetization of the African short stories on the one hand and the long narrative on the other, dramatizes the need for the writer to accept progressive development and changes in the stylistic design of his work. It also dramatizes — in the form of a triangular conjugal conflict — the need for the creative writer to remain open to change, letting himself espouse two different styles in succession, or to move back and forth between an older and a newer style within one text, as happens in *The Garden of Eden*, a long narrative in which short stories are embedded.

If we extend the allegory, David's decision to stop writing the long narrative and to stop sleeping with Catherine forms a correspondence with a second decision to start writing short stories and to move into Marita's bedroom. These correspondences result in a divorce leading to a new marriage and a new kind of writing. The text explains that "there had been too much emotion, too much damage, too much of everything and his changing of allegiance, no matter how sound it had seemed, no matter how it simplified things for him, was a grave and violent thing" (238). The Bournes are dead, long live the Bournes. One literary style is dead, long live a new one. And so on indefinitely. Marita asks, "Will they [women and/or styles] come along young new and fresh with new thing and you be tired of me? . . . They are new all the time . . . there are new ones every day. No one can ever be sufficiently warned. You most of all." The writer answers, "I know it and I love to look at you and know you are here and that we'll sleep together and be happy" (245). He can promise no more and no less; he knows he must follow his heart and the style that is closer to his emotions for the time being.

I would now like to look more closely at David's two African narratives. The first one is very generally outlined as writing in progress; we don't read the actual text of this story. The second story, which is Kibo's story, is reproduced from beginning to end and uses the two main forms of represented speech in writing: free indirect and free direct reporting styles. The combination of both styles builds a smooth transitional effect, helping to interconnect the different textual planes. The effect produced on the reader is that of continuity, and also confusion, between the fictional and the metafictional story levels. It is not easy for the reader to tell whose voice is being heard in the storytelling. Is it the voice of Hemingway (the author in the historical plane), or that of David Bourne (the author's fictional persona), or is it the voice of Davey (the young persona of an adult author's fictional persona)?

To complicate the fictional levels even further, Kibo's story starts as a dream that David dreams one night. It is so vivid that in the morning he translates it into a short story whose writing is represented along several pages (160, 163, 164–66, 171–74, 179–82, 197–202). In terms of authorship or paternity, the story is David's: the text underlines this point by having David create it thrice: when he dreams it, when he first writes it, and, after Catherine burns it, when he remembers and rewrites it again: "By two o'clock he had recovered, corrected and improved what it had taken him five days to write originally. He wrote on a while longer now and there was no sign that any of it would ever cease returning to him intact" (247). In other terms, David's Kibo's story is doubly fictional, or metafictional — a piece of African fiction written by a fictional character and embedded within a longer, non-African narrative, to produce a postmodern whole called *The Garden of Eden*. What remains to be asked is whether Kibo's story, David's only verbally available African story, represents Hemingway's short story writing in general or his African short story writing in particular. To put the question differently, what we need to determine is whether or not Kibo's story carries with it the Baudelairian subtext prevalent in Hemingway's postsafari story writing (and absent from his pre-African work). I will argue that it does.

Kibo's Story

Hemingway builds *The Garden of Eden* in intertextual and intellectual brotherhood with a literary trio of predecessors: Purchas, Coleridge, and Baudelaire, as they are intertextually associated by allusion in "The Painter of Modern Life" and in *Les Fleurs du Mal*. In Kibo's story, the mimetization of an African story in *The Garden of Eden*, we can see what is the archaeological purpose that the metanarrative representation of the African story serves within the novel. It is mainly in the context of Kibo's story that Baudelaire's code of dandyism[11] is drawn and impersonated by allegorical characters in a jocular-dramatic[12] Calderonian manner.

Kibo's story starts as an oneiric narrative, a dream that the fictional writer dreams one night and is so vivid that upon waking he can remember and write it. This type of provenance has a familiar literary precedent: Coleridge's account of the genesis of "Kubla Khan," another remembered dream put into words. Just as opium influenced the writing of Coleridge's poem, *The Garden of Eden* clearly indicates that alcohol was an important factor in David's life. Another similarity is that the book Coleridge was reading before falling asleep — *Purchas His Pilgrimage*[13] — was a travel narrative, just as the narratives that David was reading and writing before Kibo's story are travel narratives: the long narrative of his and Catherine's travels in France and Spain (the abandoned story), as well as the story about his father and himself as a child traveling on foot through lake country in Africa (the unavailable African story Catherine burned).

Kibo's Story: Beginning (*The Garden of Eden*, 163–66) — The Old Man of the Mountain

The fiction starts one night when eight-year-old David and his dog, Kibo, feel the huge dreamlike shadow of a single old elephant covering them as the elephant passes silently by. David and Kibo track the elephant to the edge of the forest, and see that it is slowly traveling to the mountain — to become The Old One in the Mountain. And David sees something else, a big moving shadow silhouetted against the moonlight, a shadow that becomes an elephant's shadow only when the projected light of the moon lets the shape of its left tusk be seen. The pursuit continues until the elephant reaches an opening in the trees. It is then that David sees the elephant in two colors: the bulk of the body is dark in the shadow, but the moonlight illuminates the elephant's head, making it silver-white. Now David sees the huge, thick right tusk that he could not see before. Only now does David turn around to come back to his father in the *shamba* (reserve).[14]

The Old Man of the Mountain — a reference originally appearing in the travel book by Purchas mentioned in Coleridge' preface to *Kubla Khan* — is a motif in Baudelaire's "The Painter of Modern Life" that recurs in altered form in Kibo's story. The Old Man of the Mountain was the leader of the Ismailite sect in medieval Syria. In Baudelaire, he serves as a mock-heroic parallel for the dandy. Just as the dandy has his followers, so the old Mohammedan is the model and ruler of a group of young sectaries who owe him perfect obedience: they must follow him *perinde ac cadaver* (as a corpse; Ignatius Loyola's precept of obedience for Jesuits), like the dead, and like the dead they cannot speak against the old man's designs. Baudelaire's Old Man of the Mountain, like Coleridge's and Purchas's Aloadine, is a creator of a fiction and a deceiving illusion. By giving the young men in his palace *garden* drugs to drink, he makes them see paradise. When they wake up from their hallucination the young men believe they have been in paradise; that is, they mistake their memory of an illusion for a memory of real experience. They become assassins able to kill if thus they can regain their lost paradise. Their leader, the Old Man, stands for the dandy unblasé, the pure artist "who has discovered unaided all the little tricks of the trade, and who has taught himself, without help or advice, [and has become a powerful master in his own way"] (Baudelaire "Painter," 396).

Through Baudelaire, Hemingway recycles The Old Man of the Mountain motif — thus connecting his work to that of older masters in the literary tradition. Two narrative details alert us to this subtext in *The Garden of Eden*. Trivial except for their value as clues, the allusive details may easily pass unnoticed; they are: (1) the wind that starts blowing when Marita stays and David starts writing his African stories comes all the way from Kurdistan (183), the area The Old Man comes from, and (2) David's remark that if he were Mohammedan (144) — like The Old Man — he could have three wives.

Thus alerted, the reader can interpret the meaning of the elephant that David and Kibo see one night in the forest. For one thing, the elephant is *old*, and for another, he is on his way to the *mountain*, to die there. He is a link in the *tradition*, for he is following a well-worn trail that many other elephants must have trodden before and will keep treading after him. But he is special too, an exceptional bull, bigger, prouder, and cleverer than all the rest except for his five-year-long dead friend, his *askari* (Swahili for soldier, guard). The old elephant still remembers his dead friend and visits his remains, his *cadaver* — skull and bones — before he follows his path to the mountain. This big old animal is imposing and admirable, dangerous to inferior competitors, but a faithful and loving friend to his equals. He is an emblem of the artist bound to become an old master after he dies, to become an emblem for excellence within a tradition, the master artist who sets the rules for other lesser and later artists to obey (*perinde ac cadaver*) while following the spoor of the powerful model within a school or a literary movement. The old elephant and the old master artist eventually die, but their achievements survive them in the work of others who revisit the master's stylistic findings and thus give him continuity within a literary line or tradition. A classic survives across generations, but even classics age, like Catherine (the longer, worn-out narrative), who says: "All of a sudden I was old this morning and it wasn't even the right time of year" (162), and is soon replaced by Marita (the new style narrative).

Kibo's Story: Middle (171–74) — Paternity and Dandyism

When David accompanies his father and Juma, two professional hunters, in their hunt for the elephant that he has told them about, he learns that the difference between a lone boy and a brotherhood of men is not one of numbers or physical strength. It has more to do with a code of behavior best explained by Baudelaire in relation to dandyism: "calmness revealing strength in every circumstance" ("Painter," 422). It has also to do with endurance — "Just last the day out, Davey," the father says to his son — stoicism, and the capacity to kill for a reason: "Ever since the tusks had grown beyond their normal size the elephant had been hunted for them and now the three of them would kill him" (*Garden of Eden*, 171, 173). In their pursuit, the men show their expertise and dexterity at providing for themselves and the child, their mutual trust, and their ability to understand and remember the signs in the world surrounding them. Juma knows what he is after, he knows the elephant well, he could only wound it five years earlier when he had killed this elephant's *askari*, an even bigger elephant than the one they are hunting now. Central to Kibo's story is David's feeling of remorse for having betrayed the elephant by telling professional killers — his father and his father's colleague — where to find him. He rejects their mercenary motivations and, when he becomes an adult, he adopts a different ethics: he is committed to truth and art in writing.

David's adult disregard of personal sacrifice as well as social and literary conventions brings him into the proud circle of those with a "burning desire to create a personal form of originality, within the external limits of social convention." This is Baudelaire's definition of the great artist and dandy:

> Indeed I was not far wrong when I compared dandism [*sic*] to a kind of religion, the most rigorous monastic rule, the inexorable commands of the Old Man of the Mountain, who enjoined suicide on his intoxicated disciples, were not more despotic or more slavishly obeyed than this doctrine of elegance and originality, which, like the others, imposes upon its ambitious and humble sectaries, men as often as not full of spirit, passion, courage, controlled energy, the terrible precept: *perinde ac cadaver*. ("Painter," 421)

Baudelaire praises the dandy's doctrine of elegance and originality that for the artist-writer crystallizes in the search for true knowledge and a simple and elegant style. In *The Garden of Eden*'s reelaboration, David repeats the idea: "Know how complicated it is and then state it simply . . . so that whoever read it would feel it was truly happening as it was read" (37, 201). In his style "the form came by what he would choose to leave out" and "the accuracy of the detail which made it believable" (211). David "disliked rhetoric and disliked those who used it" (224). The fictionalized literary precepts of the metafictional writer of *Garden of Eden*'s African short stories coincides with Hemingway's own literary credo of the 1930s, which governed his own short stories, including the African ones ("Snows" and "Macomber") — but in a Baudelairian light. Thus we can see that, although written so much later, Kibo's story represents the first period (i.e., following the first safari) of Hemingway's African short story writing.

David's father, a professional hunter, is portrayed in the role of a Baudelairian dandy, the seeker of excellence beyond good and evil, the hero possessed of "calmness revealing strength in every circumstance" ("Painter," 422). Hemingway could say of Baudelaire — his unnamed but acknowledged literary father — the same words that David says about his father:

> His father had dealt so lightly with evil, giving it no chance ever and denying its importance so that it had no status and no shape nor dignity. He treated evil like an old entrusted friend ... and evil when she poxed him, never knew she'd scored. His father was not vulnerable he knew and, unlike most people he had known, only death could kill him. Finally, he knew what his father had thought and knowing it, he did not put it in the [African] story. He only wrote what his father did and how he felt and in all this he became his father. (146–47)

As his father's son David writes a first African story about his father, who is teaching him to hunt elephants in Africa, and a second one, Kibo's story, about himself when he was eight years old and learning from his father's example. At this point in the African story (197), we see iterations of the Old Man of the Mountain/young followers' motif in its different versions: the professional hunter/his apprentice son, the big old elephant/the herd of young elephants on the same trail, David the writer/Davey the child or David's portrait of a past version of himself, and Davey/Kibo, master and dog. In the end all these correspondences procure a complex retrospective feeling of sadness caused by the child's awareness of old age and decay, the sunset of a life, a style, and a lifestyle. At the same time the memory is combined with a present feeling of elation at having witnessed and learned something great before its disappearance: "You just lose something and it's gone that's all. All we lose was all that we had. But we get some more" (118).

> All your father found he found for you too, he thought, the good, the wonderful, the bad, the very bad, the really very bad, the truly bad and then the much worse. It was a shame a man with such a talent for disaster and for delight should have gone the way he went, he thought. It always made him happy to remember his father and he knew his father would have liked his story. (129)

Like the old bull elephant going on a last visit to his dead friend and equal, his *askari*, the great writer revisits and pays homage to the great dead author, Baudelaire, bids farewell to all that is gone, but saves the memory of his findings that he honors and renews in his writing: "there are no other things [than writing]" (140). This is what the writer learns from the long-gone old masters, that fiction is all you are left with, an illusion that seems true, like the dream that made the Old Man of the Mountain's disciples continue striving for a lost paradise. Hemingway's *The Garden of Eden* is a bet on experimentalism, a play with fiction for fiction's sake and for life's sake. I see in it a literary reference to Hemingway's own literary trajectory. He could be accused of not staying with anything, of unnecessarily stepping out from modernist novel and short story writing into postmodernist experimentation — his 1920s narratives had become classics of the genre and made him famous, and then he sea-changed into nonfiction and then into postmodernity. With the success of *A Farewell to Arms* (1929), Hemingway knew that even this early in his career he had achieved fame and reputation, but this knowledge did not deter him from trying new ways of writing. The longer narratives of the 1920s and 1930s had been the fruit of his daring to step out of short story writing. But even more daring are the long narratives that Hemingway wrote in the 1940s and 1950s.

Kibo's Story: The End (197–202): The Bull, the Iceberg, Art and Illusion

When David, Kibo, Juma, and David's father catch up with the old elephant, the scene becomes a butchery: the horrific "work of chopping out the tusks and of the rough surgery on Juma disguised by mockery and railery to keep the pain in contempt and reduce its stature since there were no drugs" (200). This central and powerful scene clearly reaffirms the Baudelairian subtext of the dandy (which dominated the middle of the story), in terms of the response to pain: "A dandy may be blasé, he may even suffer pain, but in the latter case he will keep smiling, like the Spartan under the bite of the fox" ("Painter," 420). David's father and Juma do just that, when they employ "mockery and railery to keep the pain in contempt and reduce its stature."

In addition, this section of Kibo's story refers both to the Hemingway and the Baudelaire subtexts; the bullfight being the most obvious. The bullfight, of course, dominates a number of earlier Hemingway texts and is intertextualized here. In terms of the rules of bullfighting, the elephant's killing is a bad *faena*. The bull elephant is butchered; that is, he is not killed cleanly, there is no redeeming art or grace in the action, and the killer fails in his objective. Finally, it takes two men to kill him and they need to shoot repeatedly, since the initial shot is "lung and gut shot" (199) rather than a clean shot in the head. The old elephant bull takes time to die and finally he drowns in his own blood, like a bull that has been killed by a sword placed in the wrong place. This rather obvious referencing to one of Hemingway's most complex themes, the bullfight, recalls Hemingway's insistence that the bullfight is an art, just as writing is an art.

In terms of Hemingway's literary credo, the scene that dominates the end of Kibo's story follows Hemingway's early rules of good writing, in which omission (the invisible or submerged part of the iceberg) plays an important part. This explains why in his story David "put no statement of his father's intention, which had never been stated . . . but had only used the happenings, the disgusts, the events and feelings of the butchering" (200). Even more important, the elephant itself can be seen to represent the iceberg text, which is characterized by dignity of movement: "The dignity of movement of an iceberg is due to only one-eighth of it being above water" (*Death in the Afternoon*, 192). The big elephant is repeatedly described as moving with dignity till the moment of death, when this dignity is lost (200). The invisibility of the submerged seven-eighths of the iceberg has a parallel in the invisibility of the elephant in the forest when Davey meets him for the first time and sees his head only as reflected by the moonlight, while the larger body of the elephant remains invisible in the shadow.

The iceberg-elephant correspondence works in terms of color tones (dark and light, white and black) as well as visibility. External light lends the tip of the iceberg its whiteness, while the underwater ice, although part of the same block, is black for the simple reason that diminishing light causes increasing darkening in the eye of the beholder. The contrast between "whiteness" and "darkness" is thus exposed as illusory, a visual effect not based on any natural, essential, or preexisting quality. This visual illusion embodied in white/dark, or light/dark, repeatedly points the reader to the Baudelairian subtext.

The name of Davey's dog also exploits the light/dark dichotomy. The text tells us that Kibo is "the name of a mountain [Kilimanjaro]. The other part is Mawenzi" (163). *Kibo* means "the bright," as opposed to the eastern peak, *Mawenzi*, "the dark" (Lewis and Westbrook, 78). Kilimanjaro, one of Africa's most iconic landscapes, is thus a composite image.[15] Similarly, the African elephant is both grey (body) and ivory (tusks), as well as black (in shadow) and silver (in moonlight).

As we saw in the example of the iceberg, and as we see in these other instances taken from the embedded African story, color is not single, inherent, essential, or basic, but composite and illusory, or potentially illusory. This Baudelairian subtext can also be seen in the characters of the European-set frame story, who employ body darkening (extreme sun tanning) and hair lightening (repeated bleaching) techniques, producing a composite of very dark bodies and silvery heads. These characters use their bodies as the object of aesthetic manipulation, as texts of art.[16] They artificially create aesthetic effects by manipulating skin and hair color. Their beauty is artistic, an illusion, an imitation of art rather than nature. They are aesthetic texts whose light heads and dark bodies recreate the image of the iceberg text. The *Garden of Eden* is fiction about aesthetics and the results of aesthetic manipulation both in the quotidian and the literary realms. It is therefore metaliterary as well as metafictional.

In a text, and especially in an iceberg text, it is the eye of the reader, the art of the writer, and the unspoken knowledge they bring to the text that create meaning and color. In Baudelaire's "The Love of Illusion" (*Les Fleurs du Mal*), it is the triple play of reflected natural light (the sunset), artificial light (the gaslight), and the viewer's perception of an object (the woman's made-up face) that create a satisfying illusion of color and beauty.[17]

David closes his African story in a very revealing way. He sees retrospectively that the death of the elephant has become a point of inflection in his life: "The elephant was his hero now as his father had been for a long time" (201). Davey changes allegiances, he sees beyond illusions and is clear about the result of their actions: "Now all the dignity and majesty and all the beauty was gone from the elephant and he was a huge wrinkled pile" (200). He does not keep illusions either about his father being a hero, or about himself being one. But he also sees that others had a different perception. They celebrated their heroism back at the *shamba* by means of a communal illusion in which "Juma and his father and he were heroes and Kibo was a hero's dog, and the men who had carried the tusks were heroes, already slightly drunk heroes and to be drunker" (202). The story ends on a flat note: "They sat there and drank beer while the big drum started and the *Ngoma* began to build" (202). When David finishes writing his African story, he reflects on the heightened acuity of his inner and outer perception: "He felt the story was good and felt even better about Marita. Neither had been diminished by the sharpening of perception he had now, and clarity had come with no sadness" (204).

The writer in the novel, like the child in the short story, achieves a clearer understanding. They are not taken in by the surrounding world of shadow and illusion, "the unreality that reality had become," "the overpopulated vacancy of madness that had taken, now, the new turn of exaggerated practicality" (193). For David, writing a true work of fiction results in lucidity and truth, "the dreadful true understanding was all to come and he must not show it by arbitrary statements of rhetoric but by remembering the actual things that had brought it" (182). David and Davey are the adult and the child versions of the Baudelairian artist and dandy, "for the word 'dandy' implies a quintessence of character and a subtle understanding of all the moral mechanisms of this world; but, from another aspect, the dandy aspires to cold detachment" ("Painter," 399). In Kibo's story, David tells of the important event in his life when he stopped being simply a child and detached himself from paternal models to be free and progress in his path towards becoming a writer and an artist. It is the path to his own mountain, his Kilimanjaro. Africa — the dark continent — is Hemingway's metaphor for the soul of the artist, his inner landscape. Reaching the summit of art is a matter of reappropriation, of reforming the rules of art to suit new aesthetic needs. In Hemingway's African stories the appropriation of Africa by the white colonists runs on a parallel with the appropriation of "the real" by the white writer. In Africa, as in art, there is no real difference between truth and illusion. Literary truth is built on a representation, which produces the illusion of reality. This is what the African stories tell Hemingway's readers indirectly.

Postmodernist Aspects of Kibo's African Story

The embedded African narrative, David's story of Kibo, also functions as a mirror, a replica and reminder, of Hemingway's short story writing in general. Hemingway's classical short stories and novels from the 1920s had earned him fame and critical acclaim, but they had become a burden in the sense that his future writing would be compared with his early successes and would be at a disadvantage. Even so, Hemingway let himself and his writing take a risky metafictional turn, as we see, for instance, in *The Garden of Eden*, where his acclaimed writing is represented by the African short stories and made to contrast against the new kind of self-reflexive writing exemplified not so much by the long framing narrative, David's and Catherine's European travel narrative, as by the novel in full, *The Garden of Eden*. Hemingway's later, post-second-safari writing gave special emphasis to self-reflexivity in its treatment of ethical as well as aesthetic questions. At the root of his Africa-based writing lies the issue of the contrast between reality and illusion, or "the effect of the real," and of truth versus false belief in its different forms: fiction, illusion, dream, hallucination, delusion, self-delusion, deceit, compulsive lying, and the neurosis that leads to extreme confusion between illusion and fact. These versions of partial truth, or total lack of it, are made to fall within two main categories, the constructive or creative (David) and the destructive (Catherine).

Hemingway's African stories in the 1930s, after the first safari, already deal with these Baudelairian issues, but in a less radically evolved metafictional form. They show the beginnings of a gradient of self-reflexivity; the later (postsecond safari) African narratives are much more self-reflexive, both about their own form and about the cognitive processes. For instance, "The Snows of Kilimanjaro" (composed 1930s) shows a self-reflexive type of structural complexity that is analogous to *The Garden of Eden*'s (composed 1945–1961) mirror-effects, except that the later novel offers a proliferation of these and other mirrors in the fiction (Penas Ibáñez, "Looking Through"). In this short story, as in the novel, a fiction is contained within another fiction. Giving Harry, the protagonist in "Snows," the role of the writer of fictions is one way in which the 1936 short narrative becomes a metafictional statement on "the real" versus the fictional writer, and to some extent prefigures *The Garden of Eden*'s David Bourne. If David is quite a serious writer, Harry is not. Harry succumbs to the temptations of a life of luxury provided by his wife's money, wastes his time and his talents, and then regrets it. Michael Reynolds, one of Hemingway's best biographers, writes that "Hemingway, like many another American writer, was troubled by the idea of writing fiction, whose very definition included the sense of telling lies" (32).

To this I would add that Hemingway was troubled by the question of language and its use within literary representation as I have argued extensively in "Between *Melancholia* and *Jubilant Novatio*." Before his first safari, Hemingway's solution to this problem was a laconic, omissive text that minimized the shortcomings of language, as Hulme and Pound proposed. With the first African stories (1935–1936), the Baudelairian subtext operates a shift that will deepen with time, leading to the conclusion (in the work after the second safari) that good art is not an imitation of reality, that there is no need to be anxious about language and its power to represent reality. The issue is something else: the problematic quasi-Platonic status of both reality and literature as illusions, copies of copies of a world of ideas, fictions beyond truths and lies. In this new aesthetics a new type of text has to be developed. Now, the older anxiety about language and its power to represent reality is displaced by a different anxiety: the need for a famous writer to shed[18] a worn-out style, to change literary identity and transcend the limits that his success has imposed on his creativity. Having become a master early in life and having undergone the process of rejecting earlier models,[19] he now has to reject his own hard-won style and success in order to reinvent himself and his narrative. This is what *The Garden of Eden* acknowledges in its own playful manner:

> Things had changed since the war and both Monsieur and Madame had a sense of style and they wished to move with the change . . . and now there is this disregard of the established rules which can very well be the salvation of the whole coast. (167)

The long-planned and oft-postponed trip to Africa marks not only a new setting but also a new aesthetics of writing. Africa means new art. Hemingway's postsafari writings uninhibitedly show that radical iteration/replication/repetition with a difference is the root of a new kind of creativity that now we call postmodern. This new type of creativity that Hemingway saw emerging from his own late writing stemmed from an altered concept of innovation, one that was different from Hemingway's earlier modernist belief in the possibility of a more radical "making it new." As I have defended here, Hemingway's post-second-safari African writing, that is, the African stories in *The Garden of Eden* and *Under Kilimanjaro*, use new devices and techniques such as self-citation, quotation, allusion; in other words, they use intertextuality as a central mechanism for the creation of literary meaning. These are structural reforms that change the older modernist Hemingway text into a postmodernist one. Kibo's story is a representation of a modernist short story recycled within the postmodern novel *The Garden of Eden*. These structural reforms produce new effects of the real, a new kind of realism, a self-reflexive one — a text that does not mask its own fictionality, but stresses it. It is a text whose artificiality manages to strip fiction from pretensions of truth and, for that same reason, achieves the contrary of the expected effect, achieves verisimilitude and a disillusioned kind of realism: "We were going into the African world of unreality that is defended and fortified by reality past any reality there is. It was not an escape world or a day-dreaming world. It was a ruthless real world made of the unreality of the real" (*Under Kilimanjaro*, 147).

Hemingway here shows a postmodernist awareness that "reality" and its representations share something essential, being as they are signic matter, unreality, perceptual constructs, illusions — superficially comparable to The Old Man of the Mountain's artificially induced hallucinations, but essentially different and superior. Hemingway's post-second-safari African fictions are neither escapist nor complacent dreams; they are difficult designs that require much knowledge of literature and hard work, both on the part of the writer and his readers. As Harry, a character in *Under Kilimanjaro*, says to Hemingway, the homodiegetic narrator:

"Writers are supposed to understand things. That's what they implied in the book of words."
"Africa is very complicated, Harry."
"You know," he said. "That idea had occurred to me. Perhaps I was just at the point of grasping it. You were good to put it so clearly."
(200)

The post-second-safari African fictions are hard writing and hard reading and understanding — it is not that the highly omissive, modernist, non-African short stories Hemingway wrote before his safaris were at all easy. But the later ones, written upon revisiting Africa, involve a different kind of textual complexity and a higher degree of interpretative effort in response to their intertextual nature. The reader must be able to recover in them the many intertextual allusions to Hemingway's earlier life and work and to the work of other masters. *Under Kilimanjaro* is self-reflexive and explicit about a creative process — Hemingway's own — that has been developing through phases. It is also about the risks the author must run during the process of self-refashioning, the risk to make mistakes and fall prey to criticism or to misunderstanding. The self-reflexive autobiographic mood that permeates *Under Kilimanjaro* is patent in the following passage:

> I had been a fool not to have stayed on in Africa and instead had gone back to America where I had killed my homesickness for Africa in different ways. Then before I could get back came the Spanish war and I became involved in what was happening to the world and I had stayed with that for better and for worse until I had finally come back. It had not been easy to get back nor to break the chains of responsibility that are built up, seemingly, as lightly as spider webs but that hold like steel cables. I had thought about these things for a long time and about how we writers were the lowest slave laborers of the State, taxed in advance on money we could never guaranty to make. (205)

Here Hemingway (the historical author as well as his fictional avatar in *Under Kilimanjaro*) reflects on the economic pressures on the freedom of the writer. The artist needs change, he needs Africa — Africa is Hemingway's allegorical geographic cipher for his late new creative style. At the same time, Hemingway says that radical changes in style may threaten his public position as a literary authority. But still, Hemingway prefers his freedom to change his writing style even if it entailed a loss of status:

> There were enough problems of status without complicating it and I had no ambition and very few illusions. It was like all those jobs. If you did what you were asked to do well you would have the reward of doing some other job and you had certain privileges and many favors from the people that liked you. If you did anything badly you would be accused of interfering where you weren't wanted and of acting without authority. It was an old and familiar pattern and I did not mind it in the least. There were always some people who liked you very much and others who disliked you as much or more and I had drawn cards in this sort of game for so long that I had learned to feel quite impersonal about the ones who would eventually knife you. (203)

The African stories that Hemingway wrote after his second safari are daring and new. Their composition responds to Hemingway's self-conscious and confessed effort to break new ground. What increases their level of complexity is not only their self-reflexivity, that is, that they draw intertextual correspondences between Hemingway's older and newer styles, but also that the Hemingway textualities are concretely embodied by allegorical female bodies — Catherine's and Marita's in *The Garden of Eden* — that have a double function both as conventional characters in the fiction and as postmodernist allegories of writing within the writing. It is for that reason — and not because of any weakness in their design — that they end up being artificial characters. Correspondence is an intended effect that Hemingway learns from Baudelaire's praise of illusion, makeup, and artifice.

Notes

[1] Examples of this neglect are found even in cases where the critic focuses on Hemingway and French literature. Stoltzfus, for example, merely mentions Baudelaire in passing and basically in connection to spleen and the easy-going sexual mores of Paris (143–44). Also, Stoltzfus follows Baker in misquoting Baudelaire.

[2] According to Brasch and Sigman, Hemingway owned four editions of *Fleurs du Mal*: a 1894 edition with a note by Théophile Gautier, an edition for which no date is given, a 1940 edition illustrated by Rodin, and a 1944 edition published in Stockholm (25).

[3] The translation of *mensonge* as "illusion" rather than the more usual "lie" underlines the visual aspects of artificiality.

[4] I have argued these matters in three earlier essays: "Very Sad But Very Fine": *Death in the Afternoon*'s Imagist Interpretation of the Bullfight-Text," "Masters Writing on Language, Reading, and Representation," and "A Pragma-stylistic Contribution to the Study of Narrativity."

[5] I use the term "Africanism" as Toni Morrison defines it: "the denotative and connotative blackness that African peoples have come to signify, as well as the entire range of views, assumptions, readings, and misreadings that accompany Eurocentric learning about these people. As a trope, little restraint has been attached to its uses. As a disabling virus within literary discourse, Africanism has become, in the Eurocentric tradition that American education favors, both a way of talking about and a way of policing matters of class, sexual license, and repression, formations and exercises of power, and meditations on ethics and accountability" (6–7).

[6] Relying on biographical resources and the manuscript itself, Leonard clears up the confusion over when Hemingway wrote *The Garden of Eden* manuscript. With most scholars agreeing that Hemingway began working on the manuscript in 1946 and stopped working on it in 1958, Leonard contends that the central portion (chapters 13–35) was written in 1957 and that the African stories were written after the 1953–54 safari" (Leonard, "*The Garden of Eden*: A Question of Dates," 63-81.)

[7] In "Looking Through *The Garden*'s Mirrors: The Early Postmodernist Hemingway Text," I gave a first indication that the female characters in *Garden*, Catherine and Marita, are self-referential textual devices, allegorical figures allusive to the antagonistic confrontation between two Hemingway styles.

[8] Elsewhere, I have argued that *Genesis, Paradise Lost,* and *The Arabian Nights* are intertexts of *Garden*; see "Looking Through *The Garden*'s Mirrors."

[9] The surface narrative has been explored in psychoanalytical terms by Hemingway scholars, Carl Eby's rendering in "He Felt the Change" being one of the clearest.

[10] In *The Garden of Eden* we read that besides writing his two African stories, David has published *The Rift*, a "novel about being in East Africa when he was a boy" (111–12). *The Rift* would also be an African narrative, but is not represented in *The Garden of Eden*; it is only alluded to by its title and briefly commented on by Catherine, who read it.

11 Baudelaire prided himself on being a dandy. In "The Painter of Modern Life," he presents dandyism as "a kind of cult of the ego which can . . . even survive what are called illusions" (420); "dandies . . . all share the same characteristic of opposition and revolt . . . all are representatives of that need, which is too rare in the modern generation, to combat and destroy triviality" (421). "Dandyism," he writes, "is the last flicker of heroism in decadent ages" (421).

12 For instance, in *The Garden of Eden*, the references to Baudelaire's aesthetics of dandyism are made in a trivial displaced context recalling the vaudeville.

> "Sorry," David said.
> "That's another *dandy* word," Catherine said. "Explain what dandy means to your new girl. It's an Americanism."
> "I think I know it," the girl said. "It's the third word in 'Yankee Doodle *Dandy*.' Don't please be cross Catherine."
> "I'm not cross," Catherine said. "But two days ago when you made passes at me it was simply *dandy* but today if I felt that way the slightest bit you had to act as though I was an I don't know what" (134; my emphasis).

This is a characteristic strategy for Hemingway: to create ironic texts that are, but do not appear to be, part of the intellectual mainstream.

13 John Livingston Lowes extensively discussed the workings of Coleridge's creative imagination as reliant on associations created by prior readings. Lowes's analysis of "Kubla Khan" as springing from Coleridge's reading of both Samuel Purchas's travel books, *Purchas His Pilgrimage* (1617) and *Purchas His Pilgrimes* (1625), is significant here because it confirms our idea that Hemingway's *The Garden of Eden* has to be read in association to Aloadinus' paradise as described in Purchas's *Pilgrimes*. Aloadine was the Old Man in the Mountain who gave a drink to his young followers and put them to sleep during which they dreamt of a perfect paradise. When they woke they had become dangerous, suicidal assassins ready to do anything to regain their paradise lost.

14 In Swahili, the word *shamba* means "a plantation, an estate, farm, garden, plot of cultivated land." In Hemingway's use of the word, the meaning is pejorative. In *Under Kilimanjaro*, he associates the African shamba to the Indian reservation: "The reservation was rougher than the shamba. Maybe not. I did not really know but I did know that the white people always took the other people's lands away from them and put them on a reservation where they could go to hell and be destroyed as though they were in a concentration camp. Here they called the reservations the reserves" (260).

15 In "Hemingway's Ethics of Writing," I argued that Kilimanjaro was both white and dark, that Hemingway accepted the idea of the impressionists that color was not in the objects but an illusion impressed by light on the retina. In the present article I say that it was Baudelaire who explored the relevance of this general idea to literary aesthetics, and that Hemingway reappropriated Baudelaire in his African works.

[16] "Bodies are fictionalized. . . . They can be seen as living narratives. . . . The body becomes a 'text' and is fictionalized within myths and belief systems that form culture's social narratives and self-representations" (Grosz, 118).

[17] L'Amour du mensonge

> . . . Quand je contemple, aux feux du gaz qui le colore,
> Ton front pâle, embelli par un morbide attrait,
> Où les torches du soir allument une aurore,
> Et tes yeux attirants comme ceux d'un portrait, . . .
> Je me dis: Qu'elle est belle! et bizarrement fraîche!

My translation: The Love of Illusion. When I see, in the gaslight that colors it, your white forehead embellished by a morbid appeal in which the evening light lights up a pink dawn, and your eyes alluring like a portrait's, I say to myself how beautiful and fresh she is.

[18] In these years after the first safari Hemingway also "shed" bullfighting as an explicit subject and Europe as a setting. In later years, after the second safari, he revisited both the theme and the setting — and he did so in a new spiral of creativity; see my article, "A Creative Spiral: From *Death in the Afternoon* (1932) to *The Dangerous Summer* (1960)."

[19] Hemingway's formation as *homo poeticus* follows the process exposed by Harold Bloom in *The Anxiety of Influence*. Hemingway is a clear case of the strong artist who must silence his dearest sources; for instance, Baudelaire.

Works Cited

Baker, Carlos. *Hemingway: The Writer as Artist*. 4th ed. Princeton: Princeton UP, 1972.

Baudelaire, Charles. "Éloge du maquillage" ["In Praise of Makeup"]. In *Selected Writings on Art and Literature*, translated by P. E. Charvet, 424–28. Harmondsworth: Penguin, 1972.

———. *Les Fleurs du Mal. 1857–1861*. Edited by Claude Pichois. Paris: Gallimard, 1972.

———. "The Painter of Modern Life." In *Selected Writings on Art and Literature*, 390–435.

Bloom, Harold. *The Anxiety of Influence: A Theory of Poetry*. London: Oxford UP, 1973.

Brasch, James D., and Joseph Sigman. *Hemingway's Library: A Composite Record*. New York: Garland, 1981.

Eby, Carl. "'He Felt the Change So That It Hurt Him All Through': Sodomy and Transvestic Hallucination in Late Hemingway." *Hemingway Review* 25, no. 1 (2005): 77–95.

Girard, René. *To Double Business Bound*. Baltimore: The Johns Hopkins UP, 1978.

Hemingway, Ernest M. *Death in the Afternoon.* New York: Scribner's, 1932.
———. *Ernest Hemingway: Selected Letters, 1917–1961.* Edited by Carlos Baker. New York: Scribner's, 1981.
———. *The Garden of Eden.* New York: Scribner's, 1986.
———. *Green Hills of Africa.* New York: Scribner's, 1935.
———. "The Snows of Kilimanjaro." In *The Short Stories of Ernest Hemingway,* 52–77. 1938. Reprint, New York: Scribner's, 1966. First published 1936 in *Esquire.*
———. *Under Kilimanjaro.* Edited by Robert W. Lewis and Robert E. Fleming. Kent: Kent State UP, 2005.
Howell, J., ed. *Hemingway's African Stories.* New York: Scribner's, 1969.
Leonard, John. "*The Garden of Eden*: A Question of Dates." *Hemingway Review* 22, no. 2 (2003): 63–81.
Lewis, Robert W., and Max Westbrook. "'The Snows of Kilimanjaro' Collated and Annotated." *The Texas Quarterly* 13 (Summer 1970): 67–143.
Lowes, John Livingston. *The Road to Xanadu: A Study in the Ways of Imagination.* New York: Houghton Mifflin, 1927. Reprint London: Pan Books-Picador, 1978.
Morrison, Toni. *Playing in the Dark: Whiteness and the Literary Imagination.* Cambridge: Harvard UP, 1992.
Penas Ibáñez, Beatriz. "Between *Melancholia* and *Jubilant Novatio*: Ernest Hemingway's Modernist Ambivalences." In *From Baudelaire to Lorca: Approaches to Literary Modernism,* edited by José Antonio Losada-Goya and others, 637–58. Kassel: Edition Reichenberger, 1996.
———. "A Creative Spiral: From *Death in the Afternoon* (1932) to *The Dangerous Summer* (1960)." In *Hemingway in Spain: New Essays,* edited by Carl P. Eby. Kent: Kent State UP (forthcoming).
———. "Hemingway's Ethics of Writing: The Ironic Semantics of 'Whiteness' in 'The Snows of Kilimanjaro.'" *North Dakota Quarterly* 70, no. 4 (2003): 94–118.
———. "Looking Through *The Garden*'s Mirrors: The Early Postmodernist Hemingway Text." *North Dakota Quarterly* 65, no. 3 (1998): 91–104.
———. "Masters Writing on Language and Representation: T. E. Hulme's Subtext in *Death in the Afternoon.*" *North Dakota Quarterly* 73, nos. 1–2 (2006): 120–34.
———. "A Pragma-stylistic Contribution to the Study of Narrativity: Standard and Non-standard Narrativities." In *Theorizing Narrativity,* edited by John Pier and José Angel García Landa, 211–51. Berlin: Walter de Gruyter, 2008.
———. "'Very Sad, But Very Fine': *Death in the Afternoon*'s Imagist Interpretation of the Bullfight-Text." In *A Companion to Hemingway's "Death in the Afternoon,"* edited by Miriam B. Mandel, 143–64. New York: Camden House, 2004.
Reynolds, Michael. "Ernest Hemingway, 1899–1961. A Brief Biography." In *A Historical Guide to Ernest Hemingway,* edited by Linda Wagner-Martin, 15–50. Oxford: Oxford UP, 2000.

Ryan, Mary-Laure. "Narrative Cartography: Toward a Visual Narratology." In *What is Narratology? Questions and Answers Regarding the Status of a Theory*, edited by Tom Kindt and Hans-Harald Müller, 333–64. Berlin: Walter de Gruyter, 2003.

Stoltzfus, Ben. "Hemingway and French Literature: The Paris Years, 1896–1928." *North Dakota Quarterly* 73, nos. 1–2 (2006): 135–55.

5: Tracking the Elephant: David's African Childhood in Hemingway's *The Garden of Eden*

Suzanne del Gizzo

> *Africa, being as old as it is, makes all people . . . into children.*
> — Ernest Hemingway, *Under Kilimanjaro*

IN THE WAKE OF THE PUBLICATION of *The Garden of Eden*, Patrick Hemingway pointedly noted: "it may come as a surprise, but Hemingway never shot an elephant." He goes on to explain that his father "thought it was wrong — he felt that elephants were our equals" (Pooley, 1). Patrick was likely responding to readers' interest in the poignant elephant hunting episode in *Garden* that James Nagel and many other scholars have argued is the heart of the novel (330), but his statement also begins to revise the image of his father as the rugged trophy hunter, one of the many iconic images of Hemingway that *Garden* would complicate. The assumption that Hemingway might have killed an elephant, however, is far from outlandish. The elephant is one of the "Big Five" trophies that serious hunters venture to Africa to pursue, and many of the hunters Hemingway most admired, including Theodore Roosevelt, Baron Bror von Blixen, and Philip Percival, were accomplished elephant hunters. Nonetheless, the elephant appears to have occupied a particular space in Hemingway's imagination, which may account for his decision to use a traumatic elephant hunt as the centerpiece of what is arguably his most complex and challenging novel.

Many critics have explored the question of why David writes the elephant hunt story against the wishes of his wife, Catherine, who would prefer he work on their "honeymoon narrative," and how this embedded story can be read in relation to that larger narrative, but I am curious about the details of the story itself. Why does Hemingway set David's childhood in Africa? And why does he choose an elephant hunt as the formative event in David's bumpy transition into adulthood? In what follows, I will attempt to answer these questions by examining Hemingway's attitudes toward elephants doing a little tracking of my own — scholarly tracking. I will begin by exploring possible sources for the elephant hunt in *The Garden of Eden* in an attempt to account not only for the selection of the elephant as the object of the hunt but also for the particular confluence of themes in the story. My goal is to move beyond the traditional, critical emphasis on gender themes in an effort to present a reading of *Garden* that offers a fuller understanding of what is at stake in the elephant hunt story by focusing on the importance of childhood and empathy in that story in particular and in the novel as a whole. Finally, I examine the way that Hemingway's portrayal of childhood and his focus on empathy intersect with and illuminate the challenges of authorship and the rigors of the writing process in ways that deepen readers' understanding of David Bourne and his relationship to his African past.

Tracking the Sources

It is impossible to know exactly what Hemingway knew about elephants as he sat down to write the elephant hunting episode, which according to Rose Marie Burwell was originally written as an independent story in 1954 before Hemingway decided to break it up and incorporate it into the *Garden* manuscript in 1958 (101),[1] but we can gather a sense of what he knew about elephants by studying his extensive reading. There are four texts in particular, each of which addresses elephants in some detail, that we know Hemingway owned: Bror Blixen's *African Hunter*, Colonel Robert L. Scott's *Between the Elephant's Eyes!*, Beryl Markham's *West with the Night*, and W. D. M. Bell's *Wanderings of an Elephant Hunter*. Each of these works has been mentioned by previous scholars as possibly exerting an influence on Hemingway's writing about Africa.[2]

The authors of these books openly admire elephants — their complex physiology, their social organization, their excellent long-term memory, and their loyalty, including their legendary though disputed burial and visitation of their dead. Through his readings, Hemingway would have learned about elephants' powerful but agile trunks; their thick skin that must be protected from the sun through what Blixen refers to as the "elephant's toilet" (74) of mud or dust baths; their large, thin ears essential for keeping cool; and their viscous feet that narrow as the elephant takes weight off them, allowing the elephant to move easily through muddy terrain despite the handicaps of size and weight. Hemingway would have learned about their constant need for food, their ability to go without water for long periods of time, and their love of swimming. He also would have acquired information about elephant hunting techniques, from the native practice of setting trip wires so that a weighted spear would fall onto a vulnerable area of the elephant's back to the appropriate gauges of guns for elephant hunting (Bell) and where to shoot the elephant to avoid the thick, crenellated skull (Bell and Scott). In addition, we know from Hemingway's own writing that he understood the social dynamic of a herd, which is predominantly female with a few lone bulls on the periphery; and that he knew about the practice of older bulls taking young male companions or *askaris* (*Under Kilimanjaro*, 312).

What is most striking, however, when reading these books, and what may have led Hemingway to consider elephants as our equals, is the degree to which all of the authors are deeply impressed by the intelligence of elephants. Bror Blixen, the famed white hunter, husband of Karen Blixen (author of *Out of Africa*), and the man of whom Beryl Markham once said, "he has learned more about elephant [*sic*] than any other man I ever met or heard about" (206), unabashedly believed that elephants have not only sense but also reasoning power (Blixen, 56). An unrepentant elephant hunter, Blixen marvels in *African Hunter* at the elephant's intelligence and adaptability during the hunt: "When I have disturbed an elephant he has always gone down wind" (57), demonstrating a sophisticated and thoughtful response to the threat posed by the hunter. Scott, a military man and aviator, who also became an avid student of the elephant during his safari, agrees: "there are many experienced hunters and even some zoologists who say that the elephant actually possesses the power of reason" (78). Unlike Blixen, however, the more Scott learned about elephants, the more he began "to hate people who murdered this wonderful animal" (81).

Although Markham, the famed aviatrix, did not hunt elephants, she scouted them in her plane for Blixen's safaris and came to know them quite well. Like Scott and Blixen, she claims that "the elephant is a rational animal. He thinks" (206). But unlike Blixen, who "looks upon legend with a suspicious eye" (206), she is more inclined to discuss attributes of the elephant that are shrouded in lore. She recounts fascinating but unsubstantiated stories about elephants that "carry their wounded and their sick hundreds of miles, if necessary[,] to keep them out of the hands of their enemies" (208), and about elephant burial grounds (largely refuted now, although elephants do visit and caress the bones of their dead). Recognizing that her readers may be skeptical, she includes colorful, firsthand accounts in her memoir *West with the Night* of how elephants adapted to her aerial scouting efforts. She is convinced that once the elephants understood what the plane and its purpose was, they did "a good deal of thinking" (209) and developed strategies for responding to it. She explains how female elephants would gather around the bulls in the herd to frustrate her efforts to take the measure of their tusks from the air, or how a herd would use a large female with her head in the trees (effectively posing as a promising bull) as a decoy to distract Markham while the rest of the herd moved away from the area. This ploy was often successful. Markham even believes that the decoy elephant experienced a sense of triumph, explaining that often "the decoy, leering up at me out of a small, triumphant eye, would amble into the open, wave her trunk with devastating nonchalance, and disappear" (210). She cautiously concludes that "the order of intelligence in a lesser animal can obviously give rise to exaggeration — some of it persistent enough to be crystallized into legend. But you cannot discredit truth merely because a legend has grown out of it" (210).

It appears, then, that Hemingway took his cues about elephants from Scott and Markham, and chose not to hunt elephants except in his fiction. Even there, he distances himself from direct fictional responsibility for the kill by making David's father — not David himself (the writer) — kill the elephant. In fact, Michael Reynolds suggests that "through his reading . . . [Hemingway] was already identifying with the elephant [before his second safari]" (*Final Years*, 261), and he even began to compare his situation as a famous author with an aggressively interested public to that of a hunted or imprisoned bull elephant (ibid.; Burwell 214n). Clearly, the elephant was becoming a deeply personal, metatextual symbol for Hemingway. As a result, when Hemingway did finally write an elephant hunting scene, he would present the death of the elephant as a trauma, and it would become one of the most moving and complex scenes in his oeuvre.

In an effort to trace the emotional power of the scene, I want to take a closer look at the influence of Scott's and Markham's books on Hemingway. Both have been suggested but not pursued by other Hemingway scholars as sources for *Garden*. Burwell identifies Scott's *Between the Elephant's Eyes!*, a memoir of his hunt for a Samburu elephant, as a source text for Hemingway's fictional elephant hunt, and Hemingway biographers Kenneth Lynn and James Mellow have suggested that Markham's *West with the Night* influenced Hemingway's writing about Africa. Most important, these sources help focus a reading of the hunt episode in terms of not only gender, which has been the mainstay of critical approaches to *Garden*, but also in terms of empathy and childhood. In this way, they also begin to illuminate the significance of Africa as a remembered setting for David in the novel.

Several elements of Scott's hunt for his elephant surface in Hemingway's elephant hunt story. Most important, Hemingway takes from Scott a sense of the animal as a noble and intelligent creature that should not be indiscriminately killed for sport or ivory. Scott's book catalogs a hunt that was the culmination of a lifelong dream to kill an elephant, but when he finally has the elephant in the crosshairs, he finds himself unable to shoot. With his well-paid white hunter, Pitcairn Holmes, looking on, Scott explains: "My target was barely fifty feet away. I'd press the trigger and the mighty bull would slump to the ground" (231), but he is surprised to realize that "I didn't want to kill this elephant. I'd lived on his trail for too long" (232). Scott even goes so far as to shove Pitcairn's arm when he begins to take aim, thinking his client has frozen. Scott then abruptly shoots into the air and is relieved when the startled elephant makes his escape.

Hemingway borrows this narrative arc of a hunter shifting his allegiance away from the other hunters and toward the hunted elephant for the hunting story in *Garden*, where the young David ultimately comes to identify with the elephant over his father and Juma (his father's friend and tracker). But I want to focus on three aspects of Scott's hunt that appear to have direct bearing on Hemingway's fictional elephant hunt. The first is a description of an elephant after it is shot by Scott's friend, Roy Weatherby, earlier on the same safari. Scott is surprised by how disturbing he finds the body of the dead elephant:

> Even the small suaki bushes seemed higher then with the big body prone, and I was glad I had my pictures while he was alive because now, he didn't show to good advantage. There was a mighty lot of difference in that big bull striding along at seven or eight miles an hour, effortlessly and oh so quietly on those cushioned feet — and lying there crumpled and deflated forever like a spent gray balloon. (147)

Looking at the dead elephant, Scott observes that the butchered animal is "robbed . . . of all his dignity" (148) and looks like a "wrinkled gray thing" (231). Hemingway borrows both of these images for his description of the dead elephant in the story, as David notes: "Now all the dignity and majesty and all the beauty was gone from the elephant and he was a huge wrinkled pile" (199–200). Moreover, this image of the dead elephant, especially the sudden, lost vitality of the elephant — its sudden transition to thingness — haunts Scott, as it will David. Throughout the rest of the hunt, Scott will return to this memory of the "wrinkled gray thing" as he begins to shift his allegiance to the elephant he is hunting, suggesting that the experience of the large, noble creature killed so abruptly was a traumatic one.

The second aspect of Scott's story that seems to have influenced Hemingway is its outcome. Scott defies the implicitly masculine expectations and even the pressures of the hunt when he does not shoot "his" elephant. Although slightly surprised by his decision, he ultimately feels the rightness of it: "So, some day when you've found the spoor of a great bull elephant and have trailed [him]. . . . Let him live too, as I did! For I'll swear it's a far greater thrill to know he's alive and somewhere out there in the Dida Baganda than to have killed him and captured the greatest ivory teeth in Kenya!" (240). Hemingway would have agreed with this statement, which helps to explain why his ending, which effectively inverts Scott's ending as the young David is forced to witness the murder of the elephant, is rendered with such emotion. Rather than the triumphant feeling of continued connection to the elephant that Scott enjoys at the end of his story, Hemingway writes against Scott's redemptive ending and concludes his elephant hunt with the feeling that something has been irrevocably broken. David's capacity for connection with the elephant, with his father, and with others in general is severed in the hunt scene. David's age is an issue here. As a child, he is not only physically and economically dependent on his father, but he also lacks sufficient confidence or sense of self to challenge seriously his father and Juma's intention to kill the elephant. In that sense, he too is victimized by their behavior insofar as his powerlessness makes him an unwitting accomplice.

And finally, Scott's use of the hunt as a space for rebelling against traditional expectations of male behavior also surfaces in Hemingway's text. Scott knows he has perplexed his white hunter and African trackers by his decision to frighten the bull away, and he feels their scrutiny almost as keenly as he feels his own: "I stood there and tried desperately to approve of my own actions" (233). He can only bring himself to glance at Pitcairn and try "to pass the whole thing off with a grin" (233), but the fact is that Scott loses some respect, especially among the African trackers. Months later, however, he believes his masculinity is vindicated when he receives a letter from Pitcairn nominating him to honorary membership in the white hunters association (a nomination that was seconded by Philip Percival, Hemingway's white hunter). Scott's narrative of rebellion against convention and expectation worked well for Hemingway's narrative of transition from childhood to adulthood. Similarly, Hemingway uses the elephant hunt — at least in part — to highlight the expectations for masculine behavior and David's rebellion against his father and Juma's more traditional and more violent brand of masculinity, while also recognizing the capacity for expressing masculinity in the position of rebellion itself. The young David is unable to stop the slaughter of the elephant, but the older David is able to recover and give voice to the young boy's dissent. Of course, the elephant hunt in *Garden* is powerful on its own, but the effect of it is heightened by recognizing its relation to this source text with its common themes but radically different conclusion.

In addition to the particular similarities and meaningful distinctions in the narrative arc and imagery, two important issues connect Scott's book and the elephant hunt in *Garden*: first, that adult masculinity is defined as isolated and lacking empathy, and second, that the adult worldview operates in such a way that animals are more readily associated with things than with human beings. These points are distinct but related because both hinge on the idea that adult identity is self-protective and hardened against wide-reaching empathy. Lisa Tyler has explored this facet of adult masculinity in another Hemingway father-son story, "Indian Camp." Tyler observes that the young Nick is made aware of two kinds of adult masculinity — that of the Indian "father" in the top bunk, who empathizes with his wife's screams to the point of suicide, and that of his father (the doctor of the story), who "deems [the woman's] screams unimportant" (38). In this way, Tyler explains, the young Nick is presented with two options for adult masculinity: the "death of the self in endless empathy" or the loss of humanity through the "cold and instrumental rationality in which other human beings are regarded as objects" (39). Although the situation is a bit different in the elephant hunt story, again competent adult masculinity is associated with isolation and instrumental thinking about other beings, in this case the elephant. Cary Wolfe broadens the critical relevance of this observation when he criticizes the way human beings attempt to secure their specialness and excise their animal nature by purposefully designating animals as things or objects (227–28). By the dominant humanist logic, the elephant is already a thing; it becomes a simple operation of instrumental logic to associate the animal with its ivory and kill the animal for the ivory with no qualms about the ethical implications of this act. The young David, like Scott, does not find this artificial and convenient designation of animal-as-object easy to maintain; their insistence on the dead elephant's sudden "thingness" emphasizes that he was something else — a subject — before his murder. In Hemingway's work, older male figures teach their young sons or protégés what will be expected of them as competent adult men, and these scenes reveal that adult masculinity is generally associated with hierarchical, instrumental thinking that discourages wide-ranging empathy, which is usually associated with women and children, or incompetent men. One of the central questions in *Garden*, then, is to what extent does David absorb and internalize his father's understanding of adult masculinity and to what extent does he define himself against it?

The other book that I suggest influenced Hemingway's work on the elephant hunt story in *Garden* is his favorite book on Africa, a memoir by Beryl Markham.[3] Markham spent a good part of her life in Kenya and is best known as the first person to fly solo across the Atlantic from Europe to North America in 1936. Her book, *West with the Night*, which Hemingway first read almost as soon as it was published in 1942, so deeply impressed him that he wrote his editor, Maxwell Perkins, about it:

> Did you read Beryl Markham's book, "West with the Night"? I knew her fairly well in Africa and never would have suspected that she could and would put pen to paper except to write in her flyer's log book. As it is, she has written so well, and marvelously well, that I was completely ashamed of myself as a writer. I felt that I was simply a carpenter with words, picking up whatever was furnished on the job and some times [*sic*] making an okay pig pen. But this girl who is, to my knowledge, very unpleasant, . . . can write rings around all of us who consider ourselves writers. (*Selected Letters*, 541)

Although Markham's memoir[4] does not have as direct a correlation to *Garden* as Scott's book, it does seem to have influenced Hemingway insofar as he shares her assessment that "it is absurd for a man to kill an elephant. . . . It is not heroic . . .; it is just one of those preposterous things that men do" (205).

Markham's book appears to have influenced *Garden* in lesser ways as well. Early in the memoir, a young Markham recalls a hunting trip she takes with just her spear, her dog, and two Murani — a hunting party that is loosely repeated in *Garden*. Markham's dog, Buller, even recalls David's dog, Kibo, in his habit of nudging his nose against her leg during the hunt (Markham, 80; *Garden*, 159). Another interesting parallel related to Buller is that when Catherine reads the beginning of the elephant hunt story as David is writing it, she is pointedly and somewhat unreasonably afraid something will happen to Kibo. This worry may stem from Markham's story of her boar hunt in which Buller is badly gored by a boar (he is ultimately fine).

More to the point with regard to the book's impact on *Garden*'s themes, Markham acknowledges that her presence on the hunt as a young white girl was unorthodox. In fact, she recalls a conversation with a Nandi girl of about her age before the hunt. The girl marvels at the young Beryl's decision to hunt with the two warriors: "'The heart of a Murani is like unto stone,' she whispered, 'and his limbs have the speed of an antelope. Where do you find the strength and the daring to hunt with them, my sister?'" (77). Markham is respectful, but silently observes that Nandi women "were shy and they were feminine and they did the things that women are meant to do, and they never hunted" (77). This image of the young, unconventional white girl, hunting with her spear and her dog in the company of two Murani, resonates with the image of a young David and Kibo, hunting with his father and Juma. Most important, Markham's use of a hunting trip in Africa as a space to flout gender conventions and expectations likely appealed to Hemingway. Markham's book suggests — at least in part — why Hemingway would have decided to integrate the hunting story with the existing narrative of *Garden* that focused on gender and sexual reversals. Once again, as in Scott's book, the hunt is revealed as a space in which gender expectations are sharply on display and thus can be pointedly challenged and even expanded.

In addition, Markham's book highlights the significance of childhood in both stories. She explicitly presents childhood as a special period before individuals become limited and constrained by conventional expectations. This idea is reinforced by the subplot about her friendship with a black African boy named Kibii. As children, Beryl and Kibii play together as equals, but when they meet as adults after years of separation — he is now circumcised and renamed Arab Ruta — there is a painfully wide gulf between them that neither of them is able or willing to cross. Markham writes:

> What a child does not know and does not want to know of race and colour and class, he learns soon enough as he grows to see each

man flipped inexorably into some predestined groove like a penny or a sovereign in a banker's rack. Kibii, the Nandi boy, was my good friend. Arab Ruta, who sits before me, is my good friend, but the handclasp will be shorter, the smile will not be so eager on his lips, and though the path is for a while the same, he will walk behind me now, when once, in the simplicity of our nonage, we walked together. (149)

In this passage, Markham outlines one of the central themes in *The Garden of Eden* — the way societal conventions and protocols ultimately impinge upon the innocence and free-floating empathy of youth, which is also the main point in the last book that I want to mention briefly as a source for *Garden* — J. D. Salinger's *The Catcher in the Rye*.[5]

Garden and *Catcher* have radically different settings and styles, but both deal with a boy's initiation into adulthood and the way this initiation is fraught with sexual and gender anxieties. There is also a hint of the brother-sister relationship between Holden and Phoebe in the David-Catherine relationship; not only do they wear similar clothes and get similar haircuts so they will look alike, but they are also mistaken for brother and sister early in the story. For my purposes, however, the most significant connection between the two stories is the boys' nearly identical responses to their difficult transitions into adulthood. Toward the end of *Catcher*, Holden remarks: "Don't ever tell anyone anything" (214), a line Hemingway almost directly echoes as David regrets telling his father and Juma about the elephant: "Never tell anyone anything ever. Never tell anyone anything again" (181). Both boys experience — albeit for different reasons — the prospect of joining adult society as a trauma, and both respond to the pressure by shunning intimacy and refusing to share their experiences with adults, whom they regard suspiciously as narrow-minded and supercilious. Yet ironically, as they shut down and cordon themselves off in silence, they begin to espouse the very adult priorities that they wish to resist. This source, in conjunction with others, helps us see how the elephant story is ultimately, as David claims, "a very young boy's story" (201) because it captures the challenges of empathy and sharing in an adult world more interested in division and hierarchies.

"A Very Young Boy's Story"

In *Under Kilimanjaro*, which Hemingway worked on at times simultaneously with *Garden*, the main character, Ernie, notes that "Africa, being as old as it is, makes all people . . . into children" (23). It is a feeling that Hemingway appears to have welcomed: "to have the heart of a child is not a disgrace. It is an honor. A man must comport himself as a man. . . . But it is never a reproach that he has kept a child's heart, a child's honesty, a child's freshness and nobility" (23). This association of Africa with childhood is repeated in Hemingway's writing in the last decade of his career. In *The Old Man and the Sea*, Santiago recalls an image from his youth of African lions on the beach (22, 24–25, 66, 81 127);[6] in *Garden*, of course, an adult David writes about his childhood in Africa; and in *Under Kilimanjaro*, Hemingway repeatedly associates Africa with innocence and childhood, as seen in the quotation above. In all of these instances, there is nostalgia for youth, and in particular for that period before the limitations and expectations that characterize adult life. Thus, when David acknowledges upon completion of the first version of the elephant hunt story that it is "a very young boy's story" (201), this utterance may in fact be an expression of his deep satisfaction with it.

Since *The Garden of Eden* was first published in 1986, gender and sex have dominated critical discussions of the novel, and with good reason. Not only are gender and sexual role reversal pronounced themes in the novel, but they were also shocking to readers, especially given Hemingway's macho reputation at the time of publication. To the extent that the critics who have approached the book through the lens of gender wrestle with the symbolism and meaning of the elephant hunting episode, they tend to do so in terms of its relation to character development and the themes of gender and sexual role reversal in the main honeymoon narrative. In particular, they are concerned with whether or not David's writing and rewriting (after his wife, Catherine, burns the first version) of the hunt story is a betrayal of Catherine, because she insists that David work on the honeymoon narrative inspired by their life together (Burwell, Roe, Willingham), or a triumph over her destructive and controlling tendencies (Nagel, Hillman). In both cases, however, critics view David's decision to write and then rewrite the elephant hunt story as reclamation of his masculine identity and author(ity), which they see as having been challenged by Catherine and her experiments with gender and sex.

As compelling and satisfying as the gender and sex-based approach to the elephant hunt story is — and my tracking of Scott's and Markham's influences on *Garden* certainly confirms the importance of gender in the novel in general, and for the elephant hunt in particular — I have never found that it fully accounts for the raw emotional power of the hunt episode. In fact, the almost exclusive use of gender as a lens for reading the novel has arguably obscured other, equally insightful ways of approaching the text, namely, the importance of the divide between childhood and adulthood, which is highlighted in the story and its writing process. In this section, I will tease out particular points from my tracking of sources for the elephant hunt story to suggest how attention to the motifs of childhood and empathy and the details of the hunt story can add to our understanding of David's character, the dynamics of the Catherine-David relationship, and the meaning of the novel as a whole.

The elephant hunt story is most obviously "a very young boy's story," of course, in that it addresses an incident from David's childhood in Africa and his relationship as a boy with his father. But David's comment suggests that there is something specific about the elephant hunt story that earns it this designation. After all, readers are told that David is writing three stories about his experiences in Africa, but he does not describe the other two stories (although they seem to detail the same period of his life) in this way. Arguably, the specific content of this story — David's increasing empathy for and identification with the elephant, and his silent rage when the elephant is murdered[7] — makes it "a very young boy's story."

David hints at the importance of age in the story when he thinks, as he sits down to write one morning, that "it was not just the need for sleep that made the difference between a boy and men" (171). Something other than mere physical stamina divides the young from the old, and that something else is the child's capacity for wide-ranging, undiscriminating empathy with other beings. In an article on *Garden*, Wolfe examines the way cross-species identification (David's identification with the elephant) in the story serves as an "off-site" location for Hemingway's attempts to address cross-gender and cross-racial identifications in the novel (226). In the process, he tangentially notes the importance of childhood for the hunt episode, which he rightly understands as pivoting on "the child's identification with the animal" (244). His point, however, is that such an identification is considered to be illegitimate, even "perverse," by an adult culture that recognizes the animal as more closely aligned to a thing or an object than to a subject (244), and thus not an appropriate focal point for identification.[8] Wolfe observes that not only does David's father disregard the power and legitimacy of his son's identification with the elephant, but many critics of the novel do as well. He cites several critics who deem the hunt story "bad Hemingway" and a resurgence of "boyhood romanticism," as evidence of the persistent inability of adult culture to take such cross-species identifications seriously (244). As a young boy, David freely and openly identifies with the elephant in a way that his father and Juma do not (or will not) understand because of their status as adult men and as exploitative hunters. They, like some critics and readers, refuse to acknowledge David's empathy for the elephant as significant; it is childish sentiment out of touch with priorities of the adult world.

It is after all a decision to view an animal as a thing, and in *Garden*, adult logic allows the men to see the elephant as an object or thing metonymically associated with its ivory tusks and valuable only because of them. David's childhood logic and economy are different. He sees the elephant as valuable beyond his tusks, as a friend and a being in mourning for a companion killed long ago. As his dissent from the hunt grows, David pointedly expresses his disagreement along economic lines: "my father did not need to kill elephants to live" (181). This line presents the murder of the elephant as excessive and unreasonable; it rejects the instrumental logic that designates the elephant as a thing to be dominated to help men earn a living. The elephant, in this instance, is seen as a subject with dignity and rights, and thus not an object to be used at the whim of man (I am being pointedly gender exclusive here). With the murder of the elephant, the father and Juma effectively announce the dominance of the adult worldview, and the young David, powerless because dependent upon his father and Juma, is not only traumatized but also left with only silence and the refusal to speak — "Never tell anyone anything again" (181) — as his only option for registering his dissent, a dissent that in its silence ironically secures the success of the initiation experience the hunt is designed to facilitate because it initiates him to a world of isolation and detachment.

Yet as an adult and as an established writer, removed from his father's control, David finally writes (and expresses his feelings) about that traumatic hunt and thus breaks his promise to "never tell anyone anything again." Arguably, his entire career as a writer has been a violation of this oath, or put another way, a rejection of the initiation or lesson learned about adulthood during the elephant hunt. The decision to tell — in fact, the decision to make a career out of telling — suggests that David has moved into a position of power and has found other ways of registering his opinions and thoughts. Significantly, his model of adult masculinity and his vocation as a writer hinge upon his empathetic faculties, or more pointedly upon acts of *remembering*, which defy his father's *dismembering* of the elephant. David's recollection of this earlier, less restricted ability to identify and empathize with the elephant as his subject matter for the story, as well as his capacity for empathy in the writing of the story, demonstrate that empathy and the ability to re-member are essential tools in the writer's toolbox. Such observations help clarify what Hemingway might have meant when he purportedly remarked that an unhappy childhood was the best training for a writer.

A great deal hinges on the way David's work as a writer is understood. Although some critics insist that David's writing is destructive and even murderous (Burwell, Roe, Silbergleid), I would suggest that the text encourages (or at the very least supports) a different reading. As he writes, David repeatedly admonishes himself not to rush the emotions and to "*remember* the things you believed because if you know them they will be there in the writing" (166; my italics). Each day, he attempts to live in the story and "to *remember* truly how he felt and what had happened . . . and keep it untinctured by how he had felt later" (174; my italics). He must identify and empathize with his younger self as well as with the other characters in the story, including his father and Juma, in order to capture the essence of what happened. In addition, the emphasis on memory and the way David figures the story as a journey to visit the bones of that dead elephant — "He had always known the wind and sand-scoured bones but they were gone now and he was inventing all of it. It was all true now because it happened to him as he wrote and only its bones were dead and scattered behind him" (94) — work to identify him once again with the hunted elephant who remembered his dead friend and was killed because of his desire to visit the friend's burial site. But what is most curious about the quotation is the use of the pronoun "it," which seems to refer to the story. This "it" with its "bones" scattered associates the story with the elephant, whose bones are also now scattered. The writing process with its emphasis on remembering and telling (in defiance of the father) revivifies the events, just as it revivifies the elephant while he is writing. The story metonymically comes to stand for the elephant; it allows David not only to rewrite how he was but also to give voice to his protest.

Such a reading, however, is at odds with the readings of David's character by many gender critics, who have felt the need to take sides and defend Catherine at David's expense, and I would suggest at the expense of a full reading of David's character. Frequently, these critics view David as an isolated, masculine writer, who betrays or overcomes (depending on their particular view of Catherine) his wife. Burwell, Roe, Nagel, Willingham, and others, despite the differences in their readings, emphasize David as an isolated writer-figure who works in a separate room and locks his writing in a suitcase in that room. For Nagel, David's writing of the elephant hunt story against Catherine's wishes represents the artist's capacity to "transform the difficulties of his present life [with Catherine, because of her constant experimentation and descent into madness] into significant art by using present emotions to capture the feelings of the past" (337). In this case, David's ability to isolate himself from his crazy wife and to produce despite her (and her nonproductive sexual experiments) is read as a testament to his artistic determination and skill. For Burwell, David's writing and, even more important, his rewriting of the elephant hunt story after Catherine burns the first version cause him to move away from Catherine and their gender experiments and "regress" into identification with and forgiveness of his father (115); Burwell explains that David's rewriting the story is "a crystallization of his resistance to a feminine mode of experiencing, a resistance that for a time the androgynous experiences threatened to dissolve" (124). Similarly, Willingham contends that "David's development [entails] the suppression of female creativity" (296), and Roe understands David's writing as so private and destructive that he compares it to the butchered female bodies in the locked room of the Bluebeard fairy tale. In this case, David's physical isolation in his writing room is put on a par with his father's brand of isolated, brutal masculinity. As a result, his writing has also been presented as a figurative killing of Catherine, who is associated with the elephant through the nickname "ivory" (e.g., Eby, "Beach," 109, and Wolfe, 239), and even as a re-killing of the elephant with words (Silbergleid, 109).

Of critics who focus on gender, only Nancy Comley and Robert Scholes and Carl Eby see David's plight differently. Comley and Scholes have argued that "this tale of the elephant hunt is a story about separation from the father" (283), a separation that they see as linked to David's attempts to break out of Western cultural assumptions and thus akin to his rejection of "Hebrew Laws or tabus" (283) in his erotic experiences with Catherine. Although theirs is a more sympathetic reading of David, they too seem to feel an obligation to make a choice: David's writing either identifies or does not with his father. Eby, however, hints at the nuance I am seeking to address here when he argues that Hemingway (and by extension David) have a "tremendous ability to identify with others and [an] equally powerful need to fend off exactly this sort of identification" ("Beach," 107).

Still other critics, including Kathy Willingham and more recently Robin Silbergleid and Amy Lovell Strong, have argued that Catherine should be understood as a feminist character, one who is thwarted and ultimately quashed by David and the patriarchal society he comes to represent in their readings. They see Catherine as a frustrated artist, jealous of her husband's accomplishments. This approach to Catherine's character, which is extremely persuasive and compelling, suggests how sophisticated Hemingway's portrayal of women can be, but it is not clear why these critics almost invariably feel the need to bolster Catherine's feminism with overstatements about David's masculinity or the purportedly masculine and destructive nature of his writing process. After all, it is Catherine who insists that she is a "destructive type" in response to David's claim that he is "inventive" (5). These scholars contend that David's writing is portrayed as selfish and masturbatory (which is how Catherine portrays it) with little regard for whether such charges are justified or not. In nearly all instances, critics insist that David in some fundamental way aligns himself with patriarchy and masculine identity, which are figured as detached and brutal, through this writing.

This insistence on David's isolation and figurative brutality is imperfect and selective. David's writing is textually linked to empathy, a linkage reinforced by his physical movement between the privacy of his writing room and his public interactions with Catherine and Marita. In this maneuvering, readers witness his efforts to strike a balance between his life and his writing. Not only does David emerge everyday to rejoin his party after his work, but he also tries to create a bridge between the worlds when he shares his writing-in-process with Catherine and Marita, a sharing that, like young David's sharing of the location of the elephant with his father, will not go unpunished. In addition, the boundaries between

David and Catherine are fluid and permeable, and the text works against such simplistic reductions or the easy assumption of sides.

In fact many critics, including Burwell, identify Catherine and her experiments as the inspiration for the elephant hunt story. Burwell suggests that the elephant hunt story "is the objective correlative of David Bourne's independent attempt to resist the cultural constraints of family, gender, and race against which Catherine inaugurated their joint resistance in the honeymoon narrative" (99). While it may be true that Catherine's actions help David recall his early resistance to his father, it is not accurate or fair to read David's writing and rewriting of the story as activities entirely defined by isolation or simple identification with his father/the father, especially if readers acknowledge Catherine's influential role in creating the conditions that allow him to write it. Given these terms, the writing is in a sense collaborative. Moreover, David's writing requires — as I have been attempting to demonstrate — empathy and identification with all his characters. Throughout the story David's empathy and openness are highlighted through his vocation as writer. As Tyler points out, Burwell may have been right that Hemingway was a man whose "empathetic faculty" (21) was damaged in childhood because of his vexed relationships to his parents, but as Tyler goes on to explain, "no one could write as Hemingway does without extraordinary sensitivity to the feelings of others" (48). Understanding the significance of childhood and memory (specifically the act of "re-membering") in *Garden* illuminates this capacity for feeling in David's character.

Aspects of Catherine's character have been overlooked or downplayed by critics who view the book as a gender battlefield. With an emphasis on childhood and empathy, these qualities reemerge and demand closer scrutiny. For example, Catherine's behavior (or her "art," as Willingham persuasively argues, 47 *et passim*) is invested in the adult world and its sensibilities in a way that David's art simply is not. Without this adult world of restrictions and constraints, her rebellions would be meaningless. Debra Moddelmog explains this situation when she observes Catherine's efforts to escape gender divisions, "to step out of society and into a more 'natural' state is impossible because social discourses form, or at least structure, the subject.... [T]he transgressive act does not stand in opposition to the dominant order but is firmly rooted within it" (91). For Catherine, the thrill of her experiments derives from the recognition that she is transgressing taboos. A significant part of her excitement comes from public display and thus recognition of her behavior — the more public the transgression, the greater the thrill. It is not enough finally to have David as witness because he does not object to or feel particularly scandalized by her experiments. In fact, critics have frequently taken David to task for what they feel is his lack of backbone in going along with Catherine's experiments, a fact that might also be read as support for the argument that he tends toward a childlike acceptance of others.

Catherine's investment in the adult world can also be seen in her attitude toward children. She does not particularly like children, and her single expression of interest in having a child is presented as a way of securing her identity as a woman (71). Catherine even uses the designation, "child," to express disapproval or condescension, such as when she belittles David's use of "child's notebooks" (156) for his writing. She continues to attack him in ways that emphasize his childlike qualities as negative when she claims that he "makes mistakes in spelling and grammar too" (215). At the same time, however, Catherine appears interested in keeping David in a childlike position of dependence on her, a position not unlike his relationship to his father in the hunt story. She makes strenuous efforts to determine what he writes, demanding that he work on the honeymoon narrative and going so far as to burn the African stories when he disobeys her and writes them instead. Even more to the point, she seeks to control David financially; she reminds David when he writes the African stories against her wishes that she has "only tried to make it economically possible for him to do the best work of which he is capable" (156).

If Catherine has been trying to make it possible for David to do his best work, then it is curious that she should detest and destroy the story of which he is most proud. Catherine clearly feels threatened by the elephant hunt story. Arguably, she is concerned about the potential financial independence that the story (and his writing in general) represents for David. To some extent, Catherine acknowledges her motivations in this regard because after she burns the stories, she offers David money to reimburse him for the loss of the stories, which she suspects were "worth a lot" (226). But Catherine may also feel threatened by David's desire to capture a child's worldview, which renders her changes and experiments benign. David is never deeply scandalized by Catherine's desire to be a boy or by her sexual experiments as much as he is by her obsessive need to see herself through public reaction and her destruction of his manuscripts. Catherine hints that it is the child's viewpoint in the story that somehow represents a threat to her because she suggests that David can go back to Africa and "write them again when your viewpoint is more *mature*" (222; my italics). David's attempt to recover a childlike vision of the world, which is associated with Africa, and leave such valuations behind seems to be what threatens Catherine most.

Thus, although it is Catherine who is often read by gender critics as embracing multiplicity and challenging patriarchy through her gender experiments and orchestrations of sexual role reversal, when the issue is refocused around childhood and empathy, it is Catherine who appears rigid and controlling. For example, she does not understand David's attempts to manage his multiple, fluid senses of self. Early on in the novel, she asks him: "How can we be us and have the things we have and do what we do and you be this that's in the clippings [referring to press coverage of his book]?" (24). She cannot comprehend the need for David to balance his public authorial identity with his private relationship with her, which is juxtaposed to her need to have her "authentic" identity confirmed by public recognition. In another instance, she disapproves of what David has written about his father in Africa by saying: "It's bestial." She then asks: "So that was what your father was like?," to which David replies: "No. . . . But it was one way he was" (157). David is able to identify with his father's many facets, while Catherine will not or cannot recognize the father's complexity. It may, then, be a mistake to think that it is only the father who forecloses upon the process of empathetic identification when he shoots the elephant; Catherine does as well, when she metaphorically burns the father and the elephant. David resists Catherine's desire to control his writing and by extension his ability to identify with others.

My goal in pointing out these aspects of Catherine's character is not to take sides and argue that David is somehow more tortured or sympathetic than Catherine, but merely to demonstrate how a shift in attention and terms can refocus the readers' sense of their relationship. Moreover, as Moddelmog has pointed out, David's crisis in the novel is glossed over in the published version. She argues that Tom Jenks, the editor of the published version of *Garden*, saw himself as having to salvage the much-loved masculine image of Hemingway from this complex text. "To suggest that David's crisis is as serious as Catherine's . . . was more than Jenks could allow, or imagine" (113). As a result, critics working with the published version and in the shadow of Hemingway's macho persona may have had a tendency to read David less sympathetically than they do Catherine.

The essential point here, however, is that in the elephant hunting episode of *Garden*, both its original events and the representation of its writing process testify to the importance of empathy for David's character and make it clear that this childlike ability to empathize and identify freely with others is not valued in the adult worlds of his father and Catherine. In the adult world of hierarchies and restrictions, empathy and identification with others entails risk and danger, and sharing that desire for empathy with others is even more dangerous. I suggest that with both characters — David and Catherine — Hemingway was interested in complexity, instability, and contradiction, which may be why he selected "Bourne," which has its roots in the ideas of boundaries or limits, for their last name. Each character is constrained by cultural expectations and works against them in different ways.

Not the Same Old Bull

Many critics have observed that toward the end of his career and especially in his unpublished writing, Hemingway was visibly struggling with the pressures of fame and the limitations of his public persona. This aspect of *Garden* has been addressed recently by Hilary Justice and Amy Strong; they have observed that the novel might best be understood as a book about authorship that explores the danger of sharing material that departs from audience expectations. Such a reading changes the main critical lens from gender to a sense of public versus private authorship, or the tension between writing for one's public as opposed to one's self. In this case, David and Catherine can be read as manifestations of different facets of Hemingway's personality: Catherine arguably represents Hemingway's public persona and the need for public recognition (which was, like Catherine, often spinning out of control during these later years), and David represents the desire to keep his vocation as a writer clear and unencumbered by public opinion and expectation. Ultimately, however, it is valuable to make a distinction between the way *Garden* offers a meditation on the process of authorship by capturing David's writing practices, and the way the novel functions metatextually as a contemplation of Ernest Hemingway's particular conundrum as a celebrity author.

Within *Garden*, the elephant hunt story offers a glimpse into David's authorial process. The hunt story, as I am presenting it, represents the risk and danger associated with the writer's need to cultivate empathy, since the bull elephant that is the object of that empathy is killed by David's father and the story so carefully remembered about the elephant is destroyed by Catherine. In addition, David has cultivated an adult persona that privileges the power of empathy, not simply in his choice of vocation as a writer but also in his insistence on writing according to his conscience and not simply to satisfy the demands of others (represented in the text by Catherine). But it would be overly simplistic to argue that David refuses to see his writing as something that must be done to meet audience expectation and earn a living. After all, David must identify with the father as well as his younger self to produce the story. More to the point, writing requires authority and empathy, dismembering and remembering, being public and private. In other words, David identifies with the father, but not to the exclusion of identifying with others as well.

In addition, there is also an intensely personal aspect of the elephant hunt story as a part of a metatextual meditation on authorship, suggested by that fact that during this period the bull elephant became a particularly charged symbol for Hemingway not just in *Garden* but also in other manuscripts and writings as well. The symbol of the elephant finds its way into Hemingway's work and language of the period. He claimed that his degree of fame in the wake of winning the Nobel Prize often made him feel like "an elephant at the zoo" (Burwell, 214n), and in a letter to John Atkins he compared critics' interest in him to being hunted like an elephant with one hundred pounds of ivory (Reynolds, *Final Years*, 261). Remarks like these, in conjunction with Patrick Hemingway's observation that Hemingway felt elephants to be "our equals," suggest that when the father kills the elephant, it is probably not going too far to say that Hemingway, like the young David, identified with the elephant. In a sense, the story may even suggest that Hemingway's macho persona (the father) presented a threat to the skill required to be a serious writer (the son).

In *Under Kilimanjaro*, which was written around the same time, the main character, Ernie (another of Hemingway's writer-protagonists), experiences a poignant moment in which he too identifies with a large bull elephant. In the scene, which unmistakably resonates with the young David's identification with the elephant in *Garden*, Ernie notes:

> There was one old bull apart from the others who had a young bull with him. This old bull had very heavy tusks and, from the air, everything about him looked enormous. He had been standing under a tree when we first saw him and he did not move off when the others moved. When we came back for him he spread his ears out very wide and raised up his trunk. . . . This time I had a very good look at his ivory since he raised it directly toward the aircraft as we came in. It looked almost too heavy for him to lift without effort. (303)

Burwell argues that the old elephant in *Under Kilimanjaro* is "a metaphor for the heavy and destabilizing burden that the expectations of the writer's public are creating for the prematurely aging Hemingway. It is a burden as inescapable, but as essential, to the writer as tusks are to the elephant" (145). But there is also mystery to the elephant symbol in Hemingway's work; it is clear that he does not fully understand how the mechanisms of fame and public desire for his work operate. Thinking about the same large bull elephant later in the day, Ernie wonders pointedly: "I knew that the old bulls were driven out of the herds long before they were impotent but I did not know why some were still loved after they had gone by themselves and why others were not" (313). Like the abandoned old bull, Hemingway acknowledges that the machinations of his fame are unclear to him.

By recognizing that the elephant hunt story is really about empathy and the role of empathy in the writing process, we can stop trying to identify the elephant as clearly one person or the other and abandon reductive attempts to decide who is more wounded by the other or who is sacrificed by the other. The elephant is not a simple symbol for Hemingway; rather, he represents the challenge, mystery, and danger of authorship — the need to empathize freely with others but also the price of doing so. That

Hemingway should situate David's childhood in Africa and use that great giant of Africa, the elephant, as his primary symbol for the writer's process, testifies to his increasingly problematic sense of Africa as a space of contemplation where he could imaginatively work through the problems of authorship. I suspect that in part Hemingway's use of Africa for this purpose was rooted in his belief that "Africa, being as old as it is, makes all people . . . into children" (*Under Kilimanjaro*, 23). Old age and youth are curiously connected in his writings from this period. He writes in *Garden*: "[David's] own tiredness [on the hunt] . . . had brought an understanding of age. Through being too young, he had learned how it must be to be too old" (197). In the imaginative African space the old writer identifies the wellspring of his writing as the empathetic heart of his childhood.

Notes

[1] Burwell supports her suggestion that the elephant hunt story was an independent story before it was incorporated into *The Garden of Eden* with comments Hemingway made in letters from this period; but she has not found conclusive evidence that the story existed separately (214n). My essay, however, bolsters Burwell's claims, since many of the books that I explore as influences on the elephant hunt episode were published in and around the early 1950s, which is, according to Burwell, the time frame during which the elephant hunt story was first drafted (101).

[2] All four works are listed in Brasch and Sigman, *Hemingway's Library: A Composite Record*. Burwell identifies Scott's book as a potential source for *Garden* (214), Lynn suggests Markham as an influence (412), and various biographers have noted that Bror Blixen's book as well as the man himself was a key source for Hemingway on Africa and African hunting; Reynolds identifies Bell's book as one of the books Hemingway reordered as he began the revision of *Garden* after losing access to his research library in Cuba (*Final Years*, 197). In addition, it is worth noting that Hemingway met both Blixen and Markham during his 1933–1934 safari. Although he did not much care for Markham, he did strike up a friendship with Blixen, who visited Hemingway in Bimini and checked the spelling of the Swahili words in *Green Hills of Africa* (Lynn, 412; Reynolds, *1930s*, 204). It is also worth noting that Eby has cited Rudyard Kipling's *Kim* as another influence on the elephant hunt story in "Come Back to the Beach Ag'in, David Honey!" (104).

[3] Petry has also argued for Markham's influence on Hemingway, although she focuses on the connection between a scene in *West with the Night* where Markham watches a man die of black water fever and "The Snows of Kilimanjaro."

[4] I would be remiss not to mention that there have been claims (never definitively substantiated) that *West with the Night* was not written by Markham, but rather by her husband Raoul Schumacher. Schumacher was a screenplay writer in Hollywood (O'Brien, N.p.).

[5] Other critics have observed that Salinger and Hemingway, who met in Paris in 1942, influenced one another. Sandra Spanier has traced the resemblance between *Catcher* and Hemingway's short story, "The Last Good Country," and Cynthia Barron noted that Hemingway's early story, "Soldier's Home," may have influenced Salinger's *Catcher*.

[6] Manolín's age has been the subject of much debate. Recently, Jeffrey Herlihy has observed that the words for *boy* in Spanish — *chico* and *muchacho* — "can refer to males until they marry" (26). Using textual clues in *The Old Man and the Sea*, Herlihy speculates that Manolín, the "boy" of the novel, is in fact twenty-two, and that Santiago was about twenty-two when he saw the lions on the African coast. In *Reading Hemingway: The Facts in the Fictions*, Miriam B. Mandel summarizes C. Harlold Hurley's argument that Manolín is ten years old (525n). The debate hinges on the use of a pronoun with an unclear referent. In any event, even if Herlihy is correct, which would suggest a greater difference in age between the young David and the twenty-two-year-old Manolín than might initially be suspected, my main point is that Hemingway associates Africa with youth and innocence, not with a particular age range. In addition, Hemingway's insistence on age as a factor between the "old man" and "the boy" in *The Old Man and the Sea* further emphasizes that he was making a purposeful distinction about the different sensibilities of youth and age.

[7] I use the word "murdered" here intentionally to capture David's point of view that the killing of this animal is more akin to the killing of a subject deserving of rights and respect than the mere killing of an object safely removed from human beings.

[8] Wolfe's article expertly develops the debate around humans, animals, and things, and situates it in relation to twentieth-century literary theory and philosophy; see, in particular, 227–31.

Works Cited

Barron, Cynthia M. "The Catcher and the Soldier: Hemingway's 'Soldier's Home' and Salinger's *The Catcher in the Rye*." *Hemingway Review* 2, no. 1 (1982): 71–73.

Bell, W. D. M. *The Wanderings of an Elephant Hunter*. 1923. Reprint, Long Beach, CA: Safari Press, 2002.

Blixen-Finecke, Bror von. *African Hunter*. Translated by F. H. Lyon. 1938. Reprint, New York: St. Martin's Press, 1986.

Brasch, James D., and Joseph Sigman. *Hemingway's Library: A Composite Record*. New York: Garland, 1981.

Burwell, Rose Marie. *Hemingway: The Postwar Years and the Posthumous Novels*. New York: Cambridge UP, 1996.

Comley, Nancy R., and Robert Scholes. "Tribal Things: Hemingway's Erotics of Truth." *Novel: A Forum on Fiction* 25, no. 3 (1992): 268–85.

Eby, Carl P. "'Come Back to the Beach Ag'in, David Honey': Hemingway's Fetishization of Race in *The Garden of Eden* Manuscripts." *Hemingway Review* 14, no. 2 (1992): 98–117.

———. *Hemingway's Fetishism: Psychoanalysis and the Mirror of Manhood.* New York: SUNY Press, 1999.
Hemingway, Ernest. *The Garden of Eden.* 1986. Reprint, New York: Scribner's, 1987.
———. *Green Hills of Africa.* 1935. Reprint, New York: Scribner's, 1987.
———. *The Old Man and the Sea.* 1952. Reprint, New York Scribner's, 1995.
———. "To Maxwell Perkins." 27 August 1942. *Hemingway: Selected Letters 1917–1961,* 539–43. Edited by Carlos Baker. London: Panther, 1981.
———. *Under Kilimanjaro.* Kent: Kent State UP, 2005.
Herlihy, Jeffrey. "'Eyes the Same Color as the Sea': Santiago's Expatriation from Spain and Ethnic Otherness in Hemingway's *The Old Man and the Sea.*" *Hemingway Review* 28, no. 2 (2009): 25–44.
Hillman, James. "The Elephant in *The Garden of Eden.*" *Spring: A Journal of Archetype and Culture* 50 (1990): 93–115.
Justice, Hilary K. *The Bones of the Others: The Hemingway Text from the Lost Manuscripts to the Posthumous Novels.* Kent: Kent State UP, 2006.
Love, Glen A. *Practical Ecocriticism: Literature, Biology, and the Environment.* Charlottesville: U of Virginia P, 2003.
Lynn, Kenneth S. *Hemingway.* New York: Fawcett Columbine, 1987.
Mandel, Miriam B. *Reading Hemingway: The Facts in the Fictions.* Metuchen, NJ: Scarecrow Press, 1995.
Markham, Beryl. *West with the Night.* New York: Farrar, Strauss and Giroux, 1942.
Moddelmog, Debra A. "Protecting the Hemingway Myth: Casting Out Forbidden Desires from *The Garden of Eden.*" *Prospects: An Annual Journal of American Cultural Studies* 21 (1996): 89–122.
Nagel, James. "The Hunting Story in *The Garden of Eden.*" In *Hemingway's Neglected Short Fiction,* edited by Susan F. Beegel, 329–38. Ann Arbor: UMI Research Press, 1989.
O'Brien, Robert Viking. "Author and Hero in *West with the Night.*" *The Journal of African Travel-Writing* 1 (September 1996): 14–23. *JATW* web access: http://www.unc.edu/~ottotwo/authorandhero.html.
Petry, Alice Hall. "Voice Out of Africa: A Possible Oral Source for Hemingway's 'The Snows of Kilimanjaro.'" *Hemingway Review* 4, no. 2 (1985): 7–11.
Pooley, Eric. "How Scribner's Crafted a Hemingway Novel." *Narrative Magazine.* Web access: http://www.narrativemagazine.info/pages/eden.htm.
Reynolds, Michael. *Hemingway: The Final Years.* New York: Norton, 1999.
———. *Hemingway: The 1930s.* New York: Norton, 1997.
Roe, Steven C. "Opening Bluebeard's Closet: Writing and Aggression in Hemingway's *The Garden of Eden* Manuscript." *Hemingway Review* 12, no. 1 (1992): 52–66.
Salinger, J. D. *The Catcher in the Rye.* Boston: Little, Brown, 1951.
Scott, Robert L. *Between the Elephant's Eyes!* New York: Dodd, Mead, 1954.

Silbergleid, Robin. "Into Africa: Narrative and Authority in Hemingway's *The Garden of Eden*." *Hemingway Review* 27, no. 2 (2008): 96–117.

Spanier, Sandra Whipple. "Hemingway's 'The Last Good Country' and *The Catcher in the Rye*: More Than a Family Resemblance." *Studies in Short Fiction* 19, no. 1 (1982): 35–43.

Strong, Amy L. *Race and Identity in Hemingway's Fiction*. New York: Palgrave Macmillan, 2008.

Tyler, Lisa. "'Dangerous Families' and 'Intimate Harm' in Hemingway's 'Indian Camp.'" *Texas Studies in Literature and Language* 48, no. 1 (2006): 37–53.

Voeller, Carey. "'He Only Looked Sad the Same Way I Felt': The Textual Confessions of Hemingway's Hunters." *Hemingway Review* 25, no. 2 (2005): 63–76.

Willingham, Kathy. "Hemingway's *The Garden of Eden*: Writing with the Body." *Hemingway Review* 12, no. 2 (1993): 46–61.

Wolfe, Cary. "Fathers, Lovers, and Friend Killers: Rearticulating Gender and Race via Species in Hemingway." *Boundary 2* 20, no. 2 (2002): 223–57.

6: An Elephant in the Garden: Hemingway's Africa in *The Garden of Eden* Manuscript

Chikako Tanimoto

READING ERNEST HEMINGWAY'S *The Garden of Eden*, we need to ask whether, or to what degree, it presents Africa as a cultural reality, or if Africa merely forms the backdrop for what is at heart an essentially Euro-American psychological narrative. In the manuscript version of the book, David and Catherine's sexual experiments are referred to as "tribal things," which, together with the darkening of their skin from exposure to the sun, suggests what we might call "Africanization" in both physical and psychological terms. On the other hand, while the elephant hunting story David writes has its background in East Africa, it clearly reflects American literary tradition in its depiction of a little boy's initiation into manhood through the trial of gaining spiritual independence from his father. Since Tom Jenks, the editor of Hemingway's manuscript, eliminated the phrase "tribal things" and its implications, and included David's completion of the rather conventionally structured short story as a key element in the conclusion of the published novel in a way that is not apparent in the original manuscript, the edited novel could be seen to end by reemphasizing traditional white American values despite the protagonists' desire within the tale to merge with what they perceive as African culture, to become tribal. There are significant disparities between the novel and manuscript, then, that need to be taken into account if we are to attempt, as I wish to do here, to examine the complex interaction between Hemingway's American cultural background and the values he identified with the African landscape and a perceived African spirit.[1]

My aim here is to clarify the Euro-American influences surrounding Hemingway, his works, and his readers, rather than to attempt to articulate reductively what Africa and its values meant to him. Africa is an *other* space for Hemingway, which is to say that it functions in part as a place in which the writer is able to achieve a distance from certain cultural constraints he may have felt as an American, and as a particularly famous one whose discourse and behavior were subject to intense scrutiny at home and in much of the Western world. In *The Garden of Eden* manuscript, we should be able to see how much he relates Africa to freedom from gender, familial, and other, broader cultural constraints. It also seems to have meant to him freedom from the role that he was expected to assume and live out as the great American writer, Papa Hemingway. Placing the African story in the context of his larger African narratives such as *Green Hills of Africa* and *Under Kilimanjaro* will facilitate a deeper understanding of Hemingway's need to explore unconventional behaviors, transgressive identities *outside* his own America. To begin, however, some important issues surrounding the editing of Hemingway's manuscript should be attended to.

Jenks's Garden

Before *The Garden of Eden* was posthumously published in 1986, it went through considerable editing by Jenks, who instituted some very drastic cuts, reducing some two hundred thousand words of original text to a relatively short novel of seventy thousand words. As far as the structure is concerned, we must admit that the resulting work is tight and well formed. Once the narrative focus is brought into David's perspective, the central inciting event is introduced: his new bride Catherine, even as they honeymoon on the Côte d'Azur, suddenly cuts her hair and initiates an inversion of the couple's conventional sexual roles. The gender complications build as a sexually flexible woman, Marita, enters the story, resulting in a *ménage à trois*. As the endgame approaches, Catherine gradually descends into mental illness, and eventually she burns all the manuscripts of David's short stories set in East Africa. This incident forms the climax of the novel, after which she leaves a farewell letter and sets off alone on a night train for Paris. David then decides to divorce her and states his intention to marry Marita, who helps him rewrite the short story that becomes a great success, marking the ending of the novel. In other words, the novel as Jenks constructed it achieves a degree of closure by removing a woman whose deviation from normative wifely sexual and gender roles disturbed the equanimity of the male protagonist, replacing her, in effect, with a new and relatively submissive female character. In that sense, the unfolding of Jenks's story is informed by conventional patriarchal heterosexual ideology.[2]

The plot of David's African story, encased within the novel and presenting the boy's rite of passage, is itself, as I mentioned at the outset, rather conventional. Set in East Africa, where David, we learn, spent his youth, the story is inspired by his experiences of elephant hunting and depicts the psychological distance between his maturing self, who sympathizes with the elephant, and his father, who sees it as a profitable venture. If we read the story in the context of the published novel, or at least independently of Hemingway's manuscript, the young boy's loss of respect and love for his father upon the death of the elephant emerges as the central theme, and as Pamela A. Boker puts it, this theme "is the now familiar one of a boy's disillusionment with the heroic paternal ideal" (259). The boy's disappointment in the father he once saw as a hero not only signifies the end of his childhood but also implies the beginning of a deeper understanding of his father as a person. Thus, as far as its treatment of the bond between a white father and his son and the youth's initiation is concerned, the African story reflects traditional themes and underlying values of canonical American literature.

There is a paralleling, then, of the plots of the short story and the novel that envelopes it. The boy's separation and attainment of independence from his father mirror David's marital disillusionment and separation from his loved wife. In fact, the period during which David writes the African story overlaps with the period in which his marriage is beginning to fail. James Nagel argues that each segment of the hunting story reflects David's emotional situation in his married life, which gradually intensifies. In the African story, the boy realizes that he is "emotionally away from his father and away from youth" and "these realizations in the story correspond to the final events of the novel, as the marriage finally terminates" (Nagel, 337). Again, we should recognize that this neat parallel is an effect of Jenks's editorial intrusion. By placing the completion of the story at the conclusion of the novel, the editor promises to David (re)productive success both in his career as a writer and in his forthcoming marriage.

Jenks actually admitted that the guiding principle of his editing was that the resulting work was "not for any special audience, but for general readers" (30), so it is hardly surprising that he produced a well-constructed Aristotelian plot unmistakably displaying "a beginning, a middle, and an end" (Aristotle, 66): Catherine's sexual experiment is a beginning, David's conflict is a middle, and his marriage to Marita is an end. Of course, Jenks's structure also, not at all by accident, happens to correspond to a Freudian view of sexuality, which, as Judith Roof puts it, "begins with the aberrations that provide the damming stuff against which the hero of normative heterosexuality must struggle" (xix). Drawing on Roof's analysis, Robin Silbergleid argues that in *The Garden of Eden*, "the narrative of Catherine and David's relationship . . . can only function as a perverse detour from a larger narrative of artistic production and heterosexual reproduction" (Silbergleid, 103). As "Freud's story features a struggle and victory" (Roof, xx), *The Garden of Eden* depicts the hero's conflict with a devilish woman and ends with a triumph of (re)productive sexuality over perversions. If the "general readers" that Jenks had in mind means normative heterosexual readers who consider perversions as a threat, we should concede that his plot successfully achieves the "reproductive demand of the end of the story" (Roof, xxi) that these readers would presumably want.

This is Jenks's novel, however, not Hemingway's manuscript, which, among its many points of difference, does not end with the narrative closure provided by the successful completion of the African story and the launching of a new and "healthy" heterosexual coupling. In the unedited manuscript, there is a long description of the ongoing relationship between Marita and David after Catherine leaves. Hemingway also prepared a provisional ending in which Catherine returns to David. Given that the manuscript of *The Garden of Eden* "was so repetitious that it seemed interminable" to some critics (Carlos Baker, in McDowell, C21), perhaps Jenks's severe editing can be justified on aesthetic grounds, but something is lost in such a rationale. Reading these repetitions enables us to sense just how much Hemingway was possessed by ideas of sexual experimentation, along with gender and racial transgressions. The sexual role inversion undertaken by the married couple, the devices they employ to make themselves appear as twins, the darkening of their skins to become tribal, the enactment of lesbian desires, the implications of incest — these are depicted at length and in detail in the manuscript. Together, they seem to suggest an endeavor to discover some kind of truth concealed beneath sexuality by lifting the perceived social veil of common taboos, which, as Foucault would later argue, may well be a futile project.[3] This would give us at least a partial understanding of why Hemingway could not complete his novel. If there is no such thing as the truth of sexuality, any attempt to search for it, which I believe the modernist Hemingway was engaged in, necessarily remains an interminable questing, an endless deferral of and through discourse, if we want to invoke the language of French poststructuralism. Regardless of whether the reader is bored or excited by that process, Jenks's excising of content and his diminishing the sense of insistence present in Hemingway's manuscript are very deep editorial intrusions that possess some evident ideological implications.

The Tribal Things

In *Playing in the Dark*, Toni Morrison illuminates the stark contrast between David's elephant hunting story in *The Garden of Eden* and the narrative of the honeymoon by calling them the inner African story and the outer Africanist story. Her model is very useful for the further reading of Hemingway's manuscript in terms of the difference between the symbolic Africa and the African landscape.

> At the heart of *The Garden of Eden* is "Eden": the story David is writing about his adventures in Africa. It is a tale replete with male bonding, a father-son relationship, and even the elephant they track

is loyal to his male companion. This fictional, Africanized Eden is sullied by the surrounding events of the larger Catherine-David Africanist Eden. Africa, imagined as innocent and under white control, is the inner story; Africanism, imagined as evil, chaotic, impenetrable, is the outer story. (89)

Morrison makes clear that while the inner story has an African setting and American values, the outer story of the physical and spiritual Africanization of the white couple on the French Riviera suggests what from a certain American perspective of the time may be experienced as a troubling deviation from a sense of cultural order. In this outer story, David promises Catherine to write a narrative of their secret eroticism. Abandoning his promise, however, he concentrates on writing his conventional American African story. Thus, Morrison is right when she argues that Catherine is justified in destroying David's short story and thus the inner narrative. Contrary to the inner story that Morrison regards as "an old, familiar myth, Africa-as-Eden before and after its fall" (89), the outer story aestheticizes and mythologizes blackness "pulled from fields of desire and need" (90). In this sense, the American African story is "conservative," as Amy Strong argues, while David's "life is experimental" (84). The reality belies the fiction.

By eliminating the suggestive phrase "tribal things" that is used to denote the Africanization in Catherine and David's sexual experimentation in the original manuscript, Jenks relegates Africa to the status of a mere geographical backdrop for David's short story, depriving it of its symbolic significance in the larger narrative that depicts the heroine's psychosexual transformation. In the manuscript, Carl Eby argues, Hemingway "clearly associates racial otherness with a primitivism that must have struck him as only appropriate for his theme: the Garden of Eden" (160). In Hemingway's text, tanning signifies a form of erotic racial transgression. When Catherine explains the reason for her tanning by saying "white women will always bore" David (K422.1/2, chap. 4, p. 3), she refers to the Kanaka and Somali tribes as her models. It is this change that David refers to as "tribal things," insisting on their importance.

> You must not let the [white taboos (crossed out in the manuscript)] things you must not say nor write because you are white and will go back there affect you at all and you must not deny or forget all the tribal things that are as important. The tribal things are more important really and you do not have to say them if you know them. (K422.1/23, p. 10)

Acknowledging that both he and Catherine are transforming themselves into a kind of African tribe, David himself manifests "tribal scars" (Eby, 173). According to Eby, while they are the "remembrance of a long-ago plane crash" (173) on a face that has become dark under exposure to the sun, they appear as a symbol of David's own primitivism. "With his suntan, tribal scars, and ivory hair," Eby argues, "David wears the fetish objects himself in what is essentially a transvestic act" (173).[4] After Catherine leaves, Marita begins to enact the same exchange of sexual roles as Catherine had done. Like Catherine, she calls herself "African girl," a "Sahib," a "street arab," and a "Mbulu girl" (K422.1/36, pp. 4, 15, 25). David, Catherine, and Marita all expose their fetish desire, inscribing primitivism on their own bodies.

On one level, the elephant in the African story represents such fetish desire. Its ivory tusks may be readily identified with Catherine's ivory hair (Eby, 164). It also represents "David's feminine eyes" (Silbergleid, 109), which Catherine wants to protect. From this perspective, young David's desire to save the elephant from the male white hunter and Catherine's burning the stories "to keep her writer-husband from using his words — his vision — to kill the elephant again" (Silbergleid, 109) both relate to their longing for an African primitivism identified with femininity and symbolized by the elephant in Africa.

In the African story, the father and the African tracker, Juma, communicate through signs that young David cannot read. Thomas Strychacz claims that "these dumbshows of sign-reading and -interpretation constitute a discourse of masculinity" and David is "assigned a subordinate position in these dramas of signifying glances" (213). The intimacy between these sign readers could be characterized as "homosocial" in the sense that this word is used by Eve Kosofsky Sedgwick. In that context, the elephant's tusk, like a woman, is a commodity that is exchanged between men, and from which they can profit. Thus David imagines that "Juma will drink his share of the ivory or just buy himself another god damn wife" (*Garden of Eden*, 181). The important thing to notice here is that young David is alienated from this bond between men, and this situation determines his sympathy towards the elephant. Reading David's short story in the context of Hemingway's manuscript, with its unresolved desire, then, provides a more complex web of associations and a very different kind of interpretation than that which the published novel supports.

The story is set in an Africa that, by the time of the action, had already been incorporated into the Western economy; some Africans take white people on safari to make a living. The organized big game hunting of David's father brings his son safely and in relative comfort to the African wilderness, not entirely unlike Hemingway's 1933–1934 safari, underwritten by Pauline's uncle, which made it possible for him to write *Green Hills of Africa*. However, young David is inflamed with hatred toward Juma rather than against his own father. He hopes that the elephant will kill Juma, whom David considers no longer African because he earns dollars from ivory instead of protecting African nature. For David, only the elephant, with its strong odor and wrinkled grey skin, represents the true Africa.

In other words, for David, the elephant is a fetish symbol of an African primitivism that is supposed to exist outside the Western economy. Therefore, the death of the elephant represents the loss of that African innocence of which Catherine repeatedly tries to remind him through sexual experimentation in tribal things. In that case, it will be useful for us to seek the reason why he has to kill the elephant again in his own story once he has reached adulthood. In addition, if we understand that killing the elephant has the same effect for David as parting from Catherine and the tribal things that she has initiated, we might also logically ask if her reappearance in the provisional ending of Hemingway's manuscript could also imply the survival of the fetish Africa for both Catherine and David.

What Is Africa?

In Hemingway's provisional ending, Catherine and David are on the beach talking about their African trip.[5] Their conversation presents a clear contrast between the African geography and the meaning of the term "Africa." Catherine insists they "didn't go to Africa"; David answers, "We went to Africa" (K422.6, p.3). While Robert E. Fleming suggests that Catherine forgets about their trip to Africa because of her "mental illness" (268), attributing her remark to a psychologically sourced memory defect may be too quickly dismissive. It is significant that in the same passage Catherine declares Africa "was too much like Spain" (K422.6, p.3). That is to say, what is important and uniquely "African" for her is not geographical. As Hemingway observes in *Green Hills of Africa*, parts of Spain and Africa are in physical terms practically indistinguishable:

> It was a new country to us but it had the marks of the oldest countries. The road was a track over shelves of solid rock, worn by the feet of the caravans and the cattle, and it rose in the boulder-strewn un-roadliness through a double line of trees and into the hills. The country was so much like Aragon that I could not believe that we were not in Spain until, instead of mules with saddle bags, we met a dozen natives bare-legged and bare-headed dressed in white cotton cloth they wore gathered over the shoulder like a toga. (146)

The emphasis here is on the physical aspects of scenery, and in that respect there is not much difference. In contrast, it is the people and a certain spirit that define Africa for Catherine. Her insistence on not having been to Africa implies that for her they did not authentically make contact with that spirit. It seems clear that she and David actually did go to Africa, the place, as David insists. However, to Catherine, whose desire was to become a member of an African tribe, Africa is not merely a travel destination. The discord in their conversation about Africa indicates an unbridgeable gap between Catherine, who longed for a thoroughgoing immersion in African primitivism in their honeymoon narrative, and David, who fails to fulfill her wish and writes a story about Americans hunting elephants against an African scenic backdrop.

Nancy R. Comley and Robert Scholes argue that sexual mythology for Hemingway was deeply rooted in so-called primitive cultures outside the West. For these scholars, within Nick Adams's sexual fantasy in "Fathers and Sons," for example, sexual truths "lie not at the center of 'standard' heterosexual practice . . . but at the margins: in what the society of Hemingway's parents would have called perversion or miscegenation" (77–78). Similarly, Catherine considers, or constructs, the real tribal Africa as the origin of the myth of the tribal things that she wants to achieve. When she realizes that she is not able to find this in the African continent, she feels that in her sense she did not go to Africa. Of course, the real Africa does not exist as a thing, but only as an idea, feeling, or desire, in which case it represents a psychological projection and from a certain objective standpoint might even be considered illusory. Even her performance of the tribal things is a physical embodiment of her illusions about the real Africa.

Debra A. Moddelmog criticizes Catherine's attempted Africanization for its "desire to inhabit the erotic conceptual space that whites have traditionally assigned to black Africans and Americans of African descent" (100–101). The paradox of *The Garden of Eden*, with its prominent depiction of a symbolic Africa through a frame of Western cultural preoccupations, shows that a pure Africa completely independent from Western values does not exist in the world Hemingway depicts.

Yet, Hemingway in a sense attempted to place his own origins in Africa, especially in *Green Hills of Africa*, in which he refers to Africa as "home": "I loved this country and I felt at home and where a man feels at home, outside of where he's born, is where he's meant to go" (283–84). Hemingway's attempt to seek his home in a place that is not actually his home may be regarded as deconstructing the notion of the "origin" itself. However, we can better understand this in contrast with his attitude toward Oak Park, his biographical hometown. While traveling around the world, Hemingway avoided Oak Park, the suburb of Chicago in which he grew up. In a letter he sent to Mary Welsh during their engagement period, he wrote of Chicago that "[I] never have been back except to bury my Father that same fall," explaining that "it would be rude to go and not see my mother and I can't stand to see her" (*Selected Letters*, 598).

When we consider this psychological perspective in Hemingway, his identity comes to be that of an expatriate, as the protagonist Jake is explicitly referred to by his friend Bill in *The Sun Also Rises* (120). Hemingway harbored for his entire life an expatriate's sense of alienation toward his hometown, his mother's house, and his father's grave. Thus his attempt to find his own origins on the African continent is to a certain degree an attempt to escape and establish a distance from the American values he has inherited from his parents. In *Green Hills of Africa* Hemingway expresses the strong wish to preserve his "home," Africa, from Western exploitation.

> A continent ages quickly once we come. The natives live in harmony with it. But the foreigner destroys, cuts down the trees, drains the water, so that the water supply is altered and in a short time the soil, once the sod is turned under, is cropped out and, next, it starts to blow away as it has blown away in every old country and as I had seen it start to blow in Canada. The earth gets tired of being exploited. (284)

The Elephant in the Zoo

It has been argued by Rose Marie Burwell that Hemingway felt a special affinity with the elephant, that the aging elephant of the African manuscript was a projection of Hemingway himself. Hemingway likened himself to an "elephant in the zoo" in a letter to C. T. Lanham written from Cuba after he received the Nobel Prize: "Too many people know we live here and we have had too much publicity and people come like to see the elephant in the zoo. I'm very sick of it and would like to get somewhere that they don't have white peoples" (*Selected Letters*, 841).

Likening himself to an elephant is no mere offhand comment (the more commonplace expression is "*monkey* in the zoo"), especially given its association here with an escape into the "dark continent" and what we have already discerned in Hemingway's fiction. From this statement, we can see that while Hemingway was determined to be himself, it was extremely difficult for him to live independently of the public image that had coalesced around him. In that sense, the zoo represented not only Western society and media, but even the readers of his books who expected his fictional protagonists to behave like American heroes, and Hemingway to present himself as the American and resolutely masculine "Papa Hemingway."

In *Under Kilimanjaro*, Hemingway depicts himself as a character who is progressively "Africanized," and yet, no matter how he wishes to identify with the tribesmen, cannot stop being the American literary legend "Hemingway." The following conversation between Mary and Hemingway in *Under Kilimanjaro* is a quite explicit expression of how troubling that could be to the writer, albeit treated with a certain ironic distance here.

> "I wish we didn't have to go back at all. I wish we didn't have any property nor any possessions nor any responsibilities. I wish we only owned a safari outfit and a good hunting car and two good trucks."
>
> "Everybody you know would come and visit you and go on free safaris," Miss Mary said. . . . "People would turn up in their private planes and . . . say, 'Bet you can't tell me who I am. I'll bet you don't remember me. Who am I?' Sometime somebody is going to say that and I'm going to ask Charo for my bunduki and shoot the man right straight between the eyes." (125–26)

These lines remind us of the crowds who came to see Hemingway at his home in Finca Vigía. Being as famous as he was, Hemingway was unable to escape his reputation wherever he went, and in this sense, the world became for him a giant zoo, incarcerating him as one of its most popular attractions. What Hemingway longed for in "Africanization" was freedom from his public image: Africa geographically embodied and concretized that existential desire.

As Mary's speech in *Under Kilimanjaro* makes clear, however, Hemingway was never totally free from the zoo even when he was in Africa. In fact, even the elephants of Africa were not free; they were becoming major tourist attractions as East Africa was rendered more accessible as a safari destination. Still, while likening himself to those elephants, Hemingway apparently realized that he was also one of the tourists, that he himself, like David in *The Garden of Eden*, was privileged, protected, and even financially supported as a Westerner. Although he wished to immerse himself in Africa, perhaps even to become African during his second stay there, his journey was sponsored by *Look* magazine, which requested a safari report from the American legend to sell to its American readers. In *Under Kilimanjaro*, based on this expedition, he tries to become a member of an African tribe through his engagement with a Kamba girl, Debba. However, this scheme, as Suzanne del Gizzo remarks in the notes to the text, is "stunningly problematic and raises questions about his sincerity, not to mention his morality," since he "knows that he will leave Africa, that it is ultimately a 'vacation' that will end" (522). To Hemingway, Africanization does not so much mean to become African as to enjoy the white person's privilege of being able to transform oneself for a while into something different, and at some level the writer himself seems to have comprehended ironically the complexity and ambivalence in this.[6]

There are good reasons, then, for us to be at least a little skeptical of the attempts in Hemingway's texts to reach outside the normative heterosexual Western culture through African identifications and "tribal" performances. The desire of characters to be "Africanized" does not necessarily mean that they have any deep understanding of, or even interest in, the political reality of the African people. Moddelmog points out in her criticism of "The Snows of Kilimanjaro" and "The Short Happy Life of Francis Macomber" that although Hemingway loved Africa, imperialism and colonialism are at work in both pieces. To Hemingway, Africa serves the function of an "imaginative space onto which he can project white characters and conflicts without considering the ethics of their occupation of Africa or the humanity of the black people who stand before them" (113). Moddelmog sees incisively through the cynical "immobility" (117) of Hemingway the world traveler, the word "immobility" accurately suggesting that to Hemingway, who could not escape from Western values, the entire world had become a giant Euro-American zoo. In short, the African continent is to some extent functioning as an extension or annex of the zoo of Western values.

Nevertheless, we need not for this reason turn our backs on Hemingway's attempts to transgress the boundaries of gender and race, and to consider the extent to which these may be conceived as meaningful gestures of resistance or liberation from within the enclosure of a white Euro-American male-centered cultural hegemony. In studying those various unorthodox desires in Hemingway that recent critics have been eagerly taking out of the closet, perhaps it is not sufficient to say that he possessed such desires, nor enough to say that behind such desires there still exist patriarchal/imperialistic prejudices. These desires have been sometimes concealed and sometimes exposed within the critical heritage surrounding Ernest Hemingway. Jenks's edition of *The Garden of Eden* is one such example of concealment in the sense that it keeps Hemingway in the closet in order to preserve his popular public image as a heteronormative great American writer. Perhaps as far as his African narrative is concerned, it may be more important to discuss how his literary treatment of Africa casts light on the Western culture that surrounds his text rather than to focus on how he describes Africa and its people. This approach enables us to examine more closely the critical dynamics that have been positioning literary works between disclosure and concealment in relation to the desires that they invoke.

Notes

Some parts of this article first appeared in my essay, "'Afurika' ha Dokoni Arunoka" ("Where Is 'Africa'") in *Heminguuei Kenkyu* (*Hemingway Review of Japan*) 9 (2008): 15–27. I thank Professor Mark Weeks for his many useful comments on the structure and expression of this essay.

[1] According to Suzanne del Gizzo, "Hemingway often does not make clear distinctions between African geography and African cultures, which are linked for him by the idea of primitivism" (520).

[2] Reading a novel that, like *The Garden of Eden*, has been edited in a manner not in keeping with the author's intentions is an act entirely separate from discovering the intentions of the author. Instead, it is a search for the meanings spun from the manuscript by the editor. Therefore, if we want to discover what Hemingway intended when he wrote *The Garden of Eden* manuscript, we must go to the John F. Kennedy Library in Boston and directly consult the manuscript. However, even reading the manuscript is not enough to discover what Hemingway "really" meant. As Roland Barthes argues, the meaning of the text lies not with the author but with the reader — in this case, the reader who is constructing a text for him/herself across, and in the interstices between, the manuscript and the published novel.

[3] Foucault's argument here arises from his critical attitude toward the Freudian repressive hypothesis that presupposes the existence of sexual desire prior to its repression. Foucault sees desire as being generated by the repressive law itself, which, through its discursive delay of gratification, produces the very sphere for the discourses of sexuality. See Foucault, *The History of Sexuality, Volume I*. See also Butler, 65.

[4] Eby explains this transvestic act as the means of David's identification with the phallic woman. By doing so, he connects the cross-racial and cross-gender identifications with each other.

[5] Based on close study of established dates and periods relating to the writing of *The Garden of Eden* manuscript, John Leonard contends that Hemingway wrote the provisional ending in May 1958, revised the formerly written chapters in November in the same year, and then, working from this revision, spent from December 1958 to February 1959 writing the final section, which includes an alternative ending that Hemingway "intended as the conclusion for his novel" (67).

[6] The old elephant in *The Garden of Eden* is chased by a white hunter, and is at last shot with a gun. When Hemingway is likened to the elephant, those of us who know his tragic suicide by shotgun cannot help but project the death of the elephant onto the demise of Hemingway himself. When we consider the similarity between the fates of the writer and the animal, David's act of smoothly rewriting the elephant killing story becomes an ominous harbinger of the author's death. In this perspective, Catherine's destructive activity on the manuscript could be conversely understood as the remedy to prevent him from pulling the trigger. Considering what happens to David's manuscript, this interpretation is rather ironic, but it just makes us wonder if the shotgun is really the inevitable fate both for the elephant and for Hemingway.

Works Cited

Aristotle. *Poetics*. In *Classical Literary Criticism*, translated by Penelope Murray and T. S. Dorsch, 57–97. New York: Penguin, 2000.

Barthes, Roland. *Image-Music-Text*. Translated by Stephen Heath. New York: Noonday Press, 1977.

Boker, Pamela A. *The Grief Taboo in American Literature: Loss and Prolonged Adolescence in Twain, Melville, and Hemingway*. New York: New York UP, 1996.

Burwell, Rose Marie. *Hemingway: The Postwar Years and the Posthumous Novels*. Cambridge: Cambridge UP, 1996.
Butler, Judith. *Gender Trouble: Feminism and the Subversion of Identity*. New York: Routledge, 1990.
Comley, Nancy R., and Robert Scholes. *Hemingway's Genders: Rereading the Hemingway Text*. New Haven: Yale UP, 1994.
del Gizzo, Suzanne. "Going Home: Hemingway, Primitivism, and Identity." *Modern Fiction Studies* 49, no. 3 (2003): 496–523.
Eby, Carl P. *Hemingway's Fetishism: Psychoanalysis and the Mirror of Manhood*. Albany: SUNY Press, 1999.
Fleming, Robert E. "The Endings of Hemingway's *Garden of Eden*." *American Literature* 61, no. 2 (1989): 261–70.
Foucault, Michel. *The History of Sexuality, Volume I: An Introduction*. Translated by Robert Hurley. New York: Vintage, 1990.
Hemingway, Ernest. *The Garden of Eden*. New York: Scribner's, 1986.
———. "*The Garden of Eden* Manuscript." Ernest Hemingway Collection, John F. Kennedy Presidential Library, Boston.
———. *Green Hills of Africa*. 1935. Reprint, New York: Scribner's, 1987.
———. *Selected Letters, 1917–1961*. Edited by Carlos Baker. New York: Scribner's, 1981.
———. *The Sun Also Rises*. 1926. Reprint, New York: Simon & Schuster, 1954.
———. *Under Kilimanjaro*. Edited by Robert W. Lewis and Robert E. Fleming. Kent: Kent State UP, 2005.
Jenks, Tom. "Editing Hemingway: *The Garden of Eden*." *Hemingway Review* 7, no, 1 (1987): 30–33.
Leonard, John. "*The Garden of Eden*: A Question of Dates." *Hemingway Review* 22, no. 2 (2003): 63–81.
McDowell, Edwin. "New Hemingway Novel to Be Published in May." *New York Times*, December 17, 1985, C21.
Moddelmog, Debra A. *Reading Desire: In Pursuit of Ernest Hemingway*. Ithaca: Cornell UP, 1999.
Morrison, Toni. *Playing in the Dark: Whiteness and the Literary Imagination*. New York: Vintage, 1992.
Nagel, James. "The Hunting Story in *The Garden of Eden*." In *Hemingway's Neglected Short Fiction: New Perspectives*, edited by Susan F. Beegel, 329–38. Tuscaloosa: U of Alabama P, 1989.
Roof, Judith. *Come As You Are: Sexuality and Narrative*. New York: Columbia UP, 1996.
Sedgwick, Eve Kosofsky. *Between Men: English Literature and Male Homosocial Desire*. New York: Columbia UP, 1985.
Silbergleid, Robin. "Into Africa: Narrative and Authority in Hemingway's *The Garden of Eden*." *Hemingway Review* 27, no. 2 (2008): 96–117.
Strong, Amy L. *Race and Identity in Hemingway's Fiction*. New York: Palgrave Macmillan, 2008.
Strychacz, Thomas. *Hemingway's Theaters of Masculinity*. Baton Rouge: Louisiana State UP, 2003.

7: Between Ngàje Ngài and Kilimanjaro: A Rortian Reading of Hemingway's African Encounters

Frank Mehring

LIKE NO OTHER AMERICAN ARTIST, Ernest Hemingway has left his literary mark on the iconic summit of Kilimanjaro. Hemingway's admiration for the African region attracted worldwide curiosity. Particularly striking was his metaphorical use of the Masai expression *Ngàje Ngài* ("House of God") to refer to the highest mountain on the continent. With "The Snows of Kilimanjaro" (1936), Hemingway inspired readers to follow him in facing the essentials of life, either by means of an aesthetic transfer in the act of reading or quite literally by hiring a travel guide from Tanzania. Today, you can book a "Last Frontier Expedition" with Hemingway Tours & Safaris, buy "adventure clothes" from the Hemingway Travel Collection, and start your climb of Kilimanjaro at the Hemingway base camp, staying in a "tented accommodation [that] is luxuriously comfortable and spacious with en-suite bathrooms and . . . naturally, fully and tastefully furnished," as the website promises.[1] Ken Shapiro, editor of a travel magazine, has identified a trend labeled "tourism of doom" that encourages visits to endangered sites like Kilimanjaro's shrinking ice cap.[2] Hemingway's short story regains prominence in light of recent theories on global climate changes, enabling us to ask if and how the reading of "The Snows of Kilimanjaro" today could activate an ecocritical attitude in the reader. In addition, one might ask why Hemingway's African encounters are so effective in triggering a positive response to an unlikely hero such as Harry, who constantly quarrels, drinks, and blames others for his shortcomings?

This article will analyze Hemingway's African encounters by emphasizing the literary strategies he used to authenticate cultural curiosity. This analysis will reveal a hidden frame of false promises played out between urban memories and constructions of an African wilderness. Methodologically, I will combine a Rortian reading of Hemingway's African encounters with recent theories of ecocriticism. By tapping into the rich resources of aesthetics, ethics, and cultural theory, my reading will put to the test whether, as Lawrence Buell suggests, the power of imaginative literature can foster a climate of "transformed environmental values, perception and will" (vi).

Stereotypes and Means of Redemption

Texts can only answer those questions that have been put to them, and they can only answer them "as best they can" (Bode, 89). Each generation, however, asks different questions. In the wake of the "ethical turn"[3] proposed at the end of the 1980s, ethical questions such as how ought one live? and, what ought I to do? have been applied to literary texts by theoreticians such as Richard Rorty (1931–2007). Focusing on the interaction between text and reader, Rorty optimistically recognizes the process of reading imaginative literature as a starting point for a revolution or — in more modest terms — at least a change in the reader, helping him to become "a more sensitive, more knowledgeable, wiser person" ("Redemption," 244).

Because Hemingway was such a popular and authoritative figure in his time, the constructed answer to the question, how ought one to live? (as extracted from his cosmopolitan texts) defined, to a certain degree, the contemporary standard of how a man (of that period) is supposed to live. How does today's reader — the twenty-first-century individual who faces the question, how ought I to live? — relate to an American writer repeatedly described as chauvinist, racist, anti-Semitic and, in general, an immoral expatriate?[4] And when readers tend to blur the boundaries between fact and fiction, between biography and work, how can this question of self-improvement be applied to his writing, in particular to his pseudo-autobiographic narrative *Green Hills of Africa* (1935) and the two short stories "The Snows of Kilimanjaro" and "The Short Happy Life of Francis Macomber"?[5] Kurt Müller addresses precisely these questions, making a convincing argument for reevaluating Hemingway's writings in order to counteract the loss of reputation his work has suffered. By foregrounding the potential of Hemingway's texts to engage the aesthetic, moral, and political sensibilities of the reader, Müller offers a new approach to Hemingway's fiction, one that emphasizes the "moral potential that is to be realized in the act of reading" ("Modernist," 334) rather than the actual moral content. In this spirit, and within the framework of Rorty's neopragmatic readings, I would like to turn to Hemingway's "The Snows of Kilimanjaro."

To apply a Rortian approach to Hemingway's African encounters, the critic needs to overcome the powerful psychoanalytic paradigm introduced by Philip Young more than fifty years ago. According to Young's so-called wound theory, Hemingway's life and art were motivated by the trauma of his injuries in World War I. With this psychological construct, Young is able to identify a recurring "code hero" who displays "grace under pressure" as he adheres to a discipline of honor and courage. In a "life of tension and pain" these principles "make a man a man and distinguish him from the people who follow random impulses, let down their hair, and are generally messy, perhaps cowardly, and without inviolable rules for how to live holding tight" (63). Young's persuasive concept of the "code hero" made it difficult for subsequent critics "to approach Hemingway in any other fashion" (Beegel, 277). In the wake of postmodern deconstructive reading strategies as well as the traumatic loss of national naiveté occasioned by the Vietnam War, the heroic image of both Hemingway the artist and the Hemingway mirrored in his fictional protagonists came under intense scrutiny. The subsequent Hemingway industry created a paradoxical situation. On the one hand, it flooded the book market with biographies, studies about the history of ideas, contextualization, and feminist assaults on Hemingway's hostility toward women. On the other hand, guide books to Hemingway's Paris, Key West, or Cuba initiated a process of aesthetization regarding the places he had visited and wrote about.[6] Even so, the academic deconstruction of Hemingway, which has produced so many different and even contradictory readings, cannot account for the ongoing fascination with his transcultural encounters and confrontations.

I would like to advocate a Rortian reading to Hemingway's African texts because in this kind of reading the text is not reduced to the status of a tool or a fluid mass that can be molded into any form desired by the critic or biographer. Rather, with the German Americanist Kurt Müller, I argue for an "attitude of respect for the aesthetic autonomy of the work of art" ("Modernist," 318). In the case of Hemingway, this requires us to free ourselves from the stereotypes Hemingway's biographers have heaped onto the protagonists of his fiction. Following Winfried Fluck's and Wolfgang Iser's reception aesthetics, I will apply an ethics of reading, combining it with Richard Rorty's neopragmatic theory of reading in order to reevaluate the literary figure of Harry in "The Snows of Kilimanjaro." This approach generates a number of new questions regarding Hemingway's oeuvre.

According to Rorty, novels offer a "means of redemption from self-satisfaction" ("Der Roman," 49). Instead of only asking *how* something is said in order to trace back the moral effect in the reader's response, I ask how the protagonists interact with and within their cultural environment. It will become quite apparent that Hemingway's protagonists are not only incurious and inattentive "to anything irrelevant to [their] obsession about their cruelty towards other people" (Rorty, *Contingency* 163) but they also tend to be oblivious towards cultural encounters in Austria, France, Italy, Spain, or various regions in Africa. A critical scrutiny of the protagonists' self-centeredness in Hemingway's African writings will lead the reader to the heightened awareness of cultural differences.

What implications does such a reading hold for interpreting transcultural encounters? This question seems to me also relevant to Rorty's effort to focus on cultural incuriosity and its ethical implications.[7] In such an investigation, imaginative literature can play a key role. Rorty's concept of the "liberal ironist," who has "continuing doubts" about his means of expression and communication (*Contingency*, 73), challenges the reader to question the self-stylizations of, for example, the code heroes in Hemingway's African stories. Thus, cultural environments in both fiction and the reader's personal sphere become interlinked. From this perspective, literature holds an ethical potential to make us more sensitive to our fellow creatures as well as to the environment.

> It is by causing us to rethink our judgments of particular people that imaginative literature does most to help us break with our own pasts. The resulting liberation may, of course, lead one to try to change the political or economic or religious or philosophical status quo. Such an attempt may begin a lifetime of effort to break through the received ideas that serve to justify present-day institutions. But it also may result merely in one's becoming a more sensitive, more knowledgeable, wiser person. (Rorty, "Redemption," 244)

In the following pages, I will trace back various aspects of cultural incuriosity in Hemingway's African encounters to reveal the potential of a Rortian reading. Instead of trying to counterbalance the familiar image of Hemingway as the ethnocentric white racist and male chauvinist, I would like to emphasize a hidden discourse on cultural indifference ingrained in Hemingway's African stories.

Cultural Incuriosity

In "Snows of Kilimanjaro" Hemingway tells the story of Harry, an American writer, and his wife, Helen, who are on a hunting safari in East Africa. Due to a gangrenous leg, Harry faces death. While Harry and Helen wait for a rescue plane, past events of Harry's life unfold before his inner eye, revealing the critical self-reflection of a celebrated author about his loss of artistic stamina. Harry quarrels with his wife in order to blame her, her money, and their excessive drinking for his stifled creativity and feeling of "emasculation." Helen is cast as "this rich bitch, this kindly caretaker and destroyer of his talent" (60). Memories of the "dark continent" represent the happiest days of their lives (probably a period of love and creativity). The dialogues with Helen reveal the motivation for going to Africa: to enable the writer whose work has become as "rotten" as his infected wound to "work the fat off his soul" (60). Facing death, Harry remembers several stories he would have liked to write. Set apart via italics, these vignettes exemplify Harry's artistic talents to the reader.

Biographers and scholars have repeatedly pointed out the close correlation between Harry's self-condemnation and Hemingway's own increasing anxieties about his drinking, his status as a writer, and his literary fame: the critics had mostly disliked his recent *Death in the Afternoon* (1932) and had "killed" *Green Hills of Africa* (1935; *Selected Letters*, 426).[8] Jeffrey Meyers quotes Hemingway's depressed statement of January 1936, expressing fears of "impotence, inability to write, insomnia" and suicide, and argues that this, combined with the "violent and bitter break with Jane [Mason] in April 1936" led to misogynist feelings (252). Feminist discourse has also used the two African stories to shed light on Hemingway's own personality. Rena Sanderson, for example, argues that with these fictive "bitches" (Margot and Helen), Hemingway is "attacking not only or primarily the woman but rather male passivity and dependence on women — traits he found in himself" (185). The Harry/Hemingway identification has been so strong that Hemingway biographer Kenneth Lynn even suggested that Hemingway used the short story "The Snows of Kilimanjaro" as a means to rehearse his own future death and its aftermath (431). This enduring emphasis on psychology and biography shows that issues of place and the dichotomy of city and nature, featured so prominently in the flashbacks, have hardly been addressed. The matters of cultural incuriosity in the African stories, as well as the discrepancy between Harry's rhetoric about the healing powers of Africa and his status as a tourist, have also been neglected.

Wilderness, Urban Life, and African Encounters

In "The Snows of Kilimanjaro," the American artist seeks a sense of transcendental harmony. For him, as well as for the leopard, the rhetorical evocation of a sacred, mythic wilderness outside the American historical context comes at a price: death. In his African narratives, Hemingway transfers the American concept of "wilderness," as a constructed textual entity, to the African continent and blends it with elements of the frontier myth.[9] Harry embodies the traditional frontiersman who, in the sense proposed by Richard Slotkin, allegedly escaped "from civilization and its discontents" (86), driven by his love for the spirit of the wilderness. However, the construction of wilderness in Hemingway's "The Snows of Kilimanjaro" reproduces the very values and social situation from which Harry tried to escape. Harry hopes that Africa and Kilimanjaro will cure his literary flabbiness, but the all-too-familiar quarrels with his wife — an integral part of his tense, overmodernized lifestyle in various cities in Europe — come back to haunt him.[10] His memories of those cities, and of his life in those cities, exemplified in the flashbacks, also keep him from opening his senses to the African environment.

The epigraph of "The Snows of Kilimanjaro" offers an entry into Hemingway's concept of wilderness and the literary construction of his African encounters. Critics have juxtaposed the "dried and frozen carcass" of the leopard with Harry's rotting leg (e.g., Waldhorn, 145) and have generally agreed that there is a parallel between the impulse that spurred the leopard's search and the artist's drive to reach the unattainable. Moral and artistic corruption, the metaphor of the rotten body, the vultures, and the hyena, form a chain of motifs bespeaking mortality, decay, and death (Müller, *Der Mensch*, 123), against which the story has been hailed as a positive symbol of the artist exorcising his inner demons through his own imagination and his striving for perfectibility.[11] I would like to undermine this assumption by unmasking the drama of cultural indifference that has been part of other transcultural encounters in books such as *The Sun Also Rises* (1926), *Death in the Afternoon* (1932), and *Green Hills of Africa* (1935) — a drama of cultural indifference that culminates in "The Snows of Kilimanjaro," whose epigraph states:

> Kilimanjaro is a snow-covered mountain 19,710 feet high, and is said to be the highest mountain in Africa. Its western summit is called the Masai "Ngàje Ngài," the House of God. Close to the western summit there is the dried and frozen carcass of a leopard. No one has explained what the leopard was seeking at that altitude. (52)

The epigraph suggests a keen interest in a particular geographic location, as well as familiarity with the religious beliefs of the Masai and with their language. Two questions emerge. First, how deep is Hemingway's interest in the cultural "other"? Hemingway might simply have taken the information on Kilimanjaro from Samler A. Brown's *The South and East African Year Book* (1933), which was in his personal library in Key West (Brasch and Sigman, 336). One passage provides almost verbatim the information Hemingway used for his epigraph. It says that "Kibo, the western summit, is called by the Masai 'Ngàje Ngài' the House of God. The highest point of this summit was first reached by Prof. Hans Mayer and Ludwig Purtscheller in 1889" (Brown, 307). Other elements might also, and just as easily, have been gleaned from contemporary publications. The reference to the leopard, for instance, might have been taken from the article that the English mountaineer Donald Latham wrote for the *Geographical Journal* in December 1926 entitled "Kilimanjaro." Latham is the one who discovered the mummified corpse of a leopard. He wrote that a "remarkable discovery was the remains of a leopard, sun-dried and frozen, right at the crater rim. The beast must have wandered there and died of exposure" (Stewart, 87). The spot later became known as "Leopard Point." In terms of content, then, the information presented in the epigraph was easily obtainable from contemporary sources, and does not, as is often assumed, indicate that Hemingway had intimate knowledge of or sympathy for local languages, beliefs, or geography.

A second question is, what creative strategies are used to introduce the reader to the exotic locale? Hemingway brings together several stylistic elements (including journalism, guidebook information, and poetic reduction) that are important for a successful aesthetic transfer with imaginations of the concept of "Africa" at the center. The literary products of these discourses have been part of Hemingway's oeuvre since his Paris years, when he struggled to access another culture, become immersed in it, and then exploit it for creative purposes. Hemingway prided himself as a connoisseur of French culture, and the American tourist industry has accepted him as such, issuing guidebooks to Hemingway's Paris, its bars, drinks, and cuisine. The text of his first Paris-based book, however, offers many clues that reveal the superficiality of this French-American love affair. For example, in an ironic performance of notoriously conservative moralists, Bill teaches Jake about the moral fallout of being an expatriate: such a person is in limbo, out of touch with his home country, unable to grow roots, escaping from one alien nation to another. "You're an expatriate. You've lost touch with the soil. . . . You drink yourself to death. You become obsessed by sex. You spend all your time talking, not working. You are an expatriate, see? You hang around cafés." Jake's response reveals a cynic approval of such a lack of cultural communication and curiosity: "It sounds like a swell life" (*The Sun Also Rises,* 115).

In that novel, the European continent served as a metaphor for being dislocated. Later, Africa becomes another literary *objet trouvé* that Hemingway used for similar purposes. In this he is not alone. Particularly since the Harlem Renaissance, American flâneurs, flappers, intellectuals, and artists have fantasized about African culture as a rich reservoir of tropes, ideas, and imaginary spaces that might inject American modernism with a stimulating dose of energy.[12] Alain Locke's founding document of the Harlem Renaissance, the anthology *The New Negro: An Interpretation* (1925), Langston Hughes's blues poetry, Paul Robeson's iconic embodiment of the leading role in Eugene O'Neill's drama *Emperor Jones* (1920), Aaron Douglas's murals on *Aspects of Negro Life* (1934–1936), and a host of jazz musicians such as Duke Ellington, Fats Waller, and Louis Armstrong catered to white fantasies about the African jungle, primitivism, and the allegedly authentic vitality of antiurban, precivilized forms of life. Cole Porter's song, "Find me a Primitive Man," points both towards the jazz craze and the obsession with fantasies of primitivist modernist art. The reference to Cole Porter's popular musical comedy *Fifty Million Frenchmen* (1929), set in Paris, reminds Harry of his own failures to come close to "the real thing" — a trope Hemingway introduced as a goal of all artistic endeavors in *Death in the Afternoon* (2), published in 1932 before he left for his African safari the following year.

Not surprisingly, "The Snows of Kilimanjaro" uses *The Sun Also Rises* — the quintessential story of the American fantasy of and fascination with Paris — as a metatext. Having explored various spaces and places all across Europe, Harry tries to tap into the vaunted African energy promoted by the American mass media in the wake of the mass migration of African Americans from the southern states to the North in the second part of the nineteenth century, and particularly in the immediate aftermath of World War I. That migration invested the metropolitan city in the North with a glorious whiteness that became a symbol of freedom in the African American imagination — as can be seen, for example, in Aaron Douglas's idealized concept of "the city" as it appears in his *Aspects of Negro Life: Aspiration* (1936; oil on canvas, 60 x 60 in.). This painting places factories and skyscrapers at the top right of the painting: the buildings sit atop a hill from which light radiates to the aspiring people in the lower spheres, who face it longingly. In an ironic turn, Hemingway invested the image of the highest mountain in Africa with a similar mythological whiteness, turning it into a desired place of redemption for white urban travelers.[13] Hemingway seems to return to the metaphysical framework of the African setting that informed Douglas's artistic vocabulary. While Douglas emphasizes education and work as a means for African Americans to move from bondage to urban freedom, Hemingway places a literate but unproductive urban dweller at the foot of the highest African mountain.

The Changing Function of "Africa"

In the 1920s, European towns evolved as a trope and escapist landmark for young American artists looking for affordable entertainment, amusement, and transatlantic adventures. The allegedly primitive world of Africa held similar promises for wealthy travelers. Hemingway's fascination with traveling into exotic countries and big game hunting follows Theodore Roosevelt's popular travel account, *African Game Trails*, which popularized the notion of "Africa" as a new frontier for Americans, and which Hemingway owned (Brasch and Sigman, 318). The book's subtitle, *An Account of the African Wanderings of an American Hunter-Naturalist*, resonates with the notion that by the beginning of the twentieth century, adventurers, explorers, and other culturally curious intellectuals would find challenges in Africa similar to those encountered by the early discoverers of the New World such as Columbus or Vasco da Gama. Roosevelt claimed that in British East Africa, Americans might encounter the "spectacle of a high civilization all at once thrust into and superimposed upon a wilderness of savage men and beasts" (1). After seeing the snowy summit of Kilimanjaro, Roosevelt envisaged Africa as a kind of New World "of high promise for settlers of white race" (30). Hemingway was equally impressed with the promise of a new and vast country. However, for Hemingway's protagonist the African encounter proves to be more ambivalent.

In addition to naming the famous mountain in the title, Hemingway uses carefully selected and very concrete details, reminiscent of stage directions, to activate the reader's imagination to picture the African setting:

> The cot the man lay on was in the wide shade of a mimosa tree and as he looked out past the shade onto the glare of the plain there were three of the big birds squatted obscenely, while in the sky a dozen more sailed, making quick-moving shadows as they passed. ("Snows," 52)

For Harry, Africa functions as an antidote to the enervating and finally destructive rich (American) people with whom he has been spending most of his time: "Africa was where he had been happiest in the good time of his life, so he had come out here to start again" ("Snows," 59). Where does this satisfaction with Africa come from? One is tempted to argue that the intricacies of hunting, the African wildlife, the exotic landscape, and the many tribes with their specific cultural practices, languages, and music provided a rich source of inspiration, a fine antidote to the deadening habits and decorum of the *nouveaux riches* from which he had escaped. But Harry seems less concerned with these matters than with his own well being. Like a boxer training for the next season, he simply chose a remote location to try to regain his original fitness. To be sure, the safari was initiated with "the minimum of comfort," as Harry indicates in one of his inner monologues (60). Nevertheless, he admits that "there was no hardship" either (60). Hemingway puts special emphasis on Harry's well being and comfort; the narrator mentions the "personal boy" constantly at his disposal to fulfill every wish (59). Harry and Helen display imperialistic attitudes towards their African companions — and not cultural curiosity. The reader, as Debra Moddelmog has pointed out, easily becomes complicit in the colonial relationship and attitude of domination and subjugation (136).

Language functions as a tool to define the geographic and cultural environment. However, like Jake in Paris, Hemingway's Harry is hardly familiar with the local language.[14] This language barrier marks Harry as a cultural outsider who has mastered only those key words necessary for issuing commands to his Masai guides and carriers. What holds true for American visitors to Paris also applies to wealthy adventurers who book a hunting trip to Africa: "if suitable chosen, all the attendants will speak English," as a recent guide to Africa ungrammatically assures its would-be customers. Indeed, a glossary of places and vernacular expressions for Hemingway's writings set in Africa would be quite short. In "The Snows of Kilimanjaro," the vocabulary appears most often when Harry orders alcoholic beverages:

"Molo!" he shouted.
"Yes Bwana."
"Bring whiskey-soda."
"Yes Bwana." (54)

Although the next line suggests moral ambiguity (his wife critically remarks, "You shouldn't"), it becomes quite clear that her remark does not refer to his bullying attitude or his shouting at the servants. Instead, she is concerned about the level of alcohol Harry consumes.

Harry appears as a discontented racist and chauvinist who does not engage with the environment in any way. Instead of looking around him, Harry constantly ponders the past, recalling other places that he would have loved to immortalize in his fiction. The African setting never appears to hold any potential for an unwritten story. And his wife, despite her repeated insistence that she, too, "loved Africa" (62), shares her husband's attitudes, up to and including his penchant for drink that she has criticized: "*'Molo, letti dui whiskey-soda!*' she called" (63). Neither of them recognizes their disconnectedness from the African sociocultural and natural environment.[15] Instead, they spend most of their time arguing about themselves and their relationship and soothing their spirits with alcohol.

As Harry starts to realize, the promise of authenticity on a big hunt safari turns out to be both a false promise of the American tourist industry and a personal lie. "It was not so much that he lied as that there was no truth to tell. He had had his life and it was over and then he went on living it again with different people and more money, with the best of the same places, and some new ones" (59). "The Snows of Kilimanjaro" exemplifies the repetition of the same superficiality and lack of authentic cultural contacts in the flashbacks. Africa is yet another place that evokes, if anything, the same old set of emotional responses Harry had already experienced in his urban flashbacks. Thus, the juxtaposition of an "imaginary heaven" with an "African hell," as Richard B. Larsen recently argued (45), does not really apply to the story. Hemingway's notion of "Africa" is as esoteric as the construction of a Christian heaven. Paradoxically, this African safari story is dominated by narratives set in non-African urban settings.

The clever plot device of presenting Harry's memories of other, better times allows Hemingway to introduce five striking vignettes, all of them set outside Africa. The first one takes Harry to a railway station in Karagatch in 1922. He is waiting for the train to Thrace, where he traces the retreat of the Greeks during the Greco-Turkish War. This monologue features two other episodes, one set in western Austria where Harry and his first wife wintered in a scenic house, and the other featuring a World War I pilot who bragged about killing several Austrian soldiers. The second flashback transports the reader to Constantinople as Harry talks about his wild sexual encounters. His memory then takes him back to one of his favorite cities, Paris, as he remembers a discussion of Dada art and mourns the break-up with his first wife. The third flashback begins with a reference to his grandfather's log house and then moves to a fishing trip in the Black Forest. Thinking again about Paris, he recalls the whores at the *Bal Musette* as well as a French neighbor, Marie, and her complaints.

In the fourth flashback, again tied to Paris, Harry tells a short story he would have liked to write, about a gruesome murder on an American ranch. The fifth, last, and shortest flashback recalls a bombing officer named Williamson who had been hit by a "stick bomb" during World War I. Williamson had impressed Harry as a man who could stand a lot of pain without passing out. This becomes the keyword for the story's final sequence, in which Harry thinks that his pilot friend has arrived to rescue him, but, instead of flying him to the hospital in Arusha, Compton takes him towards the "square top of Kilimanjaro." However this turns out to be a delusion for both Harry and the reader.[16] The dying artist has escaped into a happy ending. When Helen awakes, she finds Harry dead on his bed.

While any of the places mentioned in the flashbacks (Germany, Austria, Bulgaria, Switzerland, and Turkey) might serve as a foil, the prominent position of Paris is remarkable. The couple's connection to Paris was established even before the first flashback, when Helen emphasizes the dissimilarities between their common time in Paris and the experience of being paralyzed at the foot of the Kilimanjaro:

> "You never would have gotten anything like this in Paris. You always said you loved Paris. We could have stayed in Paris or gone anywhere. I'd have gone anywhere. I said I'd go anywhere you wanted. If you wanted to shoot we could have gone shooting in Hungary and been comfortable." (54)

Hemingway elaborates on the metaphor of snow first introduced in the epigraph, when Harry refers to the "snow on the mountains in Bulgaria," the snow on Christmas day in Schrunz that "was so bright it hurt your eyes," or the "rush of running powders-snow on crust" in Bludenz (55–56). In the end, however, Harry's mind returns to Paris. "'Where did we stay in Paris?' he asked the woman who was sitting by him in a canvas chair, now, in Africa" (57). As if to remind the reader that the story is *not* set in Paris, Hemingway reintroduces Africa. While referring to the entire continent, the term "Africa" functions as a trope to evoke remoteness from western civilization. Paris epitomizes the dream of civilization gone right from an American perspective.

The second flashback picks up the theme of quarrelling, particularly the quarrels with his American expatriate friends that provided the substance for what Harry considers great literature. The quarrels and conversations involve Americans — Harry remembers an American poet he met in one of the Parisian cafés who talked about modern art (66) — because the language barrier as well as his drunkenness prevent serious communication with French people. This was a widespread problem, as H. L. Mencken noted: despite extensive travels and academic credentials American intellectuals abroad are "far too dull . . . to undertake so difficult an enterprise" as learning the foreign language (40). The same is true for Harry in Africa, where he is also and again a cultural outsider who describes the places he visits as if he were looking at a kitschy postcard retouched with bright colors. Consider his memory of Parisian street life:

> you could not dictate the Place Contrescarpe where the flower sellers dyed their flowers in the street and the dye ran over the paving where the autobus started and the old men and the women, always drunk on wine and bad marc; and the children with their noses running in the cold; the smell of dirty sweat and poverty and drunkenness at the Café des Amateurs and the whores at the Bal Musette they lived above. The Concierge who entertained the trooper of the Garde Republicaine in her loge, his horse-hair-plumed helmet on a chair. (69)

This trip down memory lane to Paris is followed by a reference to the successful American songwriter Cole Porter, who turned American escapist fantasies into hit Broadway plays: "Cole Porter wrote the words and the music. This knowledge that you're going mad for me" (71), Harry explains to Helen. Like Harry, Porter was a regular in the Café Society of Paris in the 1920s. In his 1929 musical comedy tour of Paris called *Fifty Million Frenchmen*, he tellingly wrote of American tourists and expatriates that they claim knowledge of Paris without having established any real ties with their cultural environment:

> You come to Paris, you come to play;
> You have a wonderful time, you go away.
> And, from then on, you talk of Paris knowingly;
> You may know Paris, you don't know Paree." (Porter, 344)

The fourth flashback follows the reference to Porter and begins with a revealing insight: "No, he had never written about Paris. Not the Paris that he cared about. But what about the rest that he had never written?" (71). The well-constructed paradox sets up the dichotomy between writing about a cultural experience and at the same time admitting that it is based on the perspective of a cultural outsider. Earlier, Harry had talked about the return of his creative strength, identifying the feeling as an illusion. His abilities to write about Paris or Africa, respectively, emerge as a white lie that allows him to continue working. "If he lived by a lie he should try to die by it" (60), Harry explains regarding his artistic talents. This reference foreshadows the rescue scene, which takes him closer to Mount Kilimanjaro. The one scene in which he finally hopes to attain a sense of purity and a sensuous overflow of powerful feelings turns out to be a hallucination of the dying artist. In a way, it is yet another lie of the writer when Harry continues the narration after his own death. In addition, the reader becomes the victim of a literary trick, which leads him or her to fallow a false storyline. The final episode is the hidden sixth vignette without the graphic identification suggested by the italics.

Thus, the overall structure of "The Snows of Kilimanjaro" resembles an artistic confession. The story deconstructs the ongoing process of Harry's self-delusion. While he blames Helen for all of his artistic failures, he admits that she has indeed been "always thoughtful" (59) and caring. There is no one to blame for his artistic and physical numbness but himself: "He had destroyed his talent himself. Why should he blame this woman because she kept him well? He had destroyed his talent by not using it, by betrayals of himself and what he believed in" (60). Another of his confessions revolves around the cultural curiosity he tried to sell as authentic in his many trips around the world. The flashbacks are a last resort to drum up support for the many transcultural encounters he experienced during his travels. However, after the fifth and final flashback the trope of cultural curiosity emerges as yet another lie.

> "You know the only thing I've never lost is curiosity," he said to her.
> "You've never lost anything. You're the most complete man I've ever known."
> "Christ," he said. "How little a woman knows. What is that? Your intuition?"
> Because, just then, death had come and rested its head on the foot of the cot and he could smell its breath. (74)

Considering the lack of curiosity in African cultures and spaces, it is ironic that Hemingway originally named the dying writer in "The Snows of Kilimanjaro" Henry Walden (Lynn, 429), with an obvious nod to the patron saint of nature writing, Henry David Thoreau. The literary strategy of "Snows," which juxtaposes the African experience with memories of urban life, reflects the dichotomy of city and nature that also plays out in *Walden*.[17] It emphasizes the tragic element encoded in Harry's love for Africa, namely, that he cannot escape his memories of urban life. Just as Thoreau ends his experiment in the "New England wilderness" (which was actually only one and a half miles outside the city of Concord) by returning to his city life, Harry's mental paralysis is doubled in physical space. Kilimanjaro, the object of his fascination, is always in clear sight, but rendered inaccessible by the spreading gangrene in his leg. Ironically, he can only hope to reach it through industrialization, by using complex machines that can transcend the limitations of the human body. Thus, the story's central act of waiting for the plane (an icon of modernization, transportation, and liberation) constantly undermines Harry's dedication to the promises of the African wilderness. In *Green Hills of Africa* Hemingway explains that he described wilderness in "an attempt to write an absolutely true book" (iii). "The Snows of Kilimanjaro" uses a fictional character to reveal the literary strategies employed in the construction of the notion of "Africa." The façade of purity and authenticity starts to crumble right after the introduction of the epigraph and continues methodically with the five flashbacks.

Hemingway's "Kilimanjaro" and the Tourist Industry

In the course of the twentieth century, the earth has urbanized at an incredible speed. As urban sociologist Mike Davis explains, cities have absorbed nearly "two-thirds of the global population explosion since 1950" (2). The German architect Thomas Sieverts predicts a new conurbation that he calls *Zwischenstadt* ("in-between city"), an almost seamless blending of rural and urban settlements (3). With the dynamics of urbanization and the creation of megacities with populations in excess of eight million or hypercities with more than twenty million inhabitants, comes the desire to leave these spatial confinements in order to confront more essential aspects of human life. In "The Snows of Kilimanjaro," the frequent flashbacks to city life seem to suggest that no matter where the urban intellectual goes, he depends on and cannot free himself of the city. A similar tendency was visible in Thoreau's account of his life in the woods at Walden Pond, from which he regularly traveled back to Concord on the railroad tracks that passed along the southwest shore. Although Hemingway was not necessarily interested in improving the ecological quality of life in the cities, Harry's dissatisfaction when he is in Africa, away from his urban environment, poses interesting questions about the relationships between urban and nonurban environments. For example, is it possible to assume an ecocritical attitude about Harry's sojourn in Africa in order to address the question of ecological footprints? Do nature and city represent an antithesis or symbiosis in "Snows"?[18]

It is crucial to understand that Hemingway turns to the quintessential constituent of city life to describe the aesthetic experience of Kilimanjaro: the house. The mountain top, the mythological House of God, recalls the mystique and symbolic status that Harlem had for the "new Negro" who was migrating from the South to the brightly lit northern "city on the hill," as depicted by Aaron Douglas in *Aspiration*. Many other works worked the same theme, transforming the city into a metaphor of self-discovery, like James Weldon Johnson's *Black Manhattan*, Alain Locke's *Mecca of the New Negro*, and Langston Hughes' *Racial Mountain*. This (African-American) experience is also at the center of Hemingway's story about the imaginary flight towards the top of Kilimanjaro. If fictive literature has, as Lawrence Buell asserts, "the power to draw its readers into its imagined scenes affectively and even sensuously, as against instilling a sense of mystified spectatorial distance,"[19] the changing image of Kilimanjaro in the age of a "tourism of doom" might activate in the reader an ecocritical attitude in the process of reading "The Snows of Kilimanjaro."

Such a reading must take John Dewey's redefinition of traditional aesthetics into account. Dewey moved away from the notion of a substantialist aesthetics, stressing the aspect of the specific experience of an object or text. The attitude towards such an object constitutes its aesthetic quality. Reception aesthetics, with Hans Robert Jauss and Wolfgang Iser as the most prominent trailblazers, focused on the various acts of reading in order to analyze the "discrepancies produced by the reader during the gestalt-forming process" (Iser, 133). In this process, the reader becomes both observer and participant because the representation of people and locations in literature is realized by a performative act in the mind of the reader. Winfried Fluck has recently transferred this reader-response model to imaginary spaces, to ask to what extent space can become an aesthetic object. In order to gain cultural meaning in an ecocritical reading of "The Snows of Kilimanjaro," I follow Fluck's assumption that "physical space has to become mental space or more precisely, imaginary space" (25). Conceptualizing the object as a carrier of an aesthetic function makes it possible, in my reading of "Snows," to transfer its implications to a new ecocritical context. I suggest a recontextualization of Hemingway's concept of "whiteness" in the metaphysical Masai term "Ngàje Ngài" (House of God) in order to concentrate on its function in a changed discourse on African safaris and the trekking industry of Kilimanjaro.

Hemingway's short story about "The Snows of Kilimanjaro" may not be part of the subgenre of environmental nonfiction that problematizes the interactions between natural and built environment. Nevertheless, the city-nature binary, which Buell identifies as the oldest and most deeply embedded metaphor to come to terms with the experience of urban life, assumes a new dimension by contrasting the immersive power of Hemingway's fiction with a close-up image of the glacier on, let's say, Google Earth™. Thus, two contrasting representations of Kilimanjaro come into focus: the mental construction produced in the reader's mind based on

Hemingway's narrative from 1936, and the mental construction created by recent satellite images that can be accessed worldwide via the internet. Fictional forms of spatial representations, as Fluck reminds us, "bring an object into our world but they are never stable and identical with itself" (31). In the case of reading Hemingway's "Snows," the fictional representation is based on a performative mode. How does this apply to an ecocritical approach?

The dramatic changes to the earth's environment during the last century have caused the ice on Kilimanjaro to recede. Mountain climbers who hope to see, with Harry, the "great, height, and unbelievable white in the sun" might be disappointed due to the loss of the ice fields on Kilimanjaro, which has been reported since the second half of the nineteenth century. Since the first tracking in 1912 until 2000, 82 percent of the icecap has been lost. Within only fifteen years, from 1984 until 1999, the glacier of Kilimanjaro lost about 300 meters of vertical ice (Stewart, 101). Predictions say that by 2015 the snow may be completely gone.[20] In short, the striking symbol of quasi-religious purification and the sense of heavenly fulfillment, which Harry envisions in his mock flight approaching the "House of God," hardly translates into a real world experience, which shows mankind diminishing its white purity.[21]

As Hemingway shows us through Harry, tourists cannot shake off their (guilty) memories of their urban pasts. Like Harry, they embark upon safaris that merely stage the encounter with wildlife within a controlled and restrained organizational grid. The guides have established safe tours, comfortable camps, and ample food supplies replete with wine and whiskey.[22] Harry's trackers took him through the bushes and after the shooting slew and skinned the animals. Hemingway used the image of the snows on the tip of Kilimanjaro in order to evoke a kind of purity that reminded Theodore Roosevelt of familiar images of the mythical American West. At the foot of Kilimanjaro, Roosevelt observed that in "many ways it reminds one rather curiously of the great plains of the West, where they slope upward to the foot-hills of the Rockies" (30). Like nineteenth century paintings that recreated a pure landscape ready to receive the imprint of civilization on the frontier, Hemingway uses fiction to superimpose the nostalgic search for a new natural purity to the African setting. The corruption of this endeavor became apparent by the fakeness of a guided safari tour and the urban memories that dominate the transcultural encounters at the foot of Kilimanjaro. Today, Google Earth™ can take one on a virtual flight from the plains towards Kilimanjaro (see fig. 7.1). The discrepancy between Harry's illusion of flying towards the "snow" and the disturbing image of the receding glacier on the internet bring into question the very reasons that led the protagonist to Africa.

Fig. 7.1. Virtual flight to Kilimanjaro via Google Earth. Accessed November 29, 2009. Image NASA, Image © 2009 TerraMetrics (2009) and © 2008 DigitalGlobe.

Conclusion

In the story's epigraph, Hemingway uses the vernacular term *Ngàje Ngài* for Kilimanjaro and provides the meaning of the phrase (House of God), thus distinguishing between cultural insiders (who know) and outsiders (who need to be told). The cosmopolitan traveler Harry claims to love the foreign world he has come to, but he is in fact completely estranged from the location, the people, the language, the African plant and animal life, and what it means to live in such an environment. Paralyzed by his infected wound, Harry escapes to other places in a series of flashbacks that indicate that he has traveled, seen many exotic places, fought bravely in several wars, and met all kinds of people. His mind is filled with stories that promise a productive future for a long literary career. But none of this has anything to do with Africa or Kilimanjaro, to which he remains an outsider.

My analysis of cultural indifference exemplified in the African encounters of "The Snows of Kilimanjaro" was not designed to revise the many readings that scholarship has produced. Nor was it my intention to counterbalance the reputation that Hemingway's work has achieved during the last decades. By following Müller's call to apply a Rortian reading to Hemingway's literary oeuvre, I am interested in the moral and ecocritical potential that a story set at the foot of the Kilimanjaro in the mid 1930s can hold in the act of reading in the new millennium. The combination of a Rortian reading with ecocritical studies shows that "Snows" can engage the reader in questions of cultural indifference and consequences for the environment. The process of coming to understand that Harry has lived by a lie and has deluded himself into thinking that he was an open-minded cosmopolitan holds a potential to engage the reader in questions of ethical and ecocritical import. The imperatives derived from my reading reveal in Harry what Rorty described as sins of incuriosity and self-satisfaction.

A transcontinental adventure marked by the tiredness of Western civilization, with the emphasis on ready-made encounters of exotic terrains, is likely to be scarred by cultural indifference. My reading of "The Snows of Kilimanjaro" liberates the text from the familiar accusation brought against Hemingway: that he brings an ethnocentric, white racist, and male chauvinist perspective to his characters who inhabit a mythical "wilderness" which, in turn, represents a problematic product of the American post–World War I landscape defined by alienation, lostness, and emptiness. Instead, by combining an ethical and ecocritical approach, the reader is led to address cultural indifference and the city-nature dichotomy as a problem in his or her very own time. With Cole Porter, Hemingway seems to tell us:

> You come to Africa, you come to play;
> You have a wonderful time, you go away.
> And, from then on, you talk of Kilimanjaro knowingly;
> You may know Kilimanjaro, you don't know Ngàje Ngài.

Notes

[1] http://www.kirurumu.com/camps_and_lodges/Hemingway's%20Camp.htm (accessed 10 November 2008).

[2] http://www.smh.com.au/travel/endangered-sites-see-boom-in-tourism-of-doom-20090206-7zbv.html (accessed 18 November 2010).

[3] The return of ethics into literary studies has been proposed at the end of the 1980s by philosophers such as Rorty, Eldridge, and Nussbaum. In literature, scholars such as Booth and Harpham have been crucial in reintroducing ethics to literary analysis.

[4] See Aiken, 4; Lynn, 242 ff.; and Fiedler, 65–117.

[5] If the ongoing concern with ethics is indeed what Theo D'Haen calls in Freudian terms "the return of the repressed" (195), the question remains, what is fresh and productive in the current debate? More concretely: what kind of new insight can be gained from Hemingway's African writings? After postmodernism's nonfunctional and playful approach to literature in the laboratory of literary criticism it comes as no surprise that the pendulum swings in a different direction where a renewed interest in the outside world unavoidably leads to a discussion of moral

issues. Literary scholars, however, should not work, in the words of Patrick Parrinder, "in an artistic vacuum" when they proclaim yet another "theoretical revolution" (13). When in close contact with literary objects, theory and criticism can be used as tools to illuminate ethical concerns.

6 See, for example, Josephs on "Hemingway's Spanish Sensibility" (221–42). Recent publications such as Hilary Hemingway's picture book about Cuba show that the heroic self-fashioning of Hemingway has not lost its fascination. And even in the latest *Cambridge Companion to Hemingway*, writers consistently exploit Hemingway's biography to draw conclusions regarding his aesthetic accomplishments. Thus, the book remains a companion to the artist rather than his writings. Müller, who has worked extensively on the connections between Hemingway's biography, his artistic aspirations, and his work in a book-length study, *Ernest Hemingway*, has successfully resisted the temptation to equate Hemingway the writer with the fictional protagonists of his stories.

7 In "Humiliation and Solidarity," Rorty accused those American fellow-citizens who supported president Bush's war against Iraq of being incurious regarding global issues. With Jürgen Habermas and Jacques Derrida, Rorty agrees that Europe must counterbalance the American hegemony in order to strive for a global confederation. He calls on Europe to activate a kind of idealism that America has lost. Namely, to create a cosmopolitan order based on the international law (*Völkerrecht*) and to defend that idealism against competing agendas. Here may also be a clue for a critical approach to Frederic Henry's fight for the Italian war effort during World War I in *A Farewell to Arms* (1929) or Robert Jordan's involvement in the Spanish Civil War of 1936–1939 in *For Whom the Bell Tolls* (1940).

8 See, for example, Fleming, 76–83. Friedman has recently pointed out and summarized the textual overlapping between Hemingway's biography and the artistic integrity of Harry in his essay "Harry or Ernest?" See also the correspondence between Hemingway and his editor regarding disappointing reports about *Green Hills of Africa* and the reception history of "The Snows of Kilimanjaro" and "The Short Happy Life of Francis Macomber" (Bruccoli, 222–41).

9 Of course, Harry is no modern day Daniel Boone frontiersman or carrier of myth-narratives about the process of leaving the imprints of civilization on the "untouched" American soil. However, Harry recreates the excitement of facing natural forces, overcoming "wilderness," and laying claim on Kilimanjaro — if only for himself.

10 Ecohistorian William Cronon has equated "wilderness" with a "flight from history" and an "escape from responsibility" (484–85).

11 The final scene leads Harry to the "House of God," the summit of Kilimanjaro, and, despite its dreamlike quality, allows him to have a triumphant epiphany. Critics overemphasized the elaborate psychological struggle and dramatic power that Hemingway derives from dissolving the orderly pattern of chronological time and the fragmented memories interspersed as interior monologues throughout the story. Here, the reader gets a glimpse of Harry as a man of "undeniable sensitivity, passionately alive to people, places, and experience" (Waldhorn, 145).

12 As Lemke points out, Hemingway worked the white fascination with "primitivist modernism" into the protagonist Catherine in *The Garden of Eden*. When

Catherine tries to make herself "darker and darker" she tries to achieve two purposes: to distinguish herself from other white people in her social surroundings, and to become more sexually attractive to her husband. With reference to Toni Morrison's *Playing in the Dark* it becomes clear that the underlying function of such references to blackness and the fictional fabrication of a black persona becomes a projection of "white desire and fear" (Lemke, 10).

[13] Douglas's murals, *Aspects of Negro Life,* on which he worked since 1933, were exhibited at the Texas World Fair at the same time Hemingway's two famous short stories about his African encounters appeared.

[14] I have pointed out the linguistic barriers in more detail in my article "'You Don't Know Paree!' Cultural Indifference." James Hinkle pointed out the struggle that Hemingway had with French and Spanish during the process of writing *The Sun Also Rises*. Looking closely at the original typescript that Hemingway sent to Scribner's on April 24, 1926, Hinkle remarked that compared to his unreliable spelling of words in English, "in French and Spanish his spelling was worse" (49).

[15] Mayer has detailed how Hemingway fashions a seemingly authentic travel experience into an African fantasy. Regarding the main protagonist in "The Short Happy Life," she reconnects the white male with Edgar Rice Burrough's *Tarzan of the Apes* and thus strips Hemingway's story of its realist African setting (248).

[16] Hays notes the resemblance between this ending and the ending of Ambrose Bierce's "An Occurrence at Owl Creek" (88).

[17] As Ross argues in her analysis of the Nick Adams stories set in Michigan, Hemingway relies on a mythic form of wilderness that in a Barthian sense is "parasitically empty" (24). His impoverished concept of wilderness becomes apparent in "The Big Two-Hearted River," where the fictive rendering of the Upper Peninsula of Michigan provides the backdrop for a paradoxical loss and regeneration of Nick Adams.

[18] Buell addressed the issue of antithesis and symbiosis in theoretical terms in a talk during the conference "Transcultural Spaces: The Challenges of Urbanity, Ecology, and the Environment in the New Millennium" at the John F. Kennedy Institute for North American Studies (30 Oct.–1 Nov. 2008), organized by Stefan Brandt and Frank Mehring.

[19] Quoted from an unpublished manuscript based on a talk Buell gave during the conference "Transcultural Spaces." I am grateful for Lawrence Buell for permission to quote from an early version of his talk.

[20] See The Ohio State University School of Earth Sciences, http://www.geology.ohio-state.edu/news_detail.php?newsId=1 (accessed 2 November 2008).

[21] According to studies on the Kilimanjaro ice fields conducted by Sheffield University in the 1950s, industrialization is not the only cause for climate change. The blame also falls on uncontrolled exploitation of planetary resources, a general indifference towards the effects of global pollution, and a slummification of the world. *Kilimanjaro: A Complete Trekker's Guide* warns those who wish to see Kilimanjaro as Hemingway did — "'great, high, and unbelievably white in the sun'" — need to hurry up (Stewart, 104). These trekkers, world travelers, and adventure seekers from Western civilizations feed the Kilimanjaro tourist industry,

which, in turn, adds to the production of greenhouse gases and waste. Their ever-increasing presence undermines the very dream of purity and cultural authenticity that is at the heart of the climbing experience.

The local communities around Kilimanjaro rely on the Hemingway tourist industry, which has taken advantage of the popularity of Hemingway's works to create, for example, Leland's *A Guide to Hemingway's Paris* (1989), or to set up safari trips promoted via the internet under the name of Hemingway. In the "Bibliography and Further Reading" section of *Kilimanjaro: A Complete Trekker's Guide*, Stewart argues that Hemingway's short story is one of the most celebrated and famous accounts of the area (250). To add to the superficial quality of the connection between authenticity and Hemingway's writings on Kilimanjaro, the name of Hemingway is misspelled consistently throughout the book as "Hemmingway."

[22] A recent travel guide to Kilimanjaro, Africa's highest mountain, encourages its audience by announcing that "it is possible to reach the 5895m summit without any technical climbing ability" (Stewart, back cover). Thus, it encourages would-be tourist mountaineers to engage in the fiction of an adventurous African encounter like the one Harry had hoped for.

Works Cited

Aiken, Conrad. "Review of *The Sun Also Rises*." *New York Herald Tribune Books*, 31 October 1926, 4.

Beegel, Susan F. "Conclusion: The Critical Reputation of Ernest Hemingway." In Donaldson, *The Cambridge Companion to Hemingway*, 269–300.

Bode, Christoph. "How Can Literary Texts Matter?" In *Why Literature Matters: Theories and Functions of Literature*, edited by Rüdiger Ahrens and Laurenz Volkmann, 87–100. Heidelberg: Winter, 1996.

Booth, Wayne C. *The Company We Keep: An Ethics of Fiction*. Berkeley and Los Angeles: U of California P, 1988.

Brasch, James D., and Joseph Sigman. *Hemingway's Library: A Composite Record*. New York: Garland, 1981.

Brown, A. Samler. *The South and East African Year Book and Guide*. Edited for the Union Castle Mail Steamship Company. 39th ed. London: Sampson Low Marston, 1934.

Bruccoli, Matthew J., with the assistance of Robert W. Trogdon. *The Only Thing That Counts: The Ernest Hemingway-Maxwell Perkins Correspondence 1925–1947*. New York: Scribner's, 1996.

Buell, Lawrence. *The Future of Environmental Criticism: Environmental Crisis and Literary Imagination*. Oxford: Blackwell, 2005.

Cronon, William. "The Trouble with Wilderness, or Getting Back to the Wrong Nature." In *The Great New Wilderness Debate*, edited by J. Baird Callicott and Michael P. Nelson, 471–99. Athens: U of Georgia P, 1998.

Davis, Mike. *Planet of Slums*. London: Verso, 2006.

D'haen, Theo. "The Return of the Repressed: Ethics and Aesthetics in Postmodern American Fiction of the 80s." In *Ethics and Aesthetics: The Moral Turn of Postmodernism*, edited by Gerhard Hoffmann and Alfred Hornung, 195–207. Heidelberg: Universitätsverlag Winter, 1996.

Donaldson, Scott, ed. *The Cambridge Companion to Hemingway*. Cambridge: Cambridge UP, 1996.

Eldridge, Richard. *On Moral Personhood: Philosophy, Literature, Criticism, and Self-Understanding*. Chicago: U of Chicago P, 1989.

Fiedler, Leslie A. "The Jew in the American Novel." In *To the Gentiles*. New York: Stein & Day, 1972.

Fleming, Robert E. *The Face in the Mirror: Hemingway's Writers*. Tuscaloosa: U of Alabama P, 1994.

Fluck, Winfried. "Imaginary Space; Or, Space as Aesthetic Object." In *Space in America. Theory — History — Culture*, edited by Klaus Benesch and Kerstin Schmidt, 25–40. Amsterdam: Rodopi, 2005.

Friedman, Norman. "Harry or Ernest? The Unresolved Ambiguity in 'The Snows of Kilimanjaro.'" In *Creative and Critical Approaches to the Short Story*, edited by Noel Harold Kaylor, Jr., 359–73. Lewiston, NY: Edwin Mellen Press, 1996.

Harpham, Geoffrey G. *Getting it Right: Language, Literature, and Ethics*. Chicago: U of Chicago P, 1992.

Hays, Peter L. *Ernest Hemingway*. New York: Continuum, 1990.

Hemingway, Ernest. *Death in the Afternoon*. 1932. Reprint, New York: Scribner's, 1935.

———. *The Garden of Eden*. New York: Scribner's, 1986.

———. *The Green Hills of Africa*. 1935. Reprint, New York: Simon & Schuster, 1996.

———. *Selected Letters, 1917–1961*, edited by Carlos Baker. New York: Scribner's, 1981.

———. "The Snows of Kilimanjaro." In *The Short Stories of Ernest Hemingway*, 52–77. 1938. Reprint, New York: Scribner's, 1966. First published 1936 in *Esquire*.

———. *The Sun Also Rises*. 1926. Reprint, New York: Scribner's, 1970.

Hemingway, Hilary, with Carlene Brennen. *Hemingway in Cuba*. New York: Rugged Land, 2003.

Hinkle, James. "'Dear Mr. Scribner' — About the Published Text of *The Sun Also Rises*." *Hemingway Review* 6, no. 1 (1986): 43–64.

Iser, Wolfgang. *The Act of Reading: A Theory of Aesthetic Response*. Baltimore: Johns Hopkins UP, 1978.

Josephs, Allen. "Hemingway's Spanish Sensibility." In Donaldson, *The Cambridge Companion to Hemingway*, 221–42.

Larsen, Richard B. "Imaginary Heaven, African Hell in 'The Snows of Kilimanjaro.'" *JAISA: The Journal of the Association for the Interdisciplinary Study of the Arts* 2, no. 2 (1997): 45–51.

Lawrence, D. H. *Studies in Classic American Literature*. 1923. Reprint, New York: Viking Press, 1984.

Leland, John. *A Guide to Hemingway's Paris.* Chapel Hill: Algonquin Books, 1989.
Lemke, Sieglinde. *Primitivist Modernism. Black Culture and the Origins of Transatlantic Modernism.* Oxford: Oxford UP, 1998.
Lynn, Kenneth S. *Hemingway.* Cambridge: Harvard UP, 1987.
Mayer, Ruth. "The White Hunter: Edgar Rice Burroughs, Ernest Hemingway, Clint Eastwood, and the Act of Acting Male in Africa." In *Subverting Masculinity: Hegemonic and Alternative Versions of Masculinity in Contemporary Culture,* edited by Russell West and Frank Lay, 247–65. Amsterdam: Rodopi, 2000.
Mehring, Frank. "'You Don't Know Paree!' Cultural Indifference in Hemingway's *The Sun Also Rises.*" In *Aesthetic Transgressions: Modernity, Liberalism, and the Function of Literature: Festschrift für Winfried Fluck zum 60. Geburtstag,* edited by Thomas Claviez, Ulla Haselstein, and Sieglinde Lemke, 337–60. Heidelberg: Universitätsverlag Winter, 2006.
Mencken, H. L. *Prejudices.* Third Series. New York: Knopf, 1922.
Meyers, Jeffrey. *Hemingway: A Biography.* New York: Harper & Row, 1985.
Moddelmog, Debra A. "Re-Placing Africa in 'The Snows of Kilimanjaro': The Intersecting Economies of Capitalist-Imperialism and Hemingway Biography." In *New Essays on Hemingway's Short Fiction,* edited by Paul Smith, 111–36. Cambridge: Cambridge UP, 1998.
Morrison, Toni. *Playing in the Dark: Whiteness and the Literary Imagination.* Cambridge: Harvard UP, 1992.
Müller, Kurt. *Ernest Hemingway: Der Mensch. Der Schriftsteller. Das Werk.* Darmstadt: Wissenschaftliche Buchgesellschaft, 1999.
———. "Modernist Point of View Technique and the Ethics of Reading: A Rortian Approach to Ernest Hemingway." In *Aesthetic Transgressions: Modernity, Liberalism, and the Function of Literature: Festschrift für Winfried Fluck zum 60. Geburtstag,* edited by Thomas Claviez, Ulla Haselstein, and Sieglinde Lemke, 337–60. Heidelberg: Universitätsverlag Winter, 2006.
Nussbaum, Martha. *Love's Knowledge: Essays on Philosophy and Literature.* New York: Oxford UP, 1990.
Parrinder, Patrick. *The Failure of Theory: Essays on Criticism and Contemporary Fiction.* Brighton: Harvester Press, 1987.
Porter, Cole. "You Don't Know Paree." In *Americans in Paris: A Literary Anthology,* edited by Adam Gopnik, 344. New York: Library of America, 2004.
Roosevelt, Theodore. *African Game Trails: An Account of the African Wanderings of an American Hunter-Naturalist.* London: Murray, 1910.
Rorty, Richard. *Contingency, Irony, and Solidarity.* Cambridge: Cambridge UP, 1989.
———. "Redemption from Egotism: James and Proust as Spiritual Exercises." *Telos* 3, no. 3 (2001): 243–63.

———. "Der Roman als Mittel zur Erlösung aus der Selbstbezogenheit." In *Dimensionen ästhetischer Erfahrung*, edited by Joachim Küpper and Christoph Menke, 49–66. Frankfurt am Main: Suhrkamp, 2003.

Ross, Patricia A. *The Spell Cast By Remains: The Myth of Wilderness in Modern American Literature*. New York: Routledge, 2006.

Sanderson, Rena. "Hemingway and Gender History." In Donaldson, *The Cambridge Companion to Hemingway*, 170–96.

Sieverts, Thomas. *Zwischenstadt — Inzwischen Stadt: Entdecken Begreifen, Verändern*. Wuppertal: Müller & Busmann, 2005.

Slotkin, Richard. "Myth and the Production of History." In *Ideology and Classic American Literature*, edited by Sacvan Bercovitch and Myra Jehlen, 70–90. Cambridge: Cambridge UP, 1986.

Stewart, Alexander. *Kilimanjaro: A Complete Trekker's Guide*. Milnthorpe, Cumbria: Cicerone Press, 2004.

Young, Philip. *Ernest Hemingway: A Reconsideration*. Rev. ed. New York: Harcourt, Brace, & World, 1966.

Waldhorn, Arthur. *A Reader's Guide to Ernest Hemingway*. Syracuse: Syracuse UP, 2002.

III: On Religion and Death

8: Memorial Landscapes: Hemingway's Search for Indian Roots

Philip H. Melling

HEMINGWAY WENT TO KENYA in 1953 to explore and understand his tribal past. It was a brave and intellectually curious journey, but it ended in confusion and, in the telling, became subject to the fantasies and inventions that Hemingway was prone to throughout his career. In a letter to Robert M. Brown written three years after the safari, he described his initiation with the Wakamba tribe, boasting that the challenge he had set himself had been fully achieved: "I was the first and only white man or 1/8 Indian who was ever a Kamba," he announced proudly, "and it is not like President Coolidge being given a war bonnet by a tame Blackfoot or Shoshone."[1] Hemingway talked a lot about his Indian blood, but without managing to prove that he knew how to trace the bloodline back to its source, or, indeed, that he was arithmetically correct in claiming for himself "a Cheyenne great-great-grandmother" (hardly one-eighth, more like one-sixteenth) and a Cheyenne son (*Selected Letters*, 695, 679).

Critics, nonetheless, remain intrigued by Hemingway's claims and refer their readers to his "Indian-consciousness" and "lifelong interest" in the Indian tribes (Lewis, 200–201), from northern Michigan to the Wind River Range. They also note the multiple references in his letters to his Cheyenne background and the ancestral origin of his "complicated blood" (*Selected Letters*, 681). Hemingway's interest in Indian affairs had a scholarly base and throughout his life he was fascinated by the work of anthropologists and writers who established themselves as pioneers in the field of primitive modernism: Ruth Benedict, Melville Herskovits, Sir James Frazer, and Sigmund Freud.[2] Their work helped him understand the aspirations and syncretic beliefs of tribal people in the different parts of the world that he visited. But it was a curious legacy. Important as these writers were, the role they played was sometimes inconsistent, their influence leavened by the disparate agendas that tended to distract him and made him feel, as they did during the time he spent in Africa in the 1950s, "very mixed up" (*Under Kilimanjaro*, 132).

The complication of primitivism set in early in Hemingway's life. In his attack on Sherwood Anderson in *Torrents of Spring* (1926), Hemingway showed himself to be deeply skeptical of the fashionable assumptions that underpinned the longing for the primitive. At the same time, Hemingway's decision to distance himself from the contemporary celebration of the noble savage took place in a kind of separate dimension from his own burgeoning interest in primitive modernism. Hemingway was particularly interested in James Frazer, a writer who devoted his intellectual life to explaining the dominance of the primitive past in the cultural traditions and dilemmas of the present. Frazer's *The Golden Bough,* published in successive editions between 1890 and 1915, was, says John B. Vickery, the preeminent cultural and intellectual work of the late nineteenth and early twentieth century and "the most encyclopedic treatment of primitive life available to the English-speaking world" (4). Hemingway owned several copies of *The Golden Bough* and was well read in the ritual objects and practices of tribal societies and ancestral religions. The ceremonies of Indian and African tribal religions, as well as the spiritual practices of Cuban *Santería,* suited his superstitious nature — the dressing up, the out-of-body experiences and precognition, the rabbits' feet and occasional fondness for earrings, the need to touch wood three times, the use of numbers, and the prayers for help (Fuentes, 84). At the Finca Vigía, Hemingway showed a fondness for the "divine mascots" and figurative statues that, according to Migene Gonzalez-Whippler, are often suggestive of primordial life in *Santería.* He was also fond of different types of stones, especially the *chinas pelonas* and *otanes* used to attract the attention of the *orishas* (spirits or deities) and thought to contain magnetic properties. In apparent emulation of a common practice in *Santería,* Hemingway carried his favorite stones around with him as if he was seeking the approval of a "spiritual guide" and acknowledging the *orishas* with a "good-luck charm" (Gonzalez-Wippler, 18). Hemingway strongly believed, as Jeffrey Meyers puts it, "that the primitive past influenced the psychology of the present" and his familiarity with totemic places — Kilimanjaro, the Gulf Stream, and the Indian swamp — is clear evidence of a long-standing interest in totemistic societies and the sanctuaries and symbols that sustained their religions ("Primitivism," 305).

Hemingway's travels and concomitant reading took him on an anthropological journey that stretched from northern Michigan (with the Ottawa and Ojibwa Indians) to Northwest Cuba (where he lived for over twenty years) to the tribal reserves of the Masai and Wakamba in East Africa. His desire to learn from Africans and Indians and to expand, as he put it, his "swamp" "knowledge" (*UK,* 439),[3] began in the virgin forests of the upper Michigan peninsula where, as a boy, he first came into contact with the tribal legacies and histories of the Ojibwa and learned to appreciate the relationship between the sacred place and the supernatural occasion. Hemingway took this sense of the sacred with him to Cuba, and, through his long exposure to Afro-Cuban religions such as *Santería*, he became aware of the shared belief structures and understandings that underlay different tribal and totemistic faiths. In *Santería* he saw the way African beliefs had been retained and adapted as a way of honoring the ancient orishas of African life. At his home in San Francisco de Paula on the outskirts of Havana, he also witnessed at first hand the "syncretisation" of African belief (Gonzalez-Kirby, 42) and the tribal interactions between primitive communities that shared one another's ancestral customs. In this quasi-African setting Hemingway became convinced of the principle that lay behind James Frazer's analysis in *The Golden Bough*; namely, that totemistic and faith-based communities saw themselves as being "of one blood, descendants of a common ancestor" and therefore "bound together by a common obligation to each other and by a common faith in the totem" (Frazer, 2–3). During this period Hemingway's interest in tribal art and sacred icons[4] played a central role in furthering his interest in tribal faiths. The time he spent in Cuba allowed him to embrace an informal philosophy that brought together his Indian ideas and their African equivalents in the Yoruba religion of *Santería*.

Hemingway's desire to reinscribe himself within the context of his tribal roots reached its apotheosis on his second safari to Kenya in 1953. The manuscript of his visit, the 850 pages of part handwritten and part typed text that he left uncompleted in February 1956, is a serious attempt to investigate the ecumenical practices of the Wakamba tribe with whom he lived and hunted. *Under Kilimanjaro* is Hemingway's last attempt to provide the reader and himself with a framework for understanding the "unfinished business" of his earlier life (*UK*, 16). The book is a study of iconic landscapes, the people who live and worship in them, and the way in which they preserve their ancient traditions and customs, focused on animals and gods, while living in the modern age. Two things in particular appear to stand out. First, the way in which Native American Indian styles of worship and religion seem to echo the cultural observances of Africa; and second, the extent to which the sacred domains of a tribal people demand acknowledgement as places of social and ceremonial importance.

In Hemingway's early work, his sense of the ecumenical was allied with the political convictions of an anti-imperialist. Hemingway's belief that indigenous communities and tribal lands were increasingly at risk from exploitation and decimation was driven home by his observations as a freelance correspondent for the *Toronto Daily Star*. The emergence of a radical, pro-nativist sensibility is evident as early as 1922. In Serbia, for example, he notes how a love of land can make men fight wars. His concern for those who have lost their land in the Balkan conflict echoes a much deeper concern for the Native American population of the United States. As he puts it:

> It is a matter of land, of fields of corn and yellowing tobacco, of flocks of sheep and herds of cattle, of heaps of yellow pumpkins in the shocked corn, of beech groves and peat smoke from chimneys, a matter of mine and thine that is the cause of all just wars — and there can never be peace in the Balkans as long as one people holds the lands of another people — no matter what the political excuse may be. ("Balkans," 225)

Hemingway's ideas on the political and economic imperatives that lead to the pursuit of territory and what Secretary of State Robert Lansing had once referred to as "the scramble for markets" changed dramatically during the 1920s (Lansing).[5] Hemingway became increasingly receptive to a postcolonial critique of empire. This critique was directed against the "African passion" of muscular Christianity, imperialist rhetoric, religious nationalism, and xenophobic adventure, all of which Hemingway's early mentor, Theodore Roosevelt, had come to personify. By the 1920s the appeal of Roosevelt's views on imperial expansion had begun to fade and Hemingway was starting to question the political imperatives on which great power politics tended to rely. He came to believe that Roosevelt was politically suspect in several ways. First, he disliked the need for countries to expand commercially, if not territorially, into the underdeveloped regions of the world (the so-called waste spaces). Second, he objected to the idea that countries like the United States should be able to transform indigenous landscapes into socially neutral places where the local people were prevented from practicing their tribal laws and indigenous customs.

The change in Hemingway's thinking on Africa occurred gradually, and it coincided with and emerged out of his intellectual coming of age in the early 1920s. Throughout his life Hemingway held many different versions of Africa in his head and not all of them by any means were applied consistently, but in the 1920s two in particular — one rooted in a political critique of French colonialism, the other a product of his burgeoning interest in cultural anthropology — far exceeded what he had learned about the African continent as a child in Oak Park.

In his 1922 review of René Maran's *Batouala* ("Black Novel a Storm Center"), Hemingway mounts a brief but vigorous challenge to the Roosevelt doctrine of "civilized domination" (Ryan, 76). René Maran was an Afro-Caribbean with years of experience in France's colonial civil service. Hemingway describes his *Batouala* as a "great novel" — it received the Prix Goncourt, the most sought after prize in French literature, for 1922 — that gives the reader an authentic sense of what it's like to "smell the smells of the village . . . [to] eat its food . . . and [to] die there." René Maran, he says, allows his reader to "see the white man as the black man sees him" ("Black Novel," 112). Hemingway is fascinated by Maran's anthropological analysis of an African village caught between the rituals of an ancient world and the demands of great power politics and empire building. The characters in *Batouala* are faithful participants in the festivals and traditions of the African village. These festivals mark the transfer of tribal authority and the revival of sacred powers during the ceremonial initiation. In primitive religions, says Vickery, such ceremonies culminate in the "ritualistic" killing of a sacred king, an ancient fertility rite in which the king's death coincides with a loss of strength "at the conclusion of a reign of preordained length." In tribal society, says Vickery, such a death is necessary to preserve the "sacred spirit" from "decay" and to pass on an inheritance so that "the continuity of power [is] maintained unimpaired" (50, 51).

In *Batouala*, Maran introduces the reader to the fertility ritual of a "peaceful" village as it prepares for the expected death of an elderly king. It is festival time in the Banda country and the novel shows us the tribe's preparation for the feast of the "Ga'nzas" (35), a nine-day celebration climaxing with a collection of dances known as "the yangba," a sexually explicit dramatization of tribal life. Here we witness the coming of age of a new generation, some of whom enter adulthood through circumcision and excision and other acts of physical mutilation. Pain gives way to erotic displays of sexual ambition. Through dance and music the feast of the Ga'nzas reenacts the archetypal myths of initiation and kingship. In a provocative display of sexuality the dancers conjure up the buried, regenerative power of the earth, and in a highly animated, theatrical performance they bring to the surface the "hidden joy" (34) of a mythic past and the latent fertility of the tribal woods.

In the ceremony that Maran describes, the reader is brought face to face with the figure of the dying god, recalling Frazer's description of the ancient practice of killing the sacred king in order to bring fertility to the earth, as detailed in *The Dying God*, the fourth volume of *The Golden Bough*. According to Vickery, this rite occurred "either when the king's 'strength' appeared to be failing him or at the conclusion of a reign of preordained length," or when the fecundity of the earth was under threat (50). This "rite of expulsion," continues Vickery, "was regarded as a statement of profound veneration" by followers of the king, an act not of murder but of primitive magic which signified on the part of his worshippers a desire to observe the "divine spirit" in a reborn world (51).

Maran refuses to allow his dancers to consummate their ritualistic desires and in so doing he provides the reader with a political commentary on the imperialist practice of the outside world. In Equatorial Africa the ancient dances of initiation and renewal lose their magic the moment the French military intervene. The traditions of the "ancestors" are undone by the "thudding of gunbutts" (Maran, 88). The old priest king — referred to by the French as a "nigger bastard" (88) — fails to satisfy the aspirations of the tribe and dies from the effects of too much

Pernod, which the French authorities introduce. The absence of ritualistic death frustrates the tribe and in the changed atmosphere the French "boundjous" are accused of having "enslaved" (70) the village and creating divisions between the tribes. The tribes that "used to be happy before the arrival of the 'boundjous'" are now considered "no more than slaves." The victims of bribery, economic exploitation, and the collaborative practices of the "tourougou," the villagers see themselves as "taxable flesh" (108, 75). Unable to take his father's place as the head of the tribe, Batouala dies, undone by tribal "ambush" (117) and sexual politics, his position in the community further compromised by military policy. Batouala's father is "planted in the ground" in accordance with the ancient ceremonies, but in spite of the possibility of "posthumous reprisals" (92) the community is demoralized, its "sacred dreams" thwarted to the point of desperation. The social aspirations of the village change. "The young," says Maran, "and in general all those who served the whites" now look on "custom with derision" (93).

It is still possible to find the political and anthropological remains of Maran's *Batouala* lodged in the entrails of Ernest Hemingway's *Under Kilimanjaro*, the account of his second safari to East Africa in 1953. The two texts are considerably different, and Hemingway has abandoned some of the political idealism that characterizes his life in Cuba and the support he gives to Fidel Castro in the later years of the 1950s. Nonetheless, he does exhibit a real concern for the tribal struggle against colonial oppression in Kenya and the failure of imperialism to serve those whose interests it claims to represent. Instead of the Banda tribe we see the Masai and Wakamba struggling to survive amid a welter of "changes" (*UK*, 43) in British colonial practice, their ancient traditions and livelihoods constantly threatened by trophy hunters and nouveau riche elites.[6] Hemingway complains about "the white people [who] always took the other people's lands away from them and put them on a reservation where they could go to hell and be destroyed as though they were in a concentration camp" (*UK*, 260). On these "reserves . . . there was much do-gooding about how the natives now called the Africans were administered." What this means, in effect, is that traditional "hunters were not allowed to hunt and the warriors were not allowed to make war" for fear it might damage the corporate interests who invest heavily in "one of the greatest rackets of all, the safari swindle" (260–61). There is also a concern that tribal hunting might scare off the "alleged sportsmen and their wives," whose behavior is lacking in "certain ethical standards" (46). These people come to Africa for the "picture lions that are accustomed to being fed and photographed" and are therefore "easily killed" with telescopic sights and "shocking pieces of ordnance" like the .300 Weatherby Magnum. In Kenya "the hunting of dangerous game" has been "corrupted and made easy"; it has become, like the country's political administration, "an invention of the whites who are temporarily occupying the country" (358). As an observer, Hemingway is angry at the way a warrior ethos has degenerated under white rule and is now subject to tight controls: "the Wakamba, who had always hunted game in the Masai country for meat, were not permitted to hunt nor take any beasts," he comments, and are themselves "hunted down as poachers by the Game Scouts," a policy that breeds tribal hatred and division, as the Game Scouts are "also, mostly, Wakamba" (129).

As an honorary or acting game warden Hemingway is convinced he can relinquish his celebrity status and behave in accordance with Wakamba tradition. From time to time he tries to do this. "The only laws are tribal laws and I was a mzee," he says at one point, "which means an elder as well as still having the status of a warrior" (*UK*, 354). In his opinion, the British are "elders" of a different kind. Although they "govern in cold blood and legal procedures," as the tribal elders do, they lack all memory or understanding of what it is to be a tribal warrior, of that vital stage of tribal life that the tribal elders know full well (23–24). The Wakamba are caught in this type of foreign rule. Not only have they lost their game to the safari hunters who are protected by the British for the revenue they generate, but they are also reduced to hunting on the Masai reserves. As a mzee, this is unacceptable to Hemingway. The colonial administration, he says, has lost its moral authority to govern in the interests of the people — especially the Wakamba, who have always remained "completely loyal to the British" even during the Mau Mau uprising (130).[7]

In 1953 Hemingway had wanted to go "somewhere" (as he wrote later to Buck Lanham) where they "don't have white peoples" (*Selected Letters*, 84). But he was disappointed in East Africa, which, in the early 1950s, was crowded with tourists and safari hunters. Hemingway despised the "ignorance and stupidity" (*UK*, 277) of this trophy brigade who lacked any real knowledge, in his opinion, of the traditions of the hunt. Trophy hunting was no longer the only thing of importance in his life. By the 1950s Hemingway saw Africa in a different way and was greatly attracted to the sacred world ignored by the hunters, a world consisting of birds, trees, animals, swamps, and the Holy Mountain, Kilimanjaro. "The time of shooting beasts for trophies [is] long past" (116), he claims, and the act of hunting as a faith or "duty" (231) must now be undertaken "cleanly" (116) and "honorably" (117). The animals of Africa could no longer be regarded as a form of amusement, as they often were in *Green Hills of Africa*, and could only be killed on the basis of strict "ethical standards." For this reason, his involvement with the "marauding lion" (44) and the "ritual leopard" (104) requires an acceptance of tribal duties underpinned by a system of "Beliefs" (271). The lion, in particular, is a "great" (42) creature endowed with the power of a sacred totem. It is a talismanic object and its home in the papyrus swamp of the Kimana region is a talismanic place, a sanctuary of great significance in the animal kingdom.

In *Under Kilimanjaro*, the swamp lies at the epicenter of an ancient ecological system. It is where many of the forests' creatures — leopard, lion, elephant, and baboon — "retire" (136) and hide — and the place from which they hunt and kill. The swamp is also close to where the Hemingways decide to set up camp. In other words, it is a place of refuge, as much for Ernest as it is for the animals he likes to study. It has a devotional importance in his life and it is one of those "mystical countries that are a part of one's childhood" (23). As such, its evocations are beautiful as well as occasionally disturbing. Normally, Hemingway contemplates his involvement with it from a "small plain in the shade of the big thorn trees at the edge of the swamp at the foot of the mountain" and he tries to make sense of it with "a child's heart, a child's honesty and a child's freshness and nobility" (23). In this mystical state he becomes, from time to time, aware of corresponding landscapes and parallel worlds. Some he may have read about, like the Indian swamps of Massachusetts; others he has known from personal experience in upstate Michigan.

Hemingway's stories "The Last Good Country," "Big Two-Hearted River," and "Now I Lay Me" are testimony to the extraordinary, haunting beauty of the swamps, as well as their importance as places of retreat and Indian acquaintance. They also show us that marshes and swamps are peculiarly susceptible to the phantasmal power of historical events, especially so when places of refuge and sanctuary are violated by interventions and acts of trespass.[8] Hemingway came to regard the swamp as a repository of knowledge and supernatural life. As a person who believed in the primacy of first-hand knowledge, he came to recognize that whatever he was looking for was under his feet: rooted in with an ancestral wisdom shared by the tribes. As Christopher Ondaatje reminds us, the Kimana swamp lay within the shadow of a mountain whose influence was beyond dispute:

> The Masai people view the mountain as holy, and the Chaga, the tribe who live on its slopes, believe its heights to be the home of Ruwa, the sun god, the great protector and provider who created nature, man and beasts. The high, flat summit known as Kibo is particularly revered by the Chaga, because it is thought to bring rain. When they wish to pray to Ruwa, they face the mountain; and their dead are buried with heads pointing towards it. (18–19)

The traditional way in which people hunt in the shadow of the mountain, and the way in which they express their relationship with the animals of the swamp, are of unique value to Ernest Hemingway. His decision to kill the lion and the leopard in accordance with ethical practice sets him apart from the trophy hunters who hit the reserves with "shocking, bone-shattering, tissue-destroying" weapons with telescopic sights and drive around in hunting cars, killing animals in ways that strip the hunt of spiritual feeling (*UK*, 276). For Hemingway, as for Maran, the hunt, when conducted properly, is a "wonderful thing" (Maran, 146). Hemingway shares with Maran that feeling of "hidden joy" that comes from trampling through the "lush growth" and "brush of the Kanyas" (Maran, 115) on a day when the hunter has nothing to rely on except his own skill. As Maran put it:

> One hunts what one finds. The hunt is the game of the strong, the fight of man against beast, of skill against brute strength. It prepares for war. Prove who can his ability, his courage, his vigor, his endurance. When chasing the beast one has wounded, it is necessary to be able to run a long time without tiring or getting winded, and to be sure of eye, agile of foot, and lithe. (129)

For Maran, "a hunting day is a festival day" in which those who participate are "crowned with feathers," their bodies "covered with red wood and greased with oil." His lament for the "few who truly hunt" (130) tallies with Hemingway's definition of the hunt as a thing of supernatural need. "When you rubbed yourself with lion fat you were," says Hemingway, "a lion in the darkness" (*UK*, 316). The ancient hunt is "a tribal thing" (360), a "ceremony" that takes him back "in the moonlight" to his "imagined" tribal origins in northern Michigan (Schedler, 64). When Hemingway hunts he heads off like an Indian with "soft moccasins" on his feet and two spears across his back (*UK*, 315). Suspended between the actual and the imaginary, he enters a quasi-mystical state in which he begins "to learn about the night" and those other landscapes, both African and Indian, with which he is "brought . . . happily in contact" (316).

This reaching out into what Alma Guillermoprieto describes as an ecumenical or parallel space is a perfect antidote for Hemingway to the pointless "stupidities" (361) of everyday life. It is, says Guillermoprieto, a shamanistic experience and typical of those in Amerindian[9] societies whose "view of the world . . . antecedes the Conquest." In these societies:

> All living beings have animal and/or spirit counterparts endowed with magical powers. These beings, and the universe they occupy, can be seen with our own eyes, provided we know how to read the signs. Frequently, a reader of the signs will have recourse to fasting, dance, or hallucinogens to reveal the parallel universe. This shaman, most often a man, is frequently titled the Speaker, and what he speaks when he is in a trance are messages from the parallel world, as well as the history of the tribe and its heroes, all of which form the chain of continuity that holds the community together — a community that includes both its present members and the ancestors who created it. (64)

Hemingway's attempt to attain the spiritual understanding of a shaman requires that he devote himself to the "spirit" presences of the Masai Mara and acquire scientific understanding of its birds and animals and an anthropological knowledge of its tribes. Denis Zaphiro comments on Hemingway's "contemplative" manner during the time he was on safari and the way Hemingway "loved Africa. He loved to sit in it and watch it. He had a natural knowledge of what animals would do" (Meyers, *Biography*, 501–2). Hemingway was adept at reading "the signs" of a "magical" world, bringing to them his own understanding of wilderness domains. As a reader of landscapes he was able to connect with the world he knew in northern Michigan and those he had read about that lay outside it. In the swamp it was possible to find "every kind of stuff" (*UK*, 19), as he puts it, including the sedimentary deposits of his own life and that of the American people for whom he was seeking to atone publicly.

The importance of reading a landscape from the inside out was an important aesthetic undertaking for Hemingway, especially so when the landscape was difficult to read, but contained information and outward "signs" that revealed something of its absent character.[10] "Signs" were like ancient deposits that, once collected, could open up the implicit identity of the hidden subject. In Hemingway's view, the landscape that was hidden was not dissimilar to the literary text in which much was unsaid or deliberately omitted. In such a text, suggests Beatriz Penas Ibáñez, Hemingway believed that what is seen and encountered (at first sight) can be enriched by that which is recovered "inferentially" from the silences and "pregnant gaps that the writer has carefully left in the text." Hemingway subscribed to this style of writing (his iceberg theory), suggesting that from the one-eighth that is stated, we can deduce the seven-eighths that were omitted (*Death in the Afternoon*, 192). In such texts, Penas Ibáñez argues, "the part omitted from the linguistic surface" is not redundant, but "is truer to life than the actually said." Thus, she adds:

> Unreadability, like invisibility, does not entail inexistence. The watcher's and the reader's imaginations, activated by an incomplete form, can infer the missing portions which although invisible exist and can be retrieved or inferred or reappropriated through personal interpretation. Hemingway's iceberg theory of writing is also a theory of reading, one that seeks to engage readers in a creative kind of reading that matches his own creativity as a writer. (156–57)

Theories of writing and theories of reading coexist in *Under Kilimanjaro*. We are invited to locate invisible worlds that the landscape and its animals represent. Each of these is a "metaphor for the invisible meanings" inside the text "as well as for the hidden, dark, invisible men and women" that inhabit those countries that Hemingway visits and the different histories he opens up (Penas Ibáñez, 157). The African landscape is redolent of hidden possibilities and lives, the fragmented inscriptions of other events, the implicit identities of distant adventures that are buried inside an equivalent world. A narrative of hunting on the "epidermic surface," *Under Kilimanjaro* is also a story whose clues reveal the symbolic importance of what William Adair calls the "interior landscape that lies underneath" (144).

Malcolm Bull describes this type of writing as a challenge to the reader's confidence. When texts are accessible only by way of their "hiddenness," says Bull, the reader is inclined to lose heart. Yet if something is hidden it is not necessarily the case, he argues, that "truth has eluded you and is unattainable." It might also be that "truth is flirting with you, simultaneously offering and withholding" its identity (19–20). In *Under Kilimanjaro* truth flirts with us in different ways, and the masked identities the story invites us to explore — a "marauding" lion whose life, like that of the dying god in *The Golden Bough*, is nearing its end, a leopard whose blood is a reminder of kinship for an old Cherokee, the hidden inscriptions of Indianness in the person of Debba, his Wakamba fiancée — each of these subjects has to be searched for and rooted out. Readers must keep their nerve in the shadows and not expect that the landscape will allow them an easy read. Hemingway, likewise, must keep his own nerve and guard against any reckless tendency to view the safari as a whimsical adventure. His ability to read the signs of the swamp and the movements of the animals that live in the forest will determine the success or failure of the trip.

Hemingway carries the additional burden of sharing the experience with a woman whose instincts are anything but analytical. When Mary uses the word "study" (*UK*, 16) in reference to the swamp, her intentions are to glimpse the lion that Hemingway has promised her and to decide what is needed for a Christmas tree. Her journey through Africa is impulsive rather than scholarly. Her instinct is to skim-read her way through the wilderness, admiring the bits that tend to appeal to her sentimental view of the natural world. Mary's agendas are Western ones. She dreams of visiting the expatriate set in Nairobi and going on trips to Abyssinia and the Belgian Congo (422). She is an avid traveler, but easily bored. A devoted consumer,[11] she doesn't remember products (or even persons) in detail. "I think but I can't remember," she says about the food she eats in Nairobi. "I don't remember," she repeats, when asked by Hemingway about people she has met (408), as if she is incapable of concentrating on anything other than the next adventure with the "Dorset" crowd (Gellhorn, 210).[12] When she asks Hemingway, "Why didn't they let me shoot that easy beautiful lion under the tree that time?" his comment exposes the jagged edges that make their relationship difficult to fathom. Women, he says, make a terrible mess when shooting lions "and the finest blackmaned lion ever shot by a woman had maybe forty shots fired into him.

Afterwards they have the beautiful pictures and then they have to live with the goddamn lion and lie about him to all their friends and themselves the rest of their lives" (*UK*, 16).

In *Under Kilimanjaro*, Mary's attitude to the African wilderness is a peculiar concoction of the utilitarian and the sublime. She admires the swamp because of the quality of its Christmas trees, while the picture lions and other animals are beautiful only in a state of repose. When the landscape of Africa isn't picturesque, it's essentially empty for Mary, and except for its meat has little to recommend it. Socially, the African wilderness is a bleak place and politically it is a dead subject. Mary's Africa is conservative, and good governance depends on white control, technological dominance, and the compliance of the tribes. For this reason possession and ownership are all important. "I have to get him," she says of the lion. "I don't need any help." And, "Everybody has something that they want truly and my lion means everything to me" (16, 19, 128). On safari Mary has an impulsive streak. Where Hemingway is "watchful," "looking back" and listening for sounds that warn him of danger (20), she prefers to charge in or, at least, stand her ground. She hates him for being "so serious and so righteous" and will not tolerate the avoidance tactics that "bore" her to death (21). Although Mary has been "guided and trained and indoctrinated . . . [and] given . . . ethics" by Philip Percival, the white hunter whom Hemingway admires (195), she hasn't been taught a spiritual understanding of the relationship between totemic landscape and sacrificial death. She describes her husband's "primitive" beliefs (271) as "superstitions" and doesn't "like to talk" about faiths that are "complicated" and "very mixed up" (132, 3). Most of all, she disagrees root and branch with his ecumenical tribal religion.

Hemingway describes his religion as a mixture of "tribal law and customs" (*UK*, 23), many of which are taken from Native American folklore and custom. He tells us how they were "revealed" to him in "the foothills of the Wind River Range," part of which is an "exact counterpart" of a mountain close to where they are camping. The "birth" of this "new religion" leaves Mary feeling "nervous" and she has no interest in its "horrible slogans and dreadful secrets" (89). They do not bear comparison with the mystery of Christmas and the birth of the baby Jesus — the focus of her attention once the lion has been shot. There is a knockabout quality to some of these exchanges, and Hemingway tries to relax his reader with gallows humor before he begins the more serious business of propitiation. Mary complains to him, "You get too tribal for your own good," and, "You don't know enough about it to practice it" properly. Hemingway ignores the accusations, merely remarking that "I learn a little every day" (433), indicating that he does not need or seek her approval.[13]

Hemingway struggles to overcome the limitation that Mary imposes on his tribal faith. He does not "want to involve" her in the discovery of tribal correspondences and the synergies that exist between different tribal practices and faiths. He prefers to undertake the investigative journey on his own, sharing with the reader those intimate moments of recollection when the sins he has committed against the tribal place and its "guardian spirit" are truly acknowledged (Frazer, in Jones, 7). We learn, for example, about his spiteful attack on some golden eagles who have fed on the flesh of a favorite horse in the Wind River Range. Hemingway realizes that a price will have to be paid for this dishonor. "I had never seen any animal or bird look at me as the eagle looked," he admits, as he kills one of them. He says that he "could not tell her [Mary] what the eagles meant to me nor why I had killed these three, the last one by smacking his head against a tree down in the timber" (*UK*, 260). Mary's reason for being in Africa is different from his, and his skepticism is fully confirmed when the lion they are hunting is finally shot. Mary reacts with "sorrow" and irritability when Hemingway intervenes to put the animal out of its misery. Her agenda does not recognize the importance of sacrificial gestures or acts of homage and propitiation in sacred domains. Her mind is not on the landscape, but on her trip to Nairobi. In contrast, Hemingway, a studious person, remains in camp to learn what he can from the animals of the forest. Because of his reluctance to travel to other places with her, Mary accuses him of having no "ambition," not knowing that his one true ambition is to "live in a place and have an actual part in the life of it than just see new strange things" (422).

Hemingway tells us clearly that what he sees in the secret places cannot be explained to someone who has never "lain under a juniper bush" *(UK,* 258) and whose sorrow is resistant to a message from the eagles. When he and Debba, his fiancée, visit the Chyulu Hills, he says that "we were all happy that Miss Mary had never been there" (337). Together he and Debba are able to enter a parallel or in-between space, a world spiritually and geographically "suspended between our new African Africa that we had dreamed and invented and the old Africa" that is represented by Miss Mary (419). This is "our country" (337), he says, meaning that what they have found is another of those "childish" places, a countryside he is able to recognize from the visits he has made to Indian country in upstate Michigan and the Wind River Range. Tribal understanding is what makes this state of suspension possible, a visionary facility that, in his opinion, Mary lacks. This complaint reappears in different guises and we don't always know how far to take it. On one occasion Hemingway jokingly suggests that Mary "is handicapped" (89) and lacks the background to understand the spiritual basis of his tribal religion. Even if the comment is made in jest, Hemingway does nothing to qualify the larger sentiment that lies behind it, returning to it in different contexts throughout the book.

Hemingway softens his frustration with those who do not "see" (*UK*, 225), as he does, the hidden inscriptions of Indianness that the birds and animals bring to his life. For him, the "marauding lion" (44) and the "ritual leopard" (104, 105) that live deep in the forest establish an important chain of continuity with the tribal past, both personal and national. Their trails are studied and the unique hiddenness they embody take him beyond the "epidermic surface" of the animal kingdom and into the world of tribal metaphor. Both creatures are condemned to die and Hemingway has no choice but to carry out the wishes of the village. Nevertheless, as acting game warden his actions are always underlined by a basic premise: to know the animals as intimately as he can and to perform his duty without dishonor. The killing is personal. Hemingway feels a kinship with the leopard when he tastes its blood on a splinter of bone. This sense of "familiarity" (327) comes from the mingling of body fluids and reminds the reader of Hemingway's knowledge of an Indian girl he knew in his youth. This wilderness experience in which sexual experience is implicitly recalled (at a hidden depth) is one of the purposes behind his journey. Interestingly, in the stories that recall the blending together of sexuality and tribal activity in the life of Nick Adams this sense of the wild comes alive forcefully, as Susan Beegel tells us, as "an erotic appreciation of nature itself" (96). The link between nature and the erotic life cannot be overstated in the later passages of *Kilimanjaro* in which Hemingway yearns for a more natural setting in order to explore his relationship with Debba, his African girlfriend.

The intensity of wilderness experience, says Hemingway, lies outside the realm of hunting, and time and again we find in his writing a quasi-mythical description of it. As the lion approaches the end of its life, the narrator describes him as an ancient monarch, surveying his kingdom "on the high, yellow, rounded mound with his tail down and his great paws comfortably before him," looking "off across his country to the blue forest and the high white snows of the big mountain" (*UK*, 218). The lion's body is colored by light — "huge black and long tawny gray-gold" (212) — and he is not only beautiful but also "wary and so intelligent. . . . He had been hunted for many years and he was very intelligent" (210, 218). He radiates majesty and kingly dominance. As he watches, the hunters behave like humble subjects, apprehensive and feeling nervous anticipation (212) as they embark upon a palace revolution. The lion's death, unfortunately, does not come from a single, well-placed shot. The "dry whack" (212) of Mary's bullet finds its target, but does little if anything to slow him down, and the lion is felled by a gang of shooters, a victim outnumbered by his attackers. This is not what anyone wants to happen, Hemingway least of all.

Hemingway's insistence on ethical standards and a neatly executed kill is a risky strategy, and because of it the reader is never certain if Hemingway believes he has fulfilled his commission. The mistake has been his, in allowing Mary to assume a proprietary interest in the lion and giving her the lead role on the day of the kill. The dilemma for Hemingway is that Mary has "a certain problem": she tends to shoot higher than she aims, partly because she is so short and partly because she "had a habit, just before she was going to shoot, of rolling up the right sleeve of her bush jacket" (*UK,* 63). Worst of all, she is in a rush to get the job done before Christmas and does not understand the importance of tradition in the killing of the lion. According to Hemingway she does not know about a lot of things, such as, for example, the way the rain falls during a downpour in East Africa. It aggravates him that "she thought she knew," when in fact "nobody could know" what Africa was like and certainly not if they had not lived there or, even worse, had been, since adolescence, "nurtured on the disasters of daily journalism" rather than the "violent . . . spectacle" Africa offers (110–11).

Hemingway goes to bed the night before the hunt worried about Mary's shooting technique and the trajectory of the bullet. The possibility of a sacred violation caused by a brutal or messy death makes him deeply uneasy. He awakes sweating "with the horrors" (*UK,* 119) from terrible nightmares that suggest that he is worried by something much more profound and difficult to resolve than his wife's shooting technique. What concerns him forms part of a recurring debate in the book about a legacy of personal and public wrongdoing that has yet to be erased from his consciousness. It's a complicated problem, bequeathed by those who went into wilderness regions — Indian ones especially — long before and found themselves unable or unwilling "to shoot and kill cleanly." In Hemingway's nightmares, the sins of these people have yet to be confronted, let alone exorcised, in order to ensure that a cleanly executed death can be "guaranteed" (116, 117). The "horrors" of the night, the terrible "sweating" that wakes him up, the gin he drinks for Dutch courage, the pistol he grasps (as if fearing an attack) — these things raise the possibility that wilderness killings in marshes and swamps belong to a history whose unresolved meanings and legacies have a particular importance in American life. Buried within the national psyche, these "cultural anxieties" are easily "reopened" when wilderness adventures, wherever they take place, incur the displeasure of primitive tribes (Lepore, xiii).

In an article entitled "Hemingway's Religious Odyssey: The Oak Park Years," Larry Grimes notes the role played by a nonconformist Protestant faith in Hemingway's upbringing in Oak Park. "The Hemingway side of the family," he says,

> were pious but not full of religious sentiment, stern moralists in favor of saving souls but not the kind of people to want a church service 'thrown open.' Their temperament was not forged in high-art, high-church Anglicanism or at emotive, triumphant, Methodist

> revivals. Rather it was gathered up from the New England of Winthrop, the Mathers, Wigglesworth, and Edwards transplanted to Oak Park by way of Wheaton College and the Wheaton Academy. Both of Hemingway's paternal grandparents, Anson and Adelaide, were educated in Wheaton's conservative, evangelical environment. In this religious tradition, *Sin* was a singular noun and required both a capital letter and capital punishment, eternal damnation. Redemption came only by the grace of God and the atoning blood of the Lamb. (45)

Hemingway was keen to learn as much as he could about the ethnic history and disposition of his family's Puritan faith and their deeply held messianic convictions. The religious environment into which he was born, and its preoccupation with the sins and errors of an uncivilized world, led him in later years to investigate the discomforting missionary role played by the church. By the time of his second safari to Africa, the place he'd been told to devote himself to in the Sunday schools of Oak Park,[14] he had long abandoned the messianic role his teachers had prepared him for, choosing instead to investigate the ritual devotions and practices of modern day tribes (*UK*, 50).

In *Under Kilimanjaro*, Hemingway repudiated the "evangelical" ideas of his youth and launched himself on an elaborate adventure with aboriginal life. He entered into what the seventeenth-century Puritan minister Cotton Mather called a state of "Criolian Degeneracy," undertaking covert actions and promiscuous engagements (well beyond the moral safety of the Puritan "Hedge") in which the risk of corruption and moral contamination was ever present (Axtell, 160). At the Kimana swamp his life resembled that of a Puritan disobedient set loose in the wilderness. Here he refuted without exception the idea of a special evangelical mission that his parents believed he was chosen to fulfill in the hinterland of Africa. As a student of Native American history Hemingway was well aware of the failure of mission and the way it had cast a large shadow in colonial New England across the seventeenth century. The Indian wars with which that century had ended were an indictment of that wilderness errand, offering spectacular proof of the failure to evangelize the Massachusetts tribes.

Hemingway was fearful of the sins of the past and keen to ensure that his own behavior not replicate the hunt for Indians in colonial New England. Hemingway was always aware of what trophy hunters in tribal terrain were liable to do when they got excited, particularly when that terrain displayed the characteristics of a colonial landscape. For example, Hemingway seems to have been aware of the correspondence between the hunt for the lion in the Kimana encampment and the memorial legacy of the hunt for King Philip in Massachusetts during The Great Swamp

Fight of 1676. It is not incidental that on two occasions Hemingway calls the area around the Chyulu hills "the great swamp" (*UK*, 405, 406), or that the lion when trapped in the open tries to make it back to his refuge in the swamp, "the heavy cover" where he (like Philip) wishes to stand and make his fight (218). The lion, we are told, "played it his own way" (218) and in some ways he shares the same tribal disposition as the leader of the Narragansett, King Philip, who died badly in his tribal "den." Sensing that history may have come back to haunt him, Hemingway is desperate to avoid a reprise, and tries to prevent the lion from making it back to his refuge so that he won't have to "dig him [the lion] out" of the swamp (as the colonists were forced to do with King Philip). The swamp — "the island of trees and thick brush" (214) — is reminiscent of the landscape where Philip died and it brings to mind the terrible atrocities that accompanied "the strange primitive ritual" of that massacre (Slotkin, 169).[15] Hemingway is eager to kill the lion in an open place, not just to avoid a repetition of the massacre in the swamp but also to prevent the lion from returning to the safety of the swamp and the animals that live there unmolested.

The lion's death turns out to be a mixed blessing for Hemingway. In one sense the villagers cannot complain about it, since he has simply complied with their request to rid them of the "marauding lion." This is in accordance with one of the most primary belief structures of ancient tribal communities, the sacrificing of the dying god whose erratic behavior starts to threaten the efficient running of the tribal place.[16] But while Hemingway succeeds in his archetypal mission to end the life of an ancient "king" (*UK*, 134), he fails to do it in a disciplined fashion. After the killing we see him in a state of anxiety, torn between the ritual death of a wayward god and the memory of a king who (like Philip in Massachusetts) has been forced to die in an unworthy manner (with too many bullets). As a result, Hemingway doubts that the dead king's blood will refresh the earth and restore the fertility of the tribal woods.

In the aftermath of the killing Hemingway does what he can to pacify the "guardian spirit" of the tribal swamp and act in accordance with its "laws and customs."[17] Among his various "anthropological studies" are those involving "the blood" (*UK*, 254) of a snake, the flesh of the lion, and the jagged edge of a leopard bone to cut his cheek. In her autobiography, *How It Was*, Mary Hemingway takes up this theme, describing how her husband wanted to show that he had become "'blood brothers' with his Wakamba friends" (391). Hemingway, she relates, demonstrated an almost overwhelming desire to go native in Africa. This involved him in "ceremonies for face-cutting and ear piercing" (391) that carried on long after his return to Cuba. Back at the Finca, Hemingway, says Mary, retained "a fever for some outward sign of his kinship with the Wakamba. He wanted to have his ears pierced and wear gold earrings in them, as I did" (426).

Hemingway's attempt to recreate a tribal lifestyle, especially in Africa, included acts of ritual observance that could have been scripted by James Frazer.[18] As well as cutting his face, he dyed his clothes "various shades of rusty pink ochre"[19] and shaved his head "to make the scalp like a Masai girl's," until it was "burned black by the sun" (Eby, 318, 173–74). Hemingway enjoyed a privileged lifestyle on safari, but disliked intensely the thought of being associated with a new generation of safari tourists that were appearing in East Africa. The changes he made to his physical appearance were a way of distancing himself from the new recreational imperialism of the West; they also pointed to the interventions that Hemingway came to associate with the breakup of indigenous landscapes and the damaging presence of colonial invaders. These changes, as well as the tribal marks he experimented with, indicate his strength of feeling for Africa and are part of an attempt to kill the homesickness that often plagued him during his absence from the country.

For a time Hemingway embraced Africa wholeheartedly. In accordance with the myth of the dying god he smeared lion fat on his body and ate lion meat. He did this not only to strengthen his nerve but also to honor the body of an extraordinary opponent. According to Richard Slotkin, the ritual eating of the body of one's enemy was widely practiced by the Tarantine Indians of New England in the seventeenth century. In all Native American history it was spiritually regenerative to invigorate the body with the flesh of the fallen at the moment of death. "Eating a bit of one's slain enemy . . . was to primitive man a ritual means of taking on the strength of that enemy. For the same reason they (the Indians) would cut a piece of a just-killed bear or wolf and eat it raw, believing that they were thus taking on the bear's strength or the wolf's cunning" (Slotkin, 90).

Hemingway's desire to imitate these old Indian practices in order to gain the strength of his enemy — what Slotkin calls a "savage Eucharist" (91) — is balanced by a need to share in the enemy's pain. In a scene that precedes his killing of the "ritual" leopard (*UK*, 104) Hemingway puts "a sharp bone fragment" from the wounded animal into his mouth. "I bit with satisfaction on the piece of shoulder bone," he says, and "the sharp end of the splintered bone had cut the inside of my cheek and I could taste the familiarity of my own blood now mixed with the blood of the leopard" (327). The spontaneity of the act enables him to feel "closer to the leopard" in much the same way that he wants to feel closer to the snake (326). Although the reason for self-mutilation is not immediately clear — "I did it without thinking" — clues are made available to us when he and Ngui follow the blood spoor "into the mangrove root patch" to find the leopard inside "the darkness of the roots" (329), where they shoot it several times until it is dead. Like the lion, the leopard has been trying to reach a place of safety by returning to its own roots.

In these "cross tangled roots" (*UK*, 329) Hemingway eventually finds the tangled remains of his own dark landscapes, including those he has not been able to come to terms with throughout his life. The leopard forces him back into the past, to those haunted remains — the "animal 'nests'" (Lepore, 87) and Indian bodies — that bring Nick Adams to the point of despair in "Big Two-Hearted River." In this story, the vegetation that thwarts Nick's progress — dark, "clotted" and "close together" — is the objective correlative of a tangled past, a place of blockage that threatens to drown him and bog him down (227, 231). Nick walks away from a difficult history, but thirty years later Hemingway decides it has to be faced. Leopard bone, lion fat, snake blood, and pieces of cloth are part of an intricate mosaic of tribal understanding that allows him access to places he has avoided. Hemingway traces the blood spoor back to a landscape difficult of access, determined to inspect those dark places in "the darkness of the roots" where much of his personal and emotional history belongs. Here he recovers something "still fresh on the dark green leaves," the memory of a wound that has not yet healed and that must be confronted once and for all. Yet, in one very specific sense, the process of recovery has already begun. Hemingway's desire to cut and scar his mouth, as we have seen, has already started the process of "familiarity," clearing away the "tangled" remains that block his way to emotional understanding. In his final moments before killing the leopard Hemingway experiences a new revelation. Traversing "the enlaced and crossed roots of the thicket" from "the left or west end" to "the other end" (*UK*, 329), he comes to the hemlock woods and secret swamps of his youth.

Hemingway has more success dealing with the leopard than he has with the lion. The killing of the lion is collaborative and Hemingway sees it as an opportunity to discharge a debt that his nation has incurred in the Indian past. The lion's death is a public occasion and always open to misunderstanding, especially so when the person who is given responsibility for the killing, Mary, is said to have defective vision. The death of the leopard, on the other hand, confirms his search for a more personal and emotional understanding of a youthful experience of Indian life, one that takes him back to the time he spent in northern Michigan. Bloody as it is, the death of the leopard is a private affair.

At the center of Hemingway's search for his tribal roots in Africa stands an Indian girl who worked in the kitchen of his parents' home in Walloon Lake on the upper Michigan peninsula. Her name was Prudence Boulton, a girl with whom Hemingway claimed his first sexual relationship. Prudence figures strongly in several short stories: as Prudence Mitchell, the Indian girlfriend of Nick Adams in "Ten Indians," and as Trudy Gilby in "Fathers and Sons." Prudence Boulton committed suicide a few months before Hemingway left for Europe in 1918. She was three months pregnant by a French-Canadian lumberjack, Richard Castle. The pair "had taken strychnine," says Peter Griffin, and according to the Indians, "their screams had been heard for hours across Susan Lake" (53).

Paul Smith argues that "it is difficult to imagine that [Hemingway] did not hear of [Prudence's] death, given his lasting memory of her part in his life. . . . He never forgot her" (68, 67), and she recurs in his letters and fiction for the next forty years. In a semi-fictional study, *Sweetgrass and Smoke* (2000), Constance Montgomery (here writing as Constance Cappel) explores the lasting impression Prudence made on Hemingway. Building on her earlier work, *Hemingway in Michigan* (1966), in which she mentions the rumor that when Prudence Boulton died "it was Ernest Hemingway's child [she] was carrying" (105), Montgomery returns to Prudence Boulton in *Sweetgrass and Smoke* and makes her the central person in Hemingway's life in the upper Michigan peninsula.

Hemingway buried his grief, refusing to elaborate on what had happened with Prudence except to say that he was very fond of her and that she took his virginity. In "Fathers and Sons" he transmuted his experience of Prudence Boulton into a fictional account, but elsewhere he found her memory difficult to deal with, hiding it where it could not be found and publicly scrutinized. By the time we reach *Under Kilimanjaro*, things have changed. Hemingway wishes to recover the past, as he tells his friends, and to reinstate the childish memory of the Michigan woods at the center of his current work, to bring together past and present aspects of his tribal experience. Prudence is central to this project. He wants to recover the bittersweet pain of his youthful affair, the memories he denied himself by blotting out the secrets of the woods.

The memory of the loss of Prudence to Richard Castle and the challenge of dealing with her unmourned death represent the "unfinished business" (*UK*, 16) he must bring to a close in Africa. The hunt for the leopard and the discovery of its body in the roots and leaves of an African thicket lead him back to Prudence Boulton, a challenge he had not wanted to undertake when he shot the lion. Since he has already been going in this direction with Debba, the discovery of the leopard gives him access to a more mystical time without the confusion he experienced with the lion.

The leopard is part of a "childhood" thing (*UK*, 23), the catalyst that brings to life the fictional identity that Hemingway gave Prudence Boulton throughout his career. When Hemingway describes his first encounter with a leopard, he thinks it "the fastest animal I had seen move" and "one of the most moving things I had ever seen" (277). The sight of a leopard evokes that same intensity of experience — it is a "soul-trying mystic moment" (276) — that Prudence Boulton brought into Hemingway's life. Just as the leopard is "a true cat . . . and a really wonderful one" (275), so, in the person of Trudy Gilby, her deputy in "Fathers and Sons," Prudence's actions are "true," "wonderful," instinctive, and unrestrained. She reminds us of the leopard who "never . . . or almost never [can be seen] in the open," so that a sighting is "a great and rare event . . . a mystical moment" (275–76).[20]

In Africa, the passion to remember Prudence Boulton is publicly and privately enacted. Her surrogate is Debba, his African fiancée, whom Hemingway describes as a "dark Indian wife" (*UK*, 383). He says that he and Debba are linked by a "not too simple trust and something else" he won't go into (30). It is not difficult to guess what Hemingway means. He wants to recover those secret places "where no white woman had ever been" (337), and in the process recover a youthful affair with an Indian girl. In a letter to Archibald MacLeish, Hemingway notes that Debba is "just like Prudy Boulton" (Baker, *Life*, 526).[21] In *Under Kilimanjaro* he is captivated by Debba's intimacy and opportunism and the way her "insolence" (372) and "impudence" (72) carry with them suggestions of promiscuity.[22] He and Debba read each other's moods. They share an affinity with the look of a place, its physical appearance, and both tend to express their feelings for each other in physical actions — touches and caresses that suggest a braillelike performance, as if their gestures are a mockery of blindness. In chapter 15 they caress each other "very lightly"; Debba responds "gently" to this "great delicacy of courtship" and the fingertip movements that "trace the outline of her nose and her lips." She in turn explores his body "very delicately." The words *carefully* and *gently* are repeated, as if Hemingway is afraid the illusion he wishes to conjure up will disappear with one wrong movement. Sometimes their movements grow in confidence and the gentle examination of surface and orifice gives way to biting, blowing, rubbing, and massaging. Scars, shoulders, earlobes are examined; even the heart is stimulated, as if there is a need to wake things up, to bring back to life a libidinous spirit that started to atrophy when Prudence Boulton ended her life.[23] The prevailing need is to access the secret places in each other's bodies. Hemingway describes how he strokes Debba's "bowed head . . . and touched the secret places behind her ears and she put her hand up, stealthily, and touched my worst scars" (72).

Debba draws attention to Hemingway's decision to mark his body with the bone of a leopard. This decision is a way of challenging the Protestant legacy that played such an important role in his youth. The scars left by the leopard bone are a product of his own free will and disobedience. They are certainly not a sign of divine appointment or, as his mother, Grace Hemingway, put it, an emblem conferred by a righteous God who had "yoked" her son "to a generation of saints" (Grimes, 49, 50). *Under Kilimanjaro* is Hemingway's final repudiation of the world of grace, both literally and figuratively. In Africa this idea of the body as a sign of Christian recognition is completely overturned. Hemingway transforms the meaning of his war wounds and the divine obscenity of God's handiwork by consciously choosing to re-mark his body. He wants that body to exhibit the features and inscriptions of an indigenous place. He can do this only by changing his appearance; in particular, through a conscious decision to rearrange the scars that pattern his body.

Hemingway's act of self-mutilation shows how far he has distanced himself from the Puritan philosophy with which he grew up. In Puritan New England, says Jill Lepore, the skin of the body was a way of marking "the boundaries of safety" in an irreligious world (like the wall of a house or a fenced-off enclave). Any wounds that caused a "breach" in the boundary of "skin" stripped the body of its Christian "civility" (81, 82). Hemingway replaces this civilized self with a belief in surgery, which "everyone [in Africa] loved" (*UK*, 376); he also does it as an act of desecration in order to violate the Christian purpose that God assigned him in the First World War. In the unsafe world Hemingway has chosen to enter, Christian grace is exchanged for "Criolian Degeneracy," and the body as a fenced and bounded site is replaced with a text whose scars and injuries are not what they were. After the leopard hunt Hemingway's head becomes a different mosaic. If the blood in his mouth is a ritual atonement for the things of the wilderness he has maimed and killed, then the surface of his skull "has much of the appearance of some plastic history of a very lost tribe" (334).

Scars and tattoos provide Debba with what Emile Durkheim calls "objective evidence" of "mechanical solidarity" with the tribe or clan (Richards, 17). Debba sees the scars on Hemingway's body and the marks on his gun holster — "carved better in Denver than anyone had ever been carved or tattooed" (*UK*, 351) — as living proof of his commitment to Africa. Hemingway describes how he and Debba "lay tight and close together" and, like Trudy Gilby with her "quick searching tongue" ("Fathers and Sons," 497), he explains how Debba "liked to play and explore" inside his mouth and that she derives sexual gratification from the mark of the scars (*UK*, 172). She presses her thigh hard against the pistol and the carved holster as if she wants to simulate an experience of pain and replicate, through the mark left by the indentation, the kind of impression a wound can leave. Scars and tattoos "give tribes their identities," says Linda Grant (15). In East Africa they also generate a sexual energy that is deeply pleasing to the opposite sex. As Hemingway notes, Mthuka is "scarred beautifully to please a girl a long time ago" (*UK*, 376). If Hemingway can please his own girl, maybe he can also retrieve the mark left on him by Prudence Boulton and, through an emotional experience that brings to mind the Michigan woods, bring about what Carl Eby calls an "easy slippage" between tribal Africa and native America (190).

In his books *Manhood* (1939) and *African Art* (1967) the French ethnographer Michel Leiris analyses the importance of pain, wounding and scarring at a time of sexual and emotional initiation into adulthood. In *African Art* he explores the link between physical disfigurement and bodily pain — from "scarification and tattooing" to "circumcision and clitoral extirpation." In particular, he examines the role played by body art in sexual initiation practices. The presence of the "erotic" during these practices signifies the arrival of manhood and an individual's "promotion to elder of the community."[24] In the case of Hemingway's promotion, these ritual markings appear to identify him, in the words of Leiris, "as a member of a definite group and designate his position in the social hierarchy" (Torgovnick, 114).

Hemingway enjoyed considerable respect in East Africa because of his willingness to exhibit his scars and make the most of his tribal features. It is because of those features that Debba responds to his courtship and demonstrates her fondness for bodily pain. When she takes his holster the "aesthetic purpose" behind the act is to mark her body in order to signify the promise of "promotion" from fiancée to bride (Torgovnick, 114). Hemingway calls her "an intelligent wife," and raises her expectations considerably as well as her self-importance with a kiss on the head. In a way, the encouragement he gives proves to be a disastrous misjudgment, and Hemingway acknowledges the mistake he has made when he prefaces the comment, "You will be an intelligent wife," with the word "stupidly" (*UK*, 337). The prediction might be a fanciful one but Debba takes it seriously. In a later scene we see her holding the carved holster and telling Hemingway, "I have all of you in the pistol" (351), as if to indicate how much she associates her new promotion with what Leiris calls the bodily "indentation of the skin" (Torgovnick, 114). Hemingway replies with "something very rude," but exonerates himself with an abstract discussion about love and "impudence" and the difficulty faced by men like him when they commit themselves to a faithful life (351–52).

Debba derives considerable status from being Ernest Hemingway's girlfriend. She rides in his car, "receiving any salutes from children or old people as though she were taking the salute from any regiment of which she might have been Honorary Colonel . . . she was patterning her public behavior after the photographs in the illustrated weeklies I had given her" (*UK*, 377). Something like a comedy of manners begins to unfold. Indeed, Hemingway teaching Debba to gesture in the fashion of the Princess Aspasia of Greece undermines much of his previous position on the acquisition of public trophies and the callous behavior of an expatriate class. We begin to see Hemingway's experiment fall apart. He becomes distracted by other agendas, in particular the return of his wife bearing gifts from Nairobi. The key role Debba has played — as a cultural ligature that enables Hemingway to connect the tribal world of East Africa with his youth in Michigan and the Native Americans he has known — is put aside. It happens almost imperceptibly within the narrative, but, nonetheless, Debba feels desperately disappointed as she realizes she has no future as Hemingway's wife.

Debba's life beyond the shamba does not lie with Hemingway, and in later scenes there are indications of Debba's uncertainty and emotional confusion that might be attributed to Hemingway's style of casual courtship. Debba finds it difficult to let go of her fetish for marks, and she allows Hemingway to "put her finger on the trigger" as together they target a Tommy ram. The collective pressure of body against body and finger against steel achieves its climax when the ram is shot. Debba cries, but the "tightened" togetherness that finds its release in the death of the ram has run its course. Debba reaches for "her royal manner," but it is no longer available and she cannot pretend any longer that things are the same. Attracted by the aesthetic impression that the bullet has made, she "put her finger into the hole where the solid had passed through" the animal, and in one last effort to hang on to her engagement, she holds "tight to the carved holster" as they drive away (378).

In the car Debba is "in a strange state" and does "not talk at all," and when they arrive at the shamba "she said nothing and went into the house" (378). It is, more or less, the end for Debba, and although Hemingway tells us "we all paid for whatever happiness or sorrow we had bought" to Africa, it's hard to see on the evidence before us what the emotional cost of the relationship has been for him. As he lies in bed, it is not Debba that is now his "best friend," but rather the pistol "lying comfortable between my legs in the carved holster that Debba had polished so many times" (381). It's a disingenuous moment. The pretence of intimacy and writerly understanding strikes the wrong note. Hemingway is "sure that [Debba] would sleep well," but it's only guesswork. The tone is patronizing and if Debba cannot or does not sleep well he would rather not know about it. He lies awake, happy in the knowledge that Mary is about to return from Nairobi, reminding himself "how lucky I was to know Miss Mary" (381–82). Who wouldn't feel lucky to have such support, one is tempted to ask, although in Hemingway's case the question of luck should do nothing to exonerate the moral ambivalence of his behavior.

In bed with Mary on the night of her return from Nairobi, Hemingway says: "I put the other Africa [Debba and the shamba] away somewhere and we made our own Africa again" (410). It is a difficult moment — Hemingway says he "felt the old splitting up my chest" — but it isn't as difficult as it ought to be for Hemingway given the likelihood of Debba's disappointment at Mary's return. Hemingway softens the pain with a lyrical burst in which he likens the act of making love with Mary to "a show of meteors on a cold night" (410). It's a curious way to raise his spirits and a curiously cold place in which to see his emotional life suddenly released. Hemingway has come to Africa to learn new things, and an explosive revelation, wrought by the beauty of an "unthinking" (410) world, suggests a kind of emotional abandon that is alien to the project he has undertaken. Hemingway has "learned not to think about Debba," and once he has "applied this bit of learning" (426) he appears content to move away.

There is one further brief meeting with Debba. She speaks politely, giggles a little, and then disappears from the book. Hemingway, with neither time nor interest, doesn't inquire where she has gone. It's a cold way to act. Debba is a woman who lights up his life, and on occasions such as these he shuts her out, confusing the one thing Debba represents — intensity of feeling — with domestic contentment and a middle-aged wife. The confusion of who means what to whom comes about because Hemingway can't face up, even in his writing, to the consequences of having to balance a tribal passion with a domestic duty, let alone make sense of the position he's been given of honorary game warden and the contract he has accepted from *Look* magazine.

At his most intriguing, Hemingway dreams up Africa and, as if by magic, makes it a part of his Michigan childhood with its hemlock woods and secret places. Africa is a way of going back home to an imagined past, and once discovered this "childhood" past offers him entry to a tribal landscape and personal atonement for the sins of his nation. The attempt to propitiate the ancestral gods with an African passion pushes Hemingway physically to his limits and challenges his beliefs and tribal passions. But his belief that it's possible to pierce the armor of a righteous skin and renew his ancient "familiarity" with things that are tribal remains unresolved. Hemingway enjoys limited success with the lion as totem, and rather more so with the "trouble leopard." But given that he raises unrealistically the hopes and aspirations of an African girl of whom he has no previous knowledge, his anthropology fails to appeal — nor does it enlist the kind of "honesty" he claims for himself in the opening pages. "Africa . . . makes all people . . . into children," he says (23); unfortunately, the kind of child Hemingway becomes by the end of the book lacks the freshness and spontaneity that ought to inform his tribal aspirations.

In the final analysis, Hemingway fails to live up to the highest standards of the hunt, whether it's with the lion or the emotion we associate with Prudence Boulton. In the case of the lion, domestic obligations interfere with the execution of a sacred duty and, in his search for Prudence, Hemingway is thoughtless of the girl who has acted as a go-between for him. Hemingway appears to discard Debba without ever knowing her well enough to explain her identity to a curious reader. Hemingway says he comes to Africa to learn about life, but the fact remains that his education is restricted to the few moments when he and Mary are apart from one another and the days when Mary is absent from camp. This constraint puts at risk the realist credo he has lived his life by: namely, that the principal qualification for writing is not talent, necessarily, but as Hamlin Garland once said, the knowledge that comes from a direct contact with life.

Hemingway believed that "you have to know what things are about before you start" to write (Reynolds, 174), and that literary knowledge was the special privilege claimed by writers whose work was rooted in direct experience. In *Under Kilimanjaro* he finds this principle increasingly difficult to uphold, and in political affairs his lack of knowledge becomes increasingly noticeable the longer he stays in country. Hemingway makes no attempt to immerse himself in the politics of East Africa or engage with the political aspirations of those in favor of independence. "It was too late to learn" (411), he says, passing comment on his lack of knowledge of English football. The comment is also an apt description of his worn-out views on the political landscape. Loneliness, mental rustiness, and the infirmities of late middle age — all of these things contribute to a patchy understanding of Kenyan politics and the movements for change that will shortly transform the country into an independent, postcolonial state.

In *Under Kilimanjaro* the question of what kind of knowledge Hemingway will carry back with him to the United States is far from clear. In one scene he goes out into the bush at night with his spear and listens to the noises made by the birds and animals. The more he travels the more wayward his thoughts become, and he begins to think of the food he must have in readiness for Mary's return. At a critical point his nerve deserts him. Fearing he would be "tempted by some animal" such as the "leopard hunting on the edge of the big swamp to the left," he deliberately "turned around and started on the worn trail back" (362). Abandoning the memorial landscapes of the jungle and the effort required by the trail, he goes back to camp, exchanging the life of an anthropologist for the dubious comforts of his own Widow Douglas.

Mary's attitude toward the hunt is a personal one, and this always puts Hemingway at a disadvantage in his search to establish an African brotherhood. But the damage is self-inflicted. The contract with Mary that brings Hemingway back to camp is signed the day he allows her to take the lead role in the hunt for the lion. Jeremiah M. Kitunda is right to argue that "pitting Miss Mary as the heroine against the king of the jungle is in a way an affront to the local men, among whom lion hunting is the province of young unmarried men, not women" (110). Just as problematical is the way Hemingway allows Mary to frame the hunt within a rigid timetable set by her in preparation for Christmas: the need for a tree, presents, decorations, the trip to Nairobi. Even worse is the way he allows her to retain a proprietary interest in the lion. When Mary says, "my lion means everything to me" (128), he does not question her assumption of ownership, but allows the conversation to continue along whimsical lines. The compromises Hemingway makes have consequences for the rest of the camp. The celebrations that accompany the lion's death are lively enough, but they tend to lack what Vickery calls the "tears and lamentations" that coincide with the death of a god (54). Mary's involvement with the hunt transforms the death of a ceremonial icon into little more than an unhappy kill. The lack of intensity among the dancers is an indication of their downbeat mood: they try to mollify an unhappy killer rather than commemorate a sacred king.

Hemingway avoids a confrontation to please his wife, and he chooses not to expose their relationship to the impact of current events. On wet days he seeks shelter in the murder mysteries of Georges Simenon instead of reading Jomo Kenyatta or André Gide or Franz Fanon. The idea that there is "nothing better" than Simenon is difficult to understand, let alone justify, given the importance and local availability of Kenyatta's analysis of the British in Kenya, *Facing Mount Kenya*. Hemingway retreats to Simenon's Paris at a time of political uncertainty in Kenya and claims he does it because he's exhausted. He says he needs Paris as a welcome distraction from a hunter's feeling of weariness, the result of an unstinting "obligation to kill, pursue, protect, intrigue, defend or participate" (110–11). This attempt to justify his escape into detective stories because he's tired of action seems, in the current political environment, somewhat hollow. It suggests exhaustion, weakness, or listlessness, a refusal to get involved in the blood and guts of African life.

Africa tires Hemingway and from time to time his stamina is low. We see this clearly in his refusal to help Debba prepare for a new political future in the country. The short, irrelevant Spanish phrases he teaches her, such as "No hay remedio" (353, 355), "La puta gloria" (353), and the misspelled "Vamanos [*sic*] a Las Vegas" (383), offer no protection, nor are they the equivalent of a revolutionary slogan or a call for independence. The excuse he offers for such frivolity is that teaching the Africans about political ideology is a waste of time. "They were not yet ready to administer nor to govern" (59), he says pessimistically of the Africans he knows. These ideas are symptomatic of an underlying confusion in Hemingway's political analysis and understanding of Kenya. Whilst he sees the country as being at risk from a weak and inept British administration, he also believes that the opponents of colonialism cannot be trusted to decide their own future. According to him political opportunists roam the country, the Masai are corrupt, and well-heeled tourists from Europe and the United States bring wasteful and destructive habits into the country. Kenya may be at risk from recreational imperialists and their lifestyles, argues Hemingway, but no amount of political independence can, in the short term, put things right. This argument is ill thought out and leaves the reader in a difficult position when trying to make sense of Hemingway's position on African nationalism and the political turmoil that enveloped Kenya during this period.

In one sense Hemingway appears to accept that the destruction of local African culture is inevitable, for throughout the book he tacitly supports the presence of Western consumer commodities that are weaning people away from their local affiliations. In his willingness to purchase and distribute Western products to rural African people he turns a blind eye to the corporate erosion of Africa's identity. He also gives unconditional support to the British settlers in Kenya who, in the early 1950s, believed that multinational companies should be given political protection and special privileges by the Colonial Office in London. According to David W. Throup,

> The settlers had vociferously supported the government's attempts to attract them [the multinationals] because they appeared to guarantee the continuation of the settler community and would provide jobs for the next generation. International capital offered the settlers their only opportunity to become Kenya's first national bourgeoisie. Without its support they would be squeezed between Asian and African entrepreneurs. The settlers believed that the multinationals would tighten the links between Britain and Kenya, guarantee Kenya's continued colonial status and protect their dominant position. (47)

Hemingway was certainly intrigued by the possibilities that existed for pharmaceutical products and the drugs that were becoming available in African markets. Indeed, he carries with him a war chest of drugs and recommends them to the people of East Africa without any warning of the chemical dependencies these drugs can create. For Hemingway, bodily weakness, bowel disorders, arthritic pain, rheumatic conditions, venereal disease, infection and virus (see *UK*, 374–76) are the important facts of life in Africa, taking precedence over political independence and the need for reform. It's a strange prognosis, given his support elsewhere for political change and his opposition to imperialism in countries like Cuba. One can only say that in the 1950s Hemingway knew Cuba from first-hand experience, but was unfamiliar with the Kenyan political landscape, especially during his time on safari. It's difficult to avoid the conclusion, however, that in Kenya Hemingway's lifelong passion for knowledge and accuracy, and the conviction, as he put it in a letter to Bernard Berenson, that "a writer should know too much" (*Selected Letters*, 780), appeared to desert him, and in general he lacked a willingness to engage with political realities.[25]

Anyone who reads *Under Kilimanjaro* for information about a country on the cusp of a political revolution and the role played by Jomo Kenyatta and his Mau Mau warriors will feel badly let down. The bigger disappointment, though, is what happens to the anthropological inquiry and the way it disappears into the background during the later stages of the narrative as he increasingly focuses on the medical equipment that has accompanied him throughout the safari and presents himself as an "amateur physician" willing to administer "massive doses of penicillin" (*UK*, 375) for the good of the country. Apparently, his answer to the virus of radical political activity is to pacify Africa with antibiotics and pharmaceuticals. These treatments and applications take us back to the remedies of his father, Dr. Clarence Hemingway. And while they may offer some relief, they are irrelevant to the concerns that Hemingway originally pursued: cultural anthropology, the work of James Frazer, and the tribal fascinations of René Maran. As we near the end of *Under Kilimanjaro* the increased reliance on medical quackery makes clear that Hemingway's interest in anthropology has run its course and the only activity he can now engage with is the shamanism of the marketplace. It's an Indian trick, not an Indian practice, and a depressing response to a developing country that could do with his help on the international stage. Hemingway gives no adequate explanation for his behavior and, instead, wanders up a blind alley. With his lotions and liniments and snake oil goods he beats a retreat to Indian Territory, a place he has always wanted to go but can only enter through his father's medicine chest. As he delves inside it Hemingway announces the arrival of a new imperialism in African life, one in which the drug companies and the multinationals — Bulmer's, Lilley's, and Gordon's Gin — are about to become the ultimate winners.

Notes

[1] Unpublished letter, Ernest Hemingway to Robert M. Brown, July 22, 1956. Ernest Hemingway Collection (1899–1961), Harry Ranson Humanities Research Center, University of Texas, Austin.

[2] Brasch and Sigman indicate that Hemingway owned Ruth Benedict's *Patterns of Culture* (1952), Melville Jean Herskovits' *Cultural Anthropology* (1955), three copies of Frazer's *The Golden Bough*, and *The Basic Writings of Sigmund Freud* (1938).

[3] These two words are not used in conjunction in *Under Kilimanjaro*, but they appear in the same context.

[4] See Fuentes, 84, and Hilary Hemingway, 106–8.

[5] This phrase was used idiomatically and widely in political circles. Among the first people to use it was Robert Lansing, American secretary of state (1915–1920) during the presidency of Woodrow Wilson.

[6] Meyers writes: "Zaphiro quoted Hemingway's ironic comment on all the young white males with pistols on their belts in the Long Bar of the New Stanley Hotel: 'only way they can feel something hard between their legs'" (*Biography*, 500).

[7] There are some exceptions, like the description of Harry Dunn, 198–99.

[8] See Melling, "'There Were Many Indians in the Story,'" 57.

[9] *Amerindian* is commonly accepted as the term for Indians throughout the Americas, North, Central, and South.

[10] See my discussion of Hemingway's article on the Rhône canal in "'There Were Many Indians in the Story,'" 45–46.

[11] She wants diamond jewelry, as well as expensive trips (398–99).

[12] The word used by Martha Gellhorn to describe the expatriate set and their struggle to remain a social elite in the nation's capital, Nairobi, during the pre- and postcolonial period. For a fuller discussion see Gellhorn's story "In the Highlands" in *The Weather in Africa* (111–235).

[13] Strong argues that "Hemingway believes Mary prevents him from fully gaining entrance into the Wakamba tribe. When he is with her, he must stifle that authenticity of his experience in Africa. With her, he becomes a visitor in the Africa constructed by British colonists, white hunters, and game wardens" (131–32).

[14] Grimes tell us that at Sunday school Hemingway was awarded a copy of Wilson Naylor's *Daybreak in the Dark Continent*, an account of missionary work in Africa (49).

[15] See my discussion on King Philip and The Great Swamp Fight in "'There Were Many Indians in the Story,'" 58–59. Philip's unclean death in the swamps has a particular relevance for Hemingway. The challenge of the lion, for whom the swamp is a place of refuge, presents Hemingway with the opportunity to reconsider his own evangelical Protestant history and to purge from it the memory of violation in the New England woods. In accepting this challenge Hemingway seeks atonement for the sins of the past and accepts responsibility for the dishonorable killing (by an ancestral church) of an ancient king. The challenge is never an easy one and the conditions attached to it are difficult to deal with. Failure with the lion risks reopening the wounds of the past as well as doing untold damage to his "complicated blood."

[16] In accordance with tribal tradition Hemingway sees it as his sacred duty, as Frazer puts it, "to save the divine life from the degeneracy of old age" (Vickery, 61).

[17] At Cambridge University, Frazer and his colleagues were literally "obsessed," argues Robert Alun Jones, "with questions about the nature of primitive religion in general and totemism in particular" (105). William Robertson Smith, Frazer's intellectual mentor at Cambridge and the person who exerted the greatest single influence on *The Golden Bough*, defined a totemic landscape as a place of sanctuary and "totemic sacrament" where the normal rights of entry, ownership, and exploitation "could not be exercised without definite restrictions." In tribal societies, argued Robertson Smith, the sanctuary was "a special place where the god is constantly present" as a "visible embodiment" of the holy. As such, it was a place where rules of trespass and "rituals of precaution are strictly enforced." The use "of a totemic sacrament," made available by a sacrificial gesture or act of homage, was a key "principle" in "governing access to the sanctuary" and a way of differentiating between those who were "holy" and those who were possessed by "commonplace" motives. In these societies a state of holiness did not amount to "morality or purity of life," but pointed us to "specific places" where "human beings came into relation with divine things" and behaved accordingly (Jones, 95).

It is important not to confuse this idea of a sacred sanctuary with the Puritan version of the sanctuary in colonial New England: the "beauty in the sanctuary," for example, with which the New England poet Edward Taylor characterized the material world of the spiritually devout; the errand, for example, to subdue a wild place and enclose it within a settlement of the elect. For Robertson Smith, the tribal sanctuary was divinely owned and "private encroachment" made it subject to the prohibitions and sacred taboos that kept it "apart" from the "ordinary" world. Those who violated the conditions of entry and avoided the godly by refusing to make "gestures of homage and words of prayers" were liable to punishment. The oldest sanctuaries, those "charged . . . with a certain supernatural energy," protected themselves against encroachment with "the curse, the ordeal, the oath of probation." These were invoked "to stamp an offender with the guilt of impiety and bring him under the direct judgement of the supernatural powers." Those, on the other hand, who approached the sanctuary as a holy place and were "motivated by respect" need have no fear of a "hostile supernatural power." In the search for "supernatural help" the exercise of "benevolent" powers could always be "relied" on, especially so if the individual sought access to the sanctuary through "magical ceremonies" and the proper use of the sacrificial (Jones, 96).

[18] According to Frazer, "the death, departure, resurrection and return of the god was celebrated . . . with ritual observances" that "took the form of sacred dramas." These involved acts of worship in which the mourners "beat their breasts and slashed their bodies with knives or sharp instruments so that they might make blood-offerings." It was also customary "for the priests and worshippers . . . to shave their heads both as a sign of their sorrow and as a sacrifice of the seat of their strength to the attempted resurrection of the god" (Vickery, 54–55). Amy Strong makes this point very clearly, arguing that Hemingway's behavior in the 1940s and 1950s, when "he shaved his head, darkened his skin, and considered cutting his face with African tribal marks," offers indisputable proof of an inner need "to alter his identity" (142).

[19] Editor's note: In answer to my query about the significance of these colors, Carl Eby wrote that "Masai warriors cover themselves in ochre and rub ochre paste into their hair for the Eunoto, when they become adult warriors (*morans*). I've read that the Masai associate the color red with power, but I don't really know much about this. I know that the blankets that are a distinctive part of traditional Masai dress (*shuka*), are usually blood red — but this often seems to wear to a rusty pink ochre" (e-mail, Eby to Mandel, 17 March 2010).

[20] In "Fathers and Sons," Prudence Boulton reappears as Trudy Gilby, a sexually active and attractive girl whose instinctive and impulsive movements in the heart of the forest replicate those of the African leopard to evoke a feeling of "joy unalloyed" (Beegel, 96). In Hemingway's mind this part of his life is associated with a golden age. In "Fathers and Sons" he puts it thus: "there was still then much forest then, virgin forest where the trees grew high before there were any branches and you walked on the brown, clean, springy-needled ground with no undergrowth and it was cool on the hottest days" (492–93).

[21] Trudy, Prudence, and the leopard itself are the victims of gossip and speculation by those who lack any knowledge of them. In the case of Prudence Mitchell

in "Ten Indians" it is Nick's father; in *Under Kilimanjaro* it is the brutal and insensitive leopard hunter.

[22] Debba is also the subject of gossip. Denis Zaphiro, a British game warden in Kenya, described Debba as an "evil-smelling bit of camp trash" (Meyers, *Biography*, 502). Hemingway ignored these rumors, something he was unable to do with Prudence.

[23] We encounter this particular psychosexual fascination as early as chapter 3.

[24] For further discussion of these ideas, see Torgovnick, chapter 5, "The Many Obsessions of Michel Leiris."

[25] Hemingway certainly does not know Africa the way Martha Gellhorn does in *The Weather in Africa*, Beryl Markham in *West with the Night*, or Karen Blixen in *Out of Africa*, writers who lived on that continent for a considerable time and whose work Hemingway admires.

Works Cited

Adair, William. "Landscapes of the Mind: 'Big Two-Hearted River.'" *College Literature* 4 (1977): 144–51.

Axtell, James. *The European and The Indian: Essays in the Ethnohistory of Colonial North America*. Oxford: Oxford UP, 1981.

Baker, Carlos. *Ernest Hemingway: A Life Story*. New York: Macmillan, 1969.

Beegel, Susan F. "Second Growth: The Ecology of Loss in 'Fathers and Sons.'" In *New Essays on Hemingway's Short Fiction*, edited by Paul Smith, 75–110. Cambridge: Cambridge UP, 1998.

Bergland, Renée. *The National Uncanny: Indian Ghosts and American Subjects*. Dartmouth: U of New England P, 1988.

Blixen, Karen. *Out of Africa*. London: Putnam, 1937.

Brasch, James D., and Joseph Sigman. *Hemingway's Library: A Composite Record*. New York: Garland, 1981.

Bull, Malcolm. *Seeing Things Hidden: Apocalypse, Vision, and Totality*. London: Verso, 1999.

Cappel, Constance [Constance Montgomery]. *Sweetgrass and Smoke*. New York: Xlibris, 2000.

Durkheim, Emile. *The Elementary Forms of the Religious Life*. New York: The Free Press, 1965.

Eby, Carl. *Hemingway's Fetishism: Psychoanalysis and the Mirror of Manhood*. Albany: SUNY Press, 1999.

Frazer, James George. *Totemism*. Edinburgh: Adam and Charles Black, 1887.

Fuentes, Norberto. *Hemingway in Cuba*. Translated by Consuelo E. Corwin. Secaucus, NJ: Lyle Stuart, 1984.

Gellhorn, Martha. *The Weather in Africa: Three Novellas*. London: Elland, 2006.

Gonzalez-Kirkby, Diana H. "Santería: African Influences on Religion in Cuba." *Negro History Bulletin* 48 (July–September 1985): 39–44.

Gonzalez-Whippler, Migene. *The Santería Experience*. Englewood Cliffs, NJ: Prentice Hall, 1982.

Grant, Linda. "Written on." *The Guardian Weekend*, April 1995, 12–20.
Griffin, Peter. *Along With Youth: Hemingway, The Early Years.* Oxford: Oxford UP, 1985.
Grimes, Larry E. "Hemingway's Religious Odyssey: The Oak Park Years." In *Ernest Hemingway: The Oak Park Legacy*, edited by James Nagel, 37–58. Tuscaloosa: The U of Alabama P, 1996.
Guillermoprieto, Alma. "A Lost World on the Map." Review of *Cave City, and Eagles' Nest: An Interpretive Journey Through the Mapa de Cuauhtinchan No 2*, edited by David Carasco and Scott Sessions. *New York Review of Books*, December 18, 2008, 63–66.
Hemingway, Ernest. "Balkans: A Picture of Peace, Not War." *Toronto Daily Star*, 16 October 1922. Reprinted in *Ernest Hemingway. Dateline: Toronto. The Complete Toronto Star Dispatches, 1920–1924*, edited by William White, 224–25. New York: Scribner's, 1985.
———. "Big Two Hearted River." In *The Short Stories of Ernest Hemingway*, 207–32. 1938. Reprint, New York: Scribner's, 1966. First published 1925 in Hemingway's *In Our Time*.
———. "Black Novel A Storm Center." Review of René Maran, Batouala, *Toronto Star Weekly*, 25 March 1922. Reprinted in *Ernest Hemingway. Dateline: Toronto. The Complete Toronto Star Dispatches, 1920–1924*, edited by William White, 112–13. New York: Scribner's, 1985.
———. *By-Line: Ernest Hemingway. Selected Articles and Dispatches of Four Decades.* Edited by William H. White. 1967. Reprint, Harmondsworth: Penguin, 1970.
———. *Ernest Hemingway: Selected Letters 1917–1961.* Edited by Carlos Baker. London: Granada, 1981.
———. *Death in the Afternoon.* 1932. Reprint, Harmondsworth: Penguin 1966.
———. "Fathers and Sons." In *The Short Stories of Ernest Hemingway*, 488–99. 1938. Reprint, New York: Scribner's, 1966. First published 1933 in Hemingway's *Winner Take Nothing*.
———. *Under Kilimanjaro.* Edited by Robert W. Lewis and Robert E. Fleming. Kent: Kent State UP, 2005.
Hemingway, Hilary, and Carlene Brennan. *Hemingway in Cuba.* New York: Rugged Land, 2003.
Hemingway, Mary Welsh. *How it Was.* New York: Knopf. 1976.
Jones, Robert Alun. *The Secret of the Totem: Religion and Society from McClennan to Freud.* New York: Columbia UP, 2005.
Kenyatta, Jomo. *Facing Mount Kenya: The Tribal Life of the Gikuyu.* London: Secker & Warburg, 1938.
Kitunda, Jeremiah M. "Ernest Hemingway's African Book: An Appraisal." *Hemingway Review* 25, no. 2 (2006): 107–13.
Lansing, Robert. "Present Nature and Extent of the Monroe Doctrine and Its Need of Restatement," 11 June 1914, File 710. 11/185 1/2. Records of the Department of State, National Archives, Washington, DC.
Leiris, Michel, and Jacqueline Delange. *African Art.* Translated by Michael Ross. Arts of Mankind Series. 1967. Reprint London: Thames & Hudson, 1968.

Lepore, Jill. *The Name of War: King Philip's War and the Origins of American Identity.* New York: Knopf, 1999.
Lewis, Robert W. "'Long Time Ago Good, Now No Good': Hemingway's Indian Stories." In *Approaches to the Short Stories of Ernest Hemingway*, edited by Jackson J. Benson, 200–212. Durham: Duke UP, 1990.
Maran, René. *Batouala.* 1922. Portsmouth: Heineman, 1987.
Markham, Beryl. *West with the Night.* New York: Farrar, Straus and Giroux, 1983.
Melling, Philip. "Cultural Imperialism, Afro-Cuban Religion, and Santiago's Failure in *The Old Man and the Sea*." *Hemingway Review* 26, no. 1 (2006): 6–25.
———. "'There Were Many Indians in the Story': Hidden History in Hemingway's 'Big Two-Hearted River.'" *Hemingway Review* 28, no. 2 (2009): 45–65.
Meyers, Jeffrey. *Hemingway: A Biography.* New York: Da Capo Press, 1985.
———. "Hemingway's Primitivism and 'Indian Camp.'" In *New Critical Approaches to the Short Stories of Ernest Hemingway*, edited by Jackson J. Benson, 301–8. Durham: Duke UP, 1990.
Montgomery, Constance. *Hemingway in Michigan.* New York: Fleet, 1966.
Ondaatje, Christopher. *Hemingway in Africa: The Last Safari.* Toronto: Harper Collins, 2003.
Penas Ibáñez, Beatriz. "'Very Sad but Very Fine': *Death in The Afternoon*'s Imagist Interpretation of the Bullfight-Text." In *A Companion to Hemingway's "Death in the Afternoon,"* edited by Miriam B. Mandel, 143–64. Rochester, NY: Camden House, 2004.
Reynolds, Michael. *Hemingway: The 1930s.* New York: Norton, 1998.
Richards, Stephen C. *The Sociological Significance of Tattoos.* New York: McGraw-Hill, 1995.
Ryan, David. *US Foreign Policy in World History.* London: Routledge, 2000.
Schedler, Christopher. "The 'Tribal' Legacy of Hemingway's Nick Adams." *Hemingway Review* 19, no. 1 (1999): 64–77.
Slotkin, Richard. *Regeneration Through Violence: The Mythology of the American Frontier, 1600–1860.* New York: Harper Collins, 1996.
Smith, Paul. "The Tenth Indian and the Thing Left Out." In *Ernest Hemingway: The Writer in Context*, edited by James Nagel, 53–74. Madison: U of Wisconsin P, 1984.
Strong, Amy L. *Race and Identity in Hemingway's Fiction.* New York: Palgrave, 2008.
Throup, David W. *Economic and Social Origins of Mau Mau.* Athens: Ohio UP, 1987.
Torgovnick, Marianna. *Gone Primitive: Savage Intellects, Modern Lives.* Chicago: The U of Chicago P, 1990.
Vickery, John B. *The Literary Impact of "The Golden Bough."* Princeton: Princeton UP, 1973.

9: Hemingway's African Book of Revelations: Dawning of a "New Religion" in *Under Kilimanjaro*

Erik G. R. Nakjavani

> *The Gods, says Epicurus, exist in the intervals of the universe. Very well; they exist only in the void space, in the abyss which is between the world of imagination and the world of reality, between the law and its application, between the action and its results, between the present and the future. The Gods are imagined beings, beings of imagination, which therefore owe also their existence, strictly speaking, not to the present but only to the future and the past.*
>
> — Ludwig Feuerbach, *The Essence of Religion*
>
> *The Gods [in African religious systems] appear as unobservable entities equivalent in many ways to the atoms, molecules and waves that feature so prominently in the explanatory statements of the sciences.*
>
> — Robert Horton, "Philosophy and African Studies"

RELIGIOUS MOTIFS CONSTITUTE a sizeable and complex body of references in Ernest Hemingway's *Under Kilimanjaro*. As the quasi-fictional narrator, Hemingway gradually prepares the reader for the birth of a "new and unknown religion" (*UK*, 168). First cautiously and then eagerly, the reader steps into the narrator's religious experiences as they unfold in the lee of Kilimanjaro. Although the narrator leavens his exploration of religion with jokes, he often feels it necessary to assure his wife, Mary, and ultimately the reader, that his "new religion" is "not a joke" (420). I do take this assurance seriously.

In what follows, I intend to explore these religious motifs, their origin, and their course of development to discover what their newness consists of and what may qualify them as "unknown." I would like to state at the outset that the essential or defining factor of this "new and unknown religion" is that it founds itself on direct, unmediated, lived experiences of what phenomenology designates as the "thing-in-itself," or what constitutes the object of our consciousness and our senses. Such experiences disclose to the narrator and eventually to the reader that the cosmos in its entirety is a sentient — that is, self-aware — series of material phenomena. In other words: all that exists, *whether it exists as organic or nonorganic matter,* possesses self-awareness. Such a sentient materialism suggests a sacral universe, and thus contrasts sharply with both speculative and Marxian materialisms. As we shall see, sentient materialism has deep roots in the history of science, philosophy, and religion. It is not at all a "new religion," but rather one whose "origin was as old if not older than the mountain although I was not sure on this point" (*UK*, 377).

The Narrator's Fantasy of Negritude

The narrator of *Under Kilimanjaro* tells us wistfully that one early morning, "watching Ngui striding lightly through the grass [I was] thinking how we were brothers," and that "for better or worse and for always I wished my skin were as dark as his and that M'Cola was my father" (251). It is a persistent fantasy in his narrative. Perhaps one may call it a fantasy of Negritude, an intense desire to be or to become African.[1] Mwindi, a member of the safari crew, asks the narrator, "Why you want to be African?" (331). His straightforward unhesitating answer is, "I'm going to be Kamba." When Mwindi doubtfully responds, "Maybe," the narrator rejects his vacillation by telling him, "Fuck maybe" (331). He means it seriously.

Of course, he does not become Kamba. However, his affinity for Africa makes him receptive to moments of optimal, fervent openness, attunement, and oneness with his surrounding world. Gradually, he experiences a vision of existence that initiates him into a semi-shaman African position or identity: he informally dispenses meat and medications, performs nominal rituals, offers advice and, from time to time, serves as an unofficial elder, diviner, and religious philosopher. He describes himself and his African coreligionists as "all bad boys" who "now . . . had the backing of a serious religion" (377).

Africa as the Generative Ground of Religious Reflections

> *We see plainly in the laws of nature that rain comes down from the heavens in the time of need. The greenness and verdure of the earth depend upon heavenly rain. If it ceases for a time the water in the upper strata of the earth gradually dries up. Thus we see that there is an attraction between the heavenly and the earthly waters. Revelation stands in the same relation to human reason as heavenly water does to the earthly water.*
>
> — Mirza Ghulam Ahmad (Al-Mahdi) (*UK*, 121)[2]

The preparation for the narrator's religious concerns and reflections in *Under Kilimanjaro* begins with evidence of his openness to Islam and Islamic practices, experienced in Africa as early as his first safari (1933–1934). In *Green Hills of Africa*, his creative nonfiction account of his first safari, the narrator mentions that his Mohammedan gunbearer, Charo, was "very serious and highly religious" (38). He observes Charo fasting from sunup to sunset during Ramadan, the ninth month of the Islamic calendar, during which fasting, prayer, and contemplation are aimed at the purification of the soul. The narrator reports that Charo was so strict about the fast that

> he never swallowed his saliva until sunset and when the sun was almost down I'd see him watching nervously. He had a bottle with him . . . and he would finger it and watch the sun . . . Charo was deadly thirsty and truly devout and the sun set very slowly. I looked at it, red over the trees, nudged him and he grinned. M'Cola offered me the water bottle solemnly. I shook my head and Charo grinned again. . . . Then the sun was down and Charo had the bottle tilted up, his Adam's apple rising and falling greedily and M'Cola looking at him and then looking away. (38–39)

The narrator adds that the Mohammedan religion or Islam was "something to believe in . . . something that gave you more complicated habits of eating, something that I understood and M'Cola [the other gunbearer] did not understand" (39). As a Christian, the narrator can see the parallels between Ramadan and the forty days of dietary restrictions and prayer that characterize Lent. He and Charo share subtle sensitivities and sensibilities that add up to certain spiritual affinities and understanding that the non-Muslim M'Cola does not share. They can therefore become "good friends," a friendship of spiritual yearnings and understanding (39). This friendship implies a genuine initiatic journey for the narrator in Africa, not merely into Islam but rather into an empathetic participation in other religious visions and practices beyond his own.

In *Under Kilimanjaro*, the narrator recalls that Charo (now Mary Hemingway's gunbearer and a *mzee*, a respected elder) "had wished to convert me to Islam some twenty years before and I had gone all through Ramadan with him observing the fast" (32). It is a remarkably decisive statement, but, in the context of *Green Hills of Africa*, whose narrator did not share the fast, an inaccurate one. Still, *Green Hills of Africa* reveals the narrator as knowledgeable about and respectful of Ramadan, accepting its religious implications as he accepts those of Lent. So here two points are clear: the narrator has long sought a connection between the material and the spiritual, and he pursues this union in Africa.

The narrator's interest in connecting the physical with the spiritual is also evident in his respect for the concept *halâl*, which derives from the extensive body of religious Islamic law. Generally, *halâl* indicates the kind of food proper for consumption by Moslems; it particularly addresses meat and the approved manner of the slaughter of animals. *Halâl* probably descends from the more familiar (to Americans of Hemingway's day) concept of *kashrut* in Judaism, which establishes not only what food is fit for consumption but also, in the case of animals, how they are to be killed, bled, and prepared. What is kosher is "clean" or "legal" in substance and manner of preparation, as opposed to what is proscribed or forbidden: *tref* in Judaism or *harâm* in Islam. The narrator's references to hunting and killing animals for meat that would be *halâl* reveal not only his knowledge of Islamic law (*shari'a*) and custom but also the focus or philosophy of his hunting. The narrator feels compelled to tell us that "the time of shooting beasts for trophies was long past with me. I still loved to shoot and to kill cleanly. But I was shooting for the meat we needed to eat" (116–17). Since the meat must be fit for consumption for Muslim members of the safari crew, the concept of *halâl* is of consequence to him. He respects the Islamic answer to the connection between bodily and spiritual needs.

The pursuit of the lion and the hunt for the proper Christmas tree also add new dimensions to the union of the religious and the corporeal, the concept of the oneness of the material, the sentient, and the sacred that in due time takes center stage in the narrative. The Christmas tree, with all its manifest implications and significations as Christian mysteries, unites the sacred and the natural. Originating in Europe, it has gained such wide popularity that it has become a sort of particular universal within the province of Christianity. Thus, Mary's search for an appropriate Christmas tree in Africa underlines the tree's symbolic mediation between the holy in Eurocentric Christianity and the numinous sentient on earth in Africanized Christianity. Additionally, it squarely fits the mood of a narrator attracted to the integrative effect of his African experience, bridging the natural and the supernatural.

Mary takes the pursuit of the Christmas tree with inordinate seriousness. She is not alone. Keiti, "the headman of [white hunter] Philip Percival's safari crew" (*UK*, 447), also "gave it a great importance. The ceremony of the tree appealed to him since in his old religion, before he had become a Moslem, a grove of trees had been of the highest importance" (45). Unbeknown to Mary, this tree produces a hallucinogenic "concoction which excited and maddened the Masai for war and lion hunting" (45). The notions of the hallucinogenic tree as sacred in Keiti's "old religion" and as a symbol of the birth of the "Baby Jesus" to Mary are not too far apart in the indigenous African religious temperament and sensibility (45). Such oneness of the earthdwelling body and the skydwelling God of Abrahamic monotheism would not be entirely alien to the ancestral African religious belief in spirit gods that bring together matter and spirit, the natural and the supernatural.

Mary Hemingway's long devotional hunt of a particular lion before Christmas also contributes to this theme. Mary herself compares the lion hunt to the "search for the Holy Grail and for the Golden Fleece" (127). The Africans also recognize its spiritual nature: "The rougher pagan element of the camp," the narrator informs us, "thought that Miss Mary's tribal religion was one of the sterner branches of religion," demanding "the slaying of a gerenuk under impossible conditions, the slaughter of a bad lion, and the worship of a tree" (45).

I believe that these early sections of the narrative — the narrator's recollection of observing Ramadan with Charo, Mary's quest for the proper Christmas tree, and the hunt for the lion that occupies so much of the narrative — indicate the narrator's familiarity with and openness to the bond between the material and the spiritual. They thus link his Eurocentric Christianity and his African/Islamic experiences, and prepare us for the emergence of his "new and unknown religion" (which actually has been some time in the making). This linkage discernibly joins the earthly and corporeal lived experiences of living human beings and the material world. One may think of this linkage as the narrator's response to the two outwardly divergent and mutually exclusive guiding principles of African religious beliefs: theism and polytheism. The narrator uses elements of his own Christian, monotheistic, and more or less Eurocentric background to invest in a mode of panpsychism, which melds various schools of religious thoughts and beliefs. Panpsychism, which claims that God and the universe are coextensive, resembles pantheism but brings to it a universal self-awareness. In this sense, panpsychism integrates the polytheism of indigenous African religions and the God of Abrahamic monotheism. According to David Skrbina, "a functional definition of panpsychism might be 'objects, or systems of objects, possess a singular inner experience of the world around them'" (16).

From this viewpoint, the narrator embarks upon an imaginative and impassioned venture into religion in *Under Kilimanjaro*. It requires of him to simultaneously invest and divest himself of his own religious background, a difficult task that only an active imagination can accomplish. For in this adventure, the narrator suggests a union of the omnipotent and omnipresent Christian God who, according to the Lord's Prayer, primarily dwells in heaven, and the constellation of gods that, in some African religions, intervene in the material world and act as symbols of human experiences and their spiritual yearnings. The import of this integration is the recognition that the single God of monotheism and the panoply of gods generally coexist in African religious beliefs. This imaginative religious endeavor opens up a fertile field of new theological perspectives. The fluidity of African religious diversities and unities is central to the narrator's later demarcation of his own "new religion."

In my view, the narrator's "new and unknown religion" evolves out of his own past religious experiences, his sensitivity and openness to meditative and contemplative responses to other religions, and his keen proclivities for all things genuinely African. This attitude drew Hemingway to *Santería* (Way of the Saints, also known as *Regla de Ocha, La Regla Lucumi*, or just *Lucumi*) as practiced in Cuba, where he mostly lived during the two decades that preceded his second safari. Afro-Cuban *Santería*, which has deep roots in the Yoruba religious system (formerly practiced in the western section of present-day Nigeria), was brought to Cuba by the slave trade (1790–1820) and grafted onto the Roman Catholicism that had been introduced by the Spanish conquistadors of the fifteenth century. The resultant new Afro-Cuban religion situated the pantheon of Yoruba gods (*Orishas*) within the interstices of Roman Catholic theology and practices. For example, Orula, the beloved *Orisha* of prophetic wisdom and divination, coincides with the Catholic Saint Francis of Assisi, the patron saint of animals, nature, and the environment, whose ecological concerns are also visionary and prophetic. In Cuba, their double feast day is celebrated on 4 October.

The more one studies *Santería*, the more one realizes that it generally functions as the Africanization of Catholicism rather than the Catholization of the Yoruba religious heritage. *Santería*'s acute awareness of the significance of natural forces in their materiality and the necessity of cooperation with them for acquiring greater human corporeal as well as spiritual strength would not have escaped Hemingway's keen mind and religious sensitivities. His interest in *Santería* may well have begun with his initial exposure to matters African during his first African safari. However, this interest gradually and naturally intensified and deepened because of the nearly two decades of his exposure to practicing *santeros* in Cuba. Clearly, Hemingway's relationship to *Santería* is relevant to the "new religion" he proposes in *Under Kilimanjaro*. Even when drawing the narrator of his earlier African narrative, *Green Hills of Africa*, he may have been making a general reference to Ogun, the Yoruba god of iron and warfare. But the allusion to Ogun appears to be even stronger in *Under Kilimanjaro*. The narrator and his African coreligionists match up well to the warrior god whose "hotheaded" followers are "impulsive, assertive, and quick to take offense; they harbor a keen sense of injustice, possess physical strength, and are actively engaged in life, sometimes to the point of self destructiveness" (Ray, 400–41).

Africa as the Necessary, Ancestral Place

For many reasons, Africa is the most suitable natural place for the narrator of *Under Kilimanjaro* to search for a religion unifying matter and spirit. Africa appears to offer him a spiritual comfort zone. Ancestral African religions resolved the dichotomy between matter and spirit by bringing into being spirit gods, such as river and tree gods, who mediate between the two spheres: the natural (material) and supernatural (sacral). In addition, as is well known, Africans have extensively adopted the beliefs and practices of monotheistic Islam and Christianity. What is less commonly known and acknowledged is that indigenous or traditional African myths and rituals have transformed the Abrahamic religions of the Middle East.[3] To a large extent, Africa seems to Africanize religious influences that are not ancestral. In *Under Kilimanjaro,* Hemingway looks at several aspects of this process of Africanization, familiar to him from his Cuban experience, as he encounters the practices and observances of African Christianity and Islam. Hence, Africa's multifaceted religious landscape is another reason for the continent to become a compelling backdrop for the narrator's exploration of religious issues as he develops his "new religion."

Above all, there are moments of passionate mystical accessibility between the world and the narrator, in which he himself seems to be a part of the multifaceted reality that is his beloved elemental African countryside. In this sense, his imagination seems to take him far beyond his own Christian religious background and puts him in touch with the reality of Africa as the ancestral home of the human species. He then gives the impression of imaginatively recapturing the child's enchantment with nature's incandescent reality to an extraordinary extent. The space of this enchanted land is unbroken and its time is the eternal present. In short, Africa represents to him what one may latently experience as the unconscious base of the imagination, creative and benign.

Being on the African continent, the narrator's imagination intimates to him the privileged but unimaginable original landscape of the world that precedes the dawn of human consciousness. It is in this specific context that we understand his "new religion" to be "as old if not older than the mountain" (377). For clearly what is older than the signifying concept of the "mountain" is the existence of the presignified and preconceptual: the mountain itself. As the unfolding site of human childhood, Africa induces in the narrator the beatific persistence of the prelinguistic stage of childhood. This privilege is available only to a lucky few men and women of active imagination who are able to envisage and relive the child's preverbal world, before linguistic differentiations and significations burst upon human consciousness. Because it requires that we imagine the existence of a material world in the absence of human consciousness, language, and thought, it suggests a *quantum leap* in our modes of thought;

what the narrator might have called a jump from "plane geometry to something far beyond calculus" (341). Such an imagined world suggests the initial awesome conceptual move toward "an awfully primitive religion" (271). It is "awfully primitive" because it induces the wonderment that precedes all our acts of thinking and comprehension of the numinous and the sacred in the midst of our everyday lives.

Touchingly, the narrator points out, "We were no longer, technically, children although in many ways *I am quite sure that we were*" (23, my italics). Here the narrator attests to the psychically all-pervasive but often repressed or latent presence of the child in us all, which presses us to go beyond the arbitrarily differentiated horizon of the known and the unknown, the truly mysterious. Childhood is the originary source of unimpeded human imagination and therefore of future human potential and possibilities. The processes of socialization, acculturation, religion, and formal education ordinarily suppress the child's active imagination.

By touching the ubiquitous child deep within him, the African setting of *Under Kilimanjaro* deeply attaches itself not only to the narrator's childhood experiences but also to humanity's ancestral and mythological childhood, whose space-time dimensions magically correspond with the creative imagination. Being in Africa sharply blends his childhood memories with the vast expanses of the psyche given to myths, folklore, and archetypal experiences. He becomes genuinely nostalgic for the purity of all beginnings because Africa not merely rejuvenates him but also constantly reminds him of all the mornings of the world, indeed of all the fearsome nights and predawns of the forgotten ancestral past. It is in the light of our momentous individual and human childhoods that the narrator reminds us that "to have the heart of a child is not a disgrace. It is an honor. A man must comport himself as a man. . . . But it is never a reproach that he has kept a child's heart, a child's honesty, and a child's freshness and nobility" (23). There is genuine freshness and nobility of spirit in such regression to childhood because the possibility of all genuine human progress resides in it.

Most of the action in *Under Kilimanjaro* takes place in the lee of Kilimanjaro, an identifiable geographic location.[4] Yet, the narrator's knowledge of the place belongs to the spatial category of phenomenology's lived space-time that may turn up in consciousness as the reality of our imagination in the absence of the real. Everyday American language refers to "lived space" in the possessive as "my space," which first and foremost personifies a qualitative rather than quantitative space. Correspondingly, the temporal dimension of the narrator's geographic African setting is "lived time" or qualitative inner time in contradistinction to chronos or clock time — as in the expression, "have a good time." The narrator makes the setting of his African narrative a part of his own lived experiences, past and present. For him it becomes inseparable from what he describes as the "mystical countries that are part of one's childhood. Those we remember and visit sometimes when we are asleep and dreaming. They are as lovely at night as they were when we were children. If you ever go back to see them they are not there. But they are as fine in the night as they ever were if you have the luck to dream of them" (23). The safari camp acquires its dreamlike poetry that makes it possible to partake once more of "the mystical countries that are part of one's childhood" (23), Elicited by the African countryside under Kilimanjaro, this poetic language works in such a way as to make the narrator's presence in Africa a mystical experience in and of itself.

The narrator then adds, "It is possible to be grateful that no one that you would willingly associate with would say, 'Be mature. Be well balanced, be well adjusted'" (23). This is so simply because being mature, balanced, and adjusted, in this restrictive sense, implies the success of wearisome conformism at the expense of liberating imagination. To be mature often implies an irreversible separation from the dream that was the visual world of our childhood, traces of which survive only in the visual poetry of dreams and in the indirect language of our unconscious. The child's psyche is so spectacularly integrative that it confers on all it encompasses a mystical sense of oneness and union. The adult's successful assumption of a mature, overly rational, differentiated attitude comes at the expense of childhood's mind-body integration and its attendant limitless freedom and creativity.

To be a conforming adult, then, more often than not interferes with genuine individual artistic, religious, and spiritual development — unfettered possibilities that exist only in the child's prelanguage stage of development. Still, the lack of language as silence in general and in literary discourse in particular often makes for a moment of creative absence, an absence that enables the creativity inherent in the imaginal space and time in childhood to surge forth. That is why the narrator as a creative man feels so extremely happy and privileged that he repeats, "Africa, being as old as it is, makes all people except the professional invaders and spoilers into children. No one says to anyone in Africa, 'why don't you grow up?'" (23). As the continent of human birth, Africa continually proffers the irreplaceable gift of childhood freedom upon those who, like the narrator of *Under Kilimanjaro*, long for that realm of unending imaginative potentials and possibilities.

That may be the reason or at least one of the truly potent reasons Africa has developed and nurtured such strong roots in the narrator's psyche as an artist. Africa is still capable of making the creative writer feel the freedom that predates societal conventions and can therefore alter it or altogether escape it. The thrust of the narrator's argument is that "the professional invaders and spoilers" are the personification of the adult world, and therefore weaken or destroy vast reservoirs of creative human energies that Africa can elicit. Thus, "the professional invaders and spoilers" become enemies of the promise of the country of childhood that may latently and magically surface from the depth of the African panorama into the creative unconscious. They steal the incomparable wealth of Africa, which resides in the primeval elements of its geography; willfully or unintentionally, they spoil everything they touch. Only an exceptional love of the world, such as the narrator's, can make up for the thievery and blight imposed on Africa.

The narrator appears to have always possessed an ample appreciation of nature and animals and to have lived passionately by his well-developed senses and their disclosures. However, his total immersion in sensual lived experiences in Africa's landscape, flora, and fauna further sensitizes him to the "miraculous," the "good magic" and "bad magic" in his encounter with nature and animals (443). The narrator's newly acquired heightened sensitivity is considerable. One may even characterize it as *hypersensitivity*. In Africa, he lives with a kind of stressful borderline hallucinatory receptivity of the senses. As we shall see later, Africa slowly transforms his hypersensitivity into a dazzling prophetic vision, so intense that it becomes nearly unbearable for him. A speculative cosmology of consequence results from it. The African earth and sky, mountains and valleys, forest and plains, bright daylight and luminous nocturnal darkness open out into a living, pulsating, sentient universe for him. Therefore, Africa serves as a catalyst to render this artist of language into a mystical seer, a visionary, and a lingual alchemist.

In Africa, the narrator's senses open up to the natural world and embrace it with total trust and with an unmistakably childlike imagination and love of the world. One may say of him that, in Wallace Stevens' words, "this man loved earth, not heaven, enough to die" (188). In this sense, one may call his love of the world *agápe*. It is an unconditional, limitless love — a love as pure and as full of awe, wonder, and reverence as one might have had for the unimaginable first flowering of conscious life on earth. Thus, the narrator's safari (from the Arabic *safar*, journey) turns into a spiritual journey of considerable magnitude. Born of heightened imagination and hypersensitivity, *agápe* leads the narrator to apprehend the natural world as sentient and sacral.

Visionary Intuition: The Union of the Seer and the Seen

This, I thought to myself, is a gaze that has substance and meaning — the look in my eyes embodies challenge. I was determined to overcome the opacity of the physical by my commitment to see. By now I had figured out that I was expected to see something other than the tree itself. Something that still was the tree, but uninvented, unmediated, pure.

— Malidoma Patrice Somé, *Of Water and the Spirit*

The narrator's maximal sensual lived experiences of nature in Africa prime his imagination to such a degree that one may consider him as a seer, in both the ordinary as well as the more mystical meanings of this word. He is a creative man of knowledge and intuition, which he calls "magic powers" (*UK*, 154). In what he sees, there are hints of the truth that the invisible always precedes the visible, both literally and connotatively. It is our common experience that the outward visual void of open spaces is the fertile womb of the visible. Without such invisibility, there would be no visibility whatsoever, as there would be no speech without silence. It is precisely in this sense that one can state that the void always and of necessity precedes creative impulses and their subsequent activities.

The narrator's visual enthusiasm as *agápe* for the natural world allows him to grasp this dual truth of all things seen. *Agápe* makes it possible for him to move from the essential surface visibility of the world to its surplus visibility of the invisible and therefore unknown, defying the unknowable in the very act of visionary intuition. The narrator is astonishingly adept at capturing this surplus visibility as subsurface multiple significations in his creative writing. No doubt, a similar process must have been at work in the painting of the quasi-fictional narrator's favorite painters. As Hemingway told George Plimpton in an interview, as a creative writer he had learned much from painters such as "Tintoretto, Hieronymus Bosch, Pieter Brueghel, Patinir, Goya, Giotto, Cézanne, Van Gogh, [and] Gauguin" ("Art of Fiction," 227). For such painters the act of looking and veritably *seeing* beyond the seen is the generative foundation of imagination in visual arts. Such acts of seeing necessitate that the seer become one with the seen, which extends the horizon of the visible to the invisible. That is how the seer *apprehends* the world in the triple signification of the verb as (1) understanding, (2) reciprocal acts of seeing and being seen, and (3) seizing and being seized by the inexhaustible truth of the visible as it emerges from the invisible. Such apprehension effortlessly unfolds in a child's imagination, which makes it both immensely valuable and rare. Defined as such, the act of seeing alchemically *transmutes* everyday lived experiences into the spiritual visions prevalent in various mystic traditions.

By the same logic, not seeing or *looking past* what one sees is an exercise in dulling, if indeed not deadening, the senses and turning them into an incomprehensible morass of dreary, mundane phenomena. The life of the spirit suffers radically from such deadly degradation of the visual life. That is why the narrator tells us that "looking but not seeing things was a great sin" (*UK*, 225), a religious or spiritual offense. In contrast, the narrator's own visionary mode of seeing often implies an agonizing visual acuity. He explains that his drinking is "not just a habit nor a way of escaping," but an antidote to his borderline hallucinatory sensitivity to visual stimuli. It is "a purposeful dulling of a receptivity that was so highly sensitized, as film can be, that if your receptiveness were always kept at the same level it would become unbearable" (225). Such overwhelming visual encounters with mystery define visionary experiences. They are always fraught with overwhelming joy and sorrow. They call for a suspension or erasure of the same-self identity, the ego, which is experienced as a fearsome loss of the self, so that a new and exceptionally larger self may be born. One needs uncommon courage to deal with such frequently intolerable visions and the rare mystical experiences they provide. I would speculate that even a single visionary experience might last a lifetime. Brave is the individual who sees it through and bears it away.

To be a visionary requires passion, an overabundance of passion. In its religious context, this passion is a suffering freely chosen. The narrator in *Under Kilimanjaro* tells us that, as a visionary, he gives the impression of being a madman to the Africans around him. Intuitively and metaphorically, the Africans he meets understand his madness to be "in the greatest tradition of Holy Men" (103). His madness conjures up images of the early Christian desert fathers and the mystics of the desert of Scetis in Egypt, whose conduct surpassed the realms of rationality and challenged everyday notions of sanity. This holy madman (the new Hemingway hero) is just as brave, if not braver, than those heroes, such as Robert Jordan of *For Whom the Bell Tolls* and Santiago of *The Old Man and the Sea*, who had come before him. The reader responds to him and his African safari with a sense of wonder and enchantment. His magical safari spreads out through expanses of reveries, visions, dreams, and mystical meditations in the lee of Kilimanjaro in Africa.

The Concept of Literary Alchemy in *Under Kilimanjaro*

> *It is common when reading alchemical texts for the reader to observe consistent references to the practice of al-Kimia [alchemy] as "our art," "this art," or "the art" or descriptions of the way to accomplish the alchemical process: "by art" or "with art." This use of the term art refers to the alchemist's understanding not only the concepts and theories of all the Arts, but also implies the plastic applications involved in undertaking any actual work of art.*
>
> — John Eberly, *Al-Kimia*

I should think that it would be difficult to comprehend the narrator's spiritual journey in Africa or the gradual development of his "new religion" in *Under Kilimanjaro* without bearing in mind the power of rituals in his daily life. Accordingly, as a writer and a seer, his vast experiences of the real and the unreal in Africa acquire the (sacramental) status of rituals.

As sacraments, these rituals or ceremonies are full of implications. Each rite, however, implies a radical alteration of certain substances, either material or spiritual. Here, I detect a connection between the rites or sacraments of the "new religion" in *Under Kilimanjaro,* and the notion of alchemy in general and literary alchemy in particular.

At first glance, the relationship between alchemy and arts, including literature, might appear tenuous. All the same, alchemy, the failed theory of transmutation of base metals into gold, works remarkably well when seen as the alteration or transmutation of lived experience into artistic expression in literature and the arts. In general, understanding the role that imaginative alteration or transformation plays in Hemingway's best fiction allows us to grasp the hermetical aspects that make his work enduring. For it is part of the extensive metaphysics and aesthetics of what we commonly refer to as the Hemingway style that comes through as felicitous but obscure, rather than manifest, in the act of reading. Certainly, that is as it should be for any appreciative, rather than critical, reading. All the same, it is always a matter of transmuting the demotic or ordinary language into the extraordinary language of various literary genres.

By its definition and function, literary alchemy joins opposites and creates new syntheses that are at once stylistic and thematic. To the extent that I have been able to identify such occasions of literary alchemy in Hemingway's work, I have associated them with acts of omission through the aesthetics of silence and of the invisible.[5] Defined as such, literary alchemy, through the associative figures of speech such as metaphor and metonymy, permits prose to acquire the full connotative features of literary language.

In his Nobel Prize acceptance speech, Hemingway identified alchemy as the originary mode of artistic transformative powers: "Things may not be immediately discernible in what a man writes, and in this sometimes he is fortunate, but eventually they are quite clear and by these and the degree of alchemy that he possesses he will endure or be forgotten." Whether such powers are at work in organic or inorganic chemistry, religion or psychology, the arts or literature, the theory of alchemy applies to each change of state and to the amelioration of their respective substances.

With its ancient African surroundings serving as a catalyst, literary alchemy greatly enriches our discussion of the concepts of the "new religion" in *Under Kilimanjaro*. The alchemical search for transmuting lead into gold is a surprisingly fundamental human desire as an archetype. As the philosopher Gershom Scholem explains, the desire to change lead into "gold fulfills all the requirements of alchemical symbolism: it represents the mystical communion of the highest principles operating in the cosmos, which come about through the medium of creation — as much God's creation of the cosmos as the alchemical completion of the Work" (22).

As a creative writer who has attained the status of a seer in Africa, the narrator is attentive to alchemy's place not only in literature but also in (among other topics) religious beliefs and practices. In *Under Kilimanjaro* creative alchemy attempts to reconcile seemingly irreconcilable opposites such as continents, races, genders, youth and old age, life and death, subjectivity and objectivity, and organic and inorganic matter — all merging in transformative prose. As practiced in *Under Kilimanjaro*, literary alchemy provides the means to bring into play the magic of a variety of narrator's lived experiences in Africa. Consequently, one does not find it wholly unexpected that often for the narrator reality and unreality merge; as happens, for example, when he speaks to faru, an imagined African animal, in an equally imagined "tongue" (based on, but not really, Spanish; 147). That is to say, Hemingway creates a semi-fictional creature called faru (Swahili for rhinoceros), situating it somewhere between the real (his knowledge of rhinoceros) and the imaginary (a beast that understands human speech, even the narrator's "invented" language) — the result being a "magical" or "marvelous" creature as one might find in a fairy tale. In other words, all that exists incessantly transforms itself or is transformed and arrives at a new ontological state with requisite new structures and functions.

Alchemy in Practice in the "New Religion" in *Under Kilimanjaro*

As I have noted, the narrator in *Under Kilimanjaro* no longer hunts for trophies, but rather focuses on "shooting for the meat we needed to eat" (116–17). The rituals of hunting, killing animals well, preparing the meat properly, and consuming it in the company of others are all acts of alchemical modifications in their largest, most inclusive sense of the adjective *alchemical*. Fasting is similarly a biophysical and spiritual transformational experience, so is drinking, which begins with the distillation of grains and grapes into alcohol, a perfect example of alchemical change. It is frequently done ritually. Ceremonial drinking reaches its highest expression with Nguili, the narrator's young mess attendant, who "loved to fill the Jinny [gin] flask almost as much as to pour beer and he always filled it as though he were serving the Mass" (78). The allusion to the ritual consumption of the consecrated wine and bread (the blood and body of Christ) points us to a sacred transformation.

Jungian psychoanalyst Marie-Louise von Franz argues that "only if the alchemist has through meditation a relationship to his inner self, that is, to the *Anthropos* in matter, can he produce the right kind of transformations" (149). This appears to be true of the narrator of *Under Kilimanjaro* as an alchemist of the art of language. I would say that the notion of transformative lingual alchemy comprises the creative matrix and the guiding principle of the quasi-fictional narrative discourse in *Under Kilimanjaro*. The narrator is not merely intuitively aware of alchemy's place within philosophy, psychology, and religion but also, and above all, of its significant place in the arts. In *Under Kilimanjaro*, creative alchemy merges the binary oppositions of the denotative and connotative lexical levels of the narrative discourse and extends this merger to the syntactic and semantic levels. *Under Kilimanjaro* even extends this merger to include human beings and nature, organic and nonorganic matter, mind and body, life and death, reality and unreality, man and woman, black and white, young and old, love and avoidable or inevitable violence, just to mention a few. As a result, the creative alchemy at work in *Under Kilimanjaro* enables the transformation of nonfiction into fiction and is capable of reversing its direction at will.

I have pointed out the narrator's transformative love for Africa, Africans, African landscape, African animals, indeed all that he encounters in Africa. The result of this transformative love is a profound aspiration to blood brotherhood with his gunbearer, tracker, and coreligionist Ngui. It is also seen in his relationship with Debba, the young Wakamba woman whom he considers his fiancée according to tribal rites, and who is therefore intimately related to him by the power of their mutual attraction. Clearly, the list of such rituals of transformation is not at all limited to these examples. Every reader can make his or her own list of such rites in *Under Kilimanjaro*.

The Seer and the Tragic Vision of Life

In *Under Kilimanjaro*, visionary encounters often occur in the dialectical fusion of beauty and grace with repulsiveness and tragedy, ecstasy and joy with pain and sorrow during the hunt, or in flashbacks, reflections, and conversations. The Spanish poet Federico García Lorca identified this kind of paradoxical, artistic, psychological, and metaphysical transformations as *duende*. Quoting Goethe's remark about the violinist Niccolò Paganini, García Lorca equates *duende* with "this 'mysterious power which everyone senses and no philosopher explains,'" adding elsewhere that *duende* "is, in sum, the spirit of the earth" that "does not come at all unless he [the spirit of the earth] sees death is possible" (57, 67). That is why *duende* as a visionary mystery is dependent on the presence of intense happiness and the sense of an inevitable ending. It appears in a dance between the luminescence of the sacred on earth and the gathering darkness of inevitable death, a truly authentic existential moment. *Duende* foretells impending death, disappearance, and oblivion in the midst of the plenitude of life and the fullness of being.

That is why I sense that in *Under Kilimanjaro duende* does not negate the promise of life; on the contrary, it hugely amplifies life. *Duende* is life affirming because it maximally intensifies the life of the senses and provides a vast horizon of sentience and transformation of states as universal, if tragic. Even if one believes that nothing is ever lost, that everything is a matter of transmutation of modes of being in the presence of death's absolute otherness, the experience of *duende* is unavoidable in extraordinary circumstances in which bliss exists side by side with anguish as an undeniably conjoined reality. In this sense, *duende* for the narrator of *Under Kilimanjaro* is still a matter of alchemical artistic transformation, but the magic in this specific sense is a darker magic; it is magic as cataclysm. Thus, in the indistinct borderline between ecstasy and sorrow, a union that comes close to the existential experience of the sacred, one feels the presence of *duende*.

Finally, I would call *duende* a powerful mode of self-disclosure of the mystical, which surpasses the duality of good and evil. It makes manifest the reality of the tragic vision of life that the seeker of truth experiences and accepts. Its significance for our concerns in the present essay is that in *Under Kilimanjaro*, many such moments occur. Psychologically, they intimate the Freudian uncanny. For the proximal and the remote, the familiar and the unfamiliar, grace and ugliness, love and cruelty coincide in many events in *Under Kilimanjaro*. The accounts of the death of beautiful and beloved animals, even when their ritual death is deliberate as it is in the corrida, link all such moments to *duende*, a gate into mysteries.

For me, with African landscape as a mnemonic background, the sorrowful account of the shooting of the beloved horse Old Kite comes as close as possible to a mode of word painting or ekphrastic sense of *duende*. The narrator tells us that as he prepared to shoot Old Kite, "he [the horse] thought it was a new game and he was learning it. He gave me a nice rubber-lipped kiss" (259). This passage of splendid prose poetry, saturated as it is with dirgelike evocations of life, love, violence, death, and irretrievable loss, lays bare a brutal truth: the inexorable destruction of certain organizations of living matter, in this case animal life. As Thomas Merton wrote in "An Elegy for Ernest Hemingway," "with one shot the whole hunt is ended" (122). *Under Kilimanjaro* is a chronicle of such endings, before the one that finally prompted Merton's elegy.

The accounts of *duende* in *Under Kilimanjaro* serve as examples that, unlike Hemingway's 1936 story "The Snows of Kilimanjaro," the narrator's "new religion" offers no salvation from decay equal to that of the frozen leopard at the sacred summit of Kilimanjaro. The death-haunted tragic sense of life that saturates all of Hemingway's writing finds no remedy in *Under Kilimanjaro*, except that now death announces the beginning of a drastic change from one form of sentient life to another. Thus, the narrator's "new religion" only holds forth the promise of an alchemical attunement to the environing numinous world. It is a demanding spiritual worldview in which there is no personal afterlife as a resurrection of the individual body. It merely holds forth the potential of our eternal oneness as sentient and therefore numinous matter.

Sentient Materialism in *Under Kilimanjaro*

> What a thing is in itself, for Goethe, is determined initially by its relation to itself. Its affinity for something else changes its self-relation, which is its self-identity.
>
> — J. Hillis Miller, *Ariadne's Thread: Story Lines*

By now, one responds to the quasi-fictional narrator in *Under Kilimanjaro* as a man who possesses an unusually, one may even say spectacularly, complex vision of life. His thoughts and emotions go far beyond his keen everyday observations on an African safari. His knowledge and insights about matters African are intricate enough. Nonetheless, the vibrant African countryside in itself augments the narrator's imagination as an evolving visionary matrix of the possible. The African reality is so stark, vivid, and poignant as to appear recurrently unreal. The narrator reports his "going into the African world of unreality that is defended and fortified by reality *past any reality there is*" (147, my emphasis). He adds that this palpable unreality was no psychological palliative for the unsupportable reality, but rather that "it was a ruthless real world made of the unreality of the real" (147).

The African reality is so piercingly real as to be unreal in its relentlessness, or, more precisely, it is *surreal*. This surreality of nature is what inspires the narrator to speak in unknown tongues. If he and Ngui "could talk to faru, who was incredible to start with, in his own tongue well enough for him to answer back and I could curse and insult faru in Spanish so that he would be humiliated and go off, then unreality was sensible and logical beside reality" (147). Indeed, unreality, as a form of dialectical antithesis to reality as we know and experience it, is always a possible alternative given to our mind by our perception of the natural world. As Adam Phillips has recognized, "it is the realities of nature that are our best sources of inspiration. Nature becomes another word for what is actually possible" (19). In addition, the opulent African reality deeply inspires the narrator of *Under Kilimanjaro* to perceive the existence of a different mode of reality in the sense that Phillips suggests.

In his three part structural model of the psyche, id, ego, and super-ego, Freud conceptualized the id or the unconscious as nature's upsurge in the mind's "apparatus." If one accepts the concept of the Freudian id, one may then maintain that the unconscious hints we receive may directly connect us with the natural world as the most intimate part of ourselves as an indivisible mind-body being. From this standpoint, it will be reasonable to infer that we as human beings are part of the material world that in its long, intricate evolutionary saga has become sentient, conscious, and *conscious of its consciousness*. As a result, one might say that the narrator of *Under Kilimanjaro* is taking a huge but *natural* speculative step forward in his belief in sentient materialism. It is fitting that he does so in Africa, which is recognized as the cradle of humanity.

The narrator's immediate lived experiences of nature in Africa lead him to believe that sentient matter constitutes all that exists, whether inorganic or organic. Thus, matter as a sentient quality or state is not restricted in any way. It may be the lowly dung beetles that the narrator watches, which "were the sacred scarabs of Egypt, in a slightly modified form." He thinks "we might find some place for them in the new religion" (439). Alternatively, it may be that "you turn and look at the sun and pray" with the intention "to live bravely, to die bravely, and to go directly to the Happy Hunting Grounds" (394). It matters not what the object is, because *everything* is in itself and *in relation to itself* sacred. The sacral is omnipresent for those whose vision is sufficiently free of preconceptions and obsessions to feel and to perceive it as such. Thus, to exist, in whatever form, is to be sentient matter. That is also the primary sense of being in the world and aware of one's own being as human. Recognizing the universal presence of sentience, and recognizing it as sacral, transforms the very act of seeing into a visionary mode of prayer.

On the plane of creation myths, the narrator's sentient cosmos intimates a spontaneous divine burst of creativity as sentience. Considering matter foundational, sentient, and universal would then situate the narrator's proposed religion in the proximity of pantheism and panpsychism, each presenting a cosmology that also endows matter with sentience and self-awareness. In a new and important context, it also opens up a whole gamut of creative vistas to artists such as the prophetic narrator himself, who works religiously in the field of language. Such vistas include an appeal to the supernatural in practicing creative magic, alchemy, divination, enchantment, and exploration of mysteries in art.

How does the narrator advance the nexus of his "new and unknown religion" as the ground of emergence of both the organic and inorganic universe? How does he formulate a possible method of elaborating on it as a reader response to his creative nonfiction? Let us examine a passage in which he criticizes vegetarians who abhor carnivorous human beings. The narrator defends Mary's hunting and killing of a "highly edible" kongoni, "which was as innocent, or more innocent, than anything could be" (129). His defense is based on her being a hunter and therefore needing "to perfect her shooting" in order "to kill without inflicting suffering" (129). He presents an apologia for the ancient activity of hunting, as a way of sustaining (and potentially creating) life. He also addresses the problem of "inflicting suffering" — a moral dilemma. Because the narrator asserts that sentience is not limited to humans, it becomes clear that animals suffer too. He rightly finds that causing unnecessary suffering is always and everywhere evil. However, anyone who struggles against violence must keep in mind that the world is irredeemably violent: violence is perpetually and inexorably present in the inevitable exercise of power. In this regard, the narrator's phrase, "no hay remedio," acquires a universal dimension. There is indeed no remedy for violence.

But why should this be so? For the narrator's "new and unknown religion" promulgates the belief in a panpsychic sentient universe as organic or inorganic matter. In the context of inexorable violence, an inherent correlate of universal sentience would be inerasable suffering always and everywhere. He asks, "who knows what the carrot feels, or the small young radish, or the used electric light bulb, or the worn phonograph disk, or the apple tree in winter? Who knows the feelings of the overaged aircraft, the chewed gum, the cigarette butt, the discarded book riddled by woodworms?" (129). In my view, these are legitimate questions. They deal with the endless desire of all that exists to continue existing, to remain inviolate and whole. But one violates the unique chemical status of the carrot and the radish when one separates them from their roots in the nourishing earth, and one alters their ontological status when one prepares and consumes them: they turn into nourishment, energy, and finally waste material. The same happens when Mary kills an edible kongoni or hunts any other animal. As a corollary to the inevitability of suffering, a moral being should minimize suffering in the exercise of power. The narrator in *Under Kilimanjaro* is primarily interested in the world as an endless series of things-in-themselves, whose identities shape themselves in the singularity of their sentient relationship with the world.

Under Kilimanjaro's "New Religion" and Lucretius's Philosophy of Matter

> *I do insist that we must recognize*
> *How small the primal atoms are that make*
> *A sentient object, I insist again*
> *That we must know their order, shape, design.*
>
> — Lucretius, *The Way Things Are*

Beyond the indispensable influence of Africa on the narrator's imagination, it is helpful to situate his reflections about his "new and unknown religion" within the context of his reading. The narrator identifies Virgil's *Georgics* as his, his wife's, and his friend Denis Zaphiro's favorite reading on their safari: "We were all reading the *Georgics* then in the C. Day Lewis translation. We had two copies then" (239).[6] I mention this because Lucretius's prose poem *De Rerum Natura* (*On the Nature of Things*, ca. 50 BCE), which draws directly from Epicurean philosophy, had a decisive influence on *Georgics*. I would suggest that the notion of the metaphysics of sentient matter presented in *Under Kilimanjaro* hints at the Epicurean physics of atoms. More specifically, it relates to Lucretius's formulation of the concept of atomic "swerve," which appears in *De Rerum Natura*.

In book 1 of *On the Nature of Things*, Lucretius declares, "Our starting-point shall be this principle: / Nothing at all is ever born from nothing" (24). Accordingly, "all things have to have the seed" or *primordia rerum* (26). He adds, "Our second axiom is this, that nature / Resolves each object to its basic atoms / But does not ever utterly destroy it" (26). For Lucretius, then, matter in its strong etymological sense of *materia* — in its double signification as the basal substance from which something originates, and as *mater*, mother, the source, the starting place — constitutes an originary version of philosophical materialism in the Western world. It is also roughly comparable to our contemporary philosophy of scientific materialism and theory of atomic physics. There is a correlative and vastly important dimension to Lucretius's concept of atomic theory. He conceptualizes the phenomenon of "atomic swerve," in Latin, *declinare* (deflection), which he adopts from Epicurean philosophy. In cognizance of Lucretius's Epicurean philosophical theory of "atomic swerve," Skrbina legitimately points out that the "willful swerving of the atoms is the basis of our own free will" (52). One may surmise that this brilliant statement, couched in such clear and concise language, would have been very appealing to the narrator of *Under Kilimanjaro*, who himself states things in a manner abundantly precise.

In his introduction to *On the Nature of Things*, Burton Feldman has written that Lucretius's "poem moves from atoms to mind, to sex, to the birth and growth of the world and society and religion, and ends with a coldly courageous and rational dissection of terror and death" (11). Feldman's description of *On the Nature of Things* comes close to our present evaluation of that other prose poem that we now know as *Under Kilimanjaro*.

Other Antecedents of Sentient Materialism in *Under Kilimanjaro*

Toward the end of *Under Kilimanjaro*, Mary Hemingway, concerned with her husband's attempt to acquire some African "poisonous shrubs and plants," has this interesting conversation with him:

> "I'm not against everything crazy or wild that you do. I just don't want anything to happen to you. And the religion does confuse me."
> "It confuses me a little. But it has a sound scientific as well as spiritual base."
> "What's the scientific base?"

"Overcoming protein deficiency."
"And the spiritual?"
"Eternal life enjoyed in happiness and things the way they were at their best. Also free beer." (438)

The narrator's responses to Mary's questions are possibly semi-humorous, but just the same thoughtful and cogent. He overcomes the deficiency of protein by the ritual of the hunt and expresses the wish for eternal happiness and ecstasy (or spiritual drunkenness) so well known to the Sufi, a mystic Shiite denomination of Islam, practiced in Africa by the Mourid brotherhood of Senegal. I find the allusion to the "sound scientific" base of the "new religion" intriguing and deserving of examination.

Consequently, very briefly, I shall mention a few of the philosophers and scientists who offer precedents of the speculative concepts of the narrator's "new and unknown" religion. I sense certain affinities between the narrator's notion of a cosmology based on a unitary concept of nature as sentient matter in *Under Kilimanjaro* and philosophers such as the Italian Giordano Bruno (1685–1753) and the Dutch Baruch (or Benedictus) Spinoza (1632–1677). For Bruno and Spinoza, as for their predecessor Lucretius, matter is the foundation of all reality. For them, too, inasmuch as God inhabits everything and everything is matter, it follows that all phenomena contain and reveal the One God. Then there is the nineteenth-century Marxian dialectical materialism, in which matter preexists all of existence and provides the guiding principles of transformation, including change in the human mind and consciousness. However, dialectical materialism refuses matter any divine origin.

In the late nineteenth and early twentieth centuries, physicists renewed their interest in the atom in the field of quantum mechanics and its studies of the physics of the subatomic structure of particles. It will considerably enlarge our perspective to make a connection between modern quantum mechanics, embedded as it is within the general context of scientific materialism, and our discussion of sentient materialism in *Under Kilimanjaro*.

In the twentieth century, the German theoretical physicist Werner Heisenberg's (1901–1976) principle of indeterminacy challenged the inert, predetermined, inalterable *thingness* of matter. He introduced the concept of a scientifically supported mode of thinking of undeniable consequence about the sentience of subatomic matter. Heisenberg detected that this indeterminacy would occur whenever he would attempt to determine separately either the electron's location or its momentum. The determination of one would reciprocally increase the indeterminacy of the other. In this context, our notion of the sentience of matter as manifested in the form of a used electric light bulb in *Under Kilimanjaro* would require no greater effort to comprehend than, say, the differing responses of subatomic particles to the varieties of measuring instruments used. Danish physicist Niehls Bohr (1885–1962) and French physicist Louis de Broglie (1892–1987) expanded this principle to include the physicist's conception of matter as either wave or particle such as an electron or atom. As a result, Stephen Toulmin and June Goodfield could conclude, by 1962, that philosophers of nature "have increased the discrimination both of their intellectual and of their practical instruments: moving from visible to microscopic, from microscopic to molecular, from molecular to electronic dimensions. At each new level, a novel type of structure has turned up" (301–2).

Now one may say confidently that the sentient materialism of *Under Kilimanjaro* defies the deterministic and mechanistic scientific materialism of the nineteenth and twentieth centuries. Perhaps it comes close to the Marxian dialectic of materialism, which declares all of existence to be matter, but matter as constantly evolving. However, it differentiates itself from such absolute materialism by endowing matter with sentience. The narrator in *Under Kilimanjaro* advances a view of the universe as originary matter or *prima materia* that defies inertness. All existents are various manifestations of such self-aware *prima materia*. Consequently, self-aware *prima materia* lays the foundation of what one may call the cosmology of a mode of mystical materialism. The consequences of such scientific and philosophical views of nature support in a new way the view of responsiveness of matter that the narrator so boldly presents in *Under Kilimanjaro*. For me, it makes known the "unknown" in the narrator's "new religion."

Above as Below in *Under Kilimanjaro*

> *Kilimanjaro is a snow-covered mountain 19,710 feet high, and is said to be the highest mountain in Africa. Its western summit is called by the Masai "Ngàje Ngài," the House of God. Close to the western summit there is the dried and frozen carcass of a leopard. No one has ever explained what the leopard was seeking at that altitude.*
>
> — Ernest Hemingway, "The Snows of Kilimanjaro"

> *In truth, certainty and without doubt, whatever is below is like that which is above. And whatever is above is like that which is below. The highest comes from the lowest and the lowest from the highest.*
>
> — Hermes Trismegistos, "The Emerald Tablet," in John Eberly, *Al-Kimia*

For Hemingway scholarship, what is new and exciting in *Under Kilimanjaro* is its thrust and directional divergence from "The Snows of Kilimanjaro" in terms of the search for the sacred. One may use the French word *sens* in this context, which indicates both direction and meaning, to differentiate the spiritual divergence in the two works separated by nearly two decades. The absolute purity and incorruptibility of the white snow at the summit of Kilimanjaro in "The Snows of Kilimanjaro" symbolically represent the sky gods. This summit is the beatific sphere where the legendary leopard sought refuge in the House of God, and towards which the writer-protagonist, Harry, seemed to be flying after his death. Nearly twenty years later, Hemingway's narrator reverses this ascensional vision of the sacral and the eternal. The "new religion" indicates a descent from on high to down below, from the purity of the white snow-covered summit to the dark fecund finite earth below. For the same reason, the verticality of the mountain ceases to be coextensive with the direction of the divine. It no longer delimits the dwelling place of the gods as it did in Hemingway's 1936 story.

In *Under Kilimanjaro*, the narrator consciously reverses the direction of sacral redemption and deliverance by conjoining the summit above and the sentient material earth below, making them both inseparable parts of a unified sentient whole. As Hermes Trismegistos observed: "In truth, certainty and without doubt, whatever is below is like that which is above" (Eberly, 82). The narrator as a seer transforms the external opacity of earthly matter into the radiant inner experience of sentient matter in the infinities of time and space.

Following an intuitive trajectory of an incorporative logic, the narrator of *Under Kilimanjaro* seems to be seeking to found a religion in which sentient matter precedes human existence and essence. That makes it possible for him to claim that the origin of his "new religion" "was as old if not older than the mountain" (377). For universal sentient matter surely predates all mountains, including Kilimanjaro. The narrator also tells us that his "new religion" is coincident with "Gitchi Manitou the Mighty versus All Others" (89). Gitchi Manitou, the Creator God of the Anishnaabeg (Odawa, Ojibwe, and Algonquin Indians of North America), is a syncretic god with immense powers of creation. The very mention of the name of Creator God Gitchi Manitou may fall into the category of *kuma*, which the Mandingo peoples associate with "special powers . . . those words uttered only at nights in the telling of myths, legends, and tales" (Abrahams, 24). *Kuma* is the language of being with the night, being immersed in its gleaming darkness with its intimations of the void, and partaking of the creative mysteries they offer.

As for Christianity, the narrator discloses that "I was not a believer but a follower and had made the pilgrimage to Compostela and it had been worth it" (338). The distinction he makes between follower and believer is salient. The believer no longer needs to seek the truth, for the simple reason that to believe is tantamount to having already found and appropriated the truth. However, the follower is still in pursuit of truth. The narrator's disclosure clarifies his statement that "we retain the best of various other sects and tribal law and customs. But we weld them into a whole that all can believe in" (89).

To conclude: under the influence of his lived experiences of nature in Africa, the narrator proposes a new vision of sentient materialism as his "new religion." In his Nobel Prize acceptance speech, Hemingway declared: "For a true writer each book should be a new beginning where he tries again for something that is beyond attainment. He should always try for something that has never been done or that others have tried and failed. Then sometimes, with great luck, he will succeed." Hemingway's *Under Kilimanjaro* is such a book, because its "new religion" is a call to a veritable homecoming, an invitation to a return to the first sacral sunrises and sunsets in the long melancholy saga of the world. It is *new* precisely because it is as old as the prerecorded history of the human race and its too-often sad and reedy music that haunts us. Happy are those who respond to the call of this speculative "new religion," for in reading *Under Kilimanjaro* they shall find the rare sense of ecstatic mystical awe, wonder, and enchantment of a luminous living universe whole and entire.

Notes

[1] As such it does not entirely coincide with what the Francophone Senegalese poet and cultural theorist Léopold Sédar Senghor and his fellow poets Martinican Aimé Césaire and Guianian Léon Damas referred to as *la Négritude* in combating French colonial racism. Damas's European, African, and American Indian (Métisse) ancestry would be of much interest to our discussion.

[2] Mirza Ghulam Ahmad (1839–1908) is the author of *The Teachings of Islam: An Exposition of the Beauties of Islam Drawn Entirely from the Holy Quran in a Very Lucid Form; The Real Key to Eternal Happiness,* of which Hemingway owned the tenth enlarged edition (Brasch and Sigman, 3, item 45). A slightly different version is available at http://aaiil.info/mga/teachings/heavenly.htm (accessed 11 December 2009).

[3] For extensive treatment of Islam and Christianity in Africa, see Ray, esp. 143–63 and 168–95.

[4] Ondaatje locates it southwest of Nairobi, "near the Kimana River and swamp" (171).

[5] See my articles, "The Aesthetics of Silence" and "The Aesthetics of the Visible and the Invisible."

[6] Hemingway had another copy of the *Georgics*, a translation into verse by John Dryden, with an introduction by George F. Whicher (New York: Heritage Press, 1953). See Brasch and Sigman, 386.

Works Cited

Abrahams, Roger D. *African Folktales.* New York: Pantheon Books, 1983.
Baker, Carlos. *Ernest Hemingway: A Life Story.* New York: Scribner's, 1969.
Brasch, James Daniel, and Joseph Sigman. *Hemingway's Library: A Composite Record.* New York: Garland, 1981.
Eberly, John. *Al-Kimia: The Mystical Islamic Essence of the Sacred Art of Alchemy.* Hillsdale, NY: Sophia Prennis, 2004.
Feuerbach, Ludwig. *The Essence of Religion.* Translated by Alexander Loos. New York: Prometheus Books, 2004.
Franz, Marie-Louise von. *Psyche and Matter.* Boston: Shambala, 1992.
García Lorca, Federico. *In Search of Duende.* Translated by Christopher Maurer. New York: New Directions, 1998.
Hemingway, Ernest. *Green Hills of Africa.* New York: Scribner's, 1935.
———. "Hemingway: The Art of Fiction." Interview in *Writers at Work: Paris Review Interviews,* edited by George Plimpton, 217–39. New York: Viking Press, 1974.
———. Nobel Prize Acceptance Speech. http://nobelprize.org/nobelprizes/literature/laureat1954/hemingway-speech.html (accessed 19 August 2009).
———. *The Short Stories of Ernest Hemingway.* New York: Scribner's, 1938.
———. *Under Kilimanjaro,* edited by Robert W. Lewis and Robert E. Fleming. Kent: Kent State UP, 2005.
Horton, Robin. "Philosophy and African Studies." In *Africa in the Wider World,* edited by David Brokensha and Michael Crowder, 266–69. Oxford: Pergamon Press, 1967.
Lucretius Carus, Titus. *The Way Things Are: "De Rerum Natura" of Titus Lucretius Carus.* Introduction by Burton Feldman. Translated by Rolfe Humphries. Bloomington: Indiana UP, 1964.
Merton, Thomas. *Selected Poems of Thomas Merton.* New York: New Directions, 1967.
Miller, J. Hillis. *Ariadne's Thread: Story Lines.* New Haven: Yale UP, 1992.
Nakjavani, Erik G. R. "The Aesthetics of Silence: Hemingway's 'The Art of the Short Story.'" *Hemingway Review* 3, no. 2 (1984): 38–45.
———. "The Aesthetics of the Visible and the Invisible: Hemingway and Cézanne." *Hemingway Review* 5, no. 2 (1986): 2–11.
Ondaatje, Christopher. *Hemingway in Africa: The Last Safari.* New York: The Overlook Press, 2003.
Phillips, Adam. *Darwin's Worms: On Life Stories and Death Stories.* New York: Basic Books, 2000.
Ray, Benjamin C. *African Religions: Symbol, Ritual, and Community.* Upper Saddle River, NJ: Prentice Hall, 2000.
Scholem, Gershom. *Alchemy and Kabbalah.* Translated by Klaus Ottmann. Putnam, CT: Spring Publications, 2006.
Skrbina, David. *Panpsychism in the West.* Cambridge: MIT Press, 2005.

Somé, Malidoma Patrice. *Of Water and Spirit: Ritual, Magic, and Initiation in the Life of an African Shaman*. New York: Penguin Books, 1994.

Stevens, Wallace. *The Collected Poems*. New York: Vantage, 1990.

Toulmin, Stephen, and June Goodfield. *The Architecture of Matter*. New York: Harper, 1962.

10: Barking at Death: Hemingway, Africa, and the Stages of Dying

James Plath

> *Since in our unconscious mind we are all immortal, it is almost inconceivable for us to acknowledge that we too have to face death.*
>
> — Dr. Elisabeth Kübler-Ross, *On Death and Dying*
>
> *Suddenly, he was afraid of dying.*
>
> — Ernest Hemingway, *The Nick Adams Stories*

In *Green Hills of Africa*, the first-person narrator says that Crane "was dying from the start" (23). In a way, so was Ernest Hemingway, whose fiction betrays what Frank Scafella described, without exaggeration, as an "extreme anxiety of death" (5). Not surprisingly, there has been a great deal written on the subject, much of it having to do with Hemingway's love of the *corrida* and most of it harking back to Phillip Young's interpretation of a famous Hemingway phrase: "grace under pressure"[1] (*Ernest Hemingway*, 7–9, 14). Young saw the emergence of a "code hero" very early in Hemingway's fiction, a hero whose message "is life: you lose, of course; what counts is how you conduct yourself while you are being destroyed" (8). For decades, critics subscribed to Young's argument that Hemingway's famous World War I wounding was the source of his alleged ambivalence toward death and the irresistible urge to confront it.

It's worth remembering, however, that Hemingway was traumatized by death even before, as a nineteen year old, he was felled by a trench mortar and machine-gun fire in Italy. As biographer Kenneth Lynn observes, Hemingway's early boyhood was haunted by death "for reasons that he could not bring himself to discuss with anyone" (22). This avoidance persisted throughout his life. Valerie (Danby-Smith) Hemingway, who became his friend and secretary in 1959, writes that Hemingway often voiced his fears to her but never talked about death (132).[2] According to Idaho hunting companion Forrest MacMullen, Hemingway broached the subject only obliquely, in a manner that could be construed as colorful behavior or jesting: he used to *bark* at the mention of death.

"He'd say, 'Woof woof,'" MacMullen recalled, "more or less acknowledging that he heard it. The first time that I was around him and death was mentioned and he said 'Woof woof,' I asked him about it. And he said, 'It's an unpleasant thing'" (Plath and Simons, 129).

Unable to talk about death to his friends, Hemingway filled his writing with it. Many scholars have noticed this, but John Killinger summarizes it best: "The most obviously recurrent motif in all of Hemingway's work has been the subject of death, or of violence, which, as Frederick Hoffman has observed, is only another form of death in which the victim survives" (17). From the accidental death and suicide in "Judgment of Manitou," Hemingway's first published high school story, to the last novel published during his lifetime, *The Old Man and the Sea* — which ends with Santiago not just dreaming of lions but also carrying his death inside him[3]— more than a few of his fictions deal with death.

In "Death and Dying: Hemingway's Predominant Theme," Mark Scheel notes that "most frequently, theories concerning the origin of Hemingway's preoccupation with death and dying take into consideration the psychology of the author" (5). So, when a young Nick Adams suddenly "realized that some day he must die. It made him feel quite sick" (*The Nick Adams Stories*, 14), critics often think of Hemingway as well — especially when this excised passage is so different from the ending Hemingway gave the published version of "Indian Camp," in which the narrator tells us that Nick was "quite sure that he would never die" (21). The statement cannot be easily dismissed as a young boy's naïveté: the author's careful revision and the fact that he has just witnessed pain, blood, and death make the line resonate. It's also a classic case of denial that typically follows the shock that accompanies the recognition of one's own mortality.

Dr. Elisabeth Kübler-Ross's seminal work, *On Death and Dying*, published eight years after Hemingway killed himself, remains the model for understanding the emotional stages that people experience when facing catastrophic loss in general and death in particular. Studying the terminally ill, the Swiss psychiatrist affirmed that fear of death was universal and that, after the initial shock, people confronting death traverse five distinct stages: denial (as young Nick appears to experience in "Indian Camp"), anger, bargaining, depression, and, finally, acceptance. What was published as a theory in 1969 was confirmed by a Yale University study in 2007: that except for acceptance — which researchers found occurring at any point in the self-grieving process, if at all — the other stages "peaked and faded in exactly the sequence of the stage theory" (Bass, 31). The implicit universality suggests, of course, that the Kübler-Ross model could be applied to Hemingway as well — especially when, as one biographer observes, "Hemingway's own death had become so real an event in his mind that he could even imagine what it might be like for his wife to find his body, and he testified to this in 'Kilimanjaro'" (Lynn, 431).

While death may be frequent in Hemingway's fiction, it is by no means a given: not all his protagonists die, and indeed, in some stories no one at all dies. But a progression takes us closer to death — a progression that points in the direction of Africa, a land that not only gave Hemingway extreme pleasure and inspiration but also helped him confront the prospect of his own mortality through his writing.

Hemingway's first trip to Africa amplified a sense of his fragility and mortality in ways that not even the famous wounding in Italy had done. That wound cannot be dismissed, but while Hemingway returned with a trunk full of souvenirs and a duffle bag full of rhetoric about how the war had changed him, and while brother Leicester later wrote that Ernest "had received some psychic shock" (56), the young man did not act the part of a traumatized veteran. He showed his scars at parties, wore his Italian officer's cape and boots around town, and shot flare pistols in his backyard for the neighborhood children (Nagel and Villard, 258). An article in the *Oak Parker* noted that Hemingway's "only voluntary comment on the war is that it was great sport and he is ready to go on the job if it happens again" (Leicester Hemingway, 53). Even before he returned to the United States, Hemingway had written his parents, with equal measures of humor and conviction, that "it has been fairly conclusively proved that I can't be bumped off," and that what makes him hate the war isn't death, but missing out on "those wonderful catches of Rainbow at the [Horton] Bay" (*Selected Letters*, 18, 16).

But fifteen years later, in Africa, there was nothing sporting or heroic about the debilitating amoebic dysentery Hemingway developed — an illness so severe that he had to be airlifted to Nairobi for eight days of hospital treatment, interrupting his much-anticipated first safari with his wife, Pauline, and their Key West friend, Charles Thompson. He did not play it down (as he had the war wound). "That's a hell of a lousy disease," he wrote his editor Max Perkins. "Your whole damn intestine tries to come out. Feels as though you were giving birth to a child" (*The Only Thing That Counts*, 206). In "A Tanganyika Letter," which was published in *Esquire*, Hemingway sounded martyred as he tried to be more poetic: "I became convinced that though an unbeliever I had been chosen as the one to bear our Lord Buddha when he should be born again on earth" (*By-Line*, 159). With factors like war, duty, patriotism, and heroism removed from the equation, a potentially life-threatening moment such as this seems to have had a serious impact on Hemingway. And there were other close calls on safari, including Hemingway's rifle falling and firing a shot past his head, as well as the realization that when Pauline tried to shoot a lion, Hemingway had remained in the car and would have been "unable to save her if the lion charged" (Reynolds, *The 1930s*, 159, 162). The entire first safari carried a subtext of accidental and nonheroic death.

By all accounts, that safari was less than a triumph. Biographers report that Hemingway's shots were so off-target it was sometimes humiliating, while their guide became sick and depressed and "the safari degenerated badly," turning into an alpha-male contest of measurements between Hemingway and Thompson in which Hemingway came up short every time (Reynolds, *The 1930s*, 162–65). Yet, none of it could dampen his enthusiasm for the long-awaited safari. Africa had such a powerful effect on Hemingway that even the memory of the dysentery that made him stagger and caused him a "fortnight of torture" (Baker, *Life*, 251) wasn't enough to keep him from gushing rhapsodically in *Green Hills of Africa*, "I loved the country so that I was happy as you are after you have been with a woman that you really love, when . . . you can never have it all and yet what there is, now, you can have, and you want more and more, to have, and be, and live in, to possess now again for always, that long, sudden-ended always" (72). As Baker writes, "Ernest's appetite and his admiration for the land were both enormous" (*Life*, 249), and that was reflected in his writing about it. Leicester Hemingway reports that his brother "had been doing twenty to twenty-two pages a day toward the end [of *Green Hills*], though his usual production was about five pages daily" (178).

The second safari in 1953–1954 also had several close calls. Michael Reynolds informs us that friends found Hemingway "incredibly changed by the two African plane crashes, his beard whiter, his eyes frequently vacant, his moods mercurial." Yet once again, working on his African book he found the words flowing at an above-average rate, producing 4,587 words the first week of February 1955 "when previously a good week would have been half that many" (Reynolds, *The Final Years*, 286). Africa was so captivating and the amount of game so unbelievably bountiful that the second trip made Hemingway "ready to give up his no longer defensible Cuban hilltop in favor of Africa" (286), despite the two crashes that almost killed him. "I never knew of a morning in Africa when I woke that I was not happy" (16), he writes in *Under Kilimanjaro*, a book composed between October 1954 and spring 1956 — that is, immediately after his experiences of observing death, inflicting death, and coming very close to his own death. In that manuscript, it's clear that Africa helped him process his thoughts on such a difficult and complex subject. Time and again an observation of an animal's death leads to a meditation on death, which in turn leads to an appreciation of life. In one such instance, Hemingway considers what would have happened had one of them been killed by a lion, wondering optimistically, "would our souls have flown off somewhere?" (220). Observing death in another quarter, he notes that "a lion after he has died and stiffened has little dignity" (224), and this leads him, on the very next page, to a happy appreciation of all the species he's ignored: "For a long time I realized I had only paid attention to the predators, the scavengers, and the birds that were good to eat and the birds that had to do with hunting," but he resolves to pay more attention to kingbirds and mockingbirds and migratory birds (225). Both safaris then, gave him direct exposure to death, heightened his feeling for life, and were followed by periods of fluent writing.

Still, it was the first safari that made the deeper impression. It was an important, emotional, and long-awaited event for Hemingway. Reynolds tells us that Ernest, at age six, "stood in awe beside two gigantic stuffed elephants in the Field Museum; at sixteen, he promised himself to do 'exploring work' in Africa; at twenty-six, he gave his character Jake Barnes the dream of hunting in British East Africa. Now, at thirty-four, Ernest was there on Roosevelt's ground" with the very guide who had led Hemingway's earliest childhood hero on his epic 1909 safari (*The 1930s*, 156). He was living out a childhood fantasy by following in Teddy Roosevelt's footsteps. To have that trip marred by pain, severe bleeding, and such a depletion of energy that "he could hardly write a letter" (Leicester Hemingway, 141) made it not just a life-threatening moment, but a life-defining one as well.

Adrenalin and youth got Hemingway through the shock of his World War I wounding, and his main concern while in the hospital in 1918 was whether he would lose his leg or if his exaggerations about his bravery would be uncovered (Reynolds, *The Young Hemingway*, 21). But in Africa, suffering far from a hospital, he feared something much worse: he knew he could die. The prospect was not leavened by any sort of spiritual or political ideology or idealism. As Hemingway the "naturalist" had written in *Death in the Afternoon*, "most men die like animals, not men." He describes "death from Spanish influenza. In this you drown in mucus, choking, and how you know the patient's dead is; at the end he shits the bed full" (139). Clearly, a slow, natural death was even more odious to Hemingway than being killed suddenly, quickly, and for an ideal, as in war.

Hemingway's treatment of death in his postsafari fiction confirms that Africa had a most profound effect on him. Before the first safari, Hemingway had only dabbled in death, keeping it at a distance. His high school fiction was as derivative of Jack London as his journalism was of Ring Lardner, and the deaths that Hemingway included in two of three stories published in his high school's literary magazine were as far removed from Hemingway's life and experiences as London's Klondike. In "Judgment of Manitou," a presumably French-Canadian trapper named Pierre plays a trick on his partner that results in poor Dick being attacked by a wolf pack. Ironically, as Pierre tries to help his friend, he gets caught in one of the traps they had set earlier, and is forced to kill himself to avoid the more unpleasant death his friend faced. Aside from the word *Manitou*, which is Ojibway for "Great Spirit" (and something Hemingway would surely have known from his summers in Michigan), nothing in the story is remotely connected to his own life. Hemingway was not a trapper, Michigan was not Canada, and the deaths in the story involved two people who were completely formed in Hemingway's (or London's) imagination. "Sepi Jingan," the other story involving death, is also a highly imaginative tale in which a dog kills an Indian. Again, while Hemingway spent time with the Ojibway in Michigan, none of the biographies or letters mentions any such incidents as the stories describe.

Likewise, of the stories Hemingway wrote in Paris following his World War I service, those that feature dying characters are far removed from the people and events in his personal life. "My Old Man" (1923), for example, tells of a jockey who dies; the story reminded critics of Sherwood Anderson, it seemed so derivative. "Indian Camp" (1925) includes the well-known suicide of the Indian husband who could not bear to hear his wife screaming during her caesarian without anesthesia — an event that Hemingway's siblings report was completely made up. "The Undefeated," "Banal Story," and Interchapter XIV from *In Our Time* (1925) feature bullfighters killed or dying, all of whose fates were totally imagined. As Reynolds reveals, while Hemingway saw Maera at the first bullfights he attended in 1923, "no matter what Hemingway saw in Pamplona and no matter what he said in letters about hanging out with bullfighters, he spoke little Spanish that summer" and did not know Maera — whom he "killed" in the bullring vignette, rather than reporting the less romantic death Maera suffered in real life from tuberculosis (*The Paris Years*, 139).

No major characters die in *The Torrents of Spring* (1926) or *The Sun Also Rises* (1926), but by this time, as Jackson Benson notes, Hemingway "began to identify very closely with his protagonists as he wrote about them, thinking of them as himself. Evidence may be found in the early manuscript of *The Sun Also Rises* wherein 'Hem' is used rather than 'Jake,' and in stories like 'Three-Day Blow' and 'Summer People' wherein Hemingway's own nickname 'Wemedge' is used as a nickname for Nick" (290). At this point, for a Hemingway haunted by death and beginning to exploit his own life in fiction, a novel that brings death closer to home is a significant step. Such a novel is *A Farewell to Arms* (1929).

Like Hemingway, Frederic Henry is a young American who is wounded below the waist while serving in the Italian ambulance corps, and, like Hemingway, young Henry has a romance with his nurse. With Catherine, Henry enjoys an Alpine idyll of love and skiing, much as Hemingway did with his first wife, Hadley. Then Catherine, like Hemingway's second wife, Pauline, has a terrible labor and a caesarian birth. Catherine dies. But while it is a major change for Hemingway to imagine the death of a character based on a composite of two real women he loved (instead of the wholly invented deaths of his previous fictions), the male protagonist still only faces the death of someone close to him, rather than his own.

Like the hyena from "The Snows of Kilimanjaro," Hemingway was gradually drawing closer to death in his fiction. Even so, although he writes about death in very graphic and grisly terms in his next book, *Death in the Afternoon* (1932), death is still kept at a safe distance because it is imagined, constructed out of knowledge acquired in observation, reading, and conversation, and not from the experience of his own flesh. The distance is reflected in the style, which assumes, as Scott Donaldson notes, the "objective tone" of a journalist or naturalist (*By Force of Will*, 283).

Then comes that first, all-important African safari that began in November 1933. The main male characters of the two famous short stories that emerged from it are clearly identifiable with Hemingway: they are on safari in Africa, they are married to rich women, and Harry is a writer. For the first time in Hemingway's writing life, his male protagonists die — Macomber an "animal" death via a hunting gun, a 6.5 Mannlicher; and Harry a "natural" death that is considerably more painful and protracted. This was a major turning point for Hemingway, for while before that safari no male protagonist had died, after Africa every main male character in every novel published during Hemingway's lifetime will die. Harry Morgan dies (1937), Robert Jordan dies (1940), Richard Cantwell dies (1950), and Santiago, if he is not dead at the end of *The Old Man and the Sea* (1952), will die soon after, having told Manolín that "in the night I spat something strange and felt something in my chest was broken" (125). According to Reynolds, "Only Mary [Hemingway]'s pleading kept Santiago alive after returning with the shark-stripped skeleton of his marlin" (*The Final Years*, 297).

In the matter of Hemingway and death, then, the fulcrum is clearly Africa, and at the apex of that fulcrum are the African stories, "The Short Happy Life of Francis Macomber" and "The Snows of Kilimanjaro." "The Short Happy Life of Francis Macomber" spawned much criticism based on the psychological necessity of facing one's fears, in this case, the fear of unmanly or unmasculine behavior. Macomber peforms poorly on safari, is consequently emasculated and cuckolded, but has his manhood (and his power over his wife) restored when he conducts himself with courage. One can point to the cuckolding as the turning point, as it leaves Macomber "grim and furious" while it strengthens the woman's power: the next morning, "Margot . . . looked younger . . . more innocent and fresher" (27). Then, when Macomber shoots well, he "felt a drunken elation," while his wife's power was reduced: she "sat very white faced" (29). Even when he discovers that one bull hadn't been killed and he has to go back in to finish the job, Macomber discovers that "for the first time in his life he really felt wholly without fear. Instead of fear he had a feeling of definite elation" (31). Later, he tells Wilson he'd like to try for another lion and adds, "I'm really not afraid of them now. After all, what can they do to you?" Macomber had learned the lesson that Africa has to teach — kill or be killed, and when you're killing you're not being killed . . . or cuckolded, which is a type of symbolic killing. "That's it," said Wilson. "Worst one can do is kill you" (32). The power in the Macombers' relationship shifts, based on who is doing the "killing." And Macomber's reward for facing death is a quick "clean kill," during which he sensed "a sudden white-hot, blinding flash explode inside his head and that was all he ever felt" (36).

It was a remarkable step for Hemingway to take, if in fact he was facing his own fears through fiction. Indeed, a good argument might be made for that position. He had long resented what he saw as his mother's emasculation of his father (explored fictionally in "The Doctor and the Doctor's Wife" and "Now I Lay Me"), which he considered a main reason for his father's suicide (revisited fictionally in *For Whom the Bell Tolls*). Closer to home, there is Hemingway's relationship with the Cuban-based Jane Mason, the beautiful young wife of Grant Mason, on whom (many critics argue) Margot and Francis Macomber are based. Biographers are divided as to whether Hemingway had an affair with Jane. Cuban writer and Hemingway scholar Enrique Cirules bases his strong case on the testimony of locals and concludes "there was an intense and scandalous love affair" (23). But even if the affair didn't happen (as Reynolds seems to feel), the couple spent an inordinate amount of time together from their first meeting in 1931 until the Hemingways' departure for Europe and Africa in late 1933. Given Hemingway's own history of adultery, and factoring in his current guilty adulterous (and therefore suspicious) thoughts, he may have, as Robert W. Lewis convincingly argues, "turned Poor Old Mama's deep affection for Pop into the adultery of 'The Short Happy Life'" (Smith, 332). Lewis "was the first and most thorough in exploring the relationship between the triangles implicit in *Green Hills* and explicit in the story" (Smith, 332). In killing Macomber, then, Hemingway had basically killed an alter ego. He had done so mercifully, in the way that seemed least offensive to him, with a bullet that comes from the outside and that kills him quickly, painlessly, and at a moment when he feels good about himself (as opposed to the more shameful self-inflicted death of his father, or the messily degrading death caused by disease). Facing his own death, and finally able to translate that into the death of a main character with whom he could identify, Hemingway gave Macomber a "good" death, not the death of a defeated man or a coward.

An even more personal, more direct and painful confrontation with death appears in Hemingway's second African story. In "The Snows of Kilimanjaro," he no longer dabbles in death, reserving the ultimate fate for characters strictly devolved from his imagination (as in the early fiction) or for secondary ones based on friends or wives (as in *A Farewell to Arms*), nor does a character psychologically close to him die a clean, quick and relatively painless death (as with Macomber). In "Snows," about which Hemingway once admitted he "never wrote so directly about myself as in that story" (Hotchner, 176), Hemingway takes an even bolder step and doesn't just try to capture the essence of a dying man; he apparently records his own progression of feelings as recalled from that grave bout with dysentery — feelings that so closely parallel the stages of the Kübler-Ross model that Harry's confronting of his own mortality must have also been Ernest's.

Always recognized as a major story, "The Snows of Kilimanjaro" has elicited much criticism, almost all of it centering on the story's symbols: the frozen carcass of the leopard in the epigraph, the vultures and hyena that close in on the dying Harry, and the great mountain itself that looms as an ethereal postscript. As Gloria Dussinger explains,

> When passing an aesthetic judgment on the symbols in 'The Snows of Kilimanjaro,' students of Hemingway follow one of three courses. The first is to grant the leopard and the mountain their full idealistic value, but to deny Harry a place among them. . . . A second critical group, accepting the metaphysical meaning of the symbols and also accepting the apotheosis of Harry, cannot reconcile the two. . . . The third approach to 'The Snows of Kilimanjaro' subscribes unreservedly to both the transcendental import of the symbols and the transfiguration of the protagonist." (55)

Other critics have found it difficult to integrate the symbols into the story. Marion Montgomery complains that "the headnote and the final two sections protrude from the story, making it an awkward iceberg" (149), while Robert O. Stephens writes, "The connection between Hemingway's riddle at the opening of 'The Snows of Kilimanjaro' and the story itself is tenuous at best" (93). Caroline Gordon and Allen Tate are even more blunt, insisting that "the symbolism seems something the writer has tacked on, rather than an integral part of the story" (144). They meant it as a complaint, but perhaps they are correct: it *is* tacked on. After all, this was a writer who once famously remarked that "all symbolism that people say is shit" (*Selected Letters*, 780), and later poked fun at critics' responses to "Snows" in a letter in which he wrote that he did not "want to be breathing down your neck like a hyena (just got these new symbols by reading reviews of The Snows of Kilimanjaro)" (782).

All this paves the way for considering the symbols as a subterfuge, as details that Hemingway inserted to draw critics' attention away from his real purpose, which would appear to be a highly personal "test run" of facing death. Such a reading would certainly help to explain why he said that of the African stories, this was the only one that was "difficult" for him (*The Only Thing That Counts*, 239), or why he was so proud of it, considering it "about as good as any of my stories" (*Conversations*, 46). "The Snows of Kilimanjaro" goes beyond what Carlos Baker called "an experiment in the psychology of a dying man." Baker writes: "Like Hemingway, the writer Harry in the story has been 'obsessed' for years with curiosity about the idea of death" ("Two Hemingway Stories," 122), but for Hemingway to write this story as accurately as he did, he had to be experiencing psychologically the very same stages as the dying Harry. As Lynn observed, the plane that was to airlift an extremely sick and suffering Hemingway that first safari "did not arrive in the morning, and the agonized waiting then began that Hemingway would recreate so brilliantly in 'The Snows of Kilimanjaro'" (414) — which may be Hemingway's first direct attempt to deal with his own physical mortality through fiction. And Harry/Hemingway's psychological journey follows the same stages in the process of facing one's own death that Kübler-Ross identified, initial shock giving way to the coping stages of denial, anger, bargaining, depression, and finally (if it occurs at all), acceptance.

As Kübler-Ross writes,

> the patient's first reaction may be a temporary state of shock from which he recuperates gradually. When his initial feeling of numbness begins to disappear and he can collect himself again, man's usual response is, "No, it cannot be me."
> ... Depending very much on how a patient is told, how much time he has to gradually acknowledge the inevitable happening, and how he has been prepared throughout life to cope with stressful situations, he will gradually drop his denial and use less radical defense mechanisms. (37)

When readers first meet Harry at the start of "The Snows of Kilimanjaro," he is already past the shock of realizing he is dying. Just as the narrative begins in medias res, so does Harry's reaction to his African death sentence. The very first line of "Snows" is an expression of denial (Kübler-Ross's second stage); Harry says, "The marvelous thing is that it's painless" (52). That sounds very much like one of Kübler-Ross's own subjects who, in the stage of denial and isolation, referred to death as a "nuisance" and wished it would come "during sleep" or "without pain" (36). "Denial functions as a buffer after unexpected shocking news, allows the patient to collect himself and, with time, mobilize other, less radical defenses," writes Kübler-Ross. She explains that denial can range from an insistent "I feel fine" or "It's not so bad" to a complete unwillingness to accept even the idea of impending death ("It can't be" or "Why me?"). "This does not mean, however, that the same patient later on will not be willing or even happy and relieved if he can sit and talk with someone about his impending death. Such a dialogue will and must take place at the convenience of the patient, when he (not the listener!) is ready to face it. The dialogue also has to be terminated when the patient can no longer face the facts and resumes his previous denial" (35).

Harry has already passed the initial and peak phases of denial and has begun to incorporate the partial acceptance that Kübler-Ross saw in patients who "may briefly talk about the reality of their situation, and suddenly indicate their inability to look at it realistically any longer" (36–37). This explains why Harry wants to talk, but only on his own terms, and as a diversion. When his wife suggests that she read to him, he quickly rules it out, saying, "I can't listen to it," and reaffirms that "talking is the easiest" (53). Harry must talk about the things that he is able to face at this stage, the odor of the wound and the three vultures "squatting obscenely" nearby, and a dozen more sailing overhead. "I'm only talking," he reiterates. "It's much easier if I talk" (52). At this stage, Harry's flippancy, humor, and mercurial changing of subjects fit the pattern of behavior Kübler-Ross discovered in dying patients:

> How do we know, then, when a patient does not wish to face it anymore? He may talk about relevant issues as far as his life is concerned, he may share some important fantasies about death itself or life after death (a denial in itself), only to change the topic after a few minutes, almost contradicting what he said earlier. Listening to him at this point may seem like listening to a patient with a minor ailment. (37)

When someone rationalizes as Harry does and considers the "bright side" of his situation, he is not only denying his impending death, he is also denying himself an emotional response to it. At this point, the closest Harry comes to acceptance of death is when he thinks about his writing: "Now he would never write the things that he had saved to write until he knew enough to write them well." But Harry quickly replaces regret with another rationalization: "Well, he would not have to fail at trying to write them either" (54).

According to Kübler-Ross, "When the first stage of denial cannot be maintained any longer, it is replaced by feelings of anger, rage, envy, and resentment. The logical next question becomes, 'Why Me?'" This can be a difficult stage for loved ones to cope with, writes Kübler-Ross, because "this anger is displaced in all directions and projected onto the environment at times almost at random," often directed at the loved ones who are not dying, who get to live (44). Harry lashes out at his wife repeatedly, rejecting her offers of help and blaming her for his failings: "If you hadn't left your own people, your goddamned Old Westbury, Saratoga, Palm Beach people to take me on —," he blusters. His comments are cruel. When she asks him, "Don't you love me?" his terse response isn't just a "no." He expands on it: "I don't think so. I never have" (55). He rejects love altogether: "'Love is a dunghill,' said Harry. 'And I'm the cock that gets on it to crow'" (57). Harry is so unrelenting that he makes her cry. "You bitch," he says to her. "You rich bitch," to which she responds, "Stop it. Harry, why do you have to turn into a devil now?" (58). Hemingway makes a point of letting readers know that the bickering was not normal for Harry and his wife: "He had never quarreled much with this woman" (64). According to Kübler-Ross, terminally ill patients often become impossible during the second stage, but "The Snows of Kilimanjaro" offers an interesting take on the lashing out. "It's trying to kill to keep yourself alive, I imagine" (58), Harry explains, which was one of the lessons that Africa had taught him. Kill, or be killed — options that, as we have seen, Hemingway explored in "Macomber."

"I did not mind killing anything, any animal, if I killed it cleanly," Hemingway writes in *Green Hills of Africa*: "they all had to die and my interference with the nightly and the seasonal killing that went on all the time was very minute and I had no guilty feeling at all" (192–93). In Africa, a not-so-peaceable kingdom full of predators and prey, the killing is constant. While stalking a bull buffalo, Hemingway thinks, "I felt the elation, the best elation of all, of certain action to come, action in which you had something to do, in which you can kill and come out of it" (80). Later he muses, "I did nothing that had not been done to me. I had been crippled and gotten away. I expected, always, to be killed by one thing or another and I, truly, did not mind that any more" (107). But he did mind. As he wrote in *Death in the Afternoon*, "when a man is still in rebellion against death he has pleasure in taking to himself one of the Godlike attributes; that of giving it" (233) — which helps to explain the "Godlike" capriciousness in Hemingway's sport killing of birds and hyena described in great detail in *Green Hills of Africa*. Africa was Hemingway's bull ring, a natural, powerful validation of a symbolic construct in which Hemingway, who was indeed "in rebellion against death" throughout most of his life, found himself joyously in his element. There was something exhilarating about being in a natural environment where death could come at any moment and one could still somehow survive, which Hemingway apparently emphasized in an interview. As a reporter for the New York *Herald Tribune* observed, "The pursuit of game having renewed his enthusiasm for life, he returned home 'to work like hell and make enough money so that I can go back to Africa and really learn something about lions'" (*Conversations*, 4). The lessons that Hemingway — and Harry — learned about kill-or-be-killed are in evidence here as Harry pounces on his wife while in the second stage of anger identified by Kübler-Ross.

But as Harry lies dying in camp, it becomes clear that all he wants is to be able to write — to write the things, finally, that he had postponed. That was the reason for this safari, in fact; Harry returns to Africa "where he had been happiest in the good time of his life" and hopes that there "in some way he could work the fat off his soul the way a fighter went into the mountains to work and train in order to burn it out of his body" (60). This is Harry entering the stage that Kübler-Ross identified as bargaining. "If we have been unable to face the sad facts in the first period and have been angry at people and God in the second phase," Kübler-Ross writes, "maybe we can succeed in entering into some sort of agreement which may postpone the inevitable" (72). In most cases, this involves bargains with God, the wish for "most always an extension of life, followed by the wish for a few days without pain or physical discomfort" (72–73). It's ironic that Harry, who had come to Africa hoping for revitalization, instead finds himself on his deathbed. But it's equally ironic that in this state Harry is finally able to accomplish something he was now bargaining for — to "write" in his head those things that he could not get down on paper before.

Critics have pronounced the italicized sections "memories" of the writer's past and the final section a "dream" or "dreamlike sequence." But these sections are much more than that. They provide evidence of a writer who has recovered his gift. Memory and detail are the writer's tools, and Harry now successfully recalls events that he could write about. These italicized, well-"written" mental compositions represent a renewed defiance of death, a relapse into Kübler-Ross's second stage. "Now in his mind he saw a railway station at Karagatch," the first italicized section begins, "and he was standing with his pack and that was the headlight of the Simplon-Orient cutting the dark now and he was leaving Thrace then after the retreat." The immersion into memory is stopped by reality — "That was one of the things he had saved to write" (55) — but immediately he returns to memory/writing, until reality interferes again: "But he had never written a line of that" (56). Yet, Harry is already composing again, with another recollection-story about Christmas in the mountains and a wartime episode with the Austrians, interrupted again by the same reality-check refrain: "he had never written a word of that" (57). That Harry is actively engaged in trying to remember, to recollect details that form the basis of his fictions, is proven by the fact that the italicized memory/writing breaks off only to enable Harry to ask his wife for more detail: "Where did we stay in Paris?" (57), a city he will "write" about later in the story. Although reality intrudes again, as he realizes not only that he hasn't written it, but also that he never will — "He had been in it and he had watched it and it was his duty to write of it; but now he never would" (66) — he is still determined to write. "You can't take dictation, can you?" he asks his wife hopefully, which reinforces even more that he's indeed engaged in the process of writing (67). No, she tells him, after which he says, "That's all right." Then the acceptance continues, as he thinks, "There wasn't time, of course," only to be followed by a return to denial: "although it seemed as though it telescoped so that you might put it all into one paragraph if you could get it right" (68). Almost instantly Harry tries to "get right" his descriptions of the Black Forest and Paris.

Another exchange, about eating, also makes clear that denial is becoming more difficult to sustain:

"Could you eat now?" [his wife asks.] . . .
"I want to write," he said.
"You ought to take some broth to keep your strength up."
"I'm going to die tonight," he said. "I don't need my strength up!"
(67)

Here a glimmer of acceptance clearly shines through, as does the brief, single episode of depression that Harry goes through: "I'm getting as bored with dying as with everything else, he thought." Then, "'It's a bore,' he said out loud" (73).

Hemingway wrote his attorney, Alfred Rice, that "if I had not been using an airplane and very near dead there would not have been any The Snows of Kilimanjaro" (*Selected Letters*, 832). The stages of dying that Harry experiences conform so closely to those that Kübler-Ross noticed in dying patients that one has to believe they were real feelings for Hemingway — stages of dying that he felt perhaps at various points in his life, but never more vividly than when he was lying weak, inwardly frightened, and in pain on a cot in Africa.

In talking with Malcolm Cowley, one of the first scholars to convince Hemingway to open up, Denis Brian says, "Part of Hemingway's do-it-yourself psychotherapy in controlling his fears of death and his nightmares of going insane, was to put them down on paper, to write about them obliquely in his fiction," to which Cowley responds, "It's his short stories in particular that seem to give a clue to his inner life" (200), adding that Hemingway "sometimes seems to regard writing as an exhausting ceremony of exorcism" (43). Donaldson saw the same thing; Hemingway used writing as therapy (to purge himself of the von Kurowsky rejection; "Therapy," 100).

In "Snows" Hemingway shows us, long before Kübler-Ross codified them, the stages a patient traverses as he or she faces death. But Hemingway adds an artist's twist, arguing that art survives death — that creation trumps the destruction of body and spirit. In *Green Hills of Africa* Hemingway writes, "A country, finally, erodes and the dust blows away, the people all die and none of them were of any importance permanently, except those who practiced the arts" (80). Art prevails. When we are first introduced to the dying Harry, we read that what takes his mind off his situation is the scene before him: "He lay then and was quiet for a while and looked across the heat shimmer of the plain to the edge of the bush. There were a few Tommies that showed minute and white against the yellow and, far off, he saw a herd of zebra, white against the green of the bush. This was a pleasant camp under big trees against a hill" (151). It's not just Africa that diverts a dying Harry; it's his writer's eye, his appreciation of detail that is the beginning of his salvation. It's the same method of overcoming so-called writer's block that Hemingway described in *A Moveable Feast*:

> I would sit in front of the fire and squeeze the peel of the little oranges into the edge of the flame and watch the sputter of blue that they made. I would stand and look out over the roofs of Paris and think, "Do not worry. You have always written before and you will write now. All you have to do is write one true sentence. Write the truest sentence that you know." So finally I would write one true sentence, and then go on from there. It was easy then.... (12)

Though it's more difficult for Harry, details and memory gradually help him recover and rediscover his ability to write, each italicized foray into narration becoming more detailed and expansive. Inexplicably, critics have been almost unanimous in pronouncing Harry a failed writer and interpreting the section in which Harry is loaded onto the plane and taken to Kilimanjaro as a "dream" or some symbol of shortcoming. Edmund Wilson wrote in an early review, "The reader is made gradually to realize that what seems to be an escape by plane with the sick man looking down on Africa is only the dream of a dying man" (630). Meanwhile, Oliver Evans — and there have been none since to refute him — complains of trickery, that "on his deathbed, [Harry] realizes that he has traded for security his integrity as a writer," and that "Hemingway has so contrived the ending that the reader is unaware, until Helen makes her discovery, that the plane trip never took place except in the mind of the dying man: the details of it are rendered with the utmost realism" (602). But that's exactly the point.

The so-called dream section features a telling typographical change: the italics disappear. This is deliberate, of course, and while readers who have come to rely on italics to denote Harry's interior monologue are led to believe that the cot-ridden writer is actually being rescued, then feel tricked when they find out that he in fact died, it's quite possible that Hemingway was trying to indicate typographically that Harry finally moves beyond interior monologue to finished-quality writing. Harry finally managed to "get it right" — so much so that the writing moves beyond description to the kind of powerful prose that Hemingway himself had been trying to perfect.

In an often-quoted letter to his father, Ernest explained, "You see I'm trying in all my stories to get the feeling of actual life across — not to just depict life — or criticize it — but to actually make it alive. So that when you have read something by me you actually experience the thing" (*Selected Letters*, 153). Harry's "writing," which he would have dictated to his wife, were she capable, is so powerful in this final scene that it literally moves him. In the final description Harry would ever write, it becomes so real for him that as he's being loaded onto the little plane it "was difficult getting him in, but once in he lay back in the leather seat, and the leg was stuck straight out to one side of the seat where Compton [the pilot] sat" (75). The power of Harry's imagination — of his writing — is that it becomes real for Harry — so real that Helen discovers her dead husband and notices his "bulk under the mosquito bar but somehow he had gotten his leg out and it hung down alongside the cot" (77). Thus, while Wilson wrote in an early review that Harry "failed to get what he had hoped," that would seem most emphatically not the case. Harry wanted rejuvenation for his dwindling powers of writing, and he found it in Africa, just as Hemingway discovered in Africa an inspiration for writing and a way to confront his own impending mortality.

The original title of "The Snows of Kilimanjaro" was "The Happy Ending" (Smith, 349), language that surfaces in Hemingway's letter to Lillian Ross of 20 February 1953: "I have no message to give Mr. Faulkner except to tell him I wish him the grace of a happy death. And I hope he will not continue to write after he has lost his talent. Don't give him that message either, but that is what I would really tell him" (807). Faulkner was also on Hemingway's mind as he first composed this story; Peter Hays points out that an odd reference in "Snows" about death coming "on bicycles" (71) is an allusion to deputy Percy Grimm's bicycle pursuit of Joe Christmas, whom he shot and brutally castrated in Faulkner's *Light in August* (434–36).[4] Harry's last act as a writer — to imagine a happy death, a scripted and painless death that's far removed from such a Grimm demise or the throes of Spanish influenza — may well be Hemingway's way of barking once more at the hyena that seemed, to him, to be coming closer year after year. Though one might argue that Harry never makes it past the bargaining stage that Kübler-Ross identified — *Please, let me write* — the writing is so vivid that it sustains Harry to the very end, as that protruding leg attests.

Hemingway, who lived longer than Harry, did make it past the bargaining stage to the next one — depression — for numerous sources explain that he was frequently depressed in the years following the African plane crashes on 23–24 January 1954. While he opted for the kind of death that Francis Macomber experienced rather than Harry's slow, natural one — perhaps because, unlike Harry (or a younger Ernest still at the height of his artistic powers), he had lost the ability to imagine a happy death for himself — there's a hint that Hemingway had at least one moment of acceptance, that final stage of dying that Kübler-Ross identified. Lloyd Arnold reports that shortly after they buried two hunting companions Mary insisted that Ernest talk on the phone to his good friend Gary Cooper, who they knew was dying. It would be the last conversation the men would have, albeit a brief one. In it, Arnold heard Hemingway say, "Well Coop, I'm sick too" (333). No one can say what went through Hemingway's mind after concussions suffered in the plane crashes, the shock therapy he endured at the Mayo Clinic, encroaching old age, or the paranoia and disease that gradually sapped his strength and powers. But in this brief, telling moment, Hemingway appears to have felt and acknowledged the weight of that hyena — death — on his own chest. And one suspects that it made him feel as uncomfortable as it did Harry.

After "Snows," the four remaining novels published during Hemingway's lifetime show a regression, but then another progression. In *To Have and Have Not* (1937) it's a step backward as death comes suddenly for the hero, as it did for Francis Macomber. And in this novel Harry Morgan never gets past the second stage of anger that Kübler-Ross identified: "No matter how a man alone ain't got no bloody fucking chance," he rails at the end (255). But the next novel finds the hero making it to the next stage. In *For Whom the Bell Tolls* (1940) Robert Jordan dies a less-sudden death and, also wounded, has a longer period of time to resign himself to his fate. "Now if the attack were only a success" (469) he thinks, then his death will not have been in vain. "*And if you wait and hold them up even a little while*," he tells himself, "*or just get the officer that may make all the difference*" (470). Finally, he bargains with a force greater than his own: "Then let me last until they come" (471). Neither Harry Morgan nor Robert Jordan were as close to Hemingway as the protagonist of "The Snows of Kilimanjaro," but by the time Hemingway writes *Across the River and Into the Trees* (1950) he's clearly had a chance to become more comfortable with the idea of describing the death of a character close to him again. Richard Cantwell knows his time on earth is limited and wants one last trip to Venice to engage in the things he has loved — duck hunting and women. After going through the stages of anger and bargaining, he arrives at a place of some acceptance: "I guess the cards we draw are those we get." Then, he adds, "You wouldn't like to re-deal, would you dealer?" (179), slipping back into the bargaining phase.

It took Hemingway sixteen years to get back to the point where he could apparently bear to bring a character to the brink of acceptance, as he had in "The Snows of Kilimanjaro." In *The Old Man and the Sea* (1952), the last novel published during Hemingway's lifetime, Santiago prays, "God help me endure. I'll say a hundred Our Fathers and a hundred Hail Marys" (87), but this little novella is otherwise full of resignation and acceptance — more so than with any other Hemingway hero since Harry lay dying on his cot in Africa. "Man is not much beside the great birds and beasts," Santiago thinks (68), the self-diminishment itself a form of acceptance, of understanding the natural order of things. "I'll stay with you until I am dead" (52), he resolves. Later comes one of the most famous lines from the book:

> "Ay," he said aloud. There is no translation for this word and perhaps it is just a noise such as a man might make, involuntarily, feeling the nail go through his hands and into the wood. (107)

Santiago may be a classic literary Christ-figure, but first and foremost he's a man who has accepted his fate while still feeling the pain of it all. And as Kübler-Ross reminds us, "Acceptance should not be mistaken for a happy stage" (100). With enough time, a person confronting his own death will "reach a stage during which he is neither depressed nor angry about his 'fate'" and he will "be tired and, in most cases, quite weak" (99). That, of course, happens to Santiago at the end of *The Old Man and the Sea*, during which he "shouldered the mast and started to climb. It was then that he knew the depth of his tiredness." It's worth noting that during his struggles at the end, there is no interior monologue for Santiago other than this single matter-of-fact statement. This too is consistent with Kübler-Ross's observations about the final stage of acceptance, which "is almost void of feelings" (100).

Santiago dreams of Africa, even though he "no longer dreamed of storms, nor of women, nor of great occurrences, nor of great fish, nor fights, nor contests of strength, nor his wife" (26–27), because at this stage Hemingway was also clearly dreaming of the Africa of his younger days. Africa enabled Hemingway to face death through fictional characters like this old fisherman who, in the final line of the last novel published in Hemingway's lifetime, was still "dreaming about the lions" (140).

Notes

[1] Hemingway first used the phrase in a 1926 letter to F. Scott Fitzgerald (*Selected Letters*, 200).

[2] Young Robert Cowley, son of writer-critic Malcolm Cowley, remembers drawing a Christmas card for Hemingway that included "a hillside with flowers, grass, birds, the sky, and some clouds. And just two feet stick out of the hill, as if a man were sleeping there hidden by the grass and pastoral scene. But to my mother it looked as if the man might be dead. She said, 'Oh God, you can't send that, because he's absolutely panicked by the idea of death!'" (Brian, 200).

[3] But he is only barely alive. He tells Manolín: "In the night I spat something strange and felt something in my chest was broken" (125).

[4] In a personal email, Hays writes that Faulkner and Hemingway often traded allusions. See also Hays's essay, "Exchange between Rivals: Faulkner's Influence on *The Old Man and the Sea*," in *Ernest Hemingway: The Writer in Context*, ed. James Nagel (Madison: U of Wisconsin P, 1984), 147–64.

Works Cited

Arnold, Lloyd. *High on the Wild with Hemingway*. Caldwell, ID: The Caxton Printers, 1968.

Baker, Carlos. *Ernest Hemingway: A Life Story*. New York: Scribner's, 1969.

———. "The Slopes of Kilimanjaro." In Howell, *Hemingway's African Stories*, 55–59.

———. "The Two African Stories." In *Hemingway: A Collection of Critical Essays*, edited by Robert P. Weeks, 118–26. Englewood Cliffs, NJ: Prentice Hall, 1962.

Bass, Carole. "Grief, by the Book." *Yale Alumni Magazine*, 70: 5 (May–June 2007): 31.

Benson, Jackson J. "Ernest Hemingway as Short Story Writer." In *The Short Stories of Ernest Hemingway: Critical Essays*, edited by Jackson J. Benson, 272–310. Durham: Duke UP, 1975.

Brian, Denis. *The True Gen: An Intimate Portrait of Ernest Hemingway by Those Who Knew Him*. New York: Grove Press, 1988.

Cirules, Enrique. *Ernest Hemingway in the Romano Archipelago*. Translated by Douglas Edward LaPrade. Havana, Cuba: Ediciones Unión, 1999.

Donaldson, Scott. *By Force of Will: The Life and Art of Ernest Hemingway*. New York: The Viking Press, 1977.

———. "'A Very Short Story' as Therapy." In *Hemingway's Neglected Short Fiction*, edited by Susan F. Beegel, 99–105. Tuscaloosa: U of Alabama P, 1989.

Dussinger, Gloria R. "'The Snows of Kilimanjaro': Harry's Second Chance." *Studies in Short Fiction* 5 (Fall 1967): 54–59.

Evans, Oliver. "'The Snows of Kilimanjaro': A Revaluation." *PMLA* 76 (December 1961): 602–7.

Faulkner, William. *Light in August*. 1932. Reprint, New York: Random House, 1959.

Fleming, Robert E. *The Face in the Mirror: Hemingway's Writers*. Tuscaloosa: U of Alabama P, 1996.

Friedman, Norman. "Harry or Ernest? The Unresolved Ambiguity in 'The The Snows of Kilimanjaro.'" In *Creative and Critical Approaches to the Short Story*, edited by Noel Harold Kaylor, Jr., 359–73. Lewiston, NY: Edwin Mellen Press, 1997.

Gordon, Caroline, and Allen Tate. "'The Snows of Kilimanjaro': Commentary." In Howell, *Hemingway's African Stories*, 142–44.

Hays, Peter. "Hemingway, Faulkner, and a Bicycle Built for Death." *NMAL: Notes on Modern American Literature* 5, no. 4 (1981): Item 28.

Hemingway, Ernest. *Across the River and Into the Trees*. New York: Scribner's, 1950.

———. *By-Line: Ernest Hemingway. Selected Articles and Dispatches of Four Decades*. Edited by William White. New York: Scribner's, 1967.

———. *Conversations with Ernest Hemingway*. Edited by Matthew J. Bruccoli. Jackson: UP of Mississippi, 1986.

———. *Death in the Afternoon*. New York: Scribner's, 1932.

———. *For Whom the Bell Tolls*. New York: Scribner's, 1940.

———. *Green Hills of Africa*. New York: Scribner's, 1935.

———. "Judgment at Manitou." 1916. Reprinted in *Hemingway at Oak Park High: The High School Writings of Ernest Hemingway, 1916–1917*, edited by Cynthia Maziarka and Donald Vogel, Jr., 93–94. Oak Park: Oak Park and River Forest High School, 1993.
———. *The Nick Adams Stories*. New York: Scribner's, 1972.
———. *The Old Man and the Sea*. New York: Scribner's, 1952.
———. *Selected Letters: 1917–1961*. Edited by Carlos Baker. New York: Scribner's, 1981.
———. "The Short Happy Life of Francis Macomber." In *The Short Stories of Ernest Hemingway*, 3–37. 1938. Reprint, New York: Scribner's, 1966. First published in 1936 in *Cosmopolitan*.
———. "The Snows of Kilimanjaro." In *The Short Stories of Ernest Hemingway*, 52–77. 1938. Reprint, New York: Scribner's, 1966. First published in 1936 in *Esquire*.
———. *To Have and Have Not*. New York: Scribner's, 1937.
Hemingway, Ernest, and Maxwell Perkins. *The Only Thing That Counts: The Ernest Hemingway-Maxwell Perkins Correspondence*. Edited by Matthew J. Bruccoli. New York: Scribner's, 1996.
Hemingway, Leicester. *My Brother, Ernest Hemingway*. Sarasota, FL: Pineapple Press, 1996.
Hemingway, Marcelline. *At the Hemingways*. Moscow: U of Idaho P, 1999.
Hemingway, Valerie. *Running with the Bulls: My Years with the Hemingways*. New York: Ballantine Books, 2004.
Hotchner, A. E. *Papa Hemingway*. New York: Random House, 1966.
Howell, John M., ed. *Hemingway's African Stories: The Stories, Their Sources, Their Critics*. New York: Scribner's, 1969.
Johnston, Kenneth G. "'The Snows of Kilimanjaro': An African Purge." *Studies in Short Fiction* 21, no. 3 (1984): 223–27.
Kashkeen, Ivan. "Alive in the Midst of Death: Ernest Hemingway." In *Hemingway and His Critics*, edited by Carlos Baker, 162–79. New York: Hill and Wang, 1967.
Killinger, John. *Hemingway and the Dead Gods: A Study in Existentialism*. Lexington: U of Kentucky P, 1960.
Kübler-Ross, Elisabeth. *On Death and Dying*. New York: Macmillan, 1969.
Lynn, Kenneth. *Hemingway*. New York: Simon and Schuster, 1987.
Montgomery, Marion. "The Leopard and the Hyena: Symbol and Meaning in 'The Snows of Kilimanjaro.'" In Howell, *Hemingway's African Stories*, 145–49.
Nagel, James, and Henry Serrano Villard. *Hemingway in Love and War*. Boston: Northeastern UP, 1989.
Plath, James, and Frank Simons. *Remembering Ernest Hemingway*. Key West, FL: Ketch & Yawl Press, 1999.
Reynolds, Michael S. *Hemingway: The Final Years*. New York: Norton, 1999.
———. *Hemingway: The 1930s*. New York: Norton, 1997.
———. *Hemingway: The Paris Years*. Oxford: Basil Blackwell, 1989.

———. *Hemingway's First War: The Making of A Farewell to Arms.* Princeton: Princeton UP, 1976.
———. *The Young Hemingway.* Oxford: Basil Blackwell, 1986.
Scafella, Frank. "I and the Abyss: Emerson, Hemingway, and the Modern Vision of Death." *Hemingway Review* 4, no. 2 (1985): 2–6.
Scheel, Mark. "Death and Dying: Hemingway's Predominant Theme." *The Emporia State Research Studies* 28, no. 1 (1979): 5–12.
Smith, Paul. *A Reader's Guide to the Short Stories of Ernest Hemingway.* Boston: G. K. Hall, 1989.
Stephens, Robert O. "Hemingway's Riddle of Kilimanjaro: Idea and Image." In Howell, *Hemingway's African Stories*, 93–94.
Wilson, Edmund. *Edmund Wilson: Literary Essays and Reviews of the 1930s and 40s.* New York: Farrar, Straus and Giroux, 1978.
Young, Philip. *Ernest Hemingway.* University of Minnesota Pamphlets on American Writers, No. 1. Minneapolis: U of Minnesota P, 1959.
———."The Hero and the Code." In Howell, *Hemingway's African Stories*, 116–18.

: What Others Have Said

11: On Safari with Hemingway: Tracking the Most Recent Scholarship

Kelli A. Larson

OVER TWO HUNDRED ESSAYS, notes, and books appear on Ernest Hemingway's life and art annually. Add the occasional posthumous publication and the critical debate rises to a feverish pitch. That Hemingway's writing continues to sustain such intense critical scrutiny proves once again that although he writes simply, Hemingway is not a simple writer. Scholars who seek to answer questions and contribute to the ever-increasing pool of Hemingway knowledge struggle to keep abreast of the latest developments in the field. Testifying to their diligence and success is the dramatic increase in the quality of Hemingway scholarship over the past two decades. Theoretical approaches, long underrepresented in traditional Hemingway criticism, are now published alongside the more conventional biographical, textual, and thematic studies, offering readers new ways of envisioning Hemingway's art. Many of these studies offer fresh and innovative ways of approaching his writings, renewing interest in even those works long considered by many to be critically exhausted. The old ways are giving rise to the new, and recent Hemingway scholarship is all the better for it.

Although the African works in general have not garnered the critical attention of such mainstays as *The Sun Also Rises* and *A Farewell to Arms*, they continue to hold their own in the critical stakes, and their underexposure to various theoretical lenses promises exciting new developments for future studies. Hemingway visited Africa twice, once in the mid-1930s and again in the mid-1950s. His publication of *Green Hills of Africa* in 1935 was meant to bolster his sagging reputation after the disappointing reception of his first nonfiction book, *Death in the Afternoon*, in 1932. However, the mixed reception of *Green Hills of Africa* only compounded Hemingway's disappointment and perhaps helps to explain the dearth of scholarly attention that haunted the book until very recently.

Currently, *Green Hills of Africa* and the two stories that followed the first safari ("The Snows of Kilimanjaro" and "The Short Happy Life of Francis Macomber") are enjoying a renascence in critical attention, due largely to the rise of postcolonial theory and the two posthumous publications based on Hemingway's second safari. These two new books, which expand the material published earlier in magazine form, are the fictional memoir *True at First Light* (1999), edited and introduced by Hemingway's son Patrick, and the longer version, *Under Kilimanjaro* (2005), which recovers passages that the first version edited out. Comparison studies of the earlier works with the later posthumous ones seem to reveal an important change in Hemingway's perspective, as evidenced by his more intense interest in African populations and cultures.

As scholars often point out, posthumous texts carved out of longer manuscript versions — such as *The Garden of Eden* and *True at First Light* — necessarily reflect the editor's vision of Hemingway's original text, and are therefore less authoritative than those texts that Hemingway himself supervised into print. The case of *Under Kilimanjaro*, however, is somewhat different, as it gives us access to a more complete version of Hemingway's original manuscript. It is to be hoped that in the future, Hemingway's other unpublished texts will also appear in their entirety, to complement the shorter, edited versions.

Despite the firestorm of criticism challenging Tom Jenks's editorial decisions in preparing *The Garden of Eden* (1986) manuscript for publication, the novel continues to elicit strong scholarly interest. Hemingway began writing *Garden* in 1946 and worked on it intermittently until leaving the project in the late 1950s, when he began revising *A Moveable Feast*. Scholars have pointed out connections between these two posthumously published texts, made all the more transparent through manuscript studies. However, manuscript studies mark only the beginning of *Garden* research. Of all the African texts, *Garden* has benefited most clearly from the application of varying theoretical approaches to the topics of gender and racial transformation, androgyny, sexuality, art, and familial relationships. Even so, it should be noted that while *Garden* continues to enjoy an increasing popularity among scholars, the portion of the novel and manuscripts devoted to Africa has been largely overlooked. Thus, the number of studies annotated here, either focusing on or including in a significant way the African stories, represents only a fraction of the overall scholarly material currently available on the novel as a whole.

The frequently anthologized "The Short Happy Life of Francis Macomber" remains at the top of the critical stakes in the short story genre, resting comfortably in that position since the 1970s. I am at a loss to explain, however, why Hemingway's other often-anthologized African story, "The Snows of Kilimanjaro," has attracted less than half of the scholarly attention devoted to "Macomber." Equally odd, while "Snows" has fostered a number of new, though admittedly limited, approaches, "Macomber" criticism continues for the most part to center on the same textual ambiguity that has frustrated scholars for decades — whether or not Margot shot at the buffalo. While this debate rages on, from a variety of critical perspectives, one is tempted to remind scholars that while gender themes are certainly central to the text, much of the "Macomber" iceberg still remains unexamined.

While the full-length works *The Garden of Eden* and *True at First Light* have been dismissed in the popular press as excessive and stylistically inferior, the positive reception of the newly published *Under Kilimanjaro* by academics and the reading public alike has done much to bolster the reputation of Hemingway's posthumous works. In addition, scholars are seizing the opportunity to read these texts as representative of an evolving writer whose vision, style, and subject matter transformed markedly over time. Like the vast and open continent they celebrate, the Africa-based texts offer scholars seemingly endless opportunities for future critical exploration. This book is a happy beginning.

An Annotated Bibliography of Hemingway's Africa-Based Work

This annotated bibliography of critical works on Hemingway's African writings begins where Larson's *Ernest Hemingway: A Reference Guide* (1990) left off and includes materials as recent as 2010. Entries are arranged alphabetically by author's last name within the year of their publication. Items unavailable to me for reading are marked by an asterisk (*), with the source of their listing given in place of the usual summary annotation. I have attempted to include all substantive contributions to scholarship focused on Hemingway in Africa and his African writings published in English (with the exception of dissertations, which are listed in *Dissertation Abstracts International*). However, I am a realist and thus apologize to those scholars I have overlooked or misconstrued.

1989

Anderson, David D. "Hemingway and Henderson on the High Savannas, or Two Midwestern Moderns and the Myth of Africa." *Saul Bellow Journal* 8, no. 2: 59–75.

Broad overview of Hemingway's experiences in Africa, pointing out parallels between such works as Hemingway's "Safari" (1954) and *Green Hills of Africa* (1935) and Bellow's *Henderson the Rain King* (1959). "Hemingway's reality, although he would deny it, is of the memory, transmuted by talent and imagination, into myth, the point at which Bellow's African reality, begins and ends" (74).

Cheatham, George. "The Unhappy Life of Robert Wilson." *Studies in Short Fiction* 26, no. 3: 341–45.

Argues for Wilson's inhumanity in "The Short Happy Life of Francis Macomber" based on Hemingway's excessive emphasis on the hunter's suntan, descriptions of his eyes (associating him with animals and machines), and questionable moral behavior. Far from exhibiting the standard of masculine courage reminiscent of characters such as Romero of *The Sun Also Rises,* Wilson more closely resembles Belmonte who has "lost the *aficion* he once had."

Dahiya, Bhim S. "Life and Art in Hemingway's *The Garden of Eden.*" *Panjab University Research Bulletin (Arts)* 20, no. 2: 17–28.

Briefly connects the writer hero of *The Garden of Eden* to Harry of "The Snows of Kilimanjaro" because both are married to women who negate their husbands' artistry. Notes that David's writing focuses mainly on his early African experiences hunting with his father.

Flora, Joseph M. *Ernest Hemingway: A Study of the Short Fiction.* Boston: Twayne.

74–88: Brief overview of "The Short Happy Life of Francis Macomber" and "The Snows of Kilimanjaro," seeing both as atypical of Hemingway's short fiction canon. Gives possible models for the Macombers, focusing specifically on the declining F. Scott Fitzgerald and his troubled marriage to Zelda. Warns against accepting Wilson's view of Margot, arguing that the story's complicated narrative structure defies an easy reading of her or her intentions when shooting. Reads "Snows" as a meditation on death, discussing its allegorical nature. Also contrasts Margot's individuality with the marginalized wife of "Snows." Concludes that "Snows" holds the deeper reality for Hemingway, serving as a warning not to squander his talent.

Gaillard, Theodore L., Jr. "Hemingway's 'The Short Happy Life of Francis Macomber.'" *Explicator* 47, no. 3: 44–47.

Contends that Macomber was murdered by Margot, who felt threatened by his newly acquired bravery. Points to Hemingway's use of animal imagery as evidence of Macomber's growing confidence, along with Margot's corresponding concern. Also draws parallels between the fallen lion and the victimized Macomber.

Hotchner, A. E. *Hemingway and his World.* New York: Vendome.

Pictorial biography, with brief references to Hemingway's two safaris and the works inspired by them, including *Green Hills of Africa,* "The Short Happy Life of Francis Macomber," and "The Snows of Kilimanjaro."

116–17: "Green Hills of Africa"
118–19: "Macomber and Kilimanjaro"
188–91: "Africa Revisited"

Nagel, James. "The Hunting Story in *The Garden of Eden.*" In *Hemingway's Neglected Short Fiction: New Perspectives*, edited by Susan F. Beegel, 329–38. Ann Arbor: UMI Research P.

Reads the elephant hunt as the formative event of David's youth, haunting him emotionally into adulthood. Discusses the interconnectedness of the two narratives, the African hunt and the marriage story, showing how each experience informs the other. By struggling with estrangement and betrayal in the present, David is able to confront the same in his past, finally enabling him to write the African story.

1990

Baym, Nina. "Actually, I Felt Sorry for the Lion." In *New Critical Approaches to the Short Stories of Ernest Hemingway*, edited by Jackson J. Benson, 112–20. Durham: Duke UP.

Feminist reading of Margot's motives in "The Short Happy Life of Francis Macomber." Taking issue with critics who read Margot as an example of the stereotypical "bitch," Baym describes a bond between the lion and Margot, arguing that the latter is innocent because of her identification with the lion as a victim of male domination and cruelty. Baym questions Wilson's hunting prowess and the presumed dangers of big-game hunting, characterizing Wilson as a man "who makes his living by manipulating the appearances of moral danger for the titillation of his clients" (114).

Bredahl, A. Carl, Jr., and Susan Lynn Drake. *Hemingway's "Green Hills of Africa" as Evolutionary Narrative: Helix and Scimitar.* Lewiston, NY: Edwin Mellen.

Close reading of the narrative, contending that *Green Hills* "results from the effort to push beyond the strictly mental in order to ask about an individual's creative energy in relation to those same energies in its environment" (20). Reads the narrative as the narrator's journey toward "physical and creative health" (50). Places *Green Hills* within its own genre since it defies the traditional categories of fiction and autobiography. Sees the images of the helix and scimitar represented in the hunt for kudu and sable as central organizing principles that argue for the narrative's overall unification. Provides an historical, social, and cultural context for the book and places it within Hemingway's oeuvre.

Cackett, Kathy. "*The Garden of Eden*: Challenging Faulkner's Family Romance." *Hemingway Review* 9, no. 2: 155–68.

Reads *The Garden of Eden* as Hemingway's thematic reworking of "The Bear" in his final attempt at one-upmanship over Faulkner. Applying Richard H. Kings' family romance theory, Cackett focuses on the epic hunt and compares how each author uses the past to inform present day experience. David Bourne and Ike McCaslin need to understand the past without repeating it.

Hays, Peter L. *Ernest Hemingway*. New York: Continuum.
Concise biography of Hemingway's life and work.
69–74: Recounts the disappointing contemporary critical reception of *Green Hills of Africa*, disparaged for its lack of social concern and weak prose style. Briefly mentions the thematic connection between the art of hunting and the art of writing. Hays concludes by criticizing the book as "garrulous" and "vapid."
84–88: Summarizes the plots of "The Short Happy Life of Francis Macomber" and "The Snows of Kilimanjaro." Characterizes "Macomber" as a series of power struggles. Comments on the resemblance of the ending of "Snows" to Bierce's "An Occurrence at Owl Creek Bridge," where both protagonists, on the brink of death, delude themselves into thinking they've been saved.

Hillman, James. "The Elephant in *The Garden of Eden*." *Spring: A Journal of Archetype and Culture* 50: 93–115.
Overview of the elephant image found in contemporary psychology, literature, and ancient animal lore. Hillman sees in Kotzwinkle's *Elephant Bangs Train*, Orwell's "Shooting an Elephant," and the African story a connection between the dying elephant and the act of writing. "The elephant hunt and the author's reflections on the writing of it become a parable for the mystical integrity of writing itself which is the soul of the book" (98).

Martin, Lawrence H., Jr. "Borges on Hemingway, Hemingway on Hemingway: Craft, Grief, and Sport." In *Hemingway in Italy and Other Essays*, edited by Robert W. Lewis, 77–84. New York: Praeger.
Explores the relationship between sport and art found in *Green Hills of Africa* to counter Borges's claim that Hemingway's regret for devoting his energies to physical adventures rather than intellectual pursuits led to his suicide. Martin suggests that for Hemingway, art and sport necessitated and mirrored one another in their emphasis on solitude and honesty, and that a life of physical activity made complete one's intellectual endeavors. See Borges, *An Introduction to Literature*. Edited and translated by L. Clark Keating and Robert O. Evans. Lexington: UP of Kentucky, 1971.

Spilka, Mark. *Hemingway's Quarrel with Androgyny*. Lincoln: U of Nebraska P.

223–48: "Tough Mamas and Safari Wives." Discusses Pauline as Poor Old Mama who provides funding for the safari and offers other emotional and financial support. Always left waiting, longing, serving, Poor Old Mama represents the wife Hemingway always leaves behind in pursuit of his own pleasures, such as fishing, drinking and writing.

279–314: "Papa's Barbershop Quintet." Drawing heavily on manuscript materials, Spilka laments Jenks's extensive editing of important scenes and subplots that tie the narrative together. Relates the themes of androgyny and lesbianism in the novel to Hemingway's own life and credits Kipling's *Jungle Books* as the source of the elephant-hunt tale. Finally, the novel is "about a writer's bravery — about Hemingway's bravery as he saw it in the daily struggle to transcend his own terrible dependencies and passivities" (306). Reprint with minor revisions of "Hemingway's Barbershop Quintet: *The Garden of Eden* Manuscript" in *Novel: A Forum on Fiction* 21 (1987): 29–55. Reprinted as "Papa's Barbershop Quintet" in *Hemingway: Seven Decades of Criticism*, edited by Linda Wagner-Martin, 349–72. East Lansing: Michigan State UP, 1998.

315–26: Appendix A: "A Source for the Macomber 'Accident': Marryat's *Percival Keene*." Suggests Marryat's influence on Hemingway by pointing out parallels between Marryat's work and "The Short Happy Life of Francis Macomber," including deadly shooting accidents, hidden motives, and cowardice. Reprint with minor revisions of "A Source for the Macomber 'Accident': Marryat's *Percival Keene*." *Hemingway Review* 3 (1984): 29–37.

Weber, Ronald. *Hemingway's Art of Non-Fiction*. New York: St. Martin's Press.

63–94: "One Central Necessity." Broad overview of *Green Hills of Africa*, beginning with a summary of the three *Esquire* letters published shortly after Hemingway's return from his first safari, and touching on the writing and publication history of the book. In his publication history, Weber discusses the author's wrangles with Maxwell Perkins over marketing and payment and addresses the book's disappointing critical reception. Comments on Hemingway's goal to create a literary landscape that defined the pattern of a month's action — captured in an artistic manner with only brief glimpses of Africa's native inhabitants.

95–108: "A First Class Life." Biographical overview of Hemingway's second African safari, including details of his itinerary, two plane crashes, and publishing agreement with *Look* magazine. Provides information on the *Sports Illustrated* excerpts edited by Ray Cave and contrasts the highly competitive Hemingway of *Green Hills of Africa* with the later, more relaxed Hemingway of the African book.

1991

Blythe, Hal, and Charlie Sweet. "Wilson: Architect of the Macomber Conspiracy." *Studies in Short Fiction* 28, no. 3: 305–9.

Gives a sinister reading of Wilson as a man so obsessed with his job that he masterminds Macomber's death to gain leverage over Margot, who subtly threatened him with her references to the illegal car chase.

Morgan, Kathleen, and Luis A. Losada. "Tracking the Wounded Buffalo: Authorial Knowledge and the Shooting of Francis Macomber." *Hemingway Review* 11, no. 1: 25–30.

Credits Hemingway's personal experience with and extensive reading in hunting and tracking for his authentic hunter's point of view and technical expertise. Considers the question of whether the shooting was accidental or not as secondary to Hemingway's creation of a credible scenario that could be interpreted either way.

Peters, K. J. "The Thematic Integrity of *The Garden of Eden*." *Hemingway Review* 10, no. 2: 17–29.

Argues that Jenks's dramatic editing of the text excised the novel's moral structure, resulting in an undeveloped and unexplainable novel. Briefly attributes David's creative recovery in writing the African stories to his newfound recognition that both he and his father share the same guilt of betrayal, thus enabling him to characterize his father more fully.

Reynolds, Michael S. *Hemingway: An Annotated Chronology, an Outline of the Author's Life and Career Detailing Significant Events, Friendships, Travels, and Achievements*. Detroit: Omnigraphics.

Extensive chronology, as the title suggests. Provides dates for Hemingway's two safaris, along with information on the writing and publishing of his African works.

73–76: First safari
123–26: Second safari
76–82: *Green Hills of Africa*
75, 81, 84–85: "The Snows of Kilimanjaro"
84–85, 108: "The Short Happy Life of Francis Macomber"
108, 115, 131–33: *The Garden of Eden*

Wagner-Martin, Linda. "A Note on Henri Rousseau and Hemingway's 'The Snows of Kilimanjaro.'" *Hemingway Review* 11, no. 1: 58–59.

Source study. Recounts the story of the needless death of French primitive painter Henri Rousseau, who died in 1910 of blood poisoning after neglecting a cut on his leg. Hemingway may have heard the story from Gertrude Stein, who had honored Rousseau's talent with a banquet in 1908.

1992

Boardman, Michael M. "Innovations as Pugilism: Hemingway and the Reader after *A Farewell to Arms*: The Reader in the Short Stories." Chapter 5 in *Narrative Innovation and Incoherence: Ideology in Defoe, Goldsmith, Austen, Eliot, and Hemingway*. Durham: Duke UP.

164–76: Contends that awkward and overwritten portions of "The Short Happy Life of Francis Macomber" were included as a duplicitous move on Hemingway's part to mislead an inattentive readership. Examines biographical sources to reveal Hemingway's authorial intentions — that Margot shot at Macomber.

Cameron, Kenneth M. "Patterson and the Blyths: The Originals of Hemingway's 'Macomber' Triangle." *Hemingway Review* 11, no. 2: 52–55.

Source study detailing the facts of the 1909 scandalous death of aristocrat James Audley Blyth while on safari with his wife and hunting guide, J. H. Patterson. Hemingway had heard the tale from his own hunting guide, Philip Percival, whose older brother had been displaced as senior game warden of the East Africa Protectorate by Patterson in 1907. It remains unknown how Percival's personal connection affected his telling of the campfire story.

Eby, Cecil D. "Hemingway's 'The Short Happy Life of Francis Macomber.'" *Explicator* 51, no. 1: 48.

Suggests Wilson's reference to Macomber as a "four-letter man" links him to high school and college athletes earning their varsity letters. For Wilson, true manhood is achieved through hunting dangerous game, not by collecting trophies on the gridiron.

Gajdusek, Robert. "A Brief Safari into the Religious Terrain of *Green Hills of Africa*." *North Dakota Quarterly* 60, no. 3: 26–40.

Traces the elaborate pattern of Christian references and allusions that underlie the hunt throughout the book. For example, Gajdusek equates the taking of the heavy heads back to camp by the old man, M'Cola, and Hemingway as a parody of Calvary, with each of the men representing a surrogate Christ. Contends that in the book a new type of religion, founded on brotherhood and bonding with nature, must replace conventional biblical authority.

Hardy, Donald E. "Presupposition and the Coconspirator." *Style* 26, no. 1: 1–11.

Semiotic approach to presuppositions in dialogue taken from three Hemingway short stories: "The Short Happy Life of Francis Macomber," "Hills Like White Elephants," and "The Doctor and the Doctor's Wife." Analyzes the presupposed solution regarding Wilson's shooting the lion. Macomber's revisionist history of the event, that Wilson saved his life, covers up his cowardice.

Mellow, James R. "*The Green Hills of Africa.*" Chapter 15 in *Hemingway: A Life Without Consequences.* Boston: Houghton Mifflin.

424–54: Biographical overview of Hemingway's book about "writings and writers," including its conception, writing, and disappointing critical reception. Agrees with Edmund Wilson's criticism of the book, that its subject matter better suited fiction. Finds numerous parallels between *Green Hills of Africa* and the later "The Short Happy Life of Francis Macomber." "The circumstances of the story — the lion hunt, the crashing charge of the wounded bull buffalo, altered for dramatic effect and whatever hidden or unconscious motives a writer uses in transmuting experience into fiction — are almost cinematic reruns of the scenes depicted in the book" (444). Reads "The Snows of Kilimanjaro" as Hemingway's "summing-up at mid-life and mid-career" (453), relating Harry's failures and regrets to Hemingway's own artistic goals and desires.

Messent, Peter. *Ernest Hemingway.* New York: St. Martin's Press.

110–23: Focuses primarily on the androgynous relationship between David and Catherine and Catherine's depiction in *The Garden of Eden,* commenting only briefly on David's rejection of his father's masculine code in the African tales.

146–61: Reads Hemingway's Africa as "constructed according to the psychological and cultural needs of an American profoundly uneasy about modern civilization and its effects" (146–47). Praises *Green Hills of Africa* as a carefully crafted and imaginative experiment in "new journalism" (148). Analyzes the closely connected themes of illness and restoration that run throughout the narrative both on a personal and national level. Also discusses the varied points of view presented in "The Short Happy Life of Francis Macomber." Concludes that Hemingway's narrative strategies defy all attempts to bring a satisfactory resolution to the ambiguous ending.

Morrison, Toni. "Disturbing Nurses and the Kindness of Sharks." Chapter 3 in *Playing in the Dark: Whiteness and the Literary Imagination.* Cambridge: Harvard UP.

61–91: Criticizes Hemingway's treatment of African Americans and African characters in his books, most specifically the silencing of Wesley from *To Have and Have Not*. Reads David's African story from *The Garden of Eden* as a "cherished masculine enclave of white domination and slaughter, complete with African servants who share David's 'guilt and knowledge'" (89). The Africanist narrative (Catherine-David as the blacked-up couple) that surrounds the African portion provides commentary on "an aestheticized blackness and a mythologized one" (90).

Roe, Steven C. "Opening Bluebeard's Closet: Writing and Aggression in Hemingway's *The Garden of Eden* Manuscript." *Hemingway Review* 12, no. 1: 52–66.

Connects David's ruthless father in the African stories to the Bluebeard archetype and reads the stories themselves as "fantasies that express aggression and contrition through an elaborate network of contrapuntal imagery, turning violent emotions into narrative energy" (58). The past becomes immersed with the present; Catherine is connected to both the Maji-Maji warriors and the elephant. Also discusses David's decreasing identification with his father through the evolution of the tales. Reprinted as "Opening Bluebeard's Closet: Writing and Aggression in Hemingway's *The Garden of Eden* Manuscript" in *Hemingway: Seven Decades of Criticism*, edited by Linda Wagner-Martin, 311–27. East Lansing: Michigan State UP.

Viertel, Peter. *Dangerous Friends: At Large with Huston and Hemingway in the Fifties*. New York: Doubleday.

218–21: Novelist and *The Old Man and the Sea* screenwriter Peter Viertel recounts learning of Hemingway's two African plane crashes.

1993

Blythe, Harold, and Charles Sweet. "The Real Philip Percival: The Mordens' View of 'Robert Wilson.'" *Hemingway Review* 12, no. 2: 78–82.

Locates an additional source of information on Philip Percival, Pop of *Green Hills of Africa* and a possible partial model for Robert Wilson. *Our African Adventure* (1954) recounts the Mordens' safari with Percival, including the retelling of a similar campfire story that Percival had told Hemingway years earlier and that later became the basis of "The Short Happy Life of Francis Macomber." Blythe and Sweet draw a number of parallels between the Mordens' descriptions of Percival and Wilson.

Davison, Richard Allan. "Hemingway's 'Homage to Switzerland' and F. Scott Fitzgerald." *Hemingway Review* 12, no. 2: 72–77.

Notes allusions to *The Great Gatsby* in "Homage to Switzerland," as well as a satirical jab made at Fitzgerald's expense. Davison questions Hemingway's motives and comments on his later inclusion of a crueler, more apparent Fitzgerald joke in "The Snows of Kilimanjaro."

Harris, Susan K. "Vicious Binaries: Gender and Authorial Paranoia in Dreiser's 'Second Choice,' Howells' 'Editha,' and Hemingway's 'The Short Happy Life of Francis Macomber.'" *College Literature* 20, no. 2: 70–82.

Feminist treatment examining the binary structures of passivity and activity in association with the female and male characters of all three stories. Reads Hemingway's construction of Margot as the most paranoid. Though excluded from the action of the story, Margot destroys not only men's lives but also men's self-concepts. "If these stories tell us anything about our culture, it is, at the very least, that male writers walk in fear that women will retaliate against male postures of author-ity" (78).

Kowalewski, Michael. *Deadly Musings: Violence and Verbal Form in American Fiction*. Princeton: Princeton UP.

154–58: Briefly analyzes Hemingway's narrative strategies in creating an ending for "The Short Happy Life of Francis Macomber" that defies easy resolution. Warns against interpreting the shifts in narrative perspective as support for any single reading of the text.

Kozikowski, S., and others. "Hemingway's 'The Short Happy Life of Francis Macomber.'" *Explicator* 51, no. 4: 239–41.

Interprets the story as a biblical allegory of Paradise Lost. The Macombers "suggest a prelapsarian Adam and Eve, created but living uncomfortably in androgyny, becoming individuated sexually after their fall, which brings destruction and death" (239). The cold and calculating Wilson symbolizes the serpent. Points out other similar androgynous couplings in Hemingway's canon, beginning with *The Sun Also Rises* and ending with *The Garden of Eden*.

Lounsberry, Barbara. "The Holograph Manuscript of *Green Hills of Africa*." *Hemingway Review* 12, no. 2: 36–45.

Manuscript study. Details the manuscript's circuitous route to the Alderman Library; excised criticisms of Stein, Fitzgerald, and others; structural changes; and serialization in *Scribner's* magazine. Reprinted as "The Holograph Manuscript of *Green Hills of Africa*" in *Hemingway: Eight Decades of Criticism*, edited by Linda Wagner-Martin, 323–35. East Lansing: Michigan State UP, 2009.

Macdonald, Alan. "Re-Writing Hemingway: Rachel Ingalls's *Binstead's Safari*." *Critique: Studies in Contemporary Fiction* 34, no. 3: 165–70.

Briefly mentions Ingalls's 1983 novel as a variation of Hemingway's "The Short Happy Life of Francis Macomber," in which the wife finds "happiness" on safari.

Saalmann, Dieter. "Hemingway's *Green Hills of Africa* and Rilke's *The Lay of the Love and Death of Cornet Christopher Rilke:* Tentative Reflections." *Germanic Notes and Reviews* 24, no. 2: 68–71.

Comparison study speculating on why Hemingway responded so positively to Rilke's minor work, the *Cornet*, in *Green Hills of Africa*. Concludes that both texts share a number of commonalities, including experimental characterization and the themes of creative pursuit and memory reconstruction.

Strychacz, Thomas. "Trophy-Hunting as a Trope of Manhood in Ernest Hemingway's *Green Hills of Africa*." *Hemingway Review* 13, no. 1: 36–47.

Reads the phallic power of trophies as ultimately subverting the code of masculinity because it shifts the focus from autonomy and individualism to performance and representation. Emphasizes the trophy hunting competition, commenting on the trophy's vulnerability as a sign of manhood that can easily be out-trophied and erased.

1994

Burwell, Rose Marie. "The Posthumous Hemingway Puzzle." *Princeton University Library Chronicle* 56, no. 1: 24–45.

Relies on information from recently opened archives to resolve unanswered questions regarding the composition dates and interrelationships of Hemingway's posthumously published writings. Hemingway began writing *A Moveable Feast* only after work on the African book stalled. Manuscripts reveal the African book's true subject matter — the authorial anxieties of a declining artist.

Comley, Nancy R., and Robert Scholes. "Tribal Things: *The Garden of Eden*." Chapter 3 in *Hemingway Genders: Rereading the Hemingway Text*. New Haven: Yale UP.

88–103: Briefly mentions Africa as that imaginative place where David in *The Garden of Eden* can recapture his authorial powers to reach his fictional truth. Notes Hemingway's focus on erotically charged fantasies involving race and gender transformation. Discusses Catherine and

Marita as African warrior chiefs, thus erotically interconnecting gender transformation with primitivism. Reprint with minor revisions of "Tribal Things: Hemingway's Erotics of Truth." *Novel* 25, no. 3 (1992): 268–85.

Fleming, Robert E. *The Face in the Mirror: Hemingway's Writers*. Tuscaloosa: U of Alabama P.

76–83: "The Snows of Kilimanjaro." Connecting the writing of "Snows" to Hemingway's bout with dysentery and increasing anxieties over his changing status as a writer, Fleming sums up the story as an examination of literary fame and authorial failure. Comments on Hemingway's careful selection of epigraphs and Harry's loss of dedication to his art. Warns against reading "Snows" as directed at any one writer, but rather should be viewed as an examination of how the creative process can be derailed for any writer.

129–58: "Posthumous Works: *The Garden of Eden*." Comments on the variant endings for the novel and its inspiration in the 1922 "lost manuscripts" incident involving Hadley. Focuses on David as a writer, his relationship with Catherine, and their growing tensions as David's artistic interests shift to the African story. As David becomes completely immersed in his fictive world, he withdraws from those around him, leaving him less than human. Reprint with minor revision of "The Endings of Hemingway's *The Garden of Eden*." *American Literature* 61, no. 2 (1989): 261–70. Reprinted as "The Endings of Hemingway's *The Garden of Eden*" in *Hemingway: Seven Decades of Criticism*, edited by Linda Wagner-Martin, 283–92. East Lansing: Michigan State UP, 1998.

Flora, Joseph M. "The Short Happy Life of Francis Macomber." In *Reference Guide to Short Fiction*, edited by Noelle Watson, 895–96. Detroit: St. James Press.

Overview of the story's composition, biographical connection to F. Scott Fitzgerald, multiple centers of consciousness, and complex characterization of Margot.

Scafella, Frank. "Beginning with 'Nothing.'" In *Hemingway Repossessed*, edited by Kenneth Rosen, 151–57. Westport: Praeger.

Reads Hemingway's works as intrapsychic struggles in which the protagonist consciously sheds the nothingness or weightlessness of the soul to achieve a new richness of feeling. Scafella draws on instances of the word "nothing" from throughout the Hemingway's canon to focus on the concept of "nothing" as a conscious state. Looks at "The Snows of Kilimanjaro," "The Sea Change," and "A Clean Well-Lighted place" in light of his theory.

Wagner-Martin, Linda. "The Snows of Kilimanjaro." In *Reference Guide to Short Fiction*, edited by Noelle Watson, 902–3. Detroit: St. James Press.

Overview of the story's composition, biographical connection to F. Scott Fitzgerald, major themes such as the destructive power of wealth, use of animal imagery, and layered endings.

1995

Bush, Lyall. "Consuming Hemingway: 'The Snows of Kilimanjaro' in the Postmodern Classroom." *Journal of Narrative Technique* 25, no. 1: 23–46.

Recounts the surprising classroom results in bringing theory to bear on a "transparent" passage from Hemingway's writing, a portion of Harry's monologue on dying. Through their application of theory, students were able to ask and answer sophisticated questions regarding gender, politics, and consumerism.

Eby, Carl. "'Come Back to the Beach Ag'n, David Honey!': Hemingway's Fetishization of Race in *The Garden of Eden* Manuscripts." *Hemingway Review* 14, no. 2: 98–117.

Psychoanalytical approach to the pervasive images of tanning in the manuscript, looking at racial transformation in light of psychosexual transformation. Looks at the male homosocial bonding between Juma and the young David, David's identification with the androgynous bull elephant, rejection of his father and Juma, and the erotically charged symbol of ivory. Reprinted as "'Come Back to the Beach Ag'n, David Honey!': Hemingway's Fetishization of Race in *The Garden of Eden* Manuscripts" in *Hemingway: Seven Decades of Criticism*, edited by Linda Wagner-Martin, 329–48. East Lansing: Michigan State UP, 1998. Reprinted with minor revision as "Ebony and Ivory: Hemingway's Fetishism of Race." Chapter 5 in *Hemingway's Fetishism: Psychoanalysis and the Mirror of Manhood*. New York: SUNY P, 1999.

Fickert, Kurt. "Two Characters in Search of an Author: Johnson's *Zwei Ansichten*." *Monatshefte* 87, no. 2: 187–202.

Thematic and stylistic comparison of Johnson's novel with *A Farewell to Arms*, focusing on each author's depiction of ill-fated lovers. Connects both to "The Snows of Kilimanjaro," contending that Harry and Helen are actually Frederic and Catherine "now grown middle-aged and bored with one another" (195).

Mandel, Miriam B. "The Garden of Eden." Chapter 9 in *Reading Hemingway: The Facts in the Fictions*. Metuchen, NJ: Scarecrow Press.

443–69: Reference guide annotating the real people, fictional characters, animals, and cultural constructs found in each of Hemingway's nine novels. Entries are arranged alphabetically and include information on such diverse topics as music, sports, politics, art, mythology, and history. Thorough index.

Meyer, William E. H., Jr. "The Hemingway Story in Its Proper American Context: The Search for the Quintessential New-World Form." *Arkansas Review* 4, no. 2: 201–19.

Classifies Hemingway's terse prose as "hypervisual" and "New-World art." Argues that his sparing use of details is American by nature, providing a model for contemporary authors to write about contemporary issues. Briefly discusses "The Snows of Kilimanjaro," "A Clean, Well-Lighted Place," *The Sun Also Rises*, and other works. Frequent comparisons to Emerson and his notion of the transparent eyeball.

Spilka, Mark. "Nina Baym's Benevolent Reading of the Macomber Story." In *Hemingway: Up in Michigan Perspectives*, edited by Frederic J. Svoboda and Joseph J. Waldmeir, 189–201. East Lansing: Michigan State UP.

Epistolary response to Baym's "benevolent" reading of Margot's motives in "Actually, I Felt Sorry for the Lion." Though he agrees with Baym's contention that the lion's point of view is transferred to Margot, Spilka objects to the rest of her reading, characterizing her logic as unfair and contradictory. Spilka takes issue, for example, with Baym's assertion that big-game hunting is dangerous only for the animal, woefully overpowered by human technology (guns and cars). See Baym (1990) in this bibliography (for annotation).

Szalay, Michael. "Inviolate Modernism: Hemingway, Stein, Tzara." *Modern Language Quarterly* 56, no. 4: 457–85.

Citing "The Snows of Kilimanjaro" and *To Have and Have Not*, Szalay looks at the relationship between human bodies and texts in light of how each responds to alteration. Examines wounded bodies in Hemingway's works, arguing that "Unlike human identities, texts do not survive change, and they do not experience their own alteration." Discusses Hemingway's allusions to Tristan Tzara and the Dada movement in "The Snows of Kilimanjaro" and his disdain for Tzara's questionable publishing practices, which Hemingway felt compromised textual identity.

1996

Atkins, John. "Dealing With the Fear of Fear." In *Readings on Ernest Hemingway*, edited by Katie De Koster, 47–54. San Diego: Greenhaven Press.

Draws on "The Short Happy Life of Francis Macomber" to argue that the hero must overcome his fear of fear, a motif central to Hemingway's writings. Reprint of "The Mechanics of Fear." Chapter 7 in *The Art of Ernest Hemingway: His Work and Personality*. London: Spring Books, 1952.

Boker, Pamela A. *The Grief Taboo in American Literature: Loss and Prolonged Adolescence in Twain, Melville, and Hemingway*. New York: New York UP.

207–13: "Ether in the Brain: Blunting the Edges of Perception in Hemingway's Middle Period." Sees "The Snows of Kilimanjaro" as Hemingway's epiphany regarding the debilitating effects of defensively repressing grief. Attempts at numbing pain through alcohol and non-thinking lead to the destruction of artistic talent for both Harry and Hemingway. Thus, because of this new-found thematic realization, Hemingway's later fiction directly addresses emotional pain and loss.

224–27: "*Green Hills of Africa*: Denial of Loss and the Resurrecting Power of Memory." Psychoanalytic approach examining Hemingway's transformation of memory into art. Hemingway's optimistic attitude that he can hold back the ravages of time and death with his art remains throughout the novel. Argues that the grief and anxiety accompanying nostalgic experience (that sense of never being able to completely recapture the past) are displaced onto Hemingway's hunting assistant, who refuses to let go of the car at the end of the safari.

255–62: "*The Garden of Eden*: Father-Hunger and Mother-Loss Revisited (Hemingway's Nostalgic Solution)." Psychoanalytic reading focused on David's desire to recapture the past and make it come alive through writing his African stories. Reads the father-son story as a familiar review of the male individuation theme found in Hemingway's earlier books, namely, *A Farewell to Arms, The Sun Also Rises,* and *In Our Time*. Suggests the hollowness and hunger felt after discovering his father's shortcomings are the same feelings David has after sex, after drinking, and after writing — thus thematically connecting this internal story to the larger narrative as a whole. Through art, David is able to recall the happiness resulting in his innocent belief in a heroic father figure, even if he must also reenact his moments of loss and disillusion within the same memory.

Bruccoli, Matthew J., with the assistance of Robert W. Trogdon. *The Only Thing That Counts: The Ernest Hemingway-Maxwell Perkins Correspondence, 1925–1947.* New York: Scribner's.

222–24, 229–31, 241 and elsewhere: Reprints selected correspondence between Hemingway and his editor, with numerous references to the writing, publication, marketing, and disappointing sales of *Green Hills of Africa* and the positioning of "The Short Happy Life of Francis Macomber" and "The Snows of Kilimanjaro" in *The Fifth Column and the First Forty-nine Stories.*

Burwell, Rose Marie. *Hemingway: The Postwar Years and the Posthumous Novels.* Cambridge: Cambridge UP.

Critical biography arguing that Hemingway's four posthumous works, *A Moveable Feast, Islands in the Stream, The Garden of Eden,* and the African journal, form a tetralogy of his vision of the artist "as writer and painter, and as son, husband and father" (1), but their publication history obscured their connection. Examines Hemingway's focus on the life of the artist from childhood through middle age, his thematic concern with the artist's growth and decline over time, and his use of memory and paired painter/writer character relationships. Hemingway's distance from his fictional artists diminished in these later works; they thereby demonstrate the author's own anxieties and fears. Yet despite his difficulties in completing the four works, Hemingway did intend them to be published after his death. Burwell devotes a chapter to each of the four posthumous works. Extensive endnotes.

95–128: "*The Garden of Eden*: Protecting the Masculine Text." Chronicles the conception, writing, and editing of the manuscript and posthumous novel. Suggests that scholarly dissatisfaction with the published version of the novel is the result of both poor editorial choices and a problematic manuscript that fails to delineate the author's own intentions for revision. Summarizes deleted manuscript portions, the second half of the chapter devoted to the African stories. Manuscript examination reveals the genesis of the African stories. Expanded version of "Hemingway's '*Garden of Eden*': Resistance of Things Past and Protecting the Masculine Text." *Texas Studies in Literature and Language* 35, no. 2 (Summer 1993): 198–225.

129–48: "The African Book: An Alternative Life." Details the writing of the book, beginning with a biography of the events leading up to Hemingway's 1953 safari. Burwell summarizes portions of the manuscript, commenting on its comic tone and connecting it thematically to other works such as *Green Hills of Africa* and "The Short Happy Life of Francis Macomber." Focuses on the love triangle of Hemingway, Debba, and Miss Mary, concluding that the manuscript reveals an aging author's anxieties over the decline of his public image and authorial status.

Fleming, Robert E. "*The Garden of Eden*." In *The Cambridge Companion to Ernest Hemingway*, edited by Scott Donaldson, 140–47. Cambridge: Cambridge UP.

Focuses primarily on the sexual theme found within the novel, remarking only briefly upon the interconnected relationship of David, Africa, and the creation of literature.

Harrington, Gary. "'A Plague of All Cowards': 'Macomber' and *Henry IV*." *Hemingway Review* 15, no. 2: 96–103.

Citing previous source studies, Harrington compares the manipulative Wilson to Shakespeare's Falstaff. "By making Wilson a much more sinister figure than his Shakespearean counterpart, Hemingway undermines that macho ethos which Wilson so emphatically, and so disastrously, embraces (101)."

Kennedy, J. Gerald. "Hemingway, Hadley, and Paris: The Persistence of Desire." In *The Cambridge Companion to Ernest Hemingway*, edited by Scott Donaldson, 210–11. Cambridge: Cambridge UP.

Compares "The Short Happy Life of Francis Macomber" with "The Snows of Kilimanjaro," pointing out several parallels, including the central focus on marital discord and self-reflection. Comments briefly on Harry's memories of Paris in "Snows," revealing Hemingway's own attachment to those early years spent there with Hadley.

Putnam, Ann. "Across the River and into the Stream: Journey of the Divided Heart." *North Dakota Quarterly* 63, no. 3: 90–98.

Comments briefly on the pastoral vision found in *Green Hills of Africa* and other works, noting the inevitable loss of the pastoral experience as the urgency of the hunt takes over the narrative.

Shaw, Samuel. "Hemingway, Nihilism, and the American Dream." In *Readings on Ernest Hemingway*, edited by Katie De Koster, 71–77. San Diego: Greenhaven Press.

Draws on "The Snows of Kilimanjaro" to argue for Hemingway's tragic and nihilistic vision of life. Differentiates the more aggressive and naïve American form of nihilism from the European version. Reprint of "Nihilism and the American Dream." Chapter 1 in *Ernest Hemingway*. New York: Frederick Ungar, 1973.

Stoltzfus, Ben. "Ernest Hemingway: *The Garden of Eden.*" Chapter 5 in *Lacan & Literature: Purloined Texts.* Albany: SUNY P.

90–102: Lacanian approach addressing the young David's rejection of his father and identification with the elephant. David as writer, however, identifies with the father and the need to kill. "Writing [language] becomes a substitute for the phallus, and it is David's assertion of maleness and difference that outrages Catherine" (95). By burning David's stories, Catherine removes the sexual difference and represses the primal scene. Reprint with minor revision of "A Post-Lacanian Reading of Hemingway's *Garden of Eden.*" *American Journal of Semiotics* 5, nos. 3–4 (1987): 381–95.

Sugiyama, Michelle Scalise. "What's Love Got to Do With It? An Evolutionary Analysis of 'The Short Happy Life of Francis Macomber.'" *Hemingway Review* 15, no. 2: 15–32.

Draws upon theories of evolutionary psychology to examine the Macombers' marital conflicts and determine Margot's motivation in murdering her husband. "Though Francis's mate value is greatly increased by his successful shooting of the buffalo, and evolutionary thinking would lead us to expect that this should benefit his wife, it is in Margot's case a threat, due primarily to her knowledge of her infidelity" (22). The newly confident Francis may divorce his wife, leaving the aging Margot with few resources (income and social status).

Tessitore, John. *The Hunt and the Feast: A Life of Ernest Hemingway.* New York: Franklin Watts.

121–25, 180–84: Brief biographical overview of Hemingway's two safaris. Geared toward young adults.

Trogdon, Robert W. "'Forms of Combat': Hemingway, the Critics, and *Green Hills of Africa.*" *Hemingway Review* 15, no. 2: 1–14.

Reads *Green Hills of Africa* as Hemingway's response to critics, addressing specific charges leveled over the years about his seemingly simple pose style, use of dirty language, and lack of political and social subject matter. Points to the mixed reception of *Death in the Afternoon* as the origin of Hemingway's feud with reviewers and literary adversaries.

1997

Brenner, Gerry. "(S)talking Game: Dialogically Hunting Hemingway's Domestic Hunters." *Hemingway Review* 16, no. 2: 35–50.

Bakhtinian reading of the hunter/hunted binary, paying particular attention to "The Short Happy Life of Francis Macomber" and *A Moveable Feast*. Focuses briefly on domestic hunters such as Harry of "The Snows of Kilimanjaro" and Phil of "The Sea Change," whose self-worth depends upon stalking and injuring others through verbal assault. In light of this type of hunter, Brenner considers animal rights activists' criticism of Hemingway myopic and naïve.

De Fusco, Andrea. "Discussing 'Macomber' in the Undergraduate Writing Seminar: What We Talk About When We Talk About Hemingway." *Hemingway Review* 17, no. 1: 72–79.

Relying on reader-response criticism, De Fusco outlines her strategies for eliciting meaningful class discussions that lead to rich and varied writing projects. Stories like "The Short Happy Life of Francis Macomber" that deal with gender "can be a good gateway topic for classes who are 'afraid to offend' the teacher or each other" (78–79). Hemingway's stories work particularly well because of his subtle and economical writing style.

Friedman, Norman. "Harry or Ernest? The Unresolved Ambiguity in 'The Snows of Kilimanjaro.'" In *Creative and Critical Approaches to the Short Story*, edited by Noel Harold Kaylor, Jr., 359–73. Lewiston, NY: Edwin Mellen Press.

Summarizes the textual ambiguities regarding Harry's artistic integrity, attitude toward wealth, Helen's role, and the function of the italicized reminiscences to show that "Snows" resists a unified resolution.

Larsen, Richard B. "Imaginary Heaven, African Hell in *The Snows of Kilimanjaro*." *JAISA: The Journal of the Association for the Interdisciplinary Study of the Arts* 2, no. 2: 45–51.

Reads the story in light of African tribal religious lore, arguing that "after his death Harry is condemned to slink along the lowlands in a new body, that of the hyena, a fittingly greedy and disreputable creature tearing at the remains of what others have left for him" (46).

Listoe, Daniel. "Writing Toward Death: The Stylistic Necessities of the Last Journeys of Ernest Hemingway." *North Dakota Quarterly* 65, no. 3: 89–95.

Marks "The Snows of Kilimanjaro" as Hemingway's first attempt at creating characters who struggle inwardly in anticipation of their eminent deaths. Unlike Harry, who possesses little hope of achieving his goals before his death, Hemingway's later three protagonists (Robert Jordan,

Richard Cantwell, and Santiago) all strive to complete their final projects, bringing in the fish in Santiago's case.

O'Meara, Lauraleigh. "Shooting Cowards, Critics, and Failed Writers: F. Scott Fitzgerald and Hemingway's Francis Macomber." *Hemingway Review* 16, no. 2: 27–34.

Argues that Hemingway based the cowardly Macomber in part upon Fitzgerald as retaliation for the latter's unsolicited critique of *Green Hills of Africa* and other works. Like Macomber with Wilson, Fitzgerald overlooked Hemingway's insults and maintained their friendship, at least superficially, until his death.

Reynolds, Michael. *Hemingway: The 1930s.* New York: Norton.

141–67: "African Game Trails." Biography of Hemingway's first African safari, recounting Pauline's efforts to shoot a lion, Hemingway's dysentery, and the growing competition over trophies.

168–93: "Pursuit Remembered." Biographical overview of the writing and publication history of *Green Hills of Africa*, "a book about writing a book" (184). Notes the author's ability to write cleanly, without the need for dramatic revision.

194–218: "Heavy Weather." Covers the final revisions of *Green Hills of Africa*, Perkins's editorial suggestions, and the novel's publication, serialization, and disappointing critical reception.

219–44: "Boxing the Compass." Biographical overview of the writing of "The Short Happy Life of Francis Macomber" and "The Snows of Kilimanjaro," noting Harry's connection to the failing F. Scott Fitzgerald and identifying the probable source for Margot as Jane Mason.

Spilka, Mark. "Abusive and Nonabusive Dying in Hemingway's Fiction." Chapter 4 in *Eight Lessons in Love: A Domestic Violence Reader.* Columbia: U of Missouri P.

210–22: Applies theories of domestic violence to "The Snows of Kilimanjaro" to show Harry as the classic verbal abuser who is rewarded with a heavenward journey. Argues that later Hemingway texts depicting nonabusive deaths, such as *To Have and Have Not* and *For Whom the Bell Tolls*, reveal the author's growing embarrassment over the earlier story's warped view of manliness.

1998

Brogan, Jacqueline Vaught. "Strange Fruits in *The Garden of Eden*: 'The Mysticism of Money,' *The Great Gatsby*, and *A Moveable Feast*." In *French Connections: Hemingway and Fitzgerald Abroad*, edited by

J. Gerald Kennedy and Jackson R. Bryer, 235–56. New York: St. Martin's Press.

Influence study connecting *The Garden of Eden* (including "An African Story"), *A Moveable Feast,* and *The Great Gatsby* to an obscure 1922 essay by Harold Loeb, whom both authors knew in Paris. Comments on Hemingway's competition with Fitzgerald to create the great American novel about money, reading *Garden* as a revision of *Gatsby*. Sees money and conquest as motivating factors in both *Gatsby* and the journey in "An African Story."

Didion, Joan. "Last words." *New Yorker* 74 (9 November): 74–80.

On Hemingway's distinct and influential writing style from the point of view of a writer. Lengthy commentary on Hemingway's difficulties in finishing the Africa book (*True at First Light*) and the problems associated with its posthumous publication.

Diguette, Richard. "The Trial of Margot Macomber: A Classroom Exercise in Fact-Finding and Literary Analysis." *Teaching English in the Two-Year College* 25, no. 2: 159–60.

Conducts a mock trial to determine Margot's guilt in "The Short Happy Life of Francis Macomber." In the process of learning how to cross-examine a text, students learn how to correctly gather and evaluate material, thus honing their analytical reading and critical thinking skills.

Eby, Carl. "Ernest Hemingway and the Mirror of Manhood: Fetishism, Transvestism, Homeovestism, and Perverse Méconnaissance." *Arizona Quarterly* 54, no. 3: 27–68.

Psychoanalytic approach to *The Garden of Eden* discussing the symbolic possibilities of David Bourne's title, *The Rift*, which alludes to East Africa's Great Rift Valley, the conflict between David and his father (similarly treated in the elephant tale), and the split between David and his "African fiancée." Reprinted with substantial revision as "Bisexuality, Splitting, and the Mirror of Manhood." Chapter 6 in *Hemingway's Fetishism: Psychoanalysis and the Mirror of Manhood*. Albany: SUNY P, 1999. 185–240.

Harrow, Kenneth W. "Gordimer Contre Hemingway: Crossing Back Through the Mirror that Subtends All Speculation." In *(Un)Writing Empire*, edited by Theo D'haen, 187–202. Amsterdam: Rodopi.

Comparison study of "The Short Happy Life of Francis Macomber" with Gordimer's "A Hunting Accident," noting striking parallels in plot that suggest Gordimer is attempting a feminist revision of Hemingway's story of domination and dependency. Gives a Lacanian reading of

"Macomber," focusing especially on Macomber's transformation in light of the Oedipal complex. Relies on the theories of Irigaray and Cixous in reading Gordimer's "response" to Hemingway.

Henn, Judy. "One Memory Does Not Destroy Another: 'The Snows of Kilimanjaro' Through the Prism of *Green Hills of Africa*." *Journal of the Department of English: Hemingway Centennial Tribute* (Rabindra Bharati University, Calcutta, India) 5: 126–35.

Reads "The Snows of Kilimanjaro" in light of *Green Hills of Africa*'s four titled parts, examining overlapping themes and motifs on the writer's vocation and creative process.

Kempton, Daniel. "Sexual Transgression and Artistic Creativity in *The Garden of Eden*." *North Dakota Quarterly* 65, no. 3: 136–42.

Relates David's sexual restoration through Marita with his newfound ability to write the African stories. Without the threatening influence of Catherine on David's heterosexual and colonial selves, the author is able to return to Africa as the place of imagination.

Kravitz, Bennett. "'She Loves Me, She Loves Me Not': The Short Happy Symbiotic Marriage of Margot and Francis Macomber." *Journal of American Culture* 21, no. 3: 83–87.

Describes the Macomber marriage as a symbiotic relationship based on fear of individuation and dependence. Macomber's new-found bravery and desire to withdraw from their marriage threatens Margot's existence, thus although she consciously shoots to save Macomber's life, she unconsciously kills him in a way out of her symbiosis without endangering her existence. Draws on Lacan's theory of desire.

Moddelmog, Debra A. "Re-Placing Africa in 'The Snows of Kilimanjaro': The Intersecting Economies of Capitalist-Imperialism and Hemingway Biography." In *New Essays on Hemingway's Short Fiction*, edited by Paul Smith, 111–36. Cambridge: Cambridge UP.

Concerned with the critical arguments surrounding Harry's artistic redemption. Contends that in both "Snows" and "The Short Happy Life of Francis Macomber," the white characters share imperialistic attitudes towards Africa and its inhabitants, thus subjecting them to domination. "Harry, Helen, Francis and Margot (not to mention Robert Wilson, who is British) all have a colonial relationship with the Africans who serve them, a relationship made possible by national ideologies in which the subjugation of a foreign land and its people is seen as just and ethical" (125–26). Warns that as we examine the works ourselves, we too must be aware of our limitations in constructing the ethical stance of the author.

Penas Ibáñez, Beatriz. "Looking Through *The Garden's* Mirrors: The Early Postmodernist Hemingway Text." *North Dakota Quarterly* 65, no. 3: 91–104.

Considers *The Garden of Eden* a metafictional narrative resurrecting Hemingway's early style. Characterizes the three African short stories as "avant-garde pieces molded within a long postmodern kind of framing narrative" (98). In her examination of the mirror motif, Penas Ibáñez contends that the dead elephant mirrors the death of a style. "The dying elephant allegorizes the doom of modernist realism through a typically modernist African motif recurring within a postmodernist text" (99).

1999

Burwell, Rose Marie. "Something's Lost and Something's Gained." *Hemingway Review* 19, no. 1: 20–23.

Mixed response to the newly published *True at First Light*, praising this latest addition for making so much of the African book available to the public, but lamenting editorial choices that, for example, distort Mary Hemingway's character in the memoir.

Catalano, Susan M. "Henpecked to Heroism: Placing Rip Van Winkle and Francis Macomber in the American Renegade Tradition." *Hemingway Review* 17, no. 2: 111–17.

Characterizing Rip and Macomber as "reluctant renegades," Catalano argues that despite marital domination both transcend their emasculation to achieve antihero status and compel reader sympathy along the way.

del Gizzo, Suzanne. "A Lie by Noon?" *Hemingway Review* 19, no. 1: 35–38.

After considering Hemingway's vacillating reputation with critics over the years, del Gizzo concludes that the African safari, like Hemingway himself, suffered from the very commercial success it sought.

Dillon-Malone, Aubrey. *Hemingway: The Grace and the Pressure*. New York: Robson.

149–54: Biographical approach briefly covering Hemingway's 1933–1934 safari. Dismisses *Green Hills of Africa* as "mediocre" but praises "The Short Happy Life of Francis Macomber" and "The Snows of Kilimanjaro" as products of the author at the "height of his creative power." Touches on the themes of catharsis in both short stories along with a diatribe against the film versions.

Eby, Carl. *Hemingway's Fetishism: Psychoanalysis and the Mirror of Manhood*. Albany: SUNY P.

119–53: "Loss, Fetishism, and the Fate of the Transitional Object." Psychoanalytical approach to Hemingway's life and writings, discussing such traditional psychoanalytical concerns as phallic symbols, fetish objects, and castration anxiety. Comments on Hemingway's interest in cats and lions, comparing them to Debba and Miss Mary, for example. While on his 1953 safari, Hemingway instinctively ate the shoulder blade of a wounded leopard. Characterizes Hemingway's desire to go native during this time as symbolic transvestism.

155–83: "Ebony and Ivory: Hemingway's Fetishization of Race." Reprint with minor revision of "'Come Back to the Beach Ag'in, David Honey!': Hemingway's Fetishization of Race in *The Garden of Eden* Manuscripts." *Hemingway Review* 14, no. 2 (1995): 98–117. See Eby (1995) in this bibliography for annotation.

185–240: "Bisexuality, Splitting, and the Mirror of Manhood." Expanded reprint of "Ernest Hemingway and the Mirror of Manhood: Fetishism, Transvestism, Homeovestism, and Perverse *Méconnaissance*." *Arizona Quarterly* 54, no. 3 (1998): 27–68. See Eby (1998) in this bibliography for annotation.

———. "Hemingway's Truth and Tribal Politics." *Hemingway Review* 19, no. 1: 23–27.

Compares portions of Mary Hemingway's diary to *True at First Light*, suggesting Papa's "fictional memoir" may be more fact than fiction. Comments briefly on Hemingway's complex and sometimes inconsistent tribal and colonial politics.

Fleming, Robert. "Africa Revisited." *Hemingway Review* 19, no. 1: 28–30.

Compares *True at First Light* to *A Moveable Feast* and especially *Green Hills of Africa*, noting similarities in subject matter, structure, and characterization. Warns scholars interested in Hemingway's later works against disregarding *True at First Light* simply because of its poor reception by the popular press.

Gajdusek, Robert. "One Blind Man Exploring a Pretty Big Elephant." *Hemingway Review* 19, no. 1: 31–34.

Praises *True at First Light* for its distinctive prose style, disciplined thematic unity, and solid depiction of complicated interrelationships. "Hemingway has brought together in a remarkable *assemblage* a complex number of themes and concerns which resonate together, and their severally developed fascinations and interests will select their readers" (31).

Hemingway, Patrick. "An Evening with Patrick Hemingway." Interview with Michael Seefeldt. *Hemingway Review* 19, no. 1: 8–16.

Editor Patrick Hemingway comments on his strategies for cutting the original manuscript of *True at First Light* by 25 percent and strengthening the memoir's two main plot lines (the love stories and hunting narratives) while maintaining his father's vision of early 1950s Africa.

Jenks, Tom. "The Old Man and the Manuscript." *Harper's* 298, May: 53–60.

Lengthy review of Hemingway's latest posthumously published book, *True at First Light*, by the editor of *The Garden of Eden* (1986), another of Hemingway's posthumously published works. Jenks characterizes *True at First Light* as a failed effort by a failing writer. Jenks outlines the events inspiring the book's conception along with Patrick Hemingway's difficulties in editing. Despite criticizing the book as "unformed, fragmentary, digressive, and anecdotal," Jenks doubts its appearance will diminish Hemingway's reputation or stem the flow of future posthumous works making their way into the marketplace.

Justice, Hilary K. "The Lion, the Leopard, and the Bear." *Hemingway Review* 19, no. 1: 39–42.

Identifies allusions to Dante's *Inferno* and Faulkner's "The Bear" in *True at First Light*, tying those references thematically to Hemingway's anxiety about himself as an aging writer, increasingly unable to write.

Kennedy, J. Gerald. "Figuring the Damage: Fitzgerald's 'Babylon Revisited' and Hemingway's 'The Snows of Kilimanjaro.'" In *French Connections: Hemingway and Fitzgerald Abroad*, edited by J. Gerald Kennedy and Jackson R. Bryer, 317–43. New York: St. Martin's Press.

Argues against the liberating influence of the expatriate lifestyle of the 1920s on both authors, suggesting instead that although Hemingway and Fitzgerald initially reveled in their revolts against convention, each paid a heavy price for their indulgences. "Babylon Revisited" and "Snows," written in the 1930s, express the authors' tragic understanding of the personal costs of these early years spent in Paris. Examines Fitzgerald's manipulation of geographical locale to reveal Charlie's conflicting attitudes toward alcohol and those crazy Paris years. Contends that Hemingway wrote "Snows" as "an analysis of wreckage and self-ruin." Harry's troubled reflections on Paris reveal the declining writer coming to terms with his own dissolution.

Kerasote, Ted. "Untouchable Wild." *Audubon* 101, no. 5: 82–86.

On the rise of ecotourism in Africa, flourishing alongside hunting safaris. Mentions Hemingway's long-held fascination with Africa, beginning with Theodore Roosevelt's much publicized safari and publication of *African Game Trails*.

Kinnamon, Keneth. "The Politics of 'The Snows of Kilimanjaro.'" In *Value and Vision in American Literature: Literary Essays in Honor of Ray Lewis White*, edited by Joseph Candido and Charles H. Adams, 15–31. Athens: Ohio UP.

Biographical approach connecting Hemingway's ambivalent feelings regarding the corrupting and oppressing power of wealth to Harry's recognition of his complicity in the destruction of his talent. Details Hemingway's financial dependence on Pauline's rich Uncle Gus while at the same time railing against the wealthy and siding with the political Left.

Lawrence, H. Lea. *A Hemingway Odyssey: Special Places in his Life*. Nashville: Cumberland House.

Biographical travelogue, briefly referencing Hemingway's African works. Only slight coverage of Kenya.

Lewis, Robert W. "'The African Book': Hemingway Major and Late in the Natural World." In *Hemingway and the Natural World*, edited by Robert Fleming, 111–24. Moscow: U of Idaho P.

Manuscript study arguing that while strong similarities exist between the African book and *Green Hills of Africa*, distinct differences mark the later comic narrative as innovative and interesting. Examines Ray Cave's editing of the *Sports Illustrated* excerpts culled from the African book and discusses that editor's identification of nine themes or plot lines within the narrative, ranging from nature and hunting to Hemingway's 'Africanization.'"

———. "Editing *True at First Light*." *Hemingway Review* 19, no. 1: 43–47.

Relies on Edmund Wilson's "The Literary Worker's Polonius" to guide his thoughts on the current critical reception of *True at First Light*. He laments editorial decisions on the part of Patrick Hemingway that distort the manuscript's narrative integrity for commercial gain.

Mandal, Somdatta. "Mount Kilimanjaro Revisited: Africa, the Lion's Roar, and Ernest Hemingway." *West Bengal: A West Bengal Government English Fortnightly* 41, no. 23: 113+.
Hemingway Review 20, no. 1: 128.

Martin, Lawrence H. "Hemingway's Constructed Africa: *Green Hills of Africa* and the Conventions of Colonial Sporting Books." In *Hemingway and the Natural World*, edited by Robert Fleming, 87–97. Moscow: U of Idaho P.

Comparison study of African books in Hemingway's collection with *Green Hills of Africa*. Despite Hemingway's vilification of earlier safari books and expressed intention to surpass them in honesty and verisimilitude, he draws heavily upon the genre's themes and conventions such as the sportsmen's rules for hunting.

Miller, Linda. "What's Funny about *True at First Light*?" *Hemingway Review* 19, no. 1: 48–52.

Describes the book as "a rollicking good read," praising the author's incorporation of humor (private jokes, wordplay, and irony) and myth in his creation of a surreal world of child's play and dream fulfillment.

Moddelmog, Debra A. "Reading Between the Lions." *Hemingway Review* 19, no. 1: 53–57.

Decries *True at First Light's* slow pace, thin plot, underdeveloped relationships, and lack of self-reflection. Moddelmog muses on whether or not the full manuscript might overcome some of these limitations and provide, for example, greater insight into Hemingway's adoption of the black African racial identity and his unceasing rejection of homosexual desire.

———. *Reading Desire: In Pursuit of Ernest Hemingway*. Ithaca: Cornell UP.

58–90: "Casting Out Forbidden Desires from *The Garden of Eden*: Capitalism and the Production of Hemingway." Comments on Jenks's editorial decision to cut most of the passages in which David, Catherine, and Marita discuss Africa and its people. "Jenks reduced the impression that Hemingway and his characters were obsessed with the African Other, especially as that Other represents an opportunity for the civilized white to transgress cultural proscriptions and discover a more 'natural' self" (67). Reprint with minor revision of "Protecting the Hemingway Myth: Casting Out Forbidden Desires from *The Garden of Eden*." *Prospects: An Annual Journal of American Cultural Studies* 22 (1996): 89–122.

100–19: "The Race of Desire and Hemingway's World-Traveling: Re-Placing Africa in 'The Snows of Kilimanjaro' and Hemingway's African Safari, 1953–1954." Expanded reprint of "Re-Placing Africa in 'The Snows of Kilimanjaro': The Intersecting Economies of Capitalist-Imperialism and Hemingway Biography" in *New Essays on Hemingway's Short Fiction*, edited by Paul Smith, 111–36. Cambridge: Cambridge UP, 1998. See Moddelmog (1998) in this bibliography for annotation. The expanded essay includes additional analysis of Hemingway's ambivalent feelings regarding white intrusion in Africa. Contends that even the 1954 *Look* pictorial article reveals the superiority of white expertise.

Oliver, Charles M. *Ernest Hemingway A to Z: The Essential Reference to His Life and Works.* New York: Facts on File.

Comprehensive guide to the facts of Hemingway's life and writings, providing biographical information along with information on the "who, what, where, and when" of the author's short stories, novels, poems, newspaper articles, and nonfiction books. Includes plot summaries for each work of fiction and synopses of the nonfiction. Entries are arranged alphabetically. Helpful appendices include maps and a chronology listing literary and historical events that place Hemingway's life and works within the larger cultural context.

128–31: *Green Hills of Africa*
301: "The Short Happy Life of Francis Macomber"
306–07: "The Snows of Kilimanjaro"
113–15: *The Garden of Eden*
333: *True at First Light*

Palin, Michael. "Africa." In *Michael Palin's Hemingway Adventure*, 158–95. New York: St. Martin's Press.

Travelogue of important Hemingway locales. Excellent photographs coupled with diary entries and notes taken while filming the television series.

Pearson, Roger L. "Ernest Hemingway: *Journal of the American Medical Association*, April 26, 1919, Volume 72, Number 17." *North Dakota Quarterly* 66, no. 2: 134–46.

Identifies a specific issue of *JAMA* as a probable source for providing Hemingway with specific and credible medical information on the progressive stages of gangrene, the disease that induces Harry's delirium in "The Snows of Kilimanjaro."

Plotkin, Stephen. "The *True at First Light* Manuscripts at the John F. Kennedy Library." *Hemingway Review* 19, no. 1: 61–63.

Announces the availability of the African book manuscripts (published in part as *True at First Light*) at both the Kennedy and Princeton University libraries.

Putnam, Ann. "Memory, Grief, and the Terrain of Desire: Hemingway's *Green Hills of Africa*." In *Hemingway and the Natural World*, edited by Robert Fleming, 99–110. Moscow: U of Idaho P.

Reads *Green Hills of Africa* as "a book about the loss of the pastoral, visionary landscape and the ultimately tragic search for redemption" (99). Discusses the sense of dividedness that marks the text at all levels — of the narrative's conflicting desires to revere the African landscape while at the same time to conquer and destroy it. The sojourner turns hunter under the ceaseless pressure of time.

Reynolds, Michael. "Night Thoughts." *Hemingway Review* 19, no. 1: 58–63.

Briefly compares *True at First Light* to *A Moveable Feast*, *Islands in the Stream*, and *Green Hills of Africa*, noting similarities in subject matter, characterization, and plot. As with many of Hemingway's earlier works, the narrator of *True at First Light* must learn how to live with dignity in a fallen world.

———. *Hemingway: The Final Years*. New York: Norton.

264–77: "The Phoenix." Biographical overview of Hemingway's final safari; catalogues his numerous injuries suffered in two plane crashes.

278–302: "Fortune and Men's Eyes" and "Intimations of Mortality." Biographical overviews detailing the writing of *True at First Light*, commenting on the narrative's comic and ironic tone. Despite its humor, however, Reynolds contends that "the Africanization of Ernest Hemingway is serious in the sense that he was looking for some way to escape from his too public life into a simpler world" (285).

303–38: "Cuba Libre" and "Exiles from Eden." Biographical overviews chronicling Hemingway's futile attempts to finish the African book and *The Garden of Eden*.

Richardson, Miles. "Place Narrative, and the Writing Self: The Poetics of Being in *The Garden of Eden*." *Southern Review* 35, no. 2: 330–37.

Briefly treats David's desire, through the writing of the African stories, to confront and understand his father's appetite for killing.

Sandison, David. "Africa, Cuba, Spain: The Great White Hunter." Chapter 5 in *Ernest Hemingway: An Illustrated Biography*. Chicago: Chicago Review Press.

102–7: Pictorial biography on Hemingway's first safari, briefly summarizing the works it inspired: *Green Hills of Africa*, "The Short Happy Life of Francis Macomber," and "The Snows of Kilimanjaro."

Theisen, Earl. "The New Safari and the Last Safari." *Audubon* 101, no. 5: 73–81.

Pictorial article noting the rise of ecotourism in Africa. Excerpts letters from Theisen to his wife detailing his time spent photographing Hemingway's 1953–1954 safari.

Trogdon, Robert W., ed. *Ernest Hemingway: A Documentary Volume* (*Dictionary of Literary Biography,* vol. 210). Detroit: Gale Group. Paperback edition: *Ernest Hemingway: A Literary Reference.* New York: Carroll & Graf, 2002.

Biographical and bibliographical guide to Hemingway's life and writings. In addition to detailed chronologies, the volume also provides scholarly criticism on individual works. Reprints letters, dust jackets, interviews, reviews, and advertisements.

109–83: "Chapter Three: 1930–1935." Covers the first safari and *Green Hills of Africa.*

184–233: "Chapter Four: 1936–1940." Covers "The Snows of Kilimanjaro" and "The Short Happy Life of Francis Macomber."

287–327: "Chapter Six: 1953–July 1961." Covers the second safari, the African book, and *The Garden of Eden.*

328–56: "Chapter Seven: 3 July 1961–1999." Covers the publication of *The Garden of Eden* and *True at First Light.*

"*True at First Light*: Special Section." *Hemingway Review* 19, no. 1: 8–63.

Significant portion devoted to commentary on the newly published memoir by its editor, archivists, and various Hemingway scholars.

Voss, Frederick. *Picturing Hemingway: A Writer in His Time.* New Haven: Smithsonian National Portrait Gallery in association with Yale UP.

Photographs of the National Portrait Gallery's exhibition, offering a visual record of Hemingway's life and career. Essay by Michael Reynolds establishes Hemingway as an American icon. Superb photographs of Hemingway on his 1953–1954 safari.

2000

Beegel, Susan F. "Eye and Heart: Hemingway's Education as a Naturalist." In *A Historical Guide to Ernest Hemingway,* edited by Linda Wagner-Martin, 53–92. New York: Oxford UP.

Treats Hemingway's lifelong interest in the natural world, frequently citing passages from *Green Hills of Africa, The Garden of Eden,* and elsewhere. Focuses on the profound influence of the Agassiz method of object-oriented science education on Hemingway's powers of observation and attention to detail, claiming that Hemingway remained an Agassiz-trained naturalist throughout his life.

Cheatham, George. "Margot Macomber's Voice in Hemingway's 'The Short Happy Life of Francis Macomber.'" *Soundings: An Interdisciplinary Journal* 83, no. 3: 739–64.

Attempts to explain how different readers arrive at different interpretations of the story, focusing primarily on narrative perspective and character consciousness. Unlike those critics who claim Macomber is finished with Margot by this point, Cheatham reads Macomber's wave as evidence that Macomber has tolerantly accepted their dysfunctional relationship. Margot's nonresponse to his wave indicates her own acceptance, thus proving she shot at the buffalo.

Clarke, Brock. "What Literature Can and Cannot Do: Lionel Trilling, Richard Rorty, and the Left." *Massachusetts Review* 41, no. 4: 523–39.

Arguing that Trilling's theories are more complex than he's been given credit for, Clarke recounts Trilling's criticism of Hemingway's *Green Hills of Africa* and other works "to remind us of the specific responsibilities of literary and cultural critics" (523). Trilling has much to teach us still concerning the vital role criticism plays in the creative writing process and the relationship between literature and politics. Accordingly, Trilling criticizes the critics of the period for not seriously reading and critiquing Hemingway's later works.

Elliott, Ira. "In Search of Lost Time: Reading Hemingway's *Garden*." In *Modernist Sexualities*, edited by Hugh Stevens and Caroline Howlett, 251–66. Manchester, England: Manchester UP.

Argues that cultural anxieties lie beneath the surface of *The Garden of Eden*, manifesting themselves in the novel's exploration of body/boundary fractures and transformations, specifically those related to gender and race. Examines Catherine's obsession with tanning and race construction and how they function within the larger text. Reads Catherine's race manipulation as an attempt to recover a lost primeval garden and also as a way to connect to the primitivism of Africa.

Hemingway, Hilary, and Jeffrey P. Lindsay, eds. *Hunting with Hemingway: Based on the Stories of Leicester Hemingway*. New York: Riverhead.

21–149. Brother Leicester reminisces about his African safari with Hemingway, hunting crocodiles and ostriches, surviving run-ins with baboons and wild dogs, observing rat fights, and saving stranded tourists who may have served as the models for "The Short Happy Life of Francis Macomber."

Jordan, Edwina. "Early 20th Century Writers in Africa." *English Record* 50, no. 3: 54–58.

Classroom approach outlining her use of Hemingway's *Green Hills of Africa*, Dinesen's *Out of Africa*, and Langston Hughes's poetry in her international studies class entitled "Africa." Contends that Hemingway's descriptions of the Kikuyu people dispel the stereotypical image of the noble African savage.

Lindsay, Creighton. "Hemingway's Nexus of Pastoral and Tragedy." *CLA Journal* 43, no. 4: 454–78.

Examination of the pastoral design of the camp in "The Short Happy Life of Francis Macomber," arguing that Macomber reaches tragic stature only through his death, and even then offers the reader little to admire beyond his ultimate sacrifice because of his insensitivity to the toll his heroic quest has exacted upon nature.

Mayer, Ruth. "The White Hunter: Edgar Rice Burroughs, Ernest Hemingway, Clint Eastwood, and the Act of Acting Male in Africa." In *Subverting Masculinity: Hegemonic and Alternative Versions of Masculinity in Contemporary Culture*, edited by Russell West and Frank Lay, 247–65. Amsterdam: Rodopi.

Traces the evolving iconic images of the white male in Africa (ape-man and white hunter), beginning with Burroughs's *Tarzan of the Apes* and concluding with Eastwood's film *White Hunter, Black Heart*. Theorizes that despite their African settings, these white protagonists, including Macomber from "The Short Happy Life of Macomber," are caught up in Western civilization's obsessions with identity, gender, autonomy, and authenticity. In "Macomber" and "The Snows of Kilimanjaro," Hemingway blends authenticity with fantasy to create African narratives in which "the notion of authenticity — being a true man — came to be intricately conjoined with the logic of escapism and the daydream — leaving the real world behind" (253). Argues that "Macomber" represents an inverted *Tarzan of the Apes* in which the action takes place within the mind of the white male, far from the African setting.

Meyers, Jeffrey. *Hemingway: Life into Art*. New York: Cooper Square Press.

21–32: "Hemingway's Second War: The Greco-Turkish Conflict, 1920–1922." Provides historical background on the Greco-Turkish War along with a brief examination of how Hemingway's involvement in the war's aftermath influenced his writing of Harry's flashbacks in "The Snows of Kilimanjaro." Reprint of "Hemingway's Second War: The

Greco-Turkish Conflict, 1920–1922." *Modern Fiction Studies* 30, no. 1 (1984): 25–36.

55–65: "A Queer, Ugly Business: The Origins of 'The Short Happy Life of Francis Macomber.'" Points to a real-life case of adultery and suicide in Africa in 1908 as the source and inspiration of Hemingway's short story. Reprint of "A Queer, Ugly Business: The Origins of 'The Short Happy Life of Francis Macomber.'" *London Magazine* 23 (November 1983): 26–37.

Mukherjee, Tutun. "Hemingway and Hollywood: An Uneasy Relationship." In *Ernest Hemingway: Centennial Essays*, edited by E. Nageswara Rao, 125–35. Delhi: Pencraft International.

Analyzing the film versions of *A Farewell to Arms* and "The Short Happy Life of Francis Macomber," Mukherjee argues that Hemingway's lean style has not translated well in Hollywood, where both critical and aesthetic dimensions have been manipulated to fit the Hollywood formula.

Nair, N. Ramachandran. "Re-Emergence of the Artist in 'The Snows of Kilimanjaro.'" In *Ernest Hemingway: Centennial Essays*, edited by E. Nageswara Rao, 90–98. Delhi: Pencraft International.

Focuses on the artist motif, reading the story as a "declaration of the triumph of art" (91). Suggests that Harry's reflection upon his failures is a necessary step toward his emergence at a higher spiritual level "as a clean artist with an uncompromising conscience" (97).

Stacy, Gerald. "Teaching Hemingway's *Short Happy Life*." *Eureka Studies in Teaching Short Fiction* 1, no. 1: 95–102.

Outlines his classroom strategies for teaching "The Short Happy Life of Francis Macomber," including three key discussion questions relating to the story's central conflicts, point of view, and sequence of events.

Strychacz, Thomas. "'Like Plums in a Pudding': Food and Rhetorical Performance in Hemingway's *Green Hills of Africa*." *Hemingway Review* 19, no. 2: 23–46.

Argues that in *Green Hills* "metaphors of food and corresponding processes of digestion and excretion articulate Hemingway's fears about irresponsible and wasteful consumption" (25). Contends that while many have lamented *Green Hills's* rhetorical excesses, scholars should in fact be reading Hemingway's prose on Africa as a rhetorical performance in light of the novel's basic themes of exploitation and consumption. In short, Hemingway's rhetorical strategies in *Green Hills* foster a reevaluation of the nature of waste itself.

Tellefsen, Blythe. "Rewriting the Self Against the National Text: Ernest Hemingway's *The Garden of Eden*." *Papers on Language and Literature: A Journal for Scholars and Critics of Language and Literature* 36, no. 1: 58–92.

Treats Catherine's experiments in racial and sexual transformation, commenting on her desire to invent a new identity beyond her unbearable self. Sees the most important connection between the African story and the honeymoon narrative to center on identity. Unlike Catherine, David's imaginative connection to Africa is based upon real experience. As he struggles to master his own identity, "David's writing, his investment in his identity as an author, can therefore be linked to his will-to-power: power to shape his own identity, to re/present his father and his father's story, and narrate/create history" (79). Also discusses David's repressed fear of his African siblings in relation to the larger myth of an American society based upon arbitrary categories of color. Reprinted as "Rewriting the Self Against the National Text: Ernest Hemingway's *The Garden of Eden*" in *Hemingway: Eight Decades of Criticism*, edited by Linda Wagner-Martin, 377–409. East Lansing: Michigan State UP.

2001

Barnhisel, Greg. "The Snows of Kilimanjaro." In *Short Stories for Students, Vol. 11: Presenting Analysis, Context, and Criticism on Commonly Studied Short Stories*, edited by Jennifer Smith, 243–55. Detroit: Gale.

Analysis of the story geared to high school students and general readers. Outlines the story's plot, characters, and major themes along with brief contextual and critical overviews.

Brogan, Jacqueline Vaught. "*True at First Light*: A New Look at Hemingway and Race." *North Dakota Quarterly* 68, no. 2: 199–224.

Drawing on Toni Morrison's criticism of Hemingway in *Playing in the Dark*, Brogan argues that *True at First Light* overtly reveals Hemingway's anxieties as an author whose continued production supported a capitalist structure permeated by sexism and racism. Together with Hemingway's other posthumous works dealing with authorial concerns, such as *A Moveable Feast* and especially *The Garden of Eden*, *True at First Light* exposes and criticizes an unethical structure that the troubled author himself participated in. Thus, these later texts show a "deeply ethical Hemingway fully conscious of his moral failings both as a writer and human being" (219). See Morrison (1992) in this bibliography (for annotation).

Hemingway, Seán, ed. *Hemingway on Hunting*. Guilford, CT: Lyons.

Compilation of excerpts by grandson Seán taken from Hemingway's books, short stories, journal articles, and letters chronicling the author's love of hunting. As can be expected, selections from the African writings, including the latest posthumous publication, *True at First Light*, dominate the collection. Includes an introduction by Hemingway's grandson Seán and a foreword by Hemingway's son Patrick expounding on his father's lifelong fascination with hunting and the outdoors.

Nesmith, Chris L. "'The Law of an Ancient God' and the Editing of Hemingway's *Garden of Eden*: The Final Corrected Typescript and Galleys." *Hemingway Review* 20, no. 2: 16–36.

Overviews the controversy regarding Jenks's extensive editing of the manuscript. Lists editorial emendations to the Cooper Library's final edited typescript.

Tyler, Lisa. *Student Companion to Ernest Hemingway*. Westport, CT: Greenwood Press.

Geared toward students and general readers. Includes extensive bibliography of reviews and criticism.

93–114: "The African Stories." After summarizing the narrative of *Green Hills of Africa*, Tyler then briefly outlines the book's largely negative contemporary reception. Speculates on the extent of Hemingway's racism as evidenced in his stereotypical depictions of the native Africans. Provides a composition history and plot summary of "The Snows of Kilimanjaro," articulating the story's major themes such as the corrupting power of money on artistic integrity and the destructive effect of Harry's inability to love. Briefly goes over the story's symbolism, including the frozen leopard. Provides an overview of the main characters of "The Short Happy Life of Francis Macomber" and their probable real life sources. Outlines the scholarly debates surrounding the story's major critical controversy of whether or not Margot aimed at the buffalo. Compares the text to an equally ambiguous story, Henry James's *Turn of the Screw*. Overview of the composition and publication history of the posthumously published *True at First Light*. Provides a plotline and brief commentary on Hemingway's changed attitudes towards race in this later novel, where he is clearly more sensitive to race issues.

146–55: "*The Garden of Eden*." Classifies *The Garden of Eden* as Hemingway's most innovative work, outlines the novel's publication history, structure, plot, and characterization. Compares the novel to Fitzgerald's *Tender is the Night* (1934) and analyzes themes such as sexual identity and betrayal (of both elephant and Catherine). Also provides an intertextual reading of the novel's allusions to the Bible, Lilith in ancient Jewish texts, and Greek mythology.

2002

Bittner, John R. "African Journeys: Hemingway's Influence on the Life and Writings of Robert Ruark." *Hemingway Review* 21, no. 2: 129–45.

Traces novelist and columnist Robert Chester Ruark Jr.'s long-term fascination with Hemingway's life and work, focusing particularly on their shared love of Africa. Concludes that Ruark's identification with Hemingway overshadowed his writing. "What Ruark had not learned, and Hemingway had, was that you can borrow from other writers, but if you want an independent literary reputation, you don't make a public display of it" (140).

Comley, Nancy R. "The Light from Hemingway's Garden: Regendering Papa." In *Hemingway and Women: Female Critics and the Female Voice*, edited by Lawrence R. Broer and Gloria Holland, 204–17. Tuscaloosa: U of Alabama P.

Laments the deletion of the racial elements from Scribner's published version of *The Garden of Eden*. Sees, for example, the tanning rituals as symbols of transformative experimentation that develop the overall thematic integrity of the work. And the references to Somali men and women (and wives) reflect Hemingway's fascination with primitivism.

Davis, Cynthia J. "Contagion as Metaphor." *American Literary History* 14, no. 4: 828–36.

Explores language's ability to hurt and heal in light of Sontag's *Illness and Metaphor* (1978). Discusses "The Snows of Kilimanjaro" as a example "that utilizes the aesthetic Sontag recommends while exploring not only their particular illness as metaphor but metaphor itself as illness — that is, when it functions as a means of evasion or implausible substitution" (832). Harry's gangrenous leg symbolizes both his rotted soul and his wasted potential as a writer. His disease has infected not only his leg but also his writing. In the end, Harry suffers from a "literal and literary death" full of rot and rotten poetry.

Eby, Carl. "Hemingway, Tribal Law, and the Identity of the Widow in *True at First Light*." *Hemingway Review* 21, no. 2: 146–51.

Straightens out the confusing relationship between Debba and the Widow. While the published version depicts Debba's mother as the Widow and Debba's father as living, the manuscripts and tribal law indicate the

Widow is not Debba's mother. Clearly Hemingway regarded the Widow as Debba's sister. Such clarity is necessary in establishing Hemingway's respect for another culture's laws and customs.

Gajdusek, Robert E. *Hemingway in His Own Country*. South Bend: U of Notre Dame P.

9–56: "Hemingway and Joyce: A Study in Debt and Payment." Study aimed at determining Joyce's influence on Hemingway in theme, structure, and technique. Gives an overview of past scholarship on the subject along with a brief look at Hemingway's associations with Joyce. Taking nearly all of Hemingway's major works into account, Gajdusek pays particular attention to how Hemingway adapts Joyce's fascination with cyclical patterns, crossover and transcendence, and ritual. Reprint of *Hemingway and Joyce: A Study in Debt and Repayment*. Corte Madera, CA: Square Circle Press, 1984.

57–73: "A Brief Safari Into the Religious Terrain of *Green Hills of Africa*." See Gajdusek (1992) in this bibliography for annotation. Reprint of "A Brief Safari Into the Religious Terrain of *Green Hills of Africa*." *North Dakota Quarterly* 60, no. 3 (1992): 26–40.

294–326: "Elephant Hunt in Eden: A Study of New and Old Myths and Other Strange Beasts in Hemingway's *Garden*." Explores Hemingway's treatment of sexual inversion and its relation to identity. Gajdusek is particularly interested in the male relinquishment of power (which is depicted not only in *The Garden of Eden* but also in almost all of Hemingway's major novels) and the need for men to balance the masculine and feminine sides of their nature. Reprint of "Elephant Hunt in Eden: A Study of New and Old Myths and Other Strange Beasts in Hemingway's *Garden*." *Hemingway Review* 7, no. 1 (1987): 15–19.

Mandel, Miriam B. "A Lifetime of Flower Narratives: Letting the Silenced Voice Speak." In *Hemingway and Women: Female Critics and the Female Voice*, edited by Lawrence R. Broer and Gloria Holland, 239–55. Tuscaloosa: U of Alabama P.

Comparison reading analyzing how Hemingway transformed his 1922 springtime visit to Chamby into four separate literary pieces reflecting his increasing discomfort and guilt over his betrayal of Hadley. Notes that in all four flower passages ("Fishing the Rhone Canal," *Green Hills of Africa*, *African Journal*, and *A Moveable Feast*) Hadley is marginalized and silenced by the guilt-ridden narrator. Yet by the final version of *A Moveable Feast*, "Hemingway enables us to resurrect the voice he had so desperately needed to silence, the voice that leads us to understand the flower narratives as consistently and painfully self incriminating" (255).

Mason, Jane Kendall. *Safari*. *Hemingway Review* 21, no. 2: 23–110.

For those interested in learning more about the woman who may have inspired Margot of "The Short Happy Life of Francis Macomber" and Helene Bradley of *To Have and Have Not*, the *Hemingway Review* publishes Jane Mason's African drama of adultery and sexual politics. Includes an introduction by her granddaughter, who provides biographical information and suggests *Safari* may well have been Mason's attempt to reclaim her own life story after "Macomber."

Putnam, Ann. "On Defiling Eden: The Search for Eve in the Garden of Sorrows." In *Hemingway and Women: Female Critics and the Female Voice*, edited by Lawrence R. Broer and Gloria Holland, 109–30. Tuscaloosa: U of Alabama P.

Argues that despite the lack of female characters in "Big Two-Hearted River," *Green Hills of Africa*, the African tale of *The Garden of Eden*, and other paradisal works, there is still a feminine presence. Examines the hunter-artist of *Green Hills* and equates the telling of the African story with Eve's story, noting the parallel themes of betrayal, suffering, and awareness.

Satterfield, Ben. "Doomed Quest: 'The Snows of Kilimanjaro.'" *Eureka Studies in Teaching Short Fiction* 2, no. 2: 40–45. Reprint of "Doomed Quest: 'The Snows of Kilimanjaro.'" *Black Mountain Review* 8 (October 1982).

Interprets the story in light of Hemingway's tragic vision, suggesting that contrary to those critics who read Harry as spiritually transcending his death, Harry's only success is with delusion. Doomed by his poor choices and carelessness, Harry has lost his chance as a writer and thus lies beyond the reach of salvation.

Trogdon, Robert W. "'This Fine, Splendid Joke': Jane Mason's *Safari*." *Hemingway Review* 21, no. 2: 125–28.

Briefly notes parallels between Hemingway's "The Short Happy Life of Francis Macomber" and *Green Hills of Africa* and Mason's *Safari*, especially in both authors' reactions to Africa. Though seeing connections between the main characters, April and Margot Macomber, Trogdon reads April as more closely attuned to Hemingway's earlier heroines in "Hills Like White Elephants" and "Cat in the Rain," women who desire a stable home.

Whitley, Edward. "Race and Modernity in Theodore Roosevelt's and Ernest Hemingway's African Travel Writing." In *Issues in Travel Writing: Empire, Spectacle, and Displacement*, edited by Kristi Siegel, 13–27. New York: Peter Lang.

Comparison study of Roosevelt's *African Game Trails* with Hemingway's later *Green Hill of Africa*, suggesting that both authors' imperialistic views of Africa represent a time of "escape from modernity." Notes their feelings of White superiority in their treatment of African primitivism.

Wolfe, Cary. "Fathers, Lovers, and Friend Killers: Rearticulating Gender and Race via Species in Hemingway." *Boundary 2: An International Journal of Literature and Culture* 29, no. 1: 223–57.

Theoretical approach. Relying on manuscript and editorial history for *The Garden of Eden*, Wolfe treats David's cross-species identification with the elephant as central to the novel. Questions Jenks's editing that resolves the ending of the novel in favor of David's reconciliation with his father. Rather, the trauma caused by the murdered elephant, and David's identification with it, connects to his later cross-gender identification with Catherine to further distance himself from his father.

2003

Breuer, Horst. "Hemingway's 'Francis Macomber' in Pirandellian and Freudian Perspectives." *Studies in American Fiction* 31, no. 2: 233–48.

Catalogues possible models for the story's main characters (including Philip Percival, Pauline Pfeiffer, and Hemingway himself) along with literary sources. Notes parallels in plot and characterization with Luigi Pirandello's novel *Quaderni di Serafino Gubbio operatore* (1915). Provides a psychoanalytic reading of Wilson as the idealized father figure, Macomber as the immature son, and Margot as "the mother-imago of the infantile scenario, emotionally cold, controlling, intrusive" (241–42).

del Gizzo, Suzanne. "Going Home: Hemingway, Primitivism, and Identity." *Modern Fiction Studies* 49, no. 3: 496–523.

Focuses on the theme of primitivism in *True at First Light* and *The Garden of Eden*, noting Hemingway's lifelong fascination with the topic and its thematic manifestation in his earlier works. In *True at First Light*, Hemingway's taking on the Kamba identity allows him the distance to critique not only himself but also Western culture. Compares Hemingway's first safari (1933–1934) and the works inspired from it (*Green Hills of Africa*, "The Snows of Kilimanjaro," "The Short Happy Life of Francis Macomber") to the later 1953–1954 safari (*True at First Light*, "Safari" article in *Look*), arguing that in his first journey personal and cultural concerns prevented him from truly experiencing Africa and its people. Reprinted as "Going Home: Hemingway, Primitivism, and Identity" in

Hemingway: Eight Decades of Criticism, edited by Linda Wagner-Martin, 479–512. East Lansing: Michigan State UP, 2009.

Donaldson, Scott. "The Averted Gaze in Hemingway's Fiction." *Sewanee Review* 111 (Winter): 128–51.

Examines Hemingway's use of the averted and direct gaze in several stories of marriage and love, including "The Short Happy Life of Francis Macomber" and "The Snows of Kilimanjaro," as an indication of the health of the couple's relationship.

Jungman, Robert E., and Carole Tabor. "Henry James on Safari in Ernest Hemingway's *Green Hills of Africa*." *Hemingway Review* 22, no. 2: 82–86.

Influence study noting a connection between Hemingway's sense of Africa as a place where he can live life to the fullest and the main theme of James's novel *The Ambassadors* and the character Strether's advice to "live all you can."

Leonard, John. "*The Garden of Eden*: A Question of Dates." *Hemingway Review* 22, no. 2: 63–81.

Relying on biographical resources and the manuscript itself, Leonard clears up the confusion over when Hemingway wrote *The Garden of Eden* manuscript. Most scholars agree that Hemingway began working on the manuscript in 1946 and stopped working on it in 1958. Leonard contends that the central portion (chapters 13–35) was written in 1957 and that the African stories were written after the 1953–1954 safari.

Love, Glen A. "Hemingway Among the Animals: Reconsidering Hemingway's Primitivism." Chapter 5 in *Practical Ecocriticism: Literature, Biology, and the Environment*. Charlottesville: UP of Virginia.

119–25: Characterizes Hemingway's primitivism in *Green Hills of Africa* as an aggressive battle against both the natural environment he reveres and his own mortality. Sees Hemingway's need as a literary modern to "make" his world, to proclaim his uniqueness, at the expense of the earth he loved so much.

Penas Ibáñez, Beatriz. "Hemingway's Ethics of Writing: The Ironic Semantics of 'Whiteness' in 'The Snows of Kilimanjaro.'" *North Dakota Quarterly* 70, no. 4: 94–118.

Contends that "Hemingway exposes the arbitrary construction of meaning as well as the positive symbolic values of 'snow' (mainly whiteness, innocence, goodness, and truth) attached to it in Western cultures"

(102). Hemingway's use of contrasting images such as whiteness and darkness remind the reader that rarely is truth achieved either in life or in art. Concludes that Hemingway is "both a modernist realist questioning the values of his time and an aesthete questioning the values of literary convention. His writing is always and simultaneously ethical and aesthetical, and, maybe for that very reason, it cannot and will not be always 'politically correct'" (111).

Stoneback, H. R. "Pilgrimage Variations: Hemingway's Sacred Landscapes." *Religion and Literature* 35, nos. 2–3: 49–65.

Begins by outlining Hemingway's commitment to Catholicism to support his contention that nearly all of Hemingway's canon, including the much later posthumously published *True at First Light*, demonstrates his Catholic vision explicitly expressed through the recurring image of the pilgrimage. For those who believe *True at First Light* reveals Hemingway's submersion into a new tribal religion and a casting away of his old Catholic identity, Stoneback urges a close reading of the manuscript's omitted passages that reveal Hemingway's continued commitment to his Catholic sensibilities. The true pilgrim "salutes all sacred landscapes, but holds fast to his own God" (64). Reprinted under same title in *Hemingway: Eight Decades of Criticism*, edited by Linda Wagner-Martin, 457–76. East Lansing: Michigan State UP, 2009.

Strychacz, Thomas F. *Hemingway's Theaters of Masculinity*. Baton Rouge: Louisiana State UP.

14–52: "Unraveling the Masculine Ethos in 'The Short Happy Life of Francis Macomber.'" Draws on performance studies, arguing that the author's awareness of an audience influenced his creation of masculine roles. Contends that audience response to Hemingway's representation of manhood reveals richness in the author's narrative strategies long overlooked by critics more interested in preserving idealized codes of masculinity. Relies on Brecht's concept of the *gest* to analyze the theatrical representations of manhood in "Macomber," concluding that "its depictions of manhood as a performance within the purview of an audience's empowering acts of watching suggest that the story will never articulate an ideal of full manhood" (52).

167–220: "Trophy Hunting as a Trope of Manhood in *Green Hills of Africa*, 'The Undefeated,' and *The Garden of Eden*." First portion reprints "Trophy-Hunting as a Trope of Manhood in *Green Hills of Africa*" from *Hemingway Review* 13, no. 1 (1993): 36–47, and "'Like Plums in a Pudding': Food and Rhetorical Performance in Hemingway's *Green Hills of Africa*" from *Hemingway Review* 19, no. 2 (2000): 23–46. See Strychacz (1993 and 2000) in this bibliography for annotations. Final portion on *Eden*, entitled "'Take a Good Look . . . Because This Is How I am': Gender Roles in *The Garden of Eden*," comments briefly on the young David's alienation during the elephant hunt, as he is forced to read the signs of "real" men, his father and Juma. Strychacz focuses primarily on the adult David's loss of manhood when Catherine enters the stage.

2004

Bender, Bert. "'Night Song': Africa and Eden in Hemingway's Late Work." Chapter 12 in *Evolution and "the Sex Problem": American Narratives During the Eclipse of Darwinism*. Kent: Kent State UP.

329–57: Evolutionary approach to *True at First Light* focusing on the essential human needs to reproduce and to kill and eat. Examines Hemingway's interest in anthropology, Mary's lion hunt, and the courtship with Debba, reading the novel as Hemingway's humorous critique of cultural practices. Many of Hemingway's writings, including stories of Native Americans and depictions of African inhabitants in *Green Hills of Africa* and *True at First Light*, "reflect his impatience with the idea that there are primitive people who are essentially different from him or that the subconscious in popular Freudianism can be meaningfully associated with the primitive" (334). Only briefly mentions David's African story in *The Garden of Eden*, focusing instead on his bisexuality and androgynous relationship with Catherine.

Flora, Joseph M. "Names and Naming in Hemingway's Short Stories." *South Atlantic Review* 69, no. 1: 1–8.

Briefly comments on the significance of the names in "The Short Happy Life of Francis Macomber" and "The Snows of Kilimanjaro," reflecting on Hemingway's allusion to Fitzgerald in the former and the confusion over missing names in the latter.

Garrigues, Lisa. "Reading the Writer's Craft: The Hemingway Short Stories." *English Journal* 94, no. 1: 59–65.

Details assignments used in a high school writing class to help students learn the craft of writing by stylistically analyzing Hemingway's short stories, including "The Short Happy Life of Francis Macomber" and "The Snows of Kilimanjaro."

Kartiganer, Donald M. "'Getting Good at Doing Nothing': Faulkner, Hemingway, and the Fiction of Gesture." In *Faulkner and His Contemporaries: Faulkner and Yoknapatawpha*, edited by Joseph R. Urgo and Ann J. Abadie, 54–73. Jackson: Mississippi UP.

Analyzes both authors' thematic fascination with "gesture," the consistent failure of purpose or empty intention. Examines Harry's final moments in "The Snows of Kilimanjaro," looking specifically at his unrealized intention to write.

Mandal, Somdatta. *Reflections, Refractions, and Rejections: Three American Writers and the Celluloid World*. Naperville, IL: Wisdom House.

59, 130, 142, 161, 165, 170–71, 177, 181–82, 210, 213, 220, 224, 238, 253, 259, 290, 306: Largely focused on Hemingway's cinematic technique, commenting on the author's use of structural, thematic, and dynamic juxtaposition. Brief references to *Green Hills of Africa*, "The Short Happy Life of Francis Macomber," "The Snows of Kilimanjaro," and *True at First Light* scattered throughout.

Meyers, Jeffrey. "Nansen and Hemingway." *Notes on Contemporary Literature* 34, no. 4: 2–4.

Provides historical background on the Greco-Turkish War to explain Hemingway's hostile allusion to Norwegian negotiator Fridtjof Nansen in Harry's first italicized flashback of "The Snows of Kilimanjaro."

Ondaatje, Christopher. *Hemingway in Africa: The Last Safari*. Woodstock, NY: The Overlook Press.

Combination biography, travelogue, interpretative study focused on Hemingway's lifelong love affair with Africa, originally inspired by magazine articles on Theodore Roosevelt's 1909 African safari. Ondaatje traces Hemingway's footsteps on his two safaris through Kenya, Tanzania, and Uganda, detailing information on the author's adventures as well as on his own present day journey. Ondaatje reads "The Short Happy Life of Francis Macomber" as a study in fear that ultimately challenges the meaningfulness of the macho hunting guide and big game hunting. He interprets "The Snows of Kilimanjaro" autobiographically to reveal Hemingway's authorial anxieties over squandered talent and opportunities, and argues for the influence of Henry James (specifically, "The Lesson of the Master" and "The Jolly Corner") and F. Scott Fitzgerald on this later story. Ondaatje sees the elephant flashback in *The Garden of Eden* as a transitional point demonstrating Hemingway's increasing sensitivity toward animal suffering. By 1953, the year of his second safari, Hemingway's view of Africa had also changed dramatically. *True at First Light* documents the author's newfound and genuine interest in the different tribes and cultures he meets while on safari. Ondaatje suspects the narrative's focus on Hemingway's courting of Debba to be exaggerated, and indeed questions the narrative's usefulness in revealing the facts of Hemingway's second safari. Frequent quotations from Hemingway's writing reveal his passion for Africa. Combines Hemingway era photographs with those taken during Ondaatje's journey.

2005

Eby, Carl P. "'He Felt the Change So That It Hurt Him All Through': Sodomy and Transvestic Hallucination in Late Hemingway." *Hemingway Review* 25, no. 1: 77–95.

Psychoanalytical approach to episodes of transvestic metamorphoses found in *The Garden of Eden*, *True at First Light*, and elsewhere, arguing that in each instance the male protagonist, after experiencing heterosexual sodomy, undergoes a momentary hallucinatory transformation into a girl.

Fantina, Richard. *Ernest Hemingway: Machismo and Masochism*. New York: Palgrave Macmillan.

Psychoanalytical approach focusing on male heterosexual masochism in Hemingway's major works, including *The Garden of Eden*, *True at First Light*, "The Short Happy Life of Francis Macomber," and "The Snows of Kilimanjaro." Finds the author's emphasis on "masculine" virtues compatible with the tradition of literary masochism (sexual submission of the male body to the female body).

96–100: "Hemingway and the Feminine Complex: 1930s: Guilt in Life and Art: 'The Snows of Kilimanjaro' and *To Have and Have Not*." Biographical approach, connecting both texts to Hemingway's guilt over his treatment of his second wife, Pauline. Fantina concludes, "The two works can be read as humiliating public confessions" (100).

129–52: "Hemingway, Race, and Colonialism." Regards *The Garden of Eden* as Hemingway's defining work in the area of masochism. Traces the reversal of traditional gender roles of dominance and submission and interprets Catherine's "Africanization" as a form of otherness. Attributes David's identification with the elephant to his masochistic relationship with Catherine. Argues that the racism depicted in *The Garden of Eden* fails to conform to Toni Morrison's earlier theoretical discussion of Hemingway's racial allusions. See Morrison (1992) in this bibliography (for annotation).

Grabher, Gudrun M. "Death in Africa in Muammar Qaddafi's 'Death' and Ernest Hemingway's 'The Snows of Kilimanjaro.'" In *North-South Linkages and Connections in Continental and Diaspora African Literatures*, edited by Edris Makward, Mark L. Lilleleht, and Ahmed Saber, 292–300. Trenton: Africa World Press.

Thematic study comparing Hemingway's treatment of the nature of death and mortality with Qaddafi's, noting that for both authors death takes many guises and is inescapable. Discusses much of the symbolism found in "Snows" (e.g., of the dark continent, snow, an infected leg); suggests that the cowardly hyena and mean vulture are representative of Harry's character on his way to die.

Rovit, Earl, and Arthur Waldhorn, eds. *Hemingway and Faulkner in Their Time*. New York: Continuum.

26–27: Reprints portion of 1936 letter from Sherwood Anderson to Ralph Church on *Green Hills of Africa*. Anderson writes: "It's really a lousy book, and the god awful thing is that he doesn't know it and never will" (26). Anderson characterizes Hemingway as an "eternal amateur" who is "too concerned with writing" (26).

66: Reprints portions of letters from Edmund Wilson to Maxwell Perkins praising "The Short Happy Life of Francis Macomber" and denigrating *Green Hills of Africa*.

Seals, Marc. "Reclaimed Experience: Trauma Theory and Hemingway's Lost Paris Manuscripts." *Hemingway Review* 24, no. 2: 62–72.

Psychoanalytic trauma theory approach contending that Hemingway's continued inclusion of the loss of his Paris manuscripts in his major posthumous works (e.g., *A Moveable Feast, Islands in the Stream, The Garden of Eden*, and *True at First Light*) helped him to deal with the traumatic episode. Considers the rewriting of the episode therapeutic for Hemingway, thus explaining the shift from bitterness and despair in the earlier *The Garden of Eden* and "The Strange Country" to forgiveness in the later posthumous work, *A Moveable Feast*.

Stolzfus, Ben. "Sartre, *Nada*, and Hemingway's African Stories." *Comparative Literature Studies* 42, no. 3: 205–28.

Reads "The Short Happy Life of Francis Macomber" and "The Snows of Kilimanjaro" in light of Sartre's existential philosophies, focusing on Macomber's transcendence and transformation and Harry's failed redemption as man and writer.

Umunç, Himmet. "Hemingway in Turkey: Historical Contexts and Cultural Intertexts." *Belleten* 69. no. 255: 629–42.

Contends that Hemingway's political and cultural biases distort his fictional representations of Turkey found in "On the Quai at Smyrna," the second interchapter of *In Our Time*, and Harry's recollections in "The Snows of Kilimanjaro." Claims Hemingway's three portraits of a savage and unpredictable Turkish character, based largely upon his own observations during a brief visit to Istanbul and information obtained from Allied sources, are "morally controversial, historically inadequate, culturally antagonistic, and politically prejudiced" (642). Umunç attempts to set the record straight with an overview of Turkey's political and military history at the time of Hemingway's writings.

Voeller, Carey. "'He Only Looked Sad the Same Way I Felt': The Textual Confessions of Hemingway's Hunters." *Hemingway Review* 25, no. 1: 63–76.

Traces Hemingway's evolving attitudes toward trophy hunting in *Green Hills of Africa*, "The Short Happy Life of Francis Macomber," "An African Story," and *True at First Light*, arguing that his compassionate treatment of animals reflects his belief regarding the "natural connection and sameness between human and animal" (64).

2006

Boese, Gil K. "*Under Kilimanjaro*: The Other Hemingway." *Hemingway Review* 25, no. 2: 114–18.

Hemingway's evolution from white hunter to naturalist.

Craig, Joanna Hildebrand. "Dancing with Hemingway." *Hemingway Review* 25, no. 2: 82–86.

On copyediting *Under Kilimanjaro*.

Fleming, Robert E. "The Editing Process." *Hemingway Review* 25, no. 2: 91–94.

On editing *Under Kilimanjaro*.

Hemingway, Ernest. "Foreword." In *Hemingway and the Mechanism of Fame: Statements, Public Letters, Introductions, Forewords, Prefaces, Blurbs, Reviews, and Endorsements*, edited by Matthew Joseph Bruccoli and Judith S. Baughman, 126–28. Columbia: U of South Carolina P.

Reprint of Hemingway's "Préface" in François Sommer, *Porquoi ces bêtes sont-elles sauvages* (1951), published as *Man and Beast in Africa*, translated by Edward Fitzgerald (London: Jenkins, 1953). Hemingway praises Sommer for his honest and vivid depiction of big-game hunting and adds his own advice to hunters on ammunition and weapons.

Howard, Jennifer. "Hemingway Autobiographical Novel is First in a Rush of Books by and About the Author." *Chronicle of Higher Education* 52, no. 34 (April).

Provides a brief publication history of *Under Kilimanjaro*, and notes its popularity among academics and the reading public alike. Also announces the forthcoming publication of new Hemingway critical studies and complete correspondence.

Justice, Hilary K. *The Bones of the Others: The Hemingway Text from the Lost Manuscripts to the Posthumous Novels*. Kent: Kent State UP.

67–72, 122–23: Using manuscript and archival materials, published texts, and posthumous novels, Justice reconstructs Hemingway's creative process and evolution from writer to professional author to reveal the fluid relationships between his texts. Justice argues that Hemingway revisits his early short fiction in the later *The Garden of Eden*, and connects both to *Death in the Afternoon*. Briefly discusses the Africa stories of *The Garden of Eden*, connecting Catherine's burning of David's manuscripts to the 1922 incident in which Hemingway's manuscripts were lost. Reads David's stories as later versions of the much earlier "Hills Like White Elephants" and "Ten Indians."

Kitunda, Jeremiah M. "Ernest Hemingway's African Book: An Appraisal." *Hemingway Review* 25, no. 2: 107–13.

Provides historical, cultural, and political context for the 1950s East African setting of *Under Kilimanjaro*.

———. "Ernest Hemingway's Safari into Kamba Culture and Language: A Note on the Geographical and Temporal Setting of *Under Kilimanjaro*." *North Dakota Quarterly* 73, no. 1–2: 156–72.

Strives to correct "some of the misunderstood ideas, misspelled words and phrases, and unlikely claims that are featured vividly throughout *Under Kilimanjaro*" (157). Kitunda pays particular attention to Hemingway's relationship with Debba, his repeated confusion of Masai and Kamba customs and traditions, and his misunderstanding of the Mau Mau movement.

Lewis, Robert W. "The Making of *Under Kilimanjaro*." *Hemingway Review* 25, no. 2: 87–90.

On editing and publishing the memoir.

Maffi, Mario. "Untender is the Night in *The Garden of Eden*: Fitzgerald, Hemingway, and the Mediterranean." In *Anglo-American Modernity and the Mediterranean*, edited by Caroline Patey, Giovanni Cianci, and Francesca Cuojati, 99–117. Milan, Italy: Conference Anglo-American Modernity and the Mediterranean.

Comparison study of *The Garden of Eden* with *Tender is the Night*, analyzing similarities in subject matter (American expatriates), theme (change, madness, money), and setting (the Mediterranean). Discusses the influence of Cézanne on Hemingway's writing. Reads Africa and David's African story as alternatives to civilization.

Maier, Kevin. "Hemingway's Hunting: An Ecological Reconsideration." *Hemingway Review* 25, no. 2: 119–22.

Hemingway's transformation from white hunter to conservationist.

Mandel, Miriam B. "Ethics and 'Night Thoughts': 'Truer Than the Truth.'" *Hemingway Review* 25, no. 2: 95–100.

Though grateful for the publication of *Under Kilimanjaro*, Mandel desires greater insight into the editorial process.

Martin, Lawrence H. "Safari in the Age of Kenyatta." *Hemingway Review* 25, no. 2: 101–06.

Comments on Hemingway's avoidance of Kenya's political unrest in *Under Kilimanjaro*.

Miller, Linda Patterson. "From the 'African Book' to *Under Kilimanjaro*: An Introduction." *Hemingway Review* 25, no. 2: 78–81.

Brief publication history.

Moore, Peter. "Hunting Hemingway." *Men's Health* 21, no. 2: 128–35.

Draws on well-known biographical details as he retraces Hemingway's footsteps through Paris, Key West, Africa, and Spain.

Müller, Kurt. "Modernist Point of View Technique and the Ethics of Reading: A Rortian Approach to Ernest Hemingway." In *Aesthetic Transgressions: Modernity, Liberalism, and the Function of Literature*, edited by Thomas Claviez, Ulla Haselstein, and Sieglinde Lemke, 315–35. Heidelberg: Universitätsverlag.

Applies Richard Rorty's neopragmatic theory of reading to the authorial silences found in "Indian Camp." Concludes that a careful and sensitive reading of the story "can make us attentive to white male racism and sexism as outstandingly cruel and destructive forms of the Rortian sins of 'incuriosity' and 'self-satisfaction'" (329–30). Comments briefly upon the much maligned Margot of "The Short Happy Life of Francis Macomber" and Robert Cohn of *The Sun Also Rises*, contending that as with the woman in labor in "Indian Camp," both characters possess the potential "for engaging the aesthetic as well as the moral political sensibilities of the reader" (334).

Nolan, Charles J. Jr. "The Importance of Hemingway's 'The Doctor and the Doctor's Wife.'" *Humanities Review* 5, no. 1 (October): 15–24.

Sees the story as "suggestive of Hemingway's life without being totally biographical" (16). Contends young Nick in this early story is imperative to our understanding of the later, more mature Nick and characters including Frederic Henry, Jake Barnes, Robert Jordan, Richard Cantwell, and David Bourne, especially in developing attitudes toward women, race, and father figures. In addition to *A Farewell to Arms*, *The Sun Also Rises*, *For Whom the Bell Tolls*, *Across the River and into the Trees*, and *The Garden of Eden*, Nolan briefly discusses "Indian Camp," "Ten Indians," and "Fathers and Sons."

Panda, Ken. "*Under Kilimanjaro*: The Multicultural Hemingway." *Hemingway Review* 25, no. 2: 128–31.

Applauds the skillful editing of this latest edition, which affords general readers and scholars alike greater insight into the author's multiculturalism.

Pope, Robert. "Faces of Fiction: Extraordinary Uses of the Obligatory Moment." *North Dakota Quarterly* 73, no. 1–2: 197–203.

Notes the reliability of Hemingway's face descriptions in "The Short Happy Life of Frances Macomber" as signs of character, e.g., Margot's faded beauty, Wilson's naturalness, and Macomber's weakness.

Putnam, Ann. "The Last Good Country." *Hemingway Review* 25, no. 2: 132–35.

Grateful for the publication of *Under Kilimanjaro*, commenting on its complexity and thematic maturity.

Sanders, Jaimé L. "The Journalistic and Philosophic Observation of Men in Hemingway's 1930s Literature." In *Florida Studies. Proceedings of the 2005 Annual Meeting of the Florida College English Association*, edited by Steve Glassman and Karen Tolchin, 157–63. Newcastle upon Tyne, England: Cambridge Scholars Publishing.

Brief discussion of *Death in the Afternoon*, *Green Hills of Africa*, and *To Have and Have Not*, connecting all three to Hemingway's growing despair over the corruption and destruction of his favorite places and people. Sees the dangers of modernism and change as ultimately leading to the loss of self reflected in Hemingway's works of the 1930s.

Stoneback, H. R. "*Under Kilimanjaro* — Truthiness at Late Light: Or Would Oprah Kick Hemingway Out of Her Book Club." *Hemingway Review* 25, no. 2: 123–27.

Compares *Under Kilimanjaro* to the much-truncated *True at First Light* and comments on Hemingway's fictionalized memoir in light of the James Frey controversy (*A Million Little Pieces*).

Tsuji, Hideo. "Cuba Libre at Odds: Hemingway, Twain, and the Spanish-American War." *Mark Twain Studies* 2 (October): 91–93.

Comments briefly on Twain's influence, suggesting that the impassioned anti-imperialism found in "The War Prayer" evolves into passive acceptance in Hemingway's works, including *Green Hills of Africa* and *The Sun Also Rises*.

"*Under Kilimanjaro*: Special Section." *Hemingway Review* 25, no. 2: 77–135.

Significant portion devoted to commentary on the newly published memoir by its editors and various Hemingway scholars.

Vejdovsky, Boris. "Wounded Bodies and Torn Canvas: Images of Life and Death in Hemingway and Picasso." In *The Seeming and the Seen: Essays in Modern Visual and Literary Culture*, edited by Beverly Maeder, Jürg Schwyter, Ilona Sigrist, and Boris Vejdovsky, 319–41. Bern, Switzerland: Peter Lang.

Discusses both Picasso's and Hemingway's fascination with pain, brutality, and sexuality, culminating in the *corrida*. Mentions briefly a number of Hemingway heroes suffering from leg traumas reminiscent of thigh wounds suffered by bullfighters: Frederic Henry (*A Farewell to Arms*), Robert Jordan (*For Whom the Bell Tolls*), and Harry ("The Snows of Kilimanjaro"). "Like Hemingway, Picasso concentrates on the mutilated body in pain, and like Hemingway, he combines this theme with an interrogation on masculinity, which reflects in both artists their conflicting relations with women" (329).

2007

Armengol, Josep M. "Gendering Men: Re-Visions of Violence as a Test of Manhood in American Literature." *Atlantis, revista de la Asociación Española de Estudios Anglo-Norteamericanos* 29, no. 2 (December): 75–92.

Opens with an overview of gender and masculinity studies in American literature. Compares Hemingway's "An African Story" (1954) with Richard Ford's "Communist" (1987) to demonstrate how the conventional concept of masculinity as violence found in Hemingway's story evolves in the much later Ford story to reveal the negative effects of male violence. Hemingway's vision of violence as a test of manhood and a symbol of heroism is challenged in Ford's "subversive re-writing of the traditional Hemingwayesque conception of hunting as proof of manly daring" (82). Ford provides alternative nonviolent images of men able to leave their negative pasts in favor of positive futures.

Dempsey, George T. "Justice for Ernest Hemingway." *Antioch Review* 65, no. 2: 239–55.

Assesses "the true state" of Hemingway's output in his final two decades, suggesting that the writer's artistic genius culminated with *The Fifth Column and the First Forty-nine Stories* (1938) and *For Whom the Bell Tolls* (1940). Laments the publication of nearly all of Hemingway's later texts, including *Across the River and Into the Trees, The Old Man and the Sea,* and *True At First Light.* Calls for the scholarly reediting of all Hemingway's posthumous works, similar to that of *Under Kilimanjaro,* "so that those of us who care can see the terrible reality of this master struggling to regain his mastery of his craft" (253).

Oliver, Charles M. *Critical Companion to Ernest Hemingway: A Literary Reference to His Life and Work.* New York: Facts on File.

Extensive revision of Oliver's *Hemingway A to Z* (1999), an encyclopedic companion to the author's life and works. Includes synopses, publication histories, and critical commentaries on the works, along with alphabetically arranged entries defining important characters, people, places, and subjects. Biographical sections provide overviews of the author's life and assess his legacy. Alphabetically listed biographical entries focus not only on family and friends but also other people, places, and things helpful for understanding the author and his work. Extensive appendices include an updated bibliography of works by and about the author.

169–85: *The Garden of Eden*
192–200: *Green Hills of Africa*
329–34: "The Short Happy Life of Francis Macomber"
337–41: "The Snows of Kilimanjaro"
400: *True at First Light*
406–7: *Under Kilimanjaro*

Trogdon, Robert W. "'You Can't Be Popular All the Time': *Winner Take Nothing* and *Green Hills of Africa.*" Chapter 5 in *The Lousy Racket: Hemingway, Scribner's, and the Business of Literature.* Kent: Kent State UP.

126–68: Covers the composition, revision, publication, marketing, mixed reception, and disappointing sales of *Green Hills of Africa*. Concludes that Hemingway turned away from the publishing of nonfiction in favor of fiction after the commercial failure of the safari book in order to maintain his popularity with critics and readers.

Wagner-Martin, Linda. "*Esquire* and Africa." Chapter 11 in *Ernest Hemingway: A Literary Life.* New York: Palgrave Macmillan.

104–11: Biography detailing Hemingway's 1933–1934 African safari financed by Gus Pfeiffer, Pauline's uncle. Covers Hemingway's debilitating bout with dysentery and hunting competition with Key West friend Charles Thompson. Suggests that Hemingway may have added commentary on the aesthetics of writing to *Green Hills of Africa* to shift reader attention away from what he perceived to be his own weaknesses while on safari. Concludes with Hemingway's growing ambivalence toward Pauline as evidenced by his labeling her P.O.M (Poor Old Mama) in the African safari book.

160–64: Covers Hemingway's second safari, with wife Mary in 1953–1954, describing his difficult recovery from injuries sustained in two plane crashes. Despite serious health concerns, Hemingway continued to work on the African safari book.

2008

Ammary, Silvia. "'The Road Not Taken' in Hemingway's 'The Snows of Kilimanjaro.'" *Connotations* 18, nos. 1–3: 123–38.

Thematically connects Frost's poem of illusory choice and lamentable chance to Hemingway's oeuvre, most specifically to "The Snows of Kilimanjaro." Focuses on Harry's sense of loss coupled with remorse over his failed writing career. Examines Hemingway's narrative style and symbolism, arguing for Harry as an unreliable narrator who projects his frustrations and regrets onto his wife.

Gray, W. Russel. "Jimmying the Back Door of Literature: Dashiell Hammett's Blue-Collar Modernism." *Journal of Popular Culture* 41, no. 5: 762–83.

Noting Hammett novels in Hemingway's library, Gray briefly compares narrative elements of "An Alpine Idyll" and "The Snows of Kilimanjaro" to Hammett's *Thin Man* and *The Maltese Falcon*.

Hediger, Ryan. "Hunting, Fishing, and the Cramp of Ethics in Ernest Hemingway's *The Old Man and the Sea*, *Green Hills of Africa*, and *Under Kilimanjaro*." *Hemingway Review* 27, no. 2: 35–59.

Hediger relies on ethical theory to redefine the traditional notion of ethics to focus on "openness to experience and to aesthetics." Examines Hemingway's evolving attitudes toward hunting and fishing, as evidenced in the two safari books and *The Old Man and the Sea*. Argues "that in Hemingway's later texts, dead animals — the number of trophies, the size of their horns, or the weight of their flesh — become less necessary as a measure or memento of his hunting or fishing experience, and ethical experience itself takes greater emphasis" (38).

Hochman, Brian. "Ellison's Hemingways." *African American Review* 42, nos. 3–4: 513–32.

Noting Hemingway's "enduring presence in Ellison's intellectual life," Hochman explores Hemingway's influence on Ralph Ellison's development as a critical reader and writer. Studies Ellison's marginalia on "Remembering Shooting-Flying" and "The Short Happy Life of Francis Macomber," arguing that "Ellison's relationship to 'technique' was constantly evolving, and the intellectual contexts shaping his understandings of 'race' and 'literature' were constantly shifting" (516). Concludes that Ellison's vision of Hemingway depended on "his own artistic and ideological interests and the time, both self and other" (529).

Just, Daniel. "Is Less More? A Reinvention of Realism in Raymond Carver's Minimalist Short Story." *CRITIQUE: Studies in Contemporary Fiction* 49, no. 3 (Spring): 303–17.

Briefly compares Hemingway's economical style with Carver's, arguing that unlike Carver, Hemingway's terse style speeds up the narrative flow. Passing references to "The Snows of Kilimanjaro."

Monteiro, George. "Traces of A. E. Housman (and Shakespeare) in Hemingway." *Hemingway Review* 28, no. 1: 122–34.

Traces the thematic influence of several Housman poems, including "Today is Friday" and "To Will Davies" on Hemingway's "Soldier's Home," *A Farewell to Arms*, and Chapter XV of *In Our Time*. Concludes with a brief comparison of Housman's "The Day of Battle" and Hemingway's "The Short Happy Life of Francis Macomber," noting that both borrow lines on cowardice and death from Shakespeare's *Henry IV, Part 2*.

Penas Ibáñez, Beatriz. "The Identitarian Function of Language and the Narrative Fictional Text: Problematizing Identity Transferral in Translation *Per Se*." In *New Trends in Translation and Cultural Identity*, edited by Micaela Muñoz-Calvo, Carmen Buesa-Gómez, and M. Ángeles Ruiz-Moneva, 47–65. New Castle upon Tyne, England: Cambridge Scholars Publications.

Translation study. Criticizes early Spanish translations of Hemingway's works, noting the poor quality overall, problems of register in dialogue, and censored passages that lead to misrepresentations of character identity, as exemplified through the characterization of Harry and Helen in "The Snows of Kilimanjaro" and Brett Ashley in *The Sun Also Rises*.

Silbergleid, Robin. "Into Africa: Narrative and Authority in Hemingway's *The Garden of Eden*." *Hemingway Review* 27, no. 2: 96–117.

Reads the published version of the novel as authored in part by Scribner's editor Tom Jenks. Concentrates on David's African story as a means for understanding the published novel's form and focus. Explores issues of narrative structure and authority, arguing that "the hunt of the novel, as it explores the Bournes' experimentation with gender and sexuality, parallels the hunt of the African story, which ultimately leads to the death of the elephant. If this sacrifice is intimately tied to the novel's gender and race politics, the resultant reading suggests that *The Garden of Eden* is not about Hemingway. Rather it sheds light on the Hemingway industry and the complex relations among biographical experience, textual construction, and interpretive practices" (97).

Strong, Amy L. *Race and Identity in Hemingway's Fiction*. New York: Palgrave Macmillan.

Examines how Hemingway's lifelong interest in race and race difference complicates his creation of the white male protagonist and helps to define American identity. "Some of the most celebrated concepts found in Hemingway's works — freedom, individuality, innocence, loss, and masculinity — are completely enmeshed and entwined with racial tropes of whiteness versus blackness, dominance versus subordination, conquest versus discovery" (12).

59–81: "Light, Snow, and Whiteness in 'The Short, Happy Life of Francis Macomber' and 'The Snows of Kilimanjaro.'" Addresses colonialism in both stories. Links Wilson's abusive power while on safari to his imperialist attitudes and desire for male dominance. Reads Harry's death as a result of his privileged status.

83–118: "Darkness in *The Garden of Eden*." Examination of race, ethnicity, and homosexuality. Suggests the novel's authorial ambivalence sets up a clear contrast between David's African story and his life with Catherine. Argues that David betrays both himself and Catherine because his story of the elephant hunt "ultimately reifies white male dominance in such a way as to deny and even condemn the very lifestyle he had been living."

119–39: "African Brotherhood in *Under Kilimanjaro*." Exploration of Hemingway's ambivalence regarding race and racial identity. Parallels Hemingway's sympathy with the Africans who have lost their land and positions of power with the Native Americans of his early stories (e.g., "Indian Camp" and "The Doctor and the Doctor's Wife").

2009

Becnel, Kim E. *Bloom's How to Write About Ernest Hemingway*. New York: Bloom's Literary Criticism.

Designed to help high school students write essays on Hemingway's works. Provides an overview of Hemingway's important themes (e.g., love and war) and stylistic techniques. Offers individual chapters on specific major works, examining theme, character, and literary elements followed by sample essay topics and open-ended questions designed to inspire students to develop their own topics for investigation. Works covered include: *The Sun Also Rises, A Farewell to Arms, For Whom the Bell Tolls, The Old Man and the Sea*, "The Short Happy Life of Francis Macomber," and "The Snows of Kilimanjaro."

Cassuto, Leonard. "Crime and Sympathy." Chapter 1 in *Hard-Boiled Sentimentality: The Secret History of American Crime Stories*. New York: Columbia UP.

Examines the roots of "hard boiled" crime fiction, primarily focusing on Dreiser's *An American Tragedy* (1925). Parallels Hemingway with Dreiser through "the way that their 'anti-sentimentality' contains a sentimentality which fundamentality informs their projects — and those of their literary descendents" (42). Looks at Hemingway's style of antisentimental sentimentality in *In Our Time, A Farewell to Arms*, "The Killers," and "The Short Happy Life of Francis Macomber."

Cushman, Stephen. "Why Didn't Hemingway Mention This Crater?" *Southwest Review* 94, no. 4: 462–77.

Attempts to explain Hemingway's omission of the Ngorongoro Crater from *Green Hills of Africa*, comparing such an omission to visiting Niagara Falls, New York and leaving out Niagara Falls. Argues Hemingway was not after geographical comprehensiveness, "but rather the transformation of northern and central Tanganyika into an eroticized paradise of pursuit and possession" (471). Suggests that by reinventing Africa, Hemingway was able to escape from an America that was old and used up. Frequently references Pauline Hemingway's unpublished journal covering the safari.

Fenstermaker, John J. "Why *Esquire*? The Multiple Voices of Hemingway's Complex Public Persona." In *Key West Hemingway: A Reassessment*, edited by Kirk Curnutt and Gail D. Sinclair, 206–19. Gainesville: UP of Florida.

Explores Hemingway's motivations behind his writing for *Esquire*. Fenstermaker argues *Esquire* gave Hemingway a means to craft his persona, document himself, and respond to negative criticism of his works. Passing references to *Green Hills of Africa* and *Death in the Afternoon*.

Müller, Timo. "The Uses of Authenticity: Hemingway and the Literary Field, 1926–1936." *Journal of Modern Literature* 33, no. 1: 28–42.

Examination of Hemingway's early work to reveal the author's ambivalent attitude toward authenticity in both his life and writings. Argues that Hemingway's depiction of authentic characters and settings fortified the authentic pose he adopted for himself. Provides an extensive comparison of the inauthentic corruption of Paris with the authentic tradition of the Spanish settings found in *The Sun Also Rises*. In connecting the construct of authenticity with the profession of writing, Müller analyzes Hemingway's depiction of literary merit and the role of writers in *The Sun Also Rises*, "The Snows of Kilimanjaro," and *Green Hills of Africa*.

Plath, James. *Historic Photos of Ernest Hemingway*. Nashville: Turner.

82–83, 160–65: Two hundred well chosen black-and-white photographs coupled with informative captions provide a pictorial biography of Hemingway from Oak Park to Ketchum. Includes photographs from both African safaris. Concludes with extensive documentation for each photograph.

Reef, Catherine. *Ernest Hemingway: A Writer's Life*. New York: Clarion.

102–106, 141–43: Biography geared to young adults. Captures Hemingway's life from Oak Park to Ketchum, including brief references to both African safaris. Numerous quotations from friends, family, and the author himself, along with black-and-white photographs, mark the passing of the years. Concludes with a selected bibliography and list of major works.

2010

Bouchard, Donald F. *Hemingway: So Far from Simple*. Amherst: Prometheus.

Argues against those who find Hemingway's writing superficial and artless, showing how Hemingway's careful attention to style and lifelong concern with his career as a writer earned him the title of one of America's most important and influential authors. Draws on Hemingway's correspondence, *A Moveable Feast*, his statements about art, and the postmodernist writings of Foucault, Deleuze, and Said to trace Hemingway's evolving style in relation to changing times. Analyzes the major works chronologically, devoting greatest attention to those suffering from critical neglect, such as *Green Hills of Africa* and *Death in the Afternoon*. In dealing with Hemingway's writings of the 1930s, Bouchard explores his shift away from modernism toward a gradually developing social and political awareness found in *Green Hills of Africa*, *Death in the Afternoon*, *For Whom the Bell Tolls*, and *To Have and Have Not*.

Brogan, Jacqueline Vaught. "Hemingway Talking to Walker Talking to Hemingway." *Hemingway Review* 30, no. 1: 122–28.

Pedagogical approach pairing *The Garden of Eden* with Alice Walker's *The Color Purple*, and focusing on issues of sexism, racism, capitalism, and environmentalism. Points out similarities of structure and theme found in each novel's "inner" story set in Africa.

Del Gizzo, Suzanne. "'Glow-in-the-Dark Authors': Hemingway's Celebrity and Legacy in *Under Kilimanjaro*." *Hemingway Review* 29, no. 2: 7–27.

Examines *Under Kilimanjaro* in relation to Hemingway's career-long struggle to reconcile his public persona with his literary output. Ties Hemingway's critique of the commodification of Africa and the safari industry to the commodification of his own image. Passing references to "The Snows of Kilimanjaro," *Green Hills of Africa*, and *The Garden of Eden*.

Ducille, Ann. "The Short Happy Life of Black Feminist Theory." *Differences* 21, no. 1: 32–47.

Advocating for the applicability of black feminist theory to the study of all literature, Ducille uses "The Short Happy Life of Francis Macomber" as her test case. Surveys critical opinion on the story, noting the lack of interest in its racial dimensions. Contends that while Margot may be a victim of white patriarchy, she is also actively engaged in and benefits from that system of oppression. Concludes that Hemingway's story of the rich, idle, and brutal is "an ugly example of what white privilege can do to those who waste it" (44).

Gordimer, Nadine. "Hemingway's Expatriates: A Way of Looking at the World." In *Telling Times: Writing and Living, 1954–2008*, 564–74. New York: Norton.

Originally delivered as a lecture. Examines Hemingway's influence on language, literature, and the creation of the expatriate persona in *For Whom the Bell Tolls* and the African short stories. Argues the African setting of "The Short Happy Life of Francis Macomber" and "The Snows of Kilimanjaro" is irrelevant because neither story engages, nor actually portrays, the Africa that Gordimer, as a native, knows. Reprint of "Hemingway's Expatriates: A Way of Looking at the World." *Transitions* 80 (1999): 86–99.

Hasan, Rabiul. *Rediscovering Hemingway in Bangladesh and India, 1971–2006*. Lanham, MD: UP of America.

Surveys the teaching, reception, and influence of Hemingway's works in Bangladesh and India, revealing the growing interest in Hemingway studies in the Indian subcontinent. Examines the cultural, social, and political factors influencing literary critics, academics, and the reading public. Includes analyses of "The Short Happy Life of Francis Macomber," "The Snows of Kilimanjaro," and other stories and novels.

Hewson, Marc. "Memory and Manhood: Troublesome Recollections in *The Garden of Eden*." In *Ernest Hemingway and the Geography of Memory*, edited by Mark Cirino and Mark P. Ott, 3–17. Kent: Kent State UP.

Explores gender roles and the autobiographical nature of David's writing within *The Garden of Eden*, paying particular attention to the African stories. Comments on Hemingway's struggle to satisfactorily conclude the novel. Hewson's study of the manuscript endings present Hemingway "as a writer no longer certain that past stability can create present stability and suggest he has moved forward significantly from his earlier beliefs about masculine and feminine identity" (15).

Lounsberry, Barbara. "Memory in *The Garden of Eden*." In *Ernest Hemingway and the Geography of Memory*, edited bt Mark Cirino and Mark P. Ott, 204–12. Kent: Kent State UP.

Extended comparison of *The Garden of Eden* with *Green Hills of Africa*, suggests that *The Garden of Eden* is a fictional reprisal of the same struggles and victories found in the earlier nonfiction volume. Draws parallels in character, setting, conflict, and the thematic treatment of memory within the artistic process. Focuses largely on the African stories.

Martin, Lawrence H. "Pursuit Remembered: Experience, Memory, and Invention in *Green Hills of Africa*. In *Ernest Hemingway and the Geography of Memory*, edited bty Mark Cirino and Mark P. Ott, 97–106. Kent: Kent State UP.

Opens with a survey of the book's negative contemporary reception before moving into a discussion of Hemingway's imaginative transformation of memory into a meditation on self and nature. "Despite his declaration about 'an absolutely true book,' *Green Hills of Africa* is about its narrator-actor's emotional state, and its mode is frequently lyric" (103).

Nakjavani, Erik. "Alchemy, Memory, and Archetypes: Reading Hemingway's *Under Kilimanjaro* as an African Fairy Tale." In *Ernest Hemingway and the Geography of Memory*, edited by Mark Cirino and Mark P. Ott, 107–16. Kent: Kent State UP.

Drawing on Jung, phenomenology, and the fairy tale tradition, Nakjavani reads *Under Kilimanjaro* as creative nonfiction, thus opening up a realm of possible interpretation. Analyzes Hemingway's use of setting, animals, and first-person narration.

Seals, Marc. "Reclaimed Experience: Trauma Theory and Hemingway's Lost Paris Manuscripts." In *Ernest Hemingway and the Geography of Memory*, edited by Mark Cirino and Mark P. Ott, 18–27. Kent: Kent State UP.

Focusing on Hemingway's posthumous works, *A Moveable Feast*, *Islands in the Stream*, *The Garden of Eden*, and *True at First Light*, Seals examines how Hemingway attempted to heal the wounds of trauma he suffered over the loss of his manuscripts in 1922 by repeatedly writing about the episode.

Contributors

SILVIO CALABI has been editor in chief of *Fly Rod & Reel* and *Shooting Sportsman* magazines and has had editorial positions at several other publications, including that of shotgun editor for *On Target*. He has written four books on sportfishing and many magazine and newspaper articles on hunting, shooting, angling, and automotive matters. Among his more esoteric distinctions are membership in the Order of Edwardian Gunners and the title of Knight of The International Order of St. Hubertus. He lives on the coast of Maine and shoots primarily in England, Scotland, Argentina, and southern Africa.

SUZANNE DEL GIZZO is Assistant Professor of English at Chestnut Hill College, Philadelphia, Pennsylvania. She has contributed chapters to several scholarly anthologies and has published articles and book reviews in peer-reviewed journals such as *Modern Fiction Studies* and the *Hemingway Review*. She serves as trustee of The Ernest Hemingway Foundation and Society, director of the Society's ALA/MLA Programs, and codirector (with Boris Vejdovsky) of the 14th Biennial Hemingway Society Conference, Lausanne Switzerland, June 2010.

JEREMIAH M. KITUNDA, Associate Professor in the Department of History at Appalachian State University, North Carolina, is an environmental historian. He has taught courses on the history of Africa and environmental history at the University of Nairobi (Kenya) and University of Oregon. He has published on Hemingway in the *Hemingway Review* and the *North Dakota Quarterly*. He is the only one of our contributors who is fluent in Kiswahili and Kikamba; he can also read French, German, Kikuyu, Ki-Meru, Ki-Tharaka, and Ki-Mbeere.

KELLI A. LARSON is Professor of English at the University of St. Thomas, St. Paul, Minnesota, and current bibliographer for *Hemingway Review*. In addition to several articles and book chapters, she is author of *Guide to the Poetry of William Carlos Williams* (1995) and *Ernest Hemingway: A Reference Guide* (1990; rpt. 1992).

MIRIAM B. MANDEL is Senior Lecturer (retired) in the Department of English and American Studies at Tel Aviv University, Ramat Aviv, Israel. She has published articles on several authors, but her main interest is the work of Ernest Hemingway. Her books include *Reading Hemingway: The Facts in the Fictions* (1995; reissued 2001), *Hemingway's "Death in the Afternoon": The Complete Annotations* (2002), and *Hemingway's "The Dangerous Summer": The Complete Annotations* (2008). She helped translate *Death in the Afternoon* to Spanish (*Muerte en la tarde*, 2005). She serves on the International Advisory Committee of *Hemingway Review* (1992–present), on the board of the Hemingway Society (2007–present), and on the team that will produce *The Cambridge Edition of the Letters of Ernest Hemingway* under the editorship of Professor Sandra Spanier. This is the second collection of essays she has edited for Camden House; the first was *A Companion to Hemingway's "Death in the Afternoon"* (2004).

FRANK MEHRING is a guest professor in the Department of Cultural Studies of the John F. Kennedy Institute for North American Studies at the Free University of Berlin, Germany. His teaching and writing are international and interdisciplinary: his books include *Sphere Melodies: Die Manifestation Transzendentalistischer Ideen in der Musik von Charles Ives und John Cage* (2003) and the biography, *Karl/Charles Follen: Deutsch-Amerikanischer Freiheitskämpfer. Studia Giessensia* (2004). He edited *Between Natives and Foreigners: Selected Writings of Karl/Charles Follen* (2007) and coedited the anthology *Transcultural Spaces* (with Stefan Brandt and Winfried Fluck, 2010). He is also a composer and performer, focusing on the nexus of music, poetry, and painting.

PHILIP H. MELLING is Professor of American Literature in the American Studies Department at the University of Wales, Swansea. He has published eighteen scholarly articles and book chapters, three plays, two novels, one biography, and two scholarly books (*Vietnam In American Literature*, 1990; and *Fundamentalism in America: Millennialism, Identity and Militant Religion*, 2000). He has also edited and coedited five books (including the three-volume *America in the 1920s: Literary Sources and Documents*, 2004), and is the founder and editor of the journal *Borderlines: Studies in American Culture* (1993–present). He has established a school in Guatemala and, when not otherwise engaged, works on Hemingway's Cuban work at the Museo Ernest Hemingway, Havana.

ERIK G. R. NAKJAVANI is Professor Emeritus of Humanities at the University of Pittsburgh and one of the founding members the Hemingway Society. His lifelong interest in psychoanalysis, philosophy, literature, and the arts has resulted in many wide-ranging publications, most recently in *Clinical Studies: International Journal of Psychoanalysis*, the *North Dakota Quarterly*, and *Ernest Hemingway and the Geography of Memory* (edited by Mark Cirino and Mark P. Ott).

BEATRIZ PENAS IBÁÑEZ is Senior Lecturer in the Department of English and German in the Faculty of Arts of the University of Zaragoza, Spain. She publishes in English and in Spanish on a variety of topics (modernism, postmodernism, interculturalism, source studies, literary pragmatics, and semiotics) as they touch the work of European and American authors. Her publications on Hemingway include articles in *Hemingway Review* and the *North Dakota Quarterly*, and essays in edited volumes such as *From Baudelaire to Lorca* (1996), *A Companion to Hemingway's "Death in the Afternoon"* (2004), *Memory, Imagination, and Desire in Contemporary Anglo-American Literature and Film* (2004), and *Theorizing Narrativity* (2008). She coedited *Interculturalism: Between Identity and Diversity*, published in English (2006) and Spanish (*Paradojas de la interculturalidad*, 2008). Most recently she has coedited *Con/texts of Persuasion* (2011).

JAMES PLATH is Professor of English, Illinois Wesleyan University, Bloomington, Illinois. His essays, interviews, short stories, poems, and reports have appeared in scholarly and popular journals, in anthologies and newspapers, in print and online. His collection of interviews, *Remembering Ernest Hemingway* (with Frank Simons) was released in 1999, and his *Historic Photos of Ernest Hemingway* was published in March 2009.

CHIKAKO TANIMOTO is Associate Professor of Gender Studies in the Graduate School of Languages and Cultures, Nagoya University, Japan. Her articles explore gender and sexuality issues in the work of several American authors; they have appeared in both American and Japanese journals. She is the author of *Kuia Monogatariron* (*Queer Narratologies*, 2009), published under the name Chikako Matsushita.

Index

Editor's Note. Only those names and concepts which appear in the text itself are indexed. The front matter, the endnotes, and the two annotated bibliographies (Chapters 1 and 11) are indexed only very lightly, mostly in connection with short stories and fictional characters that are analyzed in the text. Hemingway's fictional characters, relatives, short stories, novels, and works of nonfiction are listed individually.

Abercrombie & Fitch, 92, 96, 100
Across the River and Into the Trees, 10–11, 16, 114–15, 315; mentioned, 16
Adair, William, 249
Adams, Nick (fictional character), 26, 181, 206, 252, 257, 300, 304, 373
aesthetics, 151–58, 165–68, 172, 202–3, 212–14, 218, 225–26, 248, 285
"African Journal," xv, 18
African tribes, 5, 140, 172n14; Akamba, Kamba or Wakamba, 61, 125, 126, 130, 131, 133, 239, 240, 241, 244, 245, 255, 287; Banda, 243–44; Kanaka, 203; Kikuyu, 144n6, 356; Masai, 36n30, 126, 127, 140, 141, 217, 226, 240, 244, 245, 246, 256, 265, 269n19, 276, 294; Nandi, 183–84; Somali, 127, 203, 360; Yoruba, 241, 278
Africanism, 154, 155, 171n5, 203
Akamba. *See* African tribes
alchemist, alchemy, 282, 283, 284–90, 382
Alexander, Cecil Frances Humphreys, 128, 129
Algonquin. *See* American tribes
allegory, 131, 151, 154–59, 170
American Civil War, 26, 111
American tribes (Amerindian, Indian, Native American), 5, 239, 240–47, 251–59, 267, 304; Algonquin, 295; Cherokee, 249; Cheyenne, 239; Narragansett, 255; Ojibwa, 240, 295, 303, 304; Ottawa, 240; Tarantine, 256; Yoruba, 241, 278
Anderson, Sherwood, 11, 13, 239, 304
animals. *See* Big Five; *see also* bull; hyena; kudu; rooster; vulture; warthog
Armstrong, Louis, 218
Arnold, Lloyd R., 314
Atkins, John, 140, 194
authority, 123, 130, 133–34, 158, 170, 185, 213, 243, 245
authorship, 159, 169, 177, 192–95

Baker, Carlos, 151, 302, 308
"Banal Story," 304
Banda. *See* African tribes
Barkley, Catherine (fictional character), 8, 304, 337
Barnes, Jake (fictional character), 8, 14–15, 59, 303
Barthes, Roland, 210n2
Baudelaire, Charles, 151–68, 170
Beegel, Susan F., 42, 252, 354
Bellow, Saul, 325
Benedict, Ruth, 239
Benson, Jackson J., 304
Berenson, Bernard, 125, 266
Bierce, Ambrose, 328

Big Five, 85–89, 99, 107
  buffalo, xxii, 106, 124, 310, 324
  elephant, xxiii, xxiv, 42, 86, 92, 106, 107, 116n5, 124, 176–79, 246, 193–95, 204–5; in *Garden of Eden* (*askari*), 160–95
  leopard, xxv, 95, 245, 246, 249, 252, 255–60, 263, 264, 348; the frozen leopard, 288, 294, 295, 307
  lion, xxi, xxiii, xxiv, xxv, 95, 127, 133, 134, 140, 245, 246, 247, 249–58, 263, 264, 276–77, 301, 302, 305
  rhinoceros, xxii, xxiii, 92, 101, 109, 115n2, 135; called *faru*, 135, 286, 289; in photograph, 102
"Big Two-Hearted River," 6, 13, 137, 246, 257
Blixen, Bror, 142, 176, 177, 178
Blixen, Karen (Isak Dinesen), 140, 142
Bloom, Harold, 152, 173n19
Blyth, James Audley, 331
Bohr, Niels, 294
Boker, Pamela A., 30, 201, 339
Borges, Jorge Luis, 328
Boulton, Prudence, 257–60, 263
Bourne, Catherine (fictional character), 157, 176, 183–85, 188–93, 200–206, 333
Bourne, David (fictional character), 157–59; as child (Davey), 159–63, 165–66; name of, 192; as reader, 59; as writer, 158–59, 163, 166, 168. *See also* Bourne, David's father (fictional character)
Bourne, David's father (fictional character), 160–66, 179, 180–84, 186–94, 199–204; earlier critical readings of, 326, 330, 333, 337, 339, 342, 345, 358, 363
Brasch, James D., 44
Brian, Denis, 312
British East Africa Company, 142, 219, 303
Broglie, Louis de, 294
Brown, Robert M., 239
Bruno, Giordano, 293
Buell, Lawrence, 212, 226

buffalo. *See* Big Five
bull, bullfights, 123, 130, 288, 299, 310; EH attends, 1, 3, 8, 10, 11, 12, 13, 14, 15, 16; reads about, 45; writes about, 17
Bull, Malcolm, 249
Burroughs, Edgar Rice, 231n15
Burwell, Rose Marie, 177, 179, 188, 190, 194, 207, 340–41

Calabi, Silvio, 43
Cantwell, Richard (fictional character), 8, 305, 315
Cappel, Constance, 258
Carver, Raymond, 377
Castro, Fidel, 244
Catherine. *See* Barkley, Catherine; Bourne, Catherine
Cave, Ray, xv, 329, 350
Charo, 96, 111, 144, 208, 275, 277
Cherokee. *See* American tribes
Cheyenne. *See* American tribes
child, childhood: in *Garden*, 157, 163–66, 177, 179, 181, 184–87, 191–92, 195, 201; in *Under Kilimanjaro*, 246, 279–83; in writing by other authors, 183–84. *See also* Hemingway, Ernest, childhood of
Christianity, 221, 242, 259, 260, 275–77, 279, 286, 295, 316, 331
"Christmas Gift, The," 18, 89
Cirules, Enrique, 306
"Clean, Well-Lighted Place, A," 14
Coleridge, Samuel Taylor, 159–60
colonialism, imperialism, in Africa: 124, 129–31, 133–34, 136, 138–42, 144n14, 154, 167, 209, 219–20, 241–45, 256, 265–67, 346, 362–63, 374; in critical readings of African narratives, 346, 348, 378; decolonization, 127, 264–65; effects of, 133–34, 138–41, 265–66; opposition to, rebellion against, 16–17, 88, 127, 131, 145n24, 242–45, 264; in United States: 254–56
Comley, Nancy R., 189, 206, 335–36
Congo Civil War, 132

consumer, consumerism, 249, 266, 377
Coolidge, Calvin, 239
Cooper, Gary, 314
Cowley, Malcolm, 312
cultural incuriosity / indifference, 29–30, 214–17, 228–29

Dada, Dadaism, 222, 338
dandy, dandyism, 159–64
Dante, 349
Davis, Mike, 225
Death in the Afternoon, 12, 15, 16, 123, 128, 216, 217, 218, 303, 305, 310. See also iceberg theory
Debba, 114, 125–26, 143n6, 208, 249, 251–52, 258–63, 265, 287, 360–61
del Gizzo, Suzanne, 208, 347, 363, 381
Depression, Great Depression, 88, 95, 100, 137
Dewey, John, 226
disease, illness, 138, 266, 306, 315, 332; amoebic dysentery, xxii, 17, 34n23, 301, 302, 307, 336, 344, 376; gangrene, 225, 306, 352, 360; malaria, 26; mental illness, 200, 205; Spanish influenza, 303, 314
"Doctor and the Doctor's Wife, The," 6, 306
Dos Passos, John, 137
Douglas, Aaron, 218, 219, 226
Dreiser, Theodore, 334, 379
duende, 287–88
Durkheim, Emile, 260
Dussinger, Gloria R., 307

Eastwood, Clint, 356
Eberly, John, 284, 294
Eby, Carl, 44, 189, 203–4, 260, 337, 345, 348, 360, 368
ecocriticism, 212, 225–29
editing, editorial excisions / intrusions, 153, 200. See also Hemingway, Ernest, editors of
elephant. See Big Five

Ellington, Duke, 218
Ellison, Ralph, 377
Emerson, Ralph Waldo, 338
"End of Something, The," 6
environment, 110, 136–40, 220, 310: awareness / unawareness of, 43, 213–14, 221–29; political, 265; religious, 254, 274
Esquire. See magazines
Evans, Oliver, 313

fame, 16, 123, 164, 167, 193–94, 216
Farewell to Arms, A, 10–11, 26, 164, 230n7, 304, 306, 323; critical readings of, 337, 339, 374, 377
father, 26, 163, 181. See also Bourne, David's father (fictional character); "Fathers and Sons"; Hemingway, Clarence Edmonds (father); "Indian Camp"
"Fathers and Sons," 26, 206, 257, 258, 260
Faulkner, William, 6, 314, 327–28
Feldman, Burton, 292
feminine, feminism, 127, 129, 188–89, 204, 216, 382
Feuerbach, Ludwig, 273
Field Museum of Natural History, 140, 303
Fifth Column, The, 14
Fitzgerald, F. Scott, 326, 333–34, 344–45, 336, 337, 344–45, 349, 366, 367
Fitzgerald, Zelda, 326
Flaubert, Gustave, 130
Fleming, Robert E., xv, 18, 205, 336, 341, 348, 370
Fluck, Winifred, 226–27
For Whom the Bell Tolls, 14–15, 230n7, 284, 306, 315; critical readings of, 374; mentioned, 16, 344
Ford, Richard, 374
Foucault, Michel, 202
Francis of Assisi, 278
Franco, Francisco, 14
Franz, Marie-Louise von, 286
Frazer, James, 239, 240–41, 243, 256, 267

Freud, Sigmund, 201, 239, 288, 289, 363, 363
Frey, James, 373
Frost, Robert, 2

García Lorca, Federico, 287
Garden of Eden, The, 13, 27, 31, 153, 156–70, 176–95, 199–209; earlier critical readings of, 324, 325, 326–42, 344–48, 351–55, 358–73, 377–78, 381–83; mentioned, 18, 42
Geismar, Maxwell, 140
Gellhorn, Martha, 3, 12, 14, 270n25
gender, 126–27, 179, 183–91, 200, 202, 209, 324, 374. *See also* authority; feminine, feminism; masculinity
Gide, André, 265
Gilby, Trudy (fictional character), 257, 258–59. 260
Girard, René, 155
Gitchi Manitou, 295
Gonzalez-Whippler, Migene, 240
"Good Lion, The," xviii, 18, 28
Goodfield, June, 294
Gordimer, Nadine, 345–46, 381
Gordon, Caroline, 307
grace under pressure, 214, 299
Grant, Linda, 260
Great Swamp Fight, 255–56
Greco-Turkish War, 11, 221, 367
Green Hills of Africa, 19, 41–42, 101, 122–23, 127, 133–43, 153, 156, 204, 206, 207, 275, 278, 302, 310; earlier critical readings of, 31, 216, 306, 323, 326–44, 346–66, 369–70, 373–76, 379–82; mentioned, 18, 26, 88, 108, 109, 200, 205, 213, 217, 225, 245, 299, 312
Griffin, Peter, 258
Griffin & Howe, 98, 100, 104, 105
Guillermoprieto, Alma, 247

Hall, Ernest (grandfather), 3, 9
Hammett, Dashiell, 376
Harlem Renaissance, 218, 226
Harris, William Cornwallis, 41, 88

Harry (fictional character), 123–24, 129, 136, 167, 168, 169, 215–29, 305–17; earlier critical readings of, 326, 332, 336, 337, 339, 341–44, 346, 349, 350, 352, 356–57, 359, 360, 362, 366–67, 369, 374, 377, 378; mentioned, 130, 169, 214, 295
Havana, 3, 6, 241
Hays, Peter L., 314, 328
Heisenberg, Werner, 293
Helen (fictional character), 215, 216, 220, 222, 224, 313, 314
Hemingway, Adelaide (grandmother), 4, 254; prototype for unnamed grandmother, 26
Hemingway, Anson Tyler (grandfather), 9, 85, 115, 254
Hemingway, Clarence Edmonds (father), 3, 9, 43, 85, 176, 206, 207, 267, 306; recommends books, 43, 50, 81
Hemingway, Ernest:
accidents, wounds of, xxi, xxvi, 1, 3, 10, 17, 89, 118n29, 213, 259, 301, 303. *See also* disease
childhood of, 3–5, 9, 13, 26, 95, 136, 190, 242, 251, 258, 263, 303. *See also* Oak Park
editors of. *See* Cave, Ray; Fleming, Robert M.; Hemingway, Patrick; Hemingway, Seán; Jenks, Tom; Lewis, Robert W.; Perkins, Maxwell
homes of, 2, 3–4
marriages of, 3, 10, 12, 13, 16, 153, 301, 304
relatives of. *See individual listings*
safaris of: first, xxi–xxiii, 2, 3, 15–16, 18, 41, 153; second, xxiii–xxvi, 16–18, 26, 168–70
travels of, 1–18
works of. *See individual listings*
Hemingway, Grace Hall (mother), 3, 5, 32n3, 85, 206, 207, 259, 306
Hemingway, Gregory (son), 3, 43
Hemingway, Hadley Richardson (wife; later Mrs. Paul Mowrer), 11–13, 32n6, 304, 336, 361

Hemingway, John Nicanor (son), 11, 43
Hemingway, Leicester (brother), 93, 109, 301, 302, 355
Hemingway, Marcelline (sister; later Mrs. Sterling Sanford), 4, 5
Hemingway, Mary Welsh (wife), xxiii–xxvi, 3, 10, 12, 92, 104, 125–27, 206, 207–8, 262–65, 291, 299; and Christmas tree, 276–77; hunts in Africa, 102, 127, 249–53, 257, 290–91, 366; mentioned, 16, 30, 273, 275, 293, 305, 314; quotes from and references to *How It Was*: xxiii–xxvi, 17, 31, 86, 89, 96, 110, 255, 348; in photograph, 22
Hemingway, Patrick (son), xxiv, xxvi, 3, 12, 18, 43, 44, 89, 93, 96, 176, 194, 324, 349; comments on Hemingway's reading, 63, 64, 73; edits, introduces Hemingway's writing, xv, xix
Hemingway, Pauline Pfeiffer (wife), xxi–xxiii, 3, 11–12, 13, 14, 15, 31, 86, 92, 104, 109, 301, 344, 379; mentioned, 16, 17, 32, 34, 66, 153, 301; as parallel or prototype for character (P.O.M.), 304, 329, 363, 368, 376
Hemingway, Seán (grandson), xix, 43, 85, 359
Hemingway, Valerie Danby-Smith (daughter-in-law), 299
Hemingway Collection. *See* John F. Kennedy Library and Museum
Hemingway on Fishing, 43
Hemingway on Hunting, 43, 359
Henry, Frederic (fictional character), 26, 304
Herne, Brian, 116n11
Herskovits, Melville, 239
"Hills Like White Elephants," 14
Hoffman, Frederick, 300
Horton, Robin, 273
Hotchner, A. E., 101
Housman, A. E., 377
Howell, John M., 27

Hudson, Thomas (fictional character), 8
Hughes, Langston, 218, 226
Hulme, T. E., 152–54, 158, 168
hyena, 112, 133–34, 217, 307, 310, 314, 315, 343, 369

iceberg theory, 9, 28, 152–56, 164–66, 248, 307
illness. *See* disease
imperialism. *See* colonialism
In Our Time (1925), 144n10, 304; critical readings of, 339, 369, 377, 379; mentioned, 12
India, 88, 108, 140, 141, 382
"Indian Camp," 6, 181, 300, 304, 372
Indian tribes. *See* American tribes
Indian wars, 254
infidelity, 124–26, 306, 357, 362
Ingalls, Rachel, 335
intertextuality, 123, 128, 153–56, 159, 164, 169–70, 360
Iser, Wolfgang, 226
Islam. *See* Moslem, Muslim
Ivancich, Adriana, 10

James, Henry, 359, 364, 367
Jenks, Tom, 192, 199–203, 209, 324, 329, 342, 351
John F. Kennedy Library and Museum, iv, 20, 21, 22, 23, 24, 25, 86, 97, 102, 113, 144, 210
Jordan, Robert (fictional character), 8, 14–15, 284, 305, 315
Joyce, James, 6, 361
Judaism, 276. *See also* monotheism
"Judgment at Manitou," 300, 303
Juma, 161–62, 164, 180–81, 184, 186–87, 204, 337
Justice, Hilary, 193, 349, 371

Kamba, Wakamba, Akamba. *See* African tribes; languages
Kanaka. *See* African tribes
Keiti, 134–35, 276
Kenyatta, Jomo, 17, 266; and hunting industry, 116n10; works by, 140, 265

Kibo (fictional animal), 157, 158–67, 169, 183. *See also* Kilimanjaro
Kikuyu. *See* African tribes
Kilimanjaro, 129, 133–34, 137, 165, 172n15, 212, 217, 219, 222, 225–29, 231n21, 240, 245, 246, 280–81, 294, 295; in photographs, 97, 228
"Killers, The," 33n14
Killinger, John, 300
Kipling, Rudyard, 130, 329
Kitunda, Jeremiah M., 41, 264
Krapf, Johannes, 128, 136
Kübler-Ross, Elisabeth, 299–300, 308–15, 316
kudu, xxii–xxiii, 87, 114, 327
Kurowsky, Agnes von, 10

language, languages, 31, 42, 43, 134, 231n14, 168; Kamba, Kikamba, 130–35; Spanish, 14–15, 196n6, 265, 286; Swahili, 19, 31, 42, 88, 132, 133–36, 142, 143n6, 145n20, 161, 172n14, 286
Lansing, Robert, 242
Lardner, Ring, 303
Larsen, Richard B., 221
"Last Good Country, The," 246
Latham, Donald, 217
Leiris, Michel, 260, 261
Leonard, John, 171n6, 210n5, 364
leopard. *See* Big Five
Lepore, Jill, 260
Lewis, Robert W., xv, 18, 306, 350, 371
Life. See magazines
liminality, 2, 6, 19
lion. *See* Big Five
Locke, Alain, 218, 226
London, Jack, 303, 304
Look. See magazines
Lowes, John Livingston, 172n13
Lucretius Carus, Titus, 291, 292, 293
Lynn, Kenneth S., 179, 216, 299, 308

M'Cola, 101, 102, 126, 135 142, 274, 275
MacLeish, Archibald, 151, 152, 259

MacMullen, Forrest, 299, 300
Macomber, Francis (fictional character), 127, 231n15, 305–6, 314–15; prototypes for, 306, 326. *See also* "Short Happy Life of Francis Macomber, The"
Macomber, Margot (fictional character), 123–24, 125, 127, 216, 305, 324–25; prototypes for, 306, 326. *See also* "Short Happy Life of Francis Macomber, The"
Maera (Manuel García), 304
magazines, 41: *Esquire*, 18, 122, 301, 329, 375, 379; *Life*, 14, 17, 142, 146n25; *Look*, 16, 18, 89, 122, 208, 263, 329, 352; *Scribner's Magazine*, xv, 334; *Sports Illustrated*, xv, 18, 122, 329, 350
Manitou, Gitchi Manitou, 295, 303
Manolín (fictional character), 196n6, 305
Maran, René, xvii, 242–44, 247, 267
Marita (fictional character), 157–58, 161, 189, 200–202, 204
Markham, Beryl, 177, 178–79, 182–84, 270n25
marriage, 4, 7, 9, 13, 17, 125, 306; in *Garden*, 13, 157–58, 176, 185, 188, 201; in other Hemingway texts, 15, 136, 155, 259, 261, 263, 304, 306; in "Snows," 123–25, 215–16, 221, 300, 309, 310, 311. *See also* infidelity; monogamy; polygamy
Marsh, George Perkins, 138
Masai. *See* African tribes
masculinity, 114, 124, 127, 180–82, 185, 187–89, 192, 204, 207, 332, 365, 368; and emasculation, 204, 215, 305–6
Mason, Grant, 306
Mason, Jane, 306, 344, 362
mass migration, 139, 141, 219, 226
materialism, 274, 289–94, 296
Mather, Cotton, 254
Mau Mau uprising, 16–17, 112–14, 119n40, 131, 139–41, 266; and the Wakamba, 245

Mayo Clinic, 314
Mellow, James, 179, 33
Mencken, H. L., 223
Menocal, Mario (Mayito), 17, 93; in photograph, 20
Merton, Thomas, 288
metatextuality, 154, 157, 159, 179, 193, 219
Meyers, Jeffrey, 216, 240
Miller, J. Hillis, 289
Miró, Joan, 6
Mitchell, Prudence (fictional character), 257
Mobutu, Joseph Désiré, 132
Moddelmog, Debra, 190, 192, 206, 209, 220, 346
modernism, 153, 164, 202, 218, 239, 240
Mombasa, xxi, xxiii, xxvi, 16, 17, 18, 140
monogamy, 13, 27, 125
monotheism, 276, 277, 279
Montgomery, Constance, 258
Montgomery, Marion, 307
Morgan, Harry (fictional character), 6, 305, 315
Morrison, Toni, 171n5, 202–3, 332
Moslem, Muslim, Islamic, 160, 161, 275–77, 279, 293
Moveable Feast, A, 13, 27, 313, 324; critical readings of, 335, 340, 342–43, 344–45, 353, 358, 361, 369, 383
Müller, Kurt, 213, 214, 372
Murchison Falls, 89
mutilation, self-mutilation, 243, 256, 260. *See also* scars, tattoos
Mwindi, 274
"My Old Man," 304

Nagel, James, 176, 188, 201
Nairobi, xxi, xxii, xxiv, xxv, xxvi, 17, 18, 140, 142, 301; Mary visits, xxv, 249, 251, 261, 262, 264
Nandi. *See* African tribes
Nansen, Fridtjof, 367
Narragansett. *See* American tribes
National Board for the Promotion of Rifle Practice, 100

National Firearms Act, 90
National Rifle Association, 100, 117n21
neopragmatism, 213, 214, 372
Ngàje Ngài (House of God). *See* Kilimanjaro
Ngui, 111, 125, 256, 274, 287, 289
Nick Adams Stories, The, 26, 231n17, 299. *See also* Adams, Nick (fictional character)
Nobel Prize, 17, 194, 207, 285, 296
nonfiction, 1, 14, 15, 32n1, 43, 123, 164, 226, 275, 287, 375, 382–83
"Notes on Dangerous Game," 87
"Now I Lay Me," 246, 306

Oak Park, 3–10, 18, 26–27, 206, 242, 253–54
Ojibwa. *See* American tribes
Old Man and the Sea, The, 6, 16, 17, 185, 300, 315; critical readings of, 30, 376; mentioned, 284
Ondaatje, Christopher, 27, 140, 246, 367–68
O'Neill, Eugene, 218
Ottawa. *See* American tribes

P.O.M. (Poor Old Mama), 306. *See also* Hemingway, Pauline Pfeiffer (wife)
Pamplona, 7, 8, 13, 15, 304
panpsychism, 277, 290, 291
Park, Mungo, 128, 129, 136
Parker, Ian, 114
Patterson, John Henry, 140
Penas Ibáñez, Beatriz, 8, 248
Percival, Philip, xxi, xxii, xxiii, xxiv, xxv, 17, 87, 88, 104, 108, 176, 181, 250; in photograph, 20; as prototype for Pop, 88, 306, 333, 363; for Robert Wilson, 306, 333
Perkins, Maxwell E., 1, 182, 301
Pfeiffer, Paul and Mary (parents-in-law), 3, 95
Pfeiffer, Gustavus Adolphus (uncle-in-law), 3, 15, 88–89, 204, 350, 376
Phillips, Adam, 289
Picasso, Pablo, 374

Pirandello, Luigi, 363
Plimpton, George, 283
polygamy, 125, 126
polytheism, 277
Porter, Cole, 218, 223, 229
postmodernism, 154, 156, 159, 164, 167–70, 214
poststructuralism, 202
Pound, Ezra, 152–54, 158, 168
primitivism, 85, 203, 204–6, 218, 239; in earlier scholarship, 336, 355, 360, 363
Pulitzer Prize, 17

Raeburn, John, 123
Reynolds, Michael S., 4, 9, 44, 128, 168, 179, 302, 303, 306
rhinoceros. *See* Big Five
Rice, Alfred, 312
Rilke, Rainer, 355
Roe, Steven C., 188, 333
Roof, Judith, 201
Roosevelt, Theodore, 42, 86, 88, 99, 100, 116n8, 117n21, 176, 219, 227, 242, 303, 350
rooster (cock), 123, 130–32, 145n16, 310
Rorty, Richard, 212–15, 228, 229, 372
Ross, Lillian, 314
Rousseau, Henri, 330–31
Ruark, Robert, 92

safari, 9, 10, 17–18, 19–27, 87–89; safari reports / safari writing, 142–43, 153–57. *See also* Big Five; Hemingway, Ernest, safaris of; trophy, trophy-hunting
"Safari," 18, 325, 363
Salinger, J. D., 184, 196n5
Sanderson, Rena, 34n16, 216
Santería, 240, 241, 278
Santiago (fictional character), 33n13, 185, 284, 300, 305, 315–16
Scafella, Frank, 299, 336
scars, tattoos, 203, 204, 257, 259–61, 301
Scheel, Mark, 300

Scholem, Gershom, 285
Scholes, Robert, 189, 206, 335–36
Scott, Robert L., 74, 177, 178–82, 183, 185
Scribner's, xv, 12, 16, 44, 375
Scribner's Magazine. *See* magazines
Sedgwick, Eve Kosofsky, 204
"Sepi Jingan," 304
sexuality. *See* gender
Shakespeare, William, 341, 377
"Short Happy Life of Francis Macomber, The," xviii, 98, 123–24, 125, 127, 153, 156, 162, 209, 213, 305–7, 323, 324–25; earlier critical readings of, 31, 325–82; mentioned, 18, 122, 310
Sieverts, Thomas, 225
Sigman, Joseph, 44
Silbergleid, Robin, 189, 201, 377
Simenon, Georges, 265
Skrbina, David, 277, 292
Slotkin, Richard, 216, 256
Smith, Paul, 258
"Snows of Kilimanjaro, The," xviii, 124, 128–29, 133, 136, 156, 167, 209, 212–29, 294–95, 305–14, 315; earlier critical readings of, 323, 324, 326–28, 330–34, 336–47, 349–54, 356–69, 374–82; mentioned, 18, 30, 31, 122, 123, 153, 156, 228
"Soldier's Home," 33n14
Somali. *See* African tribes
Somé, Malidoma Patrice, 282
Sommer, François, xviii, 75, 140, 370
Sontag, Susan, 360
source studies / texts, 42, 73, 159, 177–84, 185, 217, 329, 330, 331, 341, 363. *See also* inertextuality
Spanish. *See* language, languages
Spanish Civil War, 12, 14, 16, 34n19, 170
Spanish Earth, The, 14
Spinoza, Baruch, 293, 297
Sports Illustrated. *See* magazines
Stein, Gertrude, 13, 330–31, 334
Steinbeck, John, 137, 140
Stephens, Robert, 136, 307

Stevens, Wallace, 282
Strong, Amy L., 189, 193, 203, 378
Strychacz, Thomas, 204, 335, 357, 365–66
suicide, 216, 257, 357; in fiction, 181, 300, 304; of Hemingway, 210n6, 328; of Hemingway's father, 306
"Summer People," 304
Sun Also Rises, The, 7, 12, 13, 14–15, 59, 206–7, 217, 218–19, 304; earlier critical readings of, 325–26, 334, 339, 372, 374, 377, 379–80
Swahili. *See* languages
swamp, 240, 245, 246, 248, 249–50, 253, 255, 257, 264, 268n15
symbol, symbolism, 43, 85, 114, 123, 129, 130–34, 152, 154–57, 202, 204, 219, 226, 306; of animals, 179, 185, 193–95, 204–5, 217, 307, 310, 369; of snow, 227, 295; of trees, 276

taboos, 8, 9, 27, 133, 189, 190, 202, 203, 269n17
Tarantine. *See* American tribes
Tate, Gordon, 307
tattoos. *See* scars
"Ten Indians," 257
Theisen, Earl, iv, 16, 18, 24, 37, 86, 89, 121, 353
Thompson, Charles, 17, 93, 301–2
Thoreau, Henry David, 224, 225
"Three Day Blow, The," 6, 304
Throup, David W., 266
Tiffen, Mary, 139
time, 151, 158, 279–81, 295, 316
To Have and Have Not, 6, 315; critical readings of, 333, 338, 344, 362, 368, 373, 380; mentioned, 16
Toklas, Alice B., 13
Torrents of Spring, The, 6, 12, 14–15, 33n14, 239–40, 304; mentioned, 14, 15, 323, 333, 375
totemistic objects / places /, 263, 268n17. *See also* swamp
Toulmin, Stephen, 294
transcultural, 214–15, 217, 224, 227

transgression: 190. 200, 202–3, 209. *See also* liminality
tribal: tribal past, 239–45; tribal religion, 239–43, 250–51, 255, 257–58; "tribal things," 199, 202–8, 247, 250, 256, 260, 263. *See also* scars; swamp; symbolism; totemistic objects
tribal uprising. *See* colonialism; Great Swamp fight; Mau Mau
tribes. *See* African tribes; American tribes
Trilling, Lionel, 355
Trogdon, Robert W., xv, 342, 354, 362, 375
trophy, trophy-hunting, 87, 114, 176, 244–47, 254, 276, 286. *See also* kudu
True at First Light: A Fictional Memoir, xv, 18, 63, 324, 325; earlier critical readings of, 345, 347–70, 373, 383; mentioned, 63, 122
Twain, Mark, 129–30, 140, 141, 264
Tyler, Lisa, 181, 190, 359
Tzara, Tristan, 338

"Undefeated, The," 14, 304
Under Kilimanjaro, xv, 9, 18, 26, 124–27, 132–33, 153, 155–57, 168–70, 184–85, 207–8, 241, 244–67, 273–96, 302, 324; earlier critical readings of, 370–76, 378, 381–83; mentioned, 29, 93, 122, 200
"Up in Michigan," 6

Vickery, John B., 240, 243, 265
Viertel, Peter, 80, 333
Vietnam War, 214
vulture, 217, 307, 309, 369

Walker, Alice, 381
Waller, Fats, 218
warthog, 87, 88, 126, 130, 134
Willingham, Kathy, 188, 189, 190
Wilson, Edmund, 313, 314, 350, 369

Wilson, Robert (fictional character), 105, 124, 127; critical readings of, 325–26, 327, 330, 331, 332, 333, 334, 341, 344, 346, 363, 373, 378; mentioned, 305, 306

Wolfe, Cary, 182, 186

World War I, 3, 88, 94, 99, 222, 260, 304; Hemingway injured in, 213, 299, 303; aftermath of, 219, 229

World War II, 16, 96, 99; aftermath of, 107, 127

Yoruba. *See* African tribes; American tribes

Young, Philip, 213–14, 299

Zaphiro, Denis, xxiii, xxiv, xxv, 93, 108, 291; in photograph, 22; prototype of fictional character, 103, 114; quoted, 41, 248

www.ingramcontent.com/pod-product-compliance
Lightning Source LLC
Chambersburg PA
CBHW061341300426
44116CB00011B/1945